E.C. AND U.K. COMPETITION LAW AND COMPLIANCE: A PRACTICAL GUIDE

AUSTRALIA
LBC Information Services
Sydney

CANADA and USA
Carswell
Toronto

NEW ZEALAND
Brooker's
Auckland

SINGAPORE and MALAYSIA
Sweet & Maxwell Asia
Singapore and Kuala Lumpur

E.C. and U.K. Competition Law and Compliance: A Practical Guide

PAUL M. TAYLOR BA, M.Phil, M.Jur

Solicitor of the Supreme Court;
Partner of Hewitson Becke + Shaw, Cambridge;
Formerly Barrister of Lincoln's Inn
Fellow of the Society for Advanced Legal Studies

To Rosa

With great appreciation

Paul

London
Sweet & Maxwell
1999

First edition published in 1999 by
Sweet & Maxwell Limited of
100 Avenue Road, Swiss Cottage, London NW3 3PF
(*http://www.smlawpub.co.uk*)
Typeset by Servis Filmsetting Ltd, Manchester
Printed and bound in Great Britain by
MPG Books Ltd, Bodmin, Cornwall

No natural forests were destroyed to make this product;
only farmed timber was used and replanted.

A C.I.P catalogue record for this book
is available from the British Library

ISBN 0421 68030 X

FOREWORD

The University of Cambridge Board of Continuing Education has for some years been involved in providing continuing professional development programmes for lawyers, as part of its commitment to lifelong learning in the field of professional legal education. I am therefore very pleased to write a few words about this publication.

Paul Taylor's book is designed for the very practitioners for whom we provide training. It is a useful, everyday working tool for those who will interact with United Kingdom law when the Competition Act 1998 comes into force. The text is prepared in "practitioner-friendly" terminology and contains clear explanations of difficult concepts.

The publication of this book is timely. I commend it to practitioners and students alike—the text is such that all those who have an interest in this subject will derive benefit from reading this book.

Philip Brown
Director of Legal Studies,
University of Cambridge Board of Continuing Education
Cambridge
April 1999

Competition Law has a direct impact on the transaction of business in national and European markets. No lawyer advising commercial clients, be they legal practitioners or in-house lawyers, can take the risk of ignoring the application of competition rules to their clients' transactions, or their conduct in the market place. Awareness of competition law, which may directly affect the legality of business transactions or commercial strategy, is essential knowledge.

The adoption of the Competition Act 1998, whose scope and enforcement provisions follow closely those of the E.C. competition rules, is a clear signal to undertakings operating on the United Kingdom market that United Kingdom competition authorities will enforce the new law with vigor.

This book is a timely arrival. It covers both E.C. and United Kingdom competition principles and their application to a wide range of commercial transactions relevant to a business undertaking. The book also includes chapters on the powers of investigation and the means of enforcement available to United Kingdom and E.C. competition authorities. It ends with a Chapter on compliance programmes. The book is noticeable for its clarity and practical structure. Readers who are not experts in competition law, but familiar with legal or business matters, will find this book user-friendly. Its structure enables readers to "consult the book" as and when they find it necessary. Each Chapter deals with a particular aspect of the rules, describing the relevant legislative provisions and citing appropriate case-law. A novel feature of this book is the inclusion of a Chapter on "compliance programmes". More and more undertakings are adopting in-house procedures to ensure compliance with competition law. In this final Chapter these programmes are explained and a compliance questionnaire has been prepared to facilitate undertakings contemplating introducing compliance programmes.

As far as the academic world is concerned this book will be a useful reference, particularly for those who need to grasp quickly the essential elements of the rules, and the means available to national and E.C. competition authorities to enforce them.

Rosa Greaves
Allen & Overy Professor of European Law
Durham European Law Institute
April 1999

PREFACE

Competition law is a subject that has undergone tremendous change in recent years. For those who practise in the United Kingdom, the most recent landmark has been the arrival of the Competition Act 1998 which replicates at the domestic level the E.C. model of competition law as enshrined in Articles 85 (1) and 86 of the Treaty of Rome. That Act alone will serve to highlight the fact that for decades, E.C. law has already been hard at work rendering countless agreements (or at least many of their critical provisions) void and the practices of those in a dominant position open to challenge. Two very similar systems of law (United Kingdom and E.C.) need to be grasped by the commercial practitioner.

This book is aimed at the non-specialist commercial lawyer faced with the need to understand the essentials of both United Kingdom and E.C. competition law in such a way that the similarities and differences between the two systems are readily discernible. The core provisions, considered in the early Chapters of this book, are presented so as to highlight these similarities and differences in the context of the different aims of United Kingdom and E.C. law.

The book is intended to span those aspects of competition law that are ordinarily of relevance to the practitioner, not merely those that are introduced by the Competition Act 1998. For example a strong emphasis has been placed on intellectual property agreements and the exploitation of intellectual property rights given the increased importance of intellectual property to businesses, even though the new Act makes little reference to intellectual property. Similarly, commentary on the Fair Trading Act 1973 has been included for those engaged in United Kingdom merger and acquisition work even though United Kingdom law in this area has changed relatively little recently. E.C. merger control has, however, undergone recent revision and commentary has been included to reflect these changes. The book therefore covers both United Kingdom and E.C. law, not merely the most recent reforms.

Particular forms of commercial agreement are considered in some detail in order to place competition law in context but without assuming any previous knowledge or experience of competition law. Particular agreements or practices will frequently need to be challenged or defended according to their compliance with competition law. For agreements, the accent is on establishing whether the agreement is eligible for automatic exemption and, if not, whether individual exemption was or may be granted (if reliance is to be placed on it). In the case of an abuse of dominant position, the crucial issue is whether there exists sufficient market power for dominance to be established and whether there has been any accompanying abuse. In all cases, the market context is of utmost importance and a Chapter has been devoted solely to the issue of assessing market share and market power.

In the closing Chapter the emphasis is on compliance, with a questionnaire provided by way of a "tool-kit" in order to meet the increasing demands on practitioners to provide compliance programme services. That Chapter is intended to bring the book together to enable the user to begin to set in motion a compliance programme. Detailed cross-reference is made to earlier sections of the book where the significance of each question is explained in further detail.

In short, the book has been written at a time when competition law in the United Kingdom is in transition, as a result of which new burdens are placed on the commercial lawyer. It is intended to provide access for the non-specialist to what would otherwise be an extremely daunting area of law. Reference may then more easily be made to the established specialist practitioner volumes, for which we have all been extremely grateful in the past. This book is also intended to be used by students who might appreciate single volume coverage of both United Kingdom and E.C. competition law in a level of detail that brings the subject within their immediate grasp.

I would like to express my gratitude to others who have helped with this book: Patrick Green of 2 Harcourt Buildings for his practical suggestions in Chapter 14, in the section entitled *Litigation issues*, when deploying competition law in litigation; Chris Hallam, my trainee at the time I wrote this book, for his contribution in Chapter 7 (concerning the established block exemptions for certain commercial agreements), my colleagues at Hewitson Becke + Shaw for their encouragement and assistance, Liz Akhtar for typing and caretaking the draft production of the work; Professor Rosa Greaves for her comments and valuable input, and last but not least, my wife Elisabeth for her continuous support in my writing this book.

Paul Taylor
Hewitson Becke + Shaw
Cambridge
February 1999

Table of Contents

CHAPTER 3: INFRINGEMENT BY ABUSE: ARTICLE 86 AND CHAPTER II PROHIBITIONS

CHAPTER 4: DEFINITION OF RELEVANT MARKET AND ASSESSMENT OF MARKET SHARE

CHAPTER 5: TRANSITIONAL PROVISIONS OF THE COMPETITION ACT 1998

CHAPTER 7: AGREEMENTS ELIGIBLE FOR AUTOMATIC BLOCK EXEMPTION

CHAPTER 8: AGREEMENTS COMMONLY ELIGIBLE FOR
EXEMPTION OR TO WHICH ARTICLE 85(1) DOES NOT APPLY

CHAPTER 10: EXHAUSTION OF INTELLECTUAL PROPERTY RIGHTS

CHAPTER 11: UNITED KINGDOM MONOPOLY AND MERGER CONTROL

CHAPTER 12: E.C. MERGER CONTROL

CHAPTER 13: UNITED KINGDOM INVESTIGATION AND ENFORCEMENT

CHAPTER 14: E.C. INVESTIGATION AND ENFORCEMENT

APPENDIX B

APPENDIX C

APPENDIX D

APPENDIX E

Table of E.C. Cases

Alphabetical List of Cases

NUMERICAL TABLE OF CASES BEFORE THE EUROPEAN COURT OF JUSTICE

NUMERICAL TABLE OF CASES BEFORE THE COURT OF FIRST INSTANCE

NUMERICAL TABLE OF E.C. COMMISSION DECISIONS

TABLE OF NATIONAL CASES

Table of E.C. Legislation

TABLE OF E.C. TREATIES AND CONVENTIONS

TABLE OF REGULATIONS

TABLE OF DIRECTIVES

TABLE OF COMMISSION NOTICES

TABLE OF GUIDELINES

E.C.

United Kingdom

United States of America

Table of United Kingdom Cases

Table of United Kingdom Statutes

Table of United Kingdom Statutory Instruments

CHAPTER 1

Introduction

BACKGROUND

1-01 Competition law is a daunting subject of enormous breadth and complexity. This Chapter is intended to serve as a non-technical summary of what follows in later Chapters. It also introduces the main institutions and organs of administration of competition law.

Since the United Kingdom's accession to the European Economic Community—renamed the European Community ("E.C.") by the Maastricht Treaty—two systems of law have existed in parallel in the United Kingdom: E.C. law and national law. United Kingdom law is increasingly shaped by E.C. law. This is demonstrated with striking clarity by the introduction of the Competition Act 1998 ("the 1998 Act"). For the full text of the 1998 Act see Appendix A.1 below. Although similar in content E.C. competition law and United Kingdom competition law remain distinct.

1-02 The fountainhead of E.C. competition law is the Treaty of Rome (the "E.C. Treaty"), with Articles 85 and 86 as the core provisions. Relevant extracts from the E.C. Treaty are detailed in Appendix A.2 below. Following ratification of the Treaty of Amsterdam,[1] Articles 85 and 86 of the E.C. Treaty are to be renumbered Articles 81 and 82 respectively. Appendix A.3 below, lists the Article changes effected by the Treaty of Amsterdam. This work refers throughout to the E.C. Treaty Articles before they are renumbered. Articles 85(1) and 86, together with secondary legislation, have had direct effect in the United Kingdom since 1973.[2] The impact of the E.C. Treaty was memorably described by Lord Denning in *Bulmer v. Bollinger*[3]

> "When it comes to matters with a European element, the Treaty is like an incoming tide. It flows into the estuaries and up the rivers. It cannot be held back."[4]

In parallel with the direct effect of these E.C. Treaty Articles, competition law has been regulated at the domestic level in the United Kingdom for decades by a complex matrix of enactments which have proved to be singularly ill-suited to the regulation and control of anti-competitive practices. Until that is the arrival of the 1998 Act.

---

[1] The Treaty amending the Treaty on European Union; the Treaties establishing the European Communities and certain related acts [1997] O.J. C340.
[2] European Communities Act 1972.
[3] *Bulmer v. Bollinger* [1974] 2 All E.R. 1227.
[4] *ibid.*, para. 4.

ROUGH GUIDE TO E.C. AND UNITED KINGDOM COMPETITION LAW

Legislative changes in the United Kingdom

1-03   Criticism of the United Kingdom law of restrictive practices began almost immediately following enactment of the Restrictive Trade Practices Act 1976 and Resale Prices Act 1976, as reflected in the Lisner Committee's "Review of Restrictive Trade Practices Policy".[5] More than a decade of silence followed until in 1996 a Conservative Government Green Paper proposing reform of United Kingdom restrictive trade practices law[6] led to a White Paper entitled "Opening Markets: New Policy on Restrictive Trade Practices".[7]

In line with a growing trend amongst European countries to adopt legislation reflecting Articles 85(1) and 86 of the E.C. Treaty (seven out of fifteen Member States so far have done so), pressure for similar legislation mounted and the Competition Bill was first published on October 15, 1997. It was given its second reading in the House of Lords on October 30, 1997 and its second reading in the House of Commons on May 11, 1998. The 1998 Act finally received Royal Assent on November 9, 1998.

1-04   The 1998 Act is intended as the primary source of United Kingdom competition legislation concerning anti-competitive practices and abuses of dominant position, having repealed in a single sweep the Restrictive Trade Practices Act 1976, the Resale Prices Act 1976 and much of the Competition Act 1980.[8] That will undoubtedly be welcomed by lawyers who would agree with the statement of Lord Danckwerts that the rigid, formulaic approach of certain aspects of that legislation was "calculated to drive any accurately-minded lawyer to despair".[9]

The thrust of the 1998 Act is to introduce into English law an absolute prohibition against a range of anti-competitive activities which affect trade within the United Kingdom. It was modelled on Articles 85(1) and 86 of the Treaty of Rome which continue, in parallel, to prohibit anti-competitive activities which affect trade between Member States of the Community. The effect on trade must be "appreciable". Accordingly, certain agreements and practices with insignificant effect may be disregarded. The two systems of United Kingdom competition law and E.C. competition law will therefore co-exist and there will undoubtedly be many cases where single agreements or activities infringe both United Kingdom and E.C. competition law. In other cases, only United Kingdom competition law may be infringed where the effect is felt solely within the United Kingdom (or part of the United Kingdom), and only E.C. competition law may be infringed where there is an effect on trade between Member States but no effect in the United Kingdom alone. The 1998 Act goes so far as to prohibit anti-competitive agreements or conduct where the effect is felt in only part of the United Kingdom. It will therefore catch local activities, not just those with national impact.

1-05   One significant advantage of the 1998 Act is that it has adopted almost identical language to that of Articles 85(1) and 86 in describing the key prohibitions. In doing so, its declared aim is to achieve consistency with the established principles of E.C. competition law developed over decades of experience of applying Articles 85(1) and 86. The advantage is that the business community only needs to come to grips with one set of prohibitions (albeit that as a matter of E.C. competition law they operate whenever inter-

---

[5] Cmmd 7512.
[6] "Review of Restrictive Trade Practices Policy" Cm. 331.
[7] Cm. 727.
[8] Except under the transitional provisions which will remain important for some time for the purposes of determining whether agreements caught by those provisions are void.
[9] *British Basic Slag* [1963] L.R. 4R.P. 116 at 149.

state trade may be affected, and as a matter of United Kingdom law, they operate whenever the domestic market is affected). Nevertheless, the new United Kingdom law will prohibit outright a wide range of practices and agreements that have traditionally been regarded as "commercial common sense" or "good business practice", when fending off competitors.

The consequences of infringement

1-06 The immediate consequence for agreements that infringe the prohibitions is that they are void. If particular clauses are responsible for the infringement those clauses alone will be void, if they are severable from the rest of the agreement (applying national principles of severance).

For many years those engaged in business in the Community have appreciated that enormous fines may be imposed by the Commission of the European Communities ("the Commission") for infringement of Articles 85(1) and 86. Fines may be imposed of up to 10 per cent of the annual, gross, worldwide turnover of the participating companies, including their group companies. There is no doubt that fines are used increasingly by way of deterrent. The biggest fine so far against a single undertaking was that imposed on Volkswagen recently, amounting to 102 million[10] ECUs,[11] but in the case of cartels, the total fines imposed on cartel members collectively have exceeded this level. In *Trans-Atlantic Conference Agreement*, a record fine of 273 million E.C.Us[12] was imposed.

1-07 The 1998 Act, in line with the Commission's powers, gives the Director General of Fair Trading ("the Director") power to fine undertakings up to 10 per cent of their turnover calculated on a similar basis as for infringement of Articles 85(1) and 86; except that the level of fines will be related to United Kingdom turnover only. This power itself will inevitably cause those engaged in business in the United Kingdom to examine closely whether their agreements and practices fall within the new prohibitions. The present Director, Lord Bridgeman, has declared that he will not hesitate to use these powers in enforcing the new legislation. He is assisted by the Office of Fair Trading (the "OFT") and is also given wide powers of investigation, which include the right to conduct on-the-spot dawn raids.

Of course quite apart from the disruption and cost of an investigation, anyone found to have infringed will suffer adverse publicity. The 1998 Act creates a number of criminal offences punishable by fine and up to two years' imprisonment for those who obstruct an investigation or mislead the authorities in any way.

1-08 All undertakings will therefore have to consider seriously putting in place compliance programmes to ensure that all of their activities comply both with E.C. and United Kingdom competition law. This will involve a detailed look at existing contracts (as these may become void as well as expose the parties to fines) and procedures should be adopted to ensure that new contracts are negotiated and properly vetted for compliance. Procedures should also be put in place to avoid unlawful collusion between competitors. Managers should take advantage of training available to make them aware of how best they might comply. Furthermore, senior personnel should know in advance what to

---

[10] Commission Dec. 92/273/E.C. of January 28, 1998 [1998] O.J. L124/60.
[11] Under Art. 2 of Council Regulation 1103/97 [1997] O.J. L162/1 all references to "ECU" are to be replaced by a new term, "euro". The ECU—the European Currency Unit—was introduced by Art. 109g of the E.C. Treaty (as amended by the Maastricht Treaty) and defined in Regulation 3320/94 [1994] O.J. L350/27. It was agreed at a meeting of the European Council in Madrid in 1997 that the term "ECU" should be replaced by the term the "euro" common to all Community languages. The substitution took effect from January 1, 1999, to coincide with the introduction of the single currency in many Member States. All references to ECU in this book should be construed accordingly.
[12] Commission Dec. of September 16, 1998, Commission Press Release IP/98/811.

do in the event of a dawn raid whether by the Director or the Commission. All of this may reduce an ultimate fine. The following press release in *Viho/Parker Pen*[13] bears this out.

> "The level of fine does, however, reflect the cooperative behaviour of Parker Pen during the investigation of the case and the fact that Parker has drawn up a wide-ranging competition law compliance programme for all its E.C. subsidiaries. The fine would have been significantly higher without these mitigating factors."

Although undertakings are duty-bound to co-operate fully with the authorities, there is nevertheless scope for challenging any decisions made by the authorities on the basis of the way in which they conduct investigations.

The prohibitions

1-09 The prohibitions fall into two categories. First Article 85(1) of the Treaty and Chapter I of the 1998 Act both catch a broad range of agreements and concerted practices. Article 86 and Chapter II of the 1998 Act both prohibit abuses occurring by unilateral conduct on the part of any undertaking in a dominant position.

The Article 85(1) and Chapter I prohibitions

1-10 A number of agreements and concerted practices are referred to in Article 85(1) and Chapter I by way of illustration and these include the following:

(i) Price-fixing—Collusion on prices is most harmful when it takes place between two manufacturers or two suppliers who are competitors. Price-fixing is equally prohibited when it takes place at different levels of trade such as between a supplier and distributor where, for example, both parties agree the terms on which a distributor will resell to its customers. Similar principles apply equally to setting other trading conditions, not simply prices. Of concern also will be agreements on the minimum prices to be charged, even maximum prices, and trade associations are particularly at risk of infringement where members agree the recommended prices to be charged by them. The simple exchange of price information between competitors is itself likely to raise the suspicion of price-fixing. Buying groups (where buyers pool their purchasing power) are competition-sensitive and require justification to the authorities, perhaps on the basis of the need to protect members of the group against the selling power of suppliers. Selling groups raise similar issues.

(ii) Limits on production—If parties agree to limit their own production, the scarcity of those products on the market is likely to increase price in response to demand. This may be justified in times of structural over-capacity or economic crisis in order to prevent undertakings going out of business. It may also be justified where parties need to pool their own production, for example where output is unprofitable until certain production levels are achieved. Co-operation of this sort will have to be justified individually on its merits.

(iii) Market-sharing—This frequently involves, for example the allocation of geographical territory or customers between competitors. Each agrees not to compete in relation to the other's allocated territory or customer base. The effect will be that instead of competing with each other, the parties are protect-

---

[13] Commission Dec. 92/426 [1992] O.J. L233/27.

ing each other from competition. Exclusive distribution agreements may have this effect if they are reciprocal.

(iv) Discrimination—If suppliers agree to discriminate against particular customers, those customers will be unable to compete effectively and, especially in the long-term, will be placed at a competitive disadvantage. Discrimination between customers may be justified objectively on the basis of the customer's credit risk, order volumes, payment reliability, and similar criteria.

(v) Tie-ins—When agreeing to supply one product, the supplier cannot require the customer to take other unrelated products as well, without this raising serious competition issues. A supplier of photocopiers, for example cannot force the customer to buy supplies of paper, ink and other consumables from that supplier.

Any agreement is prohibited if it adversely upsets competition by affecting trade between Member States (in the case of Article 85(1)) or within the United Kingdom (under Chapter I of the 1998 Act). It will be void, or at least the offending clauses will be void if they are severable from the rest of the agreement.

The Article 86 and Chapter II prohibitions

1-11 Article 86 and Chapter II of the 1998 Act both prohibit any abuse by a single entity (or more than one acting in concert) in a dominant position if the result is to affect trade between Member States (in the case of Article 86) or within the United Kingdom (in the case of Chapter II of the 1998 Act). As a rule of thumb, dominance may be taken to exist whenever a business represents more than 40 per cent of the relevant market but a great deal depends upon the structure of the relevant market. Some markets have been drawn extremely narrowly in the past. In general, the relevant market consists of all substitutable goods and services. Examples of particular prohibited practices are given and these include the following:

(i) Unfair purchase or selling prices or other unfair trading conditions—A common abuse would be excessive pricing when compared with the economic value of the product or service supplied. Whenever a business is dominant, there is the risk that it is exposed to insufficient competition and therefore enabled to charges prices that are excessive. Equally prohibited is predatory pricing which involves pricing below cost where the aim is to drive competitors, particularly new entrants, out of business. A large undertaking will obviously be able to weather any short-term losses either because its business activities are sufficiently widespread to cover them, or it may simply take the view that short-term losses are worth the long-term gain of driving out new competition.

(ii) Limits on production or supply—Limited availability of goods may adversely inflate prices and harm the purchaser, as well as increase costs down the supply chain. Also contemplated in this prohibition is any refusal to supply, since the purchaser may be completely dependent on that particular dominant supplier and would be easily harmed as a result. A refusal to supply must therefore be justified objectively. A common risk is the decision by a dominant company to take in-house the business activities undertaken by a customer. The customer then becomes a competitor and the supplier withholds supplies. This could harm the customer and could constitute an abuse. In exceptional circumstances, a refusal to grant an intellectual property licence may also amount to infringement, though these cases will be relatively uncommon.

(iii) Discrimination—Unilateral discrimination against particular customers is similar to discrimination resulting from agreement. Once again, any discrimination must be objectively justified and must not selectively harm or favour particular customers. Abuse must not effectively remove freedom of choice from the customers. Care must be taken with customer incentives such as loyalty rebates or discounts which escalate with volume.

(iv) Tie-ins—When supplying one product additional irrelevant obligations cannot be imposed on the purchaser unless justified. For example a software supplier cannot force the customer to take maintenance services with any software licence since an independent maintainer should be free to supply those services.

Avoiding the prohibitions

1-12 The range of prohibitions is extremely wide. The disadvantage to undertakings is that they will not know with any certainty whether any of their agreements or practices are prohibited because most infringements depend upon the effect of the agreement or conduct on trade between Member States or within the United Kingdom.

What is clear is that a limited class of agreements can in general be regarded as free of these prohibitions and they are, for example sub-contracts and pure agency agreements (where the agent undertakes no risk of its own and can be regarded as serving only an auxiliary function for the principal). Certain forms of basic co-operation in research are also not caught by the prohibitions. However in the case of other agreements, undertakings must take steps to achieve certainty by ensuring that the terms of their agreements, their market shares and surrounding circumstances do not combine to restrict competition to an appreciable extent. Agreements will be judged by their potential effects, not their proven effects. In general, any restraint on the commercial freedom of any party, or a third party, will be a potential restraint on competition for these purposes. The effect of any particular restriction depends on the type of contract concerned, as well as the market power of the participants, and it is important that those involved in contract negotiation become familiar with those agreements that are acceptable and those that are not.

1-13 If an agreement is prohibited by Article 85(1) or Chapter I, it is void unless granted exemption. Exemption is available for agreements which contain only restrictions that are indispensable for the purpose of achieving certain economic benefits. A prohibited agreement may qualify for exemption where the restrictions are necessary in order to bring corresponding advantages to consumers.

Exemption is available by one of two routes. First, exemption may be granted on application to the relevant authorities. The relevant authority for the purpose of Article 85(1) is the Commission in Brussels which grants exemption under Article 85(3). The relevant authority for the purpose of the 1998 Act is the Director, acting through the Office of Fair Trading. Secondly, in the case of Article 85(1), exemption may be conferred automatically if the agreement falls within the terms set out for that particular agreement in one of the Commission's block exemption Regulations. Each Regulation deals with a different type of agreement such as exclusive distribution agreements, exclusive purchasing agreements, research and development agreements, franchise agreements, and patent and know-how licences. These Regulations give a very clear indication of the Commission's reasoning concerning each type of agreement but it is important to note that the agreement must contain only those terms permitted by the appropriate regulation (white-listed clauses) and must not include any that are prohibited (black-listed clauses). There are also a number of preconditions which need to be met to ensure that there is still an appropriate level of competition abounding in the Community. If an agreement meets all of the requirements of a regulation then there is no need to apply for exemption. Exemption is granted automatically. Exemption will be available under the 1998 Act on similar terms in relation to Chapter I prohibitions, although at the time of writing, block exemptions have not yet been published. If an agreement is exempt under Article 85(3), either as a result of one of the Commission's block exemption Regulations or because the Commission has expressly granted exemption, then the exemption also covers any prohibition under the 1998 Act.

Third parties and contract disputes

1-14 Any third party adversely affected by an infringement of competition law (United Kingdom or E.C.) may claim damages against the parties to the agreement or concerted practice (in the case of Article 85(1) or Chapter I), and a victim may claim damages against an undertaking in a dominant position for any loss suffered by that undertaking's abuse. It is also worth bearing in mind that competition law may be used by a party to an agreement who wishes to be relieved of its unenforceable obligations.

Business valuation

1-15 Very few businesses will be unaffected by competition law. Infringement carries with it very serious consequences (including the risk of fines, unenforceability and third party claims). The value of every business will be affected according to whether its agreements and practices infringe competition law. The issue of compliance will be relevant to all transactions involving the transfer of shares or of a business, and the value attaching to the shares or business may obviously be adversely affected by non-compliance. Compliance programmes are therefore extremely important. Compliance programmes may even mitigate fines should the worst happen.

Differentiation between E.C. and United Kingdom law

1-16 The 1998 Act introduces a great deal of consistency in the application of principles of competition law in the United Kingdom with developed E.C. jurisprudence. However, it will be necessary to maintain a coherent grasp of the different aims and procedures separately operating at E.C. and United Kingdom levels, reflected in the separate sources of E.C. law and United Kingdom law. This is borne out by the textual differences (rather than similarities) between the prohibitions in Articles 85(1) and 86 of the E.C. Treaty and the equivalent prohibitions in Chapter I and Chapter II of the 1998 Act.

The essential textual differences account for the fact that Articles 85 and 86 serve the purpose of market integration (as enshrined in Articles 30 to 36 of the E.C. Treaty), in addition to the regulation of competition. The aim of market integration is clearly not relevant in the United Kingdom context. Accordingly, the Article 85(1) prohibition applies to:

> "agreements between undertakings, decisions by associations of undertakings and concerted practices which may affect trade *between Member States* and which have as their object or effect the prevention, restriction or distortion of competition *within the common market.*"[14]

Section 2(1) of the 1998 Act (containing the "Chapter I Prohibition") refers to:

---

[14] Emphasis added.

"agreements between undertakings, decisions by associations of undertakings or concerted practices which (a) may affect trade *within the United Kingdom* and (b) have as their object or effect the prevention, restriction or distortion of competition *within the United Kingdom*."[15]

These differences reflect the dual function of Article 85(1) compared with the single aim of the Chapter I prohibition. Illustrations of prohibited practices are given in both Article 85(1) and section 2(2) of the 1998 Act in identical terms intended to emphasise that precisely the same practices are targeted, even if the emphasis concerning their effect may be different.

1-17 A similar approach is taken to the anti-abuse prohibitions in Article 86 and in the 1998 Act, section 18 (containing "the Chapter II Prohibition"). Article 86 states:

"Any abuse by one or more undertakings of a dominant position *within the common market* or in a substantial part of it shall be prohibited as incompatible *with the common market* insofar as it may affect trade *between Member States*."[16]

Section 18 of the 1998 Act is strikingly similar and states:

"any conduct on the part of one or more undertakings which amounts to the abuse of a dominant position in a market is prohibited if it may affect trade *within the United Kingdom*."[17]

Section 60 of the 1998 Act is a core interpretation provision aimed at achieving consistency with Community law as interpreted by the European Court of Justice ("E.C.J"), whilst "having regard" to decisions and statements of the Commission.

E.C. LAW AND ADMINISTRATION

The E.C. Treaty

1-18 E.C. law has various sources which operate in different ways. The ultimate and originating source is the E.C. Treaty. The aims and organs of the E.C. Treaty are established in Articles 1 to 7.[18] Article 2 expresses these aims succinctly:

"The Community shall have as its task, by establishing a common market and progressively approximating the economic policies of the Member States, to promote throughout the Community a harmonious development of economic activities, a continuous and balanced expansion, an increase in stability, an accelerated raising of the standard of living and closer relations between the States belonging to it."

In order to give effect to these ambitions, Article 5 of the Treaty provides that:

"Member States shall take all appropriate measures, whether general or particular, to ensure fulfilment of the obligations arising out of this Treaty or resulting from actions taken by the institutions of the Community."

---

[15] Emphasis added.
[16] Emphasis added.
[17] Emphasis added.
[18] Now Arts 1 to 16.

This duty also includes "sincere cooperation".[19]

1-19 Part Two of the Treaty establishes the principle of free movement, the central Article being Article 30 that guarantees free movement of goods:

> "Preventative restrictions on imports and all measures having equivalent effect shall . . . be prohibited between Member States."

The Single European Act of 1986 added Article 8 which expresses the additional aim of establishing the internal market by 1992 without internal frontiers to the free movement of goods, services, persons and capital. All impediments to free trade throughout the Community must therefore be removed. Added to this are the competition principles established in Articles 85(1) and 86.

It is striking that the E.C. Treaty itself makes no mention of intellectual property other than in Article 36 which permits restrictions on free movement of goods if justified on the grounds of protection of "industrial and commercial property". The principle of free movement of goods ostensibly conflicts with the national protection afforded to goods protected by intellectual property against "importation" as an infringing act, and Article 30 resolves the conflict. The interpretation of Article 36 has given rise to considerable case law from the E.C.J to determine the extent to which intellectual property rights may be exempt from the free movement principle of Article 36.

Secondary legislation

1-20 The E.C. Treaty also gives rise (under Article 189) to secondary legislation principally in the form of Council Directives, Commission Regulations, decisions, recommendations and opinions. Directives direct Member States to enact their own legislation by a specified date to achieve a stated objective but generally they have no direct effect themselves. Commission Regulations do have direct effect, without national enactment. Decisions amount to binding rulings on particular matters, usually given a narrow sphere of competence. Recommendations and opinions are not binding but are nevertheless influential.[20] The supremacy of E.C. law is now recognised even in the case of direct conflict (*MacCarthy's Ltd v. Smith*).[21]

Organs of administration

1-21 The Treaty established as the main organs of administration, the Council of Ministers ("the Council"), the Commission, the European Parliament ("the Parliament") and the E.C.J. The Council's aim is to ensure coordination of economic policy.[22] The Commission acts as the guardian of the E.C. Treaty, monitoring compliance and also instigating legislation by means of proposals which are put to the Council for consideration. The Parliament assumes a consultative function in its legislative role, requiring the Council to consult the Parliament in draft legislation. The Court of First Instance ("CFI") was established to hear appeals against decisions by the Commission and to review

---

[19] Case 226/87 *Commission v. Greece* [1988] E.C.R. 3611; [1988] 3 C.M.L.R. 569.
[20] The status of Directives is an interesting one, in particular the extent to which they give rise to rights at a national level before their implementation. The case of *Alfons Lutticke GmbH v. Hauptzollampt Sarreloins* [1996] E.C.R. 205 established that a Directive is binding on national courts if its provisions impose a clear and precise obligation on Member States, it is unconditional (or subject to very clearly defined exceptions) and the Member State is given no discretion whether or not to apply it. These principles are not confined to Directives, but Directives are the most common source of claims for direct effect in national courts, for example where the national legislature is slow in implementing Directive obligations which favour a plaintiff.
[21] *MacCarthy's Ltd v. Smith* [1979] I.C.R. 785; [1979] 3 C.M.L.R. 44.
[22] Art. 145 of the E.C. Treaty.

Commission decisions concerning penalties (under Article 173). Finally, the E.C.J is concerned with Treaty compliance and the "interpretation and application" of the law[23] and has jurisdiction to give preliminary rulings on such matters[24] assisted by the Advocate General whose non-binding opinion is given on all cases before the E.C.J.

The list of Member States presently comprises: Austria, Belgium, Denmark, Finland, France, Germany (including the former GDR), Greece, Republic of Ireland, Italy, Luxembourg, The Netherlands, Portugal, Spain, Sweden, and the United Kingdom.

European Free Trade Association

1-22   More limited co-operation than established by the E.C. Treaty was achieved by countries comprising the European Free Trade Association ("EFTA"), formed in 1960. By 1989 the need became apparent for the inter-relation between the EFTA and E.C. countries to be formalised and in 1992 the European Economic Area Agreement ("the EEA Agreement") was signed. The parties to the EEA Agreement are the E.C., E.C. Member States and EFTA countries[25] and the geographical coverage of the European Economic Area (the "EEA") is the territory represented by those countries. The EFTA Agreement applies the basic principles of free movement of goods and services to the EFTA states (currently Iceland, Liechtenstein and Norway) by reflecting in Articles 11, 12 and 13 of the EEA Agreement the provisions of Articles 30, 34 and 36 of the E.C. Treaty. It also applies similar competition rules by reflecting in Articles 53 and 54 of the EEA Agreement the substance of Articles 85 and 86 of the E.C. Treaty.

State aids

1-23   Under Articles 92–94 of the E.C. Treaty, the Commission is empowered to control State aids that could distort competition in the common market. State aids are, potentially, incompatible with the aims of the E.C. Treaty because they afford an advantage to an undertaking which may create distortion of competition in the market. Article 92(1) provides that:

> ". . . aid granted by a Member State or through state resources in any form whatsoever which distorts or threatens to distort competition by favouring certain undertakings or the production of certain goods shall, in so far as it affects trade between Member States, be incompatible with the common market."

Articles 92(2) and 92(3) detail the circumstances under which State aids may be compatible with the common market. These Articles relate to State aids to make good damage caused by natural disasters or exceptional circumstances, to promote the economical development of deprived areas, to promote projects of common European interest or to remedy serious disturbance in the economy of a Member State, to facilitate the development of certain economic activities or economic areas, to promote cultural and heritage conservation, or such other categories of aid as may be specified by the Commission.

Coal, steel and nuclear energy

1-24   Coal and steel production within the Community is regulated under the terms of the European Coal and Steel Community (ECSC) Treaty.[26] The ECSC Treaty contains

---

[23] Art. 164 of the E.C. Treaty.
[24] Art. 177 of the E.C. Treaty.
[25] Art. 2(c) of the EFTA Agreement.
[26] Treaty of Paris, April 18, 1951.

similar competition rules to those contained in Articles 85 and 86 of the E.C. Treaty although there are major differences between the two to take account of the special nature of the coal and steel markets within the Community. In particular the ECSC Treaty specifically provides for quotas to be introduced in the event of a "manifest crisis" in either industry.[27]

The Euratom Treaty[28] provides that Articles 85 and 86 of the E.C. Treaty will apply to agreements and abuses of a dominant position in the nuclear energy industry to the extent that agreements and abuses are not already covered by the provisions of the Euratom Treaty. The Treaty deals with primary products in the nuclear industry.

UNITED KINGDOM LAW AND ADMINISTRATION

The Director General of Fair Trading, OFT and Competition Commission

1-25 The Director's functions include giving guidance and making decisions to determine whether a Chapter I or Chapter II prohibition applies to any agreement or conduct. On present predictions there are expected to be approximately 1000 applications per annum for guidance or a decision, once any initial uncertainties of the 1998 Act are settled.

The Director will also issue guidelines on matters of interpretation or general principle, intended to make the 1998 Act and its implementation as transparent as possible. Detailed procedural rules will follow, together with guidance on penalties (all subject to the approval of the Secretary of State), since the consequences of infringing the prohibitions are significant. Although the 1998 Act intends that third parties may seek damages if affected by an infringement, provision for this, significantly, is not included anywhere in the text of the 1998 Act.

1-26 The Director is given significantly enlarged powers of investigation under the 1998 Act, to make up for the weaknesses inherent in earlier legislation and it is the deterrent aspect of the 1998 Act which is seen as key to its likely effectiveness.

As Lord Bridgeman (the present Director) put it:

"It seems to me that as a general rule, compliance with the various laws relating to the conduct of business is taken most seriously in those areas where an illegal activity can result in the most severe penalties."[29]

The Director has wide powers of investigation modelled on the Commission's powers but they still fall short of equivalent powers found in the U.S. and Canada. The 1998 Act will inevitably result in a great deal more interface and co-operation between the Director and the Competition Directorate-General IV (DGIV) within the Commission.

1-27 The Director is assisted by the OFT which was established under the Fair Trading Act 1973. Its staff will be significantly enhanced in order to cope with the Director's new responsibilities and there is no doubt that these powers will be deployed rigorously as confirmed by the present Director:

"The proposed new legislation will arm me with greater powers than ever before to pursue anti-competitive activity in the market and to impose financial penalties. I

---

[27] Art. 58 of the ECSC Treaty.
[28] Treaty of Rome, March 25, 1957.
[29] IIR Conference May 19, 1998.

will not hesitate to use these powers in enforcing the new legislation. This means that the chances of being detected will be greater and the consequences of infringing the rules much more serious under the new legislation. Companies who deliberately or negligently break the law should take heed. All businesses need to guard against inadvertently falling foul of the new law's provisions."[30]

Merger control

1-28 Part III of the 1998 Act amends the monopoly provisions of the Fair Trading Act 1973 which are otherwise preserved (and therefore excluded from the ambit of the 1998 Act) but the Monopolies and Mergers Commission ("MMC") is dissolved (by Section 45(3)) on its fiftieth anniversary. A newly constituted Competition Commission will assume the role formerly undertaken by the MMC. The Director, assisted by the OFT, is also conferred enhanced powers of investigation by the 1998 Act to seek information and documents when considering any Fair Trading Act reference.

The new Competition Commission is also empowered to hear appeals from decisions of the Director, in a role similar to that of the CFI in respect of European Commission decisions. Appeals against decisions of the Competition Commission are to be made to the Court of Appeal.

Regulated industries

1-29 As a result of repealing certain key sections of the Competition Act 1980, the functions previously exercisable by the Regulators OFTEL, OFGAS, OFFER, OFWAT, ORR and OFREG, under both the Fair Trading Act 1973 and the Competition Act 1980 are no longer exercisable by them.[31] Instead, those functions are to be exercised by the Regulators under the 1998 Act. Detailed provisions of the Telecommunications Act 1984, The Gas Act 1986, The Electricity Act 1989, The Water Industry Act 1991 and The Railways Act 1993 gave the Regulators jurisdiction over specified commercial activities and supplies relating to their industries. Under the 1998 Act the Regulators will assume within their own jurisdiction many of the functions given to the Director in carrying out investigations, imposing penalties and enforcing decisions. Schedule 10 makes essential changes to the above Acts in order to reflect the transition.[32]

---

[30] IIR Conference May 19, 1998.

[31] The Office of Telecommunications, OFTEL is the regulatory body for agreements or conduct relating to commercial activities connected with telecommunications (OFTEL's powers derive from the Telecommunications Act 1984). The Office of Gas Supply, OFGAS is the regulator for agreements and conduct involving the shipping, conveyance or supply of gas and ancillary activities (OFGAS's powers derive from the Gas Act 1986). In Northern Ireland the Office for the Regulation of Electricity and Gas, OFREG has authority (OFREG's powers derive from the Gas (Northern Ireland) Order 1996). The Office of Electricity Regulation, OFFER regulates agreements and conduct concerning commercial activities connected with the generation, transmission or supply of electricity (OFFER's powers derive from the Electricity Act 1989). In Northern Ireland the Office for the Regulation of Electricity and Gas, OFREG has authority (OFREG's powers derive from the Electricity (Northern Ireland) Order 1992). Agreements and conduct relating to commercial activities connected with the supply (or securing a supply) of water or of sewage services are regulated by the Office of Water Service, OFWAT (OFWAT's powers are derived from the Water Industry Act 1991). The regulator for agreements and conduct relating to the supply of railway services is the Office of the Rail Regulator, ORR (ORR's powers derive from the Railways Act 1993). The regulators and the Director have powers in the 1998 Act to deal with anti-competitive agreements or conduct, or abuses by dominant undertakings in their designated sectors. The regulators and the Director will always consult each other before taking action in a particular case, and in some circumstances the Director may deal with a case rather than the sector's designated regulator.

[32] It is outside the scope of this particular work to address the industry-specific issues applicable to each of those sectors.

SUMMARY

1-30 There is no doubt that the 1998 Act will engender a culture of compliance, even if the threat of imprisonment is not as extensive as some might have wished. The 1998 Act is a long-overdue and much welcomed reform to the complex mosaic of historic United Kingdom competition legislation made up of the Restrictive Trade Practices Act 1976, the Restrictive Practices Court Act 1976 and the Resale Prices Act 1976—all of which have been abolished in a single stroke. The 1998 Act may not be welcomed by the business community because of the enhanced powers of investigation, the immediate prohibitions and penalties. However, it is a logical advance given the direction of the tide of Community law.

CHAPTER 2

Infringement by Co-ordination: Article 85(1) and Chapter I Prohibitions

THE AIMS: THE PURPOSE OF THE PROHIBITIONS IN ARTICLE 85(1) AND CHAPTER I

Introduction

2-01   One of the basic aims of competition law, put simply, is to place everyone in the business community on an equal footing so that businesses are able to compete on equal terms. Potential competition should not be unduly restricted by high barriers to entry into business. Pressure for low prices should enable purchasers to choose between suppliers on the basis of lowest cost matched for comparable value. This in turn should cause suppliers to increase output efficiency and increase price competition further up the supply chain. The purpose of competition law is to safeguard suppliers and purchasers at each level of supply against anti-competitive agreements or abuses of monopoly power. Competition law is aimed at creating and maintaining conditions of maximum competition.

This Chapter focuses on two provisions, Article 85(1) of the E.C. Treaty and Chapter I of the 1998 Act, which endeavour to give effect to those aims. The wording of those provisions is almost identical. However, they are intended to operate in different spheres. This Chapter therefore highlights the aims, the differences and the similarities between Article 85(1) and Chapter I.

Article 85(1)

2-02   Article 85(1) is directed at ensuring compatibility of trading arrangements within the common market in line with the Treaty purposes discussed in Chapter 1 above—of promoting throughout the Community the harmonious development of economic activities,[1] of establishing the principle of free movement of goods and services and, following the Single European Act 1986, of establishing the internal market. The competition aims of Article 85 (and Article 86 discussed in Chapter 3 below) are to prohibit trading practices that operate against those purposes. Accordingly Article 85(1) reads as follows:

"(1)   The following shall be prohibited as incompatible with the common market: all agreements between undertakings, decisions by associations of undertakings and concerted practices which may affect trade between Member States and which have as their object or effect the prevention, restriction or distortion of competition within the common market, and in particular those which:

---

[1] Art. 2 of the E.C. Treaty.

(a) directly or indirectly fix purchase or selling prices or any other trading conditions;

(b) limit or control production, markets, technical development, or investment;

(c) share markets or sources of supply;

(d) apply dissimilar conditions to equivalent transactions with other trading parties, thereby placing them at a competitive disadvantage;

(e) make the conclusion of contracts subject to acceptance by other parties of supplementary obligations which, by their nature or according to commercial usage, have no connection with the subject of such contracts."

Article 85(2) provides:

"(2) Any agreements or decisions prohibited pursuant to this Article shall be automatically void." (For further detail *see* para. 6-09 and para. 14-31 below.)

2-03 Article 85(3) sets out the criteria for declaring Article 85(1) inapplicable. If an agreement meets those criteria it may be exempt. The criteria for exemption, set out in Article 85(3), are as follows:

"(3) The provisions of paragraph 1 may, however, be declared inapplicable in the case of:

(i) any agreement or category of agreements between undertakings;

(ii) any decision or category of decisions by associations of undertakings;

(iii) any concerted practice or category of concerted practices;

which contributes to improving the production or distribution of goods or to promoting technical or economic progress, while allowing consumers a fair share of the resulting benefit, and which does not:

(a) impose on the undertakings concerned restrictions which are not indispensable to the attainment of these objectives;

(b) afford such undertakings the possibility of eliminating competition in respect of a substantial part of the products in question."

Exemption may be granted either by way of individual application to the Commission or by block exemption. The Commission is empowered to grant individual exemption pursuant to Regulation 17/62.[2] Block exemption, on the other hand, is granted automatically, without the need for individual application, if an agreement meets all of the requirements (both as to the form of the agreement and certain pre-conditions for eligibility) set out for that type of agreement in the relevant block exemption. The Commission is authorised by the Council of Ministers under Article 87(2)(b) of the E.C. Treaty to propose block exemptions, and the terms of each block exemption are determined by Council Regulation. Exemption from the prohibitions in Article 85(1) and Chapter I is examined in detail in Chapter 6 below, but is mentioned at this stage in order to put the prohibitions in context.

2-04 The consequences of infringing Article 85(1)—unless exemption is granted— are serious. First, Article 85(2) renders void the offending parts of the agreement, or if these are not severable, the entire agreement. Secondly, there is the risk of Commission investigation under Regulation 17/62.[3] Thirdly, fines may be imposed of up to 10 per cent of the turnover of each of the undertakings concerned in all its products in the business

---

[2] Art. 9(1) of Reg. 17/62, the first Regulation implementing Arts 85 and 86 of the Treaty, [1962] J.O. 204/62. For further detail see Chap. 6 below.

[3] Art. 14 of Reg. 17/62 [1962] J. O. 204/62.

year before the fine is awarded.[4] The Commission has recently demonstrated an increased willingness to fine heavily in cases of obvious infringement as illustrated by the fine of 102 million ECUs imposed upon Volkswagen on January 28, 1998 for discouraging car exports from Italy. More will be said of enforcement powers in Chapter 14.

Articles 85(1) and 86 have direct effect in the United Kingdom and breaches are actionable as torts of breach of statutory duty. National courts have the duty to enforce the rights of a plaintiff under those Articles (*BRT v. Sabam*[5]). However national courts do not have power to grant exemption from any prohibition.

Chapter I

2-05   Chapter I of the 1998 Act comprises sections 1 to 16. Section 2 contains the Chapter I prohibition and is the mirror image of Article 85(1). Although section 2 is almost a verbatim replica of Article 85(1), the 1998 Act clearly does not share the Community aims and principles that underlie Article 85(1). At the heart of Chapter I is the aim of bringing about the wholesale reform of United Kingdom competition law by repealing long-established statutes and statutory instruments which did little more than regulate the form of agreements. The 1998 Act aims to replace them with legislation that takes an economic approach to the regulation of competition in the United Kingdom. Accordingly, the Act begins in section 1 with the words:

> "The following shall cease to have effect:
>
> (a) The Restrictive Practices Court Act 1976;
> (b) The Restrictive Trade Practices Act 1976;
> (c) The Resale Prices Act 1976; and
> (d) The Restrictive Trade Practices Act 1977."

The Government's aims were put more positively by Margaret Beckett, the former President of the Board of Trade, as follows:

> "A domestic prohibition which operates and can be interpreted consistently with Article 85 itself will keep the burden of business to the minimum."[6]

2-06   The same economic and legal principles that apply to Article 85 will apply equally to the 1998 Act and thereby avoid the separate application of different principles at domestic level. Of course the 1998 Act will inevitably require separate treatment to be given to compliance with United Kingdom law but at least this will involve the application of principles similar to those under Article 85. By contrast the statutes repealed by section 1 were manifestly at odds with the economic approach of Article 85(1), basing compliance with competition law in the form, and to a lesser extent the effect, of agreements. As Lord Simon of Highbury has observed, the purpose of the 1998 Act is:

> "to ensure smooth interaction between the E.C. legal and business environment and the United Kingdom prohibitions . . . [and to] . . . reduce some of the regulatory overload and paperwork."[7]

---

[4] Art. 15(2) of Reg. 17/62 [1962] J.O. 204/62, stipulates fines of between 1000 and 1 million ECUs, irrespective of the turnover of the undertakings. For fines in excess of 1 million ECU, the fine may not exceed 10 per cent of the turnover in the preceding business year of each of the undertakings participating in the infringement.
[5] Case 127/73 *BRT v. Sabam* [1974] E.C.R. 313; [1974] 2 C.M.L.R. 238.
[6] A prohibition approach to anti-competitive agreements and abuse of dominant position, Draft Competition Bill, August 1997.
[7] Hansard, House of Lords Second Reading Debate, October 30, 1997.

This "smooth interaction" is borne out primarily in the similarity in wording between Article 85(1) and the Chapter I prohibition contained in section 2 of the 1998 Act. It is also found in the parallel exemption provisions of section 10 which confer exemption on agreements that are automatically exempt by virtue of an E.C. Commission Regulation, or are individually exempt following notification to the Commission or have passed the appropriate opposition procedure.[3] This itself will reduce the burden of dual notifications to the OFT and the Commission. Furthermore the Act dovetails neatly with one of the main concerns of the Commission as set out in its Notice on co-operation between national competition authorities and the Commission:[9]

> "to avoid duplication of checks on compliance with the competition rules . . . which is costly for the firms concerned."[10]

In that Notice the Commission urged Member States to enable national competition authorities to apply and enforce E.C. law. The Act does not go that far. Instead it achieves a domestic approach to competition law that is merely consistent with Articles 85 and 86.

2-07   The Chapter I prohibition provides, in section 2, as follows:

"(1) Subject to section 3, agreements between undertakings, decisions by associations of undertakings or concerted practices which:

    (a) may affect trade within the United Kingdom; and

    (b) have as their object or effect the prevention, restriction or distortion of competition within the United Kingdom,

are prohibited unless they are exempt in accordance with the provisions of this Part.

(2) Subsection (1) applies, in particular, to agreements, decisions or practices which:

    (a) directly or indirectly fix purchase or selling prices or any other trading conditions;

    (b) limit or control production, markets, technical development or investment;

    (c) share markets or sources of supply;

    (d) apply dissimilar conditions to equivalent transactions with other trading parties, thereby placing them at a competitive disadvantage;

    (e) make the conclusion of contracts subject to acceptance by the other parties of supplementary obligations which, by their nature or according to commercial usage, have no connection with the subject of such contracts.

(3) Subsection (1) applies only if the agreement, decision or practice is, or is intended to be, implemented in the United Kingdom.

(4) Any agreement or decision which is prohibited by subsection (1) is void."

2-08   Confidential guidance may be sought from the Director in relation both to the Chapter I and Chapter II prohibitions (under sections 13 and 21) to verify compliance with the 1998 Act which, if given, will confer limited immunity from penalties. A more formal decision may be sought (under sections 14 and 22) confirming compliance or non-compliance with the 1998 Act. In implementing this procedure, the Director will elicit the views of third parties. In addition, provision is made in section 4 for individual exemption and

---

[8] See Chap. 6 below.
[9] Commission Notice of December 19, 1977 on co-operation between national competition authorities and the Commission on co-operation between national competition authorities and the Commission [1977], O.J. C313/3.
[10] *ibid.*, para. 10.

in section 6 provision is made for block exemption of certain standard categories of agreement, similar to the Commission block exemption Regulations. In all cases, the criteria for exemption are set out in section 9 (similar to Article 85(3)), which requires that the agreement:

> "(a) contributes to:
>> (i) improving production or distribution; or
>> (ii) promoting technical or economic progress, while allowing consumers a fair share of the resulting benefit; but
>
> (b) does not:
>> (i) impose on the undertakings concerned restrictions which are not indispensable to the attainment of those objectives; or
>> (ii) afford the undertakings concerned the possibility of eliminating competition in respect of a substantial part of the products in question."

Individual exemption and block exemption are discussed at length in Chapters 6, 7 and 8 below, together with parallel exemption where the terms of an E.C. block exemption are met.

Powers of investigation are given to the Director and, following a finding of infringement, penalties may be imposed under section 36 of up to 10 per cent of the turnover of the companies concerned, as discussed in further detail in Chapter 13 below which deals generally with enforcement powers.

THE DIFFERENCES: THE KEY DIFFERENCES BETWEEN ARTICLE 85(1) AND CHAPTER I

2-09 The key differences between the Article 85(1) prohibition and the Chapter I prohibition are as discussed below.

Interpretation of the Act

Section 60

2-10 Interpretation of Part I of the Act, which embraces both the Chapter I and Chapter II prohibitions, is to be in accordance with section 60. Section 60 represents an important point of interface between United Kingdom and E.C. law. It sets out the principles to be applied in its interpretation as follows:

> "(1) The purpose of this section is to ensure that so far as is possible (having regard to any relevant differences between the provisions concerned), questions arising . . . in relation to competition within the United Kingdom are dealt with in a manner which is consistent with the treatment of corresponding questions arising in Community law in relation to competition within the Community.
>
> (2) At any time when the court determines a question arising, it must act (so far as is compatible with the provisions of this Part and whether or not it would otherwise be required to do so) with a view to securing that there is no inconsistency between:
>> (a) the principles applied, and decisions reached, by the court in determining that question; and
>> (b) the principles laid down by the Treaty and the European Court, and any rel-

evant decisions of that Court as applicable at that time in determining any corresponding question arising in Community law.

(3) The court must, in addition, have regard to any relevant decision or statement of the Commission."

Relevant differences

2-11   Section 60 establishes the aim of consistent treatment of United Kingdom law and corresponding Community law. It recognises that there will inevitably be crucial differences. Accordingly, section 60 is qualified by the words "so far as is possible", and it acknowledges the need to have "regard to any relevant differences between the provisions concerned". It will therefore be necessary to take care when examining ECJ decisions, and when having regard to a decision or statement of the Commission, to note the extent to which an issue is determined according to principles of market integration, the effect on trade between Member States, or competition within the common market. There will doubtless be many cases where it is extremely difficult to differentiate the dual aims of each of Articles 85 and 86 from the single aim of each of the Chapter I and Chapter II prohibitions, and this is likely to result in the re-examination of many established E.C.J cases to discern that difference. Numerous references under Article 177 of the Treaty are also likely to result.

Article 177 references

2-12   Article 177 confers jurisdiction on the E.C.J to give preliminary rulings concerning the interpretation of the E.C. Treaty. A request may be made of the ECJ to give a ruling on the interpretation of the E.C. Treaty if the issue is raised before any domestic court or tribunal of a Member State and a decision on the question is needed to enable it to give judgment. A reference under Article 177 may also be made where the question is raised before a domestic court or tribunal of a Member State against whose decision there is no judicial remedy under national law. In both cases, Article 177 would be available to an English court or the newly established Competition Commission seeking a ruling on the interpretation of E.C. law in order to apply national law. This is confirmed by the Opinion of the Jacobs A.G. in *Bronner v. Media Print Zeitungs- und Zeitschriftenverlag.*[11]

The judgment of the ECJ in *Giloy v. Hauptzollampt Frankfurt Am Main-Ost*[12] illustrates that:

> ". . . where, in regulating internal situations, domestic legislation adopts the same solutions as those adopted in Community law so as to provide for one single procedure in comparable situations, it is clearly in the Community interest that, in order to forestall future differences of interpretation, provisions or concepts taken from Community law should be interpreted uniformly, irrespective of the circumstances in which they are to apply."[13]

Article 177 therefore gives the Director an opportunity to seek clarification, for example concerning Commission, CFI or E.C.J decisions which he does not wish to follow, or which themselves are under appeal.

---

[11] Opinion of May 28, 1998 Case C-7/97. Examples of recent use of this power are found in ECJ judgments in Case 28/95 *Leur-Bloem v. Inspecteur der Belastingdeinst/ Ondernemingen* [1997] E.C.R. I-4161 and Case C–130/95 *Giloy v. Hauptzollampt Frankfurt Am Main-Ost* [1997] E.C.R. I-4291.

[12] Case C–130/95 [1997] E.C.R. I-4291.

[13] *ibid.*, para. 28 at 4304.

The role of the ECJ and Commission

2-13   Section 60 refers to the need to secure consistency between the decisions reached by English courts and the principles laid down by the E.C. Treaty and the ECJ. At the same time English courts must have "regard to any relevant decision or statement of the Commission". There will inevitably be occasions when decisions of the ECJ and decisions of the Commission conflict. For example the ECJ's decision in *Akzo*[14] establishes clear principles for determining issues related to predatory pricing. The President of the Board of Trade has demonstrated that section 60 adopts the principles of predatory pricing established by the E.C.J under Article 86.[15] The Commission's Notice on market definition[16] is a more up to date reflection of the Commission's approach to the issue even if the notice is not binding. The qualification in section 60(2) resolves any discrepancy by stating that the principles laid down by the Treaty and the E.C.J in any relevant decision of the E.C.J are those "applicable at the time in determining any corresponding question arising in Community law". E.C.J case law may not keep abreast with Commission practice yet at the relevant time E.C.J case law still has priority in interpretation, according to section 60, over Commission practice to which the court must merely "have regard".[17]

Rules and Guidelines

2-14   Section 52 of the 1998 Act imposes a duty on the Director to issue guidelines on interpretation and to "prepare and publish general advice and information" concerning the application and enforcement of the prohibitions "to persons who are likely to be affected by them". Guidelines are therefore intended primarily for use by the business community and are not intended to have the same legal status as formal exemptions.

Parliamentary statements

2-15   It is a striking shortcoming of the 1998 Act that it is necessary on certain fundamental issues to resort to the principles established in *Pepper v. Hart*[18] to resolve ambiguities on the face of legislation. One glaring omission from the Act is any right of private action for those adversely affected by breaches of the Act. There is no doubt from parliamentary statements that private actions are intended.[19] Given that the Act creates extensive sanctions for non-compliance, it deals at length with procedural matters and the omission of reference to injunctions and damages in favour of affected third parties is striking.

Other fundamental principles of E.C. law adopted under the same principle of *Pepper v. Hart* include the rule against self- incrimination, proportionality and non-discrimination.[20]

"Trade between Member States" compared with, "Trade within the United Kingdom"

Trade between Member States

2-16   An effect on trade between Member States is required for infringement of Article 85(1). The ECJ's statement in *Consten v. Grundig*[21] bears this out:

---

[14] Case 62/86 R *Akzo v. Commission* [1986] E.C.R. 1503; [1987] 1 C.M.L.R. 225, also Case C–62/86 [1991] E.C.R. I-3359; [1993] 5 C.M.L.R. 215.
[15] President of the Board of Trade, Hansard, House of Commons, May 11, 1998 Cols 28, 30.
[16] Commission Notice on Market Definition [1997] O.J. L372/03.
[17] A court for these purposes includes any tribunal.
[18] *Pepper v. Hart* [1993] A.C. 593.
[19] For example Lord Simon of Highbury, Hansard, House of Lords, October 2, 1997 Col. 1148.
[20] Lord Simon of Highbury, Hansard, House of Lords, November 25, 1998 Cols 960/962.
[21] Joined Cases 56 & 85/64 *Ets Consten Sarl and Grundig-Verkaufs GmbH v. E.C. Commission* [1966] E.C.R. 299; [1966] C.M.L.R. 418.

"It is only to the extent to which the agreement may affect trade between Member States that the deterioration in competition caused by the agreement falls under the prohibition of Community law contained in Article 85, otherwise it escapes the prohibition.

In this connection what is particularly important is whether the agreement is capable of constituting a threat, either direct or indirect, actual or potential, to freedom of trade between Member States in a manner which might harm the attainment of the objectives of a single market between States."[22]

The issue of inter-state trade is to be treated cautiously.

In *BNIC v. Clair*[23] an agreement to fix the minimum price of a product that was only sold within the area of Cognac, and kept well within the confines of France, was held by the ECJ to affect trade between Member States because the product constituted a raw material for another product that was marketed throughout the Community. The ECJ in *Commercial Solvents*[24] reached a similar conclusion when considering activities relating to an intermediate product with consequent impact on inter-state trade in the downstream market.

2-17   It is clear that an agreement covering the whole of a Member State may be taken to affect trade between Member States if it results in compartmentalisation of markets along national boundaries. Thus in *Vereniging van Cement Handelaren v. Commission*[25] the ECJ commented that:

"An agreement extending over the whole of the territory of a Member State by its very nature has the effect of reinforcing the compartmentalisation of markets on a national basis, thereby holding up the economic interpenetration which the Treaty is designed to bring about and protecting domestic production."[26]

Accordingly, in *Pronuptia de Paris v. Schillgalis*,[27] the partitioning effects of a franchise network, even between parties in the same Member State, could affect trade between Member States because franchisees were prevented from establishing themselves in other Member States. It will be easier to establish an effect on trade between Member States if the activities of a business that are constrained are close to continental national borders.

Agreements between parties based entirely outside the Community may also be caught by Article 85(1) if the effects of the agreement are felt within the Community. In *Woodpulp*[28] the Commission confirmed that:

"Article 85 of the E.C. Treaty applies to restrictive practices which may affect trade between Member States even if the undertakings and associations which are parties to the restrictive practices are established or have their headquarters outside the Community, and even if the restrictive practices in question also affect markets outside the E.C."[29]

---

[22] *ibid.*, p. 341.
[23] Case 123/83 *BNIC v. Clair* [1985] E.C.R. 391; [1985] 2 C.M.L.R. 430.
[24] Cases 6 & 7/73 *Commercial solvents* [1974] E.C.R. 223; [1974] 1 C.M.L.R. 309.
[25] Case 8/72 *Vereniging van Cement Handelaren v. Commisison* [1972] E.C.R. 977; [1973] C.M.L.R. 7.
[26] *ibid.*, para. 29.
[27] Case 161/84 *Pronuptia de Paris v. Schillgalis* [1986] E.C.R. 353; [1986] 1 C.M.L.R. 414.
[28] Commission Dec. 84/202[1985] O.J. L85/1; [1985] 3 C.M.L.R. 474.
[29] *ibid.*, para. 79.

Trade within the United Kingdom

2-18   Chapter I of the 1998 Act focuses on agreements which affect trade or disrupt competition "within the United Kingdom". Section 2(7) requires "United Kingdom" to be construed as the United Kingdom or any part of the United Kingdom. "Part" does not refer to substantial part (unlike the Fair Trading Act 1973 which, for merger control purposes, requires the "part" to be "a substantial part"[30]). Any part, no matter how small seemingly will suffice.

"De minimis" principles

"Appreciable effect" under Article 85(1)

2-19   Since the early case of *Völk v. Ets J Vervaeke*[31] it has been clear that an effect on inter-state trade must be "appreciable" in order for an agreement to be caught by Article 85(1). An insignificant effect is not enough, since,

> "an agreement falls outside the prohibition in Article 85(1) where it has only an insignificant effect on the market, taking into account the weak position which the persons concerned have on the market in question."[32]

Another way of putting it, as the ECJ did in *Beguelin Import v. GL Import Export*[33] is that,

> "in order to come within the prohibition imposed by Article 85, the agreement must affect trade between Member States and the free play of competition to an appreciable extent."

The Commission's 1997 Notice on agreements of minor importance[34] was intended to clarify what is meant by "appreciable", by setting quantitative criteria. The Notice expresses the threshold in terms of market share values held by the parties. Below those thresholds, the agreement might be said to have negligible effect on trade between Member States or on competition within the common market and therefore will not be caught by Article 85(1). It is also possible that parties to agreements may exceed those thresholds and yet the agreement may still have negligible effect. The agreement would then not be caught by Article 85(1). If an agreement is to benefit from the certainty provided by the Notice, the aggregate market shares held by all participating undertakings (engaged in the production or distribution of goods or in the provision of services) must not exceed, on any of the relevant markets:

(a) 5 per cent, where the agreement is made between undertakings operating at the same level of production or of marketing ("horizontal agreements") such as a joint venture between producers; and

(b) 10 per cent, where the agreement is made between undertakings operating at different economic levels ("vertical agreements") such as a distribution agreement.

---

[30] *R v. MMC ex parte South Yorkshire Transport* [1993] 1 W.L.R. 23.
[31] Case 5/69 *Völk v. Ets J Vervaeke* [1969] E.C.R. 295; [1969] 2 C.M.L.R. 273.
[32] *ibid.*, paras 5–7.
[33] Case 22/71 *Beguelin Import v. GL Import Export* [1971] E.C.R. 949; [1972] 2 C.M.L.R. 81.
[34] Commission Notice on agreements of minor importance which do not fall within the meaning of Art. 85(1) of the Treaty establishing the European Community [1997] O.J. C 372/04.

For mixed agreements where it is not clear whether they are horizontal or vertical, the 5 per cent threshold applies. The method of calculation of market share is discussed in Chapter 4 below and is critical to the issue of *de minimis* assessment.

2-20   In the Notice, "participating undertakings" refers to the parties and those entities controlling and controlled by the parties, whether directly, indirectly or jointly.

The Notice goes on to warn that even if the parties are able to satisfy these market share criteria, certain agreements may nevertheless be caught by Article 85(1) and these are:

(a) horizontal agreements which fix prices, limit production or sales, or share markets or sources of supply, and

(b) vertical agreements which fix resale prices or grant territorial exclusivity on the parties or a third party.

In general, these are agreements which should be caught by national law and the Commission would prefer intervention by national competition authorities instead of the Commission. The Notice does, however, emphasise the need for care in the case of agreements which confer territorial exclusivity.

2-21   The Notice also states that agreements between small and medium-sized enterprises (SMEs) are rarely capable of significantly affecting trade between Member States and competition within the common market. As a rule, they are therefore not caught by Article 85(1). Even if such agreements do, for some reason, infringe Article 85(1) the Commission has indicated in the Notice its unwillingness to institute proceedings preferring the matter to be dealt with instead by national authorities. The Commission may, however, wish to intervene where the agreement significantly impedes competition in a substantial part of the relevant market or there exist a number of similar agreements that constitute a network of agreements, for example, between several producers or dealers. For these purposes SMEs must satisfy the following criteria[35]:

(a) have fewer than 250 employees (calculated by reference to the number of annual working units of full-time, part-time and seasonal employees); and

(b) have either:

   (i) an annual turnover of 40 million ECUs or less, or

   (ii) an annual balance sheet total of 27 million ECUs or less (in the preceding twelve-month accounting period or, in the case of new companies which have not filed their accounts, a reliable estimate of the turnover in that financial year will suffice); and

(c) be "independent enterprises" in the sense that no more than 25 per cent of the share capital or voting rights are owned by an enterprise which itself is not an SME (whether on its own or jointly). The 25 per cent level may be exceeded by shareholdings of institutional investors (such as pension or insurance companies) or by business angels provided they do not have voting control. The 25 per cent threshold may also be exceeded if the shareholdings are so dispersed that it is impossible to identify the total shareholding of individual shareholders.

These criteria must apply for two consecutive financial years to qualify as an SME or, once qualifying, to lose that status.

---

[35] Definition of small and medium-sized enterprises adopted by the Commission [1996] O.J. L107/8.

"Appreciable Effect" under Chapter I

2-22   The guides published by the OFT entitled "The Chapter I Prohibition" and "The Major Provisions" confirm that agreements which have minimal impact on competition are excluded from the Chapter I prohibition. Chapter I, like Article 85(1), is silent on the exclusion of agreements which do not have an appreciable effect but the principle is derived from the E.C.J's decision in *Völk v. Ets J Vervaeke*.[36] The guides reiterate that only if an agreement or concerted practice has as its object or effect an "appreciable" prevention, restriction or distortion of competition in the United Kingdom will the Chapter I prohibition apply. Whether an agreement has an appreciable effect depends principally on the market power of the "participating undertakings"and whether their combined market share is small. The term "participating undertakings" is the same as that applied by the Commission as outlined above in *"Appreciable effect" under Article 85(1)*.

The Director takes the view that, in general, agreements will have no appreciable effect on competition if the participating undertakings' combined share of the relevant market is less than 25 per cent. This figure will need to be kept under careful review as it may be revised from time to time by the Director. Even if the combined market share of the parties is less than 25 per cent, an appreciable effect may still be found. There are certain types of agreement that will never be regarded as insignificant. In line with the Commission's Notice, these are agreements between competitors which directly or indirectly fix prices or share markets, or impose minimum resale prices, or form part of a network of agreements which have a cumulative effect on the market.

2-23   Market share values taken alone will not determine whether an appreciable effect results from any particular agreement. Other considerations in determining whether the effect of an agreement is appreciable include the structure of the market. If parties to an agreement have a relatively small market share when compared to that of their competitors, the combined market share of those parties may overstate their market power. The characteristics of buyers and the demand structure in the market will also be relevant. For further examples of factors that determine market power, see Chapter 11, *Investigations and orders*, below.

Section 39 of the 1998 Act confers immunity for small agreements *i.e.* agreements (other than price fixing agreements) between parties whose combined annual turnover is less than that prescribed by the Secretary of State. Below this threshold the parties will be immune from penalties. The Director has power to investigate and remove the immunity for those agreements where competition is significantly impeded in the market concerned (or in a substantial part of it) or where the cumulative effect of networks of agreements is to restrict competition.

Exclusions from Chapter I (no exclusions from Article 85(1))

2-24   Section 3 of the 1998 Act refers to a number of agreements that are excluded from the Chapter I prohibition. Exclusions are to be differentiated from exemptions. Exclusion from a prohibition means *a priori* the prohibition does not apply. On the other hand, exemption means that the prohibition does apply until it is "declared inapplicable" in the case of Article 85(3), or in the case of Chapter I, until it is declared exempt (if the criteria in section 9 are met).

Section 3 states that the Chapter I prohibition does not apply to any agreement that is excluded by virtue of Schedules 1, 2, 3 or 4. These exclusions are extensive and deserve consideration.

---

[36] Case 5/69 [1969] E.C.R. 295; [1969] C.M.L.R. 273.

Schedule 1: Mergers and concentrations

2-25   The merger and concentration provisions of the Fair Trading Act 1973 are preserved. For further detail see Chapter 11 below. The aim of Schedule 1 is to apply the Fair Trading Act 1973 provisions, instead of the Chapter I prohibitions, to agreements and their implementation which result "in any two enterprises ceasing to be distinct" (the Fair Trading Act definition of a merger).[37]

Schedule 1 also disapplies the Chapter I prohibition to any concentration which results in the Commission having exclusive jurisdiction under the Merger Regulation.[38] For further detail see Chapter 12 below.

Schedule 2: Selected business sectors

2-26   Schedule 2 lists various other exclusions from the Chapter I prohibition which relate to selected business sectors. They are excluded from Chapter I because they are already the subject of statutory regulation. These include the financial services sector, rules of companies, the broadcasting sector and certain environmental obligations.[39]

Schedule 3: General exclusions

2-27   Schedule 3 contains general exclusions from the Chapter I prohibition of which the most common are likely to be the following[40]:

(1)   Planning obligations imposed in agreements.

(2)   Agreements furnished pursuant to the Restrictive Trade Practices Act 1976 which have been given a direction under section 21(2) of that Act before commencement of the 1998 Act (that they are insignificant). However, no exclusion applies at all if there has been a material variation of the agreement, even if the variation does not relate to any competition-sensitive matter. The Director has power

---

[37]   The Director has the power to make a direction (under para. 4 of Sched. 1) withdrawing that exclusion if he considers that the merger would not qualify for unconditional individual exemption (para. 4(5) of Sched. 1). In order for the Director to disapply the exclusion, the merger must, however, not be a "protected agreement". An agreement is a protected agreement if (a) the Secretary of State has already announced a decision not to make a merger reference under s. 64 of the Fair Trading Act 1973, or (b) he has made reference of a "merger situation" which qualifies for investigation or (c) s. 65 of the Fair Trading Act 1973 applies because the agreement results in the enterprises ceasing to be distinct or (d) in the case of the water industry, a merger reference is possible under s. 32 of the Water Industry Act 1991. As the Fair Trading Act 1973 also deals (in s. 57) specifically with certain asset transfers of newspaper businesses, Sched. 1, similarly disapplies such agreements from the Chap. I prohibition.

[38]   Council Reg. 4064/89 as amended by Council Reg. 1310/97.

[39]   The exclusions in further detail are: (1) The Financial Services Sector (excluding from the prohibition agreements and other matters relating to the constitution of a recognised self-regulating organisation, a recognised investment exchange and a recognised clearing house); (2) Companies (excluding from the prohibition rules of recognised supervisory bodies or qualifying bodies and guidance issued by them); (3) Broadcasting (excluding from the prohibition agreements relating to Channel 3 licences, and networking arrangements which are already dealt with under the Broadcasting Act 1990); (4) Environmental obligations which impose "producer responsibilities" on certain entities under the Environment Act 1995.

[40]   Other exclusions under Sched. 3 are: (1) E.E.A. regulated markets concerned with investment services in the field of securities, listed by a non- U.K. EEA State; (2) Bodies undertaking services of general economic interest or entrusted with a revenue-producing monopoly are excluded insofar as the prohibition would obstruct the performance of the tasks assigned to those bodies; (3) Agreements, decisions or concerted practices made in compliance with legal requirements imposed by U.K. law or under the E.C. Treaty or EEA Agreement which have direct effect in the U.K. (even where imposed by the laws of another Member State if they have direct effect in the U.K.); (4) Agreements excluded by order of the Secretary of State if necessary to avoid a conflict between a Chapter I prohibition and an international obligation of the U.K.; (5) Agreements excluded by order of the Secretary of State for exceptional and compelling reasons of public policy; (6) Coal and steel agreements in respect of which the Commission has exclusive jurisdiction under the ECSC Treaty; (7) Agreements relating to agricultural products (unless the Director gives a direction disapplying the exclusion).

in any event to disapply the exclusion for any agreement that would not qualify for unconditional individual exemption, and he may by written notice question the parties to the agreement in order to determine that issue.

Schedule 4: Professional rules

2-28   Schedule 4 confers exemption[41] on Professional rules, regulations, codes of practices and statements of principle of specified professions provided that notification is given to the Secretary of State for the profession concerned, accompanied by a copy of the relevant rules.

Section 50: Vertical agreements and land agreements

Section 50 contemplates that further exclusions (and exemptions) may be provided from time to time by order for vertical agreements and land agreements. Draft orders have been issued for consultation by the DTI (as at February 4, 1999). In the case of land agreements, the DTI expressed concern about restrictions in leases covering the use of land but it is expected that most land agreements will ultimately benefit from an exclusion order. Restrictions on business use such as ties in brewery leases may not be excluded and are already recognised to be of concern under Community law. (See Chapter 7, *Beer supply agreements* below for further detail.) Vertical agreements are discussed further in Chapter 7, *E.C. and United Kingdom Policy Towards Vertical Restraints* below.

THE SIMILARITIES: THE COMMON ASPECTS OF ARTICLE 85(1) AND CHAPTER I

2-29   The following textual similarities exist between Article 85(1) and Chapter I. Article 85(1) is to be regarded as the model for the Chapter I prohibition and, as such, E.C. law provides the best source for interpretation, subject of course to the principles set out in *Interpretation of the Act* above for interpreting the 1998 Act under section 60.

---

[41] The professional services that are eligible for notification (described rather haphazardly) are the following: (1) Legal—the services of barristers, advocates or solicitors; (2) Medical—the provision of medical or surgical advice or attendance and the performance of surgical operations; (3) Dental—any services falling within the practice of dentistry within the meaning of the Dentists Act 1984; (4) Ophthalmic—the testing of sight; (5) Veterinary—any services which constitute veterinary surgery within the meaning of the Veterinary Surgeons Act 1966; (6) Nursing—the services of nurses; (7) Midwifery—the services of midwives; (8) Physiotherapy—the services of physiotherapists; (9) Chiropody—the services of chiropodists; (10) Architectural—the services of architects; (11) Accounting and Auditing—the making or preparation of accounts or account records and the examination, verification and auditing of financial statements; (12) Insolvency—insolvency services within the meaning of section 428 of the Insolvency Act 1986; (13) Patent Agency—the services of registered patent agents (within the meaning of Part V of the Copyright, Designs and Patents Act 1988). The services of persons carrying on for gain in the U.K. the business of acting as agents or other representatives for obtaining European patents or for the purpose of conducting proceedings in relation to applications for or otherwise in connection with such patents before the European Patent Office or the comptroller and whose names appear on the European list (within the meaning of Part V of the Copyright, Designs and Patents Act 1988); (14) Parliamentary Agency—the services of parliamentary agents entered in the register in either House of Parliament as agents entitled to practise both in promoting and in opposing Bills; (15) Surveying—the services of surveyors of land, of quantity surveyors, of surveyors of buildings or other structures and of surveyors of ships; (16) Engineering—consultants in the field of (a) civil engineering, (b) mechanical, aeronautical, marine, electrical or electronic engineering, (c) mining, quarrying, soil analysis or other forms or mineralogy or geology, (d) agronomy, forestry, livestock rearing or ecology, (e) metallurgy, chemistry, biochemistry or physics, or (f) any other form of engineering or technology analogous to those mentioned in (a) to (e); (17) Educational—the provision of education or training; (18) Religious—the services of ministers of religion.

"Undertakings"

2-30   At least two undertakings are required to form an agreement or concerted practice.

Although the E.C. Treaty does not give a definition to the term "undertaking", the Commission has on one occasion at least attempted a definition. In the *Polypropylene* case,[42] the Commission defined "undertaking" as, "any entity engaged in commercial activities".[43]

If the activities are of an economic nature, the undertaking need not be profit-making. In *Re 1990 World Cup Package Tours*[44] the Italian Football Association and the organising committee were each held to be an undertaking by virtue of their economic activities, even though none of them was profit-making. Any recognised form of legal personality is likely to be treated as an undertaking if it undertakes any commercial activities, be it an individual (*Unitel*[45]), company, partnership, co-operative (*Co-operative Stremsel-en Kleurselfabriek v. Commission*[46]), club (*P&I Clubs*[47]) or association (*Re Italian Cast Glass*[48]). Member States are not undertakings. However, Member States themselves are regulated by Article 90(1) which provides:

> "In the case of public undertakings and undertakings to which Member States grant special or exclusive rights, Member States shall neither enact nor maintain in force any measure contrary to the rules contained in this Treaty, in particular to those rules provided for in Article 7 and Articles 85–94."

2-31   State-owned corporations (*Italy v. Sacchi*[49]), quasi-government entities (*Nungesser KG v. Commission*[50]) and independent entities with particular delegated state functions are likely to be undertakings if they undertake any commercial or economic function.

Undertakings within the same group of companies will, for the purposes of Article 85(1), be treated as a single undertaking, even though each group company is a separate legal personality (*Viho Europe BV v. Commission*[51]). The general principle was stated by the E.C.J in *Centrafarm BV and de Peijper v. Winthrop BV*.[52]

> "Article 85 does not apply to agreements or concerted practices between undertakings belonging in the same group in the form of parent company and subsidiary, if the undertakings form an economic unit within which the subsidiary does not have real autonomy in determining its line of conduct on the market and if the agreements or practices have the aim of establishing an internal distribution of tasks between the undertakings."[53]

If a parent exerts control over the conduct of its subsidiary, the parent will assume liability for the acts of its subsidiary. In *Dyestuffs*,[54] the E.C.J confirmed that where a subsidiary carries out instructions given by the parent:

> "the actions of the subsidiaries may . . . be attributed to the parent company."[55]

---

[42] Commission 86/398 [1986] O.J. L230/1; [1988] 4 C.M.L.R. 347.
[43] *ibid.*, para. 99.
[44] Commission Dec. 92/521 [1992] O.J. L326/31.
[45] Commission Dec. 78/516 [1978] O.J. L157/39; [1978] 3 C.M.L.R. 306.
[46] Case 61/80 *Co-operative Stremsel-en Kleurselfabriek v. Commission* [1981] E.C.R. 851; [1982] 1 C.M.L.R. 240.
[47] Commission Dec. 85/615 [1985] O.J. L376/2.
[48] Commission Dec. 80/1334 [1980] O.J. L383/19.
[49] Case 155/73 *Italy v. Sacchi* [1974] E.C.R. 409; [1974] 2 C.M.L.R. 177.
[50] Case 258/78 *Nungesser KG v. Commission* [1982] E.C.R. 2015; [1983] 1 C.M.L.R. 278.
[51] Case C–73/95P *Viho Europe BV v. Commission* [1996] E.C.R. I-5457; [1997] 4 C.M.L.R. 419.
[52] Case 16/74 *Centrafarm BV and de Peijper v. Winthrop BV* [1974] E.C.R. 1183; [1974] 2 C.M.L.R. 177.
[53] *ibid.*, para. 32.
[54] Case 48/69 & 51–57/69 *ICI v. Commission* [1972] E.C.R. 619; [1972] C.M.L.R. 557.
[55] *ibid.*, para. 135.

2-32   Article 85(1) only applies to agreements and practices between undertakings. If the nexus between parent and subsidiary is so close that the subsidiary has no "real autonomy in determining its course of action in the market",[56] then Article 85(1) does not apply to agreements made between them, as the two entities are not treated as separate undertakings.

In the case of joint ventures, a parent company's liability for its subsidiary is well illustrated by the *Peroxygen* case[57].

"For the purpose of the present proceedings the Commission does not consider the Interox [subsidiary] grouping as an undertaking possessing an identity sufficiently distinct from that of its two parent companies so as to absolve Solvay and Laporte themselves (as opposed to Interox) from liability under E.C. competition rules. The Interox operation is simply the framework in which the activities of Solvay and Laporte in the peroxygen sector are co-ordinated and profits shared and all major policy decisions are taken by the parent companies. The Interox companies do not determine their market behaviour autonomously but in essentials follow directives issued by the parent companies."[58]

2-33   Particular care must be taken by the purchaser of a business or company which has undertaken infringing activities. The purchaser will need to ensure that these activities are not attributed to the purchaser and to some extent protection will be given in the form of typical purchase agreement warranties, intended to verify the absence of infringement. The view of the E.C.J, expressed in *CRAM v. Commission*[59] is that:

"a change in the legal form and name of an undertaking does not create a new undertaking free of liability for the anti-competitive behaviour of its predecessor when, from an economic point of view, the two are identical."

If there is continuity of any infringement, both the vendor and purchaser will be liable for infringement (if the appropriate level of control over the activities of the entity exists). The liability of the purchaser is likely to be aggravated if infringing activities are disclosed by the vendor against competition warranties and these are not corrected by the purchaser.

Similarly, in the case of pure agency agreements, both principal and agent are treated as the same entity for the purposes of Article 85(1) although the position under United Kingdom law is less certain. The Commission's Notice on exclusive dealing contracts with commercial agents 1962[60] indicates that Article 85(1) will not apply to the appointment of a commercial agent where the agent accepts no financial risks, as the agent may then be regarded as the same economic entity as the principal or an auxiliary of the principal, rather than independent. However, independence will be taken to exist in the following circumstances. First, if the agent has to maintain an after sales service or carry stocks at its own risk and expense. Secondly, where the agent carries on its own independent business. In *Pittsburgh Corning Europe*[61], the Commission decided that because the agent manufactured its own products and provided services for companies other than its principal, it was not economically dependent on its principal in spite of the name

---

[56] Case C–73/95P [1995] E.C.R. II-17 at para. 47.
[57] Commission Dec. 85/74 [1985] O.J. L35/1; [1985] 1 C.M.L.R. 481.
[58] *ibid.*, para. 49.
[59] Cases 29 & 30/83 *Compagnie Royale Asturienne des Mines SA and Rheinzink GmbH v. Commission* [1984] E.C.R. 1679; [1985] 1 C.M.L.R. 688
[60] Commission Notice of December 24, 1962 on exclusive dealing contracts with commercial agents [1962] J.O. 139/2921.
[61] Commission Dec. 72/403 [1972] O.J. L272/35.

"agency" given to the appointment. For further detail concerning agency appointments see Chapter 8 *Commercial Agents* below.

"Agreements, decisions by associations of undertakings and concerted practices"

2-34 Needless to say, for the purposes of Article 85(1) and Chapter I, agreements may take virtually any form. Agreements may therefore be non-binding (*Franco-Japanese Ballbearings*[62]), they may be recorded roughly, merely in the form a single page "Red Note" (*Peroxygen*) or unrecorded (*ACF Chemiefarma NV v. Commission*[63]). Consensus will suffice (*Polypropylene*[64]) or even a broad unwritten understanding (*Panasonic*[65]). The term "agreement" is intended to be extremely wide and the existence of agreement is readily inferred.

In the case of associations of undertakings, the reference to decisions rather than agreements entitles a finding of infringement to be made without proof of an agreement or concerted practice between the members. Even a trade association recommendation may have the same effect as a decision if members are sufficiently influenced to comply with the recommendation (*IAZ International Belgium NV v. Commission*[66]).

2-35 Once an agreement has been exposed, it is difficult for parties to maintain that the parties' independent behaviour would have been no different from that prescribed by the agreement. In *Peroxygen*[67], the parties claimed that the market structure itself (rather than the agreement) was responsible for the conduct of the parties, even though the parties had agreed to uphold that conduct in a Red note. The Commission readily concluded that the existence of the agreement would produce an effect different from the effect of free competition.

The inclusion within Article 85(1) and section 2 of the 1998 Act of concerted practices gives competition authorities room to infer co-ordination and reduces the evidential burden of proving actual agreement. Nevertheless, an inference must overcome perfectly innocuous, rational explanations for parallel behaviour that might have the appearance of collusion or concertation. In *Dyestuff's*[68], a concerted practice was defined as,

"a form of co-ordination between undertakings which, without having reached the stage where an agreement properly so called has been concluded, knowingly substitutes practical co-operation between them for the risks of competition."[69]

2-36 Conscious parallelism is a constant risk to certain businesses. Parallel conduct may on its own provide evidence of concertation and businesses must be careful to ensure that they are able to resist the suggestion of collusion. In *Woodpulp*[70], although there was no evidence of agreement, close parallel pricing over six years strongly suggested a concerted practice. This was supported by proof of information exchanges and the fact that the highly competitive structure of the market itself rendered it unlikely that price uniformity could occur without a concerted practice to fix prices. Nevertheless, the E.C.J overruled the Commission's findings of a concerted practice. The case serves as a reminder that the burden of proof still rests on the Commission and although certain inferences

---

[62] Commission Dec. 74/634 [1974] O.J. L343/19.
[63] Case 41/69 *ACF Chemiefarma NV v. Commission* [1970] E.C.R. 661.
[64] Commission Dec. 86/398 [1986] O.J. L230/1.
[65] Commission Dec. 82/853 [1982] O.J. L354/28.
[66] Case 96/82 *IAZ International Belgium NV v. Commission* [1983] E.C.R. 3369; [1984] 3 C.M.L.R. 276.
[67] Commission Dec. 85/74 [1985] O.J. 135/1; 1 C.M.L.R. 481.
[68] Cases 48/69 & 51–57/69 [1972] E.C.R. 619; [1972] C.M.L.R. 557.
[69] *ibid.*, para. 64.
[70] Commission Dec. 85/202 [1985] O.J. L85/1; [1985] 3 C.M.L.R. 474.

might be drawn from parallel conduct, if the conduct goes against expectations given the conditions of the market, those inferences may be overcome by objective explanations.

Evidence of parallel conduct will need to be "sufficiently precise and coherent . . . to justify the view that the parallel behaviour . . . was the result of concerted action" (*CRAM SA v. Commission*[71]). Examples of such objective reasons were given by Darman A.G. in *Woodpulp*:

> "Parallel conduct is not necessarily the result of prior concertation. It can be explained or even dictated by the very structure of certain markets . . . The first situation involves a concentrated oligopoly, in which undertakings are independent: each undertaking must take account in its decisions of the conduct of its rivals. Alignment on each other's conduct constitutes a rational response, independently of any concertation . . . 'Price leadership' constitutes the second situation: undertakings align themselves on a 'price leader' on account of the latter's power on the market. Mention may also be made of the spontaneous alignment on a price leader which acts as a barometer, with its decisions reflecting changes in market conditions for reasons linked, for instance to its previous knowledge of that market."[72]

2-37   Price leadership of this kind was precisely the defence used by those accused of concertation in *Dyestuffs* to explain their close parallelism. The E.C.J upheld the Commission's finding of infringement based on simultaneous identical price movement across various products in different markets. Additional evidence took the form of frequent industry meetings and similarly worded instructions issued by each company to subsidiaries when implementing the price changes. Expectations, given conditions in the market, were inconsistent with the pricing pattern.

The distinction between concertation and unilateral action ceases to be obvious in the case where the reaction of competitors to any particular "unilateral" action is predicted. In *Dyestuff's*, the E.C.J suggested that:

> "It is enough that [they] let each other know beforehand what attitude they intend to adopt, so that each of them could regulate his conduct, safe in the knowledge that his competitors would act in a similar fashion."[73]

In *Soda Ash/Solvay*[74] the Commission commented that:

> "An infringement of Article 85 may well exist where the parties have not even spelled out an agreement in terms but each infers commitment from the other on the basis of conduct."[75]

"May affect trade"

2-38   It appears from the text of both Article 85(1) and Chapter I that a possible effect on trade is all that is required and not an inevitable effect. However a remote possibility will not suffice. In *Consten and Grundig v. Commission*,[76] the E.C.J stated:

---

[71] Joined cases 29 & 30/83 *CRAM SA v. Commission* [1984] E.C.R. 1679; [1985] 1 C.M.L.R. 688 at para. 20.
[72] [1985] O.J. L85/1; [1985] 3 C.M.L.R. 474 at para. 177.
[73] Cases 48/69 & 51–57/69 [1972] E.C.R. 619; [1972] C.M.L.R. 557 at 639.
[74] [1991] O.J. L152/1.
[75] *ibid.*, para. 59.
[76] Cases 56 & 58/64 *Consten and Grundig v. Commission* [1966] E.C.R. 299; [1966] C.M.L.R. 418.

"it must be possible to foresee with a sufficient degree of probability on the basis of a set of objective factors of law or of fact that the agreement may have an influence, direct or indirect, actual or potential, on the pattern of trade."

In *Re Vacuum Interrupters Limited*[77], the test was articulated in terms of "a reasonable assumption".

An effect on trade occurs if the pattern of trade is altered whether by an increase in trade, a decrease in trade, a geographical diversion of trade, or a change in direction of trade. "Trade" refers to any commercial activities.

In *Javico International, Javico AG and Yves Saint Laurent Parfums SA*[77a], the ECJ confirmed that an effect on trade between Member States could result from an export ban in an agreement appointing a distributor for a territory outside the Community (in that case, Russia) preventing importation of products into the Community. This is only likely to be the case where sufficiently large price differentials exist between the territory of the agreement and the Community to make exports profitable.

"Object or effect the prevention, restriction or distortion of competition"

2-39   As an alternative to demonstrating that an agreement "may affect trade", reliance may instead be placed on its "object" without proving any effect. Equally, if an agreement has terminated, it may be possible to look instead to its surviving effect (*Soda Ash-Solvay*).[78]

The object and effect of an agreement are discerned from the nature of the agreement, the products or services covered by it, the market position of the parties to it, the activities undertaken by them, the economic context of the agreement, and the position of competitors and consumers.

"Directly or indirectly fix purchase or selling prices or any other trading conditions"

2-40   This encompasses a number of price-related practices.

Price-fixing

2-41   Price-fixing is one of the most flagrant infringements. Although considered throughout the first half of this century to be an acceptable form of stabilising the economy, it is now unacceptable. Horizontal price-fixing occurs primarily when agreement is reached between suppliers concerning the prices they will charge for goods or services, and less commonly between buyers concerning the prices at which they will purchase. Vertical price-fixing takes the form of agreement between a supplier and distributor on the resale price to be charged by the distributor. The term "price" for these purposes also includes any aspect of discount, allowance, rebate or credit terms offered to a customer.

The restrictive "object or effect" of price-fixing may be presumed. An appreciable effect on inter-state trade or on competition still theoretically needs to be demonstrated to amount to infringement. However, the Commission's Notice on agreements of minor importance[79] indicates that even if the market share of the parties is below the thresholds

[77] Commission Dec. 77/160 [1977] O.J. L48/32; [1977] 1 C.M.L.R. D67.
[77a] Case C–306/96 Judgment of the Court, April 28, 1998.
[78] Commission Dec. 91/299 [1991] O.J. L152/21.
[79] Commission Notice on agreements of minor importance which do not fall within the meaning of Art. 85(1) of the Treaty establishing the European Community [1997] O.J. C 372/04.

set out in the Notice for determining whether an agreement is of minor importance, Article 85(1) cannot be ruled out in the case of price-fixing agreements. The OFT's guides entitled "The Chapter I Prohibition" and "The Major Provisions" indicate that horizontal and vertical price-fixing arrangements (as well as horizontal market-sharing) arrangements cannot automatically be assumed to be *de minimis* even if they qualify as a matter of market share criteria.

2-42   Price-fixing agreements in a single Member State that do not relate to imports or exports do not usually fall within Article 85(1). However, they will be caught if they restrict competition within the Community because, for example, a national market becomes difficult to penetrate, as in *MELDOC*[80], or export patterns are affected, as in *Italian Cast Glass*[81]. Whether such an agreement affects inter-State trade is viewed on a case by case basis.

Assuming that Article 85(1) does apply, exemption is not generally available for agreements that fix selling prices. In the Tenth Report on Competition Policy, the Commission described price fixing as:

"the category of manifest infringement under Article 85(1) which it is almost impossible to exempt under Article 85(3) because of the total lack of benefit to the consumer."[82]

However, some service industries such as banking have been allowed to escape some of the rigours of Article 85 due to the special characteristics of the industry. For example in the case of *Uniform Eurocheques*[83], the Commission was prepared to exempt under Article 85(3) an agreement to maintain uniform commission charges among all the banks operating the Eurocheque system. In addition, in *Nuovo CEGAM*[84], the Commission granted exemption to an agreement between Italian engineering insurers on the basic premiums to be charged.

Price recommendations

2-43   In *Stainless Steel Producers*[85], six producers were fined 27.3 million ECUs in aggregate. In response to increases in the prices for raw materials used in stainless steel products, producers agreed to adopt a system of surcharges as part of a model for calculating prices. One participant communicated its intended surcharge to the others who followed it. This departed from previously adopted calculation methods intended to reflect fluctuations of component alloy prices in final product prices. Instead it amounted to price-fixing where a specific price recommendation was agreed between competitors.

Trade associations are particularly at risk of the accusation of price-fixing where they recommend prices. The objection is that recommendations lead to "uniform and co-ordinated conduct" (*Vereeniging van Cemanthandelaren*[86]) or, at a minimum, give competitors visibility of each other's pricing policy.[87] In *Stichting Certificatie Kraanverhuubedrijf*[88], the criteria for setting rates for crane hire, distributed by an association to its members, detailing cost calculations and rates, infringed Article 85(1). Trade associations often

---

[80] Commission Dec. 86/596 [1986] O.J. L348/50; [1989] 4 C.M.L.R. 853.
[81] Commission Dec. 80/1334 [1980] O.J. L383/19; [1982] 2 C.M.L.R. 61.
[82] Point 115.
[83] Commission Dec. 85/77 [1985] O.J. L35/43, [1985] 3 C.M.L.R. 434.
[84] Commission Dec. 84/191 [1984 O.J. L99/29, [1984] 2 C.M.L.R. 484.
[85] Not yet reported.
[86] Commission Dec. 72/22 *Vereeniging Van Cementhandelaren* [1972] O.J. L13/34; [1973] C.M.L.R. D16.
[87] Commission Dec. 72/22 [1972] O.J. L13/34; [1973] C.M.L.R. D16.
[88] Commission Dec. 95/551 [1995] O.J. L312.

protest that price-fixing agreements are not binding between the parties. In reality, price-fixing agreements rarely are enforced: the diverse interests of producers operating at different levels of efficiency drive each of them towards a different ideal price, and the resulting agreed price is frequently a compromise unsatisfactory to all of them. Departures from the agreed price are then more frequent but it is no defence that parties to the collusion have broken its terms. Article 85(1) will be infringed even if the agreement does not result in strict obligations (*TEKO*[89]).

Minimum prices

2-44   Minimum prices are clearly harmful since they rule out any price competition at all between the parties below the agreed level. In *Scottish Salmon Board*,[90] the Commission condemned an agreement to fix minimum prices between representatives of salmon producers. Likewise, producers in the *Polypropylene* case[91] were fined heavily for imposing a price floor.

Maximum prices

2-45   Less obvious, however, is the potential harm of maximum prices. There might be a tendency for parties which have agreed a maximum price to push the price to the ceiling. More commonly, the mischief of maximum prices is that they are aimed at protecting the domestic markets of suppliers. If a maximum price is set at the correct level, only the domestic supplier can achieve that price profitably, given lower transport costs. Overseas or more distant suppliers are therefore not able to compete (*IFTRA Glass Containers*[92]).

Price leadership

2-46   Genuine price-leadership of the kind described above in *Woodpulp* is permissible. However, an agreement appointing one party as the price leader for any given customer is not. In *Polypropylene*, for each customer account, one supplier was designated the "account leader". Suppliers with whom that customer had frequent dealings were merely "contenders" and other suppliers who were approached by the customers agreed to quote high prices. Another example of infringement might be the designation of the local supplier in any territory as price leader if those exporting to that territory agree not to undercut the prices of the local supplier.

Bid-rigging was the subject of fines of 92.21 million ECUs in total imposed on pipe suppliers in *District Heating Systems*.[93] For each contract tender, one participant was nominated to win the contract and the others would support it by offering higher bids. The fines were aggravated by the fact that the practices continued for nine months after the Commission investigation had begun. Also, one competitor, Powerpipe, was successfully eliminated from the market after it refused to join the bid-rigging.

2-47   Price co-ordination also resulted in fines of between 1.8 million and 39.6 million ECUs on the sugar producers, British Sugar and Tate & Lyle, and sugar merchants, Napier Brown and James Budgett,[94] apparently taking the form of "mutual certainty" over pricing and "collaborative strategy" falling short of formal price-fixing.

---

[89] Commission Dec. 90/22 [1988] O.J. L13/34; [1990] 4 C.M.L R. 957.
[90] Commission Dec. 92/444 [1992] O.J. L246/37.
[91] Commission Dec. 86/398 [1986] L230/1; [1988] 4 C.M.L.R. 3467.
[92] Commission Dec. 74/292 [1974] O.J. L160/1; [1974] 2 C.M.L.R. D50.
[93] Commission Press Release IP/917/98 October 21, 1998.
[94] Commission Press Release IP/898/98 October 14, 1998.

Other price uniformity

2-48   In an agreement between manufacturers of glass containers,[95] the Commission condemned an agreement which achieved uniformity in the "delivered price" charged by participants, regardless of the actual transport costs incurred, since this deprived local suppliers of any competitive advantage through cheaper transport costs.

Wider definitions of "Price"

2-49   Agreements that expressly fix prices are the most visible form of infringement and have been described as infringement of the "classic type".[96] Article 85 (1) covers not only agreements that fix prices in the narrow sense but also any agreement which may directly or indirectly suppress price competition by fixing discounts (*Vimtoltu*),[97] margins or credit terms (*Van Landwyck v. Commission*[98]).

Agreements which indirectly affect price

2-50   Other agreements which may indirectly restrict price competition include agreements setting target prices even where there is no evidence of an effect on the selling price, (*ICI v. Commission*[99]), and agreements not to submit quotations without prior consultation between the parties (*Cast Iron and Steel Rolls*[1]). An agreement not to depart from published list prices was found to infringe Article 85(1), not least because the parties were able to predict pricing by competitors with accuracy (*IFTRA Rules for Producers of Virgin Aluminium*[2]). Similarly with agreements not to make public any deviation from published prices or prohibiting the announcements of rebates (*Papiers Peints v. Commission*).[3]

Information agreements

2-51   The exchange of information between competitors is a sensitive issue. The risk to those that do this is the inference of price-fixing. The competition authorities will not usually object to the dissemination of purely statistical information, as confirmed by the Commission in *Vegetable Parchment*[4] and in the Seventh Report on Competition Policy 1977. In general, information exchanged between competitors should not be secret. The type of secret information of concern was identified by the Commission in *IFTRA Glass Containers*[5]:

> "It is contrary to the provisions of Article 85(1) . . . for a producer to communicate to his competitors the essential elements of his pricing policy, such as price lists, the discounts and terms of trade he applies, the rate and dates of any change to them and the special exceptions he grants to specific customers".

In short, the Commission considers that agreements, where competitors freely exchange price information will inevitably give rise to a convergence of prices and constitute infringement.

---

[95] *IFTRA Glass Containers* Commission Dec. 74/292 [1974] O.J. L160/1; [1974] 2 C.M.L.R. D50.
[96] Twelfth Report on Competition Policy (for 1982, point 62).
[97] Commission Dec. 83/361 [1983] O.J. L200/44.
[98] Case 209/78 *Van Landwyck v. Commission* [1980] E.C.R. 3125; [1981] C.M.L.R. 134, Rebates (Case 240/82 *SSI v. The Commission*) [1985] E.C.R. 3831; [1987] 3 C.M.L.R. 661.
[99] Case T–13/89 *ICI v. Commission* [1992] E.C.R. II-1021.
[1] Commission Dec. 83/546 [1983] O.J. L317/1; [1984] 1 C.M.L.R. 694.
[2] Commission Dec. 75/497 [1975] O.J. L228/3.
[3] Case 73/74 *Papiers Peints v. Commission* [1975] E.C.R. 1491; [1976] 1 C.M.L.R. 589.
[4] Commission Dec. 78/252 [1978] O.J.L70/54.
[5] Commission Dec. 74/292 [1974] O.J. L160/1; [1975] 2 C.M.L.R. D20.

The same principles apply at every level of trade. Information exchange between distributors was held to be an infringement by the Commission in *Hasselblad*,[6] where distributors exchanged information on prices and discounts to discourage parallel imports. However, a supplier is entitled to ask a distributor for price information concerning that distributor's sales, provided the supplier does not distribute the information to other distributors.

"Limit or control production, markets, technical development or investment"

Agreements to limit or control production or markets

2-52   If competitors between themselves agree to reduce output, demand is likely to increase and enable prices to rise. Restrictions on production often go hand in hand with information exchanges, price-fixing and market-sharing in order to allocate the resulting benefits between the participants. The cases of *Steel Beams*,[7] *Carton Board*[8] and *Cement*[9] are examples of agreements to limit production, combined with price-fixing and market sharing.

The Commission has acknowledged that some agreements which involve restrictions on production may be beneficial or indeed a necessity. For example, where a declining industry is faced with crippling over-capacity, the Commission may exempt an agreement to limit production. These agreements, often described as crisis cartels, may qualify for exemption if the restrictive effect of short term production limits is outweighed by the long-term benefits of a more healthy industry when it returns to dynamic competition. However, general restrictions on production without any compensating benefits will not be exempt. The agreement to limit production and the application for exemption must be made in response to the requirements of each situation. The Commission put it as follows in *Stichting Baksteen*:[10]

> "It is the primary task of individual firms to identify the moment at which their surplus capacities become untenable and take the necessary steps to reduce them".[11]

2-53   Markets may be limited in other ways. *Volkswagen*[12] were found to have infringed Article 85(1) by hindering parallel imports into Germany and Austria from Italy. Volkswagen claimed their actions were intended only to prevent active (rather than passive) sales outside allocated territories and to prevent sales to unauthorised dealers. However the evidence did not support Volkswagen's defence. If those were Volkswagen's aims, its actions were not apparently sufficiently well-targeted and instructions to dealers not sufficiently well-defined. A number of factors evidenced infringement: Volkswagen offered bonus payments conditional on sales within the dealer's territory (sales outside were subject to a limit); supplies to Italian dealers were unduly limited to stifle the export market from Italy; better payment terms were available to dealers on sales of cars registered in the dealer's territory; customers were required to give undertakings not to resell for three months or until 3000 km had been clocked; twelve dealerships had been terminated without reason where dealers exported from Italy; and finally, exports were monitored. It has been described by one Commission official[13] as "a systematic, covert

---

[6] Commission Dec. 82/367 [1982] O.J. L161/18; [1982] 2 C.M.L.R. 233.

[7] Commission Dec. 94/215 [1994] O.J. L116/1; [1994] 5 C.M.L.R. 353

[8] Commission Dec. 94/601 [1994] O.J. L243/1.

[9] Commission Dec. 94/815 [1994] O.J. L343/1.

[10] Commission Dec. 94/296 [1994] O.J. L131/5.

[11] Commission Dec. 94/296 [1994] O.J. L131/15.

[12] Commission Dec. 98/208 [1998] O.J. L124.

[13] Mr Van Miert.

operation, endorsed by the management of the company." The fine was increased as a result of the sustained duration of the infringement, the fact that Volkswagen had not heeded warnings in 1995 by the Commission and because dealers suffered greatly. The fine totalled 102 million ECUs.

Reciprocal assistance agreements

2-54   The Commission's treatment of reciprocal assistance agreements demonstrates the need for co-operation between competitors only when and for so long as it is essential. In *Compagnie Royale Asturienne Des Mines SA and Rheinzink GmbH (CRAM)* v *Commission*,[14] the E.C.J held that it was an infringement of Article 85(1) for competitors to supply products to each other or make supplies available to each other "in the event of serious technical or other disruption resulting in significant loss · of production". Deliveries between producers are obviously a common occurrence. However, in this case, the agreement did not specifically limit assistance to specific emergency situations, only for so long as they lasted, and the E.C.J held that it was an infringement. In the Commission's view, one of the dangers of reciprocal assistance between competitors (as with all agreements that limit output) is the possibility that, with reduced output, demand will increase and prices rise.

Agreements to set technical development standards

2-55   Research and development agreements are exempt if they meet the requirements of Regulation 418/85[15] because they enable products to be developed by two parties jointly which would be beyond the reach of either of them acting independently of the co-operation. The same is also true of exclusive patent and know-how licences under the Regulation 240/96.[16] Those particular Regulations indicate the limits to technical co-operation before Article 85(1) is infringed, and if Article 85(1) is infringed, whether the agreement is likely to be exempt. In its Notice on co-operation agreements,[17] the Commission indicated that it is generally supportive of joint research and development projects involving straightforward exchanges of technical information because these are thought to result in the promotion of cross-border co-operation particularly between small firms.

2-56   However, agreements must not limit technical development. In *Video Cassette Recorders*,[18] German manufacturers of video recorders agreed to converge on the technical standards set by Philips since, at that stage, Philips was the market leader in that type of equipment. The advantages of doing so would be increased compatibility of video recorders and accessories that meet the standard. However, the disadvantages would be that parties would adhere to that system and no other competing system and accordingly the Commission refused exemption under Article 85(3).

In the case of *IAZ v. Commission*,[19] a Belgian Association of washing machine manufacturers, in agreement with Belgian manufacturers and sole importers, set the technical standard for sales of washing machines in Belgium. The effect was to prevent imports and maintain artificial partitioning of the Belgian market, resulting in a significant effect on competition.

---

[14] Joined cases 29 & 30/83 *Compagnie Royale Asturienne Des Mines SA and Rheinzink GmbH (CRAM) v. Commission* [1984] E.C.R. 1679; [1985] 1 C.M.L.R. 688.
[15] Reg. 418/89 on the application of Art. 85(3) of the Treaty to certain categories of research and development agreements [1985] O.J. L53/5, see further in Chap. 9.
[16] Reg. 240/96 on the application of Art. 85(3) of the Treaty to certain categories of technology transfer agreements [1996] O.J. L31/2.
[17] Commission Notice on co-operation agreements between enterprises [1968] O.J. C75/3.
[18] Commission Dec. 78/156 [1978] O.J. L47/47; [1978] 2 C.M.L.R. 160.
[19] Case 96/82 [1983] E.C.R. 3369; [1984] 3 C.M.L.R. 276.

Agreements to limit investment

2-57   An agreement to limit investment might, for example, take the form of an agreement to limit future production such as in *Zinc Producer Group*,[20] where the exchange of plans relating to proposed investment and production cuts was held to be an infringement of Article 85(1). It may also take the form of agreement not to invest in research and development or to limit expenditure in particular areas of research.

"Share markets or sources of supply"

2-58   Geographical market-sharing is illustrated most clearly by the case of *Peroxygen Products*,[21] where the three largest producers of bulk peroxygen products in Europe operated a "home market" rule in which each producer agreed to limit sales to its traditional home market. Agreements which divide territories obviously prevent the emergence of competition in the allocated territory from other parties to the agreement and in turn lead to risks of complacency, over-pricing and stagnation in development that follow from cushioning against competition. The effect of market sharing is also to restrict the range of different sources of supply available to purchasers.

The allocation between the parties to an agreement of customers for supply by each of them (rather than the allocation of geographical territory for each to supply) is also an infringement. For example, in *BP Kemi/DDSF*[22] the parties shared out between themselves the customers which they would supply.

"Apply dissimilar conditions to equivalent transactions with other trading parties thereby placing them at a competitive disadvantage"

2-59   Price discrimination is the practice of unjustified price differentiation between customers. Customers should be treated alike and, ideally prices should be based on the true cost of supply. The mischief of price discrimination lies in the harm done to one customer when differentiated from others. Discounts may quite legitimately be given to one customer but not another based on quantities supplied where objectively justified by the corresponding reduced cost of supply. Similarly, payment terms may be extended to one customer but not another depending on their credit rating. In all cases, the different treatment given to customers must be objectively justified.

"Make the conclusion of contracts subje.c.t to acceptance by the other parties of supplementary obligations which, by their nature, according to commercial usage, have no connection with the subject of [such] contract"

2-60   "Tie-in" clauses are not uncommon in the software industry but are prohibited. For example, if software is supplied on condition that maintenance services are to be provided by the supplier, this will constitute a tie-in. If the software supplier is the only source of maintenance services, there will in practice be no need to impose the tie-in. Issues may also arise under Article 86 if the undertaking is dominant, as an unjustified tie-in is an abuse of dominant position (see Chapter 4 below).

There have been several recent high profile examples of tying practices in the software industry but they have either been settled with the Commission or are the subject of U.S. proceedings. For example *Digital*[23] settled the Commission proceedings begun under Regulation 17. The Commission alleged that hardware support was tied to software

---

[20] Commission Dec. 84/405 [1984] O.J. L220/27; [1985] 2 C.M.L.R. 108.
[21] Commission Dec. 85/74 [1985] O.J. L35/1; [1985] 1 C.M.L.R. 481.
[22] Commission Dec. 79/34 [1979] O.J. L286/32.
[23] See XXVII Report on Competition Policy (1997).

support in the sense that, though both were available separately, they were offered together as a single package at a price that was considerably less than the price for the constituents taken separately. Although there does not appear to have been any contractual or other coercion, customers were believed by the Commission to be "tied" by the attractiveness of the package to take hardware and software maintenance bundled together. Accordingly, it was considered that customers would be discouraged from seeking alternative sources for each alone.

2-61   Another example is the long-running *Microsoft* case. The first phase, which resulted in an undertaking from Microsoft in 1994, concerned Microsoft's practice of requiring OEM suppliers of Microsoft P.C.'s to pay a royalty for Microsoft's operating system software for each P.C. made, whether or not that software was included. If substitute operating system software of a third party was used instead, the OEM nevertheless had to pay the licence fee to Microsoft. This, to all intents and purposes, was regarded as a tie of the Microsoft operating system software to the P.C.'s since a double royalty was payable even if third party software was substituted. Microsoft settled the U.S. action by giving an undertaking not to enter into:

> "any Licence Agreement in which the terms of that agreement are expressly or impliedly conditional upon . . . the licensing of . . . any other product . . . (provided, however, that this provision in and of itself shall not be construed to prohibit Microsoft from developing integrated products)."[24]

The undertaking was the subject of the second phase, in which the U.S. Department of Justice claimed that the undertaking had been breached by Microsoft's marketing of the Internet Explorer browser. Microsoft had bundled its Windows 95 operating system with Internet Explorer and claimed this to be an integrated product within the terms permitted by the undertaking. The U.S. Department of Justice claim the combination of the browser software to Windows 95 and Windows 98 to be illegal tie-ins. The case continues in the U.S.

2-62   For such cases to succeed under Article 86, dominance must be found in the market of the tying product (not necessarily the tied product). Even in the case of Article 85(1), the effect of the tie-in must be appreciable (usually measured by the market shares of the parties and the foreclosing effect of the tie to prevent other suppliers competing). In both Articles 86 and 85(1), the ties must "by their nature or according to commercial usage, have no connection with the subject of such contracts".[25] In general, the Commission is not receptive to claims that tie-ins should be justified on grounds of health and safety as a means of guaranteeing product safety, since this is a matter of national legislation (*Hilti AG v. Commission*[26]) or that the tie-in is an appropriate mechanism for recouping investment in the tying product (*Vaessen/Moris*[27]).

Requirements to stock complete ranges of goods in exclusive distribution or exclusive purchasing agreements are generally permitted, even though they may fall within the description of supplementary obligations. In the exclusive distribution block exemption Regulation 1983/83,[28] and the exclusive purchasing block exemption Regulation 1984/83,[29] the Commission white-lists in each case an obligation on the reseller or purchaser to purchase complete ranges of goods. In those agreements an obligation to stock the full range of products is therefore permitted.[30]

---

[24] *United States v. Microsoft Corp* (DDC Civil Action No 94–1564), Final Judgment Section IV(E).
[25] Art. 86(d) and Art. 85(1)(e).
[26] Case T–30/39 *Hilti AG v. Commission* [1992] 4 C.M.L.R. 16.
[27] Commission Dec. 79/86 [1979] O.J. L19/32; [1979] 1 C.M.L.R. 511.
[28] Reg. 1983/83 [1982] O.J. L173/1. See Chap. 7 below.
[29] Reg. 1984/83 [1983] O.J. L173/5. See Chap. 7 below.
[30] Provided that the agreement complies with the block exemption Reg. in all other respects.

SUMMARY

2-63 The court's approach to examination of all competition restrictions was clarified in *Sociéte Technique Miniere v. Maschinenbau Ulm GmbH*.[31] A rule of reason should be adopted, requiring consideration of the economic context in which the agreement is to operate, in particular, the relevant market to see the effect on competition of particular restrictions. However certain clauses, such as export bans, will never be acceptable and certain agreements will only rarely be acceptable, such as price-fixing and market-sharing agreements. The procedure for assessing the economic context of an agreement, in particular defining the relevant market and calculating market share, is discussed further in Chapter 4 below.

---

[31] Case 56/65 *Sociéte Technique Miniere v. Maschinenbau Ulm GmbH* [1966] E.C.R. 235; [1966] C.M.L.R. 357.

CHAPTER 3

Infringement by Abuse Article 86 and Chapter II Prohibitions

THE AIMS: THE PURPOSE OF THE PROHIBITIONS IN ARTICLE 86 AND CHAPTER II

Introduction

3-01   The aim of both the Article 86 and Chapter II prohibitions, in a nutshell, is to prevent any abuse on the part of an undertaking in a dominant position. These prohibitions therefore differ from the Article 85(1) and Chapter I prohibitions in three respects.

First, no agreement or collusion is required for an abuse of dominant position. The abuse may constitute action that is entirely unilateral. Secondly, Article 86 and Chapter II only apply to undertakings that are dominant. Thirdly, no exemption is available for any infringement of Article 86. Certain practices are excluded from the Chapter II prohibition (see *Exclusions from Chapter II (no Exclusions from Article 86,*below)). There are no exclusions from Article 86.

3-02   Both measures, however, have the common aim of regulating the exercise of market power in the hands of a single entity (or, in the case of joint dominance, more than one entity). The threshold of market power for these purposes is reached, and an undertaking is taken to be dominant, when it can behave to an appreciable extent independently of its competitors and customers, and ultimately of consumers. Dominance *per se* is not harmful. It is only when unfair advantage is taken of the position of dominance by means of one or more of the practices listed in Article 86 or Chapter II, or some other recognised form of abuse, that Article 86 and Chapter II will operate to regulate that conduct.

Article 86

3-03   Article 86 has proved to be an extremely effective measure for controlling abusive conduct. The effectiveness of Article 86 is in marked contrast to equivalent pre-1998 United Kingdom measures in the form of the Fair Trading Act 1973 and the Competition Act 1980, which in the past imposed theoretical control over certain abuses of dominant position. However, those measures provided inadequate remedies for victims of abuse and inadequate mechanisms for enforcement.

Article 86, like Article 85(1), has at its heart the E.C. Treaty aims of market integration and accordingly focuses on abuses by undertakings within the common market (or a substantial part of it) insofar as those abuses may affect trade between Member States. The full text reads as follows:

> "86   Any abuse by one or more undertakings of a dominant position within the common market or in a substantial part of it shall be prohibited as incompatible with the common market insofar as it may affect trade between Member States. Such abuse may, in particular, consist in:

(a) directly or indirectly imposing unfair purchase or selling prices or unfair trading conditions;

(b) limiting production, markets or technical development to the prejudice of consumers;

(c) applying dissimilar conditions to equivalent transactions with other trading parties, thereby placing them at a competitive disadvantage;

(d) making the conclusion of contracts subject to acceptance by the other parties of supplementary obligations which, by their nature or according to commercial usage, have no connection with the subject of such contracts."

3-04   Infringement of Article 86 is not dependent upon agreement or collusion and so it is not necessary to treat any such arrangement as void (in the way that Article 85(2) renders void agreements caught by Article 85(1)). There is no possibility of exemption from Article 86 and so Article 86 does not contain a provision equivalent to Article 85(3). Either an infringement is made out by the Commission or it is not. For this reason, a great many Article 86 decisions by the Commission are contested. Given the size of entities typically accused of abuse of dominant position, it is frequently cost-effective to challenge the Commission's findings. Also if Commission findings are not refuted they might survive to haunt an undertaking long after any Commission decision is made and would prevent the undertaking from engaging in conduct that it might otherwise be able to enjoy.

Chapter II

3-05   Chapter II of the 1998 Act begins at section 17 by repealing sections 2 to 10 of the Competition Act 1980, which concerned anti-competitive practices involving the use of market strength. Those provisions are substituted by the new Chapter II prohibition.

The Chapter II prohibition, containing strikingly similar wording to Article 86, is aimed at correcting some of the previous shortcomings of United Kingdom legislation that meant that until the new Chapter II prohibition,

"serious anti-competitive behaviour [went] unchecked throughout an investigation, sometimes for a lengthy period. Competitors who [had] been damaged by such abuse [had] no redress or compensation. They [could] be driven out of business before matters [were] found, too late, in their favour."[1]

The deterrent effect of the Chapter II prohibition is intended to correct this shortcoming but its effectiveness is likely to depend upon the availability of interim measures for the victims of abuse, and the readiness of the Office of Fair Trading (OFT) to hear complaints and to initiate investigations.

3-06   Section 18 of the Act contains the Chapter II prohibition:

"(1) Subject to section 20, any conduct on the part of one or more undertakings which amounts to the abuse of a dominant position in a market is prohibited if it may affect trade within the United Kingdom.

(2) Conduct may, in particular, constitute such an abuse if it consists in:

(a) directly or indirectly imposing unfair purchase or selling prices or other unfair trading conditions;

(b) limiting production, markets or technical development to the prejudice of consumers;

---

[1] Foreword to, "A Prohibition Approach to Anti-competitive Agreements and Abuse of Dominant Position": Draft Bill, August 1997.

  (c) applying dissimilar conditions to equivalent transactions with other trading parties, thereby placing them at a competitive disadvantage;
  (d) making the conclusion of contracts subject to acceptance by the other parties of supplementary obligations which, by their nature or according to commercial usage, have no connection with the subject of the contracts.

(3) In this section:

'dominant position' means a dominant position within the United Kingdom; and
'the United Kingdom' means the United Kingdom or any part of it.

(4) The prohibition imposed by subsection (1) is referred to in this Act as 'the Chapter II prohibition'."

THE DIFFERENCES: THE KEY DIFFERENCES BETWEEN ARTICLE 86 AND CHAPTER II

Interpretation of the Act

3-07   Much has already been said in Chapter 2[2] about the interpretation of the Act in the light of section 60 and the various sources of law to be drawn upon in discerning matters of interpretation. Precisely the same principles that apply to the differences between Article 85(1) and Chapter I (as discussed above) apply equally to the differences between Article 86 and Chapter II.

Format

3-08   The text of section 18 refers to "any conduct on the part of one or more undertakings which amounts to the abuse of dominant position". Article 86, on the other hand begins more simply, "Any abuse by one or more undertakings of a dominant position".

Little is considered to turn on the textual difference. Certainly anything which amounts to exploiting customers or suppliers or which unfairly hinders competitors in their freedom to compete or which prevents the growth of competition may constitute an abuse under section 18.

"Dominant position within the common market or in a substantial part of it" compared with "Dominant position within the United Kingdom"

3-09   This difference reflects a clear divergence of the respective aims of Articles 86 and Chapter II. Article 86 requires market strength to be sufficiently widespread that it exists over a substantial part of the common market. Local dominance should be a matter primarily for national competition authorities but there will inevitably be many cases of overlap. It is clear that "substantial part of the common market" does not merely refer to geographical sales area. It will also include,

"the pattern and volume of the production and consumption of the said product as well as the habits and economic opportunities of vendors and purchasers" (*Suiker Unie v. Commission*[3]).

---

[2] Chap. 2, *Section 60*.
[3] Case 40/73 *Suikr Unie v. Commission* [1975] E.C.R. 1663 [1976] 1 C.M.L.R. 295 at para. 371.

The same case also indicates that even geographical areas forming only part of a Member State may be "a substantial part of the common market". However, there is less likely to be an effect between Member States in such cases.[4]

There is little doubt from section 18(3), that the Chapter II prohibition will apply to dominance within the United Kingdom or any part of it, and this will inevitably reach local pockets of dominance within a confined region of the United Kingdom. One such example might concern local transport.

"Trade between Member States" compared with "Trade within the United Kingdom"

3-10   The term "trade between Member States" in Article 86 will have the same meaning discussed above[5] in the context of Article 85(1), to cover any trade distortions that might result from the abuse. Anything that upsets the pattern of trade that might otherwise exist without the abuse will generally be sufficient to satisfy the "trade" dimension.

The meaning of "affect trade" will be the same in the case of section 18 except that the effect of the abuse for the purposes of section 18 must be such as to be felt within the United Kingdom or a part of the United Kingdom, rather than between Member States.

3-11   Concepts of "appreciability" and "*de minimis*" which are relevant to Article 85(1) and Chapter I are not expressly relevant to abuses of dominant position. Both Article 86 and section 18 presuppose the necessary market share criteria to be established. Furthermore, the reference in Article 86 to "a substantial part" of the common market itself imposes a certain threshold. No such reference to "substantial" is found in section 18, which merely refers to "the United Kingdom or any part of it". Thus section 18 abuses may be satisfied even if the part of the United Kingdom in which trade is affected is not substantial.

The term "significant" is relevant for the purpose of the Chapter II prohibition. Section 40 gives immunity from penalties for "conduct of minor significance", according to criteria established by the Secretary of State by reference to the annual turnover of the undertaking or undertakings (where firms are jointly dominant) concerned or the share of the market affected by the conduct. As a rule of thumb, market shares of less than 20 to 25 per cent are unlikely to result in findings of dominance.

Exclusions from Chapter II (no exclusions from Article 86)

3-12   There are a number of exclusions from the Chapter II prohibition which are set out in section 20. There are no exclusions from Article 86. Section 19 states that the Chapter II prohibition does not apply in any of the cases in which it is excluded by Schedule 1 or Schedule 3 to the 1998 Act.

Schedule 1: Mergers and concentrations

3-13   Schedule 1 to the 1998 Act excludes from the Chapter II prohibition any conduct which "results in any two enterprises ceasing to be distinct enterprises" since the control of mergers and concentrations under United Kingdom law remains the exclusive preserve of Part V of the Fair Trading Act 1973.[6]

---

[4] As to which competition authority will claim jurisdiction in cases of potential overlap—the Commission or the Director—see Chapter 14 below.
[5] In Chap. 2, "*Trade between Member States*" compared with "*Trade within the United Kingdom*".
[6] As the Fair Trading Act 1973 also deals specifically with certain asset transfers of newspaper businesses, Sched. 1 similarly disapplies those transfers from the Chapter II prohibition.

Schedule 1 also disapplies the Chapter II prohibition to any conduct giving rise to a concentration which results in the Commission having exclusive jurisdiction under the Merger Regulation.[7] See Chapter 12 below for further details.

Schedule 3: General exclusions

3-14   Schedule 3 of the Act also excludes from the Chapter II prohibition miscellaneous conduct.[8]

THE SIMILARITIES: THE COMMON ASPECTS OF ARTICLE 86 AND CHAPTER II

3-15   The following aspects of both Article 86 and the Chapter II prohibition, which are found in the text of each of these provisions, will now be examined in detail.

"Undertakings"

3-16   The term "undertakings" for the purposes of Article 86 and Chapter II will have the same meaning as under Article 85(1) and Chapter I, as discussed above in Chapter 2.[9]

"Dominant position"

3-17   The meaning given to the term dominance relates principally to the ability of an undertaking to operate independently of competitive pressure,

> "dominant position . . . relates to a position of economic strength enjoyed by an undertaking which enables it to prevent effective competition being maintained on the relevant market by affording it the power to behave to an appreciable extent independently of its competitors, its customers and ultimately of consumers."[10]

Dominance may be measured by a number of indices. Market share is the usual starting point for assessing dominance. (For details of how to assess market share, see Chapter 4 below.) The risks of dominance exist whenever a market share is held in excess of 40 per cent. Once this figure exceeds 50 per cent, in practice the burden of proving the absence of dominance shifts from the Commission to the undertaking defending a finding of dominance.[11] However, whether dominance in fact exists depends on the structure of the market. If two or three powerful competitors hold the remaining 50 per cent, they may offer severe price competition.

---

[7] Council Reg. 4064/89 on the control of concentrations between undertakings, as amended by Council Reg. 1310/97.

[8] The exclusions relate to: (1) Conduct relating to services of general economic interest or of a body possessing a revenue-producing monopoly, insofar as the prohibition would obstruct the performance of the tasks assigned to that body (Sched. 3, para. 4); (2) Conduct engaged in order to comply with a legal requirement imposed by U.K. law or under the E.C. Treaty or EEA Agreement, which has direct effect in the U.K. (or even imposed by the laws of another Member State if it has direct effect in the UK) (Sched. 3, para. 5(2)); (3) Conduct excluded by Order of the Secretary of State if necessary to avoid a conflict between a Chapter II prohibition and an international obligation of the U.K. (Sched. 3, para. 6(4)); (4) Conduct excluded by Order of the Secretary of State for exceptional and compelling reasons of public policy (Sched. 3, para. 7(4)); (5) Conduct relating to coal and steel where the Commission has exclusive jurisdiction under the Treaty establishing the European Coal and Steel Community (the ECSC Treaty).

[9] Chap. 2, *Undertakings*.

[10] Case 27/76 *United Brands v. Commission* [1978] E.C.R. 207; [1978] 1 C.M.L.R. 429 at paras 65 and 66 of the ECJ Judgment.

[11] Case 62/86R *Akzo v. Commission* [1986] E.C.R. 1503 [1987] 1 C.M.L.R. 255, also Case C-62/86 [1991] E.C.R. I-3359.

On the other hand, if the remainder of the market is fragmented and held by numerous competitors with market shares of between 1 and 5 per cent each, then a holding of 50 per cent will undoubtedly indicate dominance. Market trends are also important. A declining market share of 50 per cent as a snapshot measurement might be indicative of redundant technology or emerging competition in which that market holding does not represent strong economic power.

3-18   Emerging competition and the existence of numerous competitors with low market shares might be taken to reflect low entry barriers. High barriers to entry into a market are more likely to result in a finding of dominance by those already established in the market. The hurdles, which must be overcome by any new entrant on the market, provide protection against newcomers competing. Typical entry barriers might be represented, for example by dependence on intellectual property which either needs to be developed or acquired for a business to operate. Also high start-up costs of production requiring significant investment in plant and tooling would impose barriers to entry. These barriers exclude from competition any entity unable to take the requisite risk or make the required investment. Certain activities may only be viable for multi-national enterprises with established distribution networks of their own, or with complementary capabilities that mean that dedicated investment to the new activity is not necessary.

3-19   Three important observations should be made concerning dominance. First, there need not be any causal nexus between the dominant position and the abuse. It is sufficient to constitute infringement if the undertaking is dominant and is guilty of abuse, even if the activity constituting abuse does not stem from the undertaking's dominant position.

Secondly, infringement may occur if an undertaking which is dominant on one market, commits an abuse on another market. (More will be said of this in Chapter 4 below.) For example in *Tetra Pak II*,[12] Tetra Pak was dominant on the market consisting of asceptic packaging but committed abuses, such as predatory pricing, on markets for non-asceptic packaging. The ultimate question is whether the undertaking,

"has made use of the opportunities arising out of its dominant position in such a way as to reap trading benefits which it would not have reaped if there had been normal and sufficiently effective competition."[13]

Thirdly, since Article 86 and section 18 both refer to "one or more undertakings" there may be infringement based on "joint dominance". This was explained as follows in *Italian Flat Glass*,[14]

". . . There is nothing, in principle, to prevent two or more economic entities from being, on a specific market, united by such economic links that, by virtue of that fact, together they hold a dominant position vis-a-vis the other operators on the same market [such as] when two or more independent undertakings jointly have, through agreements or licences, a technological lead affording them the power to behave to an appreciable extent independently of their competitors, their customers and ultimately of their consumers."[15]

3-20   Economic links may be the result of company group structure, formal agreement or even collusion falling short of agreement. Nevertheless the measurement of

---

[12] Commission Dec. 92/163 [1992] O.J. L72/1; [1992] 4 C.M.L.R. 551.
[13] Case 27/76 *United Brands v. Commission* [1978] E.C.R. 207; [1978] 1 C.M.L.R. 429 at para. 249.
[14] Case T–68/89 *Societa Italiano Vetro SpA v. Commission* [1992] E.C.R. II-1403; [1992] 5 C.M.L.R. 302.
[15] *ibid.*

dominance is the same for single and joint dominance. In *Kali & Saltz*,[16] the ECJ indicated (in the context of a merger case) the method by which collective dominance should be assessed:

> "[I]n the case of an alleged collective dominant position, the Commission is . . . obliged to assess using a prospective analysis of the reference market, whether the concentration which has been referred to it leads to a situation in which effective competition in the relevant market is significantly impeded by the undertakings involved in the concentration and one or more other undertakings which together, in particular because of correlative factors which exist between them, are able to adopt a common policy on the market and act to a considerable extent independently of their competitors, customers and also of consumers".[17]

The ECJ criticised the Commission for its findings of collective dominance between two undertakings with market shares of 23 per cent and 37 per cent each. The combined market share of 60 per cent is not alone conclusive. It must be supported by other economic justifications for concluding that joint dominance exists.

3-21   Concerted behaviour taken alone does not satisfy the test of collective dominance. In *Compagnie Maritime Belge*,[18] members of a shipping conference, CEWAL, tried to exclude a competitor, G + C, by introducing "fighting ships". In order to match any sailing offered by G + C, members of CEWAL announced details of the nearest sailing on the same route offered by any member and guaranteed a price match. The members between themselves bore the cost of lost revenue. CEWAL acted on the market to all intents and purposes as a single entity, with sufficient economic links between the members, with a common structure and with members adopting the same conduct to result in a finding of collective dominance. It would be inappropriate to consider each member individually in such circumstances in assessing dominance. Joint dominance might therefore be said to exist when there are "sufficient economic links to lead to an effective single market entity."[19]

"Directly or indirectly imposing unfair purchase or selling prices or unfair trading conditions"

3-22   Most abuses under this heading concern excessive pricing and predatory pricing, although any unfair trading conditions which are unrelated to price may equally constitute abuse.

Excessive pricing

3-23   Excessive pricing by an undertaking which is not dominant does not constitute abuse, because it may be assumed that in the absence of dominance, principles of free competition will ensure that other sources of supply, offering lower prices, will be preferred. The constraining effects of competition cannot however be assumed in the case of dominance.

Excessive pricing is likely to be of concern particularly where it is sustained over time above the levels that might be expected to apply in circumstances of lively competition. Transitory high prices will be of less concern. Cases concerning excessive pricing are com-

---

[16] Cases 19 & 20/74 *Kali & Saltz* [1975] E.C.R. 499; [1975] 2 C.M.L.R. 154.
[17] *ibid.*, para. 221.
[18] Joined cases T–24, 26 & 28/93 *Compagnie Maritime Belge* [1996] E.C.R. II-1201; [1997] 4 C.M.L.R. 273, on appeal Case C–395/96P.
[19] Para. 28 of the Opinion of Advocate General Fennelly of the case in n. 18 above.

paratively rare. In *United Brands*,[20] prices of bananas varied considerably from one Member State to another according to the price which each market could bear. At first sight this might appear merely to be standard business practice. However, the price differentials indicated that in some Member States the pricing was excessive because in those countries the price had no reasonable relation to the economic value of the product. It was assumed that sales in low priced territories were profitable. The price prevailing in the highest priced countries then gave an indication of excessive pricing, without justification. The test of "excessive pricing" established in the earlier case of *Sirena v. EDA*[21] is whether prices are "unjustified by any objective criteria". This test was elaborated in *General Motors Continental*[22] to mean "excessive in relation to the economic value of the service provided".

3-24   Apart from the obvious harm of excessive pricing to any purchaser, excessive pricing may also offend Single Market principles and be used to partition countries and prevent parallel imports. In *General Motors Continental*, the ECJ held that excessive prices charged for the issue of certificates of mechanical conformity for new imported cars in Belgium was an abuse.

The ECJ applies an objective test based on the relationship between the price of goods and services and the costs of producing them. In other cases, the estimated level of profit may be a more appropriate measure of excessive pricing.

Predatory pricing

3-25   Low prices may offer benefits to the purchaser but in the case of predatory pricing, the aim is to offer prices that are so low that they cannot be matched by competitors at profitable levels, with the ultimate aim that those competitors are driven out of business. The purchaser then suffers because of the lack of competition available to constrain prices in the long term. Short-term losses made as a result of predatory pricing may then be recovered in the long term by excessive prices. In addition, predatory pricing can be used to preserve a position of high market share and to prevent potential competitors from entering the market. This technique involves the targeting of a specific competitor. For example *Easyjet*[23] have claimed that British Airways' new airline "Go" is cross-subsidised by BA such as to amount to predation, to drive Easyjet out of the market, achieved among other means by underwriting Go's aircraft leases.

In *Akzo Chemie BV v. Commission*[24] the ECJ described predatory prices as:

> "prices below average variable cost [......] such prices can drive from the market undertakings which are perhaps as efficient as the dominant undertaking but which, because of their smaller financial resources, are incapable of withstanding the competition waged against them".[25]

A finding of predation may be made even if prices exceed average variable cost of production, if they are below average total cost and the aim is to eliminate a competitor. Temporary low price promotions would not generally constitute predation (unless directed at competitor elimination) nor would pricing below cost where this is due to the miscalculation of costs or the result of some market volatility.

3-26   However, it is becoming increasingly apparent that the notion of average

---

[20] Commission Dec. 76/353 *Chiquita* (*subnom United Brands*) (1976) O.J. L95/1.
[21] Case 40/70 *Sirena v. EDA* [1971] E.C.R. 69; [1971] C.M.L.R. 260.
[22] Case 26/75 *General Motors Continental* [1975] E.C.R. 1375; [1976] 1 C.M.R.L. 95.
[23] *The Financial Times*, March 31, 1998.
[24] Case C–62/86 *Akzo Chemie BV v. Commission* [1991] E.C.R. I-3359; [1993] 5 C.M.L.R. 215.
[25] *ibid.*

variable cost is not sustainable in all circumstances, particularly in those cases where the marginal cost of providing the relevant goods or service is negligible. This was the case in *Compagnie Maritime Belge*[26] where a shipping company was already committed to its sailing schedules and merely had to make space available for the freight won by its infringing activities. Similarly in *Microsoft*[27] in which the cost of bundling software might be said to be marginal.

Other unfair trading conditions

3-27   The imposition of other unfair trading conditions may take any form. Any contractual terms imposed on buyers or purchasers which depart significantly from industry norm without any objective reason run the risk of constituting abuse.

"Limiting production, markets or technical development to the prejudice of consumers"

3-28   Examples of infringement under this heading include refusal to supply, withholding of intellectual property rights and inefficient management.

Refusal to supply

3-29   No positive duty to supply is imposed on a dominant undertaking but nevertheless a refusal to supply by a dominant undertaking may constitute an abuse if it is not objectively justified since it may be used as a mechanism to prevent others competing. The result of a refusal to supply may be to eliminate or hinder effective competition whether in the same market, a related market or an entirely unrelated market.

In *Commercial Solvents*,[28] Commercial Solvents were producers of a raw material used to make intermediate products which ultimately are required for the production of certain pharmaceutical products. Commercial Solvents decided as a matter of policy to concentrate their activities on the supply of the intermediate product rather than the raw material (as the intermediate market was more profitable) and ceased supplies of the raw material to an established customer in Italy, named Zoja. The ECJ held that Commercial Solvents decision to cease the supply of the raw material was made in order to facilitate access to the more profitable market and to eliminate competition from Zoja (and others), who were dependent upon raw material supplies from Commercial Solvents. The ECJ concluded that:

> "[a]n undertaking in a dominant position cannot stop supplying a long-standing customer who abides by regular commercial practice, if the orders placed . . . are in no way out of the ordinary". [29]

3-30   An example of an objectively justified reason to refuse to supply might be shortage of capacity, a customer's bad track record of payment or similar which may legitimately influence a supplier's decision (*Leyland DAF v. Automated Products Plc*[30]).

Similar principles apply when a dominant undertaking refuses to make available "essential facilities" without objective justification since essential facilities pose a barrier

---

[26] Joined cases T–24, 26 & 28/93 [1996] E.C.R. II-923; [1997] 4 C.M.L.R. 273.
[27] Discussed in Chapter 2, "*Make the conclusion of contracts subject to acceptance by the other parties of supplementary obligations which, by their nature, according to commercial use, have no connection with the subject of [such] contract*".
[28] Cases 6 & 7/73 *Commercial Solvents* [1974] E.C.R. 223; [1974] 1 C.M.L.R. 309.
[29] *ibid.*, para. 25.
[30] *Leyland DAF v. Automated Products Plc*, [1994] B.C.L.C 245 CA.

against those who might wish to compete, unless they are granted use of or access to those facilities. In *Port of Rodby*,[31] a finding of abuse was made against a port authority for not allowing access to routes to enable a ferry service to be operated. In *European Night Services v. Commission*[32] the CFI reviewed the case law on Article 86 (although it was an Article 85 case) and concluded that "a product or service cannot be considered necessary or "essential" unless there is no real or potential substitute".[33] Article 86 allegations based on the essential facilities doctrine will be difficult to make out in practice. Two preconditions need to be met for essential facilities. Access must be indispensable for competition to exist and duplication of the facility must be difficult if not impossible, or at least highly undesirable as a matter of public policy (*Oscar Bronner v. Mediaprint*).[34] If essential facilities are only made available at excessive prices, this may also constitute an abuse but it may prove difficult to establish excessive pricing where there exist no suitable price comparables.

Withholding of intellectual property rights

3-31   It should be remembered that dominance *per se* is not harmful, it is abuse by an undertaking in a dominant position that is prohibited. Accordingly, in *Park, Davis & Co v. Probel*,[35] the ECJ reaffirmed that ownership of a patent is not itself an abuse unless "utilisation of a patent . . . degenerate[s] into an improper exploitation of the protection".

The ECJ's attitude to the exercise of intellectual property rights was summarized in the case of *AB Volvo v. Veng*,[36] which concerned motor vehicle spare parts. The law relating to spare part designs has been overhauled in the United Kingdom since that case but the distinction between the existence of dominance and abuse is still important. The ECJ summarised the position as follows:

> "the proprietor of a protected design [may] prevent third parties from manufacturing . . . without its consent, products incorporating . . . the very subject matter of its exclusive rights. It follows that . . . even in return for a reasonable royalty, a licence for the supply of products incorporating the design would lead to the proprietor . . . being deprived of the substance of its exclusive right and that the refusal to grant such a licence cannot in itself constitute an abuse of a dominant position".[37]

The ECJ added that the exercise of the intellectual property rights could be an abuse and gave three examples:

(1) an arbitrary refusal to supply spare parts to an independent repairer; or

(2) unfair pricing of spare parts; or

(3) a refusal to continue to supply spare parts for a model of motor vehicle which was still in circulation.

Each of these examples relates to the use of products protected by intellectual property rights. This is quite different from any duty on the part of a dominant undertaking to

---

[31] Commission Dec. 94/19 [1994] O.J. L55/52; [1994] 5 C.M.L.R. 457.
[32] Joined cases T–375, 384 & 388/94 *European Night Services v. Commission* [1998] E.C.R. Judgment of September 15, 1998.
[33] *ibid.*, para. 208.
[34] Case C–7/97 *Oscar Bronner GmbH and Co v. Mediaprint Zeitungs- und Zeitschriftenverlag GmbH and Co KG*. Advocate General's Opinion paras 47 and 65.
[35] Case 24/67 *Park, Davis & Co. v. Probel* [1968] E.C.R. 55; [1968] C.M.L.R. 47.
[36] Case 238/87 *AB Volvo v. Veng* [1988] E.C.R. 6211; [1989] 4 C.M.L.R. 122.
[37] *ibid.*, para. 8.

license the use of the intellectual property rights in question. In *Magill TV Guide/ITP, BBC and RTE*,[38] the extent of any duty to grant a licence of such rights was considered. Three television companies had refused to license copyright in their TV listings for publication in a weekly guide. The issue was whether this refusal constituted an abuse of dominant position. The ECJ concluded that although the function of copyright was to protect the work from being copied, this had to be done:

> "while respecting the aims of, in particular, Article 86. Community law . . . [relating to] free movement of goods and free competition, prevails over any use of national intellectual property law in a manner contrary to those principles".[39]

An abuse was therefore constituted by the refusal to license the copyright (the TV listings) for publication in a market (TV guides) related to the one in which the TV companies were dominant (broadcasting), where the result was to prevent the emergence of that related market for which there was real consumer demand. The ECJ did acknowledge that an abuse is likely to be made out only in exceptional circumstances.

3-32 In *Magill* the ECJ therefore required the grant of a compulsory license. It is worth noting that a possible policy issue may have influenced the outcome in *Magill*. Although TV listings are protected by copyright as literary works in the United Kingdom and Ireland they would be unprotected in other Member States. The Commission may well have considered the rights not to be worthy of absolute protection, especially given the anomalies that would result in the Community.

The limited scope of the *Magill* case was illustrated recently in *Tierce Ladbroke v. Commission*[40] which concerned a refusal to supply racehorse film and soundtrack when intended for broadcast in betting shops. Betting shops could be operated without them and as such they were not regarded as essential for that purpose.

3-33 It is worth remembering that Article 86 is not a measure aimed at protecting competitors but competition, particularly the interests of the consumer. This was put as follows by Jacobs A.G. in *Oscar Bronner v. Mediaprint*[41] in an illuminating passage which also puts *Magill* in perspective:

> "It is important not to lose sight of the fact that the primary purpose of Article 86 is to prevent distortion of competition—and in particular to safeguard the interests of consumers—rather than to protect the position of particular competitors. It may therefore, for example be unsatisfactory in a case in which a competitor demands access to a raw material in order to be able to compete with the dominant undertaking on a downstream market in a final product, to focus solely on the latter's market power on the upstream market and conclude that its conduct in reserving to itself the downstream market is automatically an abuse. Such conduct will not have an adverse impact on consumers unless the dominant undertaking's final product is sufficiently insulated from competition to give it market power . . . It is on the other hand clear that refusal of access may in some cases entail elimination or substantial reduction of competition to the detriment of consumers in both the short and long term. That will be so where access to a facility is a pre-condition for competition on a related market for goods or services for which there is a limited degree of interchangeability.

---

[38] Commission Dec. 89/205 [1989] O.J. L78/43; [1989] 4 C.M.L.R. 757.
[39] Case T–69/89 *RTE v. Commission* [1991] E.C.R. II-485; [1991] 4 C.M.L.R. 586 at para. 71.
[40] Case T–504/93 *Tierce Ladbroke v. Commission* [1997] E.C.R. II-923; [1997] 5 C.M.L.R. 309, on appeal Case C–353/95 [1997] E.C.R. I-7007.
[41] Case C-7/97 Advocate General's Opinion, May 28, 1998.

In assessing such conflicting interests particular care is required where the goods or services or facilities to which access is demanded represent the fruit of substantial investment. That may be true in particular in relation to refusal to license intellectual property rights. Where such exclusive rights are granted for a limited period, that in itself involves a balancing of the interest in free competition with that of providing an incentive for R&D and for creativity. It is therefore with good reason that the Court has held that the refusal to license does not of itself, in the absence of other factors, constitute an abuse.

The ruling in *Magill* can in my view be explained by the special circumstances of that case which swung the balance in favour of an obligation to license. First, the existing product, namely individual weekly guides for each station, were inadequate, particularly when compared with the guides available to viewers in other countries. The exercise of the copyright therefore prevented a much needed new product from coming on to the market. Secondly, the provision of copyright protection for programme listings was difficult to justify in terms of rewarding or providing an incentive for creative effort. Thirdly, since the useful life of programme guides is relatively short, the exercise of the copyright provided a permanent barrier to the entry of the new product on the market. It may incidentally be noted that the national rules on intellectual property themselves impose limits in certain circumstances through rules on compulsory licensing."[42]

3-34   An Article 86 abuse constituted by a refusal to grant a licence of the intellectual property rights does not justify blanket infringement of the intellectual property withheld. This was highlighted in *Chiron Corporation v. Organon Teknika Limited*[43]:

"The fact that a person is abusing a dominant position does not mean that all wrongdoers have a defence in respect of all actions brought by that person. It is only in those cases where the exercise or existence of that right creates or buttresses the abuse will the court refuse to give effect to the exercise of the rights".[44]

Inefficient management

3-35   Inefficiency, mismanagement and even wilful neglect may conceivably amount to an abuse of a dominant position. For example in the *Port of Genoa*,[45] a refusal to adopt modern technology which led to increased costs and prolonged delays, was held to constitute an abuse of dominant position. Excessive prices may result from inefficiency. Inefficiency itself suggests lack of competitive pressure on the undertaking from other sources.

"Applying dissimilar conditions to equivalent transactions with other trading parties, thereby placing them at a competitive disadvantage"

3-36   The mischief of discrimination lies in the effect of placing one trading party at a competitive disadvantage compared with others. Discrimination more often than not relates directly or indirectly to price, but can relate to any trading term or practice.

---

[42] *ibid.*, paras 60–63.
[43] *Chiron Corporation v. Organon Teknika Limited* [1993] F.S.R. 324; [1992] 3 C.M.L.R. 813 HC.
[44] *ibid.*, para. 44.
[45] Case C–179/90 *Port of Genoa* [1991] E.C.R. I-5889.

Price discrimination

3-37   The ECJ has consistently held that substantial price differentials between customers offer a strong indication of discrimination in the absence of objective justification.[46]

Examples of price discrimination include the case of *United Brands*,[47] where the supplier imposed price differentials on distributors from different Member States set at such a level that parallel importation would not be profitable. Parallel imports would expose high-priced markets to competition and United Brands tried to discourage this. The result was rigid partitioning of the Community along national boundaries.

3-38   An example of "inclusive pricing" is *Van Den Bergh Foods Limited (Unilever)*.[48] Customers were obliged to accept ancillary products "free of charge". Those who chose not to accept the ancillary products were charged the same price as those who did. The result was discrimination against customers who chose not to accept ancillary products, and this was held to constitute an abuse. Delivered pricing may have similar results where prices are inclusive of delivery to any address, regardless of actual transport costs. In *IFTRA Glass Containers*[49] the Commission explained the ill-effects as follows:

> "This system . . . has the object of nullifying any competitive advantage which a producer . . . might gain from the proximity to his customers. It favours distant customers at the expense of those who are near; as the price is identical for both, the nearer customer pays for costs of delivery higher than those actually incurred by the seller, while the distant customer benefits from a discount on the actual freight costs. The system being of exclusive application, the sale of the products concerned is automatically tied to the user accepting their delivery to his location, a supplementary obligation which has no necessary connection with the sale of the goods".[50]

In *Compagnie Maritime Belge*[51] the distinction between competitive pricing and discriminatory pricing was spelled out by Fennelly A.G.:

> "Although a dominant undertaking is permitted to meet competition by making defensive adjustments, even aligning itself on the competitor's prices in order to keep the customers which were originally its own, it would not be legitimate for it to attempt to maintain, through a selectively offered price reduction, the customers that it has poached through below-cost pricing from its competitors unless it gives its own customers the benefit of this adjustment."[52]

Fidelity and loyalty concessions

3-39   Rebates and loyalty discounts unrelated to quantity or reduced costs of supply may constitute an abuse. They are usually aimed at securing all or an increased proportion of the business of customers. The critical issue, once again, is objective justification. In *Suiker Unie v. Commission*,[53] an association of German sugar producers granted rebates to customers which placed all of their requirements with members of the associ-

---

[46] Case 40/70 *Sirena v. EDA* [1971] E.C.R. 69; [1971] C.M.L.R. 260.
[47] Case 27/76 *United Brands v. The Commission* [1978] E.C.R. 207; [1978] 1 C.M.L.R. 429.
[48] Commission Dec. 98/531 [1998] O.J. L246/1.
[49] Commission Dec. 74/292 [1974] O.J. L160/1; [1974 2 C.M.L.R.] D50.
[50] *ibid.*, para. 48.
[51] Joined cases T–24, 26 & 28/93 [1996] E.C.R. II-1201; [1997] 4 C.M.L.R. 273, on appeal Case C–395/96P.
[52] *ibid.*, para. 128.
[53] Case 40/73 [1975] E.C.R. 1663; [1976] 1 C.M.L.R. 295.

ation. This was held to be an abuse. The effect of such concessions is to tie customers to a particular supplier, as explained in *Soda Ash—Solvay*,[54] where a rebate was:

> "[n]ot . . . treated as a quantity rebate exclusively linked with the volume of purchasers . . . but has rightly been classified . . . as a "loyalty" rebate designed, through the grant of financial advantage, to prevent customers obtaining their supplies from competing producers".[55]

Therefore an abuse may occur even if a customer is not contractually obliged to place all or even a given proportion of its requirements with a particular supplier, but has every incentive to do so. In *Hoffmann La Roche & Co AG v. Commission*,[56] an abuse was found to exist in a generous rebate scheme dependent on the quantity of orders placed but unrelated to the costs borne by the producer. In *Hoffman La Roche*, so-called "across the board" rebates were also offered which had the effect of encouraging customers to buy complete ranges of products from one producer.

3-40   The ECJ in that case also considered the position of an "English clause", which entitles a customer to purchase elsewhere if goods are available on more favourable terms. This was considered to aggravate an abuse, not excuse it, because it enables a dominant undertaking to determine information about its rivals' pricing policies.

The ECJ's strict approach to rebates is further illustrated by the case of CEWAL,[57] in which the ECJ held that an undertaking abused its dominant position where a fidelity rebate was included at the request of the customer.

Non-price related discrimination

3-41   In the case of shortages of supply, producers often have to establish a policy by which scarce resources are distributed among customers, and this carries with it the risk of discrimination. In *BPB Industries plc v. Commission*,[58] the ECJ confirmed that in such circumstances the supply criteria must be objectively justified. In this case, abuse was found in a practice adopted by a supplier of giving priority to local customers who took all their supplies from that supplier, at the expense of customers who took supplies from other Member States. This practice would result in discrimination by placing certain competitors at a disadvantage, albeit only in times of shortage.

"Make the conclusion of contracts subject to acceptance by the other parties of supplementary obligations which, by their nature, according to commercial usage, have no connection with the subject of [such] contracts"

3-42   The most obvious examples of abuse under this heading are "tie-in" clauses. For example when buying one product, a customer is obliged to take another product as well. In the case of software, a common example of an unlawful tie would be a requirement that the licensee of a software program also take maintenance services from the supplier. For further discussion see Chapter 2, "*Make the conclusion of contracts subject to acceptance by the other parties of supplementary obligations which by their nature, according to commercial usage, have no connection with the subject of [such] contracts*", above. This would be caught by Article 85(1) if reflected in an agreement but would equally be caught by Article 86 if it were a stipulation imposed by a supplier unilaterally. The

---

[54] Commission Dec. 91/299 O.J. [1991] L152/21.
[55] *ibid.*, para. 62.
[56] Case 85/76 *Hoffman La Roche & Co AG v. Commission* [1979] E.C.R. 461; [1979] 3 C.M.L.R. 211.
[57] Case C–393/92 CEWAL [1994] E.C.R. I-1477.
[58] Commission Dec. 93/82 [1993] O.J. L34/20; [1995] 5 C.M.L.R. 198.

competition danger with tie-ins is that undertakings use their market power in order to create or enhance a market for other products in which they may not yet be dominant.

In *Tetra Pak II*,[59] the Commission held that clauses requiring customers to obtain their maintenance and repair services for longer than the warranty period constituted abuse. Tetra Pak's policy was that of reserving the servicing obligations for itself rather than allowing any entity capable of supplying such services to compete with Tetra Pak. The Commission is reluctant to permit tie-ins and any objective justification must be compelling.

3-43   In *Van den Bergh Foods*[60] the Commission objected to the practice of Unilever's Irish subsidiary, HB (now Van den Bergh Foods), of providing retail outlets with free freezer cabinets on condition that they offered only HB's brand of impulse-buy ice creams from the cabinet. HB then modified its distribution practices by granting retailers favourable terms for the supply of freezers and favourable prices for ice cream products for those that had bought freezers from HB. However, the result of requiring HB's freezers to be used only for HB ice creams was equivalent to outlet exclusivity since the size of most retail outlets meant that, in general, they would only need one freezer. If the freezer had to be used only for HB ice creams, the outlet could effectively stock no other brand, unless it bought another freezer. This impeded access to the retail outlets by competitors, particularly in view of the fact that 40 per cent of the Irish market was tied. HB's total market share exceeded 70 per cent in the relevant market. The advantages of HB making freezers available on favourable terms was outweighed by the competitive restrictions on the retail outlets and the effect of excluding competitors. Accordingly the Commission (invoking both Article 85(1) and 86) prevented HB enforcing the exclusive use of HB freezers by retailers unless a second freezer was available at the outlet.[61]

Summary

3-44   Before leaving the subject of Article 86, in considering what amounts to abusive conduct, it is worth remembering that the Commission does not consider an intention even by a dominant firm to prevail over its rivals as unlawful. Nor does the Commission suggest that large producers should be under an obligation to refrain from competing vigorously with smaller competitors or new entrants."[62] As long as the price is not below average variable cost, fierce price competition should be encouraged by the authorities. In *Compagnie Maritime Belge*,[63] Fennelly A.G. commented that:

> "[p]rice competition is the essence of the free and open competition which it is the objective of Community policy to establish on the internal market. It favours more efficient firms and it is for the benefit of consumers both in the short and long run. Dominant firms not only have the right but should be encouraged to compete on price. More usually their market power tends to enable them to maintain prices above competitive levels."[64]

---

[59] Commission Dec. 92/163 [1992] O.J. L72/1.
[60] Commission Dec. of March 11, 1998 [1998] O.J. L246, on appeal Case T–65/98.
[61] The Commission's decision was suspended pending appeal.
[62] Case C–62/86 *Akzo Chemie BV v. Commission* [1991] E.C.R. I-3359.
[63] Joined Cases T–24, 26 & 28/93 [1996] E.C.R. II-1201; [1997] 4 C.M.L.R. 273, on appeal Case C–395/96P.
[64] *ibid.*, para. 117.

CHAPTER 4

Definition of Relevant Market and Assessment of Market Share

RELEVANCE OF MARKET SHARE

4-01 This Chapter sets out the principles for determining the "relevant market" for any product or service supplied by any undertaking and this in turn will enable an assessment to be made of that undertaking's market share. This Chapter will examine the relevant market and market share criteria established by the Commission in its Notice on the definition of relevant market for the purpose of Community competition law[1] and as expressed by the OFT in its guide entitled "Market Definition". Market share will need to be established for any of the following purposes.

Anti-competitive practices and agreements

Appreciability

4-02 An analysis of market power is almost always inescapable in considering whether an agreement has an "appreciable" effect on competition for the purposes of Article 85(1) and Chapter I.[2]

The Commission's Notice on agreements of minor importance[3] specifies market share thresholds of 5 per cent for horizontal agreements and 10 per cent for vertical agreements. If the parties' combined market shares are below those thresholds, their agreements are likely to be considered by the Commission to be *de minimis*.

4-03 The OFT's guide, "The Chapter I Prohibition", takes a more generous approach, indicating that an agreement is unlikely to have an appreciable effect on competition if the participating undertakings' combined market share of the relevant market does not exceed 25 per cent. A very close eye should be kept on the emerging practice of the Director as this figure may well be revised over time. There will be many circumstances in which an appreciable effect will be found at lower market shares. In both cases, market share assessments will be necessary.

Individual exemption

4-04 Any application for individual exemption under Article 85(3) or under section 9 of the 1998 Act will need to be supported by evidence that the pre-conditions for exemption have been satisfied; in particular that the agreement does not "afford the parties . . . the possibility of eliminating competition in respect of a substantial part of the products

---

[1] Commission Notice of December 19, 1997 on the definition of relevant market for the purpose of Community competition law [1997] O.J. C 372/03.
[2] See Chapter 2, *"De minimis" principles*, above on the meaning of "appreciable".
[3] [1997] O.J. C 372/04.

in question".[4] This is best demonstrated by reference to the limited market shares held by the parties.

Automatic exemption

4-05   Certain block exemptions Regulations published by the Commission contain market share thresholds which must not be exceeded by the parties, or exemption will be lost. For example, in the Technology Transfer Regulation,[5] automatic exemption is excluded[6] if the licence agreement is for the purpose of a joint venture between competitors and their combined market shares exceed a certain critical level. The threshold is 10 per cent of the market for licensed products where the licence agreement covers production and distribution, and 20 per cent of the market for licensed products where the licence covers production only. Also, Article 7(1) of the Technology Transfer Regulation withdraws exemption, as a rule, in cases where the licensee's market share is more than 40 per cent.

4-06   Market share thresholds also feature in Regulation 418/85 for research and development agreements[7] (Articles 3(2), 3(3) and 3(3)(a)) and in Regulation 417/85[8] for specialisation agreements (Articles 3(1)(a) and 3(2)(a)). See Chapter 7 for further detail.

There is little doubt that market share criteria will feature with even greater prominence in the proposed single Regulation for vertical restraints (discussed in Chapter 7 below).

Immunity from fines (Chapter I)

4-07   Section 39 of the 1998 Act confers limited immunity from fines on "small agreements" (other than price-fixing agreements). The criteria for determining whether an agreement is a "small agreement" are prescribed by the Secretary of State and expressed in terms of the combined turnover of the parties and the share of the market affected by the agreement. The immunity may, however, be withdrawn by written notice if, having investigated the "small agreement", the Director considers after all that it is likely to infringe the Chapter I prohibition. The notice must allow sufficient time to correct the agreement.

Abuse of dominant position

Dominance

4-08   The prohibitions in Article 86 and Chapter II both require dominance or joint dominance to be established. The definition of "dominance" given in *Hoffman La Roche*[9] suggests that a firm or group of firms are dominant if they are in a position to behave to an appreciable extent independently of competitors, customers and ultimately consumers. This usually occurs because a large share of the supply in any market is held by a single undertaking. Dominance *per se* is not harmful. Dominance must be coupled with an abuse to amount to an infringement of Article 86 or the Chapter II prohibition. An assessment of market share is an essential part of establishing dominance by one or more firms, because an investigation of an Article 86 or Chapter II prohibition will fail if it is established that the subject of an investigation is not dominant.

---

[4] Art. 85(3)(b) and s. 9(b)(ii).
[5] Reg. 240/96 [1996] O.J. L31/2. See Chapter 9 below.
[6] Under Art. 5.2(1) of Reg. 240/96 [1996] O.J. L31/2.
[7] Reg 417/85 [1985] O.J. L53/5, amended by Reg. 151/93.
[8] Reg. 417/85 [1985] O.J. L53/1, amended by Reg. 151/93.
[9] Case 85/76 [1979] E.C.R. 461; [1979] 3 C.M.L.R. 211.

Immunity from fines (Chapter II)

4-09 Market share will also be relevant for the purposes of section 40 of the 1998 Act, which confers limited immunity from fines for infringers of the Chapter II prohibition for "conduct of minor significance". The criteria for conduct of minor significance are determined by the Secretary of State.

As with section 40, the criteria will be turnover and market share stipulations, in this case where the relevant turnover is that of the person whose conduct is under examination, and the market share is the share of the market affected by the conduct. The immunity likewise, may be withdrawn by written notice (allowing sufficient time to correct the infringement) if, having investigated the "conduct of minor significance", the Director considers it likely that the conduct infringes the Chapter II prohibition.

Merger control

4-10 Merger policy is directed towards the control of structural changes in the supply of products or services with the aim, in E.C. legislation, of preventing the creation or reinforcement of a dominant position which might result in effective competition becoming "significantly impeded in a substantial part of the common market". As far as the Fair Trading Act 1973 is concerned, the issue is whether a merger will either result in the creation or strengthening of a "monopoly situation" in relation to goods or services in the United Kingdom or a substantial part of it, or the acquisition of assets worth more than £70 million. A "monopoly situation" exists when markets in excess of 25 per cent are held by one and the same person.[10]

It is important to remember that the market analysis will inevitably vary according to its purpose. For example when defending allegations of past infringement of any prohibition (whether Article 85(1), Chapter I, Article 86, or Chapter II) there will be a tendency to adopt a retrospective forensic style of analysis. The approach to be taken in an application for individual exemption or a merger control notification will inevitably be prospective, with a forward-looking assessment of the structural position of the market, the advantages that will result in the supply pattern and the beneficial structural changes that are likely to occur. The points to be drawn out in the analysis of the market structure in each case will be different. As the Commission has put it:

> "the different time horizon considered in each case might lead to the result that different geographic markets are defined for the same products depending on whether the E.C. Commission is examining a change in the structure of supply, such as a concentration or co-operative joint venture, or examining issues relating to certain behaviour".[11]

4-11 If an undertaking under an Article 86 investigation is dominant in one particular product market, when the same undertaking then seeks to merge with another in a related but separate market, the new product areas may enable it to increase prices still further beyond the level achievable before the merger. In this case, the relevant market would cover both the existing and the new product areas. The existing market may be relevant under Article 86 and the newly created market relevant for the purposes of examining the concentration. The principles for determining market power are otherwise substantially the same in all cases.

---

[10] See Chap. 11 below.
[11] Para. 12 of the Commission Notice on the definition of relevant market [1997] O.J. C 372/03.

COMMISSION NOTICE ON DEFINITION OF RELEVANT MARKET

Introduction

4-12   The Commission's Notice on the definition of relevant market for the purpose of Community competition law[12] is intended to apply to analyses under both Article 85 and 86. The importance of the Notice should not be underestimated given the Commission's statement that:

> "The definition of the relevant market in both its product and geographic dimensions often has decisive influence on the assessment of a competition case."[13]

The Notice has the declared aim of promoting transparency of Commission policy and decision-making. At the same time, the Commission obviously intends that anyone addressing the issue of market share to the Commission should adopt the Commission's own preferred approach and reasoning.

The Notice is to be interpreted without prejudice to any interpretation which may be given by the E.C.J or the Court of First Instance,[14] and the principles set out in the Notice are intended to be a reflection of existing case law. The Notice is therefore an extremely useful source of guidance for determining any matter related to market share. Other useful sources of guidance include Form A/B found in E.C. Commission Regulation 3385/94,[15] which sets out the information required for the purpose of applications and notifications, and Form CO relating to the notification of a concentration pursuant to Regulation 4064/8.[16] Form A/B and Form CO will be considered below.

4-13   The practical consequences of failing to address issues of market definition in the way proposed by the Commission in any application for exemption are two-fold. First, the application is more likely to be rejected. Secondly, it is easier for the Commission, or parties to a notified agreement or even third parties, to claim subsequently that all relevant information was not laid before the Commission before reaching its decision. The decision might therefore be rendered void.[17]

It is also worth bearing in mind that the Notice offers guidance to the national authorities and national courts on the methodology to be adopted in determining market shares and market power.

Relevant market

4-14   In the Notice, the Commission defines the relevant market in both its product and geographic dimensions. Relevant *product* market is defined as comprising:

> "all those products and/or services which are regarded as interchangeable or substitutable by the consumer, by reason of the products' characteristics, their prices and their intended use".[18]

---

[12] Commission Notice of December 19, 1997 on the definition of relevant market for the purpose of Community competition law [1997] O.J. C 372/03.

[13] *ibid.*, para. 4.

[14] *ibid.*, para. 6. This assists resolution of any substantive differences both in the context of E.C. law and U.K. law since the Competition Act, s. 60 expressly resolves any such differences in an identical way.

[15] Commission Reg. 3385/94 [1994] O.J. L377.

[16] Commission 4064/8 [1994] O.J. L377 amended by Commission Reg. 447/98 of March 1, 1998 on the notifications, time-limits and hearings provided for in Council Reg. 4064/89 on the control of concentrations between undertakings OJ [1998] L06 1–28.

[17] See Chapter 14 below.

[18] Para. 7 of the Notice on the definition of relevant market [1997] O.J. C372/03.

Relevant *geographic* market is defined as comprising:

> "the area in which the undertakings concerned are involved in the supply and demand of products or services, in which the conditions of competition are sufficiently homogeneous and which can be distinguished from neighbouring areas because the conditions of competition are appreciably different in those areas".[19]

The inter-relation between the two gives rise to the relevant market. Once the relevant market has been determined, an assessment may be made of the market share held by an undertaking and in turn of its market power. The market power of an undertaking is judged by the competitive constraints on it. The absence of competitive constraints on an undertaking indicates that it may be free of competitive pressure. The three main recognised sources of competitive constraints (which are referred to in the Notice) are:

(1) demand substitution;

(2) supply substitution; and

(3) potential competition.

Demand substitution

4-15 Demand substitution is a measure of the readiness of customers to switch from one supplier to another in response to price increases.

In the Commission's view, demand substitution constitutes the most immediate and effective disciplinary force on the suppliers of a product in relation to their pricing decisions.[20] If customers are able to switch easily to available substitute products in response to price increases they generally will. This is known as "cross-elasticity" of demand between the substitutable products. Market definition therefore involves identifying all effective alternative sources of supply of products or services which are readily substitutable (given their characteristics and intended use) and are readily available (given the geographic location of suppliers).

As a measure of demand substitutability, the Commission poses the hypothetical case of small, permanent price increases relative to other products. If customers decide to switch suppliers because of a permanent price increase of the order of 5 to 10 per cent, given the products and geographical areas considered, then all of the products that are substitutable in that way may be regarded as belonging to the same market. Substitution must be enough to make the price increase unprofitable to suppliers because of the resulting loss of sales in favour of other suppliers. This is very close to the "SSNIP Test" adopted by the Department of Justice in the "United States and FTC Horizontal Merger Guidelines 1992"[21] which refers to small but significant non-transitory increases in price. The cluster of products which are sensitive to price rises will result in the definition of product market.[22]

4-16 The reference price for determining customer reaction to the small, permanent price increase is the prevailing market price.[23] The starting point then is to identify the

---

[19] Para. 8 of the Notice on the definition of relevant market [1997] O.J. C372/03.

[20] Para. 13 of the Notice on the definition of relevant market [1997] O.J. C372/03.

[21] (1992) 4 Trade Reg. Rep. 13.104.

[22] The Commission has been criticised for adopting the SSNIP Test for the purposes of Art. 86 when the Guidelines themselves are not used (nor were they conceived by the U.S. authorities) for that purpose.

[23] The difficulties posed in Art. 86 cases have given rise to what is known as "the cellophane fallacy" based on the fact that even dominant firms will suffer sales losses in response to price rises. Even if the market is enlarged to cover substitutable products, the result will still understate the potential harm that may be done by a dominant entity.

type of products or services sold by an undertaking, and next the area in which they are sold or supplied. The description of product or service and the relevant geographic area must be enlarged or reduced depending on the restraining effect on price from other products or services and from other areas, until a market definition is reached according to the above test involving a price increase of between 5 and 10 per cent.

The following illustrate the application of these principles as well as other factors to be taken into account in any determination of the relevant market.

4-17   Product characteristics.   In *United Brands v. Commission*,[24] the E.C.J made a controversial decision concerning the relevant market for bananas. For certain banana consumers, all fruits are perfectly substitutable but there are apparently a great many consumers who are unable to consume hard fruit (the very old and the very young alike who have no teeth). For this reason bananas could not be said to belong to the same product market as hard fruit. As there are only a few months in each year during which soft fruits are available that might be substitutable with bananas, the Commission easily found dominance in a narrowly defined market consisting of seasonal soft fruit only. Bananas did not therefore belong in a market consisting of fruit generally, by virtue of:

> "such special features distinguishing [the banana] from other fruits that it is only to a limited extent interchangeable with them and is only exposed to their competition in a way that is hardly perceptible".[25]

Had the relevant market been defined to include all fruit, the market share of United Brands would have been dramatically reduced.

4-18   Exposure to competition.   A narrow market definition was also found in *Hilti*.[26] Hilti manufactured power actuated nail guns for use in the building industry. The Commission decided that nails for use in Hilti's guns belong in a market of their own, distinct from the market in the nail guns which fire them. Hilti was exposed to significantly greater competition in the sale of its nails (which many producers could readily supply) than it faced in the market for the guns which fire them (because the technology required to produce equivalent guns made them less readily available for manufacture by other producers). Accordingly the Commission decided that Hilti guns and Hilti nails belong in separate product markets because of the different competitive conditions faced by guns and nails.

The case of *Michelin*[27] concerned the market in tyres for heavy commercial vehicles. Although replacement tyres for vehicles when already in use are identical to tyres supplied for new vehicles, the E.C.J decided that the demand characteristics are sufficiently different between replacement and new tyres to warrant treating them as separate markets. Demand for replacement tyres was found to be quite different from the demand for tyres for new vehicles. Two markets exist for the same products intended for the same use because of differing circumstances of competition.

4-19   Single product, different uses and different markets.   Product markets can often be determined by reference to their use so that separate markets exist for the same product according to different usage. Much depends on the interchangeability of products given

---

[24] Case 27/76 [1978] E.C.R. 207; [1978] 1 C.M.L.R. 429.
[25] *ibid.*, para. 32.
[26] Case T–30/89 *Eurofix Banco v. Hilti*, [1991] E.C.R. II-1439; [1992] 4 C.M.L.R. 16.
[27] Case 322/81 *Michelin v. Commission* [1983] E.C.R. 3461; [1985] 1 C.M.L.R. 282.

their intended purpose. In *Hoffman La Roche*,[28] the importance of specific use was stressed in measuring interchangeability:

> "The concept of the relevant market in fact implies that there can be effective competition between the products which form part of it and this pre-supposes that there is a sufficient degree of interchangeability between all the products forming part of the same market insofar as a specific use of such products is concerned."

The E.C.J emphasised that separate markets may exist depending on use, according to the availability of substitutes for each use. However the E.C.J has repeatedly emphasised (for example in *Akzo*[29]) that care must be taken to weigh up all the characteristics of the relevant market and the particular circumstances of each case.

4-20   In *Commercial Solvents*,[30] a single product was differentiated into separate markets according to different uses. The Commercial Solvents group of companies produced a raw material, nitro-propane. The raw material was exploited by the Commercial Solvents group by direct sales, among others to an Italian company, Zoja. Zoja used it for producing a downstream product, ethambutol, which has pharmaceutical applications for the treatment of tuberculosis. The Commercial Solvents group also exploited the raw material by using it to make derivative downstream products. Following a policy decision only to exploit the downstream market, Commercial Solvents ceased supplies to Zoja. Zoja claimed that this constituted an abuse of dominant position (refusal to supply). Commercial Solvents claimed the relevant market to be defined widely, comprising all raw materials from which ethambutol could be produced. The E.C.J determined the relevant market narrowly as the raw material itself and not products used to produce the derivative products. This put Commercial Solvents in a dominant position. The E.C.J's reasoning was that for Zoja the relevant market was raw materials that could be substituted to serve the purpose of manufacturing ethambutol (without incurring significance expense in making the substitution). On the facts Zoja could not readily adapt production to make derivative materials using different raw materials.

4-21   Price and quality.   Luxury fur coats would obviously not belong to the same market as duffle-coats. Product descriptions might be similar (in this case, "coats") but since they cannot be regarded as substitutable or interchangeable in any conventional sense, they do not belong to the same product market.

4-22   Secondary markets.   In *Hugin v. Commission*,[31] cash registers and spare parts for cash registers were held to belong to different product markets because manufacturers of cash registers were not in a position to adapt production techniques in order to manufacture spare parts for equipment made by other manufacturers. Although various suppliers might compete for the supply of cash registers, they cannot compete for the supply of each other's spare parts.

Until the United Kingdom law of copyright and design right was overhauled in 1989[32] to allow spare parts to be manufactured by anyone without this constituting infringement, motor car manufacturers were the only source of spare parts for their cars. There therefore existed no real competition for spare part supplies. As no substitutes existed for spare parts (except to the manufacturer's specification), spare parts were held in *Volvo v. Veng*,[33]

---

[28] Case 85/76 [1979] E.C.R. 461; [1979] 3 C.M.L.R. 211.
[29] Case 62/86 *Akzo v. Commission* [1991] E.C.R. I-3359; [1993] 5 C.M.L.R. 215.
[30] Cases 6–7/73 *ICI and Commercial Solvents Corp. v. Commission* [1974] E.C.R. 223; [1974] 1 C.M.L.R. 309.
[31] Case 22/78 *Hugin v. Commission* [1979] E.C.R. 1869; [1979] 3 C.M.L.R. 345.
[32] Copyright Designs and Patents Act 1988.
[33] Case 238/87 [1988] E.C.R. 6211; [1988] 4 C.M.L.R. 122.

to belong to a separate market from the market in which the cars (to which the spare parts are fitted) belong.

Supply substitution

4-23   Supply substitution is a measure of the readiness of suppliers to switch production to new products in response to price increases by existing suppliers. The analysis in this case switches from the perspective of the buyer (on the demand side) to the producer (on the supply side). Supply substitution is described in the Notice[34] as the readiness of suppliers, in response to small and permanent changes in relative prices, to switch production to the relevant products and market them in the short term without having to incur significant additional costs or risks. The availability on the market of additional products will act as an effective and immediate price constraint on suppliers.

Supply-side substitutability is generally not found to exist if the substitution of production requires significant adjustment of tangible or intangible assets, or requires additional investment or delay. The Commission does not readily permit arguments put to it concerning supply-side substitutability, if significant costs and lead times would have to be incurred before sales can be made, or if sales are only viable if accompanied by extensive testing, advertising and distribution activities.

4-24   In *Continental Can v. Commission*,[35] the E.C.J emphasised the need to examine supply substitution. Light tin cans for fish and meat products made by Continental Can could be treated as belonging to the same market as other forms of light container made by other suppliers if those other suppliers could switch production for that purpose. The Commission was criticised by the E.C.J for its lack of reasoning in demonstrating that manufacturers of light metal containers could not make fish cans and enter the market.

In *Michelin*,[36] tyres for heavy commercial vehicles and cars belonged in different product markets since production techniques, plant and tooling needed for their manufacture were considered to be so different. Production could not readily be adapted to manufacture the substitute product, evidencing a lack of elasticity in supply. Similarly in *Hugin*,[37] even though cash registers of different manufacturers might belong in the same market, those manufacturers were not in a position to switch production in order to manufacture spare parts for another manufacturer's equipment. There was little supply substitutability in relation to spare parts, which therefore placed them in a separate market from the cash registers themselves.

Potential competition

4-25   Only if the preceding analysis gives rise to competition concerns is potential competition generally relevant. It is not normally taken into account when defining the product market. Potential competition is judged by the ease of entry into the market by would-be competitors and is generally only appropriate to the question of assessment of dominance:

> ". . . [P]otential competition is not taken into account when defining markets, since the conditions under which potential competition will actually represent an effective competitive constraint depend on the analysis of specific factors and circumstances related to conditions of entry. If required this analysis is only carried out at a subsequent stage, in general once the position of the companies involved in the relevant

---

[34]   Para. 20 of the Notice on the definition of relevant market [1997] O.J. C372/03.
[35]   Case 6/72 *Continental Can v. Commision*[1973] E.C.R. 215; [1973] C.M.L.R. 199 at paras 247–8.
[36]   Case 322/81 [1983] E.C.R. 3461; [1985] 1 C.M.L.R. 282.
[37]   Case 22/78 [1979] E.C.R. 1869; [1979] 3 C.M.L.R. 345.

market has already been ascertained, and when such position gives rise to concerns from a competition point of view."[38]

The relevant geographic market

4-26 The geographic market in which one supplier operates is not necessarily confined to the territory of sales of that supplier. In *United Brands*, the geographic market was described as the area:

"where the conditions are sufficiently homogeneous for the effect of the economic power of the undertaking concerned to be able to be evaluated."[39]

It is the area of homogeneous competitive conditions, or the area in which:

"objective conditions are the same for all traders."[40]

The Notice hints at a tendency to regard the relevant geographic market as the common market, in pursuit of its aim of market integration. With increased market integration, there should theoretically be a trend towards price sensitivity regardless of geography although obviously costs of transportation of heavy or cumbersome goods will militate against geographic markets extending across the entire Community.[41] By contrast, the readily transportable nails in *Hilti* covered a geographic market extending throughout the Community.

4-27 Evidence of diversion of trade from one geographical area to another in response to price changes is likely to be relevant,[42] although comparisons of price may be difficult due to exchange rate movements and taxation. In addition, there may be local loyalty on the part of customers, and certain products or services are incapable of export (such as power supplies and rail networks). In *Italian Flat Glass*,[43] the difficulties and risks of transporting flat glass resulted in a finding that Italy alone represented the geographic market. These issues are all acknowledged in the Notice[44] which also refers to preferences for national brands, and national preferences based on language, culture and lifestyle which limit the potential for the geographic scope of competition.

It may in appropriate circumstances be possible to define separate, isolated, geographic markets for any given product, such as in *Soda Ash—ICI*,[45] although the differentiation in that case was the result of market sharing.

Calculation of market share

4-28 Once the supplier and consumer position on any market is established, together with its geographic dimensions, the total market size and market shares for each supplier are calculated on the basis of the sales of the relevant products in the relevant area.[46]

Other indications may be relevant such as unused production capacity as a measure of

---

[38] Para. 24 of the Notice on the definition of relevant market [1997] O.J. C372/03.
[39] Paras 10 and 11 of the Notice on the definition of relevant market [1997] O.J. C372/03.
[40] Commission Dec. 89/113 *Decca Navigation System* [1989] O.J. L 43/27 para. 88–90; [1990] 4 C.M.L.R. 627.
[41] Commission Dec. 88/518 *Napier Brown/British Sugar* [1998] O.J. L 284/41; [1990] 4 C.M.L.R. 196.
[42] Para. 45 of the Notice on definition of relevant market [1997] O.J. C372/03.
[43] Commission Dec. 81/881 [1981] O.J. L326/32; [1982] C.M.L.R. 366; December 1988: [1989] O.J. L33/44; [1990] 4 C.M.L.R. 535.
[44] Para. 46 of the Notice on definition of relevant market [1997] O.J. C372/03.
[45] Commission Dec. 91/300 [1991] O.J. L 152/40; [1994] 4 C.M.L.R. 645.
[46] Para. 53 of the Notice on the definition of relevant market [1997] O.J. C372/03.

additional potential competition. Both the volume of sales and the value of sales will contribute to the analysis but in the case of differentiated products, the value of sales is usually a better reflection of market position and market power of suppliers.

Evidence

4-29 The Notice confirms that in making any decision, the Commission will follow "an open approach to empirical evidence aimed at making an effective use of all available information which may be relevant in individual cases".[47] The Commission is therefore not going to be held to the principles set out in the Notice according to any particular hierarchy and when a precise market definition is necessary, particularly in cases where a clear picture does not emerge on a straightforward analysis, the Commission will sometimes contact customers and other participants in the industry to illicit their views about the product and geographic markets, where necessary examining different levels of production or distribution both upstream and downstream. In certain cases, the Commission will request information in writing from those participants and there is some fear that greater credence might be given to third party views sought by the Commission than to the views of those making submissions to the Commission.

The Notice also speaks of carrying out visits and inspections to the premises of parties, their customers and/or competitors in order to gain better understanding of the business.[48] Consumer preferences established by marketing studies, consumer surveys and similar sources may also be relied upon. In *BBI/Boosey and Hawkes: Interim Measures*,[49] the Commission was even persuaded by statements in internal company documents describing their musical instruments as "automatically first choice", in making a finding of market power.

4-30 Examples of patterns of trade that might be relevant are those that follow "shocks". A sudden shortage of particular products or sudden price rise could provide evidence of a shift in demand. Similarly, a new product launch might indicate those products that have suffered a loss of market position. Whenever plotting historic price changes, it is vital to determine the causes of the price fluctuations before inferring anything concerning market definition.

In *European Night Services*,[50] the Commission was criticised for its lack of analysis of the market share position of the parties when applying for exemption. However, the Commission appears to have followed the terms of its Notice in *Flughafen Frankfurt/Main AG*[51] concerning a complaint by airlines about the amount of space allocated to them at Frankfurt airport for their ground handling activities. The geographic market was Frankfurt airport which, given its strategic importance, was treated as a substantial part of the common market. The market for ramp-side services was considered to be separate from the market for landing and take-off services. The two were not substitutable. The Commission recognised that in the market for certain ramp-side services, the airport was justified in retaining a monopoly and that included luggage conveyors which, if reproduced, would result in unnecessary inefficiency. For the remainder of the rampside services however the Commission decided that the airport should allow space for competitors to operate in the provision of their own ground-handling services.

---

[47] Para. 25 of the Notice on the definition of relevant market [1997] O.J. C372/03.
[48] Para. 34 of the Notice on the definition of relevant market [1997] O.J. C372/03.
[49] Commission Dec. 87/500 [1987] O.J. L286/36; [1988] 4 C.M.L.R. 67.
[50] Joined cases T–375/94, T–384/94 & T–388/94 [1998] E.C.R. Judgment of September 15, 1998.
[51] Commission Dec. 98/387 [1998] O.J. L173/32; [1998] 4 C.M.L.R. 779.

Form A/B

4-31 Form A/B sets out the structure and content of all applications to the Commission for negative clearance (to confirm that Article 85(1) does not apply) or individual exemption (under Article 85(3)).

Section 6 of Form A/B, though it predates the Notice, still provides a useful summary of the principles to be applied when establishing the relevant market for the purposes of notifications (other than those relating to structural joint ventures). Form A/B takes as the relevant product market the classic market description comprising all those products and/or services which are regarded as interchangeable or substitutable by the consumer, by reason of the products' characteristics, their prices and intended use. It then usefully lists various specific factors that are relevant including:

   (i) the degree of physical similarity between the products in question,

   (ii) any differences in the end use to which these are put,

  (iii) differences in price between two products,

  (iv) the cost of switching between two potentially competing products,

   (v) established or entrenched consumer preferences for one type or category of product over another, and

  (vi) industry-wide product classifications (*e.g.* classifications maintained by trade associations).

4-32 Form A/B describes the geographic market as the area in which the undertakings concerned are involved in the supply of products or services, in which the conditions of competition are sufficiently homogenous and which can be distinguished from neighbouring areas because conditions of competition are appreciably different in those areas. The following factors are relevant in determining the relevant geographic market:

   (i) the nature and characteristics of the products concerned,

   (ii) the existence of entry barriers (such as intellectual property and regulatory requirements),

  (iii) consumer preferences,

  (iv) appreciable differences of the undertakings' market shares,

   (v) substantial price differences between neighbouring areas, and

  (iv) transport costs.

Form A/B requires the relevant markets to be defined, giving reasons and stating all assumptions made. Even when a product market is then defined, Form A/B requires details to be given of all specific products and services directly or indirectly affected by the notified agreement, even though these products and services may fall outside the relevant market.

FORM CO

4-33   Form CO[52] is to be used when notifying a concentration pursuant to Regulation 4064/89.[53] For further detail concerning E.C. merger control see Chapter 12 below. Form CO describes, in Section 6, the relevant product market in the same way as Form A/B with the added acknowledgement that a relevant product market may in some cases be composed of a number of individual products and/or services which present largely identical physical or technical characteristics and are interchangeable. Reasons must be given in Form CO as to why products or services in these markets are included and why others are excluded, having regard to substitutability, conditions of competition, prices, cross-elasticity of demand and other relevant factors.

The description of the relevant geographic market is identical to that found in Form A/B, as is the list of factors relevant to the assessment of geographic market, save that no mention is made of transport costs in Form CO.

4-34   Information also must be given concerning "affected markets". The relevant territories are the EEA territory, the Community, the EFTA territory and, individually any Member State or EFTA State. Details must be disclosed where:

(a) two or more of the parties to the concentration are engaged in business activities in the same product market and where the concentration will lead to a combined market share of 15 per cent or more ("horizontal relationships"); or

(b) one or more of the parties to the concentration are engaged in business activities in a product market, which is upstream or downstream of a product market in which any other party to the concentration is engaged, and any of their individual or combined market share is 25 per cent or more regardless of whether there is or is not any existing supplier/customer relationship between the parties to the concentration ("vertical relationships").

Form CO therefore requires an extremely delicate analysis of relevant product and geographic markets and "affected markets" but also requires analysis of closely related upstream, downstream and horizontal neighbouring markets in which the parties to the concentration are active but which do not themselves constitute "affected markets".

OFT GUIDE TO MARKET DEFINITION

Introduction

4-35   The best source of guidance concerning market definition for the purposes of the 1998 Act is the OFT guide entitled "Market Definition".[54] The guide was issued pursuant to section 52 of the 1998 Act which requires the Director to produce general advice and information about the application of the Chapter I and Chapter II prohibitions.

The guide stems largely from the content of the Commission's Notice as well as the merger guidelines produced by the United States Department of Justice and Federal Trade Commission. The decisions of the E.C.J and (to a lesser extent) those of the E.C. Commission are relevant given that under section 60 the Director, the court and any

---

[52] Commission Reg. 447/98 on the notifications, time limits and hearings provided for in Council Reg. 4064/89 on the control of concentrations between undertakings [1998] O.J. L061/1.
[53] [1990] O.J. L257/13 amended by Council Reg. 1310/97 [1997] O.J. L180/1.
[54] "Market Definition in U.K. Competition Policy" published by the OFT, February 1999.

tribunal must ensure "consistency" with the former and must "have regard to" the latter.[55]

Relevant market

4-36 The guide explains that the purpose of the Chapter I and Chapter II prohibitions is to prevent exploitation of market power, for example, by charging higher prices or by delivering lower quality than when exposed to competitive pressure. The significance of market share is that market power exists either because a single entity possesses a high market share, or because firms which together possess high market shares collude and no longer actively compete. Market shares are therefore taken to be an index of potential market power. It is acknowledged that market power *per se* is not necessarily harmful, but it does render collusion a greater risk, affecting a significant portion of the market. There is also a greater risk that higher prices will be charged by a single entity unless it will lose sales to others as an immediate result. Much depends on the availability of existing competition to respond to the activities of those with high market shares. Potential competition is therefore obviously relevant and is more likely to exist where barriers to new market entrants are low.

4-37 In describing the concept of a "market", the OFT begins by stating that the idea of a market is familiar to businesses and is expressed in annual reports, business plans and other documents which typically refer to market shares and competitors.[56] Any documents prepared by companies whether for planning, promotional, investment or any other purpose should avoid hyperbole, and in particular, any unnecessary exaggeration of their local, European or broader market share. All statements on behalf of companies, whether made by directors or members of the sales force will be ammunition in the hands of the OFT or Competition Commission. As demonstrated in the case of *United Brands*,[57] competition authorities might be said to have considerable latitude to reach whatever conclusion they wish on the merits of each case. Other sources of information will be customers, who might be surveyed by the OFT, or competitors. Notice that the OFT comments that "common sense will normally indicate the narrowest potential market definition".[58]

Demand substitution

4-38 The concept of the relevant market begins once again with substitutability and the so-called hypothetical monopolist test posed by the question whether a "hypothetical monopolist" of these products would maximise its profits by consistently charging higher prices than it would if it faced competition. In other words, would that business be constrained by the threat of new entry?[59]

The definition of relevant market is reached by identifying the product of the entity whose market is to be established (the "key product"). The next step is to identify all product substitutes which are available to consumers to chose between, in response to the setting of prices for the key product at uncompetitive levels. A figure of between 5 and 10 per cent above competitive levels is indicated, in line with the Commission's Notice on market definition. Not all consumers need switch, only sufficient number for the business

---

[55] For additional information, the reader is referred to "Market Definition in U.K. Competition Policy", OFT Research paper 1, February 1992. "Market Definition in U.K. Competition Policy", National Economic Research Associates.
[56] Para. 2.7, "Market Definition", published by the OFT.
[57] Case 27/76 [1978] E.C.R. 207 [1978] 1 C.M.L.R. 429.
[58] Para. 3.1, "Market Definition", published by the OFT.
[59] Para. 2.9, "Market Definition", published by the OFT.

to decide not to maintain prices at the raised level for the key product. However, substitution does need to take place within a year at the longest—in many cases much less than
a year. When all the substitutes are added together with the key product, the relevant
market is established. Substitutes do not need to be identical to the key product. They may
have different properties (such as lighters and matches which the MMC determined
belong in the same product market[60]), they may also be of different price or even different quality. The important thing is that substitution occurs within the above 5 to 10 per
cent parameters. Substitution is only likely to occur if the switching costs are low relative
to the value of the key product. The hypothetical monopolist test needs to be applied in
two dimensions, product (or service) and geography.

4-39   Evidence of substitution might take the form of historic similarity of price
movement. Evidence of lack of substitutability might take the form of sustained price
divergence without accompanying product switching.

The OFT gives useful examples where a monopolist might differentiate between consumers in a "captive" section of the market from those in the remainder of the market. The
case of *United Brands* provides an illustration of "captive" consumers of bananas unable
to switch to "hard" fruit because of age or infirmity. Similarly with commuter transport.
Commuters who are time-sensitive may have to choose to travel by train as the most reliable form of scheduled transport. Buses are not generally an adequate substitute for them
between 7 and 9 a.m. or between 5 and 7 p.m. However, trains and buses may be interchangeable forms of transport for holiday travellers not dependent on published schedules.
A dominant train operator might theoretically be able to discriminate against the captive
rail commuter by charging higher prices between those hours. The crucial issue is the proportion of captive consumers to other consumers. The higher the proportion of captive
consumers, the less substitutable the service and the greater market power is held by the
train operator. In general, the proportion of captive consumers will have to be sufficiently
high to enable the dominant undertaking to take advantage of the captive consumers at a
time when the service is not exposed to competition from other sources (such as buses).

4-40   The OFT states that on occasion it will use "chains of substitution" in defining
a market.[61] A chain might be represented (using the OFT's analogy of the motor trade)
by successive increases in the size of motor cars—beginning with Volkswagen Polos, minis
and similar cars in the economy category. The next size up may represent the next link in
the chain consisting of slightly larger cars such as Volkswagen Golfs and Ford Escorts.
The next link might comprise Ford Mondeos, Lagunas and so on. Where the price differential between each link is small, purchasers might be persuaded to buy cars of the next
size up, in response to increases in the prices of cars in the category in which they usually
purchase. If an increase in price of one size of vehicle might persuade drivers instead to
purchase the next size up, a chain of substitution might then be said to exist. A price rise
applicable to a Rolls Royce, however, would not affect the market for small cars. The OFT
has expressed concern at the situation where a single entity monopolises a series of links
in the chain which enable it to increase prices across those links and thereby counteract
the competitive constraints that would otherwise exist from competition by other manufacturers in preceding or succeeding links of the chain.[62]

Supply substitution

4-41   Pressure against high prices might also be faced from potential competitors by
supply substitution. Supply substitution occurs where suppliers are able at relatively short

---

[60] Cm 1854, 1992.
[61] Para. 3.11, "Market Definition", published by the OFT.
[62] Para. 3.12, "Market Definition", published by the OFT.

notice (at most within a year) and low cost (without significant investment) to switch production and thereby compete against high prices. Supply substitution indicates the products which suppliers are prepared to make and sell in response to price increases.

The OFT gives the example of paper producers who may make paper to different grades that are not substitutable by consumers and which, applying demand substitution principles, may not fall within the same market. The different grades of paper may be consumed by entirely different groups of purchaser. Nevertheless because all grades of paper use the same raw materials and, by and large the same processes and plant, producers may readily switch from one grade to another thereby constraining the monopolist's power. It would therefore be wrong to look at demand substitution alone.

4-42 Supply substitution is a measure that is generally used to verify findings of market definition having applied first the demand substitution test. Tests of supply substitution and demand substitution may frequently produce different results. Cat food and dog food are in different demand substitution markets but readiness of producers to switch manufacture would be a measure of lack of market power and the strength of potential competition faced by any supplier of cat food or dog food. An analysis of supply substitution must always be made. In *Continental Can*,[63] the Commission was severely criticised for not carrying out that analysis. If nothing else, supply substitution will serve as a general measure of potential competition.

The OFT has indicated its readiness to seek evidence of supply substitution by enquiry of potential suppliers and their assessment of the feasibility of switching production economically in response to a 5 per cent price increase.[64] The OFT may also make enquiry concerning the spare capacity of firms, though conclusions may vary to some extent dependent on whether those firms have undertaken long-term commitments which take up capacity. If only a low level of capacity is available from producers who could potentially switch production, the market share of the entity making the hypothetical price rise may be increased. The views of customers will also be relevant since customers may not be willing to make the product switch in practice. For example a purchaser of high grade velum paper may not wish to take suppliers from a household name in the supply of toilet paper.

The geographic market

4-43 The approach to be taken to determine the geographic market is similar to the approach to be taken to determine demand substitutability and supply substitutability. The analysis begins with the geographical coverage represented by sales of the key product. The next step is to determine the area over which substitution is likely to occur.

The prime geographical constraint on demand substitution is the proximity of other sources for the key product. Much obviously depends on product value and the ease and cost of transportation. Purchasers may not travel far in order to make the product substitution. Ultimately the task is to determine the geographical area over which ready substitutes are available. The geographical area of such substitutes should be added to the geographical area of sales of the key product.

4-44 The geographical significance of supply substitution relates to the availability of substitute suppliers to supply purchasers in the same and neighbouring areas as the supplier of the key product. Much depends on the costs and other barriers to suppliers. If geographic market penetration depends on significant expenditure on product promotion, those areas which cannot be met without that expenditure would be excluded from the geographic market.

---

[63] Case 6/72 [1973] E.C.R. 215; [1973] C.M.L.R. 199.
[64] Para. 3.21, "Market Definition", published by the OFT.

Although the 1998 Act only applies to the effect on competition "within the United Kingdom", the geographic market may be much larger than the United Kingdom and this will be relevant in establishing the market shares held in the relevant market.

Miscellaneous

4-45   The OFT makes reference to various issues which may also play an important part in the ultimate determination of relevant market.

Temporal markets

4-46   The temporal nature of certain markets, such as electricity and telephone supply, is reflected in the pattern of demand throughout each day with separate consumer rates for day and night consumption.

Likewise demand may be seasonal—such as for winter or summer clothing, particularly for sports-wear. On the supply side, fruit is generally a seasonal product though less markedly so with advances in refrigerated transportation and genetically engineered crops, which have a levelling effect on seasonal differences. All of these factors may result in the differentiation of markets.

Secondary markets

4-47   The OFT identifies the inter-relation between what might be termed "primary markets", to distinguish them from "secondary markets" which depend for their existence on a viable primary market. For example the primary product in *Volvo* was cars and in *Hugin* was cash registers. In each case the primary product market was regarded as separate from the secondary product market (in *Volvo* spare parts and in *Hugin* cash register spare parts). Although primary and secondary markets are often treated as separate they may not be entirely discrete in cases where, for example the market for cars is affected by the availability of spare parts for those cars at a reasonable price. This is what the OFT describes as "the whole-life cost" of a product.[65] The availability of cheap spare parts might affect the price of those particular cars.

For example the Commission found that Kyocera, the manufacturers of computer printers, was not dominant because of the significant cost of secondary products which had a constraining effect on the market for primary printer products.[66] It is also worth noting that resistance to product switching may result either because consumers are inevitably "captive" to a primary product such as a computer for their spare parts (until it is replaced by obsolescence or age) or because they are contractually tied to maintenance agreements which in the case of computer maintenance contracts frequently have a long fixed term.

Calculation of market share

4-48   In general the OFT is likely to assess market shares on the basis of the value, rather than volume of output, preferring value as a more accurate determinant of market power. Value refers to the value of sales to customers rather than value of production or even value of sales to ultimate consumers.[67] Patterns of long-term exchange rates are used to determine the value of sales when made outside the United Kingdom.

Volume is only likely to be used in the case of homogenous markets, which should in

---

[65] Para. 5.7, "Market Definition", published by the OFT.
[66] See XXV Report on Competition Policy (1995) p. 140.
[67] Para. 4.6, "Assessment of Market Power", published by the OFT as Paper 10, "Assessment of Profitability by Competition Authorities", February 1977.

any event result in the same conclusions as the calculations made by value. The OFT will also examine trends in the market rather than assess only one particular year. Changes in the market structure will obviously be important to establish a complete picture.

4-49 The OFT has considered the extent to which internal production values by a company might be included in its market share calculations. Internal production refers to the value of intermediate products which a supplier consumes in manufacture, where an external market exists for those intermediate products. In general if a company is able to switch production easily in order to make external sales of the intermediate product the internal production values will also be included, along with the external sales values.

Ultimately, whatever arguments are deployed to minimise or maximise market share the issue for the OFT is generally the extent of market power wielded by the entities concerned. Market share does not necessarily equate with market power. Market power is determined partly by market share and partly by a number of other market factors. Reference should be made to Chapter 11, *Assessment of factors*, which highlights a number of matters that have been considered relevant in the past (albeit in the context of the Fair Trading Act 1973) when measuring market power.

4-50 Finally, it should be remembered however that the OFT's guide to market definition is only relevant in the context of the 1998 Act although in principle it does not differ from the principles set out in the Commission's Notice. It is also to be remembered that the guide is not to be interpreted as if it had statutory effect since it is intended for use by the business community as much as by lawyers.

CHAPTER 5

Transitional Provisions of the Competition Act 1998

INTRODUCTION

5-01   Schedule 13 to the 1998 Act contains the transitional provisions for phasing in the Act. These transitional provisions may be supplemented by further orders of the Secretary of State under section 75 which empowers him to make incidental, consequential, transitional or supplemental provision where necessary or expedient.

Given the extent of the changes introduced by the 1998 Act (involving the wholesale repeal of much of the existing United Kingdom competition legislation), a generous timetable has been set down to enable compliance. This is seen as necessary in view of the significant penalties that are introduced for infringement of the Chapter I and Chapter II prohibitions and in view of the Director's very clear statements that he intends to enforce the provisions of the 1998 Act to the full.

5-02   The format of this Chapter is as follows. First, the terms used throughout Schedule 13 (which contains the transitional provisions) are defined. The operation of the transitional provisions is then summarised diagrammatically. The effect of the transitional provisions is also expanded upon. When considered in conjunction with the diagrams, this may assist in determining how the transitional provisions impinge upon any agreement, depending on when it was made. The residual effect of the Restrictive Trade Practices Act 1977 and the Resale Prices Act 1977 is outlined and finally the Fair Trading Act 1973 and the Competition Act 1980 are covered. This chapter only represents a summary and detailed reference should be made to Schedule 13.

KEY DATES

5-03   It is essential to grasp the following terms:

(a) *"enactment date"* is the date on which the Act received Royal Assent (November 9, 1998);

(b) *"starting date"* is the date on which the Chapter I prohibition comes into force (March 1, 2000);

(c) *"interim period"* is the period between the enactment date and the starting date (November 9, 1998 to February 29, 2000 inclusive); and

(d) *"transitional period"* is the period within which compliance with the Chapter I prohibition is required. The period is generally one year from the starting date, but for certain agreements, such as those affecting broadcasting and financial services, the term is five years from the starting date. The transitional periods are capable of being extended on application. Special rules also apply to the utilities. It is important to note that there is no transitional period for the Chapter II prohibition, which will apply immediately from the starting date.

5-04–5-06   The diagrams on pp. 74–76 summarise the transitional provisions, depending on when the agreement was made, whether:

(i) before the enactment date (see Figure 1);

(ii) during the interim period (see Figure 2); or

(iii) on or after the starting date (see Figure 3).

THE RESTRICTIVE TRADE PRACTICES ACT 1976 ("RTPA") AND RESALE PRICES ACT 1976 ("RPA")

General

5-07   The continued application of the RTPA and the RPA depends on the date on which the agreement in question was made, *i.e.* whether before the enactment date (November 9, 1998) or during the interim period (November 9, 1998 to February 29, 2000 inclusive). Both the RTPA and the RPA are to be repealed with effect from the starting date,[1] but until that date both will continue in force, albeit in modified form. (For further guidance as to the application of the RTPA and the RPA to individual agreements see below.)

The register

5-08   The Director remains under a duty to maintain the register of agreements under section 1(2) of the RTPA for agreements already registered at the starting date and for the purpose of determining whether an agreement that was registrable was in fact registered, as this will be relevant for the purpose of determining its enforceability.

The register also has to be maintained for registrable agreements furnished for the first time before the starting date provided, of course, that they are not non-notifiable agreements.

5-09   The OFT has benefitted from a reduction in the range of agreements which are required to be furnished. Although many agreements are registrable under the RTPA they are rendered "non-notifiable" by various statutory instruments including the Restrictive Trade Practices (Sale and Purchase and Share Subscription Agreements) (Goods) Order 1989,[2] the Restrictive Trade Practices (Non-notifiable Agreements) (Turnover Threshold) Order 1996,[3] which applies to agreements (other than price-fixing agreements) where the parties (and their group companies) have an aggregate United Kingdom turnover of £20 million or less at the date of the agreement, the Restrictive Trade Practices (Non-notifiable Agreements) (Turnover Thresholds) Amendment Order 1997,[4] which increased the turnover threshold to £50 million, and the Restrictive Trade Practices (Non-notifiable Agreements) (Sale and Purchase, Share Subscription and Franchise Agreements) Order 1997,[5] which applies to certain share or business transactions and franchise agreements which contain restrictions of less than five years' duration. The category of non-notifiable

---

[1] By order of the Secretary of State bringing into force section 1 of the 1998 Act.
[2] S.I. 1989 No. 1081.
[3] S.I. 1996 No. 348.
[4] S.I. 1997 No. 2944.
[5] S.I. 1997 No. 2945.

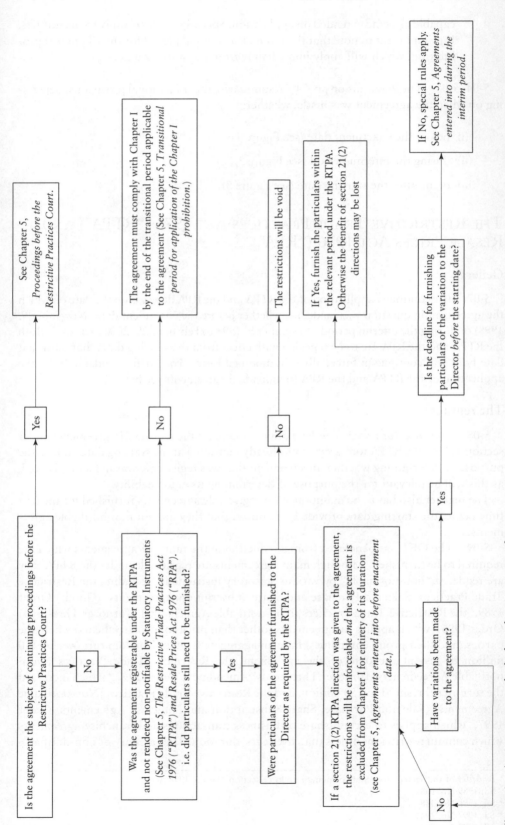

Figure 1 *Agreements made before the enactment date*

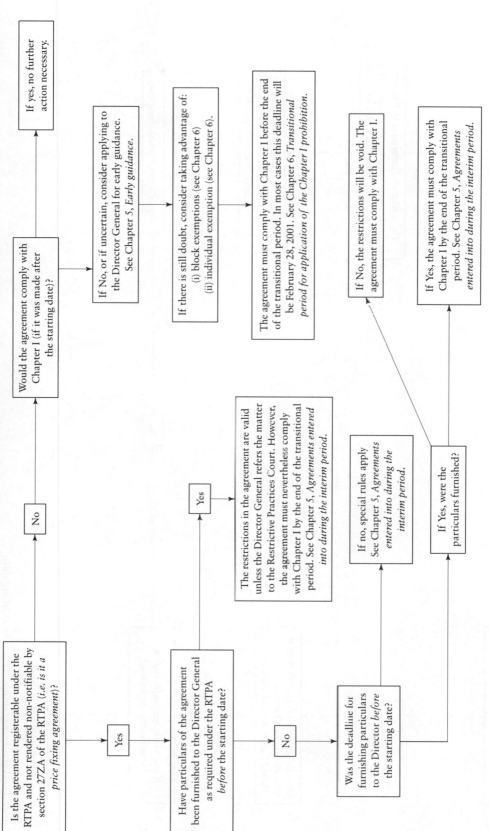

Figure 2 Agreements made in the interim period

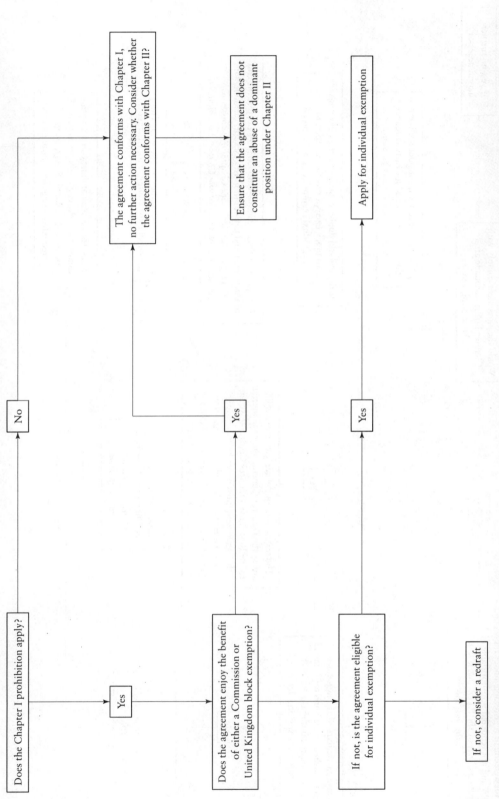

Figure 3 *Agreements made after the starting date*

agreements is to be expanded[5a] so that all agreements (with the exception of price-fixing agreements) are non-notifiable after the enactment date and this is intended to limit the number of agreements that may benefit from the transitional arrangements in relation to agreements on the RTPA register. The aim is to subject all non-notifiable agreements to the new regime of compliance with Chapter I and Chapter II of the 1998 Act.

PROCEEDINGS BEFORE THE RESTRICTIVE PRACTICES COURT

5-10 On the starting date, a number of existing applications to the Restrictive Practices Court cease, as do a number of orders by that court which are in force on the starting date.[6]

The applications which fall by the wayside are those which are not determined before the starting date and are made under the following provisions of the RTPA:

  (i) section 2(2) (for restraining orders in relation to restrictions that are contrary to public interest, including applications to vary restraining orders[7]);

 (ii) section 35(3) (for restraining orders in relation to unregistered registrable agreements);

(iii) section 37(1) (to order examination of witnesses under oath);

 (iv) section 40(1) (for a declaration whether restrictions in a registrable agreement which could not be the subject of an order under section 56 of the Fair Trading Act 1973 are contrary to public interest); and

  (v) paragraph 5 of Schedule 4 to the RTPA, concerning residual rights to make an application under section 18(2) of the Restrictive Trade Practices Act 1956.

In addition, undetermined applications under section 25(2) of the RPA are dropped on the starting date. These are civil actions on behalf of the Crown for an injunction or other appropriate relief.

5-11 The orders which are in force before the starting date and which thereupon cease are orders made under the following provisions of the RTPA:

  (i) section 2(2) (restraining orders in relation to restrictions that are contrary to public interest);

 (ii) section 29(1) (orders granting exemption from registration to agreements important to the national economy);

(iii) section 30(1) (orders approving agreements which hold down prices including orders revoking such orders[8]);

 (iv) section 35(3) (restraining orders in relation to unregistered registrable agreements); and

  (v) section 37(1) (orders for the examination of witnesses).

Any approval given under section 32(2) of the RTPA to wholesale co-operative societies will be cancelled on the starting date. In addition, orders under section 25(2) of the RPA

[5a] See n. 17 below.
[6] Sched. 13, para. 8.
[7] Under s. 4(4) of the RTPA.
[8] Under s. 33(4) of the RTPA.

are cancelled on the starting date (orders pursuant to civil actions on behalf of the Crown for an injunction or appropriate relief).

5-12   Special provision is made for other "continuing proceedings" which are those commenced by the Director making an application to the Restrictive Practices Court under the RTPA or RPA, which are not determined before the starting date. The repeal of the RTPA and RPA does not affect continuing proceedings. For as long as the proceedings continue, the Chapter I prohibition does not apply to any agreement which is the subject of continuing proceedings.[9] However, in its place, the RTPA and RPA (as appropriate) will continue to apply. Appeals against the decision made in continuing proceedings also form part of the continuing proceedings until the appeal has been dealt with, whether by disposal, withdrawal or by expiry of the period for bringing an appeal.[10] The parties may agree between themselves to discontinue continuing proceedings and, on application to the court, the effect will be as if the proceedings had never been instituted.[11]

Proceedings under sections 3 or 26 of the RTPA are not continuing proceedings.[12] Section 3 concerns interim orders made in connection with registered agreements contrary to public interest. Section 26 concerns orders to rectify the register and declarations whether the RTPA applies to an agreement. Orders under Section 3 and Section 26 are not cancelled on the starting date, unlike those in the above list. As a transitional measure, the RTPA is seen as the best mechanism for controlling agreements caught by a section 3 application or order. Any application made before the starting date for a section 3 or section 26 order which has not been determined will continue so as to allow it to be granted, whether before or after the starting date. The effective date of a section 26 application will be back-dated to before the starting date so that the register stands as amended.[13]

5-13   The right to private actions under section 35 of the RTPA and section 25 of the RPA are preserved in favour of any one who was entitled to bring a claim under either of those sections immediately before the starting date (but the claim may only relate to the period prior to the starting date).[14]

AGREEMENTS ENTERED INTO BEFORE THE ENACTMENT DATE

5-14   The RTPA applies to all registrable agreements made before the enactment date, unaffected by the 1998 Act. The statutory instruments referred to in *The Restrictive Trade Practices Act 1976 ("RTPA") and Resale Prices Act 1976 ("RPA")* above, determine whether those agreements are notifiable. For agreements entered into before the starting date (on or before February 29, 2000), the RTPA continues to apply and particulars of agreements that are registrable (and not non-notifiable) should be furnished in the normal way. The important date for determining whether the RTPA applies is the starting date.

The time limits (set out in section 24 and Schedule 2 to the RTPA) for furnishing particulars of agreements to the Director continue to apply to agreements made before the starting date (whether made before or after the enactment date). In most cases, the time limit under the RTPA is three months from the date of the agreement or the restrictions becoming effective, whichever is the earlier (see the RTPA for further details).

---

[9] Sched. 13, para. 14 (1–2). The suspension of the Chapter I prohibition in the case of the RPA applies to agreements relating to goods which are the subject of proceedings under ss. 16 or 17 of the RPA to the extent to which the agreement consists of exempt provisions *i.e.* those that are void or unlawful as a result of ss. 9 or 11 of the RPA.
[10] Sched. 13, para. 15.
[11] Sched. 13, para. 18.
[12] Sched. 13, para. 15(2).
[13] Sched. 13, para. 12(2).
[14] Sched. 13, para. 13.

5-15 Agreements which benefit from a section 21(2) direction,[15] to the effect that the agreement does not warrant an investigation by the Restrictive Trade Practices Court, are expressly excluded from the Chapter I prohibition.[16] The majority of pre-enactment date agreements which have been furnished to the Director General under the RTPA have the benefit of a section 21(2) direction. These agreements are excluded from Chapter I for their duration. However, particulars of all variations to those agreements will need to be furnished under the RTPA.

AGREEMENTS ENTERED INTO DURING THE INTERIM PERIOD

5-16 The RTPA is repealed with effect from the starting date. The RTPA therefore continues to apply to agreements entered into during the interim period. However, the category of non-notifiable agreements is to be so broad that the only new agreements which are capable of notification are price-fixing agreements.[17] The purpose of such a broad category of non-notifiable agreements

> "is intended to assist firms in readying themselves for compliance with the new regime. It is not a moratorium on the pursuit of anti-competitive activities."[18]

Even if agreements are non-notifiable, the Director may still invoke his powers under section 36 of the RTPA by way of enforcement and may also apply to the Restrictive Practices Court under section 1(2)(c) of the RTPA. Before the enactment date, the Director was under a duty to issue proceedings where appropriate but his power is discretionary during the interim period.[19] For this reason the procedure in sections 21(1) and (2) of the RTPA entitling the Director to refrain from taking proceedings to the Restrictive Practices Court in certain circumstances is no longer relevant and consequently section 21(2) directions are no longer available for agreements made after the enactment date.[20]

5-17 In the case of notifiable "price fixing" agreements (which are expected to be very few in number) the usual RTPA procedures continue to apply during the interim period, the only difference being that the discretion which the Director had before the enactment date to extend the period for furnishing particulars has been withdrawn.[21] Notifiable agreements may still be the subject of proceedings before the Restrictive Practices Court in the same way as non-notifiable agreements.

If the deadline for furnishing particulars of a notifiable agreement expires after the starting date (for example a "price fixing" agreement entered into in February 2000) special rules apply.[22] The parties have two options. First, they may (but are not bound to) furnish particulars and treat the agreement as if registered in the normal way. If the parties

---

[15] A direction made by the Secretary of State under s. 21(2) of the RTPA.
[16] Sched. 3, para. 2(1) of the 1998 Act.
[17] Sched. 13, para. 5, which renders non-notifiable any agreement made during the interim period and which satisfies the conditions in paras (a), (c) and (d) of s. 27A(1) of the RTPA, namely: (a) is subject to registration under the RTPA; (c) is not, and never has been, a price-fixing agreement; and (d) is not an agreement in respect of which the Director has entered or filed particulars under s. 1(2)(b) of the RTPA (*i.e.* it has been registered).
[18] Competition Act 1998 "Transitional Arrangements" (Formal Consultation Draft), para. 2.3.1 (produced by the OFT).
[19] Sched. 13, para. 6(a).
[20] Sched. 13, para. 6(b).
[21] Sched. 13, para. 6(c).
[22] Sched. 13, para. 25. These "special rules" apply to (a) price fixing agreements entered into in the final three months of the interim period; and (b) variations made in those final three months to both (i) interim period price fixing agreements; and (ii) pre-enactment date agreements (which continue to require furnishing as under the RTPA. See *Agreements entered into before the enactment date*, above).

register, they must do so before the starting date, and the agreement will benefit from the one year transitional period (see *Transitional period for application of the Chapter I prohibition*, below). Secondly, they may decide not to register the agreement but the agreement will not then benefit from the one year transitional period. Note however that the parties should not give effect to the relevant restrictions before the starting date as this will be prohibited under section 27ZA of the RTPA.

In relation to variations to existing registered agreements, these continue to be notifiable as they were prior to the enactment date. See *Agreements entered into before the enactment date*, above.

EARLY GUIDANCE

5-18 On application by a party, early guidance may be given by the Director General before the starting date in relation to agreements made during the interim period by means of a similar procedure to that in section 13 of the 1998 Act for post-starting date guidance. (See Chapter 6, *Guidance*, for further details). The guidance available is whether an agreement is likely to infringe the Chapter I prohibition and, if it is, whether it is likely to be granted individual exemption or block exemption. The OFT will only want to be troubled with applications for guidance where there is a real doubt, not merely in cases where the parties seek fail-safe immunity from penalties. Early guidance is not available for agreements made before the enactment date. The Director has published Directions for early guidance applications and form EG is to be used when applying for early guidance.[23]

Early guidance is intended to have the same effect (from the starting date) as guidance given under section 15 and, in particular, it will be binding on the Director to provide immunity from penalties[24] and limited protection against further action by the Director. Applications for early guidance made before the starting date may be subject to the full section 13 procedure after the starting date as if the application had been made after the starting date.[25]

TRANSITIONAL PERIOD FOR APPLICATION OF THE CHAPTER I PROHIBITION

5-19 As a rule, agreements and practices made before the starting date to which the Chapter I prohibition applies will benefit from a transitional period of one year, beginning on the starting date.[26] The Chapter I prohibition does not therefore apply during the transitional period to agreements made before the starting date. The Chapter II prohibition applies from the starting date and does not have the benefit of any transitional period.

No transitional period

5-20 There is no transitional period for the following agreements[27]:

---

[23] See Appendix B.3. The Directions "Competition Act 1998 — early guidance directions" (OFT 412) are available from the OFT. The Director is to publish Procedural Rules for notifications and guidance after the starting date (under ss. 13 and 14 of the 1998 Act) after a period of consultation.

[24] s. 15.

[25] Sched. 13, para. 7.

[26] Different transitional provisions apply to utilities.

[27] Sched. 13, para. 20.

(i) agreements to the extent that they are void under section 2(1) of the RTPA (restrictions found to be contrary to public interest) or section 35(1)(a) of the RTPA (registrable restrictions void for failure to register within time);

(ii) agreements to the extent that they are the subject of a restraining order under section 2(2) or section 35(3) of the RTPA;

(iii) agreements to the extent that a person has acted unlawfully for the purposes of section 27ZA(2) or (3) of the RTPA by giving effect to restrictions before registration under the RTPA;

(iv) agreements registrable under the RTPA where relevant particulars were not furnished by the starting date; and

(v) agreements in respect of which there are continuing proceedings, to the extent that the agreement is determined to be void or unlawful. Notice the reference to the term "to the extent that". This contemplates that an agreement may have a longer duration than the transitional period (to which only particular restrictions relate).

5-21   Schedule 13 to the 1998 Act makes no specific mention of the large category of agreements which have been furnished under the RTPA and which have received section 21(2) directions from the Secretary of State to the effect that the restrictions are not of such significance as to call for investigation by the Restrictive Practices Court. To benefit from a section 21(2) direction under the RTPA, the agreement must have been entered into before the enactment date. Agreements which have received section 21(2) directions are excluded from the Chapter I prohibition by Schedule 3 paragraph 2 of the 1998 Act for their entire duration. However, if a material variation (not necessarily one that appreciably affects competition) is made to a section 21(2) agreement, the exclusion ceases to apply from the moment that the variation is effective. In any event, the Director has power to disapply the exclusion in relation to a particular agreement and bring a section 21(2) agreement within the Chapter I prohibition. When considering whether to do so, he may require a party to the agreement to provide information. If this requirement is not met then the exclusion may be disapplied. The Director may also disapply the exclusion if he considers that the agreement, if not excluded, would infringe the Chapter I prohibition and is not likely to be a candidate for unconditional individual exemption.

In the case of continuing proceedings under the RTPA or RPA, the transitional period begins when the proceedings are determined, or earlier if they are discontinued. Agreements found by the Restrictive Practices Court not to be contrary to public interest benefit from a transitional period of five years (as do agreements within an exemption order under section 14 of the RPA).[28]

Five year transitional period

5-22   There is a five year transitional period for certain agreements regulated by the Financial Services Act 1986 or the Broadcasting Act 1990.[29] Detailed provision is also made for the utilities in Schedule 13, Chapter IV conferring transitional periods in certain cases of up to 5 years.

---

[28] Sched. 13, paras 23 and 24.
[29] Sched. 13, para. 26.

One year transitional period

5-23   The general rule[30] is that there is a transitional period of one year beginning on the starting date for agreements made before the starting date.[31] This even applies to agreements made before the starting date to which the RTPA never applied as well as to those rendered non-notifiable. Agreements made after the starting date must comply with the Chapter I prohibition immediately.

EXTENDING THE TRANSITIONAL PERIODS

5-24   The Director has power to extend the transitional periods on application by a party to an agreement provided that the application is made more than three months before expiry of the transitional period. The one year transitional period may be extended by the Director for a further year. The other transitional periods may be extended by up to six months. This may be done in response to an application or on the Director's own initiative.[32] Extensions are most likely to be granted in cases of marginal infringement of the Chapter I prohibition. Cases where exemption is likely to be granted but where the infringement is more than marginal will not be granted an extension since the appropriate course of action is to apply for individual exemption.

The application for an extension is appropriate in order to provide continuity for agreements while they are re-negotiated or are due to expire soon after expiry of the original transitional period or in order to give time to prepare an application for individual exemption. If the Director has not granted the extension within two months of the application, it will be deemed to be granted for the maximum period requested.

TERMINATION OF TRANSITIONAL PERIODS

5-25   The Director also has power to terminate the transitional period for any agreement. The Director must give a direction[33] and the circumstances in which he may do so are similar to those entitling him to withdraw the exclusion for section 21(2) agreements (see *No transition period*, above). These are where, having requested information from a party, the information has not been provided (without reasonable excuse) or where the Director considers that the agreement, but for the transitional period, would infringe the Chapter I prohibition and would not be granted unconditional exemption. The direction must be given in writing giving at least 28 days advance notice of termination.

The procedure is only likely to be invoked in cases where the parties to an agreement are taking unfair advantage of the transitional periods which are given to enable parties to bring their agreements into compliance with the newly-introduced prohibitions. The parties may then apply for individual exemption which may be granted on conditions or subject to obligations.

---

[30] See Chapter III and IV of Sched. 13 for special cases and consider the other departures from the general rule discussed above in this Chapter.
[31] Sched. 13, para. 19. Remember that the transitional periods only apply to agreements made *before* the starting date.
[32] Sched. 13, para. 36.
[33] Under Sched. 13, para. 37.

E.C. NOTIFICATIONS

5-26 An agreement which has been granted individual exemption or block exemption by the Commission under Article 85(3)[34] is automatically granted parallel exemption under section 10 of the 1998 Act. Even if an agreement is the subject of a comfort letter rather than formal exemption the Director must have regard to it. There is also an obvious need for the Commission and the Director to reach consistent decisions, as explained in the Commission's notice on co-operation between national competition authorities and the Commission in handling cases falling within the scope of Articles 85 or 86 of the E.C. Treaty.[35]

Given that the Director will decide any matter qualifying for exemption under Article 85(3) in like manner to the Commission, the Director will not deal with applications which seek confirmation of that with any high priority. The Director would prefer the appropriate decision to be sought from the Director only when the agreement is challenged in the United Kingdom courts and the application should then be for retroactive exemption.

THE FAIR TRADING ACT 1973

5-27 The 1998 Act repeals, with effect from the starting date, certain parts of the Fair Trading Act 1973 which limited the order-making powers and matters which could be given consideration in any monopoly reference or merger reference.[36] These prevented orders being made which had the effect of duplicating or enhancing the order-making provisions of the RTPA in relation to agreements caught by the RTPA.

Any order under section 54 or 73 of the Fair Trading Act 1973 (respectively, orders of the appropriate Minister on a report on a monopoly reference and orders of the Secretary of State on a report on a merger reference) may, after the starting date, also extend to agreements that would have been caught by the RTPA.

Allowance is also made for the consideration of RTPA-related matters previously excluded from consideration because of those limiting provisions.

THE COMPETITION ACT 1980

5-28 Undertakings previously accepted by the Director under section 4 or 9 of the Competition Act 1980 are cancelled with effect from the starting date. If an undertaking is given as part of continuing MMC proceedings then it will continue until the proceedings are determined.

---

[34] See Chapter 6, below.
[35] [1997] O.J. C313/03. For further detail, see Chapter 14, *Co-operation concerning national authorities*, below.
[36] Sched. 8, para. 3 to the Fair Trading Act 1973.

CHAPTER 6

Notification, Exemption and Guidance

INTRODUCTION

6-01 Given the enormous theoretical breadth of the prohibitions in Article 85(1) and Chapter I, and given also the consequences of infringement (fines, unenforceability and third party actions), a huge burden is placed on businesses to ensure compliance. Compliance may be achieved by using any one or more of the procedures described in this Chapter. An outline of these procedures would be useful at this stage by way of introduction and orientation.

Notification procedure before the commission for Article 85(1) (and Article 86) infringements

6-02 The Commission is responsible for granting exemption (under Article 85(3)) for agreements caught by Article 85(1), whether on application (for individual agreements) or by means of automatic block exemption (for certain categories of agreement which meet prescribed criteria). Instead of taking the procedure for seeking individual exemption to the point where formal exemption is granted to individual agreements, the parties may instead rely on a comfort letter which is an indication from the Commission that the agreement is eligible for exemption. It prevents the Commission taking further action against the parties for that agreement. Alternatively, the Commission may grant negative clearance on application. Negative clearance is confirmation given by the Commission that neither Article 85(1) nor Article 86 applies to any particular agreement or conduct. For further details concerning the decision-making powers of the Commission (and review of those decisions) see Chapter 14, *Introduction*, and *Review of Commission Decisions by the Court of First Instance*, below). The consequences of notification may be summarised as follows.

In relation to Article 85(1)

6-03 Notification may lead to:

   (i) individual exemption (declaring the prohibition in Article 85(1) to be inapplicable because the criteria in Article 85(3) are satisfied owing to the resulting benefits of the agreement); or

   (ii) negative clearance (certifying that the agreement is not caught by Article 85(1) in the first place); or

   (iii) a comfort letter (indicating that although Article 85(1) applies to the agreement, it would be eligible for exemption).

Agreements which satisfy all of the requirements of a block exemption Regulation do not require notification since they are granted exemption automatically. For further details of those agreements eligible for automatic block exemption, see Chapter 7 below.

In relation to Article 86

6-04 Notification of an agreement which constitutes an abuse of dominant position may not be granted exemption under Article 85(3). However, an application may be made for negative clearance.

Notification procedure before the Director (Chapters I and II)

6-05 The Director is empowered to give guidance concerning any agreement or conduct which may infringe the Chapter I prohibition or the Chapter II prohibition. Alternatively, a formal decision may be preferred which, in the case of the Chapter I prohibition, may result in exemption being granted. Provision is also made for block exemption of certain categories of agreement in a similar manner to Commission block exemptions. The consequences of notification to the Director may be summarised as follows.

In relation to the Chapter I prohibition

6-06 Notification may lead to:

(i) guidance (similar to a comfort letter if positive, but if negative would amount to a "discomfort letter"); or

(ii) a decision (if positive, equivalent to individual exemption or negative clearance given by the Commission).

Agreements which benefit from automatic block exemption do not require notification (as they are in a similar position to agreements automatically granted exemption by way of Commission Regulation).

In relation to the Chapter II prohibition

6-07 Notification may lead to:

(i) guidance; or

(ii) a decision.

In each case with similar effect as given in relation to the Chapter I prohibition. In this sense, Article 86 and Chapter II differ. Exemption is not available for any matter caught by Article 86.

NOTIFICATION PROCEDURE BEFORE THE COMMISSION FOR ARTICLE 85(1) AND ARTICLE 86 INFRINGEMENTS

Eligibility criteria for exemption of Article 85(1) infringements

6-08 Article 85(3) of the E.C. Treaty is the only gateway for the purpose of seeking exemption for agreements that fall within the Article 85(1) prohibition. It reads as follows:

"(3) The provisions of paragraph 1 may, however, be declared inapplicable in the case of:

   (i) any agreement or category of agreements between undertakings;
   (ii) any decision or category of decisions by associations of undertakings;
   (iii) any concerted practice or category of concerted practices;

which contributes to improving the production or distribution of goods or to promoting technical or economic progress, while allowing consumers a fair share of the resulting benefit, and which does not:

(a) impose on the undertakings concerned restrictions which are not indispensable to the attainment of these objectives;

(b) afford such undertakings the possibility of eliminating competition in respect of a substantial part of the products in question."

6-09   Article 85(2) renders automatically void any matter prohibited by Article 85(1). If the offending parts of an agreement cannot be severed from the rest of the agreement without making a nonsense of it, the whole agreement will be void. This was put as follows in *La Technique Minière v. Maschinenbau Ulm GmbH*[1]:

"The automatic nullity in question applies only to those elements of the agreement which are subject to the prohibition, or to the agreement as a whole if those elements do not appear severable from the agreement itself. Consequently, all other contractual provisions which are not affected by the prohibition, since they do not involve the application of the Treaty, fall outside Community law."[2]

Therefore, if the offending clauses are severable, they alone may be rendered unenforceable. The issue of severability is a matter of national law and, in the United Kingdom, much depends on what remains of the agreement after the prohibited parts have been removed. The test (as explained in *Chemidus Wavin v. TERI*[3]) is on the basis of:

"whether the contract could be so changed in its character as not to be the sort of contract that the parties entered into at all."[4]

The provisions of Article 85(3) enable Article 85(1) to be "declared inapplicable" in specified circumstances, by means either of individual exemption or automatic block exemption. The reference in Article 85(3) to any category of agreements, category of decisions or category of concerted practices is a reference to block exemption. Block exemptions apply to certain types of agreement which by their nature are considered to satisfy the criteria laid down in Article 85(3).[5]

Application for exemption

6-10   The key practical difference between individual exemption and block exemption is that a detailed application must be made for individual exemption. The Commission alone is empowered to grant exemption.[6] No court may do so, although the CFI may

---

[1] Case 56/65 *La Technique Minière v. Maschinenbau Ulm GmbH* [1966] E.C.R. 235; [1966] C.M.L.R. 357.
[2] Case 56/65 [1966] E.C.R. 235 at 250.
[3] *Chemidus Wavin v. TERI* [1978] 3 C.M.L.R. 514 CA.
[4] *ibid*. at 519.
[5] For further detail concerning the particular agreements which qualify for automatic exemption see Chap. 7 below.
[6] Reg. 17/62, Art. 9(1) [1962] J.O. 204/62.

review any Commission decision. The format of all applications is prescribed by Form A/B[7] a copy of which may be found in Appendix B.1 below. Only those who are parties to the agreement or engaging in the notified practice may apply. If more than one party is submitting an application, they should use the same form.

Form A/B is really no more than a list of headings. The substance of any application is to be set out in an Annex to Form A/B. Information must be given concerning the parties to the agreement and the groups to which they belong. Details of any other relevant submissions to competent competition authorities must also be provided. The most significant section is obviously the one that requires an explanation of the full details of the arrangements, summarising the nature, content and objectives of the notified agreement. Any provisions which may restrict the parties in their freedom to take independent commercial decisions must be identified with an assessment of the Member States[8] that may be affected by the agreement or practice, together with an assessment of any effect on trade between the Community[9] and any third country. As part of the notification process, the Commission has the right to publish in its own official publication, the Official Journal, a summary of the nature and objectives of the agreement and this will invite third party comment within a month or so of the advertisement. The notice is published as soon as possible after a notification is received. Form A/B requests that the parties provide a suitable summary of the agreement for this purpose, obviously avoiding the inclusion of any secret or confidential material.

6-11 Exemption may be granted for a period of limited validity, it may be granted subject to conditions or imposing obligations on the parties, and with provision for amendment or revocation of exemption in certain circumstances.

The effect of notification to the Commission is that it confers immunity from fines with effect from the date of notification until exemption (or negative clearance) is granted or refused.[10] Immunity may be withdrawn if the Commission, in making a preliminary investigation, determines that the prohibition in Article 85(1) applies and Article 85(3) exemption cannot be granted.[11]

6-12 Compiling a notification is a time-consuming and expensive procedure. The information given in support of a notification must be correct or there will be no immunity from fines and no exemption (*Aluminium Products*[12]). The Commission may remove any immunity from fines if incorrect or misleading information is provided in support, and penalties may be incurred for doing so.[13] It is worth remembering that any information given by a party on one occasion may be used by the Commission against that party on any subsequent occasion.

Notification using Form A/B is only as good as the information given in support of it. A considerable amount of judgement and discretion is applied when compiling supporting market information and the parties necessarily play down the potential ill-effects of the agreement notified. This does carry the risk of subsequent challenge by the Commission, by a party to the agreement or a third party. When advising the purchaser of a business to which a notified agreement is crucial, it is impossible to verify the completeness or accuracy of the notification detail without performing a repeat market analysis. Yet if the notified document was wrong when submitted, the notification is flawed and the agreement itself is potentially open to challenge. The standard warranties sought

---

[7] Commission Reg. 3385/94 [1994] O.J. L377 at 28. For full text see Appendix B.1 below.
[8] And the EFTA States.
[9] Or the EEA Territory.
[10] Reg. 17/62, Art. 15(5) [1962] J.O. 204/62.
[11] Reg. 17/62, Art. 15(6) [1962] J.O. 204/62.
[12] Commission Dec. 85/206 [1985] O.J. L92/1; [1987] 3 C.M.L.R. 813.
[13] Reg. 17/62, Art. 15(1)(a) [1962] J.O. 204/62.

by a purchaser (confirming that no infringement has taken place) will however obviously be of some value but will be subject to the usual limits on warranty liability.

Comfort letters

6-13 Having notified an agreement on Form A/B, instead of pursuing the notification procedure to a formal conclusion, the parties may instead be content to stop the procedure at the point at which the Commission issues a comfort letter. The advantage of a comfort letter, which is merely a statement of the Commission's view on the matter before it, is that it may protect the parties from a fine or other penalties but it has the shortcoming that it is not binding on any national court, nor even the parties. If a party relying on the agreement wishes to enforce it in a national court, proceedings should be stayed until the matter is formally dealt with by the Commission by way of individual exemption based on the information given at the time of seeking the comfort letter. However, it is too easy for a party challenging the validity of the agreement to claim that the information previously given is out of date and that the Commission is not entitled to grant individual exemption.[14] Even if the circumstances have not changed and individual exemption may be granted, the delay may be considerable and may be tactically fatal to the litigation. Comfort letters need to be reviewed with scepticism with these additional points in mind. There is no prescribed form for comfort letters which simply state that an agreement does not fall within Article 85(1) or is within the terms of a block exemption but it may also state limitations in relation to any comfort given such as the right to keep matters under review if the industry in question is, for example, unstable or emerging.

When publishing details of comfort letters in the Official Journal, the Commission will include an outline description of the arrangement and invite comment from third parties within, approximately, one month.[15] Once a comfort letter has been given in relation to an application for negative clearance, a notice to that effect will be posted in the Official Journal. In relation to exemption, a list detailing all comfort letters will also be included in the Commission's Annual Competition Report.

6-14 The content of comfort letters, if not binding on courts is still extremely important. In general courts may take them into account and under section 60 of the 1998 Act United Kingdom courts, must "have regard" to them. For further discussion concerning co-operation between the Commission, the courts and competent authorities, see Chapter 14, *Co-operation between the Commission, the Courts and Competent authorities*, below.

Block exemptions

6-15 The Commission is empowered (by Council Regulations 19/65 and 2821/71[16]) to grant exemption from the prohibition of Article 85(1), by way of block exemption Regulations in respect of categories of bilateral exclusive agreements and licences of intellectual property, the aim being to enable the Commission to reduce its case-load of individual notifications.

---

[14] Case T–64/89 *Automec Srl v. Commission* [1990] E.C.R. II-367; [1991] 4 C.M.L.R. 177.

[15] The Commission adopts different practices when publishing details of matters notified to it for a comfort letter depending on whether the application is for negative clearance or exemption. In the case of negative clearance, the procedure is dealt with in the Commission's 1982 Notice (Notice from the Commission on procedures concerning notifications pursuant to Art. 2 of Council Reg. 17/62[1982] J.O. C343/4). In the case of applications for exemption, the procedure is dealt with in the Commission's 1983 Notice (Notice from the Commission on procedures pursuant to notification pursuant to Art. 4 of Council Reg. 17/62 [1983] O.J. C295/6).

[16] Council Reg. 19/65 on the application of Art. 85(3) of the Treaty to certain categories of agreements and concerted practices [1965] O.J. 36/533. Council Reg. 2821/71 on the application of Art. 85(3) of the Treaty to categories of agreements, decisions and concerted practices [1972] O.J. Spec. Ed. L291/144.

Block exemptions are also an extremely useful source of guidance concerning the Commission's reasoning generally when granting individual exemption and, in particular, when granting exemption to agreements broadly of the category described in any block exemption.

6-16   In exercising its power under Council Regulation 19/65 to grant exemption by way of block exemption, the Commission has adopted a number of Regulations in recognition that it is generally supportive of certain common agreements of a recognised character that enable small companies to penetrate new markets or promote innovation. These are discussed in full in Chapters 7 and 9 below, but include the following types of agreement.

1. Regulation 1983/83,[17] which applies to exclusive distribution agreements in which one party (the supplier) appoints the other (the distributor) to act as its exclusive distributor for a given territory;

2. Regulation 1984/83,[18] which applies to exclusive purchasing agreements in which one party (the reseller) agrees with the other (the supplier) to purchase certain goods for resale only from the supplier;

3. Regulation 1475/95,[19] which applies to motor vehicle distribution and servicing agreements in which the supplier agrees to supply motor vehicles only to the other party (the reseller) or others within the distribution system within a given territory;

4. Regulation 417/85,[20] which applies to specialisation agreements in which each party agrees not to manufacture products which are allocated to the other for manufacture;

5. Regulation 4087/88,[21] which applies to franchise agreements granted on an exclusive basis for a given territory;

6. Regulation 418/85,[22] which applies to research and development agreements under which the parties undertake certain pre-agreed research obligations and then exploit the results; and

7. Regulation 240/96,[23] relating to technology transfer agreements comprising exclusive licences of patents and/or know-how for exploitation within a given territory.

6-17   The format of all block exemptions Regulations is the same. Each begins with preamble that explains the Commission's justification for granting automatic exemption to the category of agreement concerned. In the operative part of the Regulation, the Regulation identifies those restrictions that are caught by Article 85(1) but which will be allowed without jeopardising exemption (the "White List"). The Regulation then identifies those restrictions that are prohibited and will cause the agreement in all cases to lose exemption (the "Black List").

Block exemption Regulations provide all or none exemption in the sense that exemp-

---

[17] Reg. 1983/83 [1983] O.J. L173/1 amended by [1983] O.J. L281/24.
[18] Reg. 1984/83 [1983] O.J. L173/5 amended by [1983] O.J. L281/24.
[19] Reg. 1475/95 [1995] O.J. L145.
[20] Reg. 417/85 [1985] O.J. L53/1, amended by Reg. 151/93.
[21] Reg. 4087/88 [1988] O.J. L359/46.
[22] Reg. 418/85 [1985] O.J. L53/5.
[23] Reg. 240/96 [1996] O.J. L31/2.

tion is lost altogether if any restrictions on competition are included which are not white-listed or if any of the pre-conditions for exemption are not satisfied (*Delimitis v. Henninger Brau*[24]).

In general, block exemptions cannot be cumulated to exempt activities contained in one agreement that are the subject of two block exemption Regulations, because this would change the character of the agreement concerned. Exceptionally however this is permitted by the terms of certain Regulations. For example Regulation 418/85 concerns research and development agreements and permits combination with Regulation 1983/83 for agreements that cover both the development and distribution phases.

6-18 Certain Regulations contain reference to an "opposition procedure" for agreements that, strictly speaking, do not satisfy all of the terms of the block exemption. Rather than put the parties to the trouble of making a full formal notification, the opposition procedure offers an accelerated mechanism for dealing with the matter, requiring less information to be given in support and putting the Commission to the task of objecting to the agreement within the period stated in the relevant Regulation. The Regulations which incorporate an opposition procedure are Regulation 417/85 (specialisation agreements), Regulation 418/85 (research and development agreements), Regulation 4087/88 (franchise agreements) and Regulation 240/96 (technology transfer agreements). For example, in Article 4 of Regulation 417/85 if exemption is lost only because the turnover limits of the parties exceed the level permitted in Articles 3(1)(b), 3(2)(b) and 3(3), then the parties may notify the agreement, and if the Commission does not oppose it within six months, exemption will be deemed to be granted. Likewise Regulation 418/85 allows the opposition procedure to be used for agreements which contain restrictions which are not expressly white-listed. In Regulation 240/96 the opposition period is limited to four months but applies in a similar way, to allow for inclusion of such things as quality stipulations on the licensee whenever exploiting the products, and an undertaking not to contest the validity of the licensor's rights licensed under the agreement.

Negative clearance

6-19 Instead of applying for individual exemption, the parties may if appropriate seek negative clearance. Negative clearance is a Commission decision to the effect that there are no grounds for action on the part of the Commission pursuant to Article 85(1) or Article 86. The Commission is not obliged to give negative clearance and it is generally only appropriate in cases where an important problem of interpretation requires resolution. In practice parties notify borderline agreements by applying for negative clearance or exemption in the alternative. The negative clearance procedure may also be used for the purposes of Article 86 by undertakings in a dominant position but in reality this procedure is rarely used. The Commission has only made six negative clearance decisions under Article 86.

Review of Commission Decisions

6-20 Article 173 of the E.C. Treaty[25] gives the Court of First Instance:

> "jurisdiction in actions brought by a Member State, the Council or the Commission on grounds of lack of competence, infringement of an essential procedural requirement, infringement of this Treaty or of any rule of law relating to its application, or misuse of powers."

---

[24] Case C–234/89 *Delimitis v. Henninger Brau* [1991] E.C.R. I-935; [1992] C.M.L.R. 210.
[25] As amended by Art. G(53) of the Treaty of the European Union.

Furthermore, Article 173 extends that jurisdiction to the benefit of affected third parties in the following terms:

"Any natural or legal person may . . . institute proceedings against a decision addressed to that person or against a decision which, although in the form of a regulation or a decision addressed to that person or another person, is of direct and individual concern to the former."

The breadth of the term "decision" was confirmed by the E.C.J in *IBM v. Commission*[26]:

"[A]ny measure the legal effects of which are binding on, and capable of affecting the interests of the applicant by bringing about a distinct change in his legal position is an act or decision which may be the object of an action under Article 173 for a declaration that it is void."[27]

The effect is that these decisions (to grant exemption or negative clearance) may be reviewed by the CFI not only at the request of the applicant for exemption but also affected third parties.

6-21   Closely related is Article 175 which provides a mechanism to compel the Commission (or other institution) to act and this is often invoked as a means of requiring the Commission to investigate a matter which is the subject of a complaint:

"(1) Should the European Parliament, the Council or the Commission, in infringement of this Treaty, fail to act, the Member States and other institutions of the Community may bring an action before the Court of Justice to have the infringement established.

(2) The action shall be admissible only if the institution concerned has first been called upon to act. If, within two months of being so called upon, the institution concerned has not defined its position, the action may be brought within a further period of two months.

(3) Any natural or legal person may, under the conditions laid down in the preceding paragraphs, complain to the Court of Justice that an institution of the Community has failed to address to that person any act other than a recommendation or an opinion."

The case of *Bethall v. Commission*[28] demonstrates that the category of those entitled to issue an Article 175 challenge is limited to those to whom the decision is of "direct and individual concern".[29] Victims of infringement who file complaints with the Commission may therefore use Article 173 if the Commission decides not to pursue an investigation or otherwise act.[30]

6-22   A formal decision granting exemption or negative clearance is clearly a decision covered by both Articles 173 and 175. So also, in the case of Article 173, is a comfort letter as confirmed in *BAT and Reynolds v. Commission*[31] because:

"those letters have the content and effect of a decision, in so much as they close the investigation, contain an assessment of the agreements in question and prevent the

---

[26] Case 60/81 [1981] E.C.R. I-2639; [1981] 3 C.M.L.R. 635.
[27] *ibid.*, para. 9.
[28] Case 246/81 *Bethall v. Commission* [1982] E.C.R. 2277; [1982] 3 C.M.L.R. 300.
[29] *ibid.*, para. 13.
[30] Case C–39/93P *Syndicat Français de L'Express International v. Commission* [1994] E.C.R. I-2681.
[31] Cases 142 & 156/84 *BAT and Reynolds v. Commission* [1987] E.C.R. 4487; [1988] 4 C.M.L.R. 24.

applicants from requiring the reopening of the investigation unless they put forward new evidence."[32]

Non-notifiable agreements

6-23   Council Regulation 17/62[33] dispenses with any requirement to notify certain agreements for individual exemption. The category of non-notifiable agreements is small. These particular agreements are not considered to affect competition to the same extent as other agreements to which Article 85(1) applies. These are:

(1) national agreements;

(2) agreements with pricing and other restrictions on only one party;

(3) certain intellectual property transactions; and

(4) minor collaboration agreements.

National agreements

6-24   National agreements are those between undertakings from one Member State and which do not relate either to imports or to exports between Member States. The domicile of the undertakings determines the relevant Member State. It is the domicile of the party to the agreement that is important. Even if goods are imported for the purposes of an agreement, it may still not relate to imports or exports between Member States where, for example the purpose of the agreement is exclusive distribution within one Member State.[34] The agreement is still a parochial one, concerned with supply and redistribution within one country, albeit that the products are procured by the supplier from another Member State.

Needless to say steps must not be taken to protect a Member State against competition from outside by means of an export ban or market sharing which clearly are prohibited and are unlikely ever to qualify for exemption.

Agreements with pricing and other restrictions only on one party

6-25   This category of agreement is described in Article 4(2)(ii)(a) of Regulation 17/62 as agreements where:

> "Not more than two undertakings are party thereto, and the agreements only . . . restrict the freedom of one party to the contract in determining the prices for or conditions of business on which the goods which he has obtained from the other party to the contract may be resold."

If an agreement contains any restriction other than these limited ones, then notification will be necessary. The restrictions may only relate to the goods supplied, no more. Agreements under which services are supplied are not covered because it is harder to conceive of services being resold. This must be treated as an extremely narrow category to which domestic competition law (the Chapter I prohibition) will inevitably apply to prevent the control of resale prices and other resale conditions.

---

[32] *ibid.*, para. 12.

[33] Reg. 17/62 [1962] J.O. 204/62.

[34] Case 63/75 *Fonderies Roubaix-Wattrelos v. Fonderies A Roux* [1976] E.C.R. 111; [1976] 1 C.M.L.R. 538.

Certain intellectual property transactions

6-26 The particular intellectual property transactions exempt from notification under Article 4(2)(ii)(b) are agreements to which no more than two undertakings are party and:

> "Which only . . . impose restrictions on the exercise of the rights of the assignee or user of industrial property rights — in particular patents, utility models, designs or trade marks — or of the person entitled under a contract to the assignment, or grant, of the right to use a method of manufacture or knowledge relating to the use and to the application of industrial processes."

This category of agreement is narrower than it appears at first sight. It relates only to licensee or assignee restrictions and not those imposed on the licensor or assignor. The restrictions must only relate to the intellectual property itself and not ancillary matters such as products in which the rights do not subsist.[35] Even certain matters that relate directly to the intellectual property but are ancillary are not exempt, such as no-challenge clauses.[36]

Minor collaboration agreements

6-27 The category of minor collaboration agreements exempt from notification under Article 4(2)(iii) are those which:

> "have as their sole object:
>
> (a) the development or uniform application of standards or types;
> (b) joint research and development;
> (c) specialisation in the manufacture of products, including agreements necessary for achieving this;
>
> (i) where the products which are the object of specialisation do not, in a substantial part of the common market, represent more than 15 per cent of the volume of business done in identical products or those considered by the consumers to be similar by reason of their characteristics, price and use, and
> (ii) where the total annual turnover of the participating undertakings does not exceed 200 million units of account."

Regulation 17/62 predated the block exemption Regulations referred to above in relation to research and development and specialisation and to all intents and purposes this limited category of agreements exempt from notification is superseded by those block exemption Regulations particularly because the inclusion of the words "sole object" is so limiting and excludes any exploitation, distribution and similar activities in the agreement concerned.

6-28 Notice that Article 4(2) does not confer exemption on these agreements and Article 85(1) may well still apply. However, they may be granted retrospective exemption if challenged and in such circumstances will not be void for want of notification. If exemption is not granted then the Commission may prohibit the agreement if Article 85(1) applies[37] and the parties may still be fined.

---

[35] Case 193/83 *Windsurfing v. Commission* [1986] E.C.R. 611; [1986] 3 C.M.L.R. 489.
[36] Commission Dec. 79/86 *Vaessen/Moris* [1979] O.J. L19/32; [1979] 1 C.M.L.R. 511.
[37] Art. 3.

NOTIFICATION PROCEDURE BEFORE THE DIRECTOR GENERAL OF FAIR TRADING FOR CHAPTER I AND CHAPTER II INFRINGEMENTS

Criteria for exemption of Chapter I infringements

6-29   Section 4 of the 1998 Act confers power on the Director to grant exemption from the Chapter I prohibition to an agreement (in certain cases imposing conditions or obligations at his discretion) by way of individual exemption. The application for exemption is to be made by a party to the agreement. The exemption may be back-dated, possibly even as far back as the date of the agreement.[38] This is to be contrasted with the Commission's power to backdate exemption only as far as the date of notification.[39]

Section 5 entitles the Director to cancel or vary individual exemptions (or any related conditions or obligations) by giving notice if:

   (i) the Director has reasonable grounds for believing that there has been a material change of circumstances since he granted an individual exemption (in this case cancellation may not be back-dated); or

   (ii) if he has a reasonable suspicion that the information on which he based his decision to grant exemption was incomplete, false or misleading in a material particular; or

   (iii) there has been a failure to comply with an obligation attaching to the exemption.

The Director may take any of these steps on his own initiative or in response to a complaint made by any person, not necessarily the applicant or party to the agreement.

Breach of any condition attaching to exemption has the effect of cancelling the exemption without the need for the Director to give notice.

6-30   Section 6 entitles the Director to recommend that the Secretary of State make an order specifying any category of agreement suitable for block exemption. Block exemptions are likely to shadow the existing block exemption Regulations published by the Commission and will be dealt with by way of secondary legislation. There has been a great deal of debate over whether vertical agreements (such as exclusive distribution agreements, exclusive franchise agreements, exclusive licences and exclusive purchasing agreements between undertakings at different levels of trade) should fall within the Chapter I prohibition in the first place. The rationale for bringing such agreements within the ambit of Article 85(1) as a matter of Community law is that those particular vertical agreements potentially divide territories and, as such, risk compartmentalising the Community. In doing so, the Single Market aims of the E.C. Treaty are threatened. However as observed in Chapter 1 above, the 1998 Act does not share those Single Market aims and so it is arguably not appropriate to replicate the Community's treatment of such agreements.

Exclusive vertical agreements in Community law have traditionally been dealt with first of all by way of prohibition generally and, secondly, limited automatic block exemption. It remains to be seen precisely how the 1998 Act will treat vertical agreements—whether they will be excluded from the Chapter I prohibition or included within it but then granted automatically block exemption under section 6. In this context it is also worth noting that section 50 expressly contemplates that exclusions and exemptions may be provided by order for vertical agreements and land agreements, which are discussed further

---

[38] s. 4(5).
[39] Art. 6(1) of Reg. 17/62 [1962] J.O. 204/62.

in Chapter 7, *E.C. and United Kingdom Policy Towards Vertical Restraints* below and Chapter 2, *Exclusions from Chapter I No exclusions from Article 85(1)* above.

An opposition procedure is contemplated in section 7 enabling notification of agreements that do not qualify for block exemption but satisfy other criteria. Section 8 sets out the block exemption procedure requiring the Director to publish advance details of any recommendation for a block exemption and to consider any representations made in response.

6-31 Section 10 confers parallel exemption on agreements exempt by the Commission. An agreement may be granted exemption by the Commission (as set out in *Notification procedure before the Commission for Articles 85(1) and Article 86 infringements*, above) by way of individual exemption under Article 85(3), or it may qualify for exemption under any Commission block exemption Regulation or under the Commission's opposition procedure. If an agreement falls within the terms of a Commission block exemption but does not in fact need exemption from the prohibition in Article 85(1) because it does not affect trade between Member States then exemption under the 1998 Act is still conferred on the agreement in relation to the Chapter I prohibition. The exemptions in section 10 are known as parallel exemptions.

A parallel exemption takes effect on the date on which the exemption under Article 85(3) takes effect (or would have done if it had an effect on trade between Member States). A parallel exemption ceases to have effect when the corresponding Community exemption ceases to have effect, or earlier if cancelled by the Director as a result of conditions or obligations attaching to parallel exemption imposed by the Director.[40] In exercising his powers in relation to parallel exemption, the Director may require any party to the agreement in question to provide any information he may require.[41]

6-32 In all cases, the criteria for exemption contained in section 9 must be satisfied. Section 9 reads as follows:

> "This section applies to any agreement which:
>
> (a) contributes to:
>
> (i) improving production or distribution; or
> (ii) promoting technical or economic progress,
>
> while allowing consumers a fair share of the resulting benefit; but
>
> (b) does not:
>
> (i) impose on the undertakings concerned restrictions which are not indispensable to the attainment of those objectives; or
> (ii) afford the undertaking concerned the possibility of eliminating competition in respect of a substantial part of the products in question."

The deliberate similarity between the text of section 9 and Article 85(3) once again is striking. The substance and meaning of section 9 and Article 85(3) are dealt with at length in *Common Aspects of Article 85(3) and section 9*, below and in *The inter-relation between E.C. and United Kingdom exemptions*, below.

---

[40] s. 10(5) to (7).
[41] s. 11 permits the Secretary of State to grant exemption in the case of rulings under Art. 88 of the E.C. Treaty and this is likely to be of relevance principally to international airline alliances.

Guidance

6-33   Guidance is available from the Director under sections 13 and 21 concerning the status of an agreement. Guidance is the more informal alternative to a decision which may be sought under sections 14 and 22.[42]

Guidance is not formally binding on the Director or any court or other tribunal but it does confer limited immunity from penalties. Guidance also has the benefit (unlike decisions) of being given in confidence without any consultation of third parties.

Chapter I prohibition guidance

6-34   Guidance in connection with a Chapter I prohibition may be sought by a party as to whether:

1. an agreement is likely to infringe the Chapter I prohibition; if it is likely to infringe then guidance may be as to whether an agreement is likely to be exempt from the Chapter I prohibition under:

    (i)   a block exemption; or
    (ii) a parallel exemption[43]; or

2. an agreement is likely to be granted individual exemption if an application were made.[44]

Guidance gives an opportunity to parties to seek out the Director's views informally before applying for a formal decision which would involve far more paperwork. The Director is entitled to charge for giving guidance. Although it remains to be determined precisely which functions will be chargeable,[45] where guidance amounts to a substitute for taking legal advice this is likely to be subject to a fee.

Chapter II prohibition guidance

6-35   Although exemption is not available for any Chapter II prohibition, there is provision (as with the Chapter I prohibition) for seeking guidance from the Director to determine whether any conduct is likely to constitute infringement. Section 21 enables any person who is unsure, to notify the Director and apply for guidance as to whether or not in the Director's view the conduct is likely to infringe the Chapter II prohibition. The effect of guidance given under section 21 is similar to that given under section 13 concerning the Chapter I prohibition. This procedure is likely to have greatest value in cases where intended conduct, rather than existing conduct, is at issue because there is no immunity from penalties if the conduct infringes the Chapter II prohibition.

Early guidance

6-36   The 1998 Act contains a special procedure allowing for applications to be made for guidance concerning agreements made between the enactment date and the starting date of the Act.[46] The guidance procedure available is similar to that for Chapter I prohibitions and will have the same status as guidance given after the starting date. The OFT predicts that some 250 requests will be made for early guidance.

---

[42] See *Decisions*, below.
[43] Or a s. 11 exemption.
[44] s. 13.
[45] s. 53.
[46] Sched. 13, para. 7.

Decisions

6-37   Decisions are more formal than guidance and will contain detailed reasoned statements. The procedure involves publication of details of the matter and the Director will invite comment from affected third parties. Each decision will involve a detailed assessment of the circumstances of each prohibition, whether Chapter I or Chapter II. It is currently predicted by the OFT that 400 applications will be made annually for decisions, the majority of which are expected to be dealt with by means of an "administrative letter" similar to a "comfort letter" issued by the Commission. The use of administrative letters by the Director will need to avoid all the uncertainties and disadvantages experienced by Commission comfort letters over many years as outlined above.[47]

Chapter I prohibition decisions

6-38   Section 14 of the 1998 Act permits notifications to be made to the Director by any party to an agreement for a decision as to whether the Chapter I prohibition has been infringed, and if it has not been infringed, whether that is because of the effect of an exclusion or because the agreement is exempt from the prohibition. Section 14(3) provides that the application may include a request for exemption to be given to the agreement if it satisfies the Section 9 criteria. No court or tribunal other than the Director is competent to grant exemption.[48]

Once an agreement is notified, no penalty may be imposed for infringement by that agreement between the date of notification and the date of the determination of the application.

Chapter II prohibition decisions

6-39   Section 22 establishes a procedure for notifying a Chapter II prohibition for a decision as to whether it has been infringed, and if not, whether that is because of the effect of an exclusion. The conduct in question must relate to the conduct of the applicant rather than a third party. Since there is no provision for exemption to be granted, the use of this section is unlikely to be extensive.

Effect of guidance and decisions

6-40   The effect of guidance and the effect of a decision given by the Director are similar in certain respects. According to sections 15 and 16 (in relation to the Chapter I prohibition) and sections 23 and 24 (in relation to the Chapter II prohibition), the Director can take no further action with respect to the agreement or conduct concerned unless he has reasonable grounds for believing that there has been a material change in circumstances since positive guidance was given or a positive decision was made, or he has a reasonable suspicion that information on which he based his guidance or decision was incomplete, false or misleading. Finally, the Director may take further action if a complaint is made by a third party. The fact that a complaint entitles the Director to take action is obviously going to operate as a great disincentive to those who might otherwise seek guidance.

There will be limited immunity from penalties for conduct which is notified for guidance or a decision but that immunity is removed if any of the above circumstances entitle the Director to take action and he considers it likely that the agreement or conduct concerned will infringe the relevant prohibition.

---

[47] See *Comfort letters*, above.
[48] Other than a parallel exemption which derives from a Commission exemption.

6-41   The Director is required to give written notice removing the immunity, and the withdrawal of immunity may be backdated if the Director was given incomplete, false or misleading information on which to base his guidance.

Schedules 5 and 6 set out the procedures for making any notification of Chapter I and Chapter II prohibitions respectively and these reflect basic principles of natural justice.

If the application relates to an agreement between two or more parties, or the conduct of two or more persons, then the applicant must take all reasonable steps to notify all of the other parties of whom he is aware that the application has been made, indicating whether the application is for guidance or a decision. The Director will first make a preliminary investigation of an application to assess whether it is likely that the agreement or the conduct will infringe the relevant prohibition. If he makes a provisional decision he must notify the applicant, but the provisional decision will not affect the final outcome of any application.

6-42   Information given in support of a notification is to be kept confidential by the Director under section 55 except in performance of the Director's enforcement functions or those of the Commission and other officials. If the information is required to be disclosed pursuant to civil proceedings under the 1998 Act, it is excluded from this obligation of confidentiality as well as in other miscellaneous circumstances set out in section 55.[49]

The detailed procedures for determining applications both for guidance and a decision are yet to be specified. In the case of applications for a decision, the Director is obliged to arrange for the application to be published in the most suitable way for bringing it to the attention of those likely to be affected by it unless he takes the view that only a limited number are likely to be affected and it will suffice to seek information direct from them. The Director is, however, bound to take into account any representations made to him by anyone other than the applicant (whether or not they are likely to be affected). Once any decision is made, it must be published together with reasons for the decision. If the Director fails to comply with any procedural aspect of decision-making or incurs undue delay in determining an application for a decision, any person aggrieved may apply to the court to ensure that the application proceeds without further delay.

Application for guidance or a decision

6-43   When applying for guidance or a decision, the parties must use the Form N provided by the OFT. A copy of Form N may be found in Appendix B.2, below. Form N requires the applicant to indicate the purpose of the application and whether the application relates to a Chapter I or a Chapter II prohibition. If application is made for a decision the applicant must state whether the decision sought is exemption, whether it qualifies for retrospective effect (see below), whether an agreement is considered to qualify for block exemption either under Article 85(3) or under the 1998 Act, whether a prohibited matter is considered to benefit from an exclusion and, finally, why an administrative letter would not be sufficient.

The information to be provided in support must include a brief description of the arrangement or behaviour and give details of market definition (in terms of product, service and geography), the nature of the relevant goods or services, and the structure of the market (the profile of buyers and sellers, geographical extent, turn-over, the degree of competition, ease of entry and whether there are substitute products[50]). Details of the parties must be given including details of sales, the turnover of each party in relevant

---

[49]   For further details of s. 55, see Chapter 13, *Confidentiality and defamation*, below.

goods or services, in the United Kingdom, the Community, and worldwide. Details of competitors together with details of their market shares, if known, should be given. Full details of the arrangements are required, in particular, provisions which may restrict the parties in their freedom to take independent commercial decisions.[51]

6-44 If seeking "negative clearance", that is, a decision whether the Director considers that the arrangement or behaviour is or is not prohibited by Chapter I or Chapter II, an indication must be given of why the applicant considers the arrangement does not have the object or effect of preventing, restricting or distorting competition, or why its behaviour does not constitute abuse of a dominant position.

If seeking an exemption from the Chapter I prohibition, an explanation must be given how the arrangement contributes to improving production or distribution and/or promoting technical or economic progress and how a proper share of these benefits accrues to consumers, including an explanation of how all the restrictive provisions of the arrangements are indispensable to these aims, and how the arrangements do not eliminate competition in respect of a substantial part of the market for the goods or services concerned.

Other information required includes details of any relevant previous contacts with the Director, any Regulator and the Commission.

COMMON ASPECTS OF ARTICLE 85(3) AND SECTION 9

6-45 It should be remembered that Article 85(3) is significant for the purposes of United Kingdom law, not only because of the direct effect in the United Kingdom of certain E.C. Treaty provisions but because of section 60 of the 1998 Act and the need to apply similar principles of Community law when corresponding questions arise under United Kingdom law (at least in relation to sections 1 to 59 of the 1998 Act).

Article 85(3) and Section 9 both have the following textual similarities:

"Contribute to improving the production or distribution of goods or to promoting technical or economic progress"

6-46 Inevitably, it is a difficult task for the parties to a notified agreement to demonstrate such a contribution. The improved production or distribution of goods and enhanced technical or economic progress must extend beyond any benefits to be derived by parties to the agreement, ideally in the case of Article 85(3), to the Community as a whole.[52] There is a tendency on the part of the authorities to presume that an agreement containing restrictions on competition is less likely to give rise to those improvements than the market conditions prevailing in the absence of the agreement. Any detriment caused by the restrictions must be outweighed by the resulting benefits claimed. The authorities will look very closely at the restrictive effects of any agreement. The Commission will also be particularly concerned where the result is compartmentalisation of national markets or a disincentive against export. These particular concerns will be less relevant to section 9 because the 1998 Act does not share the Single Market aims of the E.C. Treaty.

The necessary positive contribution may take the form of cost reductions at any point

---

[50] For further details concerning definition of the relevant market see Chapter 4 above.

[51] *e.g.* buying or selling prices, discounts, or other trading conditions, quantities of goods to be made or distributed or services to be offered, technical development or investment, the choice of markets or sources of supply, purchases from or sales to third parties, whether to apply similar terms for the supply of equivalent goods or services, and whether to offer different goods or services separately or together (para. 3.6 of Form N).

[52] Cases 56 & 58/64 *Consten and Grundig v. Commission* [1966] E.C.R. 299; [1966] C.M.L.R.

in the chain of supply of products or services, the creation of new products that would not feasibly have been developed without the agreement (either because of lack of funds or technology), improvements that result in greater employment, particularly in depressed areas or where closure of plants is threatened, and improvements in delivery or the standard of after-sales services in distribution channels.

"While allowing consumers a fair share of the resulting benefit"

6-47   The reference to "consumer" includes any buyer at any point in the chain of supply. Benefits might take the form, most obviously, of lower prices, better quality, better response times to services, greater range of consumer choice, faster or more reliable delivery, better product guarantees, and so on. The authorities will be more easily convinced that benefits will be passed on to consumers if the suppliers concerned face competition. The presence of competition itself will act as a competitive constraint on the supplier holding on to any benefits and so it is important in any application for individual exemption to stress the existence of active competition, and lack of market power held by the parties as expressed in the form of low market shares and lively potential competition. If the parties do not face rigorous competition, the authorities will require convincing that the profits and other benefits ("the fair share") will be passed on down the supply chain.[53]

"Does not impose on the undertakings concerned restrictions which are not indispensable to the attainment of these objectives"

6-48   All of the competition restrictions must be justified on this basis, not just some or most of them. It is in relation to this requirement that often a great deal of negotiation takes place with the authorities over certain terms. Some terms will inevitably need to be shed in order to gain exemption. The link has to be maintained between the restriction on competition and the attainment of the pro-competitive objectives, or the requirement of indispensability is not satisfied. The acid test is whether the restriction is essential in order for the agreement to work. It is not enough that the restriction is merely one that the parties negotiated and require in order to protect their own commercial positions. Exclusivity restrictions are generally regarded as essential to certain types of agreement such as distribution agreements (in order for the distributor to justify the investment necessary to set up a distribution system) and technology licences (in order to justify the licensor's investment in research and patenting).

Clearly no clause that is black-listed in a block exemption Regulation is ever likely to be exempt nor, in the case of Article 85(3), are agreements which confer absolute territorial exclusivity on any party. Exemption for price-fixing or market-sharing agreements are also unlikely to be granted exemption.

"Does not afford such undertaking the possibility of eliminating competition in respect of a substantial part of the products in question"

6-49   The Commission has demonstrated a growing tendency in the terms of block exemption Regulations to disapply exemption in cases where the market shares of the parties are above certain thresholds. Once again the importance of demonstrating that low market shares are held by the parties is apparent.[54]

---

[53] Commission Dec. 78/71 *SNPE-LEL* [1978] O.J. L191/41; [1978] 2 C.M.L.R. 758.
[54] See for example the Specialisation Reg. 417/85 (Art. 3) and Technology Transfer Reg. 240/96 (Arts 5 and 7) discussed in Chapters 7 and 9, below.

In general (quite apart from the block exemption Regulations), where the parties hold a combined market share of less than 20 per cent, the agreement will either fall below the *de minimis* thresholds or is likely to be granted exemption. Market shares of between 60 per cent and 80 per cent will only result in exemption for agreements upon proof of strong competitive constraints on the parties but clearly much will depend upon the structure of the market, the nature of the agreement and its likely benefits. For further discussion on the measurement of market share and market power see Chapter 4 above.

6-50   If market share levels are sufficiently high an agreement which would otherwise be eligible for block exemption may lose it. In certain circumstances the agreement itself may constitute an abuse of dominant position. An abuse of dominant position is possible if an agreement results in the strengthening of a position of dominance to an unacceptable level. Thus in *Tetra Pak II*,[55] Tetra Pak was held to infringe Article 86 by its acquisition of a company which was the licensee under an exclusive patent licence. Even though the patent licence was given block exemption under Regulation 2349/84,[56] Tetra Pak was required to relinquish exclusivity. The patent licence, held by anyone other than Tetra Pak, was the only means of exposing Tetra Pak to competition in the market.

THE INTER-RELATION BETWEEN E.C. AND UNITED KINGDOM EXEMPTIONS

The supremacy of E.C. law

6-51   The supremacy of E.C. law remains unaffected by the Act. Any prohibition in Article 85(1) or Article 86 will not be affected by the Director granting exemption to an agreement under section 9 of the 1998 Act.[57] Equally where the Commission takes no action in respect of a matter any national authority may do so.[58] A dual system of prohibitions operates concurrently at E.C. and domestic levels.

However in the case of exemptions, it appears in general that an agreement exempt under Article 85(3) cannot still be subject to a prohibition at national level. For further discussion concerning the inter-relation between the Commission and national authorities and national courts see Chapter 14 below.[59]

6-52   Tesauro A.G. in *Bundeskartellampt v. Volkswagen and VAG Leasing*[60] put it as follows:

> "I take the view that, since the agreements in question are liable to affect trade between Member States and therefore fall in principle within the prohibition set out in section 85(1), the exemption granted to them cannot but prevent the national authorities from ignoring the positive assessment put on them by the Community authorities. Otherwise, not only would a given agreement be treated differently depending on the law of each Member State thus detracting from the uniform application of Community law, but the full effectiveness of a Community measure — which an exemption under Article 85(3) undoubtedly is — would also be disregarded."

---

[55] Commission Dec. 92/163 *Tetra Pak Rausing SA v. Commission* [1992] O.J. L72/1; [1992] 4 C.M.L.R. 551, upheld on appeal Case T–83/91 [1994] II E.C.R. 755.
[56] The patent licence block exemption Reg. that preceded the Technology Transfer Reg.
[57] Case 14/68 *Wilhelm v. Bundeskartellampt* [1969] E.C.R. 1; [1969] C.M.L.R. 100.
[58] Case 253/78 *Procureur de la Republique v. Giry and Guerlain* [1980] E.C.R. 2327; [1981] 2 C.M.L.R. 99.
[59] In particular, *Co-operation concerning national authorities.*
[60] Case 266/93 *Bundeskartellampt v. Volkswagen and VAG Leasing* [1995] E.C.R. I-3477 at 3502; [1994] 4 C.M.L.R. 478.

Consistent with this approach is section 10 of the 1998 Act, which provides for the parallel exemption of Chapter I prohibitions if they are given exemption by the Commission under Article 85(3), whether as a matter of block exemption, individual exemption or the opposition procedure:

> "10 (1) Any agreement is exempt from the Chapter I prohibition if it is exempt from the Community prohibition:
>
> (a) by virtue of a Regulation;
> (b) because it has been given exemption by the Commission; or
> (c) because it has been notified to the Commission under the appropriate opposition or objection procedure and:
>
> > (i) the time for opposing, or objecting to, the agreement has expired and the Commission has not opposed it; or
> > (ii) the Commission has opposed, or objected to, the agreement but has withdrawn its opposition or objection.
>
> (2) An agreement is exempt from the Chapter I prohibition if it does not affect trade between Member States but otherwise falls within a category of agreement which is exempt from the Community prohibition by virtue of a Regulation."

6-53 A parallel exemption takes effect on the date on which the Community exemption took effect or, in the case of agreements benefitting from block exemptions, would take effect if the agreement affected trade between Member States.[61]

A parallel exemption ceases to have effect if the Community exemption ceases to have effect. All parallel exemptions are subject to the Director's discretion in section 10(5) to:

> "(a) impose conditions or obligations subject to which a parallel exemption is to have effect;
> (b) vary or remove any such condition or obligation;
> (c) impose one or more additional conditions or obligations;
> (d) cancel the exemption."

Any breach of a parallel exemption condition will have the effect of cancelling the exemption. It is unclear whether this occurs automatically or whether the Director has discretion which must be exercised specifically to cause cancellation. In other circumstances, cancellation is effective on written notice from the Director.

6-54 Any conditions imposed by the Director must obviously "have regard" to any Commission decision or statement.[62] Accordingly, the conditions must not be inconsistent with the terms of any Commission individual exemption or comfort letter. Clearly a good deal will depend on the Commission's reasons for any decision or statement. To the extent that a decision is based on any effect on inter-state trade, or other aspect of Community law that does not give rise to a corresponding question under United Kingdom law, the Director may disregard it.

In the case of negative clearance granted by the Commission, the Director faces less risk of inconsistency in reaching a finding of infringement of the Chapter I prohibition than if the Commission had granted exemption. Negative clearance may simply have been granted because of the absence of effect on inter-State trade.

---

[61] s. 10(4).
[62] s. 60.

Dual notifications

6-55 It is essential to reduce the cost to undertakings (and the cost to the authorities) of dealing with unnecessary notifications. Maximum use should therefore be made of dual notifications.

Exemptions

6-56 Where exemption is required from both Article 85(1) and a Chapter II prohibition, the matter should be dealt with by means of parallel exemption under section 10 of the 1998 Act. This would only involve one application for exemption and this should be made to the Commission since the Commission alone may grant exemption under Article 85(3) for Article 85(1) prohibitions. If the agreement is given exemption by the Commission it will be automatically exempt under section 10 and there is no need to make a second notification to the Director. It is also worth bearing in mind that exemption by the Commission will take effect in all Member States whereas exemption by the Director only takes effect within the United Kingdom. Parallel exemptions (*i.e.* automatic exemption in the United Kingdom by virtue of any Commission individual exemption) provides provisional immunity from penalties for a Chapter I prohibition with effect from notification to the Commission, until determination of the matter.

Comfort letters

6-57 More often than not however instead of granting formal exemption from the Commission, the parties will settle instead for a comfort letter which is not binding on the courts, nor on the Director. The Commission's Notice on co-operation between national competition authorities and the Commission[63] requires the Director to have regard to Commission comfort letters when assessing agreements. The Director is likely to regard comfort letters as sufficiently authoritative to amount to a "statement of the Commission", to which the Director (and the courts) are to "have regard" under section 60 of the Act. There may however be exceptional cases where an agreement has sufficiently serious and distinct effect on United Kingdom competition to justify a departure from a Commission comfort letter, such as might be the case with local agreements involving United Kingdom breweries. Before any such departure the Director will consult with the Commission.

One of the greatest shortcomings of a comfort letter is that it is not binding on any court. When such agreements are challenged in a national court the parties should apply for a stay of proceedings and request a formal exemption from the Commission.[64]

Borderline cases

6-58 The area of greatest uncertainty concerns borderline cases where it is not apparent whether an agreement caught by the Chapter I prohibition has an effect on inter-State trade. Notification under the 1998 Act should be made to the Director, instead of to the Commission, in two situations concerning borderline agreements. The first is where the Commission informs the parties that it declines jurisdiction. The matter will not be dealt with by the Commission with any degree of priority and the outcome will remain uncertain for some time. The second is where an agreement is challenged in the United Kingdom courts. In such cases a speedy resolution is needed and, assuming the agreement

---

[63] [1997] O.J. C313/3, para. 17.
[64] For further detail see Chapter 14, *Co-operation between the Commission, the Courts and competent authorities*, below.

qualifies for exemption under section 9, the agreement may be given exemption retroactively from the date of notification.[65]

The Commission's Notice on co-operation between national competition authorities and the Commission,[66] among other things, has the aim of settling the appropriate forum for assessing agreements. While the Commission is dealing with a notification, no action is likely to be taken by the Director until the Commission has completed its assessment and informed the parties of the outcome.

6-59   If the Commission concludes the matter by exemption then parallel exemption will be granted by section 10; if by comfort letter then the effect will be as described above. If the Commission grants negative clearance confirming that Article 85(1) does not apply, the Director must obviously have regard to that decision under section 60 but there may still be room for the Director to take action if there is sufficiently serious and distinct effect on United Kingdom competition, or if the agreement involves important legal, economic or policy developments, or if for some reason the parties have a legitimate objective interest in obtaining a decision or guidance. In such cases, notification should be made to the Director as well.

It is also appropriate to notify agreements to the Director, instead of to the Commission, in the case of agreements which are not notifiable to the Commission by virtue of Regulation 17/62, Article 4(2). These are agreements in the very limited category described in *Non-notifiable agreements*, above comprising *inter alia* national agreements and certain intellectual property transactions.

---

[65] If not further back to the date of the agreement.
[66] [1997] O.J. C 313/3.

CHAPTER 7

Agreements Eligible for Automatic Block Exemption

E.C. AND UNITED KINGDOM POLICY TOWARDS VERTICAL RESTRAINTS

Introduction

7-01   Vertical agreements are those between undertakings at different levels of distribution such as between a supplier and retailer or between a retailer and customer. Their advantage is that they may be used to promote efficient distribution, particularly in overseas territories which may not otherwise be reached. They enable suppliers, for example to reach retail markets without having to invest in their own sales infrastructure, and increase efficiencies in distribution. The threat posed by vertical agreements is that they are frequently exclusive across national territories, preventing competition from other distributors for the same brand. They may also be used to divide markets geographically. Ultimately whether a particular agreement is pro or anti-competitive depends on the structure of the market in which it operates. Where there is greater inter-brand competition (competition between different brands), the greater is the likelihood that the pro-competitive effects of the agreement will be realised, since the presence of lively competition should combat any supposed anti-competitive effects of the vertical restraints. Vertical restraints will have an effect on intra-brand competition (that is, competition within a brand) because for example in the case of an exclusive distribution appointment, distributors of a particular brand will not be competing in the same territory The anti-competitive effects of the appointment will be worse where there is little inter-brand competition.

In the United Kingdom, sections 6 to 8 of the 1998 Act contemplate block exemption for agreements falling within the Chapter I prohibition, where the conditions for exemption in section 9 are satisfied.[1]

7-02   The United Kingdom block exemptions are likely to follow the pattern of the Commission block exemption Regulations, making due adjustment however for the fact that the Chapter I prohibition does not share the Single Market aims of Article 85 (1). See Chapter 2, *The Differences: The Key Differences Between Article 85(1) and Chapter I* above, for the differences between Article 85 (1) and Chapter I which are likely to be of relevance. A more liberal approach to automatic exemption is expected at the domestic level but the precise scope of the United Kingdom block exemptions remains to be seen. In the meantime, use may be made of the parallel exemption provisions of section 10 of the 1998 Act (discussed in Chapter 6, *Notification Procedure before the Director General of Fair Trading for Chapter I and Chapter II Infringements* above). The Commission block exemption Regulations discussed in this Chapter, and in Chapter 9 below, will therefore be of importance to parallel exemption under section 10.

---

[1]   At the time of writing no block exemption orders have been made by the Secretary of State under s. 6.

Vertical agreements may also benefit from exclusion orders issued by the Secretary of State under section 50 of the 1998 Act. A draft Order has been issued for consultation by the DTI (at February 4, 1999), inviting comment by April 6, 1999. The draft Order defines vertical agreements as those between undertakings operating at different economic levels in respect of the supply or purchase of goods for resale or processing, or in respect of marketing of services. According to to the draft Order, vertical agreements will be excluded from the Chapter I prohibition provided they do not have the object or effect of fixing resale prices or minimum prices. Even maximum prices and recommended resale prices will lose the benefit of the exclusion if they have the same effect as resale or minimum price fixing. The draft Order does not directly concern intellectual property agreements for which presumably a separate exclusion order, or at least separate guidance, will follow. The reason given is that the treatment of intellectual property agreements under the 1998 Act will closely follow Community law.

7-03   Section 50 refers specifically to vertical agreements, conscious of the fact that the treatment of vertical restraints under E.C. law is presently under revision. Rather than establish rules at this stage for the evaluation of vertical agreements, section 50 empowers the Secretary of State by order to provide for exclusion from the prohibitions, or exemption from the prohibitions (notably by block exemption) in relation to vertical agreements,[2] whether in general or of a prescribed description. Section 50 also contemplates orders to empower the Director to give directions to the effect that (in prescribed circumstances) an exclusion, exemption or modification should not apply in relation to an individual agreement. It is anticipated that the regime ultimately adopted for vertical agreements under the 1998 Act will follow E.C. law. However there are likely to be "claw back" provisions disapplying any exemption or exclusion in circumstances where the ill-effects of the vertical agreement may be felt on the market. The Commission's proposals in relation to vertical restraints are set out in further detail in *Commission's proposals on vertical restraints*, below.

As far as Community law is concerned, Council Regulations 19/65 and 2821/71[3] enables the Commission to adopt block exemption Regulations in respect of certain types of agreement which fulfill the conditions of Article 85(3), by virtue of being agreements

> ". . . which contribute to improving the production or distribution of goods or to promoting technical or economic progress, while allowing consumers a fair share of the resulting benefit . . ."[4]

7-04   Council Regulations 19/65 and 2821/71 emerged from concern about the considerable number of notifications of agreements submitted for individual exemption under Article 85(3). In order to facilitate the Commission's task of granting exemption it was decided:

> ". . . that it should be enabled to declare by way of regulation that the provisions of Article 85(1) do not apply to certain types of agreement and certain concerted practices."[5]

---

[2] s. 50 refers to vertical agreements and land agreements.
[3] Council Reg. 19/65 on the application of Art. 85(3) of the Treaty to certain categories of agreements and concerted practices, [1965] J.O. 533/65. Council Reg. 2821/71 on the application of Art. 85(3) of the Treaty to categories of agreements, decisions and concerted practices [1972] O.J. Spec. Ed. L291/144.
[4] Taken from the second para. of Art. 85(3).
[5] Recital 3 to Reg. 19/65 [1965] J.O. 533/65.

The Commission has exercised its powers under Council Regulation 19/65 on a number of occasions by adopting block exemption Regulations in respect of a variety of different types of agreement. This Chapter examines the following:

(i) Regulation 1983/83,[6] on the application of Article 85(3) of the Treaty concerning certain types of exclusive distribution agreements (see *Exclusive Distribution Agreements*, below);

(ii) Regulation 1475/95,[7] on the application of Article 85(3) of the Treaty concerning certain categories of motor vehicle distribution and servicing agreements (see *Exclusive Distribution Agreements*, below);

(iii) Regulation 1984/83,[8] on the application of Article 85(3) of the Treaty concerning certain exclusive purchasing agreements (see *Exclusive Purchasing Agreements*, below);

(iv) Regulation 417/85,[9] on the application of Article 85(3) of the Treaty concerning certain specialisation agreements (see *Specialisation Agreements*, below);

(v) Regulation 4087/88,[10] on the application of Article 85(3) of the Treaty concerning franchise agreements granting an exclusive territory (see *Franchising Agreements*, below).

7-05 Block exemption Regulations have also been adopted in relation to certain types of intellectual property agreements, such as research and development agreements (Regulation 418/85[11]), and exclusive patent and know-how licences (Regulation 240/96[12]), which are discussed further in Chapter 9 below.

Commission's proposals on vertical restraints

7-06 On January 22, 1997, the Commission adopted its Green Paper on Vertical Restraints in E.U. Competition Policy[13] and, on the basis of responses subsequently received, the Commission proposed (September 30, 1998[14]) amendments to Council Regulations 19/65 and 17/62 in order to substitute the existing block exemption Regulations for vertical agreements with an extended and simplified Regulation.

Economic analysis has demonstrated to the Commission that the effect of an agreement on the market is more important than its form. In particular what is now recognised as important is the type of vertical restriction used in agreements. In general a relaxation of the principles applied to vertical restraints is regarded as necessary where the parties do not possess high market shares. The Commission has already focused its attention on particular types of vertical agreement in some of its existing block exemption Regulations (for exclusive distribution agreements, exclusive purchasing agreements and franchises) but these have not reduced the Commission's case-load of individual notifications where agreements have not met the preconditions for automatic exemption set out in those Regulations. Furthermore it has become apparent that those Regulations, in practice,

---

[6] Reg. 1983/83 [1983] O.J. L173/1, amended by [1983] O.J. L281/24. For the full text see Appendix C.1 below.
[7] Reg. 1475/95 [1995] O.J. L145/25. For the full text see Appendix C.2 below.
[8] Reg. 1984/83 [1983] O.J. L173/5, amended by [1983] O.J. L281/24. For the full text see Appendix C.3 below.
[9] Reg 417/85 [1985] O.J. L53/1, amended by Reg. 151/93 [1993] O.J. L21/8. For the full text see Appendix C.4 below.
[10] Reg. 4087/88 [1988] O.J. L359/46. For the full text see Appendix C.5 below.
[11] Reg. 418/85 [1985] O.J. L53/5.
[12] Reg. 240/96 [1996] O.J. L31/2.
[13] COM (96) 721.
[14] COM (1988) 546 final.

have exempted agreements which threaten competition and have not exempted many that satisfy the general requirements of Article 85(3). The Regulations therefore need to be better focused. Block exemption Regulations also need to encourage new forms of market integration, not simply those methods covered by the existing Regulations. Finally they need to be broad enough to provide legal certainty.

7-07   The Green Paper invited comment on four options, set out below.

I Maintain current system

The first option was to maintain the current system of control of vertical restraints by means of the existing block exemption Regulations. However, given the breadth of Article 85(1) and the narrowness of the block exemption Regulations, far more agreements are still caught by Article 85(1) than is intended by the Commission and there is a continuing need to reduce the unnecessarily high case-load of the Commission in considering individual notifications.

II Wider block exemptions

The second option was to broaden the scope of the existing block exemption Regulations by exempting a greater range of particular clauses as well as clauses that are similar but less restrictive. Less attention would be given to the particular form of clauses and similar clauses to those covered by existing block exemption Regulations would benefit from exemption. This option would involve creating further Regulations for selective distribution and rendering the arrangements for beer and petrol more flexible.

III More focused block exemptions

This option addressed the anti-competitive effect of vertical restraints when coupled with market power. It was acknowledged that the effects of reduced intra-brand competition, for example by an exclusive appointment, would be less important when there is fierce inter-brand competition. When there is little inter-brand competition, automatic exemption should not be available. The market share of the parties will provide a measure of the level of the inter-brand competition on the market. Accordingly under this option the proposal was to limit exemption afforded by the current block exemptions to those with market shares below a suggested threshold of 40 per cent. This would leave great uncertainty as to the position of those with a market share in excess of 40 per cent. It was suggested that exemption may be granted in such cases only on condition that there is no price discrimination between different Member States. Nevertheless the proposal would result in a flood of notifications from those with higher market shares and this would be against the Commission's aim of case-load reduction.

IV Reduce the scope of Article 85(1)

This option proposed a rebuttable presumption of compatibility with Article 85(1) (by which negative clearance may be presumed) where the parties have a market share of less than 20 per cent. Above that threshold there are two further options. Either the existing block exemptions may be widened as suggested under Option II, or Option III may be followed which suggested wider block exemption for up to a 40 per cent market share but no block exemption above that threshold.

7-08   One of the motivating factors behind the review of vertical restraints was the fact that the block exemption Regulations for exclusive distribution agreements (1983/83), exclusive purchasing agreements (1984/83) and franchise agreements (4087/88) are due to expire on December 31, 1999. The shortcomings of these Regulations became more apparent than ever in the responses to the Green Paper and might be summarised as follows:

(i) the Regulations only apply to agreements concerning goods for resale (in a distribution or purchasing agreement) not intermediary goods, or services;

(ii) the agreements covered by the Regulations must be bilateral;

(iii) the Regulations only apply to specific forms of distribution and then only on condition that only certain typical clauses are included. For example, selective distribution agreements are not covered by the Regulations;

(iv) the narrowness of the Regulations means that far too many agreements require individual notification (most commonly resulting in a comfort letter with all the shortcomings of comfort letters); and

(v) too much emphasis is placed on the form of exempted clauses (the white-list) rather than the effect of the restrictions. This is considered likely adversely to affect innovative, perhaps even more pro-competitive forms of distribution.

The Commission's objectives in reforming its approach to vertical restraints have the goals of providing legal certainty for agreements and the need for a simplified regulatory framework to ensure that exemption is granted automatically only to agreements which pose the least threat to competition.

7-09   In its evaluation of vertical restraints the Commission has concluded as follows:

(i) Vertical restraints which reduce inter-brand competition are generally more harmful than vertical restraints that reduce intra-brand competition. Restraints that reduce inter-brand competition are achieved, for example through non-competition undertakings and incentives to carry only one brand, thereby preventing other brands reaching the market. The results are, first, that the suppliers of other brands cannot sell to those buyers who have accepted such restrictions and, secondly, fewer brands are available from the same retailer. Restraints that reduce intra-brand competition are most commonly found, for example in exclusive distribution agreements. Restraints in exclusive appointments do, however, overcome a common commercial concern with "free-riding". Free-riding between manufacturers occurs where the investment by one manufacturer in certain sales outlets attracts custom for competing goods. Free-riding between retailers occurs when one retailer makes promotional efforts to sell to a customer who purchases that product from another retailer. Vertical restraints have the advantage of protecting the investment in promotion against free-riding, especially for complex, technical and expensive goods or products with weak branding or which are not widely known to the consumer.

(ii) Exclusive agreements involving non-competition obligations are generally worse for competition than non-exclusive agreements involving minimum quantity stipulations since the latter at least allow scope for dealings in competing goods above the minimum quantity commitment.

(iii) A close eye needs to be kept on the cumulative effect of vertical restraints, particularly when practised by a number of suppliers in a given sector.

(iv) Restraints agreed for intermediate goods or services are generally less harmful than those affecting the distribution of final goods or services.

(v) Fixed and minimum resale prices are always regarded as serious restraints. If imposed in a distribution agreement price competition is likely to be eliminated across a brand (intra-brand competition is reduced) and, secondly, the clear price visibility that results permits greater collusion between suppliers. Maximum or recommended prices are not generally so restrictive unless they have the same effect as price-setting. Resale price maintenance is considered to be more restrictive than other vertical restraints.

(vi) Tying clauses are of concern because they enable market power in one market (for example sales) to be extended in another market (the "after market") such as when servicing is tied to product supply. Exclusive purchasing—requiring a purchaser to source all its requirements from one supplier—is considered to be the least serious restriction in the group.

7-10 The Commission's proposal recommends that a new broadened block exemption Regulation be adopted which covers all vertical agreements relating to the supply and/or purchase of goods, whether for resale or processing and including the marketing of services. Agreements should benefit from exemption whether they are bilateral or between more than two parties but as long as they operate at different stages of the economic process.

In general, vertical restraints between competitors would be excluded from automatic exemption. However there would be some relaxation for small and medium-sized enterprises ("SMEs"). For the meaning of "SME"s see the Annex to Commission Recommendation 96/280/E.C. and Chapter 2, *"Appreciable effect" under Article 85(1)*, above. The circumstances in which automatic exemption is likely to be granted to vertical agreement between actual or potential competitors would be where:

(i) the agreement is non-reciprocal and none of the parties has an annual turnover of exceeding 100 million ECUs; or

(ii) the agreement involves members of an association of independent retailers who are all SMEs. (Provided the horizontal aspects are not caught by Article 85(1).)

7-11 It is proposed that a single new Regulation be adopted. Instead of identifying the clauses which are contained in exempt agreements as the existing Regulations do (since this is a requirement of Regulation 19/65, Article 1(2)(b)), the new Regulation would identify only black-listed vertical restrictions, or combinations of restrictions, which would result in the loss of exemption. This approach would result in far greater flexibility since it departs from the straight-jacketing of agreements to particular forms of restriction.

In order to exempt agreements that are not regarded as harmful and to avoid exempting those that are, a wider block exemption Regulation is proposed based on departure from the identified permitted restrictions in each agreement and instead the adoption of economic criteria, such as the relevant market share accounted for by the contract goods. If the market share of the parties to the agreement exceeds a given threshold then exemption would no longer be granted. It has not yet been decided whether one or two market-share thresholds would be adopted. If a single threshold is adopted it is likely to be in the range of 25 to 35 per cent market share. If a dual threshold is adopted the first band would be 0–20 per cent market share, and the second, 20 to 40 per cent. Most Member States favour the single threshold.

7-12 There would be two grades of restriction: hardcore vertical restraints and less serious vertical restraints. Hardcore restrictions will always fall outside exemption and will include:

  (i) "fixed resale prices or minimum resale prices";

 (ii) "maximum resale prices or recommended resale prices which in reality amount to fixed or minimum resale prices";

(iii) "the prevention or restriction of active or passive sales, imports or exports to final or intermediate buyers" (except the usual restriction on active sales in the territory allocated to an exclusive distributor, the restriction on active sales to exclusively allocated customers, the restriction on members of a selective distribution system from selling to unauthorised distributors and the restriction on the buyer of intermediate goods and/or services from selling these to other direct or indirect buyers of the supplier);

(iv) "the prevention or restriction of cross-supplies between distributors at the same or different levels of distribution in an exclusive or selective distribution system or between distributors of these different systems of distribution; *i.e.* exclusive or selective distribution combined with exclusive purchasing";

 (v) "the combination, at the same level of distribution, of selective distribution and exclusive distribution containing a prohibition or restriction on active selling";

(vi) "the combination, at the same level of distribution, of selective distribution and exclusive customer allocation"; and

(vii) "an obligation on the supplier of an intermediate good not to sell the same good as a repair or replacement good to the independent aftermarket".

7-13 If the single threshold system is adopted, all the non-hardcore vertical restraints would benefit from exemption if the parties' market share is below the threshold. In the case of the dual threshold system, non-hardcore restrictions would be exempt below the 20 per cent threshold. Between 20 and 40 per cent, exemption will depend on the nature of the non-hardcore vertical restraint. Less serious restrictions would be minimum quantities in non-exclusive agreements, exclusive distribution and exclusive purchasing commitments, and agreements between SME's. For non-compete commitments a duration limit is proposed. A time limit is also proposed for exclusive purchasing agreements when combined with minimum quantity commitments.

The proposal contemplates withdrawal of exemption if, in spite of the black-list excluding certain clauses or combinations, the agreement nevertheless produces results which are incompatible with Article 85(3). It is also proposed, in line with the Commission's wish to de-centralise the implementation of competition rules to domestic level, that where an agreement manifests anti-competitive effects in a particular Member State (such that it has the characteristics of a distinct market) then the national competition authority may withdraw exemption by adopting a decision to that effect.[15]

7-14 Where agreements fall outside the block exemption, as usual, the burden of proof will remain on the Commission to prove infringement.

Certain agreements would not be covered by the new wider Regulation. These would be patent and know-how licences covered by Regulation 240/96 (presumably because that Regulation is to continue in effect) and sub-contracting agreements (because they remain subject to the existing Notice on sub-contracting agreements[16]). It is recognised that software agreements require further consideration (which is already long overdue) but that

---

[15] This would require Council Reg. 19/65 to be supplemented to stipulate the circumstances under which national authorities may withdraw exemption.

[16] [1979] O.J. C1/2. See Chapter 8, *Miscellaneous co-operation between enterprises not caught by Article 85(1)*, below.

the new Regulation would treat the intermediate supply of shrink-wrap software as the supply of goods (rather than a licence of copyright). Restrictions on the use and application of intellectual property will generally be covered by the new Regulation where the intellectual property is secondary in the sense that its use is indispensable and complementary to the performance of exempt agreements and the intellectual property provisions do not contain any further restrictions.

7-15   Legislative changes will be necessary to widen Council Regulation 19/65 (the enabling provision which empowers the Commission to declare Article 85(1) inapplicable). Its scope is limited to particular vertical restraints, namely bilateral exclusive distribution agreements, exclusive purchasing agreements (in both cases concerning goods for resale), and restrictions in relation to the assignment and use of intellectual property rights. The scope of Council Regulation 19/65 will therefore need to be widened.

Also, Regulation 17/62 Article 4(2) requires amendment in order to provide for retroactive exemption since, under Regulation 17/62, individual exemption may only be granted with effect from the date of notification. As it is intended that the new Regulation will have retroactive effect, Regulation 17/62 will require amendment to allow this. It is envisaged that the legislative changes necessary to pave the way for the new block exemption Regulation will be in place by the year 2000.

7-16   Until the new proposed programme of changes is implemented, the existing block exemption Regulations continue to apply, albeit in a manner that is not well targeted to cover only agreements appropriate for automatic exemption. The existing Regulations nevertheless are an extremely useful source for understanding the Commission's reasoning to date and, of course, still form the basis of eligibility for group exemption for particular forms of agreement.[17]

EXCLUSIVE DISTRIBUTION AGREEMENTS

Introduction

7-17   Exclusive distribution agreements and exclusive purchase agreements[18] were the first categories of agreement to benefit from block exemption. The block exemptions for both exclusive distribution and exclusive purchasing agreements were due to expire at the end of 1997, although they have now both been extended to the end of 1999[19] pending the review of the exemptions by the Commission.

An exclusive distribution agreement between a manufacturer (or supplier) and a distributor gives the distributor the exclusive right to distribute specified products of the manufacturer (or supplier) within a given geographic area.

7-18   The advantages of exclusive distribution agreements are that they encourage the distributor to focus on the promotion and sales of one particular brand or range of products to the exclusion of others. It may be difficult or expensive for the manufacturer or supplier alone to put in place the necessary sales infrastructure for all of its products in all countries, especially as the requirements of each country (such as language, labelling and consumer preferences) may vary.

Market penetration is also considered to be more effectively achieved by exclusive distributors who are generally required to devote themselves fully (by best endeavours obli-

---

[17] The Commission has also begun its process of review of horizontal restraints (Commission Competition Report 1997 points 14 and 47) by issuing preliminary questionnaires to Member States. It is expected to be some time before the Commission's reasoning on horizontal restraints is as advanced as its position on vertical restraints.

[18] Discussed in *Exclusive purchasing agreements*, below.

[19] Commission Reg. 1582/97, [1997] O.J. L214/27.

gations) to their marketing activities. The distribution of goods is therefore likely to be improved and competition between suppliers of different brands (inter-brand competition) increased, to satisfy the conditions of Article 85(3).

7-19   Exclusive distribution agreements are, however, potentially caught by Article 85(1) because they prevent the supplier appointing another distributor for the same products in the same territory and the distributor is therefore protected against the competition that might otherwise exist from other distributors of the same brand of product (intra-brand competition). There is also the risk that the common market will become compartmentalised along national boundaries since exclusive appointments are frequently made on a country-wide basis because of the characteristics that differentiate one country from another.

The block exemption for exclusive distribution agreements: Regulation 1983/83[20]

7-20   If an agreement is to be eligible for automatic block exemption it must conform in all respects with the provisions of the applicable Regulation. As with all block exemption Regulations, Regulation 1983/83 begins with a series of recitals which explain the policy of the Commission in adopting the Regulation. The recitals are themselves of legal significance as they may be referred to for the purpose of construing the substantive provisions of the Regulation where there are difficulties of interpretation.[21] As a further guide to interpretation, reliance may be placed on the Commission's Notice concerning Regulation 1983/83 and 1984/83[22] ("the Commission Notice") which may be given persuasive authority in national courts.[23]

Permitted agreements

7-21   **Object.**   The essential object of the agreement must be the appointment of the exclusive distributor and not some other purpose. (An example of an inappropriate purpose might be market sharing, achieved by the reciprocal appointment by each party of the other as its exclusive distributor. Each party would thereby agree to stay out of the other's allocated territory. Needless to say, such exemption would be unavailable under the Regulation and is unlikely to be available on individual application.)

The agreement must satisfy the requirements set out in Article 1 of the Regulation. It must be an agreement:

". . . to which only two undertakings are party and whereby one party agrees with the other to supply certain goods for resale within the whole or a defined area of the common market only to that other."

7-22   **Two undertakings.**   Exemption is only granted if the agreement is between two undertakings, one supplier and one distributor. For further discussion on the meaning of

---

[20]   Commission Reg. 1983/83, on the application of Art. 85(3) of the Treaty to certain categories of exclusive distribution agreements, [1983] O.J. L173/1 amended by [1983] O.J. L281/24. The Reg. now also applies to Art. 53 of the EEA Agreement, subject to necessary amendments (Annex XIV, para. 3 to the EEA Agreement).
[21]   Case 63/75 *Fonderis Roubaix v. Fonderis Roux* [1976] E.C.R. 111; [1976] 1 C.M.L.R. 538.
[22]   The Commission Notice concerning Commission Regs EEC 1983/83 and 1984/83: [1984] O.J. C101/02, as modified by [1992] O.J. C121/2 ('Commission Notice") (an EFTA Surveillance Authority notice has been published equivalent to the Commission's Notice for the EEA States: [1994] O.J. L153/1, as amended by [1994] O.J. L 186/57). For the full text of the Commission Notice see Appendix C.6 below.
[23]   *Cutsforth v. Mansfield Inns* [1986] 1 W.L.R. 998. However the Notice in its introduction contains a caveat expressed by the Commission that it does not "indicate the interpretation which might be given to the provisions by the Court of Justice" (para. 3 of the Notice).

"undertaking" see Chapter 2, *Undertakings*, above. The Regulation will apply even if a single supplier enters into a number of exclusive distribution agreements of this type with different distributors to form a network[24] (provided all of the other preconditions for exemption are satisfied).

7-23   Goods.   The Regulation only applies to "goods" supplied for resale and not to services. For example it would not apply to the supply of tours, which are treated as services (*Re 1990 World Cup Package Tours*[25]). However, the Commission does regard the Regulation as applying where the distributor hires or leases goods, rather than resells them.[26] There is no requirement that goods must be specified "by brand or denomination" in the agreement[27] as long as the goods are identifiable with certainty.

Furthermore the Regulation still applies where the distributor provides customer or after sales-services so long as those services are incidental to the resale of the goods and the charge for the service is not higher than the price of the goods.[28]

7-24   Resale.   It is also an absolute requirement that goods be supplied for the purpose of resale. A process of transformation affecting the economic identity of the goods, or anything other than "a slight addition in value"[29] does not constitute resale. The Commission Notice clarifies what is meant by resale as follows.

> "The notion of resale requires that the goods concerned be disposed of by the purchasing party to others in return for consideration. Agreements on the supply or purchase of goods which the purchasing party transforms or processes into other goods or uses or consumes in manufacturing other goods are not agreements for resale. The same applies to the supply of components which are combined with other components into a different product. The criterion is that the goods distributed by the [distributor] are the same as those the other party has supplied to him for that purpose. The economic identity of the goods is not affected if the [distributor] merely breaks up and packages the goods in smaller quantities, or repackages them, before resale.
>
> Where the [distributor] performs additional operations to improve the quality, durability, appearance or taste of the goods (such as rust-proofing of metals, sterilisation of food or the addition of colouring matter or flavourings to drugs), the position will mainly depend upon how much value the operation adds to the goods. Only a slight addition in value can be taken not to change the economic identity of the goods. In determining the precise dividing line in individual cases, trade usage in particular must be considered. The Commission applies the same principles to agreements under which the [distributor] is supplied with concentrated extract for a drink which he has to dilute with water, pure alcohol or another liquid and to bottle before reselling."[30]

7-25   Defined area.   It is also a requirement of exemption that the distributor be granted a defined area of territorial exclusivity in which it may distribute the products. This means that only a single distributor should be appointed for a given contract territory. The

---

[24] See para. 14 of the Commission Notice and cases 47/76 *De Norre v. Brouwerij Concordia* [1977] E.C.R. 65; [1977] 1 C.M.L.R. 378, C–234/89 *Delimitis v. Henninger Bräu* [1991] E.C.R. I-935; [1992] 5 C.M.L.R. 210.
[25] Commission Dec. 92/521 [1992] O.J. L326/31.
[26] Commission Notice para. 12.
[27] Unlike the exclusive purchasing Reg., see para. 7-64 below.
[28] Commission Notice, para. 11. Note that the Commission considers that agreements relating to hiring or leasing of goods sold to the purchaser to be within the remit of the exemption.
[29] Commission Notice, para. 10.
[30] Commission Notice paras 9 and 10. The Notice refers to a "reseller" rather than a distributor but the latter is preferred for continuity with the rest of this Chapter.

Commission confirmed this in the Seventeenth Report on Competition Policy (for 1987)[31] and in its decision in the case of *Junghans*.[32] The appointment of two distributors in a territory for identical products under separate brand names would not qualify for exemption.

The E.C.J has confirmed[33] that agreements drafted to cover the whole of the Community may be acceptable. The territorial exclusivity of an agreement must relate to a defined area, such as a Member State or a larger part of the Community, but may not relate to classes of customer (as illustrated by *Ivoclar*[34]).

Permitted restrictions on competition

7-26 Article 2 of the Regulation contains the only other restrictions on competition that may be included in the agreement (apart from the exclusive appointment).

7-27 Obligation on the supplier not to supply others. Article 2(1) permits the inclusion of an obligation on the supplier "not to supply the contract goods to users in the contract territory". The supplier cannot accept any other restrictions.

7-28 Obligation on the distributor not to compete. Article 2(2) lists the only restrictions on competition that may be imposed on the distributor. These are obligations:

(a) not to manufacture or distribute goods which compete with the contract goods;

(b) to obtain the contract goods for resale from the other party only; and

(c) to refrain, outside the contract territory and in relation to the contract goods, from seeking customers, from establishing any branch and from maintaining any distribution depot.

These provisions oblige the distributor to concentrate its efforts on distribution of the goods supplied under the contract, rather than competing products, and are also intended to prevent active sales by the distributor outside the contract territory. The distributor cannot accept any other restrictions on competition.

Non-restrictive obligations on the distributor

7-29 Article 2(3) contains examples of obligations which the Commission considers generally do not restrict competition. The parties are therefore free to include any one or more of these obligations in their agreement. However the obligations must not be drafted or applied in such a way as to amount in substance or effect to the type of restrictions that are not permitted by Article 85(1).[35]

The permitted obligations contained in Article 2(3) which may be imposed on the distributor are:

(a) to purchase complete ranges of goods or minimum quantities;

(b) to sell the contract goods under trade marks or packed and presented as specified by the other party; and

---

[31] Para. 28.
[32] Commission Dec. 77/100 [1977] O.J. L30/10; [1977] 1 C.M.L.R. D82.
[33] Case 47/76 *De Norre v. NV Brouwerij Concordia* [1977] E.C.R. 65; [1977] 1 C.M.L.R. 378.
[34] Commission Dec. 85/559 [1985] O.J. L369/1; [1988] 4 C.M.L.R. 781.
[35] The additional permissible obligations contained within Art. 2(3) are similar to those listed in the exclusive purchasing block exemption (see *Non-restrictive obligations on the purchaser*, (para. 7-71) below) except for the omission of an obligation to purchase minimum quantities of the strictly defined goods which are subject to the exclusive purchasing obligations.

    (c) to take measures for promotion of sales, in particular:

        (i) to advertise;

      (ii) to maintain a sales network or stock of goods;

    (iii) to provide customer and guarantee services; and

    (iv) to employ staff having specialised or technical training.

As part of the obligation on the distributor to take measures for promotion of sales and to maintain a distribution network ((b) and (c) above), the agreement may prevent the distributor from supplying the contract goods to unsuitable dealers. However this is subject to the proviso that admission to the distribution network is based on:

> "objective criteria of a qualitative nature relating to the professional qualifications of the owner of the business or his staff or the suitability of his business premises, if the criteria are the same for all potential dealers, and if the criteria are actually applied in a non-discriminatory manner".[36]

Inapplicability of the block exemption

7-30   Article 3 specifies a number of different circumstances in which exemption will not apply.

7-31 **Agreements between competing manufacturers.** The Regulation does not apply if the parties are manufacturers of competing goods and either:

    (i) enter into reciprocal exclusive distribution agreements in respect of those goods (because this is tantamount to market-sharing); or

   (ii) enter into a non-reciprocal exclusive distribution agreement unless one of them has a turnover of no more than 100 million ECUs. The concern is that even a non- reciprocal exclusive agreement between competitors is likely to reduce competition and to an extent give access to each other's pricing information.

Goods are competing for these purposes if they are identical or are considered by users as equivalent in view of their characteristics, price and intended use.

7-32 **No alternative supplier.** Under Article 3(c), the agreement will not benefit from exemption where:

> "users can obtain the contract goods in the contract territory only from the exclusive distributor and have no alternative source of supply outside the contract territory".

This is designed to prevent a total elimination of intra-brand competition, as explained by the Commission:

> "The block exemption cannot be claimed for agreements that give the exclusive distributor absolute territorial protection . . . the parties must ensure either that the contract goods can be sold in the contract territory by parallel importers or that users have a real possibility of obtaining them from undertakings outside the contract ter-

---

[36] Commission Notice, para. 20.

ritory, if necessary outside the Community, at the prices and the terms there prevailing."[37]

The original supplier may or may not be the alternative source of supply from outside the contract territory.[38]

7-33   Thwarting parallel imports.   Article 3(d) disapplies exemption if either party attempts to make it difficult for intermediaries or users to acquire the goods by way of parallel imports. The use of "industrial property rights", such as trade marks or patents, to achieve this aim is given by way of illustration. An example is the case of *Consten and Grundig v. Commission*[39] where the supplier assigned its trade mark to the distributor with the effect of hindering imports. However the grant of trade mark rights in an exclusive distribution agreement will not, in itself, result in the loss of the exemption.[40]

The effect of Article 3 is to limit the scope of exclusivity available to the exclusive distributor because the supplier is not able to defend its distributor from parallel imports into the contract territory from outside. For further discussion on the use of intellectual property rights to prevent parallel imports see Chapter 10 below.

Withdrawal of the block exemption

7-34   The Commission's power to withdraw exemption is contained in Article 6 of the Regulation. The Commission has power[41] to withdraw exemption in various circumstances and may do so upon its own initiative, or in response to a request from a Member State or other interested third parties if the effect of putting an exempted agreement into operation is for any reason incompatible with the conditions set out in Article 85(3).[42] The illustrations given in Article 6 of situations in which the Commission can bring proceedings to withdraw exemption are where:

(a) the contract goods are not subject, in the contract territory, to effective competition from identical goods considered by users as equivalent in view of their characteristics, price and intended use;

(b) access by other suppliers to the different stages of distribution within the contract territory is made difficult to a significant extent;

(c) for reasons other than those referred to in Article 3(c) and (d) (see *No alternative supplier* and *Thwarting parallel imports*, above), it is not possible for intermediaries or users to obtain supplies of the contract goods from dealers outside the contract territory on terms that are customary there;

(d) the distributor, without any objective justification, refuses to supply in the contract territory categories of purchasers who are unable to obtain the contract goods elsewhere on suitable terms, or applies to them differing prices or sale conditions;

(e) the distributor sells the contract goods at excessively high prices.

---

[37] Commission Notice, para. 31.
[38] *ibid.*
[39] Cases 56 & 58/64 *Consten and Grundig v. Commission* [1966] E.C.R. 299; [1966] C.M.L.R. 418.
[40] Case 170/83 *Hydrotherm v. Compact* [1984] E.C.R. 2999; [1985] 3 C.M.L.R. 224.
[41] Derived from Reg. 19/65 [1965] J.O. 533–565.
[42] The withdrawal of exemption does not have retroactive effect. See the Commission Notice, para. 24.

However, it is worth noting that the withdrawal of block exemption does not mean that the agreement is unable to qualify for individual exemption.

Individual exemption under Article 85(3)

7-35   If an agreement falls within the scope of the prohibition in Article 85(1), but outside Regulation 1983/83, the parties may apply to the Commission for individual exemption under Article 85(3). Individual exemption is covered in detail in Chapter 6 above.

Absolute territorial exclusivity is frequently sought by distributors. The Commission has stated that the only circumstance under which individual exemption would be granted for an agreement which confers absolute territorial protection would be where it is necessary to enable penetration of a new market.[43] For example, in *Johnny Walker whisky*,[44] the Commission granted exemption to an agreement that applied differential prices and terms of business for a limited period to aid the re-introduction of Johnny Walker Red Label whisky into the United Kingdom market.

Motor vehicle distribution and servicing agreements: the block exemption for motor vehicle distribution

Introduction

7-36   Motor vehicle dealership agreements have frequently been subject to scrutiny by the Commission, primarily to ensure that they are not being used to prevent the parallel importation of motor vehicles from one Member State to another. For example in *BMW Belgium*,[45] distribution arrangements for BMW cars in Belgium were said to be used to hinder parallel imports from Germany, and in *General Motors*,[46] General Motors in Belgium were alleged to have charged excessive prices for approval certificates which only General Motors were authorised to issue for parallel importation of their cars into Belgium.

The Commission's rationale for regulating motor vehicle dealerships is to ensure:[47]

(a) The consumer's right to buy a motor vehicle and to have it maintained or repaired wherever prices and quality are most advantageous, the network distributor's right to obtain any compatible spare part, whether or not manufactured by or purchased from the vehicle manufacturer, and the non-networked distributor's right to buy spare parts from the network.

(b) The promotion of competition, by facilitating parallel importation of motor cars.

The first block exemption Regulation for vehicle distribution and servicing agreements was Regulation 123/85,[48] adopted in 1985 but replaced in 1995 by Regulation 1475/95.[49]

7-37   The format of the Regulation is similar to that of other block exemption

---

[43] First Report on Competition Policy (1971) para. 49.
[44] *Distillers Company plc (Red Label)* [1983] O.J. C245/3; [1983] 3 C.M.L.R. 173.
[45] Commission Dec. 78/155 [1978] O.J. L46/33, [1978] 2 C.M.L.R. 126.
[46] Commission Dec. 75/75 [1975] O.J. L29/14; [1975] C.M.L.R. D20, see also Case 26/75 *General Motors v. E.C.* [1975] E.C.R. 1367; [1976] 1 C.M.L.R. 95.
[47] See the recitals to Reg. 1475/95 and the Commission Notice on Reg. 123/85 [1985] O.J. C17/3.
[48] Commission Reg. 123/85 [1985] O.J. L15/16.
[49] Commission Reg. 1475/95, on the application of Art. 85(3) of the Treaty to certain categories of motor vehicle distribution and servicing agreements [1995] O.J. L145.

Regulations although it is of greater length than most. Articles 1 and 2 define the types of agreement to which the exemption applies. Article 3 lists permitted restrictions on competition that may be included in the agreement. Article 4 lists those clauses which the Commission considers do not restrict competition within the meaning of Article 85(1), and may therefore also be included in an agreement. Article 5 sets out various provisions which must be included and pre-conditions which must be satisfied for an agreement to benefit from block exemption. Article 6 lists the circumstances in which exemption is not granted. Article 8 contains examples of the circumstances in which the Commission may withdraw the benefit of the block exemption from a particular agreement. Article 10 defines the terminology used throughout the Regulation. Articles 7, 9 and 11 to 13 contain ancillary administrative provisions.

Permitted agreements

7-38 Object. Article 1 of Regulation 1475/95 states that the Regulation applies to:

". . . agreements to which only two undertakings are party and in which one contracting party agrees to supply, within a defined territory of the common market:

— only to the other party; or
— only to the other party and to a specified number of other undertakings within the distribution system,

for the purpose of resale certain new motor vehicles intended for use on public roads and having three or more road wheels, together with spare parts therefor".

This provision is based upon Article 1 of the Regulation for exclusive distribution agreements[50] (discussed above in this Chapter) and some of the terminology is therefore very similar.

7-39 Two undertakings. As with Regulation 1983/83 exemption applies only if the agreement is between two parties, one supplier and one dealer.[51]

7-40 The contract territory. The contract territory is:

"the defined area of the common market to which the obligation of exclusive supply . . . applies".[52]

As with Regulation 1983/83, it is a requirement that the supplier grants to the dealer a defined area, or "contract territory", in which to distribute the motor vehicles and spare parts.

7-41 Resale. Resale in this context has an extended meaning and includes:

". . . all transactions by which . . . the [dealer] disposes of a motor vehicle which is still in a new condition and which he has previously acquired in his own name and on his own behalf, irrespective of the legal description applied under civil law or the format of the transaction which effects such resale. The term resale shall include all leasing contracts which provide for a transfer of ownership or an option to purchase

---

[50] Reg. 1983/83 [1983] O.J. L173/1, as amended by [1983] O.J. L281/24.
[51] "Parties" are the undertakings which are party to an agreement within the meaning of Art. 1: Art. 10(2).
[52] Art. 10(3).

prior to the expiry of the contract. . . . 'distribute' and 'sell' include other forms of supply by the dealer such as leasing."[53]

7-42   Contract goods: motor vehicles and spare parts.   The Regulation applies to the distribution of "new motor vehicles intended for use on public roads and having three or more road wheels".[54] The vehicles covered are new vehicles only, not second hand ones. Motorbikes are excluded as they have less than three wheels, as also are tractors, combine harvesters and the like as they are not intended for use on public roads.

The Regulation also relates to the distribution of new motor vehicles together with spare parts. "Spare parts" are:

> ". . . parts which are to be installed in or upon a motor vehicle so as to replace components of that vehicle. They are to be distinguished from other parts and accessories according to trade usage".[55]

However, agreements for spare parts only are outside the scope of the Regulation.[56]

The totality of the contract goods comprise "the contract range".[57] "Corresponding goods" are motor vehicles and cars, which are similar in kind to those in the contract range, are distributed by the manufacturer or with its consent and are the subject of a distribution or servicing agreement with an undertaking within the distribution system. They are either "corresponding motor vehicles" or "corresponding spare parts".[58]

Permitted restrictions on competition

7-43   Obligation on the supplier.   Article 2 permits the inclusion of a restriction against the supplier selling the contract goods (motor vehicles and spare parts) to final consumers in the contract territory or servicing contract goods for final consumers in the contract territory. These are the only restrictions on the supplier that are permitted under the Regulation.

7-44   Obligations on the dealer.   Article 3 of the Regulation lists the restrictions that a supplier may impose on a dealer. This list, found in Regulation 123/85, was extended by Regulation 1475/95. Most of the extensions reflect a number of decisions made by the Commission. The permitted dealer restrictions are similar to the restrictions permitted under Regulation 1983/83. They are[59]:

(1) A restriction on modifying the contract goods (or corresponding goods) without the supplier's consent (unless the modification was ordered by a final consumer and concerns a particular motor vehicle within the range covered by the contract programme, purchased by that final consumer).

(2) A restriction on manufacturing products which compete with the contract goods.

(3) A restriction on selling new motor vehicles of another make except on separate

---

[53] Art. 10(12) and (13). The Art. uses the word "reseller" rather than "dealer", but the latter is preferred for continuity.
[54] Art. 10(4).
[55] Art. 10(6).
[56] See *Fiat Spare Parts*, XXIII Report on Competition Policy (1993) at para. 229.
[57] Art. 10(5).
[58] Art. 10(11).
[59] Art. 3(1) to 3(11).

sales premises, under separate management, in the form of a distinct legal entity and in a manner which avoids confusion between makes.

(4) A ban against a third party benefiting unduly, through an after-sales service performed in a common workshop, from investments made by the supplier. In particular, this restricts the dealer from allowing a third party to benefit from the use of equipment provided by the supplier or staff trained by the supplier.

(5) A restriction on selling and/or using spare parts which compete with the contract goods (or corresponding goods) unless they match the quality of the contract goods (or corresponding goods).

(6) A ban (without the supplier's consent), on making, altering and/or terminating distribution and/or service agreements with other undertakings operating in the contract territory for contract goods or corresponding goods.

(7) If the consent of the supplier in (6) is obtained to enter into a distribution or service agreement, an obligation to impose similar terms on that other undertaking to those accepted by the dealer in its contract with the supplier.

(8) A ban outside the contract territory on making active sales by maintaining a branch or depot for distribution or soliciting customers by way of personalised advertising. As with Regulation 1983/83, the dealer may only be restricted from making active sales outside the contract territory and its right to fulfill passive orders and sales must be preserved.

(9) A ban on allowing a third party to distribute and/or service the contract goods (or corresponding goods) outside the contract territory.

(10) A ban on supplying the contract goods (or corresponding goods) to a dealer unless the dealer is an undertaking within the distribution network, or in the case of spare parts, unless the dealer uses the spare parts for the repair or maintenance of a motor vehicle.

(11) A restriction preventing sales of motor vehicles to final consumers using the services of an intermediary, unless the intermediary has the prior written authority of the consumer to purchase a specified motor vehicle or to collect it.

Non-restrictive obligations on the dealer

7-45   Article 4 of the Regulation contains a list of provisions which the Commission considers do not restrict competition, and therefore fall outside the prohibition contained in Article 85(1). Parties are therefore free to include undertakings given by the dealer to:

(1) Comply, in distribution, sales and after-sales servicing with minimum standards, regarding in particular:

(a) the equipment of the business premises and the technical facilities for servicing;
(b) the specialised technical training of staff;
(c) advertising;
(d) the collection, storage and delivery of contract goods or corresponding goods and sales and after-sales servicing; and
(e) the repair and maintenance of contract goods and corresponding goods, particularly as regards the safe and reliable functioning of motor vehicles;

(2) Order contract goods from the supplier only at certain times or within certain periods, provided that the interval between ordering dates does not exceed three months;

(3) Endeavour to sell, within the contract territory and during a specified period, a minimum quantity of contract goods, determined by the parties by common agreement;

(4) Keep in stock such quantity of contract goods as may be determined in accordance with (3);

(5) Keep demonstration vehicles within the contract range;

(6) Perform work under guarantee, free servicing and vehicle recall work for contract goods and corresponding goods;

(7) Use only spare parts within the contract range or corresponding spare parts for work under guarantee, free servicing and vehicle-recall work in respect of the contract goods or corresponding goods;

(8) Inform customers, in a general manner, of the extent to which spare parts from other sources might be used for the repair and maintenance of contract goods or corresponding goods; and

(9) Inform customers whenever spare parts from other sources have been used for the repair or maintenance of contract goods or corresponding goods.[60]

The parties are free to include any of these restrictions but there are additional requirements that must be met where the dealer has under Article 4 assumed obligations for the improvement of distribution and servicing structures (see *Distribution and Servicing Structures* below). Their inclusion is subject to the provisions contained in Article 6 which are aimed at ensuring that competition is not unduly stifled (see *Inapplicability of the block exemption*, below).

Essential provisions

7-46   Article 5 contains a list of preconditions which must be satisfied for the agreement to benefit from exemption.

7-47   The dealer.   In all cases exemption shall only apply if the dealer undertakes in respect of motor vehicles within the same contract range as its own, supplied in another Community country by a different undertaking within the distribution network:

(a) to honour guarantees and to perform free servicing and recall work, and carry out repair and maintenance work where the dealer is obliged to do so in relation to vehicles it supplies itself under the agreement[61]; and

(b) to impose the above conditions on any sub-dealers.[62]

7-48   The Supplier.   In all cases exemption shall only apply if the supplier:[63]

---

[60]   Art. 4(1)(1) to 4 (1)(9).
[61]   The obligation may be imposed under the agreement by virtue of Art. 4(1)(1)(e) and 4(1)(6).
[62]   Art. 5(1)(1)(a) and (b).
[63]   See Art. 5(1)(2).

(a) does not unreasonably withhold its consent to a request from the dealer to conclude, alter or terminate distribution and/or service agreements referred to in Article 3(6) (see para. 7-44 below);

(b) does not impose minimum requirements (such as minimum sales targets) or criteria for estimates that are discriminatory or inequitable to the dealer (without objective reason);

(c) when calculating discounts (or in other schemes based on the value of goods), distinguishes between supplies of motor vehicles within the contract range, spare parts within the contract range (where the dealer is dependant on others within the distribution network), and other goods; and

(d) for the purposes of any sale by the dealer and a consumer within the common market, supplies any passenger car which corresponds to a model within the contract range[64] and which is marketed by the manufacturer or with the manufacturer's consent in the Member State in which the vehicle is to be registered.

The last requirement is of particular importance as it is integral to the aims of the Regulation. It safeguards the consumer's right to import vehicles from other Member States by preventing manufacturers from refusing to supply dealers with vehicles on the grounds of specification variance from one country to another. It means that consumers are able to purchase new cars with the specifications they require (such as right hand drive) from official dealers in other Member States where the manufacturer sells the specific model concerned in both Member States.[65] However it is noteworthy that the dealer must have concluded a contract of sale with the consumer.

7-49   There is no obligation on manufacturers to manufacture vehicles that they would not otherwise have chosen to supply and the obligation to supply in Article 5(1)(2)(d) relates only to the supply of vehicles of a corresponding kind (*i.e.* similar) to those in the dealer's contract range. The provision does not oblige the supplier to make available to dealers in each Member State all of the models marketed by the manufacturer, but only those models which are already marketed by the dealer in that particular Member State or which correspond to such models.[66]

A supplemental charge for cars of differing specifications may be levied by the supplier but only so far as such price is reasonable and objectively justified. The supplemental charge was not found to be justified in *Peugeot*,[67] where the French manufacturer increased the cost of right hand drive vehicles in Belgium by 31 per cent with the effect of preventing parallel imports into the United Kingdom.

7-50   **Distribution and servicing structures.**   Article 5(2) lists additional requirements that must be met where the dealer has assumed obligations (as contemplated by Article 4(1))[68] for the improvement of distribution and servicing structures. Exemption will apply provided that:

---

[64] A "passenger car which corresponds to a model within the contract range" is defined in Art. 10(10) as a passenger car which is: (i) manufactured or assembled in volume by the manufacturer and; (ii) identical as to body style, drive-line, chassis, and type of motor with a passenger car within the contract range.

[65] This is illustrated by *Ford Werke AG v. Commission*, Commission Dec. 86/506 [1986] O.J. L295/19; [1989] 4 C.M.L.R. 371.

[66] *Volkswagen*, Nineteenth Report on Competition Policy (1989), para. 48.

[67] Commission Dec. 86/506 [1986] O.J. L295/19; [1989] 4 C.M.L.R. 371.

[68] See *Non-restrictive obligations on the dealer*, above.

(1) the supplier releases the dealer from the restriction contemplated in Article 3(3) (on selling new motor vehicles supplied by persons other than the manufacturer, see *Obligations on the dealer*, above) where the dealer shows that there are objective reasons for doing so;

(2) the agreement is for either: (i) a period of at least four years and each party undertakes to give the other at least six months' prior notice of its intention not to renew the agreement; or (ii) an indefinite period and terminable upon at least two years notice.

However, the notice period for termination is reduced to one year where the supplier is obliged by law or special arrangement to pay compensation on termination of the agreement or where the dealer is a new entrant to the distribution system and the period of the agreement (or notice period for termination) is the first agreed by that dealer. The conditions for exemption do not affect the supplier's right to terminate on at least one year's notice where it is necessary to reorganise the whole or a substantial part of the network, nor to the conditions affecting either party's right to terminate for breach of contract.[69]

Inapplicability of the block exemption

7-51   The following 12 points list the circumstances in which exemption is inapplicable, as set out in Article 6 of the Regulation. The effect on the agreement if any of the listed circumstances prevails is explained later in this section.

7-52   General circumstances where exemption is lost:

(1) Both parties or their connected undertakings[70] are motor vehicle manufacturers. If the parties are motor manufacturers, the risks of concerted action between competitors obviously increases.

(2) The agreement is linked or applied to stipulations concerning products and/or services other than motor vehicles and spare parts as defined by the Regulation. This is intended to prevent any inappropriate "tie-ins" to unrelated products.

(3) In respect of motor vehicles having three or more road wheels and spare parts, the parties agree to restrictions which are not expressly exempted by the Regulation.

(4) In respect of motor vehicles and spare parts, the parties make agreements or engage in concerted practices which are exempted from Article 85(1) by Regulations 1983/83 (exclusive distribution block exemption) or 1984/83 (exclusive purchasing block exemption, see *Exclusive purchasing agreements*, below) to an extent exceeding the scope of the block exemption for motor vehicle distribution.

(5) The parties agree to allow the supplier to alter the contract territory or to add specified new dealers for the contract goods.

(6) The manufacturer, supplier or another undertaking directly or indirectly restricts the dealer's freedom to determine prices and/or discounts when resell-

---

[69] Art. 5(3).
[70] "Connected undertakings" are defined in Art. 10(8) and the definition is similar to that in other block exemption Regulations.

ing contract goods or corresponding goods. This is to prevent the various kinds of "price fixing".

(7) The manufacturer, supplier or other undertaking within the network directly or indirectly restricts the freedom of final consumers, authorised intermediaries or dealers to obtain from an undertaking belonging to a network of their choice within the common market contract goods or corresponding goods or to obtain servicing for such goods, or the freedom of final consumers to resell the contract goods or corresponding goods when the sale is not effected for commercial purposes. In short, this provision prohibits the hindrance of parallel imports, and is specifically included for the sake of certainty.

(8) The supplier, without objective justification, makes payments to dealers based on the destinations of the vehicles sold or the place of residence of the purchaser. It is likely that this always would have constituted an unjustified restriction.

7-53 Circumstances relating to spare parts where exemption is lost:

(9) The supplier directly or indirectly restricts the dealer's freedom[71] to obtain from third parties spare parts which compete with contract goods and are of comparable quality.

(10) The manufacturer directly or indirectly restricts the freedom of independent suppliers of spare parts (provided that they match the quality of the contract goods) from supplying resellers of their choice, including dealers within the distribution system.

(11) The manufacturer directly or indirectly restricts the freedom of spare part manufacturers to put their trade mark and/or logo on their spare parts in an easily visible manner.

The provisions relating to spare parts ensure that competition in the market is maintained, particularly by assuring the position of independent spare parts producers to supply the market. However, the provisions are to be read subject to the obligations that may be placed on the dealer contained in Article 4(1)(7) (see *Non-restrictive obligations on the dealer*, above), permitting a dealer to be restricted in using spare parts manufactured by independent producers for use in guarantee, free servicing and vehicle recall work.

7-54 Circumstances relating to technical information where exemption is lost:

(12) The manufacturer refuses to make accessible to independent undertakings technical information needed for the repair or maintenance of the contract goods or corresponding goods or for implementing environmental protection measures.

As with (9) to (11) this provision is designed to safeguard the position of independent spare parts producers and maintainters by ensuring that they have access to the technical information required for the repair and/or maintenance of motor cars (and spare parts), although if appropriate, the supply of such information may be subject to payment. The

---

[71] The freedom provided by Art. 3(5), see point (5) in *Obligations on the dealer*, above.

requirement to give access to information is subject to an important proviso that the technical information is not covered by intellectual property rights or does not constitute identified, substantial, secret know-how (although in such a case, the information must not be withheld improperly).

7-55 Effect of exemption.   Article 6 has the effect of either rendering the whole agreement ineligible for block exemption, or in certain cases results in the nullity of the individual provision:

(i) In the case of points (1) to (5) above, all of the clauses which are restrictive of competition lose the benefit of the block exemption (and in effect the entire agreement loses exemption).

(ii) In the case of points (6) to (12) above, the block exemption will be inapplicable only to those individual clauses restrictive of competition agreed respectively in favour of the manufacturer, the supplier or another undertaking within the network engaged in the practice.[72]

There is a further proviso contained in Article 6(3), in relation to points (6) to (12) to the effect that:

". . . the inapplicability of the exemption shall only apply to the clauses restrictive of competition agreed in favour of the manufacturer, the supplier or another undertaking within the network which appear in the distribution and servicing agreements concluded for a geographic area within the common market in which the objectionable practice distorts competition, and only for the duration of the practice complained of."[73]

The Commission has explained this as setting down, "a system of sanctions as a function of the seriousness of the infringement. Only the individual dealership agreement of the dealer is prohibited and void where the effects of the misconduct are confined to the contract territory. However, if competition is distorted in a larger geographical area, the exemption is no longer available to all distributors' contracts concluded in this area."

Withdrawal of block exemption

7-56   Under Article 8, the Commission may withdraw the benefit of the block exemption[74] where it finds that an individual agreement exempted under the block exemption Regulation nevertheless has anti-competitive effects. They are:

(1) where, in the common market or a substantial part of it, the contract goods or corresponding goods are not subject to competition from products considered by consumers as similar by reason of their characteristics, price and intended use;

(2) where prices or conditions of supply of contract goods or corresponding goods are continually being applied which differ substantially as between Member States, such differences mainly being due to obligations exempted by the Regulation;

---

[72] Art. 6(2).
[73] Art. 6(3).
[74] Pursuant to Reg. 19/65 [1965] J.O. 533–565.

(3) where the manufacturer or an undertaking within the distribution system, in the supply of contract goods or corresponding goods to distributors, unjustifiably applies discriminatory prices or sales conditions.

The situations described in Article 8 are examples of the situations which may result in withdrawal of the exemption but are not to be taken as exhaustive.

Ancillary information

7-57   The Commission is committed to the regular evaluation of the application of the Regulation[75] taking into account the views of associations and experts representing interested parties and consumer associations[76] and, by January 1, 2001,[77] to drawing up a report on its evaluation. The Regulation will remain in force until September 30, 2002.[78] It may then either be extended, replaced or removed. It should be noted that the Regulation does not apply to franchise agreements[79] (which may be exempted by way of Regulation 4087/88[80]).

Individual exemption under Article 85(3)

7-58   There is no "opposition procedure" contained in the Regulation, but individual exemption may be available under the general principles discussed in Chapter 6 above.

EXCLUSIVE PURCHASING AGREEMENTS

Introduction

7-59   Exclusive purchasing agreements focus primarily on the sourcing of goods for resale by a purchaser from a particular supplier. Exclusive purchasing agreements differ from exclusive distribution agreements in that (unlike exclusive distribution agreements) they do not specifically allocate a resale territory to the purchaser. The restrictions in a purchashing agreement instead relate primarily to the purchase obligations of the purchaser and require the purchaser to source particular goods for resale exclusively from that supplier. The purchaser is not protected from competition from other purchasers which buy goods from the same supplier and no restrictions are imposed on the purchaser concerning its geographical area of resale.

The Commission defined exclusive purchasing agreements in the Seventh Report on Competition Policy (1977) as:

"Agreements under which a purchaser accepts an obligation to purchase particular goods from a single supplier only over a relatively long period."[81]

In the Commission's view, exclusive purchasing agreements may raise issues under Article 85(1) because the purchaser denies itself the freedom to buy the products from other sources, perhaps on better terms. Also different suppliers which might otherwise deal with that purchaser are denied an outlet for their products.

---

[75] Art. 11(1).
[76] Art. 11(2).
[77] Art. 11(3).
[78] Art. 13.
[79] Art. 12.
[80] See *Franchising Agreements*, below.
[81] Commission's Seventh Report on Competition Policy (1977) para. 9.

7-60   The Commission, however, recognises that reciprocal commitments given by both the supplier and purchaser, coupled with benefits associated with commercial security, justify granting exemption to such agreements in certain circumstances. As the Commission put it, exclusive purchasing agreements:

". . . have an important business function in that they give a guarantee of ensured sales to one party and a guarantee of continuous supplies to another."[82]

Regulation 1984/83 on the application of Article 85(3) of the Treaty to categories of exclusive purchasing agreements[83] specifies the terms which may be contained in exclusive purchasing agreements (and sets out the other pre-conditions which must be satisfied) in order for them to benefit from automatic block exemption.

7-61   Both the exclusive purchasing Regulation and the exclusive distribution Regulation were adopted at the same time.[84] There is considerable overlap between the two. Where this is the case, reference should be made to the commentary on the exclusive distribution Regulation in *Exclusive Distribution Agreements*, above.

Regulation 1984/83 is divided into four parts dealing separately with different types of exclusive purchase agreements under the following headings:

I.   "General Provisions", which concern general bilateral agreements, where a purchaser agrees to purchase certain products for resale only from the supplier (see *General provisions*, below);

II.   "Special Provisions for Beer Supply Agreements", which deals with agreements relating specifically to the purchase of beer and other drinks for resale, typically between a brewery and a public house (see *Beer supply agreements*, below);

III. "Special Provisions for Service Station Agreements", which deals with agreements for the purchase of motor fuel between oil companies and petrol service stations (see *Service station agreements*, below);

IV.   "Miscellaneous Provisions", which contains ancillary provisions including the Commission's powers to withdraw exemption (see *Miscellaneous provisions (withdrawal of the block exemption)*, below).

For an agreement to be eligible for automatic block exemption, it must conform with the General Provisions of the Regulation but will remain subject to the Commission's powers of withdrawal as set out in the Miscellaneous Provisions. If the agreement relates to beer or petrol supplies, it must conform with the provisions set out under the other headings. Interpretation of the Regulation is assisted by the Commission Notice concerning Regulations 1983/83 and 1984/83.[85]

---

[82] Seventh Report on Competition Policy (1977), para. 9.
[83] Reg. 1984/84 [1983] O.J. L173/5, amended by [1983] O.J. L281/24 Reg. 1984/83 now also applies to Art. 53 of the EEA Agreement, subject to necessary amendments (Annex XIV para. 3 to the EEA Agreement).
[84] Reg. 1984/83 is due to expire on December 31, 1999.
[85] "The Commission Notice" [1984] O.J. C/101 (as amended by [1992] O.J. C121/2). The Commission Notice and the Regulation refer to a "reseller" rather than to a purchaser but the latter is preferred for consistency with the rest of this Chapter.

General provisions

7-62 Articles 1 to 5 of the Regulation contains the general provisions which apply to all exclusive purchasing agreements.

Article 1 provides that automatic block exemption shall apply to:

". . . agreements to which only two undertakings are party and whereby one party, the [purchaser], agrees with the other, the supplier, to purchase certain goods specified in the agreement for resale only from the supplier or from a connected undertaking or from another undertaking which the supplier has entrusted with the sale of his goods."

Two undertakings

7-63 As with the exclusive distribution Regulation, exemption only applies if the agreement is between two undertakings, one supplier and one purchaser. However, the supplier named in the agreement need not be the entity supplying the goods, as Article 1 expressly states that in place of the supplier, this entity may be a *"connected undertaking . . . or an undertaking which the supplier has entrusted with the sale of his goods"*.[86]

Goods specified in the agreement

7-64 As with the exclusive distribution Regulation, the Regulation only applies to goods supplied for "resale". It does not apply to agreements for the supply of services.[87] However, the Regulation does apply where the purchaser hires or leases goods, rather than resells them.[88]

The contract goods must be defined with sufficient certainty. The Commission has confirmed that the goods must at least be specified "by brand or denomination in the agreement"[89] but the Commission will not permit a definition of contract goods by reference to a variable price list which may be updated from time to time. A list of goods must be defined at the date of the contract.

7-65 It is essential that the purchaser undertakes to purchase all of its requirements for those goods from the supplier. The Regulation does not exempt agreements which involve anything less than 100 per cent of the purchaser's requirements. If the commitment is less than total, it is thought that the package of commercial terms negotiated is no longer guaranteed to bring the resulting benefits to consumers. An "English Clause" might be allowed, however, without losing exemption. An English Clause entitles the purchaser to source the goods from another supplier if there is a breakdown in supply or if the other supplier is able to offer a cheaper price for the same goods. In this case the benefits of security of supply and guaranteed low price are preserved.

Resale

7-66 It is also an absolute requirement that goods be supplied for the purpose of resale. A process of transformation affecting the economic identity of the goods, or anything other than "a slight addition in value"[90] does not constitute resale.

---

[86] Art. 4 of the Reg. defines "connected undertaking". If a party owns more than half the capital or business assets or can exercise more than half of the voting rights, or has the power to appoint more than half of the members of the board, or otherwise has the right to manage its affairs, then the undertaking is connected.
[87] Commission Dec. 92/521 *Re World Cup 1990 Package Tours* [1992] O.J. L326/31.
[88] Commission Notice para. 12.
[89] Commission Notice para. 36. This is not necessary for exclusive distribution agreements, see *Goods* (para. 7-23) above.
[90] Commission Notice, para. 10.

Territory

7-67 The main distinction between the exclusive distribution Regulation and the exclusive purchasing Regulation is that the former permits territorial exclusivity in the geographical area of resale of the goods, while the inclusion of territorial exclusivity for resale in the case of exclusive purchasing will result in loss of exemption.[91] The products must be freely available for resale anywhere.

Permitted restrictions

7-68 Articles 2(1) and 2(2) contain the only other restrictions on competition that may be included in the agreement (apart from the purchase commitment referred to above).

7-69 **An obligation on the supplier not to compete.** Article 2(1) allows clauses that prevent the supplier from distributing the contract goods, or goods which compete with the contract goods, "in the [purchaser's] principal sales area and at the [purchaser's] level of distribution". "Principal sales area" is not the same as the strictly defined exclusive "contract territory" in the exclusive distribution Regulation. Principal sales area for the purpose of the exclusive purchasing Regulation is the geographical area covered by the dealer's "normal business activity".[92] Any attempt to restrict the supplier further would result in loss of exemption.

7-70 **An obligation on the purchaser not to compete.** Article 2(2) permits a restriction on the purchaser preventing it from either manufacturing or distributing goods which compete with the contract goods. The requirement to define the contract goods clarifies the range of goods which compete.

If the parties agree on obligations that are restrictive of competition, other than those in Articles 2(1) and 2(2), the agreement no longer qualifies for automatic block exemption and requires individual exemption. For example an agreement would not benefit from block exemption if the parties surrender the possibility of independently determining their prices or conditions of business, or undertake to refrain from (or even prevent) cross border trade, or impede the purchaser's freedom of choice over its customers.[93]

Non-restrictive obligations on the purchaser

7-71 Article 2(3) of the Regulation contains examples of obligations that the Commission considers generally do not restrict competition. These are the same as for the exclusive distribution exemption contained in Article 2(3) of Regulation 1983/83, with one exception. This is the addition of an obligation "to purchase minimum quantities of goods which are subject to the exclusive purchasing obligation".[94] For example an agreement may require the purchaser to purchase not less than 500 widgets per month. For an explanation of the other non-restrictive obligations, see *Non-restrictive obligations on the distributor* (para. 7-29) above.

Inapplicability of the block exemption

7-72 Articles 3, 4 and 5 set out various circumstances in which the Regulation will not apply to confer exemption.

---

[91] Art. 16 of Reg. 1984/83.
[92] Case C–234/89 *Delimitis v. Henninger Bräu* [1991] E.C.R. I-935; [1992] 5 C.M.L.R. 210.
[93] Commission Notice, para. 17.
[94] Reg. 1984/83, Art. 2(3)(b).

7-73 Agreements between competing manufacturers. Articles 3(a) and (b) are similar to Articles 3(a) and 3(b) of the exclusive distribution Regulation, (see *Inapplicability of the block exemption* (para. 7-31) above)[95] and therefore exemption will not apply to agreements between competing manufacturers.

7-74 Unconnected goods. Article 3(c) disapplies exemption where the exclusive purchasing commitment covers unconnected goods, *i.e.* "more than one type of goods where these are neither by their nature nor according to commercial usage connected to each other". An exclusive purchasing agreement which seeks to tie a purchaser into purchasing a range of unconnected goods would therefore not be covered by the Regulation. The complete range of goods which the purchaser may be obliged to purchase (as contemplated in Artice 2(3)) may not include unrelated goods, see *Non-restrictive obligations on the Purchaser* (para. 7-71) and *Non-restrictive obligations on the distributor* (para. 7-29) above.

7-75 Duration. Under Article 3(d), an agreement for an indefinite period, or even a stated period of more than five years, will not benefit from the exemption. A "rolling" agreement which is automatically renewed (unless notice to terminate is given) is considered to be for an indefinite period and will therefore not be able to take advantage of the exemption.[96] Conversely it has been suggested that an agreement which requires a positive step by either party to be renewed in order to continue after five years will comply with Article 3(d).[97]

Miscellaneous provisions (withdrawal of the block exemption)

7-76 The Commission has power to withdraw the benefit of the block exemption in the circumstances set out in Article 14 of the Regulation. The text of the Article is similar to Article 6 of Regulation 1983/83, with some minor differences to take into account the different types of agreement. These powers are further explained in *Withdrawal of the block exemption* (para. 7-34) above.

Beer supply agreements

7-77 Beer supply agreements raise particular issues under Community law.

Beer supply agreements in general: a breach of Article 85(1)?

7-78 It is important to remember that the block exemption is only needed for agreements that are caught by Article 85(1). These are most commonly agreements which include "tied houses".

In *Brasserie de Haecht (No. 1)*[98] a Belgian café agreed to purchase all of its supplies of beer and other drinks exclusively from one brewery in return for a substantial loan. The E.C.J held that this kind of "tied house agreement" was not in itself, on the particular facts, caught by Article 85(1). The E.C.J, however, did form the view that a network of agreements which together restricted competition to an appreciable extent, thereby affect-

---

[95] The wording of the two provisions differs slightly to take into account the different types of agreement, *i.e.* distribution and purchase.

[96] Case T–7/93 *Langnese-Iglo and Scholler v. Commission* [1993] E.C.R. II-131: The ECJ upheld the view of the Commission that a rolling agreement for a period of two years or less which was automatically renewable thereafter was an agreement for an indefinite period and therefore did not benefit from the exemption. This was the case even though the facts suggested that the purchasers tended to terminate the agreement after two years (or less).

[97] Bellamy & Child, *Common Market Law of Competition*, 4th ed. at 7–123 n. 31.

[98] Case 23/67 *Brasserie de Haecht v. Wilkin (No. 1)* [1967] E.C.R. 407; [1968] C.M.L.R. 26.

ing trade between Member States, may be within the prohibition contained in Article 85(1).

7-79   In *Delimitis v. Henninger Bräu*,[99] the E.C.J considered this thoroughly. An agreement between a German café owner and a brewery formed part of a network of similar agreements. The E.C.J held that the cumulative effect of a network of similar beer supply agreements constitutes only "one factor amongst others in ascertaining whether, by way of possible alteration of competition, trade between Member States is capable of being affected",[1] either in terms of barriers to entry to potential competitors to the market for beer consumption or by frustrating existing competitors from expanding their market share. The Court provided the following guidelines for determining this issue:[2]

> (i) Determine the relevant market. The relevant market is defined in terms of the nature of the economic activity in question. Thus, "off licence" sales, for consumption of beverages off the premises, should be distinguished from "on-licence" sales, where beverages are enjoyed on the premises, such as in a public house or a café bar on the grounds that "on-licence" sales consist of the purchase of beer linked with the provision of services.

Since most beer supply agreements are made at national level, rather than throughout the Community,

> "[i]t follows that . . . account is to be taken of the national market for beer distribution in premises for the sale and consumption of drinks".[3]

The market, therefore, was taken to comprise sales of beer to "on- licensed" premises in the Member State as opposed to any wider part of the Community.[4]

> (ii) Ascertain if there is a significant effect on access to the market, for which it is necessary to ". . . examine the nature and extent of the agreements in their totality".[5] This includes consideration of the following issues:
>
> (a) the duration of the agreement;
> (b) the proportion of total outlets subject to tying agreements; and
> (c) the amount of beer to which the agreements relate as a proportion of all beer sold.
>
> It is important to consider these issues in the light of the opportunities for access to the market to see how competitive the market is in relation to the tied house agreements.[6]
>
> (iii) Examine the competitive market conditions. This examination includes ". . . not only the number and size of producers, but also the degree of saturation of that market and customer fidelity to existing brands."[7]. If a small number of pro-

---

[99] Case C–234/89 *Delimitis v. Henninger Bräu* [1991] E.C.R. 935; [1992] 5 C.M.L.R. 210.
[1] *ibid.*, para. 14 of the Judgment of the ECJ.
[2] *ibid.*, paras 16–26 of the Judgment of the ECJ.
[3] *ibid.*, para. 18 of the Judgment of the ECJ.
[4] The Commission confirmed that there can be separate markets for the same type of goods in Cases of T–7 & T9/93 *Langnese-Iglo and Schöller v. Commission* [1993] II E.C.R. 131, in which there were different markets for ice cream depending upon the premises in which the ice cream was sold and the types of consumers who purchased it.
[5] *ibid.*, para. 19; see also the judgment in Case 43/69 *Bilger v. Jehle* [1970] E.C.R. 127; [1974] 1 C.M.L.R. 382.
[6] *ibid.*, paras 19 and 20 of the Judgment of the ECJ.
[7] *ibid.*, para. 22 of the Judgment of the ECJ.

ducers command significant brand loyalty, the barriers to entry are generally higher.[8]

If careful consideration along these lines fails to show that the market is difficult to enter for new national and foreign producers, the tying agreement ". . . cannot be held to restrict competition within the meaning of Article 85(1)."[9]

7-80   However, if the analysis reveals that there are substantial barriers to entry, it is necessary to analyse whether the agreement has foreclosing effects. This involves an examination of the market position of each party to the agreement having particular regard to the number of outlets that are tied, and a comparison between the length of those ties to the average on the market.[10] The E.C.J noted that both factors are important:

"A brewery with a relatively small market share which ties its sales outlets for many years may make a significant a contribution to a sealing-off of the market as a brewery in a relatively strong market position which regularly releases sales outlets at shorter periods."[11]

In summary, beer supply agreements are prohibited by Article 85(1) if two conditions are met. First, where it is difficult for potential competitors to enter the market, or for existing competitors to increase their market share for the distribution of beer in licensed premises. Secondly, where the agreement makes a significant contribution to the foreclosure of the market.[12]

7-81   Guidance is given in the case of many beer supply agreements by the Commission's Notice on beer agreements of minor importance[13-14] as well as the provisions of the purchasing block exemption which relates specifically to beer agreements.

Commission's Notice beer agreements of minor importance

7-82   Following the *Delimitis*[15] case, the Commission published a Notice on agreements of minor importance in relation to brewery networks. This laid out the criteria on which exclusive beer supply agreements are considered to be of minor importance, and therefore not within Article 85(1)[16].

In the opinion of the Commission, these agreements will fall outside the scope of the prohibition of Article 85(1) provided that:

(i)   the market share of the brewery is no higher than 1 per cent on the national market for the resale of beer in "on-licensed" premises; and

(ii)   the brewery does not produce more than 200,000[17] hectolitres of beer per year;

(iii) however the principles contained in the Notice do not apply "if the agreement

---

[8] *ibid.*, para. 22 of the Judgment of the ECJ.
[9] *ibid.*, para. 23 of the Judgment of the ECJ.
[10] *ibid.*, para. 25 which states that, when assessing "market position", the market share is that of the group of companies to which the particular brewery belongs. All similar agreements involving that group must form part of the analysis rather than merely the individual agreement with the outlet, café, public house, *etc* in question.
[11] *ibid.*, para. 26 of the Judgment of the ECJ.
[12] *ibid.*, para. 27 of the Judgment of the ECJ.
[13-14] Commission Notice of May 13, 1992 on minor brewery networks [1992] O.J. C121/2,.
[15] Case C–234/89 networks [1991] (1992) O.J. C121/2. [1991] E.C.R. 935; [1992] 5 C.M.L.R. 210.
[16] [1992] O.J. C121/2, this Notice modified the Commission Notice giving guidance on Regs 1983/83 and 1984/83, discussed earlier, and can be found at para. 40 of that Notice. The EFTA Surveillance Authority have also issued an equivalent Notice modifying its previous Notice on exclusive distribution and supply agreements [1994] O.J. L186/57.
[17] 1 hectolitre is 100 litres, so the brewery production limit is 20 million litres, or 34,129,693 pints.

in question is concluded for more than seven and a half years in as far as it covers beer and other drinks, and for fifteen years if it covers only beer.[18]

This Notice is only likely to benefit the smallest of independent brewers.

Exemption of beer agreements under the exclusive purchasing exemption: Title II of Regulation 1984/83

7-83 Scope. Exclusive beer supply agreements benefit from a more liberal treatment by the Commission than other exclusive purchasing agreements. In its Thirteenth Report on Competition Policy (1983)[19] the Commission reported that:

> "Brewery . . . agreements . . . show clear differences from other exclusive purchasing agreements so that special rules were necessary . . . Beer supply agreements entail a considerable financial involvement on the part of the supplier, which may justify binding the [purchaser] for a longer period of time than in other sectors."

To qualify for exemption, the agreements must meet all of the following conditions contained in Article 6(1) of the Regulation. The agreement must be between only two undertakings which contains special commercial or financial advantages granted by the supplier to the purchaser, and which applies to specified drinks for resale at designated premises.

7-84 The requirement that the agreement be made between "two undertakings" has already been noted in the context of exclusive distribution agreements but it is noteworthy that exemption will also apply to successors in title of either the supplier or the purchaser (*i.e.* a transferee of the business) but only for the unexpired term of the original agreement.[20]

7-85 "Special commercial or financial advantages." Examples of commercial and financial advantages accorded by the supplier are given in Recital 13 of the Regulation. Paragraph 44 of the Notice states that they are "those going beyond what the reseller could normally expect" and might involve the supplier granting loans on favourable terms, providing the purchaser with business premises, equipment and fittings, and contributing to financing. "Advantage" will be determined according to trade usage if there is any doubt whether any special advantage has been given. An example might be a low interest loan to a publican for the purchase of the lease of the public house.

7-86 "Specified drinks." To remove the temptation on the supplier unilaterally to increase the scope of the agreement, it is important to specify strictly the drinks that are to be supplied. This should be done at the time of the agreement since: "a beer supply agreement which refers . . . to a list of products which may be unilaterally altered by the supplier . . . does not enjoy [exemption]".[21] Further, to avoid any possibility of the agreement falling outside the exemption, drinks should be specified according to type and brand name.[22]

---

[18] [1992] O.J. C121/2, para. 40 of the Commission Notice.

[19] *ibid.*, para. 29. References to service station and petrol agreements have been deleted from the quote, but it applies equally to service station agreements which are discussed in *Service station agreements*, below. The Report refers to a "reseller" rather than a purchaser but the latter is preferred for continuity with the rest of this Chapter.

[20] Arts 6(2) and 8(1)(e). It is worth noting that a beer supply agreement may be drafted so that it comes within the provisions of Title I of the Reg., although in such a case it will not benefit from the more relaxed approach and under Title III (*i.e.* the agreement will be limited to a term of five years).

[21] Case C–234/89 *Delimitis* [1991] E.C.R. 935; [1992] 5 C.M.L.R. 210 at para. 36.

[22] The Commission Notice on Regs 1983/83 and 1984/83 ([1984] O.J. C/101) (para. 41) states that specification should be made by brand or denomination.

The agreement does not have to specify beer alone. Other drinks, including non-alcoholic drinks and even coffee[23] may be included, although the inclusion of other drinks will have an effect on the permitted duration of the agreement.[24]

7-87   Premises.   Exemption only applies to the resale of drinks in premises used for the "sale and consumption of drinks". This includes bars, pubs or cafés, but not off-licences, supermarkets, corner shops or other outlets where the beverages are consumed off the premises.

7-88   Extent of the permitted restrictions.   In addition to the exclusive purchase requirements contained in Article 6, by virtue of Article 7 the supplier may also:

(a) Prevent the purchaser selling beers and other drinks which are supplied by other undertakings and which are of the same type as the beers or other drinks supplied under the agreement in the designated premises.

(b) Place an obligation on the purchaser, where the purchaser sells beers of other brands than the supplier's which are of a different type from the beers supplied under the agreement, to sell such beers only in bottles, cans or other small packages unless that beer is customarily sold in draught or where that beer in draught is in sufficient demand from consumers. However, the purchaser is entitled to sell beer of other types in draught if this has been tolerated in the past.

(c) Oblige the purchaser to limit its advertisement on the premises of products of other suppliers (for example a limit on the promotion of a rival brand's beer). The advertisement of the products may be limited only in proportion to the share of those products in the total turnover realised in the premises. For example a brewery may limit the extent to which a publican (a purchaser under the agreement) may advertise a rival brand's beer to, say, 30 per cent of advertising space if that rival brand's beer accounts for 30 per cent of the turnover of the public house.

In turn, the purchaser may impose a restriction on the supplier/brewery in line with Article 2(1) not to distribute the specified drinks, or competing drinks, in the purchaser's "principal trade area" and at their level of distribution. The purchaser's principal trade area will generally be much smaller than that for other purchasers under Article 2(1), and may be as small as a single village.

7-89   Inapplicability of the block exemption.   If the agreement does not meet the requirements of Article 8 exemption is lost. In brief they are as follows.

7-90   *Drinks only.*   Only drinks may be tied. If the agreement purports to tie the purchaser to take other goods (for example crisps and peanuts) or services, or otherwise restricts the purchaser's freedom to buy goods and services from the source of its choice (except where expressly permitted above), the Regulation will not apply.

7-91   *Tenants.*   If the purchaser is the supplier's tenant (for example a publican who leases his public house from a brewery) the purchaser must benefit from additional rights. These must be expressly provided for in the agreement, otherwise the Regulation will not apply.[25] It must provide for the purchaser tenant to have the right to obtain:

---

[23] See para. 116 of the Commission's XXI Report on Competition Policy (1991).
[24] See *Inapplicability of the block exemption*, below.
[25] Art. 8(2)(b).

(a) drinks, except beer, supplied under the agreement from other undertakings who offer better terms which the supplier does not meet (for example the right to purchase wines and spirits from a third party who can provide them more cheaply than the supplier); and

(b) drinks, except beer, which are the same type as those supplied under the agreement but which bear different trade marks, from other undertakings if the supplier does not offer them.

It appears that the purchaser must inform the supplier of the better terms under which it can obtain non-beer drinks under item (a), although it need not allow the supplier the opportunity to supply the non-beer drinks that the supplier does not offer under item (b).[26]

7-92 *Duration.* If the purchaser is not a tenant the duration of the agreement must be limited to five years or less for beers and other drinks (*e.g.* wines, spirits, coffee) but can be extended to a limit of 10 years if the agreement is limited to beer alone. However, where the purchaser is a tenant, the purchasing obligations can be extended for the entire duration of the lease subject to the above right to acquire drinks other than beer from third parties on more favourable terms.

7-93 *Agreements between competing brewers/suppliers.* By Article 9 of the Regulation, Articles 3(a), 3(b), 4 and 5 apply *mutatis mutandis* to beer supply agreements, and therefore agreements between competing brewers will not benefit from the block exemption.[27]

7-94 Withdrawal of block exemption. The provisions of Article 14, as summarised above,[28] apply equally to exclusive beer supply agreements.

Service station agreements

7-95 Title III of Regulation 1984/83 applies to service station agreements. It contains similar provisions as the preceding two titles dealing with general agreements and beer agreements. A full explanation of this part of the Regulation would thus be repetitive. However, the following represents a brief summary of the most important considerations in relation to service station agreements.

The exclusive purchasing agreement must be for petroleum-based motor vehicle fuel encompassing fuels for land, water or air vehicles.[29] Service-station agreements are limited strictly to fuel, lubricants and servicing equipment products. As with beer agreements the maximum period is limited to 10 years except where the service station is let to the purchaser. In this case the agreement may extend for the period of the lease. The exemption will be inapplicable in similar circumstances to the beer agreements, and the Commission may withdraw the benefit of the block exemption in the circumstance described above.[30]

---

[26] Paras 56 to 58 of the Commission Notice on Reg 1983/83 and 1984/83.
[27] Arts 3(a), 3(b), 4 and 5 are discussed in *Agreements between competing manufacturers*, above and more particularly in *Inapplicability of the block exemption* (para. 7-30 to 7-33) above.
[28] See *Miscellaneous provisions (withdrawal of the block exemption)* (para. 7-76) and *Withdrawal of the block exemption* (para. 7-34) above.
[29] Commission Notice para. 59.
[30] See *Miscellaneous provisions (withdrawal of the block exemption)* (para. 7-76) and *Withdrawal of the block exemption* (para. 7-34) above.

Individual exemption under Article 85(3)

7-96   The parties may apply to the Commission for individual exemption if the exclusive purchasing agreement is caught by Article 85(1), but fails to qualify for block exemption under Regulation 1984/83. The general principles applicable to any application for exemption are contained in Chapter 6 of this work below. In relation to exclusive purchasing agreements, exemption has been granted by the Commission.

For example, in *Carlsberg*,[31] a beer supply agreement which was to last over 10 years was granted exemption. This was to allow Carlsberg time to develop its own sales network to enable it to become independent of other large breweries for the distribution of its output.

7-97   In *Whitbread and Moosehead*,[32] exemption was granted for an exclusive agreement of similar duration.

However, the Commission has refused to grant individual exemption in the following cases. In *Spices*,[33] restrictions were imposed on the determination of resale prices as well as limitations on the availability of competing brands. In *Schöller ice cream*,[34] the exclusive purchasing network constituted a major barrier to entry on the ice cream market in the relevant territory. In *Austrian service stations*,[35] a network of agreements significantly contributed to the foreclosure of the market.

SPECIALISATION AGREEMENTS

Introduction

7-98   Under a specialisation agreement, one party agrees to specialise in the production of one or more products to the exclusion of other products, which are to be produced by the other party. Each party may also appoint the other as its exclusive distributor in the others' primary market.

Agreements of this type help to encourage specialisation in the production of products between manufacturers. They also make it easier for the parties to the agreement to export their products since the sales' infrastructure already in existence for one party's product can be used to facilitate sales of the other party's products.

7-99   Although specialisation agreements are potentially restrictive of competition and, on the face of it, run the risk of being contrary to the prohibition contained in Article 85(1), the Commission's attitude to them is relatively favourable because such agreements enable the parties both to rationalise their production and distribution operations and to penetrate other markets more effectively:

> "Agreements on specialisation in production generally contribute to improving the production or distribution of goods, because undertakings concerned can concentrate on the manufacture of certain products and thus operate more efficiently and supply the products more cheaply."[36]

---

[31] Commission Dec. 84/381 [1984] O.J. L207/26; [1995] 1 C.M.L.R. 735.
[32] Commission Dec. 90/186 [1990] O.J. L100/32; [1991] 4 C.M.L.R. 391.
[33] Commission Dec. 78/172 [1978] O.J. L53/20; [1978] 2 C.M.L.R. 116.
[34] Commission Dec. 93/405 [1993] O.J. L183/1; [1994] 4 C.M.L.R. 51.
[35] EFTA Surveillance Authority, ESA Annual Report [1994] para. 4.9.2.
[36] Recital 3, Commission Reg. 417/85 on the application of Art. 85(3) of the Treaty to categories of specialisation agreements, [1985] O.J. L 53/1 amended by Reg. 151/93 [1993] O.J. L21/8.

Specialisation agreements have benefitted from block exemption since 1973. The current Regulation 417/85 on the application of Article 85(3) of the Treaty to categories of specialisation agreements,[37] was amended in 1993 by Regulation 151/93.[38]

The block exemption for specialisation agreements: Regulation 417/85[39]

7-100   As with the other block exemptions, an agreement will only benefit from automatic exemption if it complies in all respects with the terms of the applicable Regulation.

Permitted agreements

7-101   The Regulation applies to:

". . . agreements on specialisation whereby, for the duration of the agreement, undertakings accept reciprocal obligations:

    (a) not to manufacture certain products or to have them manufactured, but to leave it to other parties to manufacture the products or have them manufactured; or

    (b) to manufacture certain products or have them manufactured only jointly."[40]

7-102   Undertakings.   It is noteworthy that this Regulation applies to agreements between any number of undertakings, rather than the limit of two undertakings prescribed by the exclusive purchasing Regulation and exclusive distribution Regulation.

7-103   Duration of the agreement.   Unlike the Regulation for exclusive purchasing, there is no time-limit for the term of the agreement.

7-104   Reciprocal obligations.   The Regulation applies only to agreements where undertakings accept similar obligations either not to manufacture certain products, or to have them manufactured by third parties, or to manufacture them jointly. The requirement of reciprocity is essential and an agreement where only one party accepts such an undertaking will not benefit from exemption.[41]

The parties must agree completely to refrain from the manufacture of "certain products". It is, therefore, unlikely that an agreement to limit (rather than to refrain from) manufacture, would be eligible for exemption.[42]

7-105   Manufacture.   Exemption only applies to agreements relating to the manufacture of products and not to research and development agreements, which are governed by Regulation 418/85.[43] Research and development agreements are discussed in detail in Chapter 9 *Particular R&D Agreements*, below.

---

[37] [1985] O.J. L53/1.
[38] [1993] O.J. L21/8.
[39] The Regulation applies (with necessary modifications) throughout the EEA, to agreements that fall within Art. 53(1) of the EEA Agreement, the equivalent of Art. 85(1) E.C.
[40] Art. 1 of Reg. 417/85 (as amended).
[41] Such an agreement may, however, qualify for individual exemption; Commission Dec. 73/323 *Prym/Beka* [1973] O.J. L296/24; [1973] C.M.L.R. D250.
[42] Commission Dec. 82/866 *Rolled Zinc Products* [1982] O.J. 362/40; [1983] C.M.L.R. 285.
[43] As illustrated by the case of Commission Dec. *Italian Cast Glass* [1980] O.J. L383/19; [1982] 2 C.M.L.R. 61 and the XVII Report on Competition Policy (1987) para. 30.

Permitted restrictions on competition

7-106 Article 1 of the Regulation sets out the restrictions on competition that are fundamental to a specialisation agreement. Article 2 contains the only other permitted restrictions on competition that may be included in the agreement.[44] It is up to the parties to decide whether or not they wish to include any or all of the restrictions permitted under Article 2.

7-107 **Restrictions related to exclusivity.** The first three restrictions, contained in Paragraphs (a), (b) and (c) of Article 2(1), relate to exclusivity:

7-108 *Additional specialisation agreements.* The parties may agree not to enter into additional specialisation agreements with third parties in respect of identical products or products which are considered by users to be equivalent in view of their characteristics, price or intended use.[45]

7-109 *Exclusive purchase.* It is also permissible to impose a requirement that the specialisation products only be purchased from another party, a joint undertaking or an undertaking jointly charged with their manufacture, except where better terms are available elsewhere which the supplier is not prepared to match.[46]

Parties may also be required to commit to purchase minimum quantities but any attempt to impose maximum quantities for purchase will result in the loss of exemption. A requirement to purchase products that are outside the scope of the specialisation would also be outside the Regulation.[47]

7-110 *Exclusive distribution.* Under Article 2(1)(c) it is possible to grant exclusive distribution appointments of the specialisation products to the other parties for a defined territory covering the whole or a part of the common market. However, this is on the proviso that intra-brand competition is maintained. If the products are not available from other sources or if the parties make it difficult for others to obtain the products from alternative suppliers, then exemption will be lost.

7-111 **Restrictions relating to joint distribution.** The final three restrictions in Article 2(1), which (along with Article 2(1)(c)) were inserted by Regulation 151/93,[48] are contained in paragraphs (d), (e) and (f). They all relate to joint distribution.

Paragraph (d) permits an obligation to grant one of the parties the "exclusive right to distribute products which are subject to the specialisation". Paragraph (e) permits an obligation to grant exclusive distribution rights to a joint undertaking or a third undertaking. Under both paragraphs (d) and (e) the appointed distributor must not manufacture or distribute products which compete with the contract products. Paragraph (f) permits an obligation to grant the exclusive right to distribute the specialisation products within the whole or a defined area of the common market, to either a joint undertaking or a third party which neither manufactures or distributes competing products (subject, once again, to the condition that it must be possible for others to obtain the products from alternative suppliers and the parties do not make it difficult for them to do so).

Any arrangements for joint distribution under paragraphs (d), (e) and (f) must only

---

[44] Art. 2(a) states that agreements which contain restrictions on competition other than those listed in Arts 2(1) and 2(2) will not be exempt from Art. 85(1).
[45] Art. 2(1)(a).
[46] Art. 2(1)(b).
[47] Commission Dec. 69/241 *Clima-Chappée* [1969] O.J. L195/1; [1970] C.M.L.R. D7.
[48] [1993] O.J. L21/8.

relate to the products subject to the specialisation, and not other products. This is to prevent the tying of unrelated obligations.

Non-restrictive obligations

7-112   Article 2(3) lists certain obligations which the Commission considers generally do not restrict competition, and are therefore not considered to be caught by the prohibition contained in Article 85(1). These are obligations:

(a) to supply the specialisation products to other parties and to observe minimum standards of quality[49];

(b) to maintain minimum stocks of the specialisation products and spare parts for them[50]; and

(c) to provide customer and guarantee services for the specialisation products.[51]

Inapplicability of the block exemption

7-113   The Regulation was originally designed to assist small and medium-sized undertakings[52] and the grant of exemption is therefore conditional upon the parties to the agreement not exceeding the market share and turnover ceilings set out in Article 3.

7-114   Agreements generally.   Exemption only applies if:

(a) the specialisation products and the participating undertakings' other products which are considered by users to be equivalent (in view of their characteristics, price and intended use) do not represent more than 20 per cent of the market for all such products in the common market or a substantial part of it; and

(b) the aggregate annual turnover of all the undertakings participating in the agreement does not exceed 1,000 million ECUs.

7-115   Joint distribution agreements.   If distribution is entrusted to a joint undertaking or a third undertaking is involved (the circumstances referred to in *Restrictions relating to joint distribution* above), then the market share test is stricter. In these circumstances, exemption only applies only if:

(a) the specialisation products and the participating undertakings' other products which are considered by users to be equivalent in view of their characteristics, price and intended use do not represent more than 10 per cent of the market for all such products in the common market or a substantial part of it; and

(b) the aggregate annual turnover of all the participating undertakings does not exceed 1,000 million ECUs.

Participating undertakings are either parties to the agreement or parent, subsidiary and associate companies of the parties subject to 50 per cent control, and are defined in Article 7 of the Regulation. The relevant turnover includes the turnover of all such companies.[53]

---

[49] Art. 2(3)(a).
[50] Art. 2(3)(b).
[51] Art. 2(3)(c).
[52] XI Report on Competition Policy (1981), para. 31.
[53] Art. 6.

Exemption will continue to apply throughout the agreement where the turnover and market share limits are exceeded by no more than 10 per cent in any two consecutive financial years.[54] Exemption will continue to apply for a period of 6 months after the financial year during which these revised limits were exceeded.[55]

Opposition procedure

7-116   If the turnover limits are exceeded, use may be made of the "opposition procedure" referred to in Article 4. Exemption will continue to apply if the Commission does not oppose the agreement within six months of the notification.

Withdrawal of the block exemption

7-117   The Commission may withdraw the benefit of exemption where it finds that an agreement exempted by the Regulation has effects which are incompatible with the conditions set out in Article 85(3), and in particular where:

(a) the agreement is not yielding significant returns in terms of rationalisation, or consumers are not receiving a fair share of the resulting benefits; or

(b) the specialisation products are not subject in the common market (or a substantial part) to effective competition from identical products or products considered by users to be equivalent in view of their characteristics, price or intended use.[56]

FRANCHISING AGREEMENTS

Introduction

7-118   Manufacturers frequently distribute products and services through networks of franchised outlets. A franchise agreement amounts to authorisation by the owner of a business (the franchisor) to enable another (the franchise) to adopt the distinctive trading style of the franchisor comprising, for example a trade mark, trade name, get-up or other distinctive marketing package, know-how, recipes and other standardised procedures in connection with the supply of goods or services. The agreement usually provides for the franchisee to sell the goods or services through premises according to a strict format controlled by the franchisor. The franchisee remains an independent undertaking and need not necessarily purchase products from the franchisor. Further, the franchisee typically pays the franchisor a royalty for the grant of these rights.

The objective of the franchisor is generally to create a chain of outlets with standardised presentation, selling substantially the same goods or services, to give the impression that the franchised outlets are under the same ownership. This requires the franchisor to exercise considerably greater control over the outlets than would usually apply in conventional distribution arrangements. The franchisor will usually provide commercial and marketing assistance, and will generally have the right to supervise the premises and activities of the franchise to ensure the integrity of the franchisee system.

7-119   Franchise agreements are commonly used throughout the Community and can take many forms. Distribution franchises are those where the franchisee sells products from a retail outlet bearing the franchisor's name and logo, such as the "fast food"

---

[54] Art. 3(3).
[55] Art. 3(4).
[56] Art. 8.

multinationals. Other types of franchise agreements include service franchises, whole-sale franchises and production or manufacturing franchises.

In the leading case of *Pronuptia*,[57] the E.C.J recognised the benefits of franchising agreements and held that certain types of obligations in such agreements do not fall within Article 85(1) at all. On the other hand, the ECJ identified certain obligations which might bring an agreement within Article 85(1). The ruling in *Pronuptia* led to the adoption by the Commission of Regulation 4087/88 on the application of Article 85(3) of the Treaty to certain categories of franchise agreements.[58] The Regulation sets out in detail the type of franchise agreement that the Commission considers suitable for automatic exemption.

The block exemption for franchise agreements: regulation 4087/88

Scope of the exemption

7-120   The Regulation provides automatic exemption for distribution franchises, service franchises and master franchises.[59] Manufacturing and wholesale franchise agreements are outside the scope of the Regulation, although the Commission has suggested in *ServiceMaster*,[60] that the principles set out in the Regulation may equally be applicable to manufacturing franchises. Franchises that involve motor vehicles also fall outside the franchising block exemption, but may be exempt by virtue of Regulation 1475/95,[61] *Motor Vehicle distribution and servicing agreements: The block exemption for motor vehicle distribution*, above.

Definitions

7-121   Article 1(3) defines several terms used in the Regulation, in particular the terms "franchise" and "franchise agreement". The term "franchise" is defined as:

> "a package of industrial or intellectual property rights relating to trade marks, trade names, shop signs, utility models, designs, copyrights, know-how or patents to be exploited for the resale of goods or the provision of services to end users".[62]

A "franchise agreement" is a bilateral agreement where:

> ". . . the franchisor grants . . . the franchisee . . . the right to exploit a franchise; . . . it includes at least obligations relating to:
>
> (i) the use of a common name or shop sign and a uniform presentation of contract premises and/or means of transport;
>
> (ii) the communication by the franchisor to the franchisee of know-how;

---

[57] Case 161/84 *Pronuptia de Paris v. Schillgalis* [1986] E.C.R. 353; [1986] 1 C.M.L.R. 414.
[58] Commission Reg. 4087/88 on the application of Art. 85(3) of the Treaty to Categories of Franchise Agreements [1988] O.J. L359/46. The Regulation applies, subject to necessary amendments, to the EEA Agreement (Art. 53 EEA, Annex XIV, para. 8, to the EEA Agreement).
[59] Art. 1(3)(c) of Reg. 4087/88. Art. 1(3) contains definitions of various terms for use within the block exemption.
[60] Commission Dec. 88/604[1988] O.J. L332/38; [1989] 4 C.M.L.R. 581.
[61] Commission Reg. 1475/95 on the application of Art. 85(3) of the Treaty to certain categories of motor vehicle distribution and servicing agreements, [1994] O.J. L145/25. This Regulation replaced the previous Reg. 123/85 [1985] O.J. L115/1, from October 1, 1995.
[62] Art. 1(3)(a).

(iii) the continuing provision by the franchisor to the franchisee of commercial or technical assistance during the life of the agreement".[63]

Permitted restrictions

7-122 The Regulation applies to

". . . franchise agreements to which two undertakings are party, which include one or more of the of the restrictions listed in Article 2".[64]

Exemption only applies if the agreement is between two undertakings, one franchisor and one franchisee. In general, several undertakings within the same group of companies will count as one undertaking for these purposes, as with Regulations 1983/83 and 1984/83 (discussed above in *Exclusive Distribution Agreements and Exclusive Purchasing Agreements*), although care must be taken to ensure that exemption is not disapplied under Article 5 because the parties are competitors. The permissible restrictions on the franchiser and franchise contained in Article 2, are as follows.

7-123 **Restrictions on the franchisor.** The franchisee may be granted *limited* territorial protection. The agreement may contain an obligation on the franchisor, in the contract territory:

(i) not to grant the right to exploit all or part of the franchise to third parties;

(ii) not itself to exploit the franchise or otherwise market the goods or services which are the subject matter of the franchise itself under a similar formula; and

(iii) not itself to supply the franchise goods to third parties.[65]

7-124 **Restrictions on the franchisee.** The agreement may contain the following restrictions on the franchisee:

(i) to exploit the franchise only from specified premises[66];

(ii) to refrain outside the contract territory from seeking customers for the goods or the services which are the subject-matter of the franchise[67]; and

(iii) not to manufacture, sell or use in the course of the provision of services, goods competing with the franchisor's goods which are the subject-matter of the franchise.[68] This obligation (not to deal in competing goods) cannot extend to ancillary products such as spare parts or accessories.

7-125 *Master franchises.* A master franchise agreement is one in which the franchisor grants to the master franchisee (in exchange for financial consideration) the right to exploit a franchise for the purposes of concluding franchise agreements with third party franchisees (Article 1 (3)(1)). There is an additional obligation that may be placed on a master franchisee under a master franchise agreements, namely, the obligation not to conclude franchise agreements with third parties outside its contract territory.[69]

---

[63] Art. 1(3)(b).
[64] Art. 1(1).
[65] Art. 2(a).
[66] Art. 2(c).
[67] Art. 2(d).
[68] Art. 2(d).
[69] Art. 2(b).

Non-restrictive obligations

7-126   Article 3 lists these obligations which the Commission considers do not restrict competition within the meaning of Article 85(1) and are therefore permitted.

It is critical to the franchise relationship that the franchisor's intellectual property and commercial rights, such as trade marks and goodwill, are preserved. Under Article 3(1), obligations are permitted to that end, provided that they are necessary to maintain the franchisor's industrial or intellectual property rights, or to maintain the common identity and reputation of the franchised network. These include obligations on the franchisee to achieve minimum quality standards, to use or sell only goods manufactured by the franchisor or its designated third party where it is impractical to apply objective quality specifications, not to compete directly or indirectly with a member of the franchised network (even for up to a year post-termination in the case of its own franchise territory), not to acquire a material financial interest in a competitor (which would allow the franchisee to exert influence over the competitor), to use best endeavours to sell the franchise goods or supply the franchise services, to limit sales to only end users, other franchisees or other resellers; to offer a minimum range or achieve a minimum turnover, to maintain minimum stocks; to provide customer and warranty services, to contribute a portion of revenue to the franchisor's advertising campaigns, and to carry out its own advertising campaign (subject to the franchisor's approval).

7-127   Article 3(2) lists further permitted obligations. These include confidentiality undertakings, restrictions on the use of the franchisor's intellectual property for purposes other than the franchise, the grant to the franchisor and other franchisees of improvements made by the franchise (on a non-exclusive basis), obligations to support the franchisor in infringement (of intellectual property rights) actions, obligations to have staff trained and premises and operations presented in line with the franchisor's prescribed standards, commitments to the franchisor's commercial methods, submission to checks by the franchisor; a ban on changing the location of the contract premises; and restrictions on assignment of the franchise.

Essential conditions

7-128   Article 4 specifies three conditions which must be complied with for the Regulation to apply. These conditions must be met throughout the term of the agreement and failure to do so will result in loss of exemption.

7-129   Freedom of supply.   The franchisee must be free to obtain the franchise goods from other franchisees or from other authorised distributors.[70]

7-130   Guarantees.   Where the franchisor obliges the franchisee to honour guarantees for the franchisor's goods the franchisee is obliged also to honour guarantees given for the franchisor's goods, even where such goods are supplied by another member of the franchise network or other distributors which give a similar guarantee, in the common market.[71]

7-131   Status as franchisee.   The third condition provides an element of consumer protection. It obliges franchisees to indicate that they are independent undertakings, although this does not have to interfere with the common identity of the franchise.[72]

---

[70] Art. 4(a).
[71] Art. 4(b).
[72] Art. 4(c).

Inapplicability of the block exemption

7-132   The provisions contained in Article 5 set out various circumstances which will result in the loss of exemption. They are as follows.

7-133   Competitors.   Exemption will not apply if the franchise agreement is between:

> ". . . undertakings producing goods or providing services which are identical or are considered by users as equivalent in view of their characteristics, price and intended use"[73]

7-134   Alterative sources of supply.   Exemption is also unavailable if the franchisee is prevented from obtaining supplies of goods of an equivalent quality to those offered by the franchisor from other sources.[74]

7-135   Franchisor's goods.   There will be no exemption for an agreement under which the franchisee is obliged to sell (or use in providing services) goods manufactured by the franchisor (or third parties designated by the franchisor) where the franchisor refuses to approve third party manufacturers proposed by the franchisee. It is for the franchisor to justify objectively the refusal as essential for protecting the franchisor's industrial or intellectual property rights or maintaining the common identity and reputation of the franchise network.

7-136   Use of know-how.   Article 5(d) prevents a prohibition against the franchisee using know-how acquired as a result of the franchise agreement following termination of the agreement, if that know-how is publicly available (through no breach by the franchisee).

7-137   Price fixing.   The franchisor cannot, whether directly or indirectly, restrict the franchisee in the determination of sale prices, whether by setting maximum or minimum prices, or otherwise.[75] However, this does not prohibit the franchisor from recommending sale prices for the franchised goods or services.

7-138   Challenging intellectual property rights.   Exemption will not be available where the franchisor prohibits the franchisee from challenging the validity of the industrial or intellectual property rights which form part of the franchise. However, this is without prejudice to the franchisor's right of termination in response to such a challenge.[76]

7-139   Passive sales.   Under Article 5(g), there will be no exemption where franchisees are obliged not to supply within the common market the goods or services which are the subject-matter of the franchise to end users because of their place of residence. This is designed to allow end users to shop around other franchises for the goods or services in question.

---

[73] Art. 5(a).
[74] Art. 5(b).
[75] Art. 5(e).
[76] Art. 5(f).

Opposition procedure

7-140   An "opposition procedure" is provided in Article 6 of the Regulation. This is similar to that contained in the block exemption for specialisation agreements[77] discussed above in *Specialisation Agreements*. Agreements which include restrictions other than those expressly prohibited, may be granted individual exemption under Article 85(3) if they are not opposed by the Commission within six months of notification.

Withdrawal of exemption

7-141   As with other block exemption Regulations, the Commission has the power to withdraw the benefit of a block exemption under Article 8 of the Regulation. It may do so where ". . . an agreement exempted by this Regulation nevertheless has certain effects which are incompatible with the conditions laid down in Article 85(3)". The situations described by Article 8 are illustrations of the sort of situations in which the Commission may withdraw exemption. The Commission is likely to do so where the franchisee is awarded territorial protection and one or more of the following circumstances apply:

(a) Access to the market or competition in the market is significantly restricted by the cumulative effect of parallel networks of similar agreements established by competing manufacturers or distributors.[78] This is to ensure that it is not difficult for new competitors to enter the market.

(b) The goods or services do not face effective competition from identical or substitute products in a substantial part of the common market.[79]

(c) One or both of the parties to the agreement prevent end users from obtaining the products on the ground of their place of residence, or the parties use different specifications in different Member States for the goods in order to isolate markets.[80]

(d) Franchisees engage in concerted practices in relation to sale prices.[81]

(e) For reasons other than to protect the franchisor's industrial or intellectual property rights, or to maintain the common identity and reputation of the network, or to ensure that the franchisee is abiding by its contractual obligations The franchisor uses its right (under Article 3) to inspect the contract premises and/or means of transport, or refuses to consent to a change in the contract premises or to allow the franchisee to assign its rights.[82]

Individual exemption under Article 85(3)

7-142   If an agreement is caught by Article 85(1) but falls outside the franchise block exemption Regulation, the parties may apply to the Commission for individual exemption under Article 85(3). It is, perhaps, unlikely that individual exemption will be granted by the Commission if the agreement does not contain the three main conditions for exemption contained in Article 4 of the Regulation. Individual exemption will be of par-

---

[77] Commission Reg. 417/85 [1985] O.J. L53/5, see *Specialisation Agreements*, above for further details.
[78] Art. 8(a).
[79] Art. 8(b).
[80] Art. 8(c).
[81] Art. 8(d).
[82] Art. 8(e).

ticular importance to the parties to wholesale franchise agreements, which are expressly excluded from the ambit of the block exemption Regulation.[83] It is expected that the Commission would apply similar principles to those in the Regulation.[84] The general principles for individual exemption are contained in Chapter 6, above.

---

[83] Wholesale franchise agreements are excluded from the block exemption by Art. 1 of Reg. 4087/88 as noted in *Scope of the exemption*, above.

[84] Bellamy & Child, *Common Market Law of Competition* (4th ed. 1993) Sweet and Maxwell. The authors refer to an article by de Cockborne, "After the new EEC franchising block exemption regulation, which franchise agreements should still be notified?" (1989) *Journal of International Franchising and Distribution Law* 101 at 103.

CHAPTER 8

Agreements Commonly Eligible for Exemption or to Which Article 85(1) Does Not Apply

INTRODUCTION

8-01   Having considered in detail in the previous Chapter the terms of certain specific agreements that qualify for automatic exemption, this Chapter will now focus on those agreements that are not dealt with by way of block exemption Regulation—either because the agreements in question do not lend themselves to block exemption or because Article 85(1) does not apply in the first place.

Certain agreements do not lend themselves to group exemption because, for example in the case of joint ventures they take a wide variety of forms and it would be extremely difficult to describe joint ventures in terms of category. Out of a wide range of contractual terms that are commonly found in joint ventures, only a selection in the right combination given the detailed background to each agreement, will be appropriate for exemption. Block exemption Regulations cannot possibly set out the permutations that are appropriate nor the market circumstances that would support them. This Chapter therefore addresses a number of agreements that have not been covered in previous Chapters. They are not covered by block exemption Regulations but commonly qualify for individual exemption on notification. Alternatively, Article 85(1) does not apply to them in the first place, such as sub-contracts, agency agreements and even joint ventures when structured appropriately to avoid Article 85(1).

Most of this Chapter is given to the Commission's view of agreements under Article 85(1) when applying principles of Community law. These principles have direct relevance when applied under the 1998 Act in the light of section 60, as discussed in Chapter 2. The United Kingdom position is outlined in the *Relevant differences under United Kingdom law* section of this Chapter below.

JOINT VENTURES

8-02   The name "joint venture" is given to a wide variety of agreements. The competition law analysis of each agreement differs according to the type of joint venture in question. The main categories for Community law purposes are as follows:

   (1) Full-Function Joint Ventures constituting "concentrations" with a "Community dimension" within the meaning of the Merger Regulation.[1]

---

[1] Council Reg. 4064/89 on the control of concentrations between undertakings [1990] O.J. L257.

(2) Joint Ventures caught by Article 85(1) (that are not eligible for clearance under the Merger Regulation).

(3) Joint Ventures not caught by Article 85(1).

Full-function joint ventures constituting "Concentrations" with a "Community dimension"

8-03   The Merger Regulation originally distinguished "co-operative joint ventures" from "concentrative joint ventures". Until recently only concentrative joint ventures could benefit from the fast-track clearance procedures of the Merger Regulation. The Merger Regulation was updated[2] to abolish that distinction and to bring all joint ventures under the Commission's exclusive jurisdiction (under the Merger Regulation) if they are "full-function joint ventures" with a "Community dimension". The distinction between co-operative and concentrative joint ventures therefore no longer excludes co-operative joint ventures from the ambit of the Merger Regulation. A distinction however does remain between the concentrative aspects of the joint venture and its "co-ordinative" aspects. The concentrative aspects (as before) are appraised for clearance according to whether a dominant position is created or strengthened, resulting in impeded competition incompatible with the common market. This essentially requires an Article 86 analysis of dominance. The co-ordinative aspects, on the other hand, are appraised for clearance according to the principles of Articles 85(1) and 85(3).

8-04   The essence of a "concentration" in the context of joint ventures is that two independent undertakings acquire joint control of another (whether directly or indirectly) within the detailed meaning given to the term "concentration" in Article 3 of the Merger Regulation.[3] To qualify for consideration under the Merger Regulation, a joint venture concentration must be "full-function", that is it must "perform on a lasting basis all the functions of an autonomous economic entity".[4] A "Community dimension" is defined by reference to the turnover levels of the undertakings concerned in different countries.

If the joint venture is a "full-function" joint venture constituting a concentration with a "Community dimension", then within the short time-scales laid down in the Merger Regulation, it must be cleared by the Commission, whether in original or modified form, or refused. The Merger Regulation is discussed at length in Chapter 12 which also expands upon the concepts of "joint control", "full-function", "concentration" and "Community dimension".

Joint ventures caught by Article 85(1)

8-05   General guidance on the status of joint ventures was given by the Commission in its Notice concerning the assessment of co-operative joint ventures pursuant to Article 85,[5] ("the J.V. Notice") which represents a summary of its administrative practice in relation to joint ventures. Given their idiosyncratic nature, joint ventures have to be viewed for their effects on a case by case basis. The concern with Article 85(1) stems from the fact that joint ventures are under the control of separate undertakings and the co-operation established by the joint venture agreement may include restrictions either between the

---

[2] Council Reg. 1310/97 amending Reg. 4064/89 on the control of concentrations between undertakings [1997] O.J. L180.
[3] The concept of joint control is dealt with in detail in the Commission's Notice of December 21, 1989 on the notion of concentration [1994] O.J. C385/5.
[4] Art. 3(2) of the Merger Reg., amended by Art. 1(3) of the amending Reg
[5] Commisison Notice of February 16, 1993 on the assessment of co-operative joint ventures pursuant to Art. 85 [1993] O.J. C43/2.

joint venture parents, or between the parents and the joint venture itself. For the purposes of Article 85(1), the form that the joint venture takes is largely irrelevant. What is important is whether the creation of the joint venture or its activities have the effect of preventing, restricting or distorting competition.

Application of Article 85(1)

8-06   Whether Article 85(1) applies depends upon the following:

(1) the extent to which competition is affected between the parents;

(2) the scope of the restrictions between the parents and the joint venture;

(3) the effect on third parties;

(4) whether the effect of a joint venture is appreciable; and

(5) the existence of network effects.

Each of these will now be dealt with in turn.

8-07   **Competition between the parents.**   The effect of a joint venture may be to restrict competition between the joint venture parents. This is obviously most likely where the parents are actual or potential competitors. Parents will be regarded as potential competitors where each, taken alone, has the capability of performing the tasks assigned to the joint venture. The parents are potential competitors if they could each reasonably be expected to act autonomously at any stage in the production or distribution of goods (or in the provision of services) without relying on the other, and where barriers to entry do not prevent each of them entering into the market in question within a reasonable time and without undue effort or expense. The Commission has suggested that the following questions be asked to determine the extent to which the parties are actual or potential competitors.[6]

8-08   *Contribution to the J.V.*   Does each parent company have sufficient financial resources to carry out the planned investment? Does each parent company have sufficient managerial qualifications to run the J.V.? Does each parent company have access to the necessary input products?

8-09   *Production of the J.V.*   Does each parent know the production technique? Does each parent make the upstream or downstream products himself and does it have access to the necessary production facilities?

8-10   *Sales by the J.V.*   Is actual or potential demand such as to enable each parent company to manufacture the product on its own? Does each parent company have access to the distribution channels needed to sell the product manufactured by the J.V.?

8-11   *Risk factors.*   Can each parent company on its own bear the technical and financial risks associated with the production operations of the J.V.?

8-12   *Access to the relevant market.*   What is the relevant geographic and product market? What are the barriers to entry into the market? Is each parent company capable

---

[6] Originally taken from the XIII Report on Competition Policy.

of entering that market on its own? Can each parent overcome existing barriers within a reasonable time and without undue effort or cost?[7]

Where the parents are competitors, or even only potential competitors, the next step is to determine whether the effect on competition is appreciable. Even if the parties are competitors, Article 85(1) may not apply because, for example the turnover levels of the participating undertakings may be sufficiently low as not to create an appreciable effect (*Pasteur Merieux- Merck*).[8] In general the participants must be competitors, or potential competitors, in the same market for Article 85(1) to apply (*Elopak/Metal Box- Odin*[9]).

8-13   Where the parties do not have the technical or manufacturing resources immediately available but possess significant financial resources to acquire them, the Commission will more readily treat them as potential competitors (*KSB/Goulds/Lowara/ ITT*[10]). This, however, would not be justified where the time required to apply the technology or acquire the necessary skills are sufficient deterrent against proceeding with the joint venture (*Olivetti/Cannon*,[11] *Elopak/Metal Box-Odin*).

In *Elopak/Metal Box-Odin*, negative clearance was granted to a joint venture in which neither party was capable of developing the product for which the joint venture was established. Similarly in *Iridium*,[12] a new satellite communications system involving high risk investment in a range of technologies beyond the economically feasible reach of any single entity, in a wholly novel concept, was sufficient to rule out any suggestion that the joint venture restricts competition.

8-14   **Competition between the parents and the joint venture.**   The relationship between the joint venture and its parents is especially important in the case of "full-function" joint ventures because in many ways they behave on the market in the same way as independent suppliers or purchasers. Where the joint venture competes with, or is a supplier to or a customer of one or both parents, the relationship must not result in any division of the geographic market, the product market or result in the sharing out of customers if Article 85(1) is to be avoided.

The Commission is keen to examine the effects of the joint venture where, as between the parents and the joint venture, any of them are competitors. The effects of collusion and co-ordination of the market between them must be avoided as much as possible. Instead of being actively competitive, the risk is that collusion will result in the slackening of competitive effort. Of course, where there is any risk of collusion that results in a slackening of competition, Article 85(1) will apply.

8-15   **Effect on third parties.**   The effect of a joint venture on third parties may be felt in a variety of ways, even where the parties are not competitors. The most common examples are where the joint venture assumes business activities previously undertaken by each parent separately. If for example the joint venture alone undertakes the sales function of both parents, those purchasers who formerly were able to make a selection between both parents as suppliers have a more limited range of choice when dealing with the joint venture instead.

Similar principles also apply to purchasing joint ventures. Suppliers are limited to dealing with the joint venture, which is now responsible for purchases, and not (as before) two parents.

---

[7] Para. 19 of the J.V. Notice.
[8] Commssion Dec. 94/770 [1994] O.J. L309/1.
[9] Commission Dec. 90/410 [1990] O.J. L209/15; [1991] 4 C.M.L.R. 832.
[10] Commision Dec. 91/38 [1991] O.J. L19/25; [1992] 5 C.M.L.R. 55.
[11] Commission Dec. 88/88 [1988] O.J. L52/51.
[12] Commission Dec. 97/39 [1997] O.J. L16/87; [1996] 5 C.M.L.R. 599.

8-16   In the case of manufacturing joint ventures, third parties which previously supplied the products now manufactured by the joint venture will have lost custom from both parents. This applies equally to the manufacture of finished products and intermediate products. The issue is the extent to which third parties are affected. If third parties are left with sufficient choice to deal with alternative suppliers or purchasers apart from the joint venture, Article 85(1) will not apply. Where these foreclosure effects on third parties are appreciable, Article 85(1) will apply even if the parents are not competitors.

Foreclosure against third parties will be worsened by barriers to entry into the market. If large scale parents pool their market power, this may create barriers to entry against third parties who may be deterred from competing or unable to grow as a result. The effects of a joint venture on third parties will also be worsened by exclusive distribution agreements, exclusive purchasing agreements or exclusive licences of intellectual property and particular care must be taken with these additional agreements.

8-17   Joint ventures between non-competitors for R& D, production, or distribution of themselves are generally outside Article 85(1) because of the combination of complementary knowledge, products and services in the joint venture—provided that the joint venture does not create barriers to entry for others, and there are sufficient sources open to those not engaged in the joint venture to be involved in R & D activities elsewhere, or sufficient alternative sources of supply to buy from, or outlets to sell to, in spite of the joint venture. If a joint venture undertakes activities exclusively for parents which are large-scale this is likely, however, to restrict competition as third party suppliers are then barred on a sufficient scale from those activities.

8-18   Appreciable effect.   The J.V. Notice confirms that among the factors relevant to determine whether a joint venture has an appreciable effect are the market shares held by the parents and the joint venture, and the structure of the market; in particular the extent to which the parents and joint venture are exposed to competition in the sector in which the joint venture operates. The economic and financial strength of the parents and their technological lead in comparison with competitors is obviously important.

In general, the closer the activities of the joint venture are to the market, the more likely it is that competition will be affected. Also competition is more likely to be affected if the fields of activity of the parents and the joint venture are identical because the likelihood of their co-ordination through the joint venture will be accentuated. The extent to which arrangements establishing the joint venture contain express restrictions is critical. A joint venture is more likely to affect competition if it impedes access to the market by third parties, for example as a result of exclusive distribution or exclusive purchasing arrangements between the parents and the joint venture.

8-19   As to the requisite effect on trade between Member States, this may still be found even in cases where the activities entrusted to the joint venture are to be carried out within only one Member State. For example if joint venture production takes place in only one Member State, the distribution of those products may span several Member States and thereby affect the pattern of trade that might otherwise exist without the joint venture (*Mitchell Cotts/Sofiltra*[13]). An effect on inter-state trade is obviously more likely where the joint venture parents are in different Member States, such in *Ford/VW*[14] which concerned joint development in relation to Multiple Purpose Vehicles. The agreement was granted individual exemption because of the resulting increase in range of choice of M.P.V.'s available to consumers.

Even joint ventures formed outside the Community, where the effects are felt in

---

[13]   Commission Dec. 87/100 [1987] O.J. L41/31; [1988] 4 C.M.L.R. 111.
[14]   Commission Dec. 93/49 [1993] O.J. L20/14; [1993] 5 C.M.L.R. 617.

Member States may be caught by Article 85(1). In *Ansac*,[15] an export association formed between U.S. producers of soda ash prevented each producer from making independent sales to Member States. The effect would be the same as if one entity supplied Member States rather than the individual producers, which would result in a different pattern of trade.

8-20   Joint venture networks.   Where a network of joint ventures exists, care must be taken to examine the cumulative effect of the network even if the individual joint ventures comprised in the network are harmless. The J.V. Notice gives the example of a number of joint ventures established between the same two parents for the same products in different geographical areas. Where the parents are competitors, the ties between them are reinforced for each successive joint venture, each time reducing any residual competition that may exist between them. They may, alternatively, establish a similar network for complimentary products which the parents intend to process, or non-complimentary products which the parents intend to distribute. The ties between the parents are strengthened by each joint venture.

Even if the parents are not competitors, the cumulative effect of a network of joint ventures—each one harmless on its own—can be to restrict competition, for example where one of the parents establishes a joint venture with different partners for the same products. Competition between the joint ventures may then be adversely affected because of the influence that the parent which is common to all of them may bring to bear. The effects of this obviously become even more exaggerated when the partners are actual or potential competitors. In *Optical Fibres*,[16] a number of national joint ventures were set up by Corning with different partners. Corning could exercise influence on their sales and other activities to restrict competition through its 50 per cent shareholding in each of them.

Particular joint ventures involving competitors

8-21   In the case of joint ventures formed by parents who are not competitors, the main focus in the analysis of compatibility with Article 85(1) will be the third party effects outlined above (*Effect on third parties*). In the case of joint ventures formed by parents who are competitors, the following types of joint venture give rise to special considerations.

8-22   Research and development joint ventures.   R&D joint ventures will be regarded as restrictive of competition and caught by Article 85(1) if research activities by the parents are precluded in the field of the joint venture research work. R&D joint ventures may also restrict competition (between the parents) in relation to the resulting products, where the joint venture assumes the function of exploiting the newly-developed technology.

The J.V. Notice emphasises that whether the restrictions on competition, and possibly the secondary effects on third parties, are appreciable can only be decided on a case by case basis. Block Exemption Regulation 418/85 gives a good illustration of the terms of R&D agreements that are acceptable between two parties and will be automatically exempt, and the market share pre-conditions in that Regulation give an indication of the extent to which the parties are able to occupy the market before exemption is lost.[17] Even if the terms of the block exemption regulation are not met, the Commission will generally regard R & D Agreements favourably under Article 85(3).

---

[15] Commission Dec. 91/301 [1991] O.J. L152/54.
[16] Commission Dec. 86/405 [1986] O.J. L236/30.
[17] See Reg. 418/85 concerning R&D agreements [1985] O.J. L53/5, discussed in Chap. 9 below.

8-23   Selling joint ventures.   Selling joint ventures are established for the purpose of undertaking certain selling activities of the parents. Competition is likely to be restricted on the supply side, to limit the choice of suppliers with whom purchasers may deal. In addition the effect may be that the parents no longer compete with each other (particularly on price but also other indices of competition) in order to win business since they no longer operate independently. The parents may also restrict the volume of products available to their customers and thereby influence prices.

Selling joint ventures fall within Article 85(1) if the effect on competition is appreciable and will generally be regarded unfavourably by the Commission. The exceptional case might be a sales joint venture between manufacturers concluded in the form of reciprocal specialisation agreements to enable the parents to offer to their customers the widest range of products available, that each parent could not offer alone.

8-24   Purchasing joint ventures.   Where competitors establish a joint venture for the purpose of purchasing supplies for the parents then competition on the demand side is restricted. The position of suppliers may be particularly badly affected where the parents are competitors and hold a significant market share, since the joint venture can exercise influence and competitive pressure over the suppliers through its purchasing power. The purchasing power of the joint venture over suppliers, however, may be limited where there is a wide range of customers that those suppliers are able to service by way of alternative outlets.

Much also depends on the importance of the jointly-purchased products to the activities of the parents. Where the purchase price is a significant part of the ultimate price of products or services when supplied by the parents, the effects of joint purchasing are more acute. The prices charged by the parents after the jointly-purchased goods are incorporated may become similar.

The advantages of purchasing joint ventures are that the cost of administering orders and transportation costs may be reduced and these cost reductions may be passed down the supply chain. Only in exceptional circumstances are purchasing joint ventures granted exemption under 85(3) and on condition that the parents are free to purchase independently of the joint venture.

8-25   Production joint ventures.   Similar principles apply where a joint venture manufactures primary or intermediate products for supply to the parents before incorporation and resale by the parents. The effect on competition will depend on the proximity to the market of the production stage. The closer to the market, the greater the likelihood that prices will be aligned, most obviously where the parents are merely distributors competing for the resale margin. Possible advantages of production joint ventures include the pooling of investment in production, thereby avoiding duplication. A production joint venture may also be a defensive measure in times of over-capacity.

8-26   Full-function joint ventures.   Full-function joint ventures deserve favourable treatment provided the joint venture does not facilitate collusion between the parents and does not result in creating or strengthening market power, with resulting threats to third parties. Low aggregate market shares will prevent any ill-effects to third parties provided there are no significant barriers to market entry, and as long as effective competition still prevails. If these criteria are not satisfied, Article 85(1) will apply and the matter should definitely be considered for individual exemption. As a rule of thumb where the aggregate market share of the parties is less than 10 per cent, the foreclosing effect on third parties and resulting barriers to entry should be small enough that Article 85(1) should not apply.[18]

---

[18] Para. 64 of the J.V. Notice.

Competition is most likely to be affected where a joint venture undertakes the same activities as the parents, or even related activities. Where the parents are not competitors, the issue is whether the parents occupy a position of sufficient market strength to produce the third party ill-effects described in *Effect on third parties* above. In the case of a joint venture operating up-stream from the activities of the parents, the effect will be the same as a purchasing or production joint venture, if the parents are dominant. In the case of a joint venture operating down-stream from the activities of the parents, the effect will be the same as a sales joint venture, if the parents are dominant. In the case of neighbouring or adjacent markets, competition will be more likely to be adversely affected where there is inter-dependence between the two markets. The example given in the J.V. Notice is of a joint venture which manufactures products complimentary to those of the parents. If the activities of the joint venture are upstream of one parent and downstream of another, this multi-level vertical integration may well exclude third parties from supplying or purchasing to a significant extent. In any event the effect on third parties in any analysis must not be forgotten.

8-27   Finally, as with all joint ventures between competitors, the ultimate question is whether the effect is to restrict, prevent or distort competition. This is not taken to be the case:

> "where co-operation in the form of J.V. can effectively be seen as the only possibility for the parents to enter a new market or to remain in their existing market provided that their presence will strengthen competition or prevent it from being weakened. Under these conditions the J.V. will neither reduce the existing competition nor prevent potential competition from being realised. The prohibition in Article 85(1) will therefore not apply."[19]

Ancillary restrictions

8-28   A distinction must be made between restrictions that arise from the creation and operation of a joint venture, and extraneous restrictions. Restrictions that are directly related to and necessary for the establishment and operation of the joint venture and cannot be dissociated from it without jeopardising its existence are assessed on the basis that they are part and parcel of the joint venture itself and will be considered according to the above criteria. These restrictions are "necessary" to the creation and operation of the joint venture in the sense of being normally required taking account of the nature, duration, subject-matter and geographical scope of the joint venture.

If the joint venture does not fall within Article 85(1) according to the above criteria[20] then neither do these ancillary restrictions. Conversely, if a joint venture is caught by Article 85(1) then so are the ancillary restrictions.

Restrictions that are not ancillary to the joint venture are generally caught by Article 85(1) even if the joint venture itself is not, and they must be separately justified on individual exemption under Article 85(3).

8-29   **Restrictions on the joint venture.**   Examples of ancillary restrictions on the joint venture may include clauses that specify the product range of the joint venture or the place of production of the joint venture. These restrictions give expression to the object of the joint venture and are regarded as ancillary, as long as they do not impose limits on quantities or restrictions on the prices to be charged or customers to be supplied.

If a joint venture is established to create production capacity or exploit technology of

---

[19] Para. 42 of the J.V. Notice.
[20] Set out in this section—*Joint Ventures*.

the parent for specified licensed products, an undertaking on the joint venture not to manufacture or sell goods that compete with the licensed products is likely to be regarded as ancillary on the basis that the joint venture must itself ensure the success of the new production unit without depriving the parents of their control over the use and disclosure of the licenced technology.[21] In *Mitchell Cotts/Sofiltra*[22] a ban on the joint venture to prevent it manufacturing and selling competing products was regarded as ancillary. Field of use restrictions when imposed on the joint venture's application of technology licensed by the parents will be regarded as part and parcel of the existence of the joint venture for specified activities. An exclusive licence granted to the parents by the joint venture of its own technological developments will not be ancillary (*Olivetti/Cannon*). In *BBC/Brown Boveri*,[23] exclusive licences granted by the joint venture to the parents for different territories were not regarded as ancillary but were granted exemption under Article 85(3).

Where the joint venture undertakes certain stages of the production or manufacture of products then restrictions on the joint venture to prevent it supplying or purchasing from anyone other than the parents may be justified if only for the joint venture start-up period.

8-30   Restrictions on the parents.   Non-compete undertakings may be required from the parents to prevent them competing with the joint venture in its allocated field of activities (*Rockwell International Corp and Iveco International Corp. BV*[24]) and these will frequently be regarded as ancillary during the joint venture start up period. The start-up period is generally five years or so.[25] Any non-competition undertakings given by the parents which go beyond this will certainly require justification and exemption under Article 85(3). Post-termination, non-competition clauses will require strong justification for exemption. Restrictions on the parents concerning quantities, prices and customers, as well as export bans, will not easily be justified.

An exclusive technology licence may be justified without limit in time if indispensable to the creation and operation of the joint venture (for example if the parent is not active in the same field of application of the licensed technology and the parents are not competitors). In general however, exclusive technology licences granted by parents to the joint venture are not ancillary restrictions (*Optical Fibres*[26]).

Exemption under Article 85(3)

8-31   In applying the criteria of Article 85(3), the following must be satisfied:

(1) the joint venture must contribute to improving the production or distribution of goods (or services) or to promoting technical or economic progress;
(2) consumers must be allowed a fair share of the resulting benefit;
(3) the parents and the joint venture, or the parents between themselves, must not be subject to any restrictions that are not indispensable for the attainment of the pro-competitive objectives of the joint venture; and
(4) the co-operation in the joint venture must not afford the undertakings concerned the possibility of eliminating competition in respect of a substantial part of the products or services in question.

---

[21] Para. 72 of the J.V. Notice.
[22] Commission Dec. 87/100 [1987] O.J. L41/31; [1988] 4 C.M.L.R. 111.
[23] Commission Dec. 88/541 [1988] O.J. L301/68; [1989] 4 C.M.L.R. 410.
[24] Commission Dec. 83/390 [1983] O.J. L224/19; [1983] 3 C.M.L.R. 709.
[25] Commission Dec. 88/496 *Iveco/Ford* [1988] O.J. L230/39; [1989] 4 C.M.L.R. 40.
[26] Commission Dec. 86/405 [1986] O.J. L236/30.

Advantages may take the form of new or improved products[27] or technology,[28] regardless of whether the resulting products or technology are exploited by the joint venture or by a third party under licence. Also market penetration into a new territory or wider product range would be an advantage, since the range of choice to purchasers would thereby be enhanced. Indispensability arguments for joint ventures frequently relate to the achievement of aims that would be unfeasible by any parent alone, for example in order to enter a new market or create a new technology. Joint ventures may be indispensable in order to achieve accelerated timescales for achieving the joint venture objectives.[29] Increased production, in general, increases availability and competition. Where necessary as a means of consolidation in a diminishing market, rationalisation may produce consumer benefits and other means of cost savings in order to preserve the existence of competition. Likewise, distribution may yield reduced costs and in turn lower prices. In times of structural over-capacity, prices may be reduced by reducing unprofitable production.

8-32   The Commission will not view favourably any agreements that masquerade as joint ventures where in reality they are established for the purpose of price-fixing between the parents, quota sharing or merely to divide the market. The Commission will also view with concern joint ventures where the parents possess high market shares or where the market is held by means of joint venture networks or oligopolies. Joint ventures which strengthen a dominant position are generally not granted exemption. In granting exemption, non-competition covenants by the parents have been justified,[30] as have exclusive licences granted by the parents to the joint venture[31] and purchase commitments given to the joint venture by the parents.[32]

Joint ventures not caught by Article 85(1)

8-33   Article 85(1) does not apply to joint ventures which are either *de minimis* or are established between companies within the same group.

Joint ventures of minor importance

8-34   The Commission's Notice on agreements of minor importance[33] indicates that there will be no appreciable restriction on competition if the market share thresholds of the parents taken together with the joint venture itself are not exceeded.[34]

Joint ventures between group members

8-35   Joint ventures established by parents in the same group are not caught by Article 85(1) provided the parents are not able to determine their own market behaviour independently of each other. In these circumstances, the joint venture is merely a matter of internal organisation.[35]

---

[27] Commission Dec. 86/405 *Optical Fibres* [1986] O.J. L236/30.
[28] Commission Dec. 93/49 *Ford/VW* [1993] O.J. L20/14; [1995] 5 C.M.L.R. 89.
[29] Commission Dec. 91/562 *Eirepage* [1990] O.J. L306/22; [1991] 4 C.M.L.R. 233.
[30] Commission Dec. 83/390 *Rockwell International Corp and Iveco Industrial Vehicles Corp BV* [1983] O.J. L224/19; [1983] 3 C.M.L.R. 709.
[31] Commission Dec. 88/88 *Olivetti/Cannon* 1988] O.J. L52/51; [1989] 4 C.M.L.R. 940.
[32] *ibid.*
[33] [1997] O.J. C372/04.
[34] See Chap. 2, *"De minimis" principles,* for the application of that Notice.
[35] See Chap. 2, *"Undertakings"*, on the meaning of "undertakings".

Joint Selling Agreements

8-36   Joint selling arrangements readily give rise to concern under Article 85(1). They involve agreements between various suppliers to entrust sales to a single entity. As with selling joint ventures,[36] the risk of entrusting sales to a single entity is that price competition between the participants will be reduced, if not eliminated. This may not be the case if the parties are not competitors (*Wild-Leitz*[37]). The ill- effects of joint selling arrangements will certainly be more acute where the suppliers possess high market shares (*Nederlandse Cement Handelsmaatschappij*[38]) unless the market shares of other suppliers are sufficiently high to keep competition active. Of course the harmful consequences of joint selling would be reduced if the participants are not bound to commit their sales to the joint enterprise.

Joint selling arrangements may, however, be justified if necessary to counter-balance the purchasing power of dominant buyers, or to compete more effectively against dominant competitors.

A joint sales agreement where the sales territory is only one Member State may still affect trade between Member States because the parties are less likely to compete with each other outside that territory as well (*Centra Stikstof Verkoopkantoor*[39]). Article 85(1) may still apply if the market shares of the parties are small, as in *Floral*,[40] where three large producers in France jointly sold to Germany where their market share was 2 per cent. Exemption will depend upon the market shares of the parties and the extent to which the parties are exposed to lively competition. Exemption is unlikely to be granted where the parties could adequately make sales independently of each other (*Bayer/BP Chemicals*[41]).

Joint Purchasing Agreements

8-37   Joint purchasing occurs when two or more purchasers act together in their dealings with suppliers. The aim is usually to receive greater discounts when ordering combined quantities. It often results in uniformity in price or other terms when applied to the purchasers.

Some of the anti-competitive effects of joint purchasing have already been discussed in the context of purchasing joint ventures,[42] principally in terms of the influence that purchasers may bring to bear upon suppliers where the purchasers taken together possess market power. Sellers may not readily find an alternative outlet for the products where the bargaining power of the joint purchasers is strong enough to undermine the competitive position of the sellers. The economic power wielded by the purchasers depends upon their aggregate purchasing requirements when compared with the alternative outlets available to sellers in the event that sales to those purchasers are uneconomic.

8-38   Joint purchasing is particularly restrictive of competition when applied to items which represent a significant proportion of the purchasers' cost of finished goods. There will be greater price uniformity for those finished goods among the members of the purchasing group, particularly if they sell similar products. This of course will not happen where the purchasers buy for different purposes, as was the case in *National Sulphuric Acid Association*.[43]

---

[36]   See *Selling joint ventures*, above.
[37]   Commission Dec. 72/108 [1972] O.J. L61/2; [1972] C.M.L.R. D36.
[38]   Commission Dec. 72/68 [1972] O.J. L22/16.
[39]   Commission Dec. 78/732 [1978] O.J. L242/15; [1979] 1 C.M.L.R. 11.
[40]   Commission Dec. 80/182 [1980] O.J. L39/51; [1980] 2 C.M.L.R. 285.
[41]   Commission Dec. 88/330 [1988] O.J. L150/3; [1989] 4 C.M.L.R. 24.
[42]   See *Purchasing joing ventures*, above.
[43]   Commission Dec. 80/917 [1980] O.J. L260/24; [1980] 3 C.M.L.R. 429.

Joint purchasing agreements are therefore caught by Article 85(1) but may be regarded favourably by the Commission, for example if necessary to enable enterprises to penetrate into overseas markets which would otherwise be inaccessible because of size and lack of purchasing power when compared to other purchasers, or where others are vertically integrated and effectively procure their supplies internally at comparatively low cost. Exemption is most likely to be granted when it can be shown that the price advantages of pooled purchasing will be passed on to consumers. The suppliers should not be adversely affected and, ideally, it should be shown that suppliers are dominant (*EEIG Orphe*[44]).

Where the market shares of the purchasers are sufficiently low, Article 85(1) may not apply through lack of appreciable effect (*Socemas*[45]). In *National Sulphuric Acid Association*,[46] a joint purchasing arrangement was granted exemption under Article 85(3) to members of an association but only on condition that they were not obliged to procure all their requirements through the purchasing arrangements. In that case, the Commission only permitted 25 per cent of their requirements to be committed, leaving them free to purchase 75 per cent of their requirements from other sources. The Commission also prohibited use and resale limitations on the sulphur procured through the group.

SELECTIVE DISTRIBUTION AGREEMENTS

8-39   Selective distribution is practised by certain brand owners as a means of limiting the retail outlets that are entitled to stock their products. This is usually done for the purposes of brand protection where retailer selection is made on the basis of the retailers' ability to meet technical and other standards. Selective distribution has the potential to introduce competitive distortions since the products sold through the selective distribution system may have a tendency towards higher prices and may not be exposed to rigorous undercutting from retailers with lower overheads. However, selective distribution networks may be compatible with Article 85 (1) in certain circumstances. The ECJ's view of selective distribution is illustrated by the case of *Metro v. Commission (1)*[47] in which the ECJ commented that a selective distribution "accords with" Article 85 (1):

> "provided that resellers are chosen on the basis of objective criteria of a qualitative nature relating to the technical qualifications of the reseller and its staff and the suitability of its training premises and that such conditions are laid down uniformly for all potential resellers and are not applied in a discriminatory fashion".[48]

Article 85 (1) will apply unless a number of conditions are met. The products must be of a type which justify limitation on the retail outlet selected. Highly complicated electronic equipment, cameras and computers require advice from expert staff during product selection by the customer as well as after the product has been purchased. Luxury goods such as perfumes, though not requiring customer support, are dependent upon brand image and this would suffer if the product were available without careful retailer selection. The product characteristics of certain consumer electronic goods justified the selective distribution network in *Grundig*.[49] The case of *Kruidvat BVBA v. Commission*[50] concerned the Givenchy selective distribution network which had been notified to the

[44] XX Report on Competition Policy 1990, para. 102.
[45] Commission Dec. 68/318 [1968] O.J. L201/4.
[46] Commission Dec. 80/917 [1980] O.J. L260/24; [1980] 3 C.M.L.R. 429.
[47] Case 26/16 *Metro v. Commission* [1977] E.C.R. 1875; [1978] 2 C.M.L.R. 44.
[48] *ibid.*, para. 21.
[49] Commission Dec. 94/29 [1994] O.J. L 20.
[50] Case C–70/97 *Kruidvat BVBA v. Commission*, Judgment of the Court November 17, 1998.

Commission and received a favourable indication. Retailers were selected according to the professional qualifications of their staff, the training of their staff, the location and fittings of the outlet and other similar factors including the availability of competing brands that reflect the image of Givenchy products. Although the Commission required certain aspects of the agreement to be changed, the Commission accepted the justifications for a selective distribution network in the case of perfume.

8-40   As a rule (though one not consistently applied) the selection criteria must be qualitative in nature and not quantitative. Quantitive criteria, for example might relate to turnover or minimum purchase quantities and the holding of certain stocks (*Grundig*). No quantitative criteria should be applied. Qualitative criteria, though permitted, must only go so far as are justified by the product characteristics. They must, however, be applied without discrimination. No one should be refused admission to a distribution network if they meet the qualitative criteria. Finally, competition must be enhanced by the selective distribution network to justify the potential that exists to use a network as a means of sustaining higher prices.

As it is notoriously difficult to balance these criteria with certainty and given the ECJ's inconsistent treatment of selective distribution networks, application for individual exemption and negative clearance (in the alternative) remains the safest option in most cases.

MISCELLANEOUS CO-OPERATION BETWEEN ENTERPRISES NOT CAUGHT BY ARTICLE 85(1)

8-41   It is necessary to distinguish between conduct that is restrictive of competition and conduct that is competition-neutral. The Commission's Notice on co-operation between enterprises[51] (the "Co-operation Notice") treats the following types of co-operation as non-restrictive of competition.

8-42   *Agreements having as their sole object:*

(a) an exchange of opinion or experience;

(b) joint market research;

(c) the joint carrying out of comparative studies of enterprises or industries; and

(d) the joint preparation of statistics and calculation models.

Agreements of this sort to gather information for the own independent use of participants are harmless provided that they go no further. If they involve any subsequent co-ordination or joint implementation of recommendations or conclusions reached by the parties on the basis of the information exchanged then they may restrict competition.[52]

8-43   *Agreements having as their sole object:*

(a) co-operation in accounting matters;

(b) joint provision of credit guarantees;

---

[51] Commission Notice of July 29, 1968 on co-operation agreements between enterprises [1968] O.J. C75/3, amended by Corrigendum [1968] O.J. C84/14.
[52] See Chap. 2, *Information agreements*, above, concerning the risks of exchanging information.

(c) joint-debt collecting associations; and

(d) joint business or tax consultant agencies.

These arrangements contemplate such things as the use of standardised forms for handling accounting work and not co-ordination concerning the supply of goods or services or economic decisions of the enterprises involved. They do not generally result in restrictions on competition, as long as they do not include fixing of prices or the terms on which services are to be supplied.

8-44 *Agreements having as their sole object:*

(a) the joint implementation of research and development projects;

(b) the joint placing of research and development contracts; and

(c) the sharing out of research and development projects among participating enterprises.

The straightforward exchange of research results, as a rule, is harmless to competition. Even the joint execution of research work or the joint development of the results of research work is neutral, but only up to the stage of industrial application. Similarly with the sharing-out of fields of research if the results are available to all participating enterprises.

The real issue is whether any party is restricted in its own R & D activities or the use of jointly-developed results. The parties must have complete freedom in their activities outside any joint projects, including the use of their own independently developed results. In particular, restrictions imposed on parties that do not carry on R & D under a joint venture, to restrict their research work in given fields, will be restrictive of competition. Even the sharing-out of research activities between the parties may be restrictive unless all parties have clear mutual access on unrestricted terms to all of the results.

As to the exploitation of results, Article 85(1) will apply where the parties agree to manufacture only products of the type jointly-developed or allocate production between themselves. The Cooperation Notice indicates that exploitation by the parties must be in proportion to their participation, by which the Notice means that results may be made available to certain enterprises to a limited extent if, for example they only contributed within a narrow section of the research or only gave a financial contribution. In the case of licences to third parties, where this is excluded or limited, for example because one party is given the exclusive right to grant licences, then competition may be restricted. Where research is jointly undertaken, an agreement to grant licences only with unanimous consent may conceivably be justified. The cautious approach must be to regard any restrictions on licensing as caught by Article 85(1).

8-45 *Agreements which have as their only object the joint use of production facilities and storing and transport equipment.*

These arrangements relate only to the use of facilities and are not caught by Article 85(1) unless they relate to joint production or the sharing-out of production, or if they establish a joint enterprise.

8-46 *Agreements having as their sole object the setting up of working partnerships for the common execution of orders, where the participating* *enterprises do not compete with each other as regards the work to be done or where each of them by itself is unable to execute the orders.*

If they do not compete and there is no foreseeable likelihood of them competing, enterprises may form working partnerships or associations for supplying goods or services. Enterprises may do so even if they do compete where, given lack of resources or experience, they have no chance of carrying out the requisite work alone. They must, however, at all times be free to do other work and to act independently from each other for other purposes that do not satisfy these criteria.

8-47   *Agreements having their sole object:*

(a) joint selling arrangements; and

(b) joint after-sales and repair service, provided the participating enterprises are not competitors with regard to the products or services covered by the agreement.

In general, co-operation between non-competitors of itself does not restrict competition. Joint selling by small and medium-sized enterprises, even if they are competitors, may well not result in an appreciable restraint on competition but much depends on the facts of each case and the Commission in the Co-operation Notice did not feel able to recite the facts and circumstances of the agreements that would not be caught by Article 85(1).

8-48   *Agreements having as their sole object joint advertising.*

These agreements are caught by Article 85(1) if one or more parties are restricted in their own independent advertising activities. The purpose of joint advertising is to draw the buyer's attention to the products of an industry or to a common brand.

8-49   *Agreements having as their sole object the use of a common label to designate a certain quality, where the label is available to all competitors on the same conditions.*

The right to use the label must not, however, be linked to obligations concerning production, marketing or other commitments. Anyone whose products meet the stipulated requirements must be free to use the quality label.

Agreements falling within any of these eight categories are regarded as competition-neutral and are not caught by the prohibition in Article 85(1) because they relate to procuring non-confidential information needed for the parties to make their own independent decisions, or they relate only to management co-operation or organisation arrangements without further co-ordination, or the co-operation relates to matters that are remote from the market, or they concern non-competitors. Where they do concern competitors they must not limit the parties' competitive conduct or their relations with third parties. The words "sole object" appear repeatedly in these eight headings to emphasize that they cannot be used as a cloak for other arrangements, nor can any restrictions be imposed on the parties which serve other purposes.

The Co-operation Notice emphasizes that joint ventures that do not fall clearly within any of those categories must be individually examined to see whether they have the object or effect of restricting competition.

SUB-CONTRACTS

8-50   The Commission's Notice concerning its assessment of certain subcontracting agreements in relation to Article 85(1) of the E.E.C. Treaty[53] ("the Subcontracting Notice") expresses the Commission's view on the status of subcontract agreements where one party (the contractor) contracts to another (the subcontractor) various tasks, be they the manufacture of goods, the supply of services or other work under the contractor's instructions.

Where the contractor provides technology or equipment that is necessary to enable the subcontractor to complete the work, the contractor may impose limitations or restrictions on its use, in order to preserve the value of the equipment or technology, without the restrictions being caught by Article 85(1). The contractor may impose any of the following restrictions on the subcontractor:

(1) a ban on using the technology or equipment for any purpose other than performance of the subcontract obligations;

(2) a ban on making the technology or equipment available to any third party; or

(3) a requirement that all goods, services or work resulting from the use of the technology or equipment only be supplied to the contractor (or performed on behalf of the contractor) and no one else.

8-51   The rationale for saying that Article 85(1) does not apply is that the subcontractor is merely carrying out the contractor's instructions and is using the contractor's own technology or equipment that is essential for the task. The subcontractor is not acting as an independent supplier in the market. The necessary technology may take the form of intellectual property, secret know-how or manufacturing processes, or documentation such as process flows that the contractor might prepare. The equipment may take the form of dies, patterns or tools that are distinctive to the contractor. Those items must be non-generic. They must be particular to the contractor but need not be protected by intellectual property rights.

The Subcontracting Notice goes on to deal with the circumstances in which these restrictions are not justified and these are where the subcontractor already has access (or could gain access on reasonable conditions) to the relevant technology or equipment in order to carry out the work. Where, for example the contractor only provides general information describing the work to be done, the subcontractor should not be restricted in developing its own business in that field as a provider of the type of services covered by the subcontract.

8-52   Additional conditions may be imposed on the subcontractor without infringing Article 85(1) and these include:

(1) an undertaking on either party to keep confidential all secret know-how, manufacturing processes and other confidential information received by that party in the course of the negotiation or performance of the agreement, but only for so long as it remains confidential;

(2) a ban on the subcontractor using any manufacturing processes or other secret know-how even after termination of the agreement, but only for so long as the information remains confidential;

---

[53] Commisison Notice of December 18, 1978 concerning its assessment of certain subcontracting agreements in relation to Art. 85(1) of the E.C. Treaty [1979] O.J. C1/2.

(3) an undertaking by the subcontractor to grant a non-exclusive licence of technical improvements to the contractor's technology made during the term of the agreement. If the subcontractor creates any patented invention that improves upon an invention of the contractor then the licence may be for the patent life of the original invention. Where the improvements made by the subcontractor in performing the contract are not severable, in that they cannot be exploited independently of the technology of the contractor, the licence back of improvements from the subcontractor may be exclusive. That is not considered to impose any appreciable restriction because the improvement has no independent value. However, any restriction on the results of the subcontractor's own research and development work which are capable of independent exploitation, would be restrictive of competition; and

(4) restrictions on trade mark use. The Subcontracting Notice clarifies the position of trade marks by stating that the contractor is entitled to grant only limited rights to the subcontractor, to enable the subcontractor to apply the contractor's trade marks for the purpose of supplying goods or services to the contractor. The restriction on further use of the trade mark is not caught by Article 85(1).

Commercial Agents

8-53 The appointment of certain commercial agents falls outside Article 85(1). The Commission's Notice on exclusive agency contracts made with commercial agents[54] ("the 1962 Notice") sets out the nature of the agent's functions if Article 85(1) is not to apply. The agent must merely undertake the following tasks and must not undertake or engage in the activities of an independent trader. The agent may:

(1) negotiate transactions on behalf of the principal; or

(2) conclude transactions in the name and on behalf of the principal; or

(3) conclude transactions in its own name but on behalf of the principal.

The critical issue is whether the representative bears any responsibility for the financial risks associated with any agency appointment. The description "agent" is largely irrelevant. The agent should not assume any risks itself under any transaction on behalf of the principal or will be regarded as an independent trader and Article 85(1) may then apply. The following factors will render it more likely that the representative is, in fact, an independent trader:

(1) if the representative is required to hold stocks of products (or in fact does so);

(2) if the representative is required to organise and maintain a support service to customers free of charge; or

(3) if the representative is free to determine prices or terms of business.

Article 85(1) applies to the exclusive appointment of representatives that are not true agents in the sense of the Notice because of the restrictions inherent in the exclusive appointment. The appointment of true commercial agents is not caught by Article 85(1)

---

[54] Commission Notice of December 24, 1962 on exclusive agency contracts made with commercial agents [1962] J.O. 139/62.

because the agent in those circumstances only performs an auxiliary function. The agent only acts on the instructions and in the interests of the principal and is neither a purchaser nor vendor in the negotiation and conclusion of contracts.

8-54   If agency appointments fall outside these strict confines, as frequently they do, they should be notified to the Commission for negative clearance, or individual exemption if the effect on competition may be appreciable.

In *Pittsburgh Corning Europe/Formica Belgium/Hertel*,[55] the absence of economic dependence on the principal was decisive. Formica was sufficiently independent of the so-called principal to resist its demands and could not be regarded as an agent within the terms of the 1962 Notice. A major portion of Formica's earnings were from sales of its own products and those of third parties. The sensitivity with a selling agent in such circumstances is the risk that prices may be manipulated by collusion. A similar conclusion was reached in *Suiker Unie v. Commission*.[56]

Care must be taken that additional restrictions are not imposed in any agency appointment especially if the agent is not a true agency within the terms of the 1962 Notice. A non-competition clause imposed on a true agent within the 1962 Notice would be acceptable but otherwise not. Further, a non-competition clause imposed on an "agent" who is in fact treated as an independent dealer might also infringe Article 86 if the principal is in a dominant position (*Suiker Unie*). The effect may be to prevent others finding a suitable representative to promote their products or services.

8-55   In *1990 World Cup package Tours*,[57] 90 Tour Italia were granted the exclusive right to sell World Cup tours on behalf of the organising committee but because of the level of commercial risk accepted by 90 Tour Italia, it could not be regarded as an agent.[58]

The 1962 Notice is presently under review by the Commission. The draft guidelines prepared by the Commission focus on the issue of integration. This bears out that the agent must be dedicated to serving the principal's interests and not its own, so that those dealing with the agent identify with the principal and do not expect the agent to act autonomously. The agent may have certain peripheral interests of its own, as long as these are kept to a certain level and do not place the agent in any conflict of interest with the principal. Unintegrated agents will be treated as independent traders and Article 85(1) will apply.

RELEVANT DIFFERENCES UNDER UNITED KINGDOM LAW

Joint ventures

8-56   The Fair Trading Act 1973 may apply to a joint venture in one or both of the following ways. If the joint venture constitutes a "merger situation qualifying for investigation", because the criteria in section 64 are satisfied, then the Secretary of State may refer the matter to the Competition Commission to determine whether it operates against public interest. The joint venture may alternatively qualify for investigation if the long-term result is to create a "monopoly situation" within the meaning of sections 6 to 11 of the Fair Trading Act 1973. This Act is discussed at length in Chapter 11 below. The Fair Trading Act 1973 is concerned primarily (though not entirely) with the structural changes that result from joint ventures. There is overlapping jurisdiction between the Fair Trading

---

[55] Commission Dec. 72/403 [1972] O.J. L272/35; [1973] C.M.L.R. D2.
[56] Joint Cases 48/50, 54–56, 111, 113 & 114/73 *Suiker Unie v. Commission* [1975] E.C.R. 1663; [1976] 1 C.M.L.R. 295.
[57] Commission Dec. 92/521 [1992] O.J. L326/31.
[58] An inconsistent decision with these principles was made in Commission Dec. 88/84 *ARG/Unipart* [1988] O.J. L45/34; [1988] 4 C.M.L.R. 513.

Act 1973 and the 1998 Act but given the relatively cumbersome procedures of the former, the procedures and powers available under the 1998 Act are likely to be preferred when controlling any anti-competitive effects that result from co-ordination of joint venture parents between themselves or with the joint venture.

Other agreements

8-57   The Commission's approach to the various agreements outlined above in this Chapter is likely to be followed by United Kingdom courts and authorities when considering the effect of those agreements in the United Kingdom, particularly in the light of section 60 of the 1998 Act which requires consistent treatment with corresponding questions arising in Community law.[59] The position in the United Kingdom will be clarified with the advent of block exemptions under the 1998 Act, in particular those concerned with vertical restraints. Even if particular agreements do not qualify for automatic exemption, the terms of the block exemptions will lend clarity to the reasoning to be applied when seeking individual exemption or when determining whether the Chapter I or Chapter II prohibitions apply.

---

[59] For further detail concerning s. 60 see Chap. 2, *Interpretation of the Act*, above.

CHAPTER 9

Intellectual Property Agreements

INTRODUCTION

9-01 This Chapter will focus on the Community law approach to intellectual property agreements. As far as United Kingdom law is concerned, it is anticipated that the 1998 Act will follow Community law although perhaps with greater relaxation for intellectual property agreements. As noted in Chapter 7 (*E.C. and United Kingdom Policy Towards Vertical Restraints*, above) the question of vertical restraints is still being debated at Community (and national) level with a view to a single block exemption for vertical restraints dependent on the market share of the parties and the nature of the restrictions. It remains to be seen whether in the United Kingdom a similar block exemption will follow. Intellectual property agreements will either be dealt with by way of block exemption (consistent with the E.C. block exemption Regulations) or by way of exclusion from the prohibitions. Only when the implementing secondary legislation is drafted will the final position be known.

9-02 The traditional approach to intellectual property agreements under the Restrictive Trade Practices Act 1976 has largely been to regard them as benign, on the basis that in general they confer freedom to do things that would otherwise be prevented by the intellectual property owner. In that sense, they have been regarded as similar to property agreements such as leases. All of this will change and an analysis of intellectual property agreements, similar to that applicable under Community law, will be necessary in future when considering the compatibility of intellectual property agreements (and the exercise of intellectual property rights) with the Chapter I and Chapter II prohibitions. This is confirmed by the following recent statement of the DTI:

> "Our present view on intellectual property rights under a prohibition-based approach is that the boundaries of what is acceptable and what is anti-competitive is best established directly from European jurisprudence. Different treatment for intellectual property rights under the Competition Act regime and European regime seems neither necessary nor desirable and is likely to increase the burden on business of compliance. To the extent to which they are covered by the proposed E.C. block exemption (or would be if there were an effect on trade) they will be parallel exempt under the Act; the same applies to agreements covered by the technology transfer block exemption."[1]

Even before the position under the 1998 Act is clarified by block exemptions and exclusion orders, it is already clear that intellectual property agreements will benefit from parallel exemption under section 10 of the 1998 Act (see Chapter 6, *Notification Procedure. Before the Director General of Fair Trading for Chapter I and Chapter II Infringements*, above). For this reason, the Commission block exemption Regulations discussed in this

---

[1] Competition Act 1998. Exclusion of Vertical Agreements, Consultation on draft Order, para. 22.

Chapter and in Chapter 7 above, will be relevant. It is worth noting that the Commission's proposals for a single block exemption covering vertical restraints (discussed in Chapter 7, *E.C. and United Kingdom Policy Towards Vertical Restraints*, above) do not at this stage contemplate changes that will apply to intellectual property agreements. For the time being, the existing block exemption Regulations for intellectual property agreements will continue. Even where there is no prospect of automatic exemption for an intellectual property agreement, the remaining sections of this Chapter concerning the Commission's view of intellectual property transactions will serve as a guide to whether an agreement is likely to be granted individual exemption. The likely status of an agreement under the 1998 Act should be considered in the light of Community law, once again, bearing in mind all relevant differences between Article 85 (1) and Chapter I (as discussed in Chapter 2, *The Differences: The Key Differences Between Article 85(1) and Chapter I* above).

As a matter of Community law, Articles 85(1) and 85(3) together define in general terms the extent to which an intellectual property proprietor and licensee may enter into agreements conferring or reserving territorial exclusivity or which are otherwise potentially restrictive of competition. As discussed in Chapter 2 above, an agreement prohibited by Article 85(1) is automatically void and unenforceable unless granted exemption under Article 85(3). If the offending clauses are severable they alone may be rendered unenforceable.[1a] Also infringement exposes undertakings to the risk of considerable fines. Infringement therefore has important consequences for any purchaser of a business which operates under agreements potentially caught by Article 85(1). Even if extensive indemnities are given by the vendor of the business to cover the costs of any fine, the purchaser will nevertheless risk being involved in lengthy proceedings and will suffer the uncertainty of not knowing the outcome of any Commission investigation. Meanwhile the enforceability of any intellectual property agreement acquired remains in question.

9-03   The prohibitions are cast in such broad language and have such far-reaching effect that inevitably conscientious parties to intellectual property agreements should modify them for exemption. Regulation 19/65,[2] empowers the Commission to grant block exemption. The Director has similar powers under section 6 of the 1998 Act. Regulation 19/65 specifically refers to agreements or concerted practices which:

> "include restrictions imposed in relation to the acquisition or use of intellectual property rights—in particular patents, utility models, designs or trade marks—or to the rights arising out of contracts for assignment of, or the right to use, a method of manufacture of knowledge relating to use or to the application of industrial processes".[3]

In exercising this power, the Commission has adopted the following Regulations in recognition that it is generally supportive of intellectual property agreements that enable small companies to penetrate new markets or promote innovation:

(1) Regulation 2349/84[4] relating to patent licensing agreements (the "Patent Regulation");

(2) Regulation 418/85[5] relating to research and development agreements (the "R&D Regulation");

[1a] *Chemidus Wavin v. TERI* [1978] 3 C.M.L.R. 514 CA, on appeal from [1976] 2 C.M.L.R. 387 HC.
[2] Reg. 19/65 [1965] J.O. 533–65.
[3] Art. 1.
[4] Reg. 2349/84 [1984] O.J. L219/15.
[5] Reg. 418/85 [1985] O.J. L53/5. For the full text see Appendix D.1 below.

(3) Regulation 556/89[6] relating to know-how agreements (the "Know-How Regulation"); and more recently

(4) Regulation 240/96[7] relating to technology transfer agreements (the "Technology Transfer Regulation").

9-04   The Technology Transfer Regulation went beyond the usual aim of caseload reduction and additionally was aimed at simplifying the existing block exemptions. It repealed the Know-How Regulation and the Patent Regulation (except for transitional purposes) in order to accommodate technological advances:

"The rules governing patent licensing agreements and agreements for the licensing of know-how ought to be harmonised and simplified as far as possible, in order to encourage the dissemination of technical knowledge in the Community and to promote the manufacture of technically more sophisticated products".[8]

The Commission acknowledges that exclusive licences may be incompatible with Article 85(1) because of the undertakings by the licensor not to exploit the licensed territory and not to grant further licences in the exclusive territory.[9] However, in certain circumstances, exclusive licences may be regarded as satisfying the conditions for exemption in Article 85(3) where they concern the introduction and protection of new technology in the territory and are justified by the research investment required and the increased level of competition that is likely to result from the dissemination of innovation within the Community. Exclusivity is seen as a necessary incentive for the intellectual property proprietor to grant licences and for the licensee to invest in manufacture and marketing in the allocated territory.[10] As such, exclusive licences generally contribute to improving the production of goods and to promoting technical progress but only if the exclusivity and other restrictions are kept within justifiable bounds, as described in the above Regulations.

PATENT AND KNOW-HOW LICENCES (THE TECHNOLOGY TRANSFER REGULATION)

Introduction

9-05   It is perhaps telling that the Technology Transfer Regulation emerged in anticipation of the pending expiry of the Patent Regulation which was to occur on December 31, 1994,[11] rather than a wholesale examination of how best the exemption of all forms of intellectual property licences might be achieved. Its main emphasis was unification of the Patent Regulation and Know-how Regulation. The Commission's draft which was first circulated in April 1994 met with vehement criticism and was rejected as unworkable largely due to the incorporation of market share criteria as pre-conditions for exemption. As originally drafted, territorial exclusivity would only be available to a party if it had a market share of less than 40 per cent. The market share test is still present in Article 7(1) in diluted form when compared with the original proposals, in such a way that exemption

---

[6]   Reg. 556/89 [1989] O.J. L61/1.
[7]   Reg. 240/96 [1996] O.J. L31/2. For the full text see Appendix D.2 below.
[8]   Recital (3) Reg. 240/96.
[9]   Recital (1) Reg. 240/96.
[10]   Recital (12) Reg. 240/96.
[11]   Extended to June 30, 1995 by Commission Reg. 70/95 [1995] O.J. L12/13. The Know-how Reg. was due to expire on December 31, 1999.

conferred by the Regulation is withdrawn if the effect of the agreement is to prevent the licensed products being exposed to effective competition in the exclusive territory from the same or similar products "which may in particular occur where the licensee's market share exceeds 40 per cent".[12]

Scope of the technology transfer regulation

9-06   The Technology Transfer Regulation applies to licences of patents on their own ("pure" patent licences), licences of non-patented technical information ("such as descriptions of manufacturing processes, recipes, formulae, designs or drawings"[13]), ("know-how licences"[14]) and combinations of both, ("mixed licences"). The licences may cover other ancillary intellectual property,[15] in particular trade marks, design right and copyright, especially software[16] but it is only appropriate to include this ancillary intellectual property when the additional licensing contributes to the achievement of the objects of the patent or know-how technology and the provisions relating to these items are only ancillary (*i.e.* the provisions relating to these additional items only contain restrictive obligations which attach equally to the licensed patents or know-how[17]). Ancillary intellectual property is therefore narrowly defined, emphasising the limits of the Regulation to catch primarily only patent and know-how rights but not other intellectual property.

The significant step made by the Commission in creating a combined Regulation for patent and know-how licences recognises that in reality the two rights are essentially similar in nature and in practice are licensed together. The combination is creditable also in the transitional treatment of the earlier Know-how Regulation and Patent Regulation because any licence that would have been exempt under either of those two Regulations would also be exempt under the more relaxed regime of the new Regulation.

9-07   Another positive result of the Regulation is that it did away with the artificial analysis that had to be made in the past to determine in the case of a licence which included know-how whether the know-how was ancillary to patents, and covered by the Patent Regulation, or was more than ancillary and therefore eligible for exemption only under the Know-how Regulation. The two are now combined in a more flexible form but still differentiating between core patents and know-how for the purpose of determining the scope of permissible territorial restrictions.[18]

Pure patent licences

9-08   Article 1(2) deals with the duration of territorial restrictions in pure patent licences. The licensor may be prevented from granting equivalent patent licences to others in the allocated territory[19] and may be prevented from exploiting the patent itself[20] for the duration of the patents (*i.e.* for so long as they are maintained).[21] Similarly, for the duration of the patents, the licensee may be prevented from exploiting by any means the licensed patent in the licensor's territory[22] and may be prevented from exploiting the

---

[12]   Market share assessment is nevertheless still relevant for the purposes of Regs 417/85, 418/85, 2349/84 and 556/89—see also Reg. 151/93 [1993] O.J. L21/8 in the context of joint ventures.
[13]   Recital (4).
[14]   Art. 1(1).
[15]   Art. 1(1).
[16]   Recital (6).
[17]   Art. 10(15).
[18]   See Art. 1 and Recitals 3–9 and 12.
[19]   Art. 1(1)(1).
[20]   Art. 1(1)(2).
[21]   Art. 1(2).
[22]   Art. 1(1)(3).

patent by manufacture or use[23] or by active sales and marketing[24] in territories licensed to other licensees of the licensor.

In addition, the licensee may be prevented even from making passive sales against unsolicited orders[25] in territories licensed to other licensees but only during the period of five years from the date when the licensed product is first marketed within the common market by one of the licensees[26], and then only to the extent that there is protection in those territories by parallel patents. Notice that the timescale is set by reference to first marketing by one of the licenses. The licensor should ensure that the date of first marketing is properly communicates to it.

Pure know-how licences

9-09   The position of pure know-how licences is dealt with in Article 1(3), permitting the same restrictions on the licensor and licensee except that the maximum duration of those restrictions differs. It is confined to a period not exceeding 10 years from the date when the licensed product is first put on the market within the common market by one of the licensees except that this period ends five years from that date in the case of the restriction on the licensee putting licensed products on the market in territories licensed to other licensees in response to passive orders. (One aspect of the Regulation that is particularly welcomed is that the commencement date for the time limits is now the date of first marketing, rather than under the Patent Regulation and the Know-how Regulation, the date of the agreement. If the change had not been made, the life of those restrictions might well have expired too early to be of practical value.) It may not be within the knowledge of the licensor or any licensee precisely when first marketing occurred, as this may be known only by another licensee who has not communicated this to the licensor. The date of first marketing is the critical trigger event for the permissible period of these restrictions. Each licence agreement should therefore require the licensee to communicate the date of first marketing.[27]

An important proviso to exemption is that it only applies if the parties clearly identify all licensed know-how and subsequent improvements and exemption only applies for so long as the know-how remains secret and substantial.[28] This is consistent with the definition of know-how in Article 10 as "a body of technical information that is secret, substantial and identified in appropriate form". The terms "secret", "substantial" and "identified" in turn are defined in such a way as to result in a requirement that the know-how must be secret in the sense that it confers a market lead (even if all component parts are publicly available) and it must be "useful" in conferring competitive edge, and verifiable (so that it is distinguishable from the licensee's own technology which is to be kept free of restrictions). The licensed know-how must therefore be documented accurately, though ideally not in a form that discloses any know-how that is secret.[29]

---

[23] Art. 1(1)(4).

[24] Art. 1(1)(5).

[25] Art. 1(1)(6).

[26] Art. 1(2).

[27] The parties to know-how licences are possibly on risk that they are giving effect to restrictions beyond their permissible end-date if the date of first marketing is not known. They might therefore be conducting themselves under the agreement contrary to Art. 85(1) even if the form of their agreement is compliant with the Reg.

[28] Art. 1(3).

[29] If the parties have documented the know-how, but inaccurately or incompletely, they may be operating the limited restrictions that are only permissible in relation to qualifying documented know-how, in relation to undocumented know-how. Although the undocumented know-how may be capable of qualifying for exemption, it does not if it is not identified. Even though the document on its face may comply with the Reg., the unidentified know-how that is licensed *de facto* would not be licensed within the exemption and the conduct of the parties may therefore still infringe Art. 85(1).

Mixed licences

9-10   The duration permitted for the same restrictions in mixed licences reflects a combination of the rules separately applicable to patents and know-how licences. The permissible period is the same 10 year period as for know-how or, if longer, the duration of "necessary patents" in Member States where they are held.[30] Article 10(5) defines "necessary patents" rather inelegantly as:

> "patents where a licence under the patent is necessary for the putting into effect of the licensed technology in so far as, in the absence of such a licence, the realisation of the licensed technology would not be possible or would only be possible to a lesser extent or in more costly or difficult conditions. Such patents must therefore be of technical, legal or economic interest to the licensee".

This test of whether a patent is a "necessary patent" depends on the capability of each licensee and may vary from one licensee to another.[31] The concept of "necessary patents" is one newly introduced by the Regulation and is found nowhere else in any other Regulation or Directive. It also unintentionally has the potential of putting unnecessary constraints on both licensor and licensee in relation to improvements.

Improvements

9-11   If technical progress is to be made (as contemplated by the Regulation) the licensor should be encouraged to disclose and license improvements in order to keep the technology at its cutting edge and most competitive. If the improvements are patented and yet are not sufficiently "core" to a product to constitute "necessary patents", the licensor runs the risk that the permissible restrictions may only be applied for a period of 10 years.[32] The licensee, on the other hand, itself may wish to be clear that the restrictions only apply for 10 years by claiming that the improvements patents are not "necessary patents". In doing so the licensee risks termination of the agreement if it contains a white-listed clause envisaged by Article 2(1)(16), reserving to the licensor the right to terminate the licence agreement of a patent if the licensee raises the claim that such a patent is not necessary.[33]

It is also worth bearing in mind in the same context that improvements clauses that extend the licence life are no longer black-listed[34] unless a territorial restriction on either the licensor or licensee is extended.[35] Article 2(1)(4) directly addresses improvements in the white list by confirming as non-restrictive:

> "an obligation on the licensee to grant to the licensor a licence in respect of his own improvements to or his new applications of the licensed technology",

with two important provisos. The first is that where the improvements are severable, the licence must be non-exclusive so that the licensee is free to exploit them elsewhere freely (insofar as the licensor proprietary information is not thereby disclosed). If improvements

---

[30] Art. 1(4).

[31] The same technology in the hands of one licensee may result in a 10 year period of protection while, in the hands of another, the period of protection will be the patent term. Even in cases of a single licensee, an assessment of whether a patent is a "necessary patent" cannot be made by examining the documentation alone although an indication is likely to be given on questioning of the licensee.

[32] Though when the 10 year period commences may be uncertain.

[33] This is consistent with the white-listing of "no-challenge" clauses in Art. 2(1)(15) entitling the licensor to terminate a licence if the licensee contests the secret or substantial nature of the know-how or challenges the validity of licensed patents even though these clauses were black-listed in the Know-how Reg. and Patent Reg.

[34] These were previously black-listed under Art. 3(2) of the Patent Reg. and Art. 3(10) of the Know-how Reg.

[35] Art. 3(7).

are not severable, it is arguable (with some risk) that the licence back may be taken on an exclusive basis although Article 2(1)(4) does not expressly say so. In any event the question of severability is one of fact and would require care in examination. The second proviso is that any grant-back of improvements must be reciprocal, *i.e.* the licensor must undertake to grant an exclusive or non-exclusive licence of improvements to the licensee. No explanation for the second proviso is given in the Recitals and it is considered that the requirement in Article 2(1)(4) on the licensor to grant the corresponding licence of improvements is unusual. It is potentially restrictive of competition since it prevents the most effective application of the technology by the licensor and this may not necessarily be justified by a licence of improvements made by the licensee. Article 3(6) confirms that an obligation on the licensee to assign its improvements to the licensor is black-listed.

Quantity limits

9-12   Article 1(1)(8) expressly exempts an obligation on the licensee to:

> "limit production of the licensed product to the quantities that the licensee requires in manufacturing its own products and to sell the licensed product only as an integral part of or a replacement part for his own products",

provided that such quantities are freely determined by the licensee. White-listed in Article 2.1(12), is a clause with similar effect which permits an obligation on the licensee not to use the licensor's technology to construct facilities for third parties.

The purpose of this is explained in Recital 8, the objective being to facilitate the dissemination of technology and improvement of manufacturing processes, in this instance, where the licensee itself manufactures the licensed products or sub-contracts manufacture. It therefore excludes agreements solely for the purpose of sale. The Commission clearly permits a restriction intended to confine the licence scope only to the licensee's own requirements, whatever those might be. However, quantity restrictions in the case of sales agreements are not countenanced, and even measures to monitor "own" or "domestic" requirements, as in *Adalat*,[36] risk being treated as Article 85(1) infractions.

The white list and the black list

9-13   The white and black lists are always crucial to block exemption Regulations. Among the clauses permitted in Article 2 are post-termination confidentiality and non-use undertakings[37]; a ban on sub-licensing or assignment[38]; licensee minimum quality requirements or tie-ins to designated suppliers[39]—but only if necessary on the grounds of the proper exploitation of the technology or uniformity with licensor or other licensee products (formerly blacklisted[40])—undertakings concerning assistance with infringement actions[41]; calculation of royalties beyond expiry of secrecy or patent life of the licensed rights[42] (formerly blacklisted[43]), field of use limitations[44]; minimum royalties or minium production obligations[45]; undertakings to grant no less favourable terms than to later

---

[36] Commission Dec. 96/478 [1996] O.J. L201/1; [1996] 5 C.M.L.R. 416.
[37] Art. 2(1)(1) and (3).
[38] Art. 2(1)(2).
[39] Art. 2(1)(5).
[40] Art. 3(9) of the Patent Reg., Art. 3.3 of the Know-how Reg.
[41] Art. 2(1)(6).
[42] Art. 2(1)(7).
[43] Art. 3(4) of the Patent Reg., Art. 3.5 of the Know-how Reg.
[44] Art. 2(1)(8).
[45] Art. 2(1)(9).

licensees[46]; marking obligations to indicate the licensor[47]; obligations not to construct facilities for third parties[48]; limitations on second source supplies[49]; a reservation of the licensor's right to oppose exploitation outside the licensed territory[50]; no challenge clauses[51]; termination on claims that a patent is unnecessary[52]; best endeavours licensee undertakings[53]; and revocation of exclusivity and improvements rights if the licensee competes with the licensor.[54]

Article 3 refers to various clauses which are black-listed (to the extent not expressly white-listed) and these include restrictions on price determination,[55] wide non-compete restrictions against research and development, production or distribution,[56] quantity limitations,[57] assignment of licensee improvements,[58] and extension of territorial restrictions by licensing improvements.[59]

9-14   These provisions, on the whole, are self-evident and their scope may be matched, word for word or in substance, to determine the status of the clause. If any clauses exist which are not expressly exempt under Article 1, which are not white-listed under Article 2 or black-listed under Article 3, they may be presumed to be eligible for block exemption within the Regulation if the Commission confirms this under the stream-lined opposition procedure established under Article 4. The requirements for formal notification using Form A/B will usually be waived at the Commission's discretion if the text of the agreement is submitted together with an analysis of market structure and an estimate of the licensee's market share requiring considerably less information than Form A/B. Exemption may be claimed unless the Commission opposes it within four months, two months shorter than the six month period under the Patent Regulation and Know-how Regulation.[60] At present the opposition procedure is in limited use by parties to such agreements with under a dozen or so submissions in each year.

Matters not apparent on the face of the document

9-15   Even if the form of an agreement meets all the requirements of Article 1, contains any number of white-listed clauses in Article 2 and no black-listed clauses in Article 3, and even if grey-listed clauses (*i.e.* neither white-listed nor black-listed) are passed under the expedited opposition procedure, exemption may still be jeopardised and the parties exposed to the full consequences of infringement of Article 85(1) for reasons that are not apparent on document inspection alone.

For example under Article 3 exemption is lost where there exists a concerted practice (or unjustified requirement) between the parties resulting in refusal by one party to meet demand from users or resellers in its allocated territory who would market the products in other territories within the common market.[61] Exemption is also lost where the parties

---

[46] Art. 2(1)(10).
[47] Art. 2(1)(11).
[48] Art. 2(1)(12).
[49] Art. 2(1)(13).
[50] Art. 2(1)(14).
[51] Art. 2(1)(15).
[52] Art. 2(1)(16).
[53] Art. 2(1)(17).
[54] Art. 2(1)(18).
[55] Art. 3(1).
[56] Art. 3(2).
[57] Art. 3(5).
[58] Art. 3(6).
[59] Art. 3(7).
[60] Art. 4.
[61] Art. 3(3)(a).

make it difficult for users or resellers to obtain the products from other resellers within the common market, in particular by the exercise of intellectual property rights or other measures which:

"prevent users or resellers from obtaining outside, or from putting on the market in the licensed territory products which have been lawfully put on the market within the common market by the licensor or with his consent".[62]

9-16 The similarity of this wording to the case law on Articles 30 and 36 of the E.C. Treaty is clear and it may be taken as adopting certain basic principles of exhaustion of intellectual property. (See Chapter 10 below, for further commentary on Articles 30 to 36.) Article 3(3) reflects the Commission's eagerness to ensure that products are freely available to resellers "within the common market". Reliance no doubt will be placed by licensors on the expression "without any objectively justified reason" in Article 3(3).

It is worth noting also that Article 2(1)(14) contains an important provision which permits:

"a reservation by the licensor of the right to exercise the rights conferred by a patent to oppose the exploitation of the technology by the licensee outside the licensed territory".

This might be taken to clarify the position of direct sales by a licensee outside its allocated territory.

9-17 Similarly, Article 3(4) disapplies exemption if the parties to an agreement (which is otherwise perfectly compliant with the Regulation) were competing manufacturers at the time of the agreement, if the agreement contains customer or user limitations, *i.e.* where:

"the parties were already competing manufacturers before the grant of the licence and one of them is restricted, within the same technical field of use or within the same product market, as to the customers he may serve, in particular by being prohibited from supplying certain classes of user, employing certain forms of distribution or, with the aim of sharing customers, using certain types of packaging for the products, save as provided in Article 1(1)(7) and Article 2(13)."

Article 5 disapplies exemption to the following: agreements between members of patent or know-how pools (which relate to the pooled technologies), licences involving a joint venture where the parents are competitors[63] (except where the parties' combined market share for the relevant product is less than 20 per cent for production licences and 10 per cent for production and distribution licences[64]), and reciprocal arrangements between competitors under which the licence is granted in exchange for an intellectual property or marketing licence.

9-18 Under Article 7 exemption is withdrawn in a wide range of circumstances, namely where the effect of the agreement is to prevent the licensed products being exposed to effective competition in the licensed territory from identical or similar goods. This is said, in Article 7(1), to occur where the licensee's market share exceeds 40 per cent. As

---

[62] Art. 3(3)(b).
[63] Because this is covered by Reg. 151/93 [1993] O.J. L21/8.
[64] Art. 5(2)(1).

with all market share criteria, this adds uncertainty to the status of agreements expressly drafted to benefit from exemption. The Commission included market share criteria both in Article 5(2) and 7(1) in spite of the fact that it was the aspect of market share that raised so much protest against early drafts of the Regulation and delayed its progress. Further, under Article 7(2), matters solely within the conduct of the licensee may result in loss of the exemption. Exemption is lost if the licensee refuses, without objectively justified reason, to meet unsolicited orders from users or resellers in the territory of other licensees. This is beyond the power of the licensor to prevent and it cannot be verified on document inspection alone. The matter may even not be within the knowledge of the licensor and so oral enquiry may not reveal it. Nevertheless, as a party to the agreement which does not thereby benefit from exemption, the licensor is exposed to the consequences of unenforceability, and so on.

Article 7(3), similar to Article 3(3), disapplies exemption if the parties, without apparent justification, and without it being a requirement present in the agreement, refuse to meet demand in the territory where the product would be bought for resale outside the territory for other common market countries or where the parties otherwise make it difficult for users or resellers to acquire the products from other common market sources (whether by means of intellectual property rights or otherwise).

9-19   Article 7(4) deprives an otherwise exempt agreement of sanctuary if the parties are competitors at the date of the licence and the best endeavours or minimum quantity marketing obligation on the licensee has the effect of preventing the licensee from using competing technologies. This is not a matter that can easily be tested even at the stage of entering into the agreement and yet the status of the agreement, particularly if reliance is placed on territorial restrictions, is critical.

Finally, when an agreement is challenged and a decision is to be made, whether its terms comply with those of a block exemption, the agreement must comply in each and every respect if it is to be enforceable by a national court.[65]

Conclusion

9-20   The single most important criticism of the Regulation is its uncertainty. Criticism initially focused on the use of market share criteria in the body of the white-list and black-list of clauses. Market share calculations are most uncertain when new technologies emerge yet it is precisely these technologies that will contribute most to technical and economic progress. The market in which fledgling science is first licensed is often extremely narrow and specialised and a reference to market share alone to determine market power is inappropriate where no sales of a given technology have taken place. The Commission itself is aware, for example of the sensitivities of defining markets in which pharmaceutical products are to be put because they do not face direct competition and might be said to possess 100 per cent market share before a single penny of research money is recouped by sales. Nevertheless the stipulations of market share remains in various places in the Regulation, albeit not in the core Articles 1 to 4. However the preconditions for exemption and circumstances of withdrawal in Articles 5 and 7 are equally, if not more, undesirable since they concern matters that are incapable of verification except by extremely detailed enquiry and even then the result would continue to be uncertain. The process of making a market share assessment is not straightforward. The Commission has published its Notice on Market Definition[66] as a useful guide to the measurement of market share in terms of demand substitutability (*i.e.* the ability of cus-

---

[65] Case 234/89 *Delimitis v. Henninger Brau* [1991] E.C.R. I-935; [1991] 4 C.M.L.R. 329.
[66] Commission Notice of December 19, 1997 on Market Definition [1997] O.J. C372/03. See Chap. 4 above, for further discussion.

tomers to switch from one product to another in response to price rises) supply substitutability and potential competition.

Another shortcoming of the Regulation is that it is limited in scope, confined as it is to patent and know-how and ancillary rights. The Commission has in certain circumstances adopted Regulations which deal with all categories of intellectual property, namely the Specialisation Regulation and R&D Regulation but these likewise are limited in ambit and are not wide enough to cover licensing arrangements typically found in industry. It is perhaps because the Technology Transfer Regulation in its draft state met with such opposition that the Commission was reluctant to be too ambitious in its reforms even if the result is unsatisfactory both for lawyers and industry.

9-21   For example there is no block exemption dealing with trade marks or copyright even though exclusive trade mark licences may be caught by Article 85(1).[67] In order to determine whether particular clauses in licences of trade marks or copyright infringe Article 85(1) a detailed review must be made of the case law concerning that particular right. In *Moosehead v. Whitbread*[68] the Commission's reasoning provides extremely useful guidance but of course offers no exemption, leaving the parties with no choice when entering into exclusive arrangements potentially caught by Article 85(1) than to go to the trouble, expense and uncertainty of notifying them.

Finally, it is interesting to observe the comparison with the U.S. intellectual property guidelines adopted by the U.S. antitrust enforcement agencies.

"The E.C. Block Exemption and the USIP Guidelines reflect their very different jurisprudential ancestry. In the E.C., the strict construction of the complementary roles of Article 85(1) and Article 85(3), coupled with a virtual anathema for provisions which restrict free movement of trade between Member States has resulted in much less balancing of such purpose and effect factors than in the United States. In contrast, the USIP Guidelines place great emphasis on the factual context in which the licensing operates, that is, its purpose and effect".[69]

COPYRIGHT LICENCES

Copyright generally

9-22   It is clear that the Commission considers that, in principle, the rules of patent and know-how licensing apply also to copyright licensing, even if copyright licences that meet the rigours of the Technology Transfer Regulation are not themselves exempt.[70] However, certain types of licence will be outside Article 85(1) and no exemption will be necessary. Even certain exclusive licences may be outside Article 85(1) if they are "open", and exclusivity is indispensable to the launch of newly developed products on which considerable research and development expenditure has been invested, for reasons of market penetration.[71]

A licence is "open" where the licensor agrees not to grant further licences and agrees not to compete with the licensee in its exclusive territory, provided that no protection is given against competition from other licensees or parallel importers. The ECJ established in *Nungesser v. Commission*[72] that such an open licence would avoid Article 85(1) if the

---

[67] Commission Dec. 90/186 *Moosehead v. Whitbread* [1990] O.J. L100/32; [1991] 4 C.M.L.R. 391.

[68] *ibid.*

[69] Howard W Togt and Ilene Knable Gotts. "A Tale of Two Continents: European Technology Transfer Block Exemption Takes Different Approach From U.S. Counterpart Guidelines" [1996] 6 E.C.L.R. 327.

[70] *Neilson-Hordell/Richmark* XII Report on Competition Policy, p. 73.

[71] *Nungesser v. Commission*, on appeal Case 258/78 [1982] E.C.R. 2015; [1983] 1 C.M.L.R. 278.

[72] *ibid.*

product licensed is new and unfamiliar, if it requires market penetration by exclusivity to recoup significant research costs, and the licence is not for excessive duration.

9-23   These matters are impossible to determine with any certainty and must be treated with care (as illustrated by *Knoll-Hille Form* in which product investment was not considered sufficient to justify exclusivity, although the Commission may have been influenced by the fact that both parties held sizable market shares[73]).

Market share may also be an issue under Article 86 if the licensor is dominant. Similarly, where barriers to entry exist and a copyright owner withholds valuable data which would open a market in such things as compatible products (*IBM Settlement Case*[74]), or TV programme listings (*Magill TV Guide*[75]).

As far as software licensing is concerned, when it was considered at the time of the Council Directive on the legal protection of computer programs ("the Software Directive"[76]) the opportunity was not taken of providing any further clarification or indeed block exemption for agreements relating to copyright in spite of the burgeoning industries in the software, multimedia and entertainment sectors.

Software

9-24   The Commission has stated[77] that it regards products protected by copyright in the same as it regards products protected by patents. Even though software distribution may take the form of product distribution exempt under Regulation 1983/83,[78] software distribution will nevertheless not be exempt because Regulation 1983/83 only applies to "goods for resale".[79] In any event, the nature of software distribution is sufficiently different from that of other products that it typically requires restrictions concerning enforcement of intellectual property, confidentiality and post-term use which, though exempt under the R&D Regulation or Technology Transfer Regulation, are not mentioned in Regulation 1983/83. The supplier will want to ensure that the user enters into contractual relations either with the supplier or the distributor (for the supplier's benefit) to confine software use to particular hardware, limited users, and to prevent reverse engineering or decompilation beyond the limits permitted by statute.[80] All software agreements which contain any such clauses should be treated with care.

Similarly there is no automatic exemption for software under the Technology Transfer Regulation. Use restrictions in the case of exploitation are frequently imposed on the licensee, taking the matter outside the Technology Transfer Regulation. Also software transactions of this sort will not merely be ancillary to the licensing of patents and know-how. Reliance will therefore need to be placed on open exclusivity, following *Nungesser*,[81] but only if justified by the investment in the product in question required in order to promote technical progress (which will be difficult to discern case by case).

9-25   There is some uncertainty concerning the status of licensee restrictions which prevent disclosure and use by a third party, commonly needed to ensure the protection of the software. Such restrictions though common, have been put in doubt in *Société du*

---

[73] Thirteenth Report on Competition Policy (1983) p. 91.
[74] Commission Dec. 84/233 [1984] O.J. C118/24 [1984] 2 C.M.L.R. 345.
[75] Commission Dec. 89/205 [1989] O.J. L78/43; [1989] 4 C.M.L.R. 757.
[76] Council Dir. 91/250 on the legal protection of computer programs [1992] O.J. L122/42.
[77] XII Report on Competition Policy (1982) para. 162.
[78] Commission Reg. 1983/83 on the application of Art. 85(3) of the Treaty to categories of exclusive distribution agreements [1983] O.J. L173/1, amended by [1983] O.J. L281/2.
[79] Art. 1.
[80] S.I. 1992 No. 3233 implementing Council Dir. 91/250.
[81] Case 258/78 *Nungesser v. Commission* [1982] E.C.R. 2015; [1983] 1 C.M.L.R. 278.

Vente de Ciments et Betons v. Kerpen and Kerpen[82] and *Bayo-on-ox*[83] as similar to restrictions that prevent resale. The restrictions should be justifiable on the basis of the ease of copying of software and also the lack of privity of contract between the initial supplier and ultimate user. On the other hand, site restrictions are generally justified since they form the basis of the charging structure and the licence fee.[84]

TRADE MARK LICENCES

9-26   As with copyright, the Commission has confirmed that guidance may be found in the Technology Transfer Regulation to exemptible terms and there is every reason to suppose that the principles of permissible "open licences" established in *Nungesser* will equally apply to trade mark licences. However, the case of *Moosehead v. Whitbread* serves to highlight that in reality the need for caution continues as, in that case, the Commission decided that the exclusivity of the licence was caught by Article 85(1) because it had the consequence of excluding third parties from exploiting the licence where they had the interest and ability to do so.

No block exemption exists for trade mark licences and so parties to unnotified exclusive trade mark licences are at risk. Guidance on particular clauses has been given in the case of *Campari*.[85] Exemption was granted to restrictions guaranteeing quality control, an obligation to purchase essential secret raw materials from the licensor (herbs and colouring), obligations of confidentiality, a ban on sub-licensing or assignment, an export ban outside the Community (but only where reimportation was unlikely), and obligations on the licensee actively to promote the product. The Commission also emphasised that exemption must be sought for non-competition undertakings by the licensor.[86]

9-27   In *Moosehead v. Whitbread*, the Commission exempted an obligation to comply with the licensor's manufacturing instructions to preserve quality, an obligation to obtain raw materials with specific properties (yeast) only from the licensor, obligations of confidentiality and requirements for joint advertising (provided independent advertising is not excluded). However, in that case, the Commission refused to exempt a no-challenge clause although the Commission appears to be relaxing its position on no-challenge clauses over the years, as reflected in the Technology Transfer Regulation.

In short, the position of trade mark licences is as undeveloped as that of copyright licences. Any guidance offered by the Technology Transfer Regulation is only as good as that Regulation itself, which as has been noted is open to criticism.

JOINT VENTURES

Commission measures

9-28   Joint ventures are discussed at greater length in Chapters 8 (above) and 12 (below). This section deals primarily with the Commission's treatment of intellectual property aspects of joint ventures.

The Commission's Notice on co-operation between enterprises[87] did little more than express the view that the exchange of experience with cost-sharing of research and

---

[82] Case 319/82 *Société du Vente de Ciments et Betons v. Kerpen and Kerpen* [1983] E.C.R. 4173; [1985] 1 C.M.L.R. 511.
[83] Commission Dec. 90/38 [1990] O.J. L22/71; [1990] 4 C.M.L.R. 930.
[84] Case 262/81 *Coditel v. Cine Vog Films* [1982] E.C.R. 3381; [1983] 1 C.M.L.R. 49.
[85] Commission Dec. 78/253 [1978] O.J. L70/69; [1978] 2 C.M.L.R. 397.
[86] *Campari* para. 73, *Moosehead* para. 16.2.
[87] [1968] O.J. C75/3. See Chap. 8 above for further discussion.

development falling short of industrial application are outside Article 85(1). However, Article 85(1) will apply where independent research and development activities are restricted in any way or utilisation of the results is limited. These are precisely the terms on which parties to research and development agreements will want clarification. While the Notice has some value, it is limited by virtue of having been largely superseded by the R&D Regulation.

9-29 Competition law considerations arise in joint ventures for various reasons although clearly much depends upon the structure of the joint venture, the form and substance of the particular licensing and other contractual arrangements between the joint venture and the joint venture parents, and the economic context in which it is to operate. First, if the joint venture parents are competitors, the result of cooperation might be to prevent them competing with each other in the field of the activities of the joint venture—if each parent alone is in a position to fulfil the tasks assigned to the joint venture (based on its own resources and technical and financial risk). If they forfeit their capability to do so, competition may be adversely affected. Secondly, third parties who traditionally supply or purchase from the parents might be adversely affected by the joint venture where the selling or purchasing power of the joint venture is strengthened by combining the supplying or purchasing capability of the parents. Also, on the supply side (sales joint venture) the choice available to purchasers would be limited; on the demand side (purchasing joint ventures) the outlets available to suppliers would be limited. Thirdly, if the joint venture activities concern manufacturing rather than purchasing or sales, the result would be fewer manufacturers, therefore less product choice and competition. The competition justification for joint ventures in these cases is often that it is impossible economically to enter the market or to stay competitive without operating though a joint venture.

As joint ventures can take any form they do not readily lend themselves to automatic exemption by way of block exemption Regulation although the Commission has provided it in the form of the R&D Regulation and Specialisation Regulation. As those Regulations are specific to particular forms of agreement the Commission has issued more general guidance in the form of the Notice concerning the assessment of co-operative joint ventures.[88] The Commission distinguishes between the competition effects of the creation of the joint venture, which result from its mere existence, and the effects of ancillary contractual arrangements that surround it and which might be restrictive of competition. If the creation of the joint venture itself is outside Article 85(1), so also are the ancillary restrictions if they are a necessary means of achieving the joint venture aims.[89] The emphasis in determining whether restrictions are permitted is on whether they limit the freedom of action in the market of the participating undertakings.[90] Justified restrictions might include the following:

    (a) Where the joint venture is granted a licence by the parents:

        (i) licence exclusivity (usually) if limited in duration[91];

        (ii) a ban on the joint venture dealing in products that compete with the licensed products[92]; and

        (iii) field of use reservations.

---

[88] [1993] O.J. C43/2. For further detail see Chap. 8 above.
[89] Paras 66 and 67 of the Notice.
[90] Para. 65 of the Notice.
[91] However great, care should always be taken with exclusivity restrictions in joint ventures.
[92] Commission Dec. 87/100 *Mitchell Cotts/Sofiltra* [1987] O.J. L41/31, [1988] 4 C.M.L.R. 111. Para. 72 of the Notice.

These define the limits to the cooperation and ensure that it is not jeopardised by other activities.

(b) Where the joint venture concerns production, an obligation to supply to or purchase from the parents, provided this is of limited duration.[93]

(c) Non-competition covenants from the parents in the activities of the joint venture.

The range of unjustified restrictions would include:

(d) Restrictions on quantities, prices or customers; and

(e) Export bans.

Research and development generally

9-30 The obvious reasons why research and development joint ventures should be treated sympathetically by the Commission are that innovation is risky and expensive and would be wasted if duplicated by different entities. Joint venture research simulates and speeds innovation. Research and development joint ventures more than any other joint ventures will be formulated by issues of intellectual property ownership and licensing. The Commission is concerned about controlling the terms of exclusive licences and this is already apparent from the terms of the R&D Regulation. Concern stems from the fact that often research and development joint ventures are between large firms at a similar level of production, in the same industry sector. The Commission therefore aims to ensure that technical progress results and does not serve to produce monopoly profits for the participants. The Commission has repeated a preference for separate research and development activities by independent entities, since this is bound to result in greater consumer choice (assuming separate products emerge), and is concerned also to ensure that parties are not prevented by joint research and development from getting a competitive advantage over each other. For example a cross-licence of research results carried out independently of the joint venture would eliminate the competitive edge and be unnecessarily restrictive.[94] This is clearly only likely to occur where the parties are competitors, and the matter must be dealt with by exemption. Even if the parties are not competitors, the Commission will still wish to preserve freedom of action on the part of the participants. A reasonable restriction on independent research activities confined to the joint venture sphere of activities is likely to be exempt but any restriction going beyond those activities is unlikely to be exempt.

Joint venture licensing

9-31 The Commission will certainly favour a research and development joint venture between non-competitors where independent product development by either of them is unlikely. The case of Elopak[95] concerned joint production in such circumstances. ODIN was the joint venture vehicle of two carton suppliers—Elopak and Metal Box—established to carry out research and development to develop a particular carton for UHT products. ODIN was also to produce and sell the developed product. The parents granted ODIN licences of their own technology which were exclusive for the scope of project

---

[93] Para. 74 of the Notice.
[94] Commission Dec. 76/172 *Bayer/Gist-Brocades* [1976] O.J. L30/13; [1976] 1 C.M.L.R. D98.
[95] Commission Dec. 90/410 [1990] O.J. L209/15; [1991] 4 C.M.L.R. 832.

activities. The parents would in turn be granted non-exclusive licences of the results for activities other than those given to ODIN. The Commission held that the exclusive licences to ODIN were a necessary and ancillary restriction to the start-up and functioning of the joint venture and were suitably confined to a narrow field relevant to the project.

Licences granted to the joint venture

9-32   The exclusive licences to ODIN were justified according to the Commission as a guarantee by each parent to the other that it would devote its full effort to the project, whose success required this level of commitment to compensate for the accompanying financial, technical and commercial risks. The duration of the exclusive licence went beyond the start-up period of the joint venture operations (covering the life of ODIN itself) and this was considered not to infringe Article 85(1) because:

(i)   the combination of both parents' technology, added to the research and development work of ODIN, was required for the project work and even for subsequent project manufacture and marketing (in order to keep the product technology at a competitive edge);

(ii) there were no unnecessary restrictions on ODIN such as controls on price, volume, customer or territory; and

(iii) the exclusivity was limited in scope to the closely defined field of the agreement and the parents were not restricted in research and development activities in products closely related or even competing with the ODIN products.

Licences granted by the joint venture to its parents

9-33   The extent to which research and development joint ventures may go further than the research and development stage to cover licensing of the research and development results to the parents has been the subject of the R&D Regulation which grew out of developments in Commission reasoning over many years as reflected in a number of cases.

In *Brown/Boveri* and *NGK*,[96] the Commission exempted a licence of project results granted by the joint venture to its parents which, for the European parent, was exclusive in the Community and USA.

9-34   Post-termination licences may be granted of restrictive scope when a partner leaves the joint venture provided that the outgoing partner is not restricted in the use of technology it was previously entitled to use (as it should be able to use this to compete freely).[97] A ban on use of joint venture project results following withdrawal by a parent would in all likelihood constitute a restriction essential to the existence of the joint venture.

Royalty payments between partners on independent exploitation of project results by them would infringe Article 85(1). However, remuneration for the research and development expenditure and risk would not be caught by Article 85(1), nor would royalty payments only by one of the parties where the other is not technically capable of exploiting (*Beecham/Parke Davis*).[98]

---

[96] *Re the Agreements between BBC Brown and Boveri and NGK Insulators Limited* Commission Dec. 88/541 [1988] O.J. L301/68; [1989] 4 C.M.L.R. 610.
[97] Commission Dec. 86/666 *Carbon Gas Technologie* [1983] O.J. L376/67; [1984] 2 C.M.L.R. 275.
[98] Commission Dec. 79/298 [1979] O.J. L70/11; [1979] 2 C.M.L.R. 157.

Licences granted by joint venture parents to third parties

9-35   Any restriction on the ability of joint venture participants to license the project results to third parties will be caught by Article 85(1) but if confined to the field of activities of the joint venture it should be exempt (*EMI/Jungheinrich*).[99] This would include a general requirement that the consent of a party be given before another may grant such a licence.

Summary

9-36   These cases and principles illustrate the complexity and uncertainty of the status of research and development agreements even if the Commission is generally supportive of them. Emphasis correctly is placed on the economic reality of the market place in which agreements operate, including market shares, market power and similar. Nevertheless, for the purchaser of a company or business participating in joint venture research, whether as parent or investor in the joint venture, or the joint venture vehicle itself, the position concerning the enforceability of the essential commercial intellectual property restrictions is uncertain. Analysis will not produce a definitive answer, as the economic context cannot be easily assessed and the Commission's reasoning is still developing. In order to clarify these principles in the case of certain commonly found research and development agreements the Commission published the R&D Regulation as a means of conferring automatic exemption on a limited range of research and development agreements.

PARTICULAR R&D AGREEMENTS

9-37   The R&D Regulation applies to agreements for the joint research and development of products or processes with or without joint exploitation of the results. It therefore differs from the Notice on co-operation between enterprises[1] in that it deals with "applied" research and development agreements (*i.e.* dealing also with the exploitation of results) rather than "pure" research agreements. The scope of exploitation originally permitted in the R&D Regulation was broadened by Regulation 151/93 and is seen as a useful extension to what would otherwise have been a Regulation of such narrow application that it would have been of little practical value. Another useful aspect of the R&D Regulation is that Recital 14 expressly permits exploitation within the scope of other block exemptions with the result that (within the limits stated in the body of the R&D Regulation) these may (in appropriate circumstances) in effect be bolted on to span both the research and development phase and subsequent exploitation phases with third parties, whether by way of patent licence or exclusive distribution.

The preconditions of exemption in Article 2 require the research and development work to be carried out according to a clearly defined programme, setting out its objectives and field.[2] All the parties must have access to the results.[3] If it is a pure research and development agreement, all parties must be unrestricted in their exploitation of the results (except to the extent exempt under Articles 4 and 5).[4] Joint exploitation (and any exempt restrictions) must relate only to "results" which are protected by intellectual property rights or constitute know-how which substantially contribute to technical or economic

---

[99] *EMI/Jungheinrich* XXVII Report on Competition Policy (1987) point 119 [1978] 1 C.M.L.R. 395.
[1] Commission Notice of July 29, 1968 on co-operation between enterprises [1968] O.J C75/3.
[2] Art. 2(a).
[3] Art. 2(b).
[4] Art. 2(c).

progress such that the results are decisive for the manufacture of the contract products or the application of the contract process.[5] Background technology will be included in this if "decisive" for manufacture.

9-38   Article 3 deals with the duration of exemption for agreements, depending on whether the parties are competing manufacturers. This itself is a matter of judgement and difficult to verify and could well change rapidly over time. It might even be precipitated by a change of control resulting from acquisition.

If the parties are not competing manufacturers of products that will be improved or replaced by the contract products, then exemption will be for the duration of the research and development programme and, if the results are jointly exploited, five years following first product marketing within the common market. If the parties are competing manufacturers, exemption is only allowed for the above duration (by virtue of Article 3(2)) if at the time of entering into the agreement the parties' combined market share is less than 20 per cent in the common market or a substantial part (for products that are improved or replaced by the contract products). Following expiry of that period, exemption will continue under Article 3(3), but only for so long as the parties' market share does not exceed 20 per cent of production of the contract goods.

9-39   The Regulation underwent amendment in 1992[6] such that if product distribution is entrusted to one of the parties, a joint undertaking or a third party, exemption may still apply (for five years) but only if the parties' production of those products is less than 10 per cent of the market for all such products in the common market or a substantial part.[7]

The list in Article 4 permits a ban on independent research in the programme field or closely related field[8]; a ban on similar research and development agreements with third parties in that field[9]; an obligation to procure products from the parties or designated third party[10]; a ban on the manufacture of contract products in territories reserved for other parties[11]; field of use restrictions on manufacture (if the parties are not competitors)[12]; a ban on active product sales for five years from first marketing in territories reserved for other parties[13]; distribution restrictions when one party has exclusive distribution rights (but only if the distributor does not sell goods competing with the joint venture goods)[14]; similarly with the appointment of a joint undertaking or third party undertaking[15]; the grant of exclusive distribution rights for particular territories within the common market to joint or third parties but only if they do not manufacture or sell competing goods[16]; and finally, a reciprocal obligation to disclose and license improvements non-exclusively.[17]

9-40   The list in Article 5 goes further and permits an obligation to disclose technology for the purpose of carrying out the project and exploiting the results[18]; a corresponding obligation on the recipient to confine its use to those purposes[19]; an obligation to

---

[5] Art. 2(d).
[6] Group Exemptions (Amendment) Reg. 151/93 [1993] O.J. L21/8; [1993] 4 C.M.L.R. 151.
[7] Art. 3(3)(a).
[8] Art. 4(1)(a).
[9] Art. 4(1)(b).
[10] Art. 4(1)(c).
[11] Art. 4(1)(d).
[12] Art. 4(1)(e).
[13] Art. 4(1)(f).
[14] Art. 4(f)(a).
[15] Art. 4(f)(b).
[16] Art. 4(f)(c).
[17] Art. 4(1)(g).
[18] Art. 5(1)(a).
[19] Art. 5(1)(b).

maintain intellectual property rights[20] and inform each other of infringements,[21] and confidentiality obligations for received or jointly-developed technology during and after expiry of the agreement.[22] Article 5 also permits royalty obligations but only to compensate for unequal project contributions[23] provided this does not result in any disincentive to making sales,[24] an obligation to share royalties received from third parties with other parties[25] and an obligation to supply other parties with minimum quantities or observe minimum standards.[26]

Blacklisted in Article 6 are restrictions on the parties' freedom to carry out independent research and development in unconnected fields or even connected fields after project completion[27]; no challenge clauses after project completion relating to contributed or developed technology[28]; quantity restrictions on manufacture or processing[29]; price restrictions on products sold to third parties[30]; restrictions on customers to be served[31]; restrictions[f] on active marketing after expiry of the period in Article 4(1)(f)[32]; restrictions against parties contracting manufacture to third parties,[33] and finally (as with the Technology Transfer Regulation) any agreement or arrangement which requires the parties to refuse without objective reason to meet demand from those who wish to market products in the common market or make it difficult for users or dealers to obtain the products from each other within the common market. Parallel imports must therefore not be impeded and this is the mirror image of Articles 3(3) and 7(2) of the Technology Transfer Regulation.

As with the Technology Transfer Regulation, exemption may be withdrawn in a wide range of circumstances[34] equivalent to those in the Technology Transfer Regulation.[35]

NOTIFICATION PROCEDURE

9-41 Mention of Articles 85(1) and 85(3) would be incomplete without reference to the notification procedure and its shortcomings. Form A/B requires detailed information that its preparation frequently occupies weeks of management time which may be regarded as disproportionate in the case of undeveloped or newly-launched technology, particularly when owned by start-up companies. The Commission's Notice on agreements of minor importance[36] provides a reason in such circumstances for not notifying an agreement but the uncertainties of market share definition and calculation are such that an agreement may easily be challenged as being above the market share *de minimis* levels if it concerns technology that is sufficiently innovative to be in a market of its own (or at least not directly substitutable with other products).

---

[20] Art. 5(2)(c).
[21] Art. 5(1)(e).
[22] Art. 5(1)(d).
[23] Art. 5(1)(f).
[24] Commission Dec. 79/298 *Beecham/Parke-Davis* [1979] O.J. L70/11; [1979] 2 C.M.L.R. 157.
[25] Art. 5(1)(g).
[26] Art. 5(1)(h).
[27] Art. 6(a).
[28] Art. 6(b).
[29] Art. 6(c).
[30] Art. 6(d).
[31] Art. 6(e).
[32] Art. 6(f).
[33] Art. 6(g).
[34] Art. 10.
[35] Art. 7.
[36] Commission Notice of September 3, 1986 [1986] O.J. C231/2, amended by Commission Notice of December 7, 1994 on agreements of minor importance [1994] O.J. C368/20.

ARTICLE 86

9-42   Quite apart from considerations of Article 85(1), an exclusive licence may fall foul of Article 86 if granted to a licensee which is dominant. Even if granted to a licensee which is not dominant at the date of the agreement, if the licence is subsequently acquired by a company that is dominant or which owns alternative technology, this may result in infringement of Article 86.[37] For further examples of agreements and practices concerning the use or exploitation of intellectual property that may infringe the Chapter II prohibition or Article 86, see Chapter 2, "*Make the conclusion of contracts subject to acceptance by the other parties of supplementary obligations which, by their nature, according to commercial usage, have no connection with the subject of [such] contracts*" and Chapter 3, "*Limiting production, markets or technical development to the prejudice of consumers*" above.

---

[37] Case T–51/89 *Tetra Pak Rausing SA v. Commission* [1990] E.C.R. II-309; [1991] 4 C.M.L.R. 334.

CHAPTER 10

Exhaustion of Intellectual Property Rights

INTRODUCTION

10-01　The doctrine of exhaustion has emerged because of significant differences that have existed (and continue to exist) in the national laws of Member States, not only concerning activities within national boundaries (infringement) but activities outside as well. While the harmonisation process continues, the ECJ interprets and enforces the provisions of the E.C. Treaty in such a way as to balance the free movement requirements of Article 30 of the E.C. Treaty with the requirements of intellectual protection recognised in Article 36.

Articles 30 and 36 of the E.C. Treaty

10-02　The scope of any monopoly (or quasi-monopoly) conferred nationally by means of intellectual property protection must be read subject to the principles of free movement established in Article 30 of the E.C. Treaty. Article 30 has already been referred to in Chapter 1 above, but requires elaboration. It contains a simple prohibition against quantitative restrictions on imports and exports between Member States as well as measures having equivalent effect. The language is so broad ("all restrictions on imports and measures having equivalent effect shall . . . be prohibited between Member States") that it is necessary to make an exception for intellectual property rights which typically include as infringing acts the act of importation. For example infringement occurs on the importation of infringing copies of a design in the case of copyright and design right works,[1] the importation of infringing products falling within product or process patent claims of the country of importation,[2] the importation of goods bearing a registered trade mark of the country of importation[3] or the importation of goods to which a registered design of the country of importation has been applied.[4] The ban on importation without the consent of the rights holder is clearly a matter caught by Article 30.

Article 36 of the E.C. Treaty provides the necessary gateway for the exercise of intellectual property rights. Article 36 reads:

> "The provisions of Article 30 . . . shall not preclude prohibitions or restrictions on imports, exports or goods in transit justified on grounds of public morality, public policy, or public security; the protection of health and life of humans, animals or plants; the protection of national treasures possessing artistic, historic or archaeological value or the protection of industrial and commercial property. Such

---

[1]　ss. 22 and 227 of the Copyright Designs and Patents Act (CDPA) 1988.
[2]　ss. 60(1)(a) and 60(1)(c) of the Patents Act 1997.
[3]　s. 10(4)(c) of the Trade Marks Act 1994.
[4]　s. 7 of the Registered Designs Act 1949, as amended by s. 268 CDPA 1988.

prohibitions or restrictions shall not, however, constitute a means of arbitrary discrimination or a disguised restriction of trade between Member States."

10-03   At the heart of what is termed the "doctrine of exhaustion" is the inter-relation between the non-importation restrictions of intellectual property rights and Articles 30 and 36. In the early case of *Deutsche Grammophon Gesellschaft mbH v. Metro-SB-Grossmarkte GmbH & Co KG,*[5] the ECJ stated:

> "If a right . . . is relied upon to prevent the marketing in a Member State of products distributed by the holder of the right or with his consent on the territory of another Member State on the sole grounds that such distribution did not take place on the national territory, such a prohibition, which would legitimise the isolation of national markets, would be repugnant to the essential purpose of the Treaty, which is to unite national markets into a single market".[6]

It is to be noted that Article 222 of the E.C. Treaty preserves the national effect of intellectual property law by stating that it shall "in no way prejudice the rules in Member States governing the system of property ownership".

National intellectual property laws

10-04   Intellectual property is territorial in nature, formulated and enforced by the laws of the state which confers protection. For example a patent offers protection on the patentee only in the country in which the patent has been granted. At its widest, a patent is only national in scope (to prevent things being done in that state) in spite of the European Patent Convention ("EPC") harmonisation measures and even terminology which refers to a "European Patent". Protection is merely conferred state by state in territories according to the rules of each state which confer monopoly or quasi-monopoly protection.[7]

Each state has also historically developed principles concerning the point at which those rights are said to be exhausted. For example in the United Kingdom, once a patented product is sold, the purchaser could deal with it anywhere in the world subject only to restrictions of which the purchaser is given notice (*Betts v. Willmott*)[8]:

> "When a man has purchased an article he expects to have control over it, and there must be some clear and explicit agreement to the contrary to justify the vendor in saying that he has not given the purchaser his consent to sell the article, or to use it wherever he pleases as against himself".[9]

Betts v. Willmott is clearly an old case and must now be read subject to the limits on the freedom of patentees to impose contractual restrictions within the constraints of Articles 85(1) and 85(3) of the E.C. Treaty and the developed case law of the ECJ in connection with Articles 30 and 36.

10-05   The principles stated in *Betts v. Willmott* (and in subsequent cases[10]) have been

---

[5] Case 78/70 *Deutsche Grammophon Gesellschaft mbH v. Metro-SB-Grossmarkte GmbH & Co KG* [1971] E.C.R. 487; [1971] C.M.L.R. 631.
[6] *ibid.* para. 12.
[7] The only Community-wide right is the Community Trade Mark which became obtainable in 1996. Council Reg. 40/94 on the Community trade mark [1994] O.J. L 11/1.
[8] [1870] L.R.6 Ch. App 239.
[9] Penultimate para. of the Judgment in *Betts v. Wilmott* at p. 245.
[10] *National Phonographic Co of Australia v. Merck* [1911] 28 R.P.C. 229; *Gillette v. Bernstein* [1942] 1 Ch.D. 45.

confirmed more recently in *Roussel Uclaf SA v. Hockley International Limited & Another*[11] in which Jacob J. stated that it is open to the patentee to stipulate limitations on any implied licence and these will be binding on the person supplied, as well as on subsequent dealers in the product, provided that notice of those limitations is brought to the attention of every person down the chain. This judgment is not immune from criticism[12] and reflects a Common Law approach to the doctrine of exhaustion. Applied at the national level, the doctrine in effect resulted in worldwide exhaustion, subject only to limits on any implied licence that are effectively imposed by notice to prevent export or reimportation.

By contrast, many continental European countries (such as Germany) have resisted any concept of international exhaustion of patents, preferring instead to entitle the patentee to resist imports of products first sold outside their borders.

Inconsistency has therefore developed across the national laws of Member States concerning the application of principles of exhaustion; in particular whether international exhaustion is to be recognised and, if so, to what extent. In some countries (again Germany) international exhaustion has not been applied in the case of patents but has in the case of trade marks (at least until the implementation of Council Directive 89/104 to approximate the laws of Member States relating to trade marks[13] (the "Trademark Directive")).

The emergence of exhaustion under Articles 30 to 36

10-06 The doctrine of exhaustion developed by ECJ case law on the subject of Articles 30 to 36 historically focused little attention on the operation of the national law. The case of *Silhouette Internationale Schmied GmbH and Co KG v. Hartlauer Handelsgesellschaft mbH*[14] ("the *Silhouette* Case") highlighted the fact that the effect of inconsistent national treatment of international exhaustion would be that:

> "the same products could be the subject of parallel imports into one Member State but not into another, a result incompatible with the internal market".[15]

The following sections of this Chapter will analyse the effect of the application of Articles 30 to 36 upon the value and scope of intellectual property protection and the need to establish a marketing strategy that takes best advantage of Articles 30 to 36 taking in turn patents, copyright, registered designs and trade marks.

PATENTS

10-07 The commercial pressure for parallel imports and patent protection are best illustrated by the market factors that apply in the pharmaceutical industry, for three main reasons. First, the costs of research, development and of obtaining regulatory approval are considerable for bringing a medicinal product to market and accordingly the price of pharmaceutical products (and therefore potential profit) is generally high. The start up costs and other barriers to entry for a would-be parallel importer are low. Secondly,

---

[11] [1996] R.P.C. 441.

[12] For example, it is at odds with the decision in *Badische Anilin und Soda Fabrik v. Isler* [1906] R.P.C. 173 that "if a person innocently buys a patented invention from a licensee and uses it not knowing that there are limits on the licence . . . he is equally an infringer".

[13] Council Dir. 89/104 [1989] O.J. L 40/1.

[14] Case 355/96 *Silhouette International Schmied GmnH & Co. KG v. Hartlauer Handelsgesellschaft mbH* [1998] E.C.R. Judgment of the Court Transcript July 16, 1998.

[15] Para. 42 of the Opinion of Jacobs A.G. delivered on January 29, 1998 in the *Silhouette* case.

pharmaceutical products are generally small, light and easily transported, making them a ready candidate for cross-border trade. Thirdly, the incentive for parallel importation exists in many countries because of price differentials that have resulted from government price control measures adopted pursuant to their national healthcare policies. The price of products in one country may therefore be fixed at a level considerably higher than that in a neighbouring country.

An essential part of the formulation of any marketing strategy will be the selection of countries for patent protection and subsequent maintenance. The patent strategy is crucial to research and development in the pharmaceutical industry in which product development may last a decade or more before a single sale is made, in which the number of drug "hits" is extremely low when compared to the "misses" and where the patent term is relatively short given that the underlying inventions are often made, and the patent term commences, many years before the product may be marketed. The result is that a significant proportion of the patent term and corresponding patent filing and maintenance expense is occupied with pre-sales research and development, clinical trials, regulatory approval and similar. Supplementary Protection Certificates under Regulation 1768/92[16] go some way towards extending the life of pharmaceutical patents beyond their normal term in recognition of the long gestation period of patented pharmaceutical products. Regulation 1768/92 was aimed at prospering the pharmaceutical industry but in line with a programme of harmonisation heralded by the EPC.[17] Nevertheless, the lack of uniformity in the national patent law of Member States, compounded by government price intervention has led to the testing of the principles of exhaustion in a number of cases concerning pharmaceutical patents. The ECJ has traditionally applied Article 30 by reference to notions of the "specific subject matter" of intellectual property".

The "specific subject matter" of patents

10-08 In *Centrafarm BV et Adriaan de Peijper v. Sterling Drug Inc*[18] ("*Centrafarm v. Sterling Drug*"), the ECJ held that a claim of patent infringement could only be used as the basis of preventing importation of goods if necessary to protect the "specific subject matter" of the intellectual property. The "specific subject matter" of a patent differs from what might be described as the "function" of a patent. The function of a patent has been described as "a temporary exclusive right on a new product or process to reward . . . creative effort".[19] The limits to the exercise of that exclusive right were spelled out in *Centrafarm v. Sterling Drug* in the statement by the ECJ that:

> "a derogation from the principle of free movement is not, however, justified where the product has been brought onto the market in a lawful manner by the patentee himself or with his consent in the Member State from which it has been imported, in particular in the case of a proprietor of parallel patents".[20]

The issue of consent has its origins in the recognition that the patentee alone has the right to do, or authorise others to do, anything that would otherwise amount to patent infringement, including sales and importation. The right to first market (which encompasses both sales and importation) is not however exercised when the patentee does not

---

[16] Council Reg. (1768/92 concerning the creation of a supplementary protection certificate for medicinal products [1992] O.J. L182/1.
[17] See for example the measures discussed in *Trade Marks* below.
[18] Case 15/74 *Centrafarm BV et Adriaan de Peijper v. Sterling Drug Inc* [1974] E.C.R. 1147; [1974] 2 C.M.L.R. 480.
[19] I Govaere "The Use and Abuse of Intellectual Property Rights in E.C. Law" 1996 para. 4.24.
[20] Issue 2, para. 11 of the Judgment of the ECJ in *Centrafarm v. Sterling Drug*.

make that marketing choice voluntarily, as in *Pharmon v. Hoechst*,[21] in which the reimported goods had been marketed pursuant to a compulsory patent licence, because:

> "such a measure deprives the patent proprietor of his right to determine freely the conditions under which he markets his products".[22]

10-09 Consent is obviously adequately given by a proprietor by means of a licence or assignment. Consent is also considered to be given between entities under common control (*Centrafarm v. Sterling Drug*).

The cases of *Merck & Co Inc., Merck Sharp & Dohme Ltd and Merck Sharp & Dohme International Services BV v. Primecrown Ltd, Ketan Himatlal Mehta, Bharat Himatlal Mehta and Necessity Supplies Ltd and Beecham Group plc v. Europharm of Worthing Ltd*[23] ("*Merck v. Primecrown*"), raised a number of fundamental issues concerning the scope and extent of the doctrine of exhaustion and gave the ECJ the opportunity to review its existing policy.

10-10 The review began with the interpretation of the ECJ's judgment in the case of *Merck & Co Inc v. Stephar BV and Petrus Stephanus Exler*[24] ("*Merck v. Stephar*"). In that case, Merck held patents in the Netherlands for a pharmaceutical product, but not in Italy, where patents were not then available. Merck claimed to be entitled to prevent imports from Italy on the basis that no rights can be said to be exhausted where they do not exist. The ECJ rejected this argument on the grounds that Merck had freely chosen to market the products in Italy. Patent rights could not be invoked to prevent parallel importation of goods sold, even in unpatented territories, by the patent proprietor or with his consent. Considerable emphasis was placed on the choice of first marketing in that case:

> "It is for the proprietor of the patent to decide, in the light of all the circumstances, under what conditions he will market his product, including the *possibility* of marketing it in a Member State where the law does not provide patent protection for the product in question. If he decides to do so he must then accept the consequences of his choice as regards the free movement of the product within the common market, which is a fundamental principle forming part of the legal and economic circumstances which must be taken into account by the proprietor of the patent in determining the manner in which his exclusive right will be exercised.".[25]

The fundamental issue in *Merck v. Primecrown* was whether *Merck v. Stephar* was good law. Similar facts arose in *Merck v. Primecrown* except that Merck relied on patents held in the United Kingdom to prevent importation from Spain and Portugal where pharmaceuticals were not at the relevant time patentable under the laws of those countries in spite of their accession to the Community. Maximum prices were set at extremely low levels. Although the products were marketed in Spain and Portugal with their consent, Merck argued that patent rights could not thereby be said to be exhausted. They also claimed that the principle in *Merck v. Stephar* should be limited in the case of pharmaceutical manufacturers because:

---

[21] Case 19/84 *Pharmon v. Hoechst* [1985] E.C.R. 2281; [1985] 3 C.M.L.R. 775.
[22] Issue 2, para. 25 of the Judgment of the ECJ in *Pharmon v. Hoechst*.
[23] Joined Cases C–267/95 & C–268/95 *Merck v. Primecrown* [1996] E.C.R. I-6285.
[24] Case 187/80 *Merck v. Stephar* [1981] E.C.R. 2063; [1981] 3 C.M.L.R. 465.
[25] Para. 11 of the Judgment of the ECJ in *Merck v. Stephar*. Emphasis added.

(i)   the effects of price control legislation in one country are otherwise exported to other Member States (following *Pharmon v. Hoechst*)[26];

(ii) the monopoly revenues of the pharmaceutical industry would be sufficiently undermined at a time when E.C. measures had been supportive of the industry by means of the Supplementary Protection Certificate; and

(iii) there is at least an ethical obligation to make medicinal products available which does not leave pharmaceutical companies free choice to withhold them from unpatented countries as part of a marketing strategy.

10-11   The ECJ ruled that the fact that the products were unpatentable in Spain and Portugal but were in the United Kingdom could not be the basis for preventing imports of products from Spain and Portugal into the United Kingdom. The ECJ adopted what might be said to be a formal and legalist approach to these issues and refused to adjust the ratio of the *Merck v. Stephar* decision founded on the principle that the patentee has free marketing choice and must bear the consequences of that choice. The special circumstances pleaded for pharmaceutical companies did not qualify for a derogation from the rule in *Merck v. Stephar*. However the ECJ commented that exceptions would be allowed in the case of marketing in a Member State under genuine existing legal obligations. Mandatory price control in Member States did not fall within that exception, nor did a mere ethical obligation.

At this point two observations should be made. First, the ECJ is likely to have been persuaded that the problem caused by the transitional provisions relating to the accession of Spain and Portugal was one unlikely to dog the pharmaceutical industry for long since all Member States now allow for patentability of pharmaceutical products and the facts of *Merck v. Primecrown* are unlikely to be repeated. However, the effects of the *Merck v. Primecrown* decision are likely to be felt for the patent life of those products which are caught by the transitional provisions relating to the accession of Spain and Portugal, or any other country in the future acceding with patent laws which are unharmonised. Anomalies of accession are likely to be significant given that at present 10 countries from Central and Eastern Europe have applied for membership of the European Union.[27] Secondly, the ECJ did not pursue an issue canvassed at some length by Fennelly A.G. in *Merck v. Primecrown* concerning the consequences of their decision in relation to the marketing plans of pharmaceutical companies. This is especially important given that the central issue in *Merck v. Primecrown* is not purely an historic one.

"The current logical implications of *Merck v. Stephar* not only encourage pharmaceutical companies to partition Spain and Portugal from the rest of the Community by withdrawing from those markets, but this also constitutes a potential copyists' charter for those two markets which will last at least until research orientated pharmaceutical companies are able to bring through to the marketing stage on those markets novel and therefore patentable products".[28]

---

[26] It was noted in Case 19/85 *Pharmon v. Hoechst* [1985] E.C.R. 2281; [1985] 3 C.M.L.R. 775 that schemes for compulsory licences are a matter for national legislation and that if the doctrine of exhaustion were to apply to permit exports of products made under a compulsory licence it would amount, in effect, to exporting the national patent legislation concerning compulsory licences.

[27] "Agenda 2000: For a Stronger and Wider Europe 1997", European Commission.

[28] Para. 112 of the Opinion of Fennelly A.G. in *Merck v. Primecrown*.

The significance of market conditions

10-12   In *Merck v. Primecrown*, the ECJ stated that:

"although the imposition of price controls is indeed a factor which may, in certain conditions, distort competition between Member States, that circumstance cannot justify a derogation from the principle of free movement of goods. It is well settled that distortions caused by different price legislation in a Member State must be remedied by measures taken by the Community authorities and not by the adoption by another Member State of measures incompatible with the rules of free movement of goods".[29]

Numerous Community harmonisation measures have been taken specifically in the pharmaceutical sector. (For example Council Directives 65/65 and 93/39[30] and Council Regulation 2309/93[31] created a European Agency concerned with Community-wide standards of quality, safety and efficacy and for product authorisation, Council Directives 92/28[32] and 92/27[33] were directed at marketing standards for the advertising and labelling of products, and Directive 87/21 offers an abridged procedure enabling the applicant to refer to "essentially similar" results from pre-existing medicinal product authorisations of other proprietors to avoid repetition of pharmacological and toxicological tests and clinical trials.) Nevertheless, national regulatory regimes remain in place for pharmaceutical products. In *Merck v. Primecrown*, Fennelly A.G. perceived that the effect is:

"to export not merely the product but also the commercial consequences of the legislative choice made by the exporting State to the importing State because the patentee has made a commercial choice to sell the product even in a less protected environment".[34]

10-13   The economic structure of the market was dismissed by the ECJ in *Merck v. Primecrown* and pharmaceutical companies were reminded by the ECJ of their decision to choose a marketing strategy to take account of the E.C. rules of exhaustion. The risks of running directly into claims based on Article 85(1)and 86 are clear, and have recently been illustrated by the case of *Merck, Organnon, Glaxo v. Commission*.[35] In that case, a sales system applied a 12 per cent discount to wholesalers on sales of products destined for the United Kingdom. The discount was structured merely to reflect a scheme operated by the United Kingdom government and therefore did not apply to sales destined for other countries where no similar scheme exists. Following the threat of Commission proceedings, the discount scheme had to be abandoned. A similar situation arose in the case concerning the drug *Adalat*[36] ("*Adalat*"). Nevertheless, the Commission fined Bayer AG a total of three million ECUs for imposing a system of monitoring exports of their Adalat drug and limiting supplies to wholesalers to meet domestic demand only. The

---

[29] *ibid.*, para. 47 of the Judgment of the ECJ.
[30] Council Dir. 93/39 amending Dirs 65/65, 75/318 and 75/319 in respect of medicinal products[1993] O.J. L214/22.
[31] Council Reg. 2309/93 laying down community procedures for the authorisation and supervision of medicinal products for human and veterinary use and establishing a European agency for the evaluation of medicinal products [1993] O.J. L214/1.
[32] Council Dir. 92/28 on the advertising of medicinal products for human use [1992] O.J. L113/13.
[33] Council Dir. 92/27 on the labelling of medicinal products for human use and on package leaflets[1992] O.J. L113/8.
[34] Para. 108 of the Opinion of Fennelly A.G. in *Merck v. Primecrown*.
[35] Order of the CFI of June 3, 1997, Case T–60/96 [1996] E.C.R. II-849.
[36] Commission Dec. 96/478 [1996] O.J. L201/1; [1996] 5 C.M.L.R. 416.

Commission inferred an agreement between Bayer and the wholesalers contrary to Article 85(1) on the grounds that the latter understood and were influenced by Bayer's "true motives" in imposing the monitoring system. That was in spite of the fact, as the Commission recognised, that:

> "differences in price fixing methods and refund arrangements mean that there are wide disparities in pharmaceutical product prices in Member States".[37]

The significance of the judgment in *Merck v. Primecrown*, in the light of these cases is three-fold. First, it would appear that enterprises are not as free as the ECJ might suggest, to adopt a market strategy that takes account of the economic market conditions of the pharmaceutical sector. Even if adopted unilaterally, the risks of inference of an agreement caught by Article 85(1) are high. Secondly, even if a strategy is devised with the intention of protecting the proprietor against the effects of exhaustion, this will inevitably involve the risk of market partitioning to which the Commission is likely to take exception. Thirdly, it is to be expected that such a strategy, if not constituting arbitrary discrimination, may constitute a disguised restriction on trade between Member States.

COPYRIGHT

10-14 The function of copyright has been stated to be "to protect the moral rights in the work and ensure a reward for the creative effort"[38] of the author. By contrast, the specific subject matter of copyright is "the exclusive right to reproduce the protected work".[39] It will be seen that many of the issues already discussed in the context of patents are equally relevant to copyright although on occasion the ECJ has differentiated between the two in its analysis. In *Merck v. Primecrown*, the ECJ differentiated between forms of exploitation at least to separate the reproduction right from the rental right. This enabled the ECJ to decide in favour of free movement of goods on the facts of *Merck v. Primecrown* on policy grounds and to provide an answer to arguments based on the earlier case of *Warner Bros Inc and Metronome Video ApS v. Erik Viuff Christiansen*[40] ("*Warner v. Christiansen*"). Warner were proprietors of the copyright in the James Bond film, "Never Say Never Again". Christiansen purchased a video cassette of the film in London and took it to Denmark to rent it to the public. Although rental right did not exist in the United Kingdom at that time, a rental right separate from the reproduction right did exist in Denmark (and had already been granted to Metronome). Warner relied on this right to prevent rental of the cassette in Denmark. The ECJ held that:

> "where national legislation confers on authors a specific right to hire out video cassettes, that right would be rendered worthless if its owner were not in a position to authorise the operations for doing so. It cannot therefore be accepted that the marketing by a film maker of a video cassette containing one of his works, in a Member State which does not provide specific protection for the right to hire it out, should have repercussions for the right conferred on that same film maker by the legislation

---

[37] Para. 55. However, the President of the CFI suspended the decision because there did not appear to be "at first sight" sufficient participation on the part of the wholesalers: Case T–41/96R *Bayer v. Commission* [1996] E.C.R. II-381.

[38] Para. 5 Judgment of the CFI of July 10, 1991, Case T–69/89 *Radio Telefis Eireann v. Commission* [1991] E.C.R. II-485.

[39] Commission Dec. 89/205 *Magill/Television Listings* [1989] O.J. L78/43; [1989] C.M.L.R. 757.

[40] Case 158/86 *Warner v. Christiansen* [1988] E.C.R. 2605; [1990] C.M.L.R. 684.

of another Member State to restrain, in that State, the hiring out of that video cassette".[41]

The point was argued in *Merck v. Primecrown* that patent rights cannot be taken to be exhausted by sales in Spain and Portugal where no such rights exist. The flaw in this argument was said, by the ECJ, to be found in the "specific subject matter" of copyright which distinguishes it from patent rights. According to Fennelly A.G. in *Merck v. Primecrown* (which in this respect the ECJ followed):

"the specific subject matter of a patent right may not be divisible in the same way as copyright into several individual acts restricted by copyright. But each of the several rights is an item of industrial or intellectual property whose existence flows from the law of a Member State".[42]

In other words, only the right of reproduction was exhausted in *Warner v. Christiansen* but not the different and separate performance right (which in any event would be dealt with under the free movement of services provisions of Articles 59 to 66 of the E.C. Treaty). He went on:

"The essence of the rights (if, admittedly not the extent) conferred in two parts on a copyright owner (the exclusive right to reproduce and to perform) and in one part in respect of a single act of marketing by a patentee are indistinguishable".[43]

10-15 Similarly, in the case of *Coditel SA v. Ciné Vog Films SA*,[44] Ciné Voq was granted exclusive film and television rights to the film "Le Boucher" in Belgium and Luxembourg which excluded television showing for 40 months from film release. A parallel licence was granted by the same licensor to a German broadcast company who showed it on German television during the 40 month period binding Ciné Voq. A third party, Coditel, recorded and retransmitted the film shown on German television to cable subscribers in Belgium. It was held that television transmission was a performing right (a service falling within Article 59 of the Treaty), not dependant on physical deliverables, on which revenues are based on the number of broadcasts made. The owner therefore had a legitimate interest to protect when it decided to authorise a television broadcast of the film only after it had been exhibited in cinemas for a certain period of time. The right to insist on fees for broadcasting the film was said to be part of the "specific subject matter" of the right. Strategies demarcated along national boundaries with royalties based on usage were therefore held to be necessary to enable the proprietor to regulate royalty collection as part of the specific subject matter of the performance right.

This distinction is likely to be maintained in future harmonisation measures. The Proposal for a Directive entitled "Copyright and Related Rights in the Information Society"[45] has the aim of harmonising rights of distribution and exhaustion within the Community of tangible forms of the work of authors such as CD's, tapes and CD-ROM. One shortcoming of the Proposed Directive is that it excludes altogether from its scope delivery of material on-line, treating non-tangible delivery perhaps artificially as a service or akin to a performance.

---

[41] *ibid*., para. 18.
[42] Para. 133 of the Opinion of Fennelly A.G. in *Merck v. Primecrown*.
[43] *ibid*.
[44] Case 62/79 *Coditel SA v Ciné Vog Films SA* [1980] E.C.R. 881; [1981] 2 C.M.L.R. 362.
[45] COM (97) 628 Final.

10-16   It is noteworthy in the case of *Warner v. Christiansen* that Warner had deliberately withheld sales of the video cassette in Denmark. The fact that the ECJ found in favour of Warner does perhaps lend some support to the view that the intellectual property proprietor does have the power to make marketing decisions, which the ECJ will respect, in order to avoid the adverse market consequences of the right being exhausted. The free choice of the intellectual property proprietor might then be maintained in such a way that it may act in its own best interests in making marketing decisions. This is a theme consistently threaded through the cases ending in *Merck v. Primecrown*, extending back to the case of *Musik-Vertrieb Membrau GmbH et K-tel International v. GEMA-Gesellschaft für Musikalische Aufführungs und Mechanische Vervielfaltigungsrechte*[46] from which came the statement that the intellectual property proprietor (in that case an author acting through a publisher):

> "is free to choose the place, in any of the Member States, in which to put his work into circulation. He may make that choice according to his best interests, which involve not only the level of the remuneration provided in the Member State in question but also other factors such as, for example, the opportunities for distributing his work and marketing facilities which are further enhanced by virtue of the free movement of goods within the Community".[47]

In other words, it is apparently open to the proprietor to make the point of first marketing the most propitious, but as with all intellectual property, it is not open to the proprietor to object to the subsequent free movement across other states that follows from exhausting that intellectual property right. The critical trigger point remains that of exploitation by the proprietor or with the proprietor's consent. Marketing consent in the case of copyright occurs by way of licence or assignment (as with other intellectual property) but it was not considered to be given in the case of expiry of protection. In *EMI Electrola GmbH v. Patricia Im-und Export and others*,[48] reliance was successfully placed on copyright subsisting in Germany, to prevent reimportation from Denmark where the copyright had expired (since the Danish sales were not made with the proprietor's consent).

REGISTERED DESIGNS

10-17   The principles of exhaustion as applied to copyright apply equally to registered designs (although the decided cases are fewer in number). This has been confirmed in *Keurkoop BV v. Nancy Kean Gifts BV*.[49] However, those cases concerning motor car spares (for example *Consorzio italiano della componentistica di ricambio per autoveicoli and Maxicar v. Regie nationale des usines Renault*[50]), which upheld national law giving a design proprietor protection against spare parts importation, must be regarded with some suspicion. In the same context, the case of *AB Volvo v. Erik Veng (U.K.) Ltd*[51] is relevant but largely superseded given the sweeping changes to European design laws that fol-

---

[46] Joined Cases 55/80 and 57/80 *Musik-Vertrieb Membrau GmbH et K-tel International v. GEMA-Gesellschaft für Musikalische Aufführungs und Mechanische Vervielfaltigungsrechte* [1981] E.C.R. 147 [1981] 2 C.M.L.R. 44.

[47] *ibid.*, para. 25 of the Judgment of the ECJ.

[48] Case 341/87 *EMI Electrola GmbH v. Patricia Im-und Export and others* [1989] E.C.R. 79; [1989] 2 C.M.L.R. 413.

[49] Case 144/81 *Keurkoop BV v. Nancy Kean Gifts BV* [1982] E.C.R. 2853; [1983] 2 C.M.L.R. 47.

[50] Case 53/87 *Consorzio italiano della componentistica di ricambio per autoveicoli and Maxicar v. Regie nationale des usines Renault* [1988] E.C.R. 6039; [1990] 4 C.M.L.R. 265.

[51] Case 238/87 *AB Volvo v. Erik Veng (U.K) Ltd* [1988] E.C.R. 6211; [1989] 4 C.M.L.R. 122.

lowed. In that case however, design "specific subject matter" was defined as "the right of the proprietor of a protected design to prevent third parties from manufacturing and selling or importing, without its consent, products incorporating the design".[52]

TRADE MARKS

The subject matter and function of trade marks

10-18 Principles of exhaustion relating to trade marks are determined by the fact that the function of a trade mark is said to be that of identifying the origin of the goods i.e. the manufacturer.

In *Centrafarm BV et Adriaan de Peijper v. Winthrop BV*[53] ("*Centrapharm v. Winthrop*") (the trade mark equivalent to the patent case *Centrafarm v. Sterling*), the essence of a trade mark (apparently combining both its specific subject matter and function) was said to be:

> "the guarantee that the owner of the trade mark has the exclusive right to use that trade mark for the purpose of putting products protected by the trade mark into circulation for the first time, and it is therefore intended to protect him against competitors wishing to take advantage of the status and reputation of the trade mark by selling products illegally bearing that trade mark".[54]

It was held that the proprietor of the Dutch trade mark was not entitled to prevent importation of goods bearing that mark which had already been marketed by it in the United Kingdom. The ECJ stated that trade mark rights could not be relied upon to prevent importation:

> "when the product has been put on the market in a legal manner in the Member State from which it has been imported, by the trade mark owner himself or with his consent, so that there can be no question of abuse of infringement of the trade mark".[55]

This issue of consent, once again, is a critical one but has been restated differently in different cases.

Consent

10-19 In *Van Zuylen Freres v. Hag AG*[56] ("*Hag I*"), the ECJ ruled on the basis (now seen to be wrongly reasoned) that trade mark rights could not be used to prevent importation of goods with the same mark, "having the same origin". It was then considered by the ECJ that confusion could be avoided by measures that would not affect the free movement of goods (presumably labelling and similar devices) and would not otherwise lead to market partitioning.

In *SA CNL-SUCAL v. Hag AG*[57] ("*Hag II*") the ECJ took the opportunity of restating the principles established in *Deutsche Grammophon v. Metro*, *Centrafarm v. Winthrop*, and *Pharmon v. Hoechst*, focusing again on the absence of consent on the

---

[52] *ibid.*, para. 2 of the Judgment of the ECJ.
[53] Case 16/74 [1974] E.C.R. 1183; [1974] 2 C.M.L.R. 480.
[54] *ibid.*, Issue 2, para. 8 of the Judgment of the ECJ.
[55] *ibid.*, Issue 2, para. 8 of the Judgment of the ECJ.
[56] Case 192/73 *Van Zuylen Freres v. Hag AG* [1974] E.C.R. 731; [1974] 2 C.M.L.R. 127.
[57] Case C–10/89 *SA CNL-SUCAL v. Hag AG* [1990] E.C.R. I-3711; [1990] 3 C.M.L.R. 571.

part of the trade mark proprietor as the determining factor (rather than a concept of common origin). Likewise, in the case of *IHT International Heiztechnik GmbH and Uwe Danzinge v. Ideal-Standard GmbH and Wabco Standard GmbH*[58] ("*Ideal Standard*") concerning the voluntary separation of trade mark ownership by means of express trade mark assignment, in line with *Hag II*, the critical importance of consent was emphasised. However, in *Ideal Standard* the ECJ drew a useful distinction between the "essential function of the trade mark" and "the specific subject matter of the trade mark". The "essential function" of the trade mark was said to be that of identifying origin and protecting the consumer assumption that goods bearing the same mark are made by a single source responsible for quality control. The "specific subject matter" was said to protect trade mark proprietors against competitors' theft of goodwill and reputation.

Trade mark legislation

10-20   The above cases were decided before trade mark law had become harmonised in the Community. Council Directive 89/104 to approximate the laws of Member States relating to trade marks[59] ("the Trade Mark Directive") contains the following requirements:

"(1)   The trade mark shall not entitle the proprietor to prohibit its use in relation to goods which have been put on the market in the Community under that trade mark by the proprietor or with his consent.

(2)   Paragraph 1 shall not apply where there exist legitimate reasons for the proprietor to oppose further commercialisation of the goods, especially where the condition of the goods is changed or impaired after they have been put on the market".[60]

The Trade Mark Directive was implemented substantially in this form into the United Kingdom law by means of section 12 of the Trade Marks Act 1994. Section 12 states:

"(1)   A registered trade mark is not infringed by the use of the trade mark in relation to goods which have been put on the market in the European Economic Area under that trade mark by the proprietor or with his consent.

(2)   Sub-section (1) shall not apply where there exist legitimate reasons for the proprietor to oppose further dealings in the goods (in particular, where the condition of the goods has been changed or impaired after they have been put on the market)".

The similarity between the Trade Mark Directive and the Act is striking.

10-21   Owing to different labelling requirements and pharmaceutical practices in Member States, trade mark protection might be used by a trade mark proprietor to prevent a change of condition necessary to allow products to be sold from one country into another. The ECJ has therefore been keen to ensure that trade marks are not used as a device for doing so and has developed clear principles concerning repackaging and trade mark substitution.

---

[58] Case C–9/93 *IHT International Heiztechnik GmbH and Uwe Danzinge v. Ideal-Standard GmbH and Wabco Standard GmbH* [1994] E.C.R. I-2789.
[59] Council Dir. 89/104 [1989] O.J. L40/1.
[60] Art. 7.

Change of condition

Repackaging

10-22 At the heart of the repackaging cases has been the extent to which Article 36 may entitle a trade mark proprietor to rely on principles of trade mark infringement to prevent importation of goods which have been repackaged but nevertheless bear the proprietor's trade mark.

In *Hoffman-La Roche & Co AG v. Centrafarm Vertriebsgesellschaft Pharmazeutischer Erzeugnisse mbH*[61] ("*Hoffman-La Roche*"), Centrafarm acquired "Valium" marketed in the United Kingdom by Hoffmann-La Roche and repackaged it using the same Hoffmann-La Roche trade mark (owned by Hoffmann-La Roche in the United Kingdom and Germany) for sales in Germany. The ECJ emphasised the trade mark function (following *Centrafarm v. Winthrop*) to be that of guaranteeing for the consumer (or ultimate user) the identity of the origin of the product so that the consumer:

> "can be certain that a trade marked product which is sold to him has not been subject at a previous stage of marketing to interference by a third person, without the authorisation of the proprietor of the trade mark, such as to affect the original condition of the product. The right attributed to the proprietor of preventing any use of the trade mark which is likely to impair the guarantee of origin so understood is therefore part of the specific subject matter of the trade mark right".[62]

Accordingly, the ECJ decided that the first sentence of Article 36[63] would entitle a trade mark proprietor to prevent unauthorised importation of repackaged goods. However, the ECJ stated that any ban on imports could constitute a disguised restriction on trade caught by the proviso to Article 36[64] and the ECJ listed the criteria which would prevent reliance on trade mark rights by the proprietor. The proprietor's use of the mark would be caught by the proviso, if the proprietor were to adopt a registration policy or marketing strategy which contributes to the artificial partitioning of the markets between Member States, if the original condition of the product is not adversely affected by repackaging, and if the fact of repackaging is disclosed on the package itself and to the trade mark proprietor. In these circumstances, the trade mark proprietor could not object to reimportation based on trade mark rights.

10-23 The significance of the proprietor's own marketing strategy is obviously critical in determining whether it imposes a "disguised restriction". The matter, once again, is to be resolved by reference to the subject matter and function of the intellectual property right in question.

The criteria laid down in *Hoffmann-La Roche* were applied in the case of *Pfizer Inc v. Eurim-Pharm GmbH*.[65] The importer, Eurim-Pharm, placed substitute external wrapping on the product "Vibramycin", which had already been marketed by Pfizer in the United Kingdom in blister strips, in such a way as to indicate both the manufacturer and the fact of rewrapping. Pfizer was unable to rely on its trade mark in Germany (where the prevailing price was considerably higher) to prevent importation because in these

---

[61] Case 102/77 *Hoffman-La Roche & Co AG v. Centrafarm Vertriebsgesellschaft Pharmazeutischer Erzeugnisse mbH* [1978] E.C.R. 1139; [1978] 3 C.M.L.R. 217.
[62] *ibid.*, Issue 2, para. 7 of the Judgment of the ECJ.
[63] "The provisions of Art. 30 shall not preclude prohibitions or restrictions on imports, exports or goods in transit . . . justified on the grounds of . . . the protection of industrial or commercial property".
[64] "Such prohibitions or restrictions shall not, however, constitute a means of arbitrary discrimination or a disguised restriction of trade between Member States".
[65] Case 1/81 *Pfizer Inc v. Eurim-Pharm GmbH* [1981] E.C.R. 2913; [1982] 1 C.M.L.R. 406.

circumstances, "no use of the trade mark in a manner liable to impair the guarantee of origin takes place".

10-24   The issue of "artificial partitioning" came under scrutiny in the more recent line of repackaging cases, *Paranova*.[66] The crucial parts of the judgment summarise the essential function of the trade mark:

> "which is to guarantee to the consumer or end-user the identity of the trade-marked product's origin by enabling him to distinguish it without any risk of confusion from products of different origin. That guarantee of origin means that the consumer or end-user can be certain that a trade marked product offered to him has not been the subject at a previous stage of marketing to interference by a third person, without the authorisation of the trade mark owner, in such a way as to affect the original condition of the product".[67]

The trade mark owner may therefore prevent any use which interferes with the guarantee of origin.

The ECJ related the issue of "artificial" market partitioning to the essential trade mark function by saying that partitioning is not artificial if it is done in order to preserve the guarantee of origin:

> "By stating that the partitioning of the market must be artificial, the court's intention was to stress that the owner of a trade mark may always rely on his rights as owner to oppose the marketing of repackaged products when such action is justified by the need to safeguard the essential function of the trade mark, in which case the resultant partitioning could not be regarded as artificial".[68]

10-25   The test of artificial partitioning is to be applied objectively, judged at the time before enforcement (presumably at the stage of formulation of a strategy for trade mark registration). The ECJ also concluded that the condition of a product would not be adversely affected (applying *Hoffmann-La Roche*) by the application of self-adhesive labels to flasks, phials, ampoules or the translation of written instructions for use in different Member States.[69] The ECJ also took the opportunity of addressing the position of the parallel importer, extending the *Hoffmann-La Roche* requirements of identification of the manufacturer to cover also a requirement that the new packaging must state the identity of the repackager and the manufacturer (to whom specimens must be made available upon request) in a form of print and language intelligible to a normally attentive person with normal eyesight, identifying additional items for which the trade mark owner is not the source. Also, the presentation of the packaging must not damage the reputation of the trade mark or its proprietor.[70] Finally, the extent to which a parallel importer may repackage is obviously important, as the judgment only permits repackaging "insofar as the repackaging undertaken by the importer is necessary to market the product in a Member State of importation".[71]

---

[66] Joined Cases C–427/93 *Bristol-Myer Squibb v. Paranova A/S and CH Boehringer Sohn*, C–429/93 *Boehringer Ingelheim KG and Boehringer Ingelheim A/S v. Paranova A/S* & C–436/93 *Bayer Aktiengesellschaft and Bayer Danmark A/S v. Paranova A/S* [1996] E.C.R. I-3457.

[67] *ibid.*, para. 47 of the Judgment of the ECJ.

[68] *ibid.*, para. 57 of the Judgment of the ECJ.

[69] In any event, it has been established in Case C–238/89 *Pall v. Dahlhausen* [1990] E.C.R. I-4827 that national laws concerning packaging requirements will contravene Art. 30 if they prevent the marketing of products because they are not packed or marked in a particular way.

[70] Paras 67–78 of the Judgment of the ECJ in *Paranova*.

[71] Para. 56 of the Judgment of the ECJ in *Paranova*.

Relabelling

10-26 The case of *Frits Loendersloot v. George Ballatine and Sons LTD*[72] ("*Loendersloot v. Ballantine*") appears recently to have confirmed the ECJ's willingness to permit relabelling, in that case of whisky bottles with the removal of the identification number of the bottle, the name of the importer and the word "pure", provided the relabelling does not defeat another legitimate purpose of the original label such as the identification of the manufacturer and chain of supply for product liability purposes and provided the relabelling causes "as little prejudice as possible to the specific subject matter of the trade mark right".[73]

Trade mark substitution

10-27 Different rules appear to apply in the case of trade mark substitution rather than repackaging. Substitution may be relevant where the mark originally applied is confusing, is not lawful in the territory of importation, is not passed by the drug approval authorities, or is unfamiliar to pharmacies and doctors prescribing them.

In *Centrafarm v. American Home Products Corporation (AHP)*,[74] quantities of the sedative "Oxazepamum", which had been sold by the proprietor of that mark, AHP, in the United Kingdom under the mark "Serenid D" were purchased by a parallel importer and resold under the mark "Serestra" in the Netherlands. In the Netherlands, AHP marketed the product under its mark "Seresta" with the same pharmacological properties but with a different taste. AHP successfully claimed infringement of the trade mark "Seresta" since this had been applied in the Netherlands without the consent of the proprietor. The ECJ confirmed that only the trade mark proprietor is entitled to give its products their identity by fixing the trade mark, and the guarantee of origin principle would be offended by anyone else doing so. The Court acknowledged that the deliberate use of two different marks to achieve *artificial* partitioning would amount to "a disguised restriction on trade between Member States" under Article 36 but that valid (not "artificial") justifications for the use of different trade marks in Member States might exist. Examples would be the existence of trade marks in a country of proposed sale, differences in the pharmaceutical packaging laws of Member States, or other plausible, explicable, cultural, environmental, political, social or legal variations.

10-28 It is significant that rules of confusion for the purpose of trade mark law differ considerably from country to country. In *Hag II*, Jacobs A.G.[75] noted the abundance of confusingly similar marks and the likelihood that intra-Community trade would be significantly impeded. He noted that confusion judged by the German standard in *Societe Terrapin (Overseas) Ltd v. Societe Terranova Industrie CA Kapferer & Co*[76] would not amount to confusion in the United Kingdom. Therefore a German exporter could sell in the United Kingdom but a United Kingdom exporter could not sell in Germany. Rules of confusion still appear to be a matter to be determined at national level, as confirmed more recently in *Deutsche Renault AG v. Audi AG*[77]:

"Community law does not lay down any criterion requiring a strict interpretation of the risk of confusion".[78]

---

[72] Case C–349/95 *Frits Loendersloot v. George Ballantine & Son Limited* [1997] E.C.R. I-6227.
[73] *ibid.*, para. 46 of the Judgment of the ECJ.
[74] Case 3/78 *Centrafarm v. American Home Products Corporation* [1978] E.C.R. 1823; [1979] 1 C.M.L.R. 326.
[75] Para. 591 of the Opinion of Jacobs A.G in *Hag II*.
[76] Case 119/75 *Societe Terrapin (Overseas) Ltd v. Societe Terranova Industrie CA Kapferer & Co* [1976] E.C.R. 1039; [1976] 2 C.M.L.R.
[77] Case C–317/91 *Deutsche Renault AG v. Audi AG* [1993] E.C.R. I-6227.
[78] *ibid.*, para. 31 of the Judgment of the ECJ.

Advertising

10-29 In order to permit the practical implementation of the developed principles of exhaustion, it has now been clearly established that the parallel importer may undertake ancillary activities such as advertising. In *Christian Dior SA and Parfums Christian Dior BV v. Evora BV*[79] ("*Christian Dior v. Evora*") the ECJ affirmed the practice of advertising Christian Dior products by a company which held less of a "luxury image" than Christian Dior, provided that it did not "seriously damage" the reputation of the trade marks used or the goods. A luxury brand would not however be treated as "seriously damaged" merely by sales at a cheaper price than those chosen by the trade mark proprietor for a given territory.

TERRITORIAL EXTENT OF THE DOCTRINE OF EXHAUSTION

10-30 The implementation of the Trade Mark Directive has been the catalyst for important clarification of whether, at least in the trade mark context, rights are exhausted when first marketed outside the Community. Article 7 of the Trade Mark Directive is ambiguous insofar as it relates to the position of goods which have been first put on the market outside the Community. Article 7 may be interpreted as merely setting a minimum standard, requiring Member States to apply principles of exhaustion throughout the Community but leaving them free to decide whether to apply principles of international exhaustion beyond that. (Those favouring this interpretation maintain that Article 7 is merely a modification of existing ECJ case law, since the Court itself has stressed that Article 7 is to be interpreted in the same way as the Court's case law on Articles 30 and 36. It is maintained that the aim of the Trade Mark Directive was limited and, in the absence of clear wording to the contrary, the discretion that countries previously had to apply international exhaustion, should remain.) Alternatively, Article 7 may be interpreted as a maximum standard, requiring Member States to apply principles of exhaustion only within the Community and not internationally beyond the Community. (Those arguing in favour of a maximum point to the third recital of the Directive's preamble, which refers to the approximation of national provisions of law which most directly affect the functioning of the internal market and maintain that international exhaustion is one such principle which the Trade Mark Directive aimed to harmonise.)

The Trade Mark Directive has been interpreted by the Federal Supreme Court of Germany to mean that exhaustion in the EEA does not occur as a result of first sales outside the EEA (*Levi Strauss v. Knecht*[80]). According to that decision, legislation enacted in 1995 in Germany pursuant to the Trade Marks Directive may be relied upon to prevent importation into Germany of jeans first marketed in the USA. That legislation represented a clear reversal of the principles of international exhaustion which had been developed in Germany prior to its enactment. Before the Trade Marks Act 1994, the United Kingdom took an inconsistent approach to exhaustion in the United Kingdom by non-EEA sales. It appears that the Court of Appeal in *Colgate Palmolive v. Markwell Finance*[81] permitted reliance on United Kingdom trade mark rights to prevent imports of an inferior quality toothpaste where that amounted to misrepresentation of quality and consent could not be implied. However, consent to worldwide sales was found to be present in *Revlon v. Cripps & Lee*[82] in the marketing strategy of the trade mark proprietor under the well known slogan, "New York, Paris, London".

---

[79] Case C–337/95 *Parfums Christian Dior SA and Parfums Christian Dior BV v. Evora BV* [1997] E.C.R. I-6013.
[80] GGH, Urt v. 14. 12. 1995—1ZR 210/93.
[81] [1989] R.P.C. 497.
[82] [1982] F.S.R. 85.

10-31 The historical disparities in national trade mark law are therefore crucial to an understanding of the importance of *the Silhouette Case*.[83] Jacobs A.G. recognised that in view of these disparities, it was necessary for the Trade Mark Directive to transform the impact of Community law on trade mark protection.[84] Jacobs A.G. appealed to the aims and scope of the Directive having determined that the terms of the Directive themselves are not conclusive. In spite of the fact that there are obvious limits to the scope of the Trade Mark Directive, as it was not intended as a measure of total harmonisation, it nevertheless did set out to harmonise the essential conditions and consequences of trade mark protection and he recognised that the scope of the exhaustion principle is central to the content of trade mark rights. Turning to the effect of national disparities concerning international exhaustion, Jacobs A.G. concluded that:

> "The Directive regulates the substance of trade mark rights, and its provisions are designed to be substituted for the diverse national laws across the whole range of its provisions . . . If some Member States practise international exhaustion while others do not, there will be barriers to trade within the internal market which it is precisely the object of the Directive to remove".[85]

Accordingly, he agreed with the submission of various countries (which argued against any discretion to apply international exhaustion) that the same products could be the subject of parallel imports into one Member State but not into another and that this was clearly against the aims of the internal market.

10-32 In his opinion, Jacobs A.G. referred also to the text and intention of the Community Trade Mark Regulation[86] ("Community Trade Mark Regulation"). The Community trade mark is perhaps the most developed of the Community's harmonisation measures because of its unique emphasis on "unitary character":

> "A Community Trade Mark shall have a unitary character. It shall have equal effect throughout the Community, it shall not be registered, transferred or surrendered or be the subject of a decision revoking the rights of the proprietor or declaring it invalid, nor shall its use be prohibited save in respect of the whole Community".[87]

Article 13 of the Community Trade Mark Regulation is a mirror image of Article 7 of the Trade Mark Directive, providing for exhaustion only for goods which have been put on the market "in the Community". Jacobs A.G. concluded that it is impossible to construe the Regulation as imposing international exhaustion; similarly with the Trade Mark Directive. The original Proposal for the Directive expressly provided for international exhaustion and was subsequently changed to limit it only to the Community. The Trade Mark Regulation, given its unitary character, cannot be intended to give Member States discretion whether or not to permit international exhaustion. In view of the history of the Directive, its purpose and the identical wording to the Regulation, Jacobs A.G. concluded that Article 7(1) of the Trade Marks Directive is to be interpreted to entitle a trade mark owner to prevent a third party using the mark when importing goods into an EEA country after first marketing in a country outside the EEA.

10-33 The ECJ followed the Opinion of Jacobs A.G. by concluding as follows:

---

[83] Case C–355/96 *Silhouette International Schmied GmbH & Co. KG v. Hartlauer Handelsgescellschaft mbH* [1998] E.C.R. Judgment of the Court Transcript July 16, 1998.
[84] Para. 39 of the Opinion of Jacobs A.G. in the *Silhouette Case*.
[85] *ibid.*, paras 39 to 41.
[86] Council Reg. 40/94 on the Community trade mark [1994] O.J. L 11/1.
[87] Art. 1(2).

"[T]he Directive cannot be interpreted as leaving it open to the Member States to provide in their domestic law for exhaustion of the rights conferred by a trade mark in respect of products put on the market in non-member countries . . . This . . . is the only interpretation which is fully capable of ensuring that the purpose of the Directive is achieved, namely to safeguard the functioning of the internal market. A situation in which some Member States could provide for international exhaustion while others provided for Community exhaustion only would inevitably give rise to barriers to the free movement of goods and the freedom to provide services."[88]

The level of clarification, although given in the context of trade marks, is of great value. However, the extent to which it applies to other rights remains to be decided. As national disparities in the treatment of international exhaustion of any intellectual property right will inevitably result in barriers to trade within the internal market, the reasoning of the ECJ may be applicable to other intellectual property rights—though further ECJ decisions are awaited to confirm this.

---

[88] Paras 26 and 27 of the Judgment of the ECJ in the *Silhouette Case*.

CHAPTER 11

United Kingdom Monopoly and Merger Control

LEGISLATIVE BACKGROUND

The Fair Trading Act 1973

11-01   The Fair Trading Act 1973 gives separate treatment to "monopoly situations" and "mergers". In spite of fundamental changes brought about by the 1998 Act to dissolve the Monopolies and Mergers Commission ("MMC") and replace it with the newly constituted Competition Commission, the Fair Trading Act 1973 is preserved largely in tact. (See Appendix E.1 below for relevant extracts from the Fair Trading Act 1973.) This will enable structural aspects of the market to be controlled, not merely those concerned with specific agreements or conduct regulated by Chapters I and II of the 1998 Act.

The MMC was established under section 1 of the Monopolies and Restrictive Practices (Inquiry and Control) Act 1948.[1] The principal functions now assigned to the Competition Commission under the Fair Trading Act 1973 are the investigation and reporting on questions referred to the Competition Commission concerning monopoly situations and mergers qualifying for investigation. For further commentary on the composition, functions and powers of the Competition Commission see Chapter 13 below.

The Fair Trading Act 1973 is an extremely long statute involving a great deal of duplication. Part IV (sections 44 to 56) is concerned with "monopoly situations", Part V (sections 57 to 77) with "mergers". *Monopolies*, below will focus on "monopoly situations". Mergers will be dealt with below in *Mergers*.

The Competition Act 1980

11-02   The Competition Act 1980 ("the 1980 Act") was created to address a number of shortcomings of the Fair Trading Act 1973. Anti-competitive practices were controlled by sections 2 to 10 of the 1980 Act but these sections are repealed by the 1998 Act.[2]

To put the 1980 Act in context, it was targeted at anti-competitive practices implemented by conduct rather than by agreement. An anti-competitive practice is defined by section 2(1) to cover any:

"course of conduct which . . . has or is intended to have or is likely to have the effect of restricting, distorting or preventing competition in connection with the production, supply or acquisition of goods in the United Kingdom or any part of it or the supply or securing of services in the United Kingdom or any part of it."

---

[1] It was initially named the Monopolies and Restrictive Practices Commission but was renamed the Monopolies Commission. Only on commencement of the Fair Trading Act 1973 did it become known as the Monopolies and Mergers Commission.
[2] s. 17 of the Competition Act 1998.

11-03   From a swift reading of section 2(1), it will be apparent that the Chapter I prohibition and Chapter II prohibition engulf practices previously caught by section 2(1) and that the 1998 Act will provide a speedier mechanism for investigation and enforcement. The mechanisms for controlling anti-competitive practices under the 1980 Act were cumbersome. The Director was empowered to initiate investigations of anti-competitive practices and would usually try to resolve them by means of undertakings from those engaged in them. The Director could refer the matter to the MMC which in turn would determine whether the practice operated against public interest. Only if this did not result in undertakings by the parties involved or modification of their practices would the MMC make an appropriate order to correct the offending practice. There has always been a substantial overlap between the Fair Trading Act 1973 and the 1980 Act, and in many cases the Director could investigate activities under either of them. In general the Fair Trading Act 1973, with wider coverage, better enabled the Director to investigate entire industries rather than individual practices. Most practices previously giving rise to investigation under the 1980 Act will now be caught by the Chapter II prohibition because anti-competitive practices primarily concern unilateral conduct. However, certain practices caught by the Competition Act 1980 may conceivably fall within the Chapter I prohibition if the course of conduct is the result of concertation.

MONOPOLIES

Monopoly situations

11-04   The term "monopoly situation" is defined in sections 6 to 11 of the Fair Trading Act 1973 to differentiate between the following:

(1) a monopoly situation in relation to the supply of goods (sections 6 and 11);

(2) a monopoly situation in relation to the supply of services (sections 7 and 11);

(3) a monopoly situation in relation to exports (section 8); and

(4) a monopoly situation limited to only part of the United Kingdom (section 9).

A Monopoly situation in relation to the supply of goods (sections 6 and 11)

11-05   A monopoly situation is taken to exist in relation to the supply of goods in four cases. First, where at least one quarter of all the goods of any description which are supplied in the United Kingdom are supplied by one and the same person, or are supplied to one and the same person. This amounts to a market share of 25 per cent on the supply side or demand side for goods of the relevant description.

A monopoly situation similarly exists, secondly, where that 25 per cent market share is held by members of the same group of inter-connected companies, where the group consists of parents and subsidiaries.[3]

11-06   Complex monopolies (so described by section 11) arise, thirdly, in relation to the supply of goods when the 25 per cent market share for those goods is held by two or more persons (not being group companies) who conduct themselves, whether deliberately or through inadvertence, in such a way as to prevent, restrict or distort competition in connection with the production or supply of those goods. Those persons need not be affected by the competition which they upset and it does not matter whether those that are affected are producers, suppliers, customers or others.

---

[3] Defined by s. 736 of the Companies Act 1985.

Fourthly, a monopoly situation in relation to the supply of goods may exist, more simply, if one or more agreements operates in such a way that goods of the relevant description are not supplied in the United Kingdom at all.

A monopoly situation in relation to the supply of services (sections 7 and 11)

11-07   The four situations giving rise to a monopoly situation in relation to the supply of goods apply to a monopoly situation in relation to the supply of services. There may, however, be some doubt when dealing with certain services, such as electronic services delivered on-line, whether they are supplied in the United Kingdom for the purpose of determining whether they should count toward the one quarter figure. In general, the place of supply will be the United Kingdom where the supplier has a place of business in the United Kingdom or controls the relevant activities from the United Kingdom or, in the case of companies, where the supplier is incorporated in Great Britain or Northern Ireland.[4]

A monopoly situation in relation to exports (section 8)

11-08   A monopoly situation is taken to exist in relation to exports of goods of any description from the United Kingdom if at least one quarter of all goods of that description which are produced in the United Kingdom are produced by one and the same person or inter-connected companies. The focus of section 8 is on production within the United Kingdom of the goods exported and not merely the export market of goods. The monopoly situation, once established, is taken to exist both in relation to the United Kingdom export market generally, and in relation to individual export markets taken separately.

Export monopolies are also taken to exist by way of agreements which operate in such a way as to prevent, restrict or distort competition in relation to the export of goods of the relevant description from the United Kingdom, provided the agreements operate in relation to at least one quarter of all the goods of that description which are produced in the United Kingdom.

Section 8 may well operate to catch export practices which fall outside the Chapter I prohibition or Chapter II prohibition of the 1998 Act by virtue of not having an effect on trade within the United Kingdom. In practice, there are comparatively few investigations of export monopoly situations.

A monopoly situation limited to part of the United Kingdom (section 9)

11-09   Section 9 applies the principles of sections 6 and 7 (monopoly situations in relation to the supply of goods and the supply of services) to local monopolies to catch, for example, the activities of local bus companies, builders or other businesses which are often parochial in nature. Given that the 1998 Act is to control agreements and conduct with effects felt even within a part of the United Kingdom, less reliance is likely to be placed on the cumbersome mechanism of the Fair Trading Act 1973. Instead, the Chapter I and Chapter II prohibitions of the 1998 Act will be favoured as tools for investigation and enforcement of local monopolies.

In sections 6 to 9, monopoly situations are defined by reference to "the United Kingdom". This refers to part of the United Kingdom (*Buildings in the Greater London Area*[5]).

The difference between the definitions of the four types of "monopoly situation" and the definition of "dominance" for the purposes of the Chapter II prohibition is striking.

---

[4]   s. 7(3).
[5]   HCP 1953–54, 264.

The 25 per cent threshold for monopoly situations is seemingly arbitrary and departs from what economists conventionally regard either as a monopoly or dominant position, especially when a monopoly situation may exist irrespective of the market power of competitors (which may be considerable) and, in the case of complex monopolies, a monopoly situation may exist where tiny market shares are held separately by each of the participants.

11-10   The criteria for establishing the market share of "goods of the same description" according to section 10(6) are to be the " most suitable in all the circumstances". Suggested criteria include "value or cost or price or quantity or capacity or number of workers employed". In practice, the method of calculation will be as set out in detail in Chapter 4 above.

Unlike the 1998 Act and Articles 85(1) and 86, which require some effect to be felt either within the United Kingdom (or part of it) or between Member States, the Fair Trading Act 1973 requires public interest to be threatened before a reference may be made. Whatever may be said against the Fair Trading Act 1973, it is at least "effects-based" and catches complex monopolies that might otherwise fall through the net. It may therefore be distinguished from the Restrictive Trade Practices Act 1976 and Resale Prices Act 1976 which focused primarily on the form of agreements irrespective of their effect.

11-11   The Fair Trading Act 1973 is not aimed at preventing the existence of a monopoly situation, only the resulting harm. Even if procedurally the Fair Trading Act 1973 might be cumbersome, it has been used to good effect in the past. For example, against a finding that Bryant and May held a market share of 78 per cent in the retail sales of matches and was making excessive profits, the MMC recommended price controls.[6] High profitability does not necessarily indicate excessive pricing and harm to public interest. In 1991 the MMC measured Nestlé's market share in coffee sales at 56 per cent but put its high profitability down to better performance against its competitors.[7] Even traditional practices in particular industries may be open to challenge. For example tied houses owned by breweries were found to harm public interest until the ties were ordered to be relaxed.[8] In the case of oil companies, their ownership of retail outlets was not, however, found to harm public interest.[9]

The threat of further action is usually sufficient to bring any harmful effects under control. For example when Grey-Green Coaches offered free bus services which in the Director's view could have eliminated new competition, the free offer was withdrawn.[10] Similarly, a refusal by a local bus company in the Isle of Wight (Southern Vectis) to give access to the central bus station to competitors was corrected in order to prevent any further action by way of investigation.[11] Where there is the prospect of flourishing competition, particularly in industries with low barriers to entry, the authorities are less likely to take action (*Tampons*[12]).

The Director's investigative powers

11-12   One advantage of the changes to the administration of the Fair Trading Act 1973, introduced by the 1998 Act, is that the number of different institutions involved in the implementation of United Kingdom competition legislation is reduced primarily to the Director (and the OFT), the Competition Commission and the Secretary of State.

---

[6] MMC Report March 5, 1992 Cm. 1854 (1992).
[7] MMC Report March 8, 1991 Cm. 1459 (1991).
[8] MMC Report March 21, 1989 Cm. 651 (1989).
[9] MMC Report February 14, 1990 Cm. 972 (1990).
[10] OFT Press Release January 24, 1985.
[11] OFT Report February 17, 1988.
[12] Cmnd 8049 (1980).

The Director's powers under section 44 of the Fair Trading Act 1973 have been extended by the 1998 Act. Section 44 empowers the Director to call for information where it appears there are grounds for believing,

"that a monopoly situation may exist in relation to the supply of goods or services of any description, or in relation to exports of goods of any description from the United Kingdom."[13]

The purpose of requiring the information must be to assist the Director in determining:

(a) whether to make a monopoly reference to the Competition Commission with respect to the existence or possible existence of the situation [see *Monopoly References* below]; or

(b) whether, instead, to make a proposal under section 56A for the Secretary of State to accept undertakings (see *Undertakings* below).[14]

11-13   The Director may require anyone who supplies or produces goods or services, or purchases goods or services of the description in question, to produce to the Director at a time and place notified in writing by him, specified documents or categories of document within that person's custody or control which are relevant. The Director may copy them and demand explanations from officers and employees of that entity or, if a document cannot be produced, to demand to know its whereabouts.[15] The Director may also require other information to be provided. Evidence of authorisation is required by those enforcing the Director's powers.

The Director's powers of investigation under the Fair Trading Act 1973 have been brought in line with his powers to investigate infringement of any Chapter I or Chapter II prohibition, enabling him in the context of an investigation of a monopoly situation to enter any business premises used by a producer, supplier or purchaser of the goods or services in question and require delivery up of documents within their custody or control, or to demand an explanation of those documents.

11-14   There are limits to the Director's powers of investigation. He is not empowered to compel production of a document from anyone who could not be compelled to produce it in civil proceedings before the High Court (or in Scotland the Court of Session) or, so far as information is concerned, who could not be compelled to give that information in evidence in civil proceedings. Furthermore, the documents to be produced are only those that are relevant to the Director's decision whether to make a monopoly reference or to propose instead that undertakings be accepted. The Director may only exercise his powers for the purpose of those decisions.

The amendments to the Fair Trading Act 1973 made by sections 66 and 67 of the 1998 Act are to apply equally to the jurisdiction of the following, as well as the Director, in order to enable them to fulfil their regulatory functions:

(a) the Director General of Telecommunications;

(b) the Director General of Electricity Supply;

(c) the Director General of Electricity Supply for Northern Ireland;

(d) the Director General of Water Services;

---

[13] s. 44(1)(a) of the Fair Trading Act 1973.
[14] s. 66(3) of the 1998 Act, amending s. 44(1) of the Fair Trading Act 1973.
[15] s. 66(4) and (5) of the 1998 Act, amending s. 44(2) of the Fair Trading Act 1973.

(e) the Rail Regulator;

(f) the Director General of Gas Supply; and

(g) the Director General of Gas for Northern Ireland.[16]

11-15   Section 45 of the Fair Trading Act 1973 previously dealt with the investigation of complex monopoly situations and has been repealed.

Section 46 of the Fair Trading Act 1973 (amended by section 67 of the 1998 Act) created a number of offences committed by those who refuse or wilfully neglect to comply with any section 44 requirement of the Director, or who intentionally obstruct the Director in the exercise of his section 44 powers, or who alter, suppress or destroy documents which are required to be produced. These offences are punishable by a fine and (in the case of conviction on indictment) up to two years imprisonment. Defences are available to those who do not have the documents in their possession or control, to those who have a reasonable excuse for not complying with the Director's requirements, and to those for whom compliance with any of the Director's requirements is not practicable.

Monopoly references

11-16   References concerning monopoly situations are made either by the Director under section 50 or by the Secretary of State under section 51 of the Fair Trading Act 1973.

Part I of Schedule 5 and Part I of Schedule 7 to the Fair Trading Act 1973 specify those monopoly situations which only the Secretary of State can refer to the Competition Commission (whether on his own or in conjunction with the relevant Minister when required to do so by section 51(2)). At one stage, the list of matters which only the Secretary of State could refer concerned rail transport, the postal system and the supply of telecommunications, electricity and gas services but the list has dwindled with successive repeals that have been part and parcel of the privatisation of various utilities. Certain agricultural goods and services are the exclusive preserve of the Secretary of State (and relevant Minister).

11-17   When making a reference, the Director and Secretary of State have wide discretion concerning the scope of the reference. Section 47 requires the reference to specify the description of goods or services to which it relates (in the case of goods, stating whether it relates to supply or export). The scope of the reference may be confined to only part of the United Kingdom, where only part of the United Kingdom is affected, although this is not mandatory. The reference may be so framed so as to exclude from consideration, or confine consideration to, specified agreements or practices. A reference may be framed to require the Competition Commission only to investigate and report on particular facts. This is known as a "monopoly reference limited to the facts" (which will steer the Competition Commission to investigate and report on the question whether a monopoly situation exists in relation to specific matters set out in the reference). Alternatively, a reference may be framed more generally, known as a "monopoly reference not limited to the facts", which enables the investigation to be more wide-ranging, and enables the Competition Commission to make findings on any facts (not limited specific facts) found by the Competition Commission.

In each case, the reference may require the Competition Commission to investigate and report on the following questions:

(1) whether a monopoly situation exists in relation to the matter set out in the reference; and if so,

---

[16] Sched. 10, Part I of the 1998 Act.

(2) by virtue of which provisions of sections 6 to 8 of the Fair Trading Act 1973 that monopoly situation is to be taken to exist;

(3) in whose favour the monopoly situation exists (as the Act quaintly puts it);

(4) whether steps are taken by that person to exploit or maintain the monopoly situation, identifying "uncompetitive practices" and other means for doing so; and

(5) whether any activities (or lack of them) by that person are attributable to the monopoly situation.

In the case of a monopoly reference not limited to the facts, the investigation and report may also require determination of whether any act or omission by any person in whose favour a monopoly situation exists, operates or may be expected to operate, against the public interest.

11-18 A monopoly reference not limited to the facts may be framed more generally to require an investigation and report on whether a monopoly situation exists, if so, identifying in whose favour the monopoly situation exists and (instead of examining the issues referred to in items 4 and 5 above) whether that person's activities (or lack of them) operates or may be expected to operate against public interest. This is more common and generally more effective. In *Chlordiazepoxide and Diazepam*[17] the issue under investigation was extremely broad, namely whether the prices for certain pharmaceuticals were excessive.

A monopoly reference limited to the facts may be varied to become a monopoly reference not limited to the facts (but not vice versa). Other variations are allowed (provided they do not in effect result in a reference of the type from which the Director is precluded from making).

11-19 In the case of all monopoly references (and variations) the Director or Secretary of State making the reference must arrange for it to be published in full in the London, Edinburgh and Belfast Gazettes to invite comment from those likely to be affected by it.

The report by the Competition Commission is to be made to the Director or Secretary of State making the reference and it must contain definite conclusions on the questions comprised in the reference, giving an account of the Competition Commission's reasons for the conclusions reached and a survey of the general position concerning the subject-matter of the reference and of developments that led up to that position. In the case of a monopoly reference not limited to the facts, followed by a finding of a monopoly situation operating or expected to operate against the public interest, the Competition Commission must particularise the adverse effect on public interest and must consider what action (if any) should be taken to remedy those effects. The report may include recommendations for action, whether by a Minister, public authority or the person in whose favour the monopoly situation exists.

Each monopoly reference contains time-limits within which the Competition Commission must report, unless the time-scale is extended.

Undertakings

11-20 The Director may (by virtue of section 56A of the Fair Trading Act 1973) propose that the Secretary of State accept undertakings in lieu of the Director making a monopoly reference, if the Director considers that a monopoly situation exists and that there are facts relating to the monopoly situation which may already or in the future operate against the public interest. The purpose of accepting undertakings is pre-emptive

---

[17] HCP (1972–73) 197.

and, if successful, the exercise is less time-consuming and less costly. Undertakings may only be accepted if a monopoly reference would otherwise be made. However, the reference must be a monopoly reference not limited to the facts and not a monopoly reference limited to the facts. The Director must also be of the view that undertakings would deal sufficiently with the harm to public interest. The proposal must include the terms of the undertakings to be given, identifying those who are to give them, together with a statement of the facts relating to the monopoly situation which the Director considers poses a threat to public interest.

Before making a proposal under section 56A, the Director must publish an appropriate notice to bring it to the attention of those likely to be interested and must consider any representations made to him in response.

If the proposal is accepted by the Secretary of State then for a period of 12 months from giving the undertakings, no monopoly reference may be made of the matters published by the Director unless an undertaking has been breached or requires variation.

Assessment of factors

11-21   The procedures of the Competition Commission in carrying out its investigations and the orders that may be made following investigation are similar for monopoly situations and mergers and are dealt with in *Investigations and Orders* below.

In assessing any matter before it, the Competition Commission is likely to take account of a number of factors.[18] The focus will primarily be on the current and future structure of the market. The recent history of the industry is also important in indicating the extent of competition and in identifying trends, such as profitability levels, price movements both in relation to costs and in response to price changes by competitors, adjustments in market shares held by competitors, the likely threats posed by imports, the record of attempts by those trying to break into a given market and the reasons why contenders have left the market. Past anti-competitive practices may well suggest greater risk of future anti-competitive practices.

11-22   In examining the structure of the market and the relative strength of competitors, it is important to see whether competitors are evenly balanced and whether there are sufficient number of them to indicate strong competition. If few dominate, then collusion between them is more likely. If there are a few with similar market shares, they may constitute an oligopoly.

The level of resources available to each competitor is a measure of its strength and ability to compete. Profitability is obviously an important measure of strength.[19]

11-23   Potential competition from imports will be more likely if transport costs are low relative to value but the potential for competition from imports may be overstated if in fact there is no market for imports due to preferences for home-branded products or cultural differences that influence purchasers. Consumer preferences for particular brands even within a given country may produce narrow, niche markets which limit competition across different brands.

Although price is a good index of competition with low prices implying strong competition, prices alone may not take account of such factors as product quality and competition on the level of after sales support. Published prices may in reality not be adhered to at all and significant discounts may routinely apply to obscure the true price position.

11-24   Any strength that may be found on the part of a supplier must be considered in the light of the power of its purchasers. Multiple retailers are notoriously powerful pur-

---

18   These have been set out in detail in the MMC's publication "Assessing Competition". MMC, 1993.
19   Low profitability is likely to be sustained if the costs of leaving the market are high, for example, due to extensive past investment in plant which is irrecoverable.

chasers. Purchasers may be able to exert power over suppliers if they buy in high volume in relation to the seller's overall output or if the product in question represents a high proportion of the buyer's costs because the buyer will be under greater pressure to seek out the lowest price. This is particularly so if there is little to distinguish between the different suppliers (little "brand differentiation"). Equally, the supplier may face pressure from the threat that the purchaser will undertake manufacture in-house.

On the other hand, if the purchaser is dependent on one particular supplier and there are few alternative sources, the balance will shift in favour of the supplier. Equally, if the supplier is readily able to adapt products to suit other purchasers then the supplier will face less pressure to reduce price (and offer other competitive terms) to get the business.

11-25 In general, all suppliers may be constrained to one degree or other by the threat of new entrants to the market or the loss of market share in favour of competitors. A great deal depends on the cost of breaking into the market and whether there are other obstacles in the path of potential competitors such as intellectual property, regulatory compliance or approvals. Brand loyalty may be another entry barrier if buyers prefer existing suppliers.

Other barriers may be lack of economies of scale, economies of scope or economies of integration. Economies of scale may be needed in order to operate efficiently above a given scale of operation. Economies of scope (rather than scale) refers to economies that result from being able to share costs of production between different products or other activities. Economies of integration refer to the ease with which any supplier may reach distribution outlets either because they are already part of the organisation or are established by distribution arrangements. By contrast, barriers to newcomers may be posed by existing exclusive distribution agreements which prevent access to the market.

11-26 Another barrier to entry may be that control of an essential facility is held by another who denies access to it. An example might be a port controlled by the port authority, or transport network system to which access is indispensable in order to compete and where duplication of the resources is highly undesirable (*Oscar Bronner v. Mediaprint and others*[20]).

Sunk costs will act as a deterrent against market entry if it is known that these cannot be recovered in the event of a decision to withdraw from the market. Advertising is an example of sunk costs, another might be investment in specialist plant which cannot easily be deployed for other purposes.

11-27 Potential competition may also stem from excess capacity held by an existing competitor who is ready to respond to changes in the market. Also, the risks of retaliation in response to entry into the market must be considered.

All of these factors will influence the Competition Commission in drawing its conclusions whenever it is required to report on the structure of the relevant market and potential harm to public interest.

Bearing in mind the importance of the description given to the relevant goods or services and the assessment of market power, the criteria for establishing the relevant market and market share should be considered, as discussed in Chapter 4 above. It is worth noting, however, that the 25 per cent market threshold of goods or services of the relevant description is only important for the purposes of determining whether a monopoly situation exists or a merger qualifies for investigation. The real issues on examination of a reference are the extent of market power and harm to public interest.

---

[20] Case C-7/97 *Oscar Bronner GmbH and Co KG v. Mediaprint Zeitungs- und Zeitschriftenverlag GmbH and Co KG* [1998].

MERGERS

Merger situations qualifying for investigation (not relating to newspapers)

11-28   Mergers offer a number of potential advantages. They may enable economies of scale and corresponding efficiencies to be reaped in relation to part or even all of the activities undertaken. Given both the business pressure to compete and the creation of competitive conditions intended by competition legislation, the need for greater efficiency is obvious. Mergers may also be beneficial in times of crisis affecting a particular market or in times of generally economic adversity, to prevent businesses from ceasing to exist. The loss of a business would mean the loss of a source of supply. Consumer choice may then be more limited and ultimately competition may suffer.

However, mergers pose a potential threat in that they may enable an entity with significant market power to strengthen its position further by eliminating a competitor. Rationalisation that follows a merger may also result in closure of facilities and local redundancies. For these reasons, the Fair Trading Act 1973 regulates mergers by means of procedures not dissimilar to those applicable to monopoly situations.

11-29   Sections 64 to 75 of the Fair Trading Act 1973 apply to merger references other than those relating to newspapers (to which sections 57 to 62 apply). Section 64 is the crucial provision which defines those merger situations that qualify for investigation. If the following three criteria are satisfied, a merger reference may be made to the Competition Commission by the Secretary of State:

(1)   two or more enterprises must have ceased to be distinct;

(2)   one of the enterprises must carry on trade in the United Kingdom; and

(3)   the value of the acquired assets must exceed £70 million or a monopoly situation be created or enhanced.

For the purpose of merger references (but not monopoly situations) "part of the United Kingdom" has been taken to mean "a substantial part" of the United Kingdom (*R v. Monopolies and Mergers Commission, ex parte South Yorkshire Transport LTD*[21]).

Two or more enterprises must have ceased to be distinct enterprises

11-30   For the purposes of section 64(4) of the Fair Trading Act 1973, enterprises are taken to cease to be distinct enterprises:

(a)   if they did so within the period of four months prior to the date of the merger reference[22]; or

(b)   if they did so pursuant to transactions concluded without prior notification to the Secretary of State or the Director and without the material facts surrounding the transaction being made public. The time-limit for making a merger reference in this case is four months from notifying the Secretary of State or the Director, or four months from the material facts being made public. "Made public" means so publicised as to be generally known or readily ascertainable.

---

[21] [1992] 1 All E.R. 257; [1993] 1 W.L.R. 23.
[22] Deregulation (Fair Trading Act 1973) (Amendment) (Merger Reference Time Limits) Order 1996, (S.I. 1996 No. 345).

In spite of these statutory time-limits, the Secretary of State is to avoid uncertainty by making a determination as soon as is reasonably practicable.

The term "cease to be distinct enterprises" is important. Section 63(2) defines "enterprise" to mean the activities, or part of the activities, of a business. It therefore excludes altogether any transfer of bare assets. "Activities" are more likely to be inferred where assets are coupled with goodwill and live contracts. The words, "cease to be distinct" are clarified in section 65 which treats two enterprises as ceasing to be distinct if either:

(a) they are brought under common ownership or common control; or

(b) pursuant to the transaction, either of the enterprises ceases to be carried on at all (in order to bury any competition from that enterprise).

Section 65 deals at disproportionate length with what is meant by "common control". It refers to enterprises belonging to "inter-connected bodies corporate",[23] enterprises carried on by separate companies controlled by the same person or group, and enterprises carried on separately by a company and the person that controls that company.

11-31 Control is given a wide meaning to include the ability, whether directly or indirectly, to control or materially influence the policy of any company or person in carrying on the enterprise, even if a controlling interest by way of board representation or share-holding is not held. A shareholding of as little as 20 per cent may be enough to exert sufficient influence and, on occasion, even less. In *P+O/European Ferries Group plc*,[24] a shareholding of 16.1 per cent was sufficient given that the other shareholdings were relatively low and fragmented. Section 65(4) goes further to regard enterprises as ceasing to be distinct if control, already held by virtue of being able materially to influence policy, is enhanced to the point where the purchaser acquires a controlling interest either in the enterprise or the company owning it, or becomes able to control the policy of the person carrying on the enterprise. Depending on the circumstances, policy may be said to be controlled at the 30 per cent shareholding threshold (*Minorco Consolidated Goldfields*[25]).

Sections 66 and 67 are concerned with timing and creeping mergers involving successive transactions. Section 66 treats successive events or transactions as having occurred simultaneously if they occur within a period of two years of each other and would qualify for investigation if they had occurred simultaneously. The time at which the enterprises cease to be distinct enterprises in such circumstances is the time when the parties to the arrangements or transactions become contractually bound to give effect to them. Options are therefore not relevant for these purposes until they are actually exercised. (Section 66A deals with the circumstances in which enterprises cease to be distinct by reason of the acquisition of successive rights over a period of two years which result in an enterprise being brought under the control of a person or group, and for this purpose too, the common control provisions of section 65 will apply to determine whether this has occurred).

One of the enterprises must carry on trade in United Kingdom

11-32 The second of the three criteria to be met before a merger reference may be made is that at least one of those enterprises must carry on business in the United Kingdom, whether by itself or under the control of another.

---

[23] s. 137(5).
[24] Cmnd 31 (1986).
[25] Cmnd 587 (1989).

The value of the acquired assets must exceed £70 million or a monopoly situation be created or enhanced

11-33   Thirdly, the value of the assets taken over must exceed £70 million,[26] or the result of the merger must be that a monopoly situation then exists where it did not exist before, or the monopoly situation is aggravated.[27] The term, "monopoly situation" is not referred to in section 64 although that section does refer to circumstances where at least one quarter of all the goods or services of a given description in the United Kingdom (or a substantial part of the United Kingdom) are supplied by one and the same person, or are supplied to one and the same person. A monopoly situation must therefore be created or exist to a greater extent.

The value of the assets taken over, according to section 67, is the total asset value of the enterprises which cease to be distinct (*i.e.* the target) on the date that this occurs or, if earlier, on the date of making a merger reference to the Competition Commission. Total asset value refers to the book value of the business, whether held in the United Kingdom or not, less depreciation, renewals or any diminution in value. Adjustments in value may be necessary in the case of transactions that result in creeping mergers and these adjustments will be made where appropriate by the Secretary of State or Competition Commission.

Merger references

11-34   On making a merger reference, the Secretary of State must publish details of the merger in the most suitable way for bringing it to the attention of those who, in his opinion, are likely to be affected by it so that they are offered the opportunity to respond.

As to the timing of any reference, for those references that are made after a merger has taken place, section 64(4) imposes a time limit on the Secretary of State of four months following the merger. If material facts about the merger had not been given either to the Secretary of State or the Director by prior notice or had not been made public, then the four month period runs from the date of such notification or publication.

Section 75 expressly provides, alternatively, a fast-track procedure for statutory pre-notification of mergers.

Statutory pre-notification

11-35   Although parties to a merger are under no obligation to notify the Secretary of State or the Director, they frequently do so under section 75 in advance, in order to avoid the uncertainty and disruption of a reference by the Secretary of State after the merger has taken place.

One of the risks of pre-merger notification is that the existence of a monopoly situation will be brought to the attention of the Director and, in the process of providing information by way of justification of the merger, the Director may have access to information which might not otherwise be available to him. Even if no further action is taken following a pre-merger notification, there is always the risk that the activities of the merger parties will be kept under review by the Director. A monopoly reference always remains a possibility after a merger has taken place, unless of course the merger qualified for investigation only by virtue of exceeding the assets value threshold. The provisions inserted into the Fair Trading Act 1973 by section 149 of the Companies Act 1985[28] should be

---

[26] s. 64(1)(b), updated by the Merger References (Increase in Value of Assets) Order 1994 (S.I. 1994 No. 72).
[27] s. 64(1)(a).
[28] ss. 75 4(A) to 4(H), 4(J) to 4(M) of the Fair Trading Act 1973.

noted as they make certain share dealings unlawful in companies controlling any enterprise to which a reference under section 75 relates.

Pre-notification to the Director under section 75 serves three functions. First, it triggers the time-limits within which the Secretary of State may make a reference. Once the Director receives a merger notice in the prescribed form, the Secretary of State must make a reference within 20 working days, extendable by a further 15 days,[29] failing which no reference may subsequently be made by the Secretary of State in relation to the same transaction. If the section 75 procedure is not adopted, the time-limits inherent in section 64 will nevertheless apply to limit the time within which a reference must be made by the Secretary of State to four months following the giving of notice to the Director.[30] One drawback of the statutory pre-notification procedure is that section 75B(1) requires the Director to publish details of the merger in order to attract comment from affected third parties. In addition, the Director will rely on the fact-finding resources resident in the OFT. This is particularly important given that it is one of the prime functions of the Director under section 76(1) to keep himself informed about actual or intended transactions that may result in merger situations qualifying for investigation.

Confidential guidance

11-36 An alternative to statutory notification under section 75 is the use of informal guidance available from the OFT. This avoids publicity but lacks the advantages of the tight time-scales for a decision under section 75. In giving confidential guidance, the OFT requires sufficient information to be provided in support or it will decline to give guidance. Confidential guidance is not binding on the OFT.

A turnaround time of six weeks may be anticipated. Even though advice is given in confidence, the OFT is nevertheless made aware of the existence of a potential monopoly situation or merger situation qualifying for investigation. Parties to a merger may prefer instead to place the onus of uncovering transactions which are not of a high profile on the Director or the Secretary of State.

Undertakings

11-37 If it is apparent that the Secretary of State will make a reference, as a last resort, the parties may offer in negotiation with the Director to give undertakings to the Secretary of State under sections 75G to K of the Fair Trading Act 1973. The merger must be one which qualifies for investigation. Once undertakings are accepted then no reference may subsequently be made to the Competition Commission in relation to the same transaction, unless of course the undertakings are breached.[31] The Director must keep under review compliance with those undertakings and their appropriateness given changing circumstances. Details of undertakings given to the Secretary of State are published.

Investigation

11-38 It is the Secretary of State who alone is responsible for making any merger reference and for deciding what action should follow a Competition Commission report. The Secretary of State (though he is not duty-bound to) will invariably follow any recommendation from the Director that a reference be made.

---

[29] s. 75B(3) of the Fair Trading Act 1973.
[30] There is some doubt whether these time limits would apply in the case of confidential guidance (see *Confidential Guidance* below).
[31] In which case the Secretary of State may exercise limited powers relating primarily to divestment.

A merger reference requires the Competition Commission to investigate and report on one or both of the following two questions:

(1) whether a merger situation qualifying for investigation has been created; and if so

(2) whether the creation of that situation operates, or may be expected to operate, against the public interest.

The reference may be framed in such a way as to require the Competition Commission only to address one or other of the two limbs, (a) and (b), of section 64(1).[32] If the relevant asset value exceeds £70 million, it would be unnecessary to ask the Competition Commission to address the issue of whether a monopoly situation is created or strengthened. Similarly, if the figure is manifestly not exceeded, the Competition Commission need not be required to investigate asset value further but instead may be asked to focus on the status of the monopoly situation.

11-39 An investigation, where appropriate, may be confined only to activities within a part of the United Kingdom. Once a finding is made that the merger does qualify for investigation, the investigation may then be confined to specific elements or consequences that have public interest implications.

Each merger reference must specify a deadline, within six months of the reference, for making a report. No action may be taken by the Secretary of State in relation to a reference until the report is made, which must be made in time, unless the deadline is extended by the Secretary of State at the Competition Commission's request. Only one extension may be made and that must be of less than three months. There is provision for varying merger references, but these time-scales may not be varied.

11-40 On making a merger reference, the Secretary of State will also make arrangements for details to be published.

The Competition Commission in making its report must give definite conclusions on the questions comprised in the reference, together with a reasoned account of its conclusions and a survey of the general position concerning the subject matter of the reference and the developments that gave rise to it. In making a finding that a merger situation qualifying for investigation has been created which may, or threatens to, harm public interest, the Competition Commission must particularise the adverse impact on public interest and consider remedial action by Ministers or public authorities or those running the enterprises and may, if appropriate, make recommendations.

11-41 If the Competition Commission determines that the merger does not harm public interest, no further action may be taken by the Secretary of State. If, on the other hand, the Competition Commission concludes that the merger does threaten public interest, extensive powers are available to the Secretary of State as described below in *Investigations and Orders*. These are set out in full in Parts I and II of Schedule 8.[33] More often than not, the matter is resolved by means of undertakings negotiated with the Director but given ultimately in favour of the Secretary of State. Civil remedies are available to any third party adversely affected by a breach of such an undertaking.[34]

Historically, there has been great unwillingness on the part of the Secretary of State to exercise his powers, particularly in relation to divestiture, although divestiture orders are being made or threatened with greater frequency (unless undertakings are given).

---

[32] See *Merger Situations qualifying for investigation (not relating to newspapers)* above.
[33] s. 73(2).
[34] s. 93A.

11-42 The likely outcome of a Competition Commission investigation may be predicted to some extent by the MMC's past approach.[35]

Competition is likely to be regarded as most at risk in the case of horizontal mergers involving overlapping markets. Competition is less likely to be affected if the merger participants are only vertically linked (because they operate at different stages of production or supply of the same goods or services). Where no connection or overlap exists between the activities of the merger parties, competition will rarely be affected. Ultimately, the purpose of each analysis will be to determine whether the merger would result in higher prices, lower quality or other harm to public interest. Once again, issues of market definition and market share are relevant.[36] Those aspects of market structure highlighted in *Assessment of factors* above will apply to an assessment of each merger to determine, in particular, whether the result of the merger is to create or increase market power, depending on the market shares of the parties, other competitors and their market shares. The extent to which there exist barriers to entry (in terms of investment, intellectual property or distribution hurdles), potential competition and other constraints on the ability of the dominant players, will all be relevant.

The Competition Commission will certainly be influenced where market shares will reach unacceptable levels as a result of a merger, such as 70 per cent in *European Ferries/Sealink*,[37] or will result in control of essential facilities such as ports, or where high prices are unlikely to be constrained by competition (*Great Universal Stores/Empire Stores (Bradford)*),[38] unless counter-vailing economic benefits are available such as enhanced employment (*Weidman/Whitely*[39]). There is an increased tendency to view matters more strictly in narrowly-drawn markets such as shoe polish (*Sara Lee Corp/ Reckett and Colman*[40]) or matches (*Swedish Match A/B/Allegheny International Inc*[41] and *The supply of Matches and Disposable Lighters*[42]).

Newspaper mergers

11-43 Special consideration is given to newspaper mergers under sections 57 to 62 of the Fair Trading Act 1973. They are dealt with according to a stricter regime than other mergers. The consent of the Secretary of State is required under section 58 to the transfer of a newspaper or newspaper assets to a newspaper proprietor whose newspapers have an average daily circulation, when combined with that of the target newspaper, of 500,000. Newspapers are defined as daily, Sunday or local newspapers. The transfer is defined to include transactions involving the acquisition of controlling interests (described more broadly than for the purpose of other mergers). Before giving his consent, the Secretary of State must receive a favourable report from the Competition Commission (within a three month time-scale) except in cases of urgency and except where the target newspaper is not economic as a going concern. Penalties may be incurred by those involved in newspaper mergers in breach of the Act.

Issues of public interest are to be investigated by the Competition Commission and reasoned conclusions must be given, together with conditions that might be appropriate in the case of an adverse finding. The political sensitivity which requires newspaper mergers to be treated differently from other mergers is illustrated by the way in which harm to

---

[35] As set out in the MMC's publication "Assessing Competition. MMC, 1993.
[36] See Chap. 4 above.
[37] HCP 1981–82.
[38] Cmmd 8777 (1983).
[39] HCP (1971–72) 490.
[40] Cmmd 2040 (1992).
[41] Cmmd 227 (1987).
[42] Cmmd 1854 (1992).

public interest is to be examined by the Competition Commission under section 59(3), which requires particular account to be taken of:

"the need for accurate presentation of news and free expression of opinion."

11-44   Most references involve local newspapers which pose no threat to public interest although concern has been expressed over the increasing concentrations of ownership of local newspapers (*West Somerset Free Press/Bristol United Press Limited*[43]) and the risk that editorial independence would thereby be lost.

OTHER REFERENCES BY THE SECRETARY OF STATE

General references

11-45   Section 78 of the Fair Trading Act 1973 empowers the Secretary of State (whether alone or in conjunction with the relevant Minister) to require the Competition Commission to report on the general effect on public interest (with a report on the desirability of corrective action) of practices of a specified class which are commonly adopted either as a result of, or for the purpose of, preserving a monopoly situation or of any specified practices which appear to be "uncompetitive practices". Section 137 defines "uncompetitive practices" as "practices having the effect of preventing, restricting or distorting competition in connection with any commercial activities in the United Kingdom", and these powers therefore theoretically extend considerably beyond monopoly situations and merger situations. However, given the breadth of the Chapter I and Chapter II prohibitions introduced by the 1998 Act, the Secretary of State is less likely to need to resort to general references.

References as to restrictive labour practices

11-46   The Secretary of State may also make a reference under section 79 of the Fair Trading Act 1973 (either alone or jointly with the appropriate Minister) concerning restrictive labour practices and their adverse effect on public interest, whether in relation to commercial activities in the United Kingdom generally or the supply (or export) of goods or services of a description chosen by the reference. A "restrictive labour practice" is a practice resulting in restrictions or requirements (other than as to pay) concerning the employment of workers or work done by them which are either unnecessary, or are more stringent than necessary, given the commercial activities to which they relate. References under section 79 are comparatively rare.

INVESTIGATIONS AND ORDERS

11-47   Parts VII and VIII of the Fair Trading Act 1973 (sections 81 to 93) deal with the procedures for carrying out investigations and making references to the Competition Commission, whether in relation to monopoly situations or mergers.

The Competition Commission is to take into consideration any representations made by those who appear to have a substantial interest in the subject matter of the reference, or by bodies that represent interested parties, and to permit oral representations to be made unless it is not necessary or is impracticable. The Competition Commission may determine its own procedures for carrying out any investigation on a reference under the

---

[43] HCP (1979 — 80) 546.

Fair Trading Act 1973, including the extent to which interested parties may be present in proceedings and cross-examine witnesses giving evidence to the Competition Commission. The Competition Commission must, however, act in accordance with directions given by the Secretary of State.

11-48 The Competition Commission must also pay regard (within practical limitations) to the need to exclude from any report matters relating to the private affairs of an individual where publication would prejudice that person, and matters concerning any body of people (including a company) if its interests would likewise be prejudiced by publication.[44]

Section 84 of the Fair Trading Act 1973 set out those matters that are relevant to a determination of whether public interest may be harmed. The Commission must take into account all matters which appear in the particular circumstances to be relevant and, among other things, shall have regard to the desirability:

(a) of maintaining and promoting effective competition between persons supplying goods and services in the United Kingdom;

(b) of promoting the interests of consumers, purchasers and other users of goods and services in the United Kingdom in respect of the prices charged for them and in respect of their quality and the variety of goods and services supplied;

(c) of promoting, through competition, the reduction of costs and the development and use of new techniques and new products, and of facilitating the entry of new competitors into existing markets;

(d) of maintaining and promoting the balanced distribution of industry and employment in the United Kingdom; and

(e) of maintaining and promoting competitive activity in markets outside the United Kingdom on the part of producers of goods, and of suppliers of goods and services, in the United Kingdom.

11-49 Witnesses may be required to give evidence upon the order of the Competition Commission and others may be required by notice to produce documents described in the notice within their custody or control, provided they are relevant to the investigation. The Competition Commission may also require other information to be provided.

Witnesses are not compellable in proceedings before the Competition Commission if they are not compellable in civil proceedings and the production of documents and information may only be compelled to the same extent as in civil courts.

As with section 44 of the Fair Trading Act 1973, which applies to investigations by the Director, it is an offence to wilfully alter, suppress or destroy a document which is required to be produced or to fail to comply with a notice under section 85. Nevertheless, the offences created under section 85 do not exactly match those created under section 44.

11-50 If a report by the Competition Commission concludes that public interest is or may be expected to be adversely affected, extensive powers as set out in Schedule 8, Parts I and II are available. Under section 56(2), in the case of a monopoly reference not limited to the facts, the Secretary of State may by order made by statutory instrument exercise any of those powers for the purpose of remedying or preventing the adverse effects specified in a Competition Commission report laid before Parliament. However, an Act of Parliament is required before any of the powers in Part II may be exercised as these are more draconian. Schedule 8, Part I includes the power to make an order:

---

[44] s. 82 of the Fair Trading Act 1973.

(1) requiring termination of any agreement specified in any order; or

(2) declaring it unlawful:

    (i) to make or carry out any agreement specified or described in the order;

    (ii) to refuse to supply, to threaten to refuse to supply or to agree not to supply specified services;

    (iii) to require as a condition of supplying goods or services, the buying of other goods or making unrelated payments;

    (iv) to discriminate between customers buying goods or services;

    (v) to offer certain preferential business terms when supplying goods or services;

    (vi) to depart from published prices (or an order may alternatively require prices to be published or accounting details relating to price to be published);

    (vii) to issue price recommendations;

(3) prohibiting or restricting the acquisition of shares or assets;

(4) requiring activities to be carried on separately from each other.

Schedule 8, Part II includes power to make any of the following orders for divestment by a single undertaking or group:

(1) the transfer or vesting of property, rights, liabilities or obligations;

(2) the adjustment of contracts, whether by discharge or reduction of any liability or obligation or otherwise;

(3) the creation, allotment, surrender or cancellation of any shares, stocks or securities;

(4) the formation or winding up of a company or other association, corporate or unincorporate, or the amendment of the memorandum and articles or other instruments regulating any company or association;

(5) the continuation, with any necessary change of parties, of any legal proceedings.[45]

11-51 In addition, section 51 of the Patents Act 1977 empowers the Comptroller of Patents to cancel or modify any patent licence term or grant a licence of right following a report from the Competition Commission justifying such action. Similarly, section 144 of the Copyright Designs and Patents Act 1988 confers equivalent powers on the Secretary of State in relation to copyright works.

In reality, the powers under the Fair Trading Act 1973 are rarely invoked. It is ultimately up to the Secretary of State whether to follow any recommendations in a report issued by the Competition Commission. The Director in any event may keep matters under review even if no action is taken. Matters are resolved in practice by means of undertakings. Further powers are found in Schedule 8 to correct breaches of undertakings and a breach in any event will entitle a further reference to be made by the Director.

11-52 At the end of the day, the Fair Trading Act provides a framework for discretion to be exercised by the Director and the Secretary of State.

The Act preserves the right to pursue civil remedies (under section 93) for any breach

---

[45] Para. 14.

of any order. Nevertheless, monopoly situations and mergers are not themselves prohibited. Given the regime of the Chapter I and Chapter II prohibitions, the Fair Trading Act 1973 is likely to be side-lined except for the purpose of regulating the biggest United Kingdom mergers and few, if any, monopoly situations.

INTERFACE BETWEEN THE COMPETITION ACT 1998 AND THE FAIR TRADING ACT 1973

11-53   Schedule 1 to the 1998 Act[46] addresses the inter-relation between the Chapter I and Chapter II prohibitions on the one hand, and the Fair Trading Act 1973 on the other. The Chapter I prohibition does not apply to the extent that agreements result in two enterprises ceasing to be distinct. because these are intended to be caught by the Fair Trading Act 1973 only. The exclusion also extends to those provisions that are directly related and necessary to the implementation of the merger.

However, considerable discretion is reserved to the Director in paragraph 4 of Schedule 1 to disapply that exclusion and require any party to the agreement in question to provide any information he may require, if he considers that the agreement would infringe the Chapter I prohibition and not be eligible for unconditional individual exemption. For the Director to do so, the agreement must not be a protected agreement, *i.e.* one which is the subject of an announced decision by the Secretary of State not to make a merger reference (under section 64 of the Fair Trading Act 1973) or, following a merger reference is one that the Competition Commission has found constitutes a merger qualifying for investigation, or otherwise results in enterprises ceasing to be distinct within the meaning of sections 65 of the Fair Trading Act.[47]

11-54   Similarly, the Chapter II prohibition does not apply to conduct otherwise caught by Chapter II, to the extent that it results in two enterprises ceasing to be distinct, or is directly related and necessary to achieving the merger in question. Similar principles apply to newspaper mergers.

---

[46] Para. 1.
[47] There is a specific provision applicable to mergers the subject of references under s. 32 of the Water Industry Act 1991, which are also "protected agreements".

CHAPTER 12

E.C. Merger Control

INTRODUCTION

12-01 Mergers under E.C. law are controlled primarily by means of Council Regulation 4064/89 on the control of concentrations between undertakings[1] (the "Merger Regulation"), which underwent revision by Council Regulation 1310/97 (the "Amending Regulation")[2] in the light of some seven years of experience. The control of mergers is required to supplement Articles 85(1) and 86 of the E.C. Treaty because those Articles are not sufficient to control all operations that result in structural changes to the market which create or strengthen market power in such a way that competition is significantly impeded. The Merger Regulation is only concerned with mergers with a "Community dimension" which have the result of impeding competition within the Community. "Community dimension" is defined by reference both to geography and turnover.

The Merger Regulation requires concentrations with a Community dimension to be notified to the Commission. The Commission is given exclusive jurisdiction to determine their compatibility with the common market. Unlike mergers qualifying for investigation under the Fair Trading Act 1973, notification under the Merger Regulation is mandatory. The Commission is then given time to consider whether or not the merger should proceed. Provision is made for the suspension of concentrations for a limited period and, where necessary, for any suspension to be extended or waived. This is to be balanced against the need for certainty concerning the legal validity of transactions. Very clear time-scales are laid down for the Commission to make its decision, as well as strict time-scales for initiating proceedings in relation to notified mergers. The advantage of the Merger Regulation is that it provides for swift clearance of concentrations.

12-02 The thrust of the Merger Regulation, as revised, is to decentralise the task of merger control by giving jurisdiction to the Commission only in the clearest cases of impact on competition in the Community. The intended result is to place control of other mergers in the hands of the national competition authorities and to reduce the unnecessary caseload of duplicate notifications to the Commission and national authorities, by establishing a "one-stop shop" system of notification.

The Merger Regulation deals primarily with structural changes to the market that result from concentrations. Joint ventures in certain circumstances may be concentrations if they bring about lasting changes and qualify as full-function joint ventures.

SCOPE OF THE MERGER REGULATION

The meaning of "Concentration" and "Community dimension"

12-03 All "concentrations" with a "Community dimension" must be notified to the Commission. According to Article 3(1), a "concentration" arises where:

---

[1] Council Reg. 4064/89 [1990] O.J. L257/13.
[2] Council Reg. 1310/97 [1997] O.J. L180/1.

"(a) two or more previously independent undertakings merge, or

(b) — one or more persons already controlling at least one undertaking, or

— one or more undertakings

acquire, whether by purchase of securities or assets, by contract or by any other means, direct or indirect control of the whole or parts of one or more other undertakings."

A concentration may also result from the creation of a joint venture performing on a lasting basis all the functions of an autonomous economic entity (as discussed further in *Full-Function Joint Ventures* below).

The term "control" refers to "the possibility of exercising decisive influence on an undertaking", whether by virtue of ownership of shares, assets or contractual or voting rights.[3]

12-04 Concentrations will be reviewed by the Commission within the general framework of achieving the fundamental objectives in Article 2 of the E.C. Treaty namely of establishing and maintaining the common market and with the aim of strengthening the Community's economic and social cohesion. Article 2 of the Merger Regulation requires the Commission to take account of the following:

"(a) the need to maintain and develop effective competition within the common market in view of, among other things, the structure of all the markets concerned and the actual or potential competition from undertakings located either within or outwith the Community;

(b) the market position of the undertakings concerned and their economic and financial power, the alternatives available to suppliers and users, their access to supplies or markets, any legal or other barriers to entry, supply and demand trends for the relevant goods and services, the interests of the intermediate and ultimate consumers, and the development of technical and economic progress provided that it is to consumers' advantage and does not form an obstacle to competition."

Articles 2(2) and 2(3) confirm that concentrations which create or strengthen a dominant position as a result of which effective competition would be significantly impeded in the common market (or substantial part) are to be declared incompatible with the common market and those that do not are to be declared compatible. Having said that, the Merger Regulation only applies to concentrations with a "Community dimension", defined by various turnover thresholds in Article 1(2).

12-05 A concentration has a Community dimension where:

"(a) the combined aggregate worldwide turnover of all of the undertakings concerned is more than 5,000 million ECUs; and

(b) the aggregate Community-wide turnover of each of at least two of the undertakings concerned is more than 250 million ECUs

unless each of the undertakings concerned achieves more than two-thirds of its aggregate Community-wide turnover within one and the same Member State."[4]

This reflects the "two-thirds rule" which excludes from a Community dimension mergers between undertakings where each derives more than two-thirds of its Community-wide turnover from a single Member State. The aim is to exclude from the Community's jurisdiction those mergers which are essentially national in character. However, jurisdiction is clawed back by Article 1(3) if the merger results in national mergers in at least three Member States. Article 1(3) was newly introduced by the Amending Regulation and

---

[3] Art. 3(3).

[4] Art. 1(2) of the Merger Reg.

stipulates that even if a concentration does not meet the thresholds of Article 1, a concentration nevertheless still has a Community dimension where:

"(a) the combined aggregate worldwide turnover of all the undertakings concerned is more than 2,500 million ECUs;

(b) in each of at least three Member States, the combined aggregate turnover of all the undertakings concerned is more than 100 million ECUs;

(c) in each of at least three Member States included for the purpose of point (b), the aggregate turnover of each of at least two of the undertakings concerned is more than 25 million ECUs; and

(d) the aggregate Community-wide turnover of each of at least two of the undertakings concerned is more than 100 million ECUs;

unless each of the undertakings concerned achieves more than two-thirds of its aggregate Community-wide turnover within one and the same Member State."[5]

12-06–12-07   This might be represented as shown in Figures 4 and 5[6] pp. 227 and 228.

Turnover

12-08   Turnover is defined in Article 5 by reference to sales (whether of products or services or from other ordinary activities of the undertakings) in the preceding financial year after deduction of sales rebates, VAT and other taxes on turnover. Relevant turnover is that of the undertakings and those they control or are controlled by whether directly, indirectly or jointly (with due apportionment of turnover in the case of jointly-held entities). However, turnover from sales between those entities is excluded.

Special provision is made in the Amending Regulation for the calculation of turnover for certain credit institutions, other financial institutions and insurance companies which deal in and hold securities on behalf of others on a temporary basis.[7]

Notification

12-09   "Concentrations" with a "Community dimension" must be notified to the Commission within a week following the agreement, announcement of the public bid or acquisition of a controlling interest giving rise to the concentration. Notification is to be made jointly by the parties to the merger or those acquiring joint control as appropriate, using Form CO.[8] Details of all notifications that qualify under the Merger Regulation are published by the Commission specifying the parties, the nature of the concentration and the economic sector involved. In publishing those details, the Commission must take account of the legitimate interests of the undertakings in the protection of their business secrets.[9]

PROCEDURE ON NOTIFICATION

12-10   The Commission is required by Article 6 to examine each notification as soon as it is received and to decide whether the notified concentration is within the scope of the

---

[5] Art. 1(3) of the Merger Reg. amended by Art. 1(1)(b) of the Amending Reg.

[6] Diagram prepared by Raymond Gay for papers presented by the author at a conference in Cambridge on January 29, 1998.

[7] Art. 5(3) of the Merger Reg. amended by Art. 1(4) of the Amending Reg.

[8] Form CO was amended by Commission Reg. 447/98 on the notifications, time limits and hearings provided for in Council Reg. 4064/89 on the control of concentrations between undertakings [1998] O.J. L061/1–28—the "Implementing Reg.".

[9] Art. 5(3).

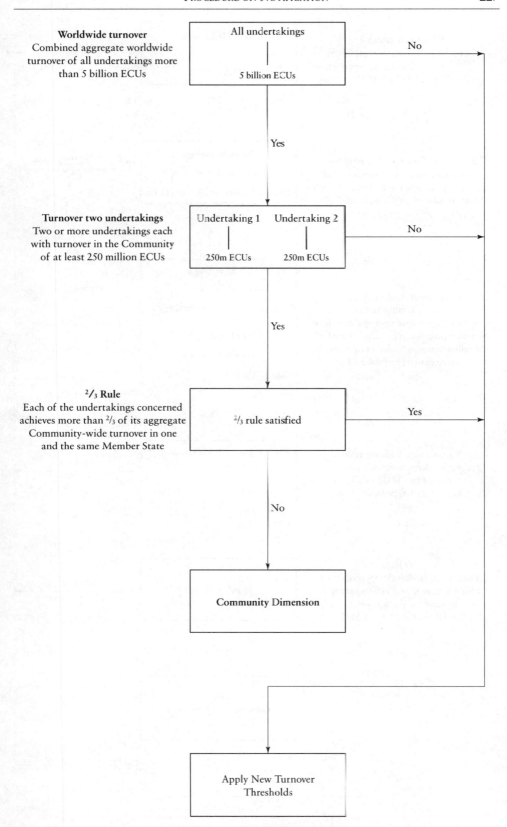

Worldwide turnover
Combined aggregate worldwide turnover of all undertakings more than 5 billion ECUs

All undertakings

5 billion ECUs

No

Turnover two undertakings
Two or more undertakings each with turnover in the Community of at least 250 million ECUs

Undertaking 1   Undertaking 2

250m ECUs   250m ECUs

No

Yes

²/₃ Rule
Each of the undertakings concerned achieves more than ²/₃ of its aggregate Community-wide turnover in one and the same Member State

²/₃ rule satisfied

Yes

No

Community Dimension

Apply New Turnover Thresholds

Figure 4   E.C. Merger Control Current Turnover Thresholds

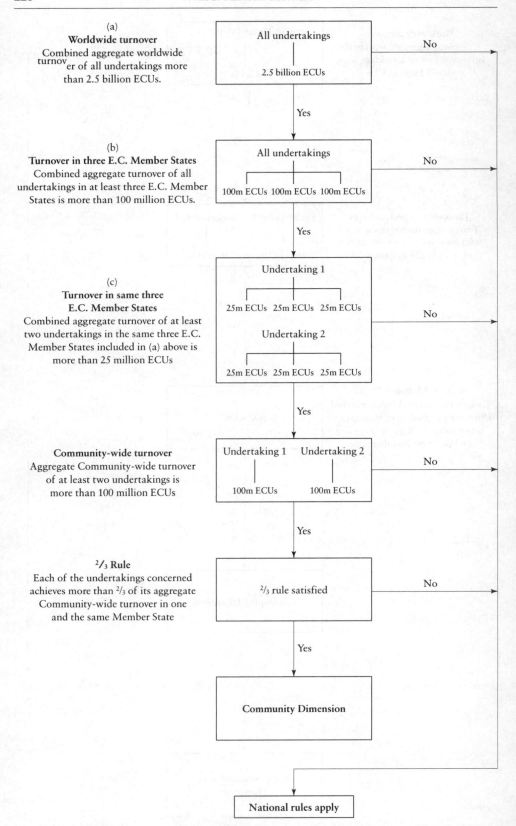

Figure 5   E.C. Merger Control Regulation New Supplemental Turnover Thresholds

Regulation. If it finds that a qualifying concentration does not raise serious doubts as to its compatibility with the common market, it must clear it by declaring it to be compatible with the common market, together with the restrictions directly related and necessary to the implementation of the concentration.[10] If the Commission decides that it does raise serious doubts, the Commission must initiate proceedings. In each case, the Commission must notify its decision to the authorities of the relevant Member States without delay.

Phase I

12-11   Article 6(2)[11] provides for modification of agreements in order to achieve clearance and for the Commission to attach conditions and obligations to any clearance given, to ensure that the undertakings comply with commitments given to the Commission to render the merger acceptable. This formalises an existing practice of the Commission. However, the Amending Regulation stipulates that this is appropriate only "where the competition problem is readily identifiable and can easily be remedied".[12] (Proposed commitments must be submitted to the Commission within three weeks of notification.[13]) In any event, the Commission must notify its decision both to the undertakings themselves and to the competent authorities within the relevant Member State without delay.[14]

No qualifying concentration may be put into effect before it has been notified and been cleared.[15] Until then the merger is suspended. However, the Commission has power under Article 7(4)[16] to grant a derogation from the suspension of the merger upon a well-reasoned request, taking into account "the effects of the suspension on one or more undertakings concerned by a concentration or on a third party and the threat to competition posed by the concentration". Derogation will be particularly important for rescue mergers which need to process with speed.

12-12   Article 10(1) requires the Commission to make its decision concerning compatibility with the common market under Article 6 within one month at the most from notification. This period is extendable to six weeks either where the undertakings submit suitable commitments or upon request by a Member State.[17] This request may be made by a Member State in response to referral of the merger by the Commission to relevant Member States under Article 9.

Article 9 enables the Commission, by means of a decision, to refer a notified concentration to the competent authorities of Member States. Within three weeks of receipt of a notification, a Member State may inform the Commission (who must pass this on to the undertakings concerned) that the concentration affects competition in a distinct market within the territory of that Member State in that it either:

(a)   threatens to create or strengthen a dominant position with resulting impact on competition within that Member State, which presents all the characteristics of a distinct market; or

(b)   affects competition on a market within that Member State, which presents all the characteristics of a distinct market and which does not constitute a substantial part of the common market.[18]

---

[10]   Art. 6.1(b) of the Merger Reg. as amended.
[11]   Inserted by Art. 1(5)(b) of the Amending Reg.
[12]   Recital 8 of the Amending Reg.
[13]   Implementing Reg. Art. 18.
[14]   Art. 6(5).
[15]   Or deemed clearance.
[16]   Amended by Art. 1(6)(d) of the Amending Reg.
[17]   The request by a Member State will only be made in exceptional circumstances.
[18]   Art. 9(2) of the Merger Reg. amended by Art. 1(8)(a) of the Amending Reg.

12-13 If a Member State informs the Commission that a concentration affects competition in a distinct market within its territory that does not form a substantial part of the common market, the Commission is to refer all or part of the case to the national authority, with a view to the application of that State's national competition law. Otherwise the Commission may deal with the matter itself either entirely or in part.

The decision whether or not to refer to the national authority must be made within the extended six week period[19] or within three months at most of notification in cases where the Commission has decided to initiate proceedings[20] following a finding that the concentration raises doubts as to its compatibility with the common market.

12-14 Liaison with national competition authorities goes further in Article 19 by requiring the Commission to transmit to competent authorities of Member States copies of notifications within three working days of their receipt together with copies of the most important documents lodged with the Commission, as well as any commitments given to the Commission under Articles 6(1)(a) or 8(2). Close and constant liaison is also to be maintained between the Commission and those authorities in all proceedings covered by the Merger Regulation in order to give the authorities the opportunity to express their views on those procedures.

If the Commission does not act within these timescales, the concentration is deemed to be cleared. Unless incomplete information is given in support of a notification.

One of the most important changes introduced into Article 9 by the Amending Regulation relates to the case-load division between the Commission and the authorities of Member States. This is consistent with the aims set out in the Commission Notice on co-operation between national competition authorities and the Commission in handling cases falling within the scope of Article 85 or 86 of the E.C. Treaty,[21] in particular, that of enhancing the role of national competition authorities in order to boost the effectiveness of Articles 85 and 86 and to avoid duplication by national authorities and the Commission.

12-15 An Advisory Committee on concentrations, consisting of representatives of the authorities of the Member States is to be consulted before any decision is made under Article 8(2) to clear a merger after proceedings have initiated, or to revoke such a decision under Article 8(5), or to impose a fine. The Advisory Committee may deliver an opinion on the Commission's draft decision and the Commission must take "the utmost account" of that opinion.[22]

In summary the Commission may clear a qualifying merger without modification. Secondly, the merger may be modified where necessary before clearance is given as provided in the amended Article 6(2). The clearance may contain conditions and obligations to ensure that the undertakings comply with commitments to the Commission to render the merger compatible with the common market. Thirdly, the merger might be referred to relevant Member States under Article 9. Fourthly, the Commission may decide not to permit the merger and instead to initiate proceedings under Article 6(1)(c).[23] Phase II will then commence.

Phase II

12-16 All proceedings, once initiated, must be resolved by one of the following decisions:

---

[19] Under Art. 10(1).
[20] Under Art. 6(1)(c) as amended by Art. 1(5) of the Amending Reg.
[21] Commission Notice of October 15, 1997 on co-operation between national competition authorities and the Commission [1997] O.J. C 313/03, discussed further in Chap. 14 below.
[22] Art. 19(6).
[23] Art. 10(3).

(1) A decision may be taken under Article 8(2) declaring the concentration to be compatible with the common market, following modification if necessary by the undertakings. The basis of the decision would be that the concentration satisfies the Article 2(2) criteria[24] or, in the case of to joint venture concentrations, the Article 85(3) criteria are satisfied in relation to the co-ordination of competitive behaviour between the joint venture parents. Conditions and obligations may be attached to the Commission's decision, to ensure compliance with commitments given by the undertakings to the Commission in order to render the concentration compatible. Any clearance given also extends to restrictions directly related and necessary to the implementation of the concentration.[25] The Commission must make a decision under Article 8(2) as soon as it appears that the serious doubts referred to in Article 6(1)(c) have been removed[26] and, at the latest, within four months of the date on which proceedings were initiated unless, in exceptional circumstances for which one of the undertakings is responsible, the Commission has to request information under Article 11[27] or the Commission has decided to order an investigation under Article 13;

(2) A decision may be taken under Article 8(3) (as amended) to refuse to clear the merger by declaring that the concentration is incompatible with the common market because the Article 2(3) criteria are satisfied[28] or, in the case of joint venture concentrations, the Article 85(3) criteria are not satisfied in relation to the co-ordination of competitive behaviour between the joint venture parents; or

(3) As part of the decision referred to in (2) above, under Article 8(4) the Commission may require, after completion of a merger, that the undertakings or assets or joint control be separated or the Commission may require any other appropriate action to restore competition.

Any clearance given by the Commission under Article 8 may be revoked if given on the basis of incorrect information for which one of the undertakings is responsible or if any of the undertakings given is breached. In such cases, the Commission is not bound by the timescales for deciding to refuse a merger.

12-17 In *Boeing Company/McDonnell Douglas Corporation*,[29] the Commission estimated that Boeing's market share of fleet aircraft would increase from approximately 60 per cent to 85 per cent and it only allowed the merger to proceed on condition that all exclusive supply contracts with certain airlines cease (and there be no more in the future to tie airlines to Boeing). Also certain intellectual property rights were required to be made available for exploitation by competitors.

In *Tesco/ABF*,[30] the acquisition by Tesco of retail outlets in Ireland would result in strengthened purchasing power in Ireland owing to Tesco's market position in the United Kingdom but as Tesco's presence in Ireland was weak, it was not likely to result in dominance. The transaction was cleared.

12-18 In *Coca-Cola Enterprises Inc./Amalgamated Beverages*[31] the acquisition by

---

[24] That the concentration does not create or strengthen a dominant position as a result of which effective competition would be significantly impeded in the Common Market or a substantial part of it.
[25] For further detail see *Ancillary Restrictions* below.
[26] Art. 10(2).
[27] See *Requests for information and investigation* below.
[28] That the concentration creates or strengthens a dominant position as a result of which effective competition would be significantly impeded in the Common Market or a substantial part of it.
[29] Commission Dec. 97/816 [1997] O.J. L336/16.
[30] [1997] O.J. C162/3 [1997] 4 C.M.L.R. 981 (1P) May 5, 1997.
[31] Commission Dec. 97/540 [1997] O.J. L218/15 [1997] 4 C.M.L.R. 368 (1P) January 22, 1997.

Coca-Cola of a bottling plant gave rise to concerns of dominance in view of the pre-existing high market share of Coca-Cola in the United Kingdom in a market comprising cola-flavoured soft drinks. The operation would be vertically integrated combining a powerful brand and economies of scale at all levels of production and distribution. Undertakings were given not to impose tying restrictions, exclusively obligations or long-term target rebates. Similarly in *Coca-Cola/Carlsberg A/S*,[32] concerns were expressed about a joint venture that would result in greater vertical integration of Coca-Cola in bottling and distribution, and the loss of competition from Carlsberg that would result from licences of its soft drinks to Coca-Cola. Undertakings were given that would result in Carlsberg's divestiture of its interests in companies which bottle or produce Pepsi or other cola products in Denmark.

Divestiture was also required in order to clear the *Guinness/Grand Metropolitan*[33] merger. One of the issues was the effect of "portfolio power" *i.e.* market strength achieved through complementary brand portfolios. Market strength may increase beyond that merely reflected in increased market shares. Distribution of Bacardi was required to be ended in Greece even though there was no resulting increase in market share. Concerns about portfolio power stem from the risk that where a single entity controls a portfolio of "must stock" products, its bargaining strength increases disproportionately. It may also piggy-back secondary brands, in effect forcing them on the purchaser.

12-19 The existence of market power in secondary markets was also of concern in *Hoffman-La Roche/Boehringer Mannheim*.[34] It concerned one aspect of the combined businesses, namely *in vitro* (out of body) diagnostic tests. Diagnostic tests comprise two components: diagnostic equipment and the chemical reagents used in the equipment. The combined market share of the parties and their established strengths in diagnostic equipment were considered to enable them to exert power in the chemical reagents "after-market", where purchasers have a preference for taking supplies of chemical reagents from the supplier of the corresponding equipment. Clearance was given against undertakings to divest the business in certain instruments in particular Member States and to grant licences of intellectual property.

Kali and Salz[35] illustrates that the burden is on the Commission to establish, as a matter of evidence, the effects of the concentration in question, in that case that collective dominance would result. The case also confirms that a merger is likely to be cleared if the target would no longer exist in the market if the merger were not to proceed and the market share of the outgoing business in such circumstances would transfer to the acquiring company, provided there are no less anti-competitive solutions available.

Procedure Following Notification

Requests for information and investigation

12-20 The Commission is empowered by Article 11 to make wide-ranging requests for information including from governments, the competent authorities of Member States, third parties and obviously from the undertakings themselves. Any request from a private entity must also be copied to the competent authority of the Member State in which the entity is situated.

Article 13 is concerned with the investigative powers of the Commission to examine the

---

[32] Commission Dec. 98/327 [1998] O.J. L145/41 [1997] 5 C.M.L.R. 564 (1P) September 11, 1997.
[33] Commission Dec. 98/602 [1998] O.J. L288/24 [1997] 5 C.M.L.R. 567 (1P) October 15, 1997.
[34] Commission Dec. 98/526 [1998] O.J. L234/14.
[35] Joined Cases C–68 & C–30/95 *French Republic and Société Commerciale des potasses et de l'atoze (SCPA) and Enterprise Minière et Chimique (EMC) v. Commission* [1998] E.C.R. I-1375.

books and records of undertakings, to ask for on the spot oral explanations and to enter their premises. These investigations, where necessary, are to be carried out by the competent authorities of the Member States upon the Commission's request under Article 12.

Fines

12-21   Fines of between 1,000 to 50,000 ECUs may be levied for intentionally or negligently failing to notify a concentration, for supplying incorrect or misleading information in any notification or in response to an Article 11 request, for not complying with an Article 11 request on time, and for supplying incomplete documents during an investigation.

Far greater fines may be imposed, according to the gravity of the infringement, of up to 10 per cent of the aggregate turnover of the undertakings concerned for putting into effect a concentration which is declared incompatible with the common market, or for breach of the terms of any obligation relating to derogation from suspension under Article 7(4), or breach of any commitment to the Commission under Article 8(2) given as a condition of clearance.

12-22   In addition, periodic penalties of up to 25,000 ECUs for each day may be levied for failure to provide complete and correct information requested under Article 11 or for failure to submit to an investigation ordered under Article 13. In addition, periodical penalties may be imposed on a daily basis of up to 100,000 ECUs for non-compliance with any Article 8(2) commitment given as a condition of clearance or an Article 8(4) order made by the Commission after the merger has taken place. All penalties are subject to review by the ECJ which may increase, cancel or reduce fines.

Professional secrecy is to be maintained under Article 17 for information acquired pursuant to Articles 11, 12 or 13 or in hearings involving the undertakings and even third parties under Article 18. Information is to be used only for the purpose of the relevant request, investigation or hearing.

Hearings

12-23   Before the Commission makes any decision under Article 7(4) to derogate from the usual suspension period or, after initiating proceedings, before it makes a decision under Article 8(2) to clear a merger following commitments, or decides under Article 8(3) to refuse a merger, or decides under Articles 8(4) or 8(5) to reverse a merger, or decides to revoke a previous decision, the Commission will give the undertakings concerned the opportunity of expressing their views on the objections against them.[36] The Commission must only make its decision on the basis of the objections on which the undertakings have had the opportunity to submit their observations. The parties directly involved will be allowed access to the files subject to the need to respect the confidentiality of business secrets in order to protect the legitimate business interests of undertakings. Others may also be heard if they have sufficient interest, including members of management and employee representatives.

Publication

12-24   Finally, decisions by the Commission pursuant to Articles 8(2) to (5) are published in the Official Journal stating the names of the parties and the main content of the decision, having regard once again, to the legitimate interests of the undertakings in relation to their business secrets.

---

[36] The Commission may instead, in the case of an Art. 7(4) decision, notify the undertakings after the decision has been made.

FULL-FUNCTION JOINT VENTURES

12-25 Certain joint ventures, known as "full-function joint ventures", are now assessed under the Merger Regulation if the parents jointly control the joint venture and satisfy the turnover thresholds for a Community dimension referred to above. The amendments introduced by the Amending Regulation simplify the treatment of joint ventures. Article 3(2) of the Merger Regulation[37] now provides as follows:

> "The creation of a joint venture performing on a lasting basis all the functions of an autonomous economic entity shall constitute a concentration."

The test for determining whether a joint venture should be refused is two-fold. First, as with all concentrations, a dominance test applies to determine whether it

> "create[s] or strengthen[s] a dominant position as a result of which effective competition would be significantly impeded in the common market or in a substantial part of it."[38]

Secondly, an assessment must be made applying Article 85(1) and 85(3) criteria, since Article 2(4)[39] provides as follows:

> "To the extent that the creation of a joint venture constituting a concentration pursuant to Article 3 has as its object or effect the co-ordination of the competitive behaviour of undertakings that remain independent, such co-ordination shall be appraised in accordance with the criteria of Article 85(1) and (3) of the Treaty, with a view to establishing whether or not the operation in question is compatible with the common market."

12-26 When applying the Article 85(1) and (3) criteria, two factors in particular must be taken into account. The first is the extent to which two or more parent companies retain to a significant extent activities in:

(a) the same market as the joint venture; or

(b) in a closely-related market which is downstream or upstream from that of the joint venture; or

(c) in a closely-related neighbouring market.[40]

The greater the range of common activities between the parents, the more likely it is that Article 85(1) will apply and the joint venture be regarded as co-ordinative between the parents. If common activities are confined to upstream, downstream or neighbouring markets then the effects are less directly felt.

12-27 The second factor to be taken into account when applying the Article 85(1) and (3) criteria is whether the co-ordination which is the direct consequence of the joint venture affords the undertakings concerned the possibility of eliminating competition in respect of a substantial part of the products or services in question. The determination

---

[37] Amended by Art. 1(3)(b) of the Amending Reg.
[38] Arts 2(2) and 2(3) of the Merger Reg.
[39] Introduced by Art. 1(2) of the Amending Reg.
[40] Art. 2(4).

of issues concerning Articles 85(1) and (3) will involve the participation of the Article 85 Directorate of the Commission at the request of the Merger Task Force.[41]

In this respect, the Amending Regulation made a significant change. Previously only concentrative, rather than co-operative, joint ventures were controlled by the Merger Regulation. The Commission went to some lengths in its Notice on the distinction between concentrative and co-operative joint ventures[42] to provide guidance on the distinction between the two. The purpose at that time was to exclude co-operative joint ventures from the Merger Regulation, leaving them to be considered in relation to Article 85(3) for individual exemption and not the Merger Regulation. The result of the Amending Regulation is now to treat as concentrations certain co-operative joint ventures that were previously outside the scope of the Merger Regulation, as long as they are full-function joint ventures. The advantage of a full-function joint venture constituting a concentration is that clearance must be given or refused according to strict timescales set out in the Merger Regulation, without the parties having to face the uncertainties and indefinite delays of notification under Article 85(3).

12-28 The Notice on the distinction between concentrative and co-operative joint ventures has been replaced, in the light of the Amending Regulation, by the Commission's Notice on the concept of full-function joint ventures.[43]

The Notice on the concept of full-function joint ventures sets out the requirements of a concentration by reference to principles of joint control and the structural change of the undertakings. Joint control must be acquired by two or more undertakings.[44] The Notice deals at greater length with the structural changes brought about by joint ventures and the requirement that for a joint venture to be eligible for consideration under the Merger Regulation it must perform, on a lasting basis, all the functions of an autonomous economic entity. The joint venture must perform the functions normally carried out by other undertakings operating on the same market. In order to do so, the Notice indicates that the joint venture:

> "must have a management dedicated to its day to day operations and access to sufficient resources including finance, staff[45] and assets (tangible and intangible)[46] in order to conduct on a lasting basis its business activities within the area provided for in the joint venture agreement."[47]

12-29 If the joint venture takes over only one specific function within the parents' activities and does not itself have access to the market then it is not "full-function". An example might be a company that undertakes only R&D, or only production, or only sales. However, a joint venture may utilise distribution networks of the parent without being disqualified as a full-function joint venture.[48]

---

[41] For further discussion on the principles of evaluating joint ventures under Art. 85(1), see Chapter 8, *Joint ventures caught by Article 85(1)*, above.

[42] Commission Notice of December 21, 1989 on the distinction between concentrative and co-operative joint ventures under Council Reg. 4064/89 on the control of concentrations between undertakings [1994] O.J. C385/1.

[43] Commission Notice of March 2, 1998 on the concept of full-function joint ventures under Council Reg. 4064/89 on the control of concentrations between undertakings [1998] O.J. C66/01.

[44] The concept of control is set out in Art. 3(3) of the Merger Reg. and the principles of determining joint control are set out in the Commission's Notice on the concept of a concentration [1998] O.J. C66/5. Closely related is the Commission's Notice on the concept of undertakings under Council Reg. 4064/89 on the control of concentrations between undertakings [1998] O.J. C66/14.

[45] Case IV/M-585 *Voest Alpine Industrieanlagenbau GmbH/Davy International LTD* [1995] 5 C.M.L.R. 135 July 7, 1995.

[46] Case IV/M-527 *Thomson CSF/Deutsche Aerospace* [1995] 4 C.M.L.R. 160 (1P) December 2, 1994.

[47] Para. 12 of the Notice.

[48] Case IV/M–102 *TNT/Canada Post* December 2, 1991.

Heavy reliance by a joint venture on sales to its parents or purchases from its parents may make a finding of full-function less likely unless this is only for a start- up period of about three years.[49] If sales to the parents are made on a long-term basis, much depends on whether the joint venture is able to play an independent role on the market, on the proportion of sales to the parents when compared to its other activities, and whether it sells to (or buys from) the parents on arm's length terms.[50] Where the joint venture makes purchases from the parents and resells them, the likely conclusion will be that a joint sales agency is established. This will be the case if the joint venture does not add value to the product unless, for example it sells and distributes a range of products from different sources of supply, ideally also investing in its own facilities and sales infrastructure.[51]

12-30   Dependence on intellectual property is obviously important. Irrevocable, perpetual licences of intellectual property granted by the parents for all of the activities of the joint venture will obviously help in considering it as a full-function joint venture but it may not be in the interests of the parents to do so as this will prevent them from granting subsequent exclusive licences. By contrast, licences that are too restrictive or temporary may prevent a joint venture from being treated as full-function. The issue for the purposes of the Merger Regulation is whether the joint venture brings about a lasting change in the structure of the undertakings concerned. If a joint venture does that, it is appropriate to treat it as a concentration falling within the Merger Regulation.

The term "lasting change" may vary according to different circumstances. If the joint venture is terminable at will within a period of three to five years it is not likely to be regarded as lasting. A period of more than six years has been considered sufficient (*BA/TAT*).[52] Termination for insolvency or breach should not jeopardise the lasting nature of the joint venture unless, for example termination for breach may be triggered easily.

12-31   Joint ventures raise a number of issues of procedure and jurisdiction in the context of the Merger Regulation. The Merger Regulation only applies to concentrations, including full-function joint ventures, and the Commission is given exclusive jurisdiction to clear those with a Community dimension. Joint ventures inevitably require ongoing co-operation between the parents, which will be considered by applying the principles applicable to Articles 85(1) and 85(3). Only those aspects of the joint venture parents that are structural will be cleared by the Merger Regulation. This includes "restrictions directly related and necessary to the implementation of the concentration".[53] The other aspects of co-operation will need to be the subject of separate notification to the Commission for individual exemption (and will not benefit from the accelerated clearance timescales of the Merger Regulation).

Joint ventures that do not meet the criteria for a "Community dimension" are not eligible for clearance under the Merger Regulation and, if caught by Article 85(1), will need to be the subject of an application for individual exemption without the benefit of the time-scales set out in the Merger Regulation.[54]

12-32   The Commission's Press Release of March 3, 1998 confirms that full-function joint ventures which fall below the turnover thresholds of the Merger Regulation may require notification to Member States in accordance with the national laws of those Member States. In addition, full-function joint ventures which fall below the turnover thresholds, and all partial-function joint ventures which affect trade between Member

---

[49] Case IV/M–560 *EDS/Lufthansa* May 11, 1995.
[50] Case IV/M–556 *Zeneca/Vanderhave* [1996] 4 C.M.L.R. 734 (1P) April 9, 1996.
[51] Case IV/M–788 *Agrevo/Marubeni* [1996] 5 C.M.L.R. 521 (1P) September 3, 1996.
[52] [1992] O.J. C326, para. 10; [1993] 4 C.M.L.R. 10.
[53] Arts 6(1)(b) and 8(2).
[54] However, the Commission is expected to expedite the Reg. 17 procedures in such cases.

States will need to be notified to the Commission under Regulation 17 for individual exemption. However, the Press Release re-iterates the Commission's policy by which the focus for the treatment of such cases should be with the Member States concerned, referring to the Commission's Notice on co-operation between national competition authorities and the Commission in handling cases falling within the scope of Article 85 or 86 of the E.C. Treaty.[55]

ANCILLARY RESTRICTIONS

12-33   The Commission's Notice regarding restrictions ancillary to concentrations[56] ("the Ancillary Restrictions Notice"), though issued in 1990, may arguably still be helpful for the purpose of determining those aspects of full-function joint ventures which are to be considered as "directly related and necessary to the implementation of the concentration", and therefore cleared together with the other structural aspects of the merger. Articles 6(1)(b) and 8(2) of the Merger Regulation both refer to "restrictions directly related and necessary to the implementation of the concentration". The same restrictions are referred to as "ancillary restrictions" in the Ancillary Restrictions Notice. That Notice may also be helpful for the purpose of determining whether Article 85(1) applies to those concentrations that are not eligible for consideration under the Merger Regulation for any reason, as an indication of the extent to which Article 85(1) will apply.

The Restrictions must be necessary. "Restrictions" are those agreed between the parties which limit their own freedom of action in the market (rather than restrictions to the detriment of third parties). For restrictions to be considered "directly related", they must be ancillary to the implementation of the concentration, *i.e.* subordinate in importance to the main object of the concentration. Also the restrictions must be "necessary to the implementation of the concentration". That is to say, the concentration could not be implemented (or not readily) without them. Of relevance, of course, are such matters as the duration and subject-matter of the restrictions, and their geographical scope. As a rule, the undertakings should seek out alternative, less restrictive, means of achieving what the concentration requires without imposing express contractual restrictions. Acceptable ancillary restrictions include the following.

Non-competition clauses

12-34   Non-competition restrictions accepted by the vendor of an undertaking (or part) are commonly acceptable because they guarantee to the purchaser the full value of the assets transferred (whether physical assets or intangible assets such as goodwill, or rights in the form of know-how). Non-competition restrictions are not only directly related to the concentration but also its implementation. Without them the full value of those assets is not transferred to the purchaser if the purchaser is not protected against the activities of the vendor, whether in response to customer loyalty or the fact that the vendor possesses key know-how relating to the business. Non-competition clauses are not generally necessary (and not justified) in the case of a transfer merely of physical assets (because no goodwill is assigned) or in the case of the transfer of certain intellectual property (where the intellectual property confers a monopoly which may be asserted against the vendor such as patents, trade marks and registered designs).

In all cases, the scope of any non-competition clause must not exceed what is

---

[55] [1997] O.J. C313/03 discussed further in Chapter 14 below.
[56] [1990] O.J. C203/05 The Ancillary Restrictions Notice was replaced in the context of joint ventures by the Commission Notice on the distinction between concentrative and co-operative joint ventures, which in turn was replaced by the Notice on the concept of full-function joint venture.

reasonably necessary in terms of duration, geography, subject-matter and those to whom the restriction applies. As a rule of thumb, five years is generally recognised as appropriate in the case of the transfer of an undertaking transferred with both goodwill and know-how, and two years only in the case of the transfer of an undertaking involving goodwill on its own. The geographic scope of the restriction must be confined to the area in which the vendor had established its products or services before the transaction and the restriction must relate only to the activities transferred on the sale of the undertaking.

12-35   The Ancillary Restrictions Notice states[57] that in the case of a partial transfer of assets, the purchaser does not on the face of it need protection against the retained activities of the vendor. There has been increasing use of reverse non-competition clauses in recent years in which the purchaser (rather than vendor) gives non-competition undertakings to protect the retained activities of the vendor. The Ancillary Restrictions Notice does not comment upon the restrictions justified to protect the vendor.

Non-competition restrictions when given by a vendor may bind the vendor, its subsidiaries and commercial agents but should not go further to bind others.

Licences of intellectual property

12-36   Where the undertaking transferred is dependent on intellectual property rights then obviously, in order for the purchaser to exploit the assets transferred, some intellectual property rights will need to be granted. If the vendor has no further need of the intellectual property for any retained business, the rights may be assigned. Otherwise they will need to be licensed, or assigned to the purchaser subject to a licence back to the vendor. Licence restrictions may be included to limit the licensee's field of use, to match the activities of the undertaking transferred or retained. However the Ancillary Restrictions Notice is unclear on the scope of territorial restrictions that may be imposed on the use of intellectual property (other than that it confirms that territorial limits on manufacture would not generally be acceptable). Licence exclusivity does appear to be contemplated as necessary in certain circumstances though these are not spelled out other than by way of reference to the block exemption Regulations 2349/84[58] and 559/89[59] concerning licences of patents and know-how respectively, which have been superseded by the Technology Transfer Regulation 240/96. There is no block exemption Regulation for trade marks or copyright but similar principles to those found in those Regulations may be applied by analogy.

Exclusive licences exclude the licensor from licensed activities for the duration of the licence. If an exclusive licence is granted by the vendor of a business, then the effect might in substance be equivalent to a non-competition undertaking, at least in relation to the activities that utilise the licensed technology. The licence must not be such as to restrict unduly either the vendor or the purchaser. For further discussion concerning intellectual property and joint ventures see Chapter 8 above.

Purchase and supply agreements

12-37   In order to ensure continuity of procurement and supply following the transfer of an undertaking, it is frequently necessary to establish agreements concerning purchase or supply, and ancillary restrictions may be accepted either by the vendor or purchaser. The aim of those restrictions must be to ensure continuity of supply to one or other party of products or services in sufficient quantity needed by them for the retained or acquired business, at least for a transitional period. For example, obligations relating to fixed quan-

---

[57] Para. III A4.
[58] Reg. 2349/84 [1984] O.J. L219.
[59] Reg. 559/89 [1989] O.J. L61.

tities may be necessary but, in general, there does not appear to be justification for exclusive purchase or supply obligations, unless exceptional circumstances apply such as where the products are very specific or there is no available market for them. It is generally considered that alternative means of securing supplies (such as the fixing of quantities required) are sufficient and exclusivity is not necessary.

Any procurement and supply obligations must be objectively justified and no longer than necessary to overcome any transitional period of dependency following the transaction.

Joint venture ancillary restrictions

12-38   In the case of long-term joint ventures involving no ongoing co-ordination between the parents and where, in effect, the parents have withdrawn from the market assigned to the joint venture, non-competition undertakings pose little difficulty since they merely express the reality that the parents have withdrawn from those activities as part of the transaction. Similarly, licences of intellectual property should obviously not be limited in time or territory but may more readily be exclusive, reflecting an arrangement closer to an assignment of intellectual property (except for the scope of retained activities). The Ancillary Restrictions Notice is, once again, less committed on the status of purchase and supply obligations other than to say that they must be examined in accordance with the above principles that apply in the case of the transfer of an undertaking.[60]

It should be remembered that the Ancillary Restrictions Notice is aimed at identifying those cases where, in general, issues of Article 85(1) are avoided. There always remains the possibility of exemption under Article 85(3) for those restrictions that go beyond the scope of those that are purely ancillary.

INTERFACE BETWEEN THE COMPETITION ACT 1998 AND THE MERGER REGULATION

12-39   Schedule 1 to the 1998 Act[61] deals with the inter-relation between the Chapter I and Chapter II prohibitions, on the one hand, and concentrations which are subject to the Merger Regulation.

The 1998 Act clarifies that neither the Chapter I prohibition nor the Chapter II prohibition applies to the extent to which an agreement or conduct gives rise to a concentration with a Community dimension over which the Commission has exclusive jurisdiction under the Merger Regulation.

---

[60] For further discussion on the subject of joint ventures and Art. 85(1) see Chapter 8, *Joint Ventures*.
[61] Para. 6.

CHAPTER 13

United Kingdom Investigation and Enforcement

INVESTIGATIONS

Introduction

13-01 The approach taken by the 1998 Act to investigation and enforcement is in marked contrast to certain continental systems. The Act covers in great detail the procedures and powers governing investigation and enforcement by the Director, due largely to the penalties that may be incurred as a result of infringement of any Chapter I or Chapter II prohibition and the offences created for failure to comply with the Director's requirements.

Chapter III of Part I of the 1998 Act (sections 25 to 44) sets out the Director's powers, both to initiate and conduct investigations and to enforce directions, all under the threat of criminal sanctions for non-compliance.

13-02 The Act is intended to correct many of the manifest shortcomings of the Restrictive Trade Practices Act 1976, the Resale Prices Act 1976 and Competition Act 1980 and to enhance the limited powers of the Director under the Fair Trading Act 1973, all of which contributed to produce a regime of United Kingdom competition law (until the 1998 Act) which did little to correct or deter anti-competitive practices or conduct, or punish those that engaged in them. This is borne out by Lord Bridgeman's statements quoted in Chapter 1, *United Kingdom Law and Administration*. For example, the Director's powers of investigation has been enlarged considerably when compared with those found under section 36 of the Restrictive Trade Practices Act 1976 which merely entitled him to serve a notice on a person whom he had "reasonable cause to believe" was a party to a registrable agreement. Section 37 of the Restrictive Trade Practices Act 1976 enabled the Director to enforce section 36 by an application to the court ordering cross-examination of officers and current employees (but not former employees). The procedure was seldom used because section 36 notices were normally met with plausible responses given after taking legal advice which ensured that the matter was taken no further. Another shortcoming of the Restrictive Trade Practices Act 1976 was its sheer complexity which often left room for parties to a registrable agreement to claim, on their own interpretation, that it was not registrable and to answer any section 36 request accordingly.

The Director now has extensive powers to carry out investigations, to enter premises and to order the production of documents in line with the Commission's powers under Community law.

Grounds for investigation

13-03 Under the 1998 Act the Director may not conduct an investigation at whim. He may only do so if there are "reasonable grounds for suspecting" that either the Chapter I prohibition or the Chapter II prohibition has been infringed. The words, "reasonable grounds for suspecting" are, at first sight, similar to the words, "reasonable cause to believe" in section 36(1) of the Restrictive Trade Practices Act 1976 which posed difficulties for the Director in the past. However, there is a crucial difference which has improved the Director's position considerably. In *Registrar of Restrictive Trading Agreements v. W H Smith*[1] the Registrar was unable to prove "reasonable cause to believe" under section 14(1) of the Restrictive Trade Practices Act 1956. The parallel conduct of competitors could be explained on grounds other than the existence of a restrictive agreement. Lord Denning pointed out[2] that the words are not, "if the Registrar thinks he has reasonable cause to believe". There must in fact have existed such reasonable grounds, known to the Registrar, before he could validly serve such a notice. The subjective test of "suspicion" now overcomes that hurdle.

In practice, infringements come to the Director's attention because of complaints by competitors (or would-be competitors), by disgruntled employees or by victims of infringement. There has always been a practical threshold to overcome before persuading the Director to take up a complaint. It is obviously necessary for the Director to treat complaints with scepticism and to allocate resources properly to the most important demands on the OFT's resources.

13-04 There is no statutory procedure for making a complaint, nor any form or stationery issued by the Director to assist complainants. The Director is unlikely to act on any complaint without knowing the identity of the complainant. As much detail should be provided to the Director concerning the complaint, including any relevant correspondence, notes of meetings or telephone discussions and, ideally, information concerning market structure and the position of the alleged infringer in the market. The harm to public interest, especially harm to the consumer, should be given particular attention. The Director will make the most effective approach to the target if he is able to produce evidence of infringement. Any evidence which accompanies a complaint is likely to be made available to the target unless the complainant expressly requests that it be kept confidential. This may be done by identifying the relevant evidence in a separate schedule when writing to the Director.

Complainants should expect to be revealed as the source of a complaint, although if this will upset the future business relations between the complainant and target, the Director will be sympathetic about requests for anonymity. The Director will keep informants advised of the outcome of decisions made by him. He is not bound to explain why a complaint has been rejected but will frequently do so.

13-05 The Director, of course, not only acts in response to complaints, but frequently takes action on his own initiative. It is one of the Director's primary duties to:

> "keep under review the carrying on of commercial activities in the United Kingdom, and to collect information with respect to those activities, and the persons by whom they are carried on, with a view to becoming aware of, and ascertaining the circumstances relating to, monopoly situations or uncompetitive practices."[3]

When conducting an investigation, the Director is empowered to demand the production of documents and to enter premises, with or without a warrant, depending on the circumstances. These powers closely resemble (and are moulded by) the Commission's powers of enforcement under Community law under Regulation 17/62 Article 11,[4] although there do remain some crucial differences.

---

[1] [1969] 3 All E.R. 1065.
[2] At p. 1070.
[3] The Fair Trading Act 1973, s. 2(2).
[4] See Chap. 14 below.

Production of documents

13-06   In ordering document production, the Director exercises his power by written notice specifying the subject-matter and purpose of the investigation. The notice must warn that offences are committed for non-compliance.[5] It must specify or describe the required document or information required.[6] The time, place, manner and form of production may also be stated but this is not mandatory.[7] The Director may take copies of documents or extracts, as he wishes, and he may demand explanations from the person required to produce the documents and from any past or present officers or employees. ("Person" when referred to in section 26(6) presumably refers to legal persons, including companies and unincorporated associations, otherwise it would be difficult to interpret the reference to "a person who is a present or past officer of his".) If a document is not produced then the Director may demand to know its whereabouts.

The notice which orders document or information production is crucial and defines the scope of the investigation. It will define what is relevant for the purpose of the investigation. Only relevant documents and information are required to be produced. There may well be a difference of opinion between the Director and the recipient of the notice concerning the relevance of certain documents or information and these should be screened for relevance by those under investigation. Documents in dispute should be put to one side pending appeal to the Competition Commission. In practice they may be left with the solicitors acting for the person investigated, against suitable solicitors' undertakings. The decision as to whether a document or information required to be produced is relevant is to be made by the investigating officer rather than the recipient of the request. Section 26(1) refers to "a specified document . . . or specified information, which the Director considers relates to any matter relevant to the investigation". It might be said that until he has examined a document or other information, he will not know its relevance. Nevertheless, even if the contents are not known, it may be specified for production if he considers it relevant. There is nothing to be gained by withholding irrelevant documents or information that would do no harm if made available to the Director. However, there may be items which might be regarded as prejudicial in the sense that, though not relevant, nevertheless create an unfavourable impression. At all times the need for compliance must be paramount and an atmosphere of courtesy and co-operation must be maintained with the authorities.

13-07   Given that infringement of a Chapter I or Chapter II prohibition may incur significant penalties and given that the Act creates certain criminal offences,[8] it is obviously important that the Director follows properly all of the procedures laid down in the Act for the exercise of his powers. Any decisions made in cases where these procedures have not been properly followed may, in appropriate circumstances, be challenged. It is therefore important that anyone investigated should at all times check that the procedures set out in this Chapter are complied with by the Director since a failure to comply may give rise to grounds for appeal.

There are one or two points of departure from Community law. The Commission's powers of enquiry under Article 11 of Regulation 17/62 are significantly wider than section 26. Also the privilege against self-incrimination under Community law may differ from that under United Kingdom law. The principle established in *Orkem v. Commission*[9] is that in Article 11 requests, no question may be put which requires admission of infringement; only questions intended to elicit evidence of infringement. In the United Kingdom,

---

[5] See *Penalties for non-compliance* below.
[6] ss. 26(3) and (4).
[7] s. 26(5).
[8] See *Penalties for non-compliance* below.
[9] Case 374/87 *Orkem v. Commission* [1989] E.C.R. 3283; [1991] 4 C.M.L.R. 502.

a different rule against self-incrimination applies under section 14 of the Civil Evidence Act 1968 in civil proceedings, extending a broader privilege than exists under Community law. At the same time it is important to bear in mind that employees are encouraged under United Kingdom law to provide relevant information to the authorities and are protected by the *Public Interest Disclosure Act 1998*[10] in relation to the Employment Rights Act 1996[11] which treats resulting job losses as unfair dismissal. Employers who dismiss employees in such circumstances may be required to pay compensation of up to £45,100 in each case.

The European Convention on Human Rights and the Human Rights Act,[12] though also relevant, will not prevent the Director from compelling document production (*Saunders v. United Kingdom*[13]).

Entry without a warrant

13-08 Any authorised officer of the Director may enter any premises in connection with an investigation.[14] Written notice must be given by the investigating officer at least two working days before the date of intended entry, once again indicating the subject-matter and purpose of the investigation, with a reminder that non-compliance may incur criminal liabilities and penalties.

Notice need not be given in certain circumstances in which the element of surprise would in all likelihood result in loss of critical evidence. These circumstances are where the Director has reasonable suspicion that the premises are (or have been) occupied by the target of an investigation, that is, by a party to an agreement under investigation or the undertaking whose conduct is under investigation. In addition, the Director may enter premises without notice if he has taken all steps reasonably practicable to give notice but has not been able to do so. In this case, the premises need not be occupied by the target of the investigation. Whenever entering premises without a warrant, the investigating officer must on arrival at the premises produce evidence of authorisation and a document containing the same information that the written notice would have contained if it had been served.

13-09 The investigating officer may also take with him "such equipment as appears to him to be necessary",[15] which refers primarily to equipment needed for scanning and copying documents and computer discs rather than equipment needed to gain access to the premises, since forcible access may not be gained without a warrant. Once at the premises, the investigating officer may require anyone there to produce and explain documents relating to the investigation or say (to the best of their knowledge and belief) where the relevant documents may be found. Copies or extracts may be taken from those documents and, in the case of data held on any computer accessible from the premises (even if off-site), hard copies may be required so that they can be taken away.

As with any request for document production, the person faced with an investigating officer must be prepared to challenge whether any document requested is relevant to the investigation. This will be indicated by the notice served in advance or on arrival. The investigating officer would be acting *ultra vires* by asking for documents (or information about them) which are not relevant to the investigation. Of course, full compliance is required even if those investigated firmly believe that no Chapter I or Chapter II prohibition has been infringed, and even if those investigated are not themselves the alleged infringers.

---

[10] 1998 c.23.
[11] 1996 c.18.
[12] 1998 c.42.
[13] [1997] 23 E.H.R.R. 313.
[14] s. 27(1).
[15] s. 27(5).

13-10   A very careful note must be made of all documents (and document-related information) requested so that at a later stage a careful analysis may be made of those items in the Director's possession. A note must also be made of everything said, whether by the investigating officer or by way of response, as well as any other surrounding circumstances that may be relevant. At all times compliance should be offered in a helpful manner. Although the officer may not demand the use of a photocopier, copying facilities should be made available. It is advisable to offer to photocopy documents for the officer, as a courtesy.

Entry with a warrant

13-11   In addition to the section 27 powers to enter the suspected infringer's premises without a warrant, section 28 provides for entry without warning to premises occupied by someone other than the suspected infringer (as well as those occupied by a suspected infringer), with broader powers of search and seizure. Where the premises investigated are used by the suspected infringer, the powers of entry under section 27 may be exercised without a warrant and this will be preferable, partly because of the additional cost of investigation to the OFT under section 28 in getting the warrant and partly because of the added disruption of forcible entry under section 28. The threat of criminal sanctions for non-compliance with a section 27 request may also be sufficient to ensure that section 28 powers are used infrequently. Furthermore, co-operation on the part of those under investigation under section 27 will require less manpower.

Under section 28, the Director may apply to the court for a warrant if "there are reasonable grounds for suspecting" that on the premises there are documents which:

(a) have been required to be produced when exercising the section 27 powers but which were not then produced[16]; or

(b) could be required to be produced when exercising the section 27 powers but would be concealed, removed, tampered with or destroyed[17]; or

(c) remain in spite of an unsuccessful attempt to enter the premises in exercise of the section 27 powers.[18]

In the case of (b), the warrant may extend to other documents relating to the investigation if the judge is satisfied that it is reasonable to suspect that they are also on the premises.[19]

13-12   The warrant will authorise a named officer of the Director (and other accompanying named officers) to enter the premises specified in the warrant, using such force as is reasonably necessary for the purpose and to search those premises, taking copies of documents and extracts from documents of the kind referred to in (a) to (c) above in respect of which the application was granted. The original documents may be taken if it is necessary to preserve them, or to prevent interference with them, or if it is not a practical proposition to copy them on the premises.[20] The warrant is only effective for a period of one month. Original documents may be kept for a maximum of three months. Any other steps necessary to preserve or protect documents from interference may be taken.

As with sections 26 and 27, the officers may demand explanations of the relevant documents or demand to know where (to the best of their knowledge and belief) they might

---

[16] s. 28(1)(a).
[17] s. 28(1)(b).
[18] s. 28(1)(c).
[19] s. 28(3).
[20] s. 28(2).

be found. Information held on computer, accessible from the premises and relating to any matter relevant to the investigation, may be required in hard copy or disk form so that it may be taken away.

13-13   Anyone authorised by the warrant to enter premises "may take with him such equipment as appears to him to be necessary",[21] presumably in this case, not only to read and copy documents but also to gain access to the premises by using such things as crow-bars, jacks and gemmies provided that the premises are left secure if the officers leave the premises unoccupied.

In practice the officers may ask to see the contents of filing cabinets, cupboards, shelves, drawers, desks and briefcases. Vehicles arguably are not premises unless they are specified in the warrant. However, the premises concerned need not be business premises and company directors may be at risk of investigation at home if there are reasonable grounds for suspecting that the relevant documents are kept there.

13-14   The warrant, with a section 26 or section 27 notice, must state the subject-matter and purpose of the investigation and a reminder of the criminal offences for non-compliance. The section 28 powers may only be exercised on production of a warrant. The warrant should therefore be carefully inspected by anyone investigated and an eye kept on all the procedural requirements of investigations.

If no one is present at the premises at the time proposed for executing it then "such steps as are reasonable in the circumstances" must be taken to inform the occupier. If it is not possible to inform the occupier, a copy of the warrant should be left in a prominent place. These steps obviously need not undermine the element of surprise which is at the very heart of the section 28 powers. Once informed, the occupier should be given the opportunity to have a legal or other representative present during execution. The OFT officers are unlikely to wait more than an hour or two for representatives to arrive, not least because of the risks that the lost time might prejudice the investigation. Note that the same opportunity to take legal advice is not given in relation to section 26 or 27 matters.

Privilege

13-15   Privilege attaches to certain communications and, as a result, they cannot be required to be produced or disclosed in an investigation. The category of privileged communications is confined to those between professional legal advisers and their clients and to those made in connection with or in contemplation of litigation, provided in both cases that these would be protected from disclosure in High Court proceedings (or in Scotland, Court of Session proceedings).

It is a long-established principle of Community law that only communications with external legal advisers are privileged and not those from in-house counsel (*AM&S v. Commission*[22]), unless those communications merely summarise the advice of external legal advisers. The external legal advisers, furthermore, must be qualified in an EEA country. Any commentary given by in-house counsel on a privileged communication is not itself privileged. The same principles do not apply in the United Kingdom where communications both to and from in-house counsel will be given privileged status. There may be some doubt as to whether any particular documents are privileged. The OFT is likely to accept the word of a solicitor (whether in-house or external) concerning the privileged status of documents. All privileged communications should be kept separate from all other documents and each should contain a cover sheet indicating its privileged status to prevent it being examined further.

---

[21] s. 28(4).
[22] Case 155/79 *AM&S v. Commision* [1982] E.C.R. 1575; [1982] C.M.L.R. 264.

13-16 A clear distinction needs to be made between the OFT's investigations under Part I of the 1998 Act, which relate to Chapter I and Chapter II prohibitions, and those under Part II which relate to Article 85(1) and 86 infringements. The principles applicable to privilege and relevance in each case are different.[23]

Penalties for non-compliance

13-17 Section 42 creates the offence of non-compliance with any requirement imposed under section 26, 27 or 28. Defences are available on the basis that any document required to be produced was not in the possession or control of the person charged or for some reason it was not practicable to comply with the requirement. A "reasonable excuse" is a defence to failing to explain a document (or state where it might be found) or failing to provide information.

If the investigator has failed to act in accordance with section 26 or 27, a failure to comply with his requirements under those sections is not an offence. A very careful check on procedures should therefore be maintained throughout an investigation. The range of offences is broadened in section 42(5) to include intentional obstruction of an officer in exercising any of his powers under section 27.

13-18 Intentional obstruction of an officer in the exercise of his powers under warrant under section 28 is an offence. The intentional or reckless destruction, disposal, falsification or concealment of documents required to be produced under sections 26, 27 or 28 is an offence under section 43(1). Section 44 is of general application (to Part I of the Act) and makes it an offence knowingly or recklessly to provide to the Director any information that is false or misleading in any material respect, whether that information is provided direct or through someone else knowing that it will be used by the Director.

All of these offences are punishable on summary conviction by a fine which is limited, and on conviction on indictment are punishable by an unlimited fine and/or up to two years' imprisonment.

Article 85(1) and Article 86 investigations

13-19 Sections 61 to 65 of the 1998 Act contain provisions dealing with co-operation on the part of the United Kingdom authorities with Commission investigations concerning infringement of Articles 85(1) or 86, consistent with the spirit of the provisions of the Commission's Notice on co-operation between national authorities and the Commission in handling cases falling within the scope of Article 85 or 86 of the E.C. Treaty.[24]

If the Commission's investigation of an Article 85(1) or Article 86 infringement is being obstructed, or is likely to be obstructed, the Director may apply to the High Court under section 62 for a warrant authorising a named officer of the Director (and accompanying officers) and an official of the Commission to enter premises, to search for books and records and to use necessary force in doing so.

13-20 The Commission's investigation is taken to be "obstructed" where there are reasonable grounds for suspecting that there are books or records on the premises, which the Commission is entitled to examine and either the Commission's official was unable to enter those premises under his powers of investigation following an attempt or, in spite of exercising his powers of investigation, those books and records have not been produced as required by the official. An investigation is "likely to be obstructed" where there are reasonable grounds for suspecting that if the authorised Commission official attempted his powers of examination, those books and records would be concealed, removed, tampered with or destroyed.

---

[23] See *Article 85(1) and Article 86 investigations* below.
[24] [1997] O.J. C 313. For further details of the Notice, see Chapter 14 below.

In almost identical terms section 63 concerns the Director's own special investigations which are investigations conducted by the Director at the Commission's request in connection with a Commission investigation. The difference between a Commission investigation under section 62 and a Director's special investigation under section 63 is that the former is conducted by the Commission and the latter is conducted by the Director at the Commission's request.[25]

13-21 In both cases anyone entering premises must produce their warrant. They may take along any necessary equipment and, on leaving, the premises must be secured if they are left unoccupied. The warrant only lasts for one month. The warrant must indicate the subject-matter and purpose of investigation together with warnings of criminal sanctions for offences committed by non-compliance. Penalties, once again, consist of a limited fine on summary conviction and an unlimited fine on conviction on indictment and/or up to two years' imprisonment.

Before executing a warrant under sections 62 or 63, reasonable steps must be taken to inform the occupier, allowing due opportunity for him or a representative to be present.

Criminal liability

13-22 Under section 72, criminal liability is imposed on certain individuals for their part in the criminal activities of companies. Those individuals are "officers" of a company which has committed an offence with the "consent or connivance" of the officers or where the offence is attributable to negligence on the part of the officers. Both the officers and the company are guilty of the offence in such circumstances. "Officer" is defined very broadly to mean a "director, manager, secretary or other similar officer" as well as members if they manage the affairs of the company.

Although the Crown is bound by the Act, the Crown cannot be criminally liable, nor liable to pay any penalty.[26] Powers exercisable under section 28 to enter premises under a warrant may not be exercised in relation to land occupied by a government department, or occupied for Crown purposes when the suspected infringer is not the Crown or a public servant. Powers under section 27 to enter those premises without a warrant may only be exercised with the permission of the person specifically authorised to give it by the Secretary of State. Powers under sections 27 and 28 are unrestricted where the suspected infringement is by the Crown or a public servant.

However, specific provision may be made in the interests of national security to prevent entry to Crown property under section 27, 28, or in the case of Commission investigations, sections 62 or 63.

ENFORCEMENT

Decisions

13-23 The Director is given decision-making powers under section 31. Primarily he may make a decision:

(a) that the Chapter I prohibition has been infringed; or

(b) that the Chapter II prohibition has been infringed.

Before making any decision, the Director must give written notice to those likely to be affected by the proposed decision, in order to give them an opportunity to make representations.

---

[25] Also, the procedures under s. 63 require production of authorisation by the Director's officials.
[26] s. 73.

Under section 51 the Director may make rules of procedure (which require Secretary of State approval). In Schedule 9 these are contemplated in further detail.[27]

Directions

13-24   Under sections 32 and 33, after deciding that a Chapter I or Chapter II infringement has occurred, the Director may give such directions as he considers appropriate to bring that infringement to an end irrespective of whether the decision was made on his own initiative or in response to an application made to the Director. The most common directions will be to require offending agreements or conduct to be modified or terminated.

In the event of non-compliance with any section 32 or 33 directions without reasonable excuse, the Director may apply to the court for enforcement by means of an order requiring any default to be made good (within any time-limit specified in the order) or an order requiring the matter directed to be carried out by the undertaking concerned, or its officers. An order for the costs of the application may be made against the defaulter, or an officer of an undertaking in default.

Interim measures

13-25   Interim measures are available under section 35 when the Director has a reasonable suspicion that a Chapter I or Chapter II prohibition has been infringed but he has not yet completed his investigation. Where he considers it necessary to act as a matter of urgency in order to prevent serious, irreparable harm to certain persons or to protect public interest, he may give appropriate directions but must first notify those to whom he proposes to give the direction, to give them the opportunity to make representations, (indicating with sufficient clarity the nature of the direction proposed and the reasons for considering it necessary). Directions given by way of interim measure under section 35 may, in due course, be replaced by final directions under sections 32 and 33.

Penalties for substantive infringement

13-26   The core enforcement measures are the penalties for infringement of a Chapter I or Chapter II prohibition. Once the decision has been made that an agreement has infringed the Chapter I prohibition or conduct has infringed the Chapter II prohibition, the Director may impose a penalty in respect of that infringement of up to 10 per cent of the turnover of the undertaking concerned, as determined in accordance with any order made by the Secretary of State. The relevant turnover for these purposes is expected only to be United Kingdom turnover but at the time of writing this has not been formalised by Order. The Director may only impose a penalty if he is satisfied that the infringement has been committed intentionally or negligently by the undertaking concerned.

Due account must be made of the amount of any fine imposed by the Commission or another court or body in another Member State in respect of the same agreement or conduct.

13-27   Payment of the penalty may be required at any time after the period has expired for bringing an appeal under section 46 against the Director's decision. (The rules for bringing an appeal are determined in accordance with Schedule 8).

---

[27] The rules referred to in para. 5 concern the form and manner of decisions, those to whom notice of decisions should be given, publication of decisions and action to be taken after a decision has been taken that an agreement or conduct does not infringe a Chapter I or Chapter II prohibition. The rules referred to in para. 12 contemplate the circumstances in which the Director should disclose information given to him by a third party when exercising any function under Part I and para. 14 contemplates rules to establish the procedure to be followed when the Director takes action under ss. 32 to 41 when enforcing his decisions.

The Director is required to publish guidance (which he may subsequently update) concerning the appropriate awards of penalties, after consultation with others (including the Regulars which have concurrent jurisdiction to impose penalties). Any guidance given must first be approved by the Secretary of State. When imposing any penalty, the Director must adhere to the terms of any guidance then in force.

13-28 Limited immunity is offered under section 39, in the case of the Chapter I prohibition, for small agreements (other than price-fixing agreements). The category of small agreements is as prescribed by the Secretary of State and therefore may change, the main criteria being that they are agreements between parties with a turnover below a given threshold or where the share of the market affected by the agreement is below a threshold value. Immunity may, however, be withdrawn if following investigation of a small agreement, the Director considers that the agreement is likely to infringe the Chapter I prohibition. The Director's notice of withdrawal must state the effective date of withdrawal, which must follow the date of the notice, and must take account of the time necessary to correct the infringement.

13-29 Likewise immunity from penalties is available under section 40 for "conduct of minor significance" in the case of a Chapter II prohibition. The category of conduct is as prescribed by the Secretary of State, the criteria being principally that the turnover of those whose conduct is in question and the market share affected by the conduct are below given thresholds.

Immunity may be withdrawn by notice by the Director following investigation of particular conduct if he considers the Chapter II prohibition is likely to be infringed. Similar principles as in section 39 apply to the Director's notices withdrawing immunity under section 40.

Finally, provisional immunity is available for agreements after they have been notified to the Commission for exemption under Article 85(3), since the Commission confers provisional immunity on those agreements. However, the Director may withdraw immunity from penalties once the Commission's provisional immunity is withdrawn. Notification to the Commission for individual exemption does not preclude investigation by the Director.

Confidentiality and defamation

13-30 Section 55 imposes general restrictions on the disclosure of information obtained as a result of any investigation or enforcement measures, where it relates to the affairs of any individual or to any business of an undertaking. The information is not to be disclosed during the life-time of the individual or while the business trades unless consent is given by the person who provided it and (if different) the person to whom the information relates (or the person who carries on the business to which the information relates).

The restriction on disclosure does, however, not apply to prevent disclosure for the purpose of "facilitating the performance of any relevant functions of a designated person".[28] (This primarily refers to the Director but the designated person could also be one of a long list of Regulators and others in Schedule 11.[29])

13-31 Other purposes for which the restrictions on disclosure are disapplied are facilitating the performance of any of the Competition Commission's Community law functions principally under Part II (sections 62 and 63) but also when co-operating with

---

[28] s. 55(3).
[29] Their functions are also listed in Sched. 11 to include those under Part I of the Competition Act 1998, the statutes which empower the industry Regulators, the Fair Trading Act 1973, and, for transitional purposes, the legislation repealed by Part I (the Competition Act 1980 ss. 2 to 10, the Restrictive Trade Practices Act 1976 and the Resale Prices Act 1976).

the European Commission.[30] Also disclosure is allowed for the purposes of criminal proceedings in any part of the United Kingdom.[31]

The restriction does not apply to disclosure:

"(b) made with a view to the institution of, or otherwise for the purpose of, civil proceedings brought under or in connection with this Part; or
(c) made in connection with the investigation of any criminal offence triable in the United Kingdom or in any part of the United Kingdom; or
(d) which is required to meet a Community obligation."[32]

Once information is public, further disclosure may be made by anyone for other purposes.

Section 55(8) creates an offence committed by anyone who breaches confidentiality in contravention of section 55 punishable with a limited fine on summary conviction and with an unlimited fine and/or up to two years' imprisonment on conviction on indictment.

13-32 Section 56 relates to disclosure by the Secretary of State and any information he acquires under Part I of the Act (in relation to the Chapter I and Chapter II prohibitions). He must have regard to the public interest impact of disclosure and the need to avoid, so far as practicable, disclosure of commercial information which might damage an undertaking's legitimate business interests or information concerning the private affairs of an individual which might harm his interests. The Secretary of State must bear in mind the extent to which disclosure is necessary given the purposes of disclosure.

Section 57 attaches absolute privilege against defamation to any advice, guidance, notice or direction given or decision made by the Director in exercising his functions.

Miscellaneous

13-33 Under section 58 a finding of fact by the Director "which is relevant to an issue arising in Part I proceedings" is binding once the time for bringing an appeal has passed without an appeal being made, or where an appeal tribunal confirms the finding. These, most commonly, are civil proceedings in the courts, where the Plaintiff may be a party to an agreement of contested validity, a victim of abuse or a third party adversely affected by infringement. The exception is where circumstances have changed sufficiently for the Director to take action under section 16(2) or section 24(2) following a decision that there is no infringement of a Chapter I or Chapter II prohibition, or where he was misled in making the finding.

The findings of fact that are binding are those made by the Director in the course of determining an application for a decision under section 14 or section 22 or when conducting an investigation under section 25.

13-34 Section 52 requires the Director to prepare and publish general advice and information about the application of the Chapter I prohibition and the Chapter II prohibition, as well as the enforcement of those prohibitions, with a view to explaining them to the business community, extending awareness, and indicating how the Director expects Part I of the Act to operate. The Director must make appropriate consultation when preparing any such advice and information. Any Regulator doing so must consult with the Director and other Regulators as well.

Section 53 entitles the Director to charge fees for exercising any of his Part I functions, which may be turnover-related. Different amounts may be charged for different functions and provision may be made for repayment in appropriate circumstances. The most likely fee-earning functions will be applications for individual exemption and other decisions.

---

[30] See Chap. 14 below.
[31] s. 55(3)(a).
[32] s. 55(3).

THE COMPETITION COMMISSION

Functions

13-35 The name, "the Competition Commission" makes for ready confusion with the European Commission (especially since sections 61 to 65 refer to the European Commission as "the Commission" and Schedule 7 refers to the Competition Commission as "the Commission").

The MMC was dissolved by section 45(3) of the 1998 Act and its functions transferred to the newly-formed Competition Commission whose functions and procedures are set out in Schedule 7 of the Act. These include hearing appeals against decisions by the Director, hearing third party appeals and undertaking all the previous functions of the MMC in relation to the Fair Trading Act 1973 which by and large remains in force as before. For further details concerning the functions of the Competition Commission in relation to the Fair Trading Act 1973, see Chapter 11 above.

Appeals

13-36 Under section 46 an appeal may be made against any of the following decisions of the Director (and any directions given under sections 32, 33 or 35):

(a) whether the Chapter I prohibition has been infringed;

(b) whether the Chapter II prohibition has been infringed;

(c) whether to grant an individual exemption and if so:

   (i) whether to impose any condition or obligation when granting an exemption (under section 4(3)(a) or 5(1)(c)) and if so;

      (i) the condition or obligation imposed;
      (ii) the period during which the exemption is effective; and
      (iii) the date from which exemption granted is effective;

(d) whether to extend the duration of any individual exemption and if so the period of any extension;

(e) the cancellation of an exemption;

(f) the imposition of any penalty under section 36 for substantive infringement including the amount of the penalty; and

(g) the withdrawal or variation of any of the above decisions (apart from the last, relating to penalties) following a third party appeal.

An appeal made against any of those decisions under section 46 does not suspend the effect of the decision that is appealed (except in the case of appeals relating to penalties). The procedures relating to appeals are dealt with in Schedule 8 Part I.

13-37 Third party appeals may be made under section 47 in relation to any of the above decisions (except those relating to penalties), asking the Director to withdraw or vary his decision. The third party appeal must be made in writing giving the applicant's reasons for considering that the Director's decision should be withdrawn or varied. The Director may, having considered the third party appeal, decide that the third party applicant (or those represented by or representing the applicant) do not have a sufficient interest in the decision. The Director may alternatively decide that the third party appeal does not contain sufficient reason to withdraw or vary any decision. In each case the Director must notify the applicant to that effect and those decisions themselves may be appealed (without suspending the effect of any decision under appeal).

All appeals to the Competition Commission under section 46 or 47 are determined by the allocated appeal tribunal of the Competition Commission.

Procedure on appeal to the Competition Commission

13-38   Notice of appeal must be given to the Competition Commission setting out the grounds of appeal in sufficient detail to indicate under which provisions of the 1998 Act the appeal is brought, to what extent (if any) the appellant considers that the decision under appeal was based on an error of fact or was wrong in law and to what extent (if any) the appellant is appealing against the Director's exercise of his discretion in making the disputed decision. An appeal tribunal, constituted by the President of the Competition Commission Appeal Tribunals,[33] determines the appeal on its merits by reference to the grounds of appeal set out in the Notice of Appeal. (The Notice of Appeal may be amended with the tribunal's leave).

The tribunal may confirm or set aside any decision appealed (or any part of it). It may then remit the matter back to the Director. The tribunal may impose a penalty or revoke or vary the amount of an existing penalty. It may grant, cancel or vary any exemption. The tribunal may make any other decision which the Director could himself have made, which also means that a penalty may be increased,[34] and may give such directions, or take such other steps or make any other decision as the Director could himself have effected.

13-39   Decisions of the tribunal on appeal have the same effect as decisions of the Director (except as to appeal). Any tribunal decision need not be unanimous. A majority decision will suffice but the decision itself must state whether it was unanimous or taken by a majority. A statement of the reasons for the tribunal's decision must be documented and signed by the tribunal Chairman having proper regard to the need to exclude information, as provided in section 56, where disclosure would be contrary to public interest. The President of the Competition Commission Appeals Tribunal must arrange for each tribunal decision to be published.

Further appeals

13-40   An appeal against a decision of an appeal tribunal of the Competition Commission may be made (either on a point of law or as to the amount of any penalty) to the Court of Appeal, with leave of that tribunal or the Court of Appeal, at the instance of a party to the proceedings or a third party who has a sufficient interest in the matter.[35]

Composition of the Competition Commission

13-41   Members of the Competition Commission are appointed by the Secretary of State for specific functions. The function may be to handle appeals, to determine newspaper references (for which members are appointed from a special newspaper merger panel[36]), or for any of the general functions of the Competition Commission. Members

---

[33] See *Composition of the Competition Commission* below.
[34] By contrast in the case of a successful appeal to the CFI, the Commission is left to comply with the judgment of the Court where appropriate administrative proceedings may continue. A further distinction with the Community system is the power of the tribunal to grant exemption. Only the European Commission is entitled to do that and not the CFI or the ECJ.
[35] The time-limits for doing so are to be determined under s. 48. This contrasts with the Community system in that no leave is required to appeal to the CFI but the grounds of appeal are confined to points of law. However, the manifest disregard of essential facts constitutes a point of law.
[36] Maintained under Sched. 7, para. 22.

may also be appointed to the Competition Commission in the case of the regulated industries by virtue or the Water Act 1991,[37] the Electricity Act 1989,[38] the Telecommunications Act 1984[39] and the Electricity (Northern Ireland) Order 1992.[40]

There are three types of member—an appeal panel member, a reporting panel member and a specialist panel member. Each member may also be appointed to be a member of one or more of the other kinds.

The Chairman of the Competition Commission is chosen by the Secretary of State from among the reporting panel members, as are deputy chairmen each of whom may act as chairman in the Chairman's absence. The Chairman and deputy chairmen only hold office for as long as they are members.

13-42 In relation to appeals, one of the appeal panel members is appointed to preside over the Competition Commission's appeal functions, and is known as the "President of the Competition Commission Appeal Tribunals". He is appointed by the Secretary of State after consultation with the Lord Chancellor and must be of long-standing legal qualification. The management board of the Competition Commission is known as the "Competition Commission Council".

In general, the Commission has power to do anything (other than to borrow money) "calculated to facilitate the discharge of its functions" or "incidental or conducive to the discharge of its functions".[41]

All general functions of the Commission are performed through a group consisting of at least three selected for the purpose by the Chairman and including the Chairman himself. Certain groups must be constituted with special panel members or members from the newspaper merger panel. Each group may be attended by any reporting panel member who is not a member of that group upon the invitation of the chairman of the group. The reporting panel member may take part in the proceedings, but may not vote (or have any dissent recorded).

13-43 Each group may determine the extent to which those interested or claiming to be interested in the subject-matter of the proceedings may be present, be heard (either by themselves or through their representatives) or may cross-examine witnesses or otherwise take part in proceedings. Each group may also determine the extent to which its sittings are held in public. The group will be guided by the Chairman (after consultation with the members of the Competition Commission) and, needless to say, such procedures are subject to Secretary of State directions.

Anything transacted by a group is to have the same effect as if done by the Competition Commission. However, a two thirds majority is required for the purposes of the Fair Trading Act 1973, sections 56 and 73 which concern reports by the Competition Commission on monopoly references and merger references.[42]

---

[37] s. 12(4) or 14(8).
[38] s. 12(9).
[39] s. 13(10).
[40] Art. 15(9).
[41] Para. 8 of Sched. 7.
[42] See Chap. 11 above.

CHAPTER 14

E.C. Investigation and Enforcement

INTRODUCTION

14-01   This Chapter will examine the procedures by which the E.C. Treaty provisions relating to competition are enforced by the Commission and how national courts might be used to defend or attack agreements or conduct caught by Articles 85(1) or 86, given that those Articles have direct application in the United Kingdom.

Article 9 of Regulation 17/62[1] confers on the Commission its essential powers including the power to apply Articles 85(1) and 86.[2] The Commission also has sole jurisdiction under Article 9(1) to grant exemption from Article 85(1) if the criteria of Article 85(3) have been satisfied.[3] Furthermore, it is the Commission's duty under Article 89 of the E.C. Treaty to "ensure the application of the principles laid down in Articles 85 and 86".

14-02   United Kingdom courts may apply Articles 85(1) and 86 in proceedings before them and are expressly encouraged to do so by the Commission as part of the Commission's aim of decentralising the enforcement of E.C. competition law from the Commission to the national authorities. Article 9(3) of Regulation 17/62 confirms their authority, as long as the Commission has not begun proceedings under Articles 2 or 4 of Regulation 17/62 (following application for negative clearance or individual exemption) or Article 3 (to terminate any infringement). The Commission has offered advice to the National Courts in its Notice on co-operation between National Courts and the Commission in applying Articles 85 and 86 of the E.C. Treaty.[4]

In deciding which matters to investigate the Commission has discretion. It is not bound to take up any complaint, and in allocating its limited resources will focus on those matters which are of major importance or policy such as where a "Community interest" exists, preferring to avoid those for which an adequate remedy already exists in any national court (*Automec v. Commission* (No. 2)[5]). The Commission will also bear in mind the role of Member States as established in the Commission Notice on co-operation between national competition authorities and the Commission in handling cases

---

[1] Reg. 17/62 [1962] J.O. 204/62, applies to all sectors other than transport (to which separate Regs apply depending on the transport sector concerned).

[2] Even if the time limits for notifying individual agreements have not expired.

[3] Notifications represent approximately 60 per cent of the Commission's workload, the vast majority of which are determined by way of a comfort letter rather than formal exemption. Complaints represent about 25 per cent, and 15 per cent is attributable to proceedings begun on the Commission's own initiative (Twenty third Report on Competition Policy (1993), para. 208). The procedures for applying for individual exemption are dealt with in depth in Chapter 6 above.

[4] Commission Notice of February 13, 1993 on Co-operation between National Courts and the Commission in applying Articles 85 and 86 of the E.C. Treaty [1993] O.J. C39/6.

[5] Case T–24/90 [1992] E.C.R. II-2223; [1992] 5 C.M.L.R. 431. For further detail see *Co-operation Between the Commission, the Courts and Competition Authorities* below.

falling within the scope of Articles 85 or 86 of the E.C. Treaty.[6] The scope of "Community interest" is illustrated by *Bureau Européen des Medias de'l Industrie Musicale (BEMIM) v. Commission*[7] which concerned a complaint by discotheque owners against the French copyright collecting society in which the impact of the alleged infringement was felt only in France. The matter was already being heard before the French courts. In such circumstances, the CFI held that the Commission was entitled to drop its investigation, as adequate safeguards already existed in France. The result may be different if for some reason the national courts are unable to accumulate the necessary evidence to establish an infringement. This might be the case, for example where the evidence is held in different countries, given that a national court is not empowered to carry out its own investigations abroad. It is always assumed that national courts are technically competent to handle matters relating to Articles 85 and 86, as it is always open to any national court to refer a question to the ECJ for determination under Article 177.

14-03   In the case of a complaint, the Commission will isolate the relevant factual and legal issues in a preliminary examination of the complaint, which may involve dialogue between the Commission and complainant. If the Commission rejects a complaint, the complainant will be given an opportunity to respond within timescales fixed by the Commission.

The fact-finding powers of the Commission are found primarily in Articles 11 (requests for information) and 14 (investigations) of Regulation 17/62.

Broad principles of natural justice bind the Commission to the extent that any person affected by a Commission decision is entitled to a hearing (*Transocean Marine Paint Association v. Commission*[8]) and the Commission must apply the principle of proportionality, which prevents the imposition of any measure on undertakings (notably fines) which is excessive in order to protect public interest. The Commission must also make findings on the basis of the facts available to it.

ARTICLE 11 REQUESTS FOR INFORMATION

14-04   Article 11(1) of Regulation 17/62 entitles the Commission to obtain "all necessary information from the Governments and competent authorities and from associations of undertakings" in carrying out its duties under Article 89 of the E.C. Treaty. Article 89 requires the Commission to investigate cases of suspected infringement of Articles 85 and 86 and if it finds an infringement to propose appropriate measures to bring it to an end.

When any Article 11 request is addressed to an undertaking, a copy is sent to the competent authority in the Member State in which the undertaking is situated. In all requests, a reminder must be given of the penalties for supplying incorrect or misleading information, or for supplying information late.[9] In the event of non- compliance, the Commission may by decision under Article 11(5), require the information to be supplied, specifying the information required and the timescale for supplying it (usually within a month). A penalty warning must again be given for non-compliance. A copy of that decision must simultaneously be forwarded to the relevant Member State.

14-05   Under Article 12, the Commission may conduct a general enquiry into any economic sector where competition appears to be restricted or distorted within the common

---

[6] Commission Notice of October 15, 1997 on Co-operation between national competition authorities and the Commission in handling cases falling within the scope of Articles 85 or 86 of the E.C. Treaty [1997] O.J. C313/3.
[7] Case T–114/92 *Bureau Européen des Medias de'l Industrie Musicale (BEMIM) v. Commission* [1995] E.C.R. II-147.
[8] Case 17/74 *Transocean Marine Paint Association v. Commission* [1974] E.C.R. 1063; [1974] 2 C.M.L.R. 459.
[9] See *Fines* below for further detail concerning penalties.

market and in doing so the Commission may request undertakings in that sector to supply information on the same basis as any Article 11 request or order.[10]

Requests for information must not be couched in such terms that the answer results in an admission of infringement, since it is for the Commission to prove infringement (*Orkem v. Commission*[11]).

14-06 An Article 11 request must be for the purpose of investigating the suspected infringement and no other purpose or it will be *ultra vires*.

In responding to an Article 11 request, it is generally best to respond to requests as quickly and as fully as possible. If any information is beyond reach within the time-scales available then a response should be given identifying the information that is still sought with an explanation of why it is not readily available. Care should obviously be taken to ensure consistency across all statements. Any significant inconsistency and any late response is likely to suggest concealment and result in a further order under Article 11(5) or an order for full-scale investigation under Article 14.

ARTICLE 14 INVESTIGATIONS

14-07 Article 14 empowers the Commission (in carrying out its Article 89 duties) to undertake "all necessary investigations" and in doing so:

"(a) to examine the books and other business records;
(b) to take copies of or extracts from the books and business records;
(c) to ask for oral explanations on the spot; and
(d) to enter any premises, land and means of transport of undertakings."[12]

Investigations may be undertaken with the co-operation of the undertakings concerned, or alternatively the undertakings may be ordered by the Commission to submit to investigation. In exercising any of its powers of investigation, the authorised officials of the Commission must produce their written authorisation specifying the subject-matter and purpose of the investigation. The authorisation will also contain a reminder of the penalties under Article 15(1)(c) for producing incomplete books and other business records. In the case of an order requiring submission to an investigation, the authorisation will also contain a reminder of the penalties for refusing to submit to an Article 14 investigation, together with a reminder of the CFI's powers to review any Commission decision.[13] The Commission must inform the competent authorities in the Member State of the investigation and the identity of the officials. Article 14(4) requires consultation with national authorities before the decision is made to investigate under order.

14-08 Officials from the competition authorities of relevant Member States may assist the Commission in the investigation either at the request of the authority or at the request of the Commission.

It is increasingly common for officials from national authorities to attend Commission investigations, and the authorities may even be requested to undertake the Commission investigation themselves. Article 13 includes the procedure for competent authorities of Member States to undertake the Commission's investigations (where necessary with the

---

[10] The commission may also ask for details of agreements or decisions made by these undertakings or concerted practices in which they are involved even if they are non-notifiable agreements under Art. 4(2). The Commission may ask for details of market structure to be provided by those undertakings which appear to be dominant.
[11] Case 324/87 *Orkem v. Commission* [1989] E.C.R. 3283.
[12] Art. 14(1).
[13] See Thirteenth Report on Competition Policy 1983 (p. 270) for details of the explanations that accompany the authorisation.

assistance of the Commission). In the United Kingdom, sections 61 to 65 of the 1998 Act enact the procedural aspects of such investigations.[14]

The term "documents" is given a broad meaning to render irrelevant the medium in which information is held. It covers computer-stored items, emails, and documents held on microfiche or CD-ROM. The Commission's document search will depend on the nature of the infringement. The Commission may be in search of agreements that reveal anti-competitive terms on their face, or alternatively marketing documents that reflect practices intended to deter exports and protect the home market as part of a market-sharing arrangement. Diary entries may evidence meetings and collusion between competitors. The evidence may take any form.

14-09 Upon arrival of any investigating officials, legal advisers should obviously be asked to attend immediately. Although Commission officials will wait for some time (up to about four hours at most) they will not wait longer than is necessary and an hour or two is more the expected length of delay. The absence of a legal adviser does not jeopardise any investigation and the Commission will in any event not delay if in-house legal advisers are present.

If at any stage of an investigation the target undertaking raises an objection to the Commission taking any particular document, the undertaking should submit to the request and dispute the matter before the CFI. Most disputes concern the relevance of documents or their privileged status. It is generally better to appeal to the CFI, rather than risk penalties and disapproval for obstruction. If the Commission is dissatisfied with the level of access it is given to books and records requested, the Commission may invoke the assistance of the OFT by seeking an *ex parte* injunction from the High Court. The power is enshrined in Article 14(6), which requires Member States to assist Commission officials in their investigation whenever an undertaking opposes an investigation. It has been invoked in the case of *Ukwal*.[15]

14-10 The Commission cannot force entry (*Hoechst v. Commission*[16]) but may require the target undertaking to submit to the investigation or risk an injunction requiring it to do so (in addition to the penalties for obstruction). Submission to an investigation generally requires the undertaking merely to produce the documents requested and to provide access to filing cabinets and cupboards in which they are held. In general, only straightforward questions will be asked to enable the investigation to continue in the most effective way. Commission officials should be monitored closely throughout the investigation. Notes should be made of everything they do and say, in particular any questions asked by them and the answers given in response. This will help any subsequent challenge if the Commission's procedures are breached. Copies of all documents taken by the Commission should also be kept in order to build up a picture of the case which the Commission may make against an undertaking. In asking any questions the Commission may not require any answer which amounts to an admission of infringement.[17] Given the ease with which photocopying facilities may be made available failure to offer them is likely to be regarded as unhelpful if not obstructive. Document concealment or destruction will almost certainly result in a fine.

PRIVILEGE AND CONFIDENTIALITY

14-11 Legal professional privilege attaches only to communications between an undertaking and independent outside counsel. In-house counsel are not subject to

---

[14] See Chapter 13 above.
[15] Commission Dec. 92/237 [1992] O.J. L121/45; [1993] C.M.L.R. 632.
[16] Cases 47/87 & 227/88 *Hoechst v. Commission* [1989] E.C.R. 2859; [1991] 4 C.M.L.R. 410.
[17] See Case 374/87 *Orkem v. Commission* [1989] E.C.R. 3283; [1991] 4 C.M.L.R. 502, in the context of Art. 11.

uniform, professional rules of conduct throughout all Community countries and no privilege attaches to their communications (*AM&S Europe v. Commission*[18]). However, if in-house counsel passes on the advice by internal memorandum, that will also be protected. Further limits on professional privilege are inherent in the fact that it attaches to the defence of the Commission's allegations of infringement. It therefore only applies principally to correspondence after Commission proceedings have been initiated. However, items written before commencement of Commission proceedings will also be protected if they relate to "the subject-matter of that procedure".[19]

If an undertaking raises an argument concerning the privileged status of a document, the undertaking is not required to disclose it but should try to satisfy the Commission of its status. If unsuccessful the matter may then be contested before the CFI.

14-12   Undertakings will undoubtedly be concerned about the confidentiality of material in the hands of the Commission. Article 20 of Regulation 17/62 reassures them that information acquired in response to a request for information under Article 11 or as a result of an Article 14 investigation (even information given to competent national authorities if they are involved in investigations under Article 13) may only be used for the purpose of the relevant request or investigation. Confidentiality is binding on the employees of the Commission and the authorities of those Member States. However, it obviously does not prevent the disclosure of decisions which the Commission is obliged to publish under Article 21 (giving the names of the parties and the content of the decision) although in doing so, the Commission must "have regard to the legitimate interest of undertakings in the protection of their business secrets". If the matter is to be resolved by way of granting negative clearance or individual exemption then within a month of that decision a summary of the relevant application must be published, inviting third party comment.

Publication may also be necessary under Article 19 in hearings involving the undertakings but also third parties "where they show significant interest". If aspects of a hearing are to be kept confidential they should therefore be separated from the rest of the proceedings.

STATEMENT OF OBJECTIONS, ACCESS TO THE FILE AND HEARINGS

14-13   If sufficient evidence of infringement exists, proceedings are opened by the Commission, the competent authorities of Member States are notified and, unless the Commission decides to proceed informally, the undertakings themselves will receive a statement of objections. A statement of objections must be issued in all cases where there is the possibility that the Commission will fine an undertaking. In cases where the Commission does not contemplate a fine, a notice in the Official Journal will suffice.

The statement of objections contains a short summary of the facts. It is not legally binding and, unlike a decision, cannot be reviewed by the CFI. However, once a statement of objections is received, the undertakings may have access to their file in order to enable them to make representations to the Commission. The list of documents to which access is granted is attached to the statement of objections but excluded will obviously be the business secrets of other undertakings, documents of the Commission prepared for internal purposes and anything which will disclose the identity of a complainant (if the complainant wishes to remain anonymous). All other documents should be made available by the Commission. The hearing officer determines any dispute concerning access to the file.

14-14   Apart from these exceptions, the Commission has a duty to provide access to

---

[18] Case 155/79 *AM&S Europe v. Commission* [1982] E.C.R. 1575; [1982] 2 C.M.L.R. 264.
[19] XII Report on Competition Policy paras 50–54.

its files to the undertakings concerned (*Hercules v. Commission*[20]) whether or not the documents disclosed are relevant to the defence (since the decision of relevance is to be made by those defending the statement of objections). The Commission may not rely on any evidence to which the undertakings do not have access. The Commission may also not take action concerning activities that are not covered by the statement of objections.

The statement of objections requires a response within a stated period, usually two months or so. The matter may then be dealt with by way of hearing. Hearings are regulated by Article 19. All hearings are presided over by the hearing officer who, though part of the Directorate General for Competition (DG-IV), is not involved in the conduct of the case. The hearing officer is independent and oversees the procedural aspects of the hearing.

ORDERS TERMINATING INFRINGEMENT

14-15 Article 3(1) of Regulation 17/62 empowers the Commission either on application or on its own initiative, to order an infringement of Article 85 or Article 86 to be brought to an end. Those entitled to make an application for an order are Member States or "natural or legal persons who claim a legitimate interest". This may be done by way of interim order or final order.

Interim orders

14-16 An interim order might be likened to an interlocutory injunction. No cross-undertakings in damages are required by the applicant although the Commission may require undertakings to be given if appropriate.

Interim orders under Article 3(1) are extremely rare. The Commission may only order by way of interim measure those things that it could order by way of a final decision. In *Distribution System of Ford Werke AG Interim Measures*,[21] the Commission responded to the notification of distribution arrangements by Ford by making an interim order that right hand cars be supplied in Germany. A refusal to supply right hand drive cars would not be an infringement. The order to supply could not have been the subject of a final order. Instead the Commission should have withdrawn immunity from fines by notifying Ford to that effect under Article 15(6).

14-17 An interim order is not a speedy measure and is only available:

> "to avoid a situation likely to cause serious and irreparable damage to the party seeking their adoption, or which is intolerable for the public interest" (*Camera Care v. Commission*[22]).

A *prima facie* case for such irreparable damage needs to be made out (*La Cinq v. Commission*[23]). For example interim measures were adopted in *Sealink/B&I—Holyhead: Interim Measures*[24] to alter Sealink's schedules at Holyhead which threatened to disrupt B&I's Summer ferry service and would have resulted in substantial loss of business reputation.

The procedures for hearings set out in Article 19 apply equally to hearings concerning

---

[20] Case T–7/89 *Hercules v. Commission* [1991] E.C.R. II-1711; [1992] 4 C.M.L.R. 84.
[21] Commission Dec. 82/628 [1982] O.J. L256/20; [1982] 3 C.M.L.R. 267. On appeal, Cases 228 & 229/82 *Distribution System of Ford Werke AG Interim Measures* [1984] E.C.R. 1129; [1984] 1 C.M.L.R. 649.
[22] Case 792/79 R *Camera Care v. Commission* [1980] E.C.R. 119; [1980] 1 C.M.L.R. 334, para. 19.
[23] Case T–44/90 *La Cinq v. Commission* [1992] E.C.R. II-1; [1992] 4 C.M.L.R. 449.
[24] [1992] 5 C.M.L.R. 255.

interim measures. This renders them more cumbersome than United Kingdom interlocutory measures which allow *ex parte* injunctions to be granted to the applicant and for orders to be issued without a hearing. Instead of using interim measures, however, most cases are resolved by way of an undertaking by those concerned.[25]

Final orders

14-18   Article 3(1) also empowers the Commission to make a final order terminating an infringement. This will be after the statement of objections has been issued and the undertakings concerned, as well as third parties where appropriate, have been heard.

The burden of proof for a finding of infringement is high and must amount to "sufficiently precise and coherent proof" of infringement (*Cie Royale Asturienne des Mines and Rheinzing v. Commission*[26]). Final orders may be negative (restraining conduct or the implementation of agreements) or may be positive (requiring supplies to be maintained such as in the event of a refusal to supply (*ICI and Commercial Solvents v. Commission*[27])). A positive order may also, for example require a licence to be granted of intellectual property rights (*Magill TV Guide*[28]).

Fines

14-19   The Commission may impose a fine for procedural irregularities under Article 15(1) of between 100 and 5000 ECUs for intentionally or negligently:

(1)   supplying incorrect or misleading information when applying for negative clearance or individual exemption; or

(2)   suppling incorrect information in response to a request for information under Article 11 (whether on initial request or as required by order); or

(3)   not supplying the information within the stipulated time-limits specified in an order under Article 11(5); or

(4)   producing books and records during an investigation in incomplete form; or

(5)   refusing to submit to an investigation.

Fines for substantive infringement may be imposed under Article 15(2) of:

(1)   between 1000 ECUs and 1 million ECUs; or, if greater

(2)   up to 10 per cent of the turnover in the preceding business year of each of the undertakings participating in the infringement,

where either undertaking intentionally or negligently infringes Article 85(1) or Article 86 or breaches an undertaking given to the Commission as a condition of exemption. When imposing any fine for substantive infringement, the Commission must have regard to the gravity and the duration of the infringement. Article 15(4) expressly provides that these sanctions are not to be taken as criminal in nature. Fines may only be levied on the undertakings concerned and not the individuals participating in them.

---

[25]   For example Commission Dec. 88/138 *Eurofix-Bauco v. Hilti* [1988] O.J. L65/19.

[26]   Case 29–30/83 *Cie Royale Asturienne des Mines and Rheinzing v. Commission* [1984] E.C.R. 1679 at 1702; [1985] 1 C.M.L.R. L88 at 711.

[27]   Case 67/73 *ICI and Commercial Solvents v. Commission* [1974] E.C.R. 223; [1974] 1 C.M.L.R. 309.

[28]   Commission Dec. 89/205 [1989] O.J. L78/43; [1989] 4 C.M.L.R. 757 (upheld on appeal).

In addition periodic penalties may be incurred under Article 16(1) on a daily basis of between 50 ECUs and 1,000 ECUs per day:

(1) to compel termination of infringement of Articles 85(1) and 86 when ordered under Article 3; or

(2) to prevent any act prohibited by the Commission whenever there has been any revocation or amendment of any decision under Article 8. Article 8 entitles the Commission to vary its previous decisions where the circumstances under which exemption has been granted have changed, where any undertaking given to the Commission as a condition of exemption has been breached, if exemption was granted on the basis of false information or deceit or where the parties abuse any exemption granted to them;

(3) to compel undertakings to supply complete and accurate information whenever requested by the Commission under Article 11(5); and

(4) to compel undertakings to submit to an investigation ordered under Article 14(3).

14-20   The Commission's readiness to impose high levels of fine is reflected in its decision to fine *Volkswagen* a total of 102 million ECUs.[29] The next largest fine imposed on a single undertaking was in *Tetrapak II*[30] at 75 million ECUs. The largest fines in total have been imposed in the case of cartels. In *Cartonboard*,[31] 19 cartel members were fined 132 million ECUs in aggregate. In *Trans-Atlantic Conference Agreement*, the cartel members were fined a total of 273 million ECUs.[32] The fine will reflect the level of participation by each undertaking in the infringement and the degree of co-operation given to the Commission. Given that awareness of competition law is now widespread, there is less room to claim unwitting involvement in an infringement (*Michelin v. Commission*[33]). In *Cartonboard,* the Commission provided a useful summary of the considerations which it took into account in that case and these included the serious nature of the infringement (price collusion and market-sharing), the geographical scope of the cartel (the entire Community), the value of the industry sector affected (2,500 million ECUs per annum), the fact that the participating undertakings accounted for nearly the whole market, the infringements themselves were explicit, institutionalised meetings regulated the market in explicit detail, steps were taken to conceal infringement (such as the avoidance of minute-taking and stage-managing of price increases to support false claims of price leadership), and finally the success of the cartel.[34] In general the closer the effects of an infringement to the market, particularly the consumer market, the greater the fine.

There is no doubt that fines are increasingly deterrent in nature, particularly where the rewards for infringement are high and will be aggravated by concealment, which itself clearly demonstrates guilt. In *Cast Iron and Steel Rolls*[35] an alarm procedure operated to warn participants of a visit by the authorities.

14-21   Fines may be mitigated by co-operation with the Commission, especially in providing information which the Commission did not already have, or where positive

---

[29] Commission Dec. 92/273 [1998] O.J. L124/60.
[30] Commission Dec. 92/163 [1992] O.J. L72/1; [1992] 4 C.M.L.R. 551.
[31] Commission Dec. 94/601 [1994] O.J. L243/1; [1994] 5 C.M.L.R. 547.
[32] Commission Press Release IP/98/811.
[33] Case 322/81 *Michelin v. Commission* [1985] E.C.R. 3461.
[34] *Cartonboard*, paras 168–169.
[35] Commission Dec. 83/546 [1993] O.J. L317/1 [1984] 1 C.M.L.R. 694.

measures to reverse the infringement are taken (such as in *Cartonboard* where one under-taking assisted in disbanding the cartel). In *John Deere*,[36] the Commission was explicit in mitigating a fine on the basis of a compliance programme instituted by the undertaking.

The Commission published its "Leniency Notice" in 1996[37] as a means of encouraging whistleblowers in cartel cases to terminate their involvement. The Notice sets out the con-ditions under which those who co-operate with the Commission in this way may be exempt from fines or may suffer reduced fines. The conditions are that the enterprise must:

(a) inform the Commission about a secret cartel before the Commission has under-taken an investigation (ordered by decision) of the cartel, provided that the Commission does not already have enough evidence to establish the existence of the cartel. (This is something which may not be known to the cartel participant before informing the Commission and therefore carries a risk);

(b) be the first to adduce evidence of the cartel's existence. (This likewise may not be known to the participant);

(c) put an end to its involvement in the cartel on or before disclosing it;

(d) provide the Commission with all relevant information, documentation and evi-dence available to it relating to the cartel and maintain co-operation throughout the investigation; and

(e) not have compelled another participant to take part in the cartel or have acted as instigator or played a determining role.

These conditions will qualify for a reduction in fine of at least 75 per cent or entire exemp-tion. If conditions (b) to (e) are satisfied but the co-operation begins only after an inves-tigation then the fine may be reduced by between 50 per cent and 75 per cent.

14-22   Lesser reductions of fines, of between 10 per cent and 50 per cent are available for those who co-operate less extensively. Non-exhaustive examples given in the Notice are where an enterprise, before a statement of objections is sent, provides information, documents or evidence which materially contributes to establishing the existence of infringement, or having received a statement of objections informs the Commission that it does not substantially contest the facts on which the Commission bases its allegations.

To benefit from the Notice, these steps may only be taken by those who are expressly authorised to take action. The outcome of the co-operation, in terms of fine reduction, will not be known until the end of the administrative procedure. The leniency offered by the Commission will not, however, protect against civil actions that may result from the infringement. In fact, given that the enterprise offering co-operation and benefitting from a reduction in fine will be named, it may in fact facilitate third party litigation against that co-operating enterprise. If a reduction in fine is granted on the basis that the enterprise did not contest the Commission's findings, the Commission will apply to increase the fine if the enterprise subsequently appeals to the CFI to annul the Commission's decision.

14-23   In *Stainless Steel Producers*,[38] the Commission followed its Leniency Notice and allowed a 40 per cent reduction of the fine in favour of one participant who dissented from the calculation system adopted by the others. Another received a 40 per cent reduc-tion for informing the Commission of the crucial meeting at which price- fixing consen-

[36] Commission Dec. 85/79 [1985] O.J. L35/58; [1985] 2 C.M.L.R. 554.
[37] Commission Notice of July 18, 1996 on the non-imposition or reduction of fines in cartel cases [1996] O.J. C207/4.
[38] Not yet reported.

sus was reached. The others benefitted from a 10 per cent fine reduction for co-operating by ready admission of the practices.

14-24 The guidelines published by the Commission[39] on the method applicable to the setting of fines under Article 85 and 86 of the E.C. Treaty and Article 65.5 of the ECSC Treaty offer further guidance.[40] According to the guidelines, a new method of determining the amount of a fine will apply according to the following rules, which start from a basic amount that will be increased to take account of aggravating circumstances or reduced to take account of attenuating circumstances.

(1) **Basic amount**—The basic amount will be set on the basis of the gravity and duration of the infringement:

(a) *Gravity*—Three categories of gravity may be distinguished according to the following criteria:

(i) minor infringements—typically these will be vertical restrictions with limited market impact, affecting only a substantial but relatively limited part of the Community market. Likely fines: 1,000 ECUs to 1 million ECUs;

(ii) serious infringements—these will include horizontal or vertical restrictions more rigorously applied, with a wider market impact, and with effects in extensive areas of the common market. They might also be abuses of a dominant position (refusals to supply, discrimination, exclusion, loyalty discounts made by dominant firms in order to force competitors out, etc.). Likely fines: 1 million ECUs to 20 million ECUs; or

(iii) very serious infringements—these will include classic horizontal restrictions such as price cartels, market-sharing, compartmentalisation of national markets and clear abuses of a dominant position by undertakings holding a virtual monopoly. Likely fines: above 20 million ECUs.

(b) *Duration*—the duration of the infringement will impact as follows:

(i) infringements of short duration (in general, less than one year): no increase in amount;

(ii) infringements of medium duration (in general, one to five years): increase of up to 50 per cent in the amount determined for gravity;

(iii) infringements of long duration (in general, more than five years): increase of up to 10 per cent per year in the amount determined for gravity.

(2) **Aggravating circumstances**—the basic amount determined under 1) above will be increased where there are aggravating circumstances such as:

(i) repeated infringement of the same type by the same undertaking(s);

(ii) refusal to co-operate with or attempts to obstruct the Commission in carrying out its investigations;

(iii) role of leader in or instigator of the infringement;

(iv) retaliatory measures against other undertakings with a view to enforcing practices which constitute an infringement;

---

[39] Guidelines on the method of setting fines imposed pursuant to Art. 15(2) of Reg. 17 and Art. 65(5) of the ECSC Treaty [1998] O.J. C9/03 January 14, 1998.

[40] Paraphrasing the text closely.

(v) need to increase the penalty in order to exceed the amount of gains improperly made as a result of the infringement when it is objectively possible to estimate that amount.

(3) **Attenuating circumstances**—the basic amount will be reduced where there are attenuating circumstances such as:

(i) an exclusively passive or "follow-my-leader" role in the infringement;
(ii) non-application in full of the agreements or practices which constitute the infringement;
(iii) termination of the infringement as soon as the Commission intervenes (in particular when it carries out checks);
(iv) existence of reasonable doubt by the undertaking as to whether the restrictive conduct does indeed constitute an infringement;
(v) infringements committed as a result of negligence or not intentionally;
(vi) effective co-operation by the undertaking in the proceedings, outside the scope of the notice of July 18, 1996 on the non-imposition or reduction of fines in cartel cases.

REVIEW OF COMMISSION DECISIONS BY THE COURT OF FIRST INSTANCE

14-25 The Commission is coming under increasing pressure to be rigorous in its fact-finding and its economic analysis when making decisions. For example, *European Night Services*[41] concerned an application for exemption for a joint venture involving European rail operators in the provision of night rail services between the United Kingdom and mainland destinations. Exemption was granted by the Commission on condition that the parties offer services to the joint venture's competitors. Exemption would only last eight years. The parties appealed to CFI on the basis that the Commission had failed to give any analysis concerning market shares which the parties claimed would not exceed 5 per cent. In such circumstances the Commission should have reasoned why Article 85(1) applies. Also the condition imposed by the Commission was not reasoned. The Commission did not explain why the condition was necessary, nor why exemption would be granted only for eight years when the evidence was that the investment in the joint venture would not be recouped over less than twenty years.

An appeal may be made to the CFI against a Commission decision to impose a fine or periodic penalty. It may cancel, reduce or increase the fine or periodic penalty. The CFI's jurisdiction is conferred by Article 172 of the E.C. Treaty.[42]

14-26 Article 173 of the E.C. Treaty gives the CFI wider jurisdiction to review the legality of acts of the Commission encompassing any of the above decisions under Articles 11 to 16 concerned with investigation and enforcement, as well as any of the following decisions:

(1) The decision to grant negative clearance under Article 2 on application by the undertakings concerned (certifying that there are no grounds under Article 85(1) or Article 86 for action on the part of the Commission).[43] If the application is refused the Commission may serve a statement objections.

---

[41] Cases T–375, 384 & 388/94 *European Night Services* [1998] E.C.R. Judgment of September 15, 1998.
[42] Amended by Art. G(52) of the Treaty of the European Union. Although both Arts 172 and 173 refer to the "Court of Justice" (ECJ), jurisdiction was given to the CFI by Council Dec. 88/591 Establishing a Court of First Instance of the European Communities [1998] O.J. L319/1.
[43] If the application is refused the Commission may serve a statement of objections.

(2) The decision to grant individual exemption under Article 6 specifying the effective date of exemption and, if appropriate, attaching conditions or obligations as part of its decision.

(3) The decision to remove the immunity from fines that would otherwise be available in relation to the period between notification and the Commission's decision on an application for individual exemption (insofar as the notified activities are concerned). The Commission must inform the undertakings concerned of its conclusion that exemption under Article 85(3) is not justified.

The CFI has jurisdiction in actions which challenge the Commission on grounds of lack of competence, infringement of an essential procedural requirement, infringement of the E.C. Treaty or of any rule of law relating to its application, or misuse of powers. Article 173 of the E.C. Treaty provides as follows:

"Any natural or legal person may . . . institute proceedings against a decision addressed to that person or against a decision which, although in the form of a regulation or a decision addressed to another person, is of direct and individual concern to the former".

This would include, for example an application under Article 3(2) by any person with a "legitimate interest" to see that an infringement is terminated (*Metro SB Grossmarkte v. Commission*.[44]

14-27 Proceedings must be instituted within two months of the publication of the Commission measure or of its notification to the plaintiff. This procedure is not intended to substitute for participation by interested third parties in hearings or for responses to notices published by the Commission when the Commission is required to invite third party comment. Use should therefore be made of those procedures before reliance is placed on Article 173 of the E.C. Treaty.

In addition, Article 175 provides for a right of review by the CFI, should the Commission "fail to act" in infringement of the E.C. Treaty, within two months of being called upon to do so. The Commission does not have a duty to act in cases where there is no Community interest (*Automec v. Commission* (No. 2[45])but where a Community interest does exist the most likely use of it will be by complainants applying under Article 3 of Regulation 17/62 to terminate an infringement. The "act" required need not be a decision (*GEMA v. Commission*[46]).

It should also be noted that Article 215 renders "the Community" liable for damage caused by its institutions or by its servants in the performance of their duties. However, no proceedings have yet succeeded in relation to the application of this Article to competition law.

THE USE OF NATIONAL COURTS

14-28 The Commission has sole jurisdiction in relation to granting exemption[47] but in other respects Articles 85 and 86 are to be applied by both the Commission and the national courts since those Articles have direct effect. In fact the Commission has for

---

[44] Case 26/76 *Metro SB Grossmarkte v. Commission* [1977] E.C.R. 1875; [1978] 2 C.M.L.R. 1.
[45] Case T–24/90 *Automec v. Commission* (No. 2) [1992] E.C.R. II-2223; [1992] 5 C.M.L.R. 431.
[46] Case 125/78 *GEMA v. Commission* [1979] E.C.R. 3173; [1980] 2 C.M.L.R. 177. For discussion concerning the status of comfort letters see Chapter 6, *Comfort letters*, above.
[47] Reg. 17/62, Art. 9(2).

many years encouraged national courts to apply Articles 85 and 86 because the result will be to relieve the Commission's own workload and to breed a culture of enforcement throughout the Community.[48]

Actions for infringement of Articles 85 and 86 may be divided into two categories— actions between the parties (including for these purposes the victims of abuse of dominant position) and actions involving third parties.

Actions by the parties to infringement

14-29 If a party to an agreement wishes to contest its validity, it must first determine whether the agreement is void under Article 85(2). However, matters are complicated in the case of notified agreements which have not yet been granted exemption.

Article 85(2) renders void any agreements or decisions prohibited by Article 85(1). No decision is required by the Commission to prohibit them.[49] The only hope of enforceability for agreements caught by Article 85(1) lies in individual exemption and automatic block exemption, in both cases, where the criteria for exemption in Article 85(3) are satisfied.[50]

14-30 Article 6 of Regulation 17/62 clarifies the position of agreements once they are notified. Whenever the Commission grants exemption pursuant to Article 85(3), it is required to state the effective date of the exemption. Exemption does not apply at the date of notification, only once a positive decision has been made, although the effect of the decision may be backdated as far as the date of notification. Article 8(1) states that exemption under Article 85(3) will apply for a specified period (typically between five and 10 years) and the Commission may attach conditions or obligations to the exemption such as may require the parties to report market or pricing information to the Commission. Decisions are renewable[51] and may be revoked or amended (or specified acts prohibited) in certain circumstances. These are where fundamental facts underlying the decision change, where the parties breach an obligation attaching to the exemption,[52] where the decision was based on incorrect information or deceit or where the parties abuse the exemption granted to them. Breach of those obligations imposed may itself result in a fine.[53]

Time limits for notification apply to agreements that already existed when Regulation 17/62 came into effect but otherwise no time limits exist for notification. The advantages of early notification are driven by the above consequences.

14-31 These principles make the enforcement of notified agreements in national courts more complex during the period before a formal decision is made by the Commission. The courts cannot act in conflict with any decisions by the Commission (*Delimitis v. Henninger Brau*[54]) and yet are bound to give effect to Articles 85 and 86.

The national court deciding on the enforceability of an unnotified agreement must determine first of all whether Article 85(1) applies to it. It may decide that Article 85(1)

---

[48] See, for example the Notice on Co-operation between National Courts and the Commission in Applying Art.s 85 and 86 of the EEC Treaty [1993] O.J. C 39/6 and, more recently, the Commission's Notice on Co-operation between national competition authorities and the Commission in handling cases falling within the scope of Arts 85 or 86 of the E.C. Treaty [1997] O.J. C 313/3. The Commission may also offer guidance in its Annual Report on Competition Policy.
[49] Reg. 17/62, Art. 1.
[50] The category of agreements referred to in Art. 4(2) of Reg. 17/62 are the exception to the general principle, and do not require notification. For further details of non-notifiable agreements see Chapter 6, *Non-notifiable agreements* above.
[51] Art. 8(2).
[52] In this case the decision may have retrospective effect.
[53] Art. 15(2)(b).
[54] Case C –234/89 *Delimitis v. Henninger Brau* [1991] E.C.R. I-935; [1992] 4 C.M.L.R. 546.

does not apply in clear cases and may continue on that basis. The court may decide that a notifiable agreement clearly infringes Article 85(1) and it must then decide upon its eligibility for block exemption. If an agreement is eligible under a block exemption, the block exemption must be applied. If it is not eligible according to all the pre-conditions and other criteria for exemption in any block exemption Regulation then, bearing in mind that the Commission has sole jurisdiction to grant exemption under Article 85(3), the court must rule that the agreement is void. In doing so the court will apply rules of severance that are relevant as a matter of national law (*Chemidus Wavin v. TERI*[55]). If an entire agreement is rendered void, the consequences may be significant. For example, an intellectual property licensor or franchisor may then be unable to recover royalties by enforcing the terms of the void agreement.

14-32 Further uncertainty is introduced by the Commission's practice of issuing "comfort letters" as a means of foreshortening the full procedure for granting individual exemption. Their status before national courts is that they are not binding. Comfort letters represent the Commission's view on any matter but it is open to a national court to depart from the Commission's conclusion. The court may be influenced by the circumstances in which a comfort letter is issued (for example whether third party comment had been invited by a notice in the Official Journal, the basis on which the Commission provided the comfort letter, and in particular whether there have been any changes to the circumstances which formed the basis of the letter). If there has been a change of circumstances, the national court will be more willing to depart from the terms of the comfort letter. However, the national court is not at liberty to depart from the terms of an individual exemption, once granted, even if circumstances underlying it change. That issue should be raised before the Commission rather than the national court.

Before leaving the subject of actions between the parties (as opposed to third party actions), it is worth remembering that an agreement may be void where it constitutes an abuse of dominant position, for example by means of unlawful contractual tie-ins or discrimination which puts the party affected at a competitive disadvantage. Alternatively, a victim of abuse may simply seek damages for the loss it suffers as a result of the abuse in the same way as if it were a third party.

Actions by third parties

14-33 The most common remedies sought by a third party are injunctions and damages and these may be claimed without the involvement of the Commission. The Commission expressly encourages such actions because of the deterrent value against infringement. The Commission is not empowered to award damages to third parties. In the landmark case of *Garden Cottage Foods v. Milk Marketing Board*,[56] the House of Lords refused to grant an injunction because damages were seen to be an adequate remedy. This principle has been applied in numerous cases (for example *Plessey v. GEC and Siemens*[57]) but in reality damages are not often awarded because the vast majority of cases settle. Damages should be available for any breach of Article 85 or 86, as confirmed by the ECJ in *Brasserie du Pecheur v. Germany*.[58]

The basis of the action is generally taken to be breach of statutory duty. According to Lord Diplock in *Garden Cottage Foods v. Milk Marketing Board*, the relevant statute is the European Communities Act 1972 in relation to those provisions which have direct effect in the United Kingdom, such as Articles 85 and 86. The difficulty of any claim by a

---

[55] [1978] 3 C.M.L.R. 514 CA.
[56] [1984] A.C. 130.
[57] [1990] O.J. C239/2.
[58] Case C–46/93 *Brasserie du Pecheur v. Germany* [1996] E.C.R. I-1029; [1996] 1 C.M.L.R. 889.

party to an unnotified agreement caught by Article 85(1) is that the breach of statutory duty (infringement of Article 85(1)) is committed equally by all the parties to the agreement.[59] Damages are not available to one party to an agreement that is void by reason of Article 85(2) if the other party gives effect to it (*Trent Tavern v. Sykes*[60]).

14-34   Claims may also be made against Member States themselves for any breach of their obligations under the E.C. Treaty or secondary legislation. In *Francovich v. The Italian Republic*,[61] the ECJ held that the failure by Italy to implement a Directive as required could give rise to a claim in damages by individuals affected. The full scope of this principle remains unclear but action may nevertheless be taken against governments for breaches of their Treaty obligations, if not by way of breach of statutory duty then as misuse of public office (*Bourgoin v. Ministry of Agriculture, Fisheries and Food*[62] (which concerned a breach of Article 30 of the E.C. Treaty)).

It is striking that the 1998 Act does not expressly provide for a remedy for a breach of the Chapter I and Chapter II prohibitions by way of a breach of statutory duty especially since the Commission's Notice on co-operation between national competition authorities and the Commission in handling cases falling within the scope of Article 85 or 86 of the E.C. Treaty encourages national courts to provide private remedies for infringement. The opportunity for doing so was available in the drafting of the 1998 Act in which this issue was side-stepped.

14-35   It has been suggested[63] that another cause of action may be that of causing loss by unlawful means, following the judgment of Lord Denning in *Acrow (Automation) LTD v. Rex Chainbelt*[64]:

> "If one person, without just cause or excuse, deliberately interferes with the trade or business of another, and does so by unlawful means, that is, by an act which he is not at liberty to commit, then he is acting unlawfully. He is liable to damages, and, in a proper case, an injunction can be granted against him."[65]

The real hurdle in such a claim is proving deliberate interference directed at the Plaintiff.

The standard of proof in satisfying any claim based on Article 85 or 86 is higher than the standard of proof (balance of probabilities) in normal civil actions. Because of the risk of fines, the appropriate standard is "a high degree of probability" (*Shearson Lehman Hutton Inc v. McLaine Watson Co LTD*[66]). The difficulties in discharging the evidential burden are high.

14-36   It is striking that very few actions result in an award of damages. The application of Articles 85 and 86 still give rise to inconsistencies and results are unpredictable. The remedies available may therefore be summarised as follows:

(1)   damages; and/or

(2)   an injunction (interlocutory or permanent). For an interlocutory injunction the requirements established in *American Cyanamid v. Ethicon*[67] must be proved,

---

[59] The same however may not be said of agreements which infringe Art. 86 where one party is the victim of the abuse of dominant position.

[60] Judgment of the High Court, David Steel J.

[61] Cases 6 & 9/90 *Francovich v. The Italian Republic* [1991] E.C.R. I-565; [1993] 2 C.M.L.R. 66.

[62] [1985] 3 All E.R. 585.

[63] Green and Robertson *Commercial Agreements and Competition Law Practice and Procedures in the U.K. and EC*, Kluwer, (2nd Ed. 1996).

[64] [1971] 3 All E.R. 1175.

[65] Para. 1181.

[66] [1989] 3 C.M.L.R. 429 HC.

[67] [1975] A.C. 396.

namely there must be a triable issue, damages alone would be an inadequate remedy, irreparable harm would be done to the plaintiff pending full trial and the balance of convenience must favour the plaintiff. Cross-undertakings to damages will be expected to be given by the plaintiff;

(3) a declaration as to whether or not an agreement infringes Article 85(1) or 86, or is exempt by a block exemption Regulation, or whether or not specified conduct contravenes Article 86.

The potential range of plaintiffs are:

(1) victims of abuse of dominant position under Article 86

(2) parties to an agreement which infringes Act 86; or

(3) third parties affected by infringement of Article 85(1) or Article 86.

The potential range of defendants are:

(1) dominant undertakings guilty of abuse under Article 86;

(2) parties to agreements that infringe Article 85(1) or Article 86; or

(3) governments of Member States which do not give effect to their obligations.

Given the need to avoid conflict between national courts and the Commission (*Delimitis v. Henninger Brau*[68]) when there are parallel proceedings at the Commission, it is appropriate to stay the proceedings in the national court until their outcome is known. However, the court does not necessarily have to stay proceedings, as demonstrated by *MTV Europe v. BMG Records (U.K.) LTD and others*[69] which concluded:

"There is in my Judgment, nothing which suggests that in a case where the answer is not clear in favour of the Plaintiff or the Defendant, the national court must at once stay the proceedings pending a decision by the Commission. The Court's concern is to avoid inconsistent decisions. There is no ground for seeking to prohibit the preparation of an action for trial for so long as it does not lead to a decision in advance of a decision by the Commission."[70]

14-37 It may be difficult for a plaintiff to succeed in Order 14 applications[71] given the complexities of fact and law that typically converge in competition law cases. Furthermore, an application for security of costs against non-United Kingdom residents within the EEA would now amount to discrimination on grounds of nationality (*Mund & Fester v. Hatrex*[72]).

Finally, there is the possibility that vexatious litigation may possibly constitute abuse under Article 86 if it threatens the viability of a new market entrant (*BBI/Boosey and Hawkes Interim Measures*[73]). The view expressed by the Commission in *ITT Promedia NV v. Commission*[74] and confirmed by the CFI is as follows:

---

[68] Case 234/89 [1991] E.C.R. I-935; [1992] 4 C.M.L.R. 546.
[69] [1997] E.U. L.R. 100.
[70] *per* Sir Thomas Bingham M.R.
[71] Order 14 of the Rules of the Supreme Court (currently subject to change).
[72] Case C–398/92 *Mund & Fester v. Hatrex International Transport* [1994] E.C.R. I-467.
[73] Commission Dec. 87/500 [1987] O.J. L286/36; [1988] 4 C.M.L.R. 67.
[74] Case T–111/96 *ITT Promedia NV v. Commission*, Judgment of the CFI of July 17, 1998.

"[I]n principle the bringing of an action, which is the expression of a fundamental right of access to a Judge, cannot be characterised as an abuse unless an undertaking in a dominant position brings action (i) which cannot reasonably be considered as an attempt to establish its rights and can therefore only serve to harass the opposite party, and (ii) which is conceived in the framework of a plan whose goal is to eliminate competition."[75]

Litigation issues

14-38   There are a number of practical points which arise in cases where either or both of Articles 85 and 86 are relied upon in a claim or defence. It is as well for the practitioner to have these in mind from the outset, before proceedings are issued. These procedural considerations are further complicated by the new Civil Procedure Rules. The purpose of this section is to highlight these considerations to practitioners.

The litigation of alleged breaches of the provisions of Articles 85 and 86 almost invariably involves careful dissection and analysis a substantial body of commercial information. Fishing expeditions are not uncommon in such cases[75a] They are often unwelcome. Modern practice tends towards limiting discovery[75b] whilst always focusing on the pleaded issues between the parties. In these circumstances, careful consideration should be given to pleadings and forum before proceedings are issued.

14-39   Parties defending an allegation of anti-competitive behaviour will generally have an interest in minimising the scope of issues on the pleadings (particularly by making any proper admissions) and minimising the scope of the consequent discovery obligation. Conversely, parties alleging such behaviour may have an interest in obtaining fuller discovery.

Practitioners will be aware that the Civil Procedure Rules ("CPR") provide for different procedures to govern certain types of proceedings and those brought in certain divisions of the High Court, particularly the Commercial Court, the Technology and Construction Court and the Patents Court.[75c] Importantly, differences in the requirements for the content of pleadings may survive. CPR will generally require fuller particulars of all claims, defences, non-admissions and denials, clear statements of any positive case and statements of truth verifying them.[75d]

14-40   Cases decided under the Rules of the Supreme Court ("RSC") prior to the introduction of the CPR may continue to have some authority where the provisions of the RSC or their spirit continue to apply under the CPR or are in fact applied by the judiciary.

The Commission's role will always be an important consideration. A complaint to the Commission may have practical advantages and disadvantages. The cost of investigation will be borne by the Commission not the complainant. In some circumstances, the Commission may be prepared to keep the identity of the complainant confidential. This is not available in litigation and may be a real advantage to the small company complainant which depends on doing business with the undertaking allegedly behaving anti-competitively.

14-41   The practical disadvantages of a complaint mainly arise from the complainant's loss of control of the process. The Commission may decide not to investigate or may reach an accommodation with the accused undertaking which, while improving conditions for competition in the industry, leave the complainant unsatisfied.

---

[75]   Para. 30 of the Judgment of the CFI.
[75a]   British Leyland Motor Corp. Ltd v. Wyatt Interpart Co. Ltd [1979] F.S.R. 39.
[75b]   CPR and the attendant Practice Directions; and, for example OCo. v. MCo. [1996] 2 Lloyd's Rep. 347.
[75c]   CPR Part 49, Specialist Proceedings.
[75d]   Contrast CPR Pt 16.4, 16.5 and 22 with RSC O.18, r.13.

The Commission's involvement may also affect the procedure and progress of parallel litigation in the courts. In *Fichera v. Flogates Ltd and British Steel Ltd*,[75e] an application to strike out the action for want of prosecution failed because the proceedings had been delayed while the Commission carried out investigations.

The fact that the Commission has formed a view of a *prima facie* violation of Article 85 or 86 was critical to the scope of discovery to which the Defendant was entitled in *Aero Zipp Fasteners Ltd v. YKK Fasteners (U.K.) Ltd*.[75f] YKK pleaded a general defence alleging a breach of the provisions of Articles 85 and 86 and sought discovery before giving further particulars. The plaintiff contended that this was a fishing expedition which should not be allowed. The Commission's preliminary view and the plaintiff's unique knowledge of its own behaviour were decisive in the court allowing YKK the discovery it sought.

14-42 Any view formed or steps taken by the Commission on competition issues affecting the parties to litigation, may be relevant on any application for summary judgment in that litigation.[75g]

The question of privilege against self-incrimination raises further issues. This privilege may excuse a party from answering questions or giving discovery of documents which might incriminate or expose that party to a penalty. This issue may therefore arise frequently in competition litigation. By section 14(1) of the Civil Evidence Act 1968, the privilege only extends to offences or penalties provided for under United Kingdom law. By virtue of the European Communities Act 1972, it is clear that penalties which might be imposed by the European Commission for infringement of Articles 85 and 86 are penalties provided for by United Kingdom law. Proceedings under the 1998 Act obviously raise a similar issue on this question of privilege.

14-43 Equally, public policy may restrict the use of documents making complaint to the European Commission of a breach of Article 85. This was recognised by the Court of Appeal in *Hasselblad (G.B.) Ltd v. Orbinson*[75h] which refused to allow a letter of complaint to the Commission to be used as the basis for a libel action.

The importance of these issues of discovery and privilege will substantially depend on the commercial sensitivity of the information contained in the documents sought. However, despite the intention to simplify litigation in Lord Woolf's reforms, these questions of discovery and privilege are likely to remain important and to be hotly and expensively contested well into the future.

14-44 The last practical point addressed in this section is the alternative to any proceedings at all, namely mediation. In some cases, competition issues will arise where relations between the parties have already broken down, if they ever existed. That does not make the dispute unsuitable for mediation. However, where the dispute involves any consideration of the terms upon which the parties continue to deal, it may be peculiarly well suited to mediation, quickly and cheaply resolving the dispute, whilst preserving the business relationship in a way that protracted litigation would not. Mediation may often be appropriate in competition cases, whether in parallel with other enforcement proceedings or not.

CO-OPERATION BETWEEN THE COMMISSION, THE COURTS AND COMPETENT AUTHORITIES

14-45 The Commission has issued two important notices aimed at enhancing co-operation between the Commission on the one hand and national courts and national

---

[75e] [1992] F.S.R. 48.
[75f] [1973] F.S.R. 580.
[75g] *Joseph Francis Dymond v. G.B. Britton & Sons (Holdings) Ltd* [1976] F.S.R. 330.
[75h] [1985] Q.B. 475.

competition authorities on the other. The Notice on co-operation between national courts and the Commission in applying Articles 85 and 86 of the EEC Treaty[76] deals with the allocation of tasks to assist national courts in closer co-operation with the Commission in individual cases. The Commission Notice on co-operation between national competition authorities and the Commission in handling cases falling within the scope of Article 85 or 86 of the E.C. Treaty[77] is the counterpart, dealing with co-operation between the Commission and competition authorities, in the United Kingdom, the OFT.

Co-operation concerning national courts

Powers of national courts

14-46   The Co-operation Notice concerning national courts recognises that the different powers of the Commission and national courts are exercised with different objectives. They are exercised by the Commission in accordance with the procedures set out in Regulation 17/62 and by national courts, which are required to give direct effect to Community law in Member States, in accordance with national procedural law.

The Notice confirms that national courts are entitled to adopt their own procedures in order to bring infringement of Community competition rules to an end, and to provide remedies such as compensation for infringement in private actions. All the procedural remedies available as a matter of national law in the event of a breach of national law, should apply equally to any breach of Community law. However, if this gives rise to any conflict with Community law then the latter takes precedence.

Division of function between the Commission and national courts

14-47   In exercising the Commission's powers, its resources are inevitably limited and it is bound to prioritize its activities. In doing so, the Commission concentrates primarily on notifications (because it has sole jurisdiction to grant exemption), complaints and own-initiative proceedings that have a particular political, economic or legal significance to the Community.[78] In the Commission's view, complaints are better dealt with by national authorities or national courts unless of course they raise particular issues of Community interest. The advantages are that the Commission, unlike national courts, cannot award damages for infringement, although it can fine infringers. Local enforcement of Community competition rules is also likely to result in better compliance. The range of interlocutory measures available to national courts are far speedier and more effective than the interim measures available to the Commission. However, in practice, in the United Kingdom courts, it will be difficult to overcome the "triable issue" hurdle in Order 14[79] proceedings. In addition, costs may be awarded by national courts but not by the Commission.

Application of Articles 85 and 86 by national courts

14-48   The most common applications of Articles 85 and 86 in national courts are first, contract disputes, defended on the basis of voidness by virtue of Article 85(2), and secondly, damages claims by victims of infringement on the basis of breach of statutory

---

[76] [1993] O.J. 93/C 39/05.
[77] [1997] O.J. C313/03.
[78] The Commission prefers to foreshorten the notification procedures by dealing with them by way of administrative or comfort letters.
[79] Order 14 Rules of the Supreme Court (currently subject to change).

duty. In exercising their powers to apply Articles 85 and 86. national courts need to avoid making any decision that would conflict with any Commission decision, and should do so by means of the following principles.

National courts should check that any decision they are about to make concerning an infringement of Article 85(1) or Article 86 has not already been the subject of a decision, opinion or some other official statement by the Commission. Even if a particular statement is not binding on a national court, it nevertheless is useful as information which, if nothing else, the courts should bear in mind. Certain statements are particularly significant such as comfort letters, which are issued by the Commission in place of a decision. Though not binding, comfort letters express a clear opinion on the part of the Commission and the national courts should take these into account in determining the status of agreements under Article 85. National courts should also be guided by the case law of the ECJ and existing Commission decisions and Notices where the Commission has not itself ruled on a particular agreement, and this should be sufficient to enable the courts to determine compatibility with Articles 85(1) and 86.

14-49   In the interests of certainty, once the Commission has initiated a procedure in relation to a matter which is before a national court, proceedings in that court should be stayed pending the outcome of the Commission action (*BRT v. Sabam*[80]). Proceedings may also be stayed by a national court while it seeks the Commission's views on a particular matter[81] or where it has some persistent doubts on questions of compatibility which it wishes to raise by way of an Article 177 reference.[82]

If a national court decides that there is no infringement of Article 85(1) or 86, it may proceed on that basis even if the court's decision relates to an agreement that has been notified. However, where the court decides that there has been an infringement, national courts must then apply the appropriate measures available under national law that render the infringement actionable. In the United Kingdom, infringement is actionable as a matter of breach of statutory duty.

14-50   Particular care must be taken with agreements that qualify for exemption under Article 85(3). If a national court makes a finding that Article 85(1) applies, it must then check with the Commission whether it has been (or will be) granting exemption. National courts must respect any exemption decisions of the Commission, giving effect to them in any civil actions. Given that the majority of applications for individual exemption are dealt with by way of comfort letters, and because the Commission states in them that the conditions of eligibility are met for exemption under Article 85(3), comfort letters must be taken into account in national courts "as factual elements"[83] even if they are not legally binding on the courts.

Clearly national courts must apply any block exemption Regulation in determining the status of an agreement without any need for a comfort letter or individual exemption by the Commission. In the absence of any Commission comfort letter, decision or block exemption Regulation, the national court must first find out whether the agreement in question has been formally notified. If not, and if exemption can be ruled out, then the court may decide that the agreement or its severable parts are void under Article 85(2).[84]

If notification has been made to the Commission, the national court may make an assessment of the chances of it succeeding. If the conclusion is that the agreement is not eligible for exemption, the court may apply Articles 85(1) and 85(2). If exemption is a possibility, then the court should suspend its proceedings until the outcome of the

---

[80] Case 127/73 *BRT v. Sabam* [1974] E.C.R. 51; 2 [1974] C.M.L.R. 238.
[81] See *Co-operation between national courts and the Commission* below.
[82] See Chap. 2 *Article 177 references* above.
[83] Para. 25(a) of the Notice.
[84] Assuming it is not in the category of non-notifiable agreements under Reg. 17/62, Art. 4(2).

Commission's decision. However, even if the national court does suspend its proceedings, it remains free to adopt any appropriate interim measures that are available to it as a matter of national law.

Co-operation between national courts and the Commission

14-51   Article 5 of the E.C. Treaty requires Member States to,

> "take all appropriate measures, whether general or particular, to ensure fulfilment of the obligations arising out of this Treaty or resulting from action taken by the institutions of the Community. They shall facilitate the achievement of the Community's tasks. They shall abstain from any measure which could jeopardise the attainment of the objectives of this Treaty".

This duty is described by the Commission as one "of constant and sincere co-operation" between the Community and the judicial authorities of Member States. Co-operation is seen as essential to guarantee the strict, effective and consistent application of Community competition law, leaving the Commission in a better position to steer competition policy.

For its part in the process of co-operation, the Commission undertakes to continue to give guidance by means of block exemption Regulations, Notices and its Annual Reports on Competition Policy. The courts are further assisted, obviously, by developing ECJ and CFI case law and ongoing Commission decisions to enable them to decide individual cases with certainty.

14-52   In addition national courts are encouraged if these are not sufficient, to ask the Commission for information of a procedural nature to identify whether any particular case is pending before the Commission, whether a particular agreement has been notified or whether the Commission has initiated any procedures or taken a position by way of an official decision or comfort letter. National courts may also ask for an indication of the timing of any decision granting or refusing exemption, so that it knows whether it is appropriate to suspend its proceedings pending the Commission's outcome or to adopt interim measures.

National courts may also consult the Commission on points of law in particularly difficult cases. Examples are most likely to relate to whether there is an appreciable effect on trade between Member States and eligibility for exemption. If the Commission indicates that an agreement is unlikely to qualify for exemption, the national courts will be able to waive a stay of proceedings and give a ruling on the validity of the agreement.

14-53   Any answers given by the Commission under these procedures are non-binding and it is open for the national court to make an Article 177 reference at any time. National courts may ask for factual data from the Commission (or ask to be referred to the appropriate sources) such as statistics, market studies or analyses, if they are at the Commission's disposal and are not subject to procedural restrictions such as confidentiality.

Finally, it should be noted that all judgments by national courts when applying Community rules are covered by the Convention on jurisdiction and the enforcement of judgments in civil and commercial matters[85] which facilities reciprocal enforcement of judgments in different Member States.

---

[85] Convention signed at Brussels on September 27, 1978 [1978] O.J. L304.

Co-operation concerning national authorities

Power of authorities

14-54 The Commission Notice on co-operation between national competition authorities and the Commission in handling cases falling within the scope of Articles 85 or 86 of the E.C. Treaty[86] describes the practical co-operation between the Commission and the national authorities and the allocation of functions between them, given in particular, that national authorities must apply domestically the prohibitions in Articles 85(1) and 86, even though the Commission has sole power to grant exemption from Article 85(1) and to issue comfort letters. The relevant national authority in the United Kingdom is the OFT. The more readily it is that national authorities apply Articles 85(1) and 86, the more effective will be the application of Community competition law throughout the Community, not least because national authorities are often in a better position to enforce competition law than the Commission. Detection of infringement is obviously more likely at national level. National authorities have a better knowledge of the relevant markets and the businesses concerned. In addition, where the Commission and national authorities co-operate on procedural matters, there is scope for avoiding duplication particularly where there is the risk of parallel proceedings before the Commission and at national level, which is obviously costly to those concerned and a waste of public resources. Where a single procedure is adopted in place of parallel procedures, there is also less room for divergence in the decisions made, which is a particular risk where one procedure offers advantages over the other.

Decisions and exemptions

14-55 National authorities are encouraged to apply Articles 85 and 86 in conjunction with their own national competition laws. The case law of the ECJ and CFI over many years is now sufficiently developed for this to be practicable. However, there is still room for divergence where a Member State applies national law rather than Community law. When applying Community law, national authorities are in the same position as national courts who must comply with any Commission decision taken in the same proceedings. In the case of comfort letters which are non-binding on national courts, the courts and national authorities must merely have regard to the comfort letter. However, the Commission requires national authorities to consult with the Commission before they adopt a different decision from the indication given in a comfort letter, whether applying Community law or national law.

14-56 The following principles may assist in determining how to resolve a conflict between Community law and decisions by national authorities:

(1) If a Commission decision establishes an infringement of Article 85(1) or 86, no domestic legal measure may operate to authorise what is prohibited.

(2) A comfort letter does not prevent a finding nationally that the matter constitutes an infringement of national competition law based on its national effects.[87]

(3) In cases where national law is more stringent than Community law, the status of individual exemption, according to the Notice is that:

---

[86] [1997] O.J. C313/03.

[87] Joined cases 253/78 & 1–3/79 *Procureur de la République v. Giry and Guerlain* [1980] E.C.R. 2327; [1981] 2 C.M.L.R. 99, para. 1.

"[t]he uniform application of Community law would be frustrated every time an exemption granted under Community law was made to depend on the relevant national laws . . . a given agreement [would] be treated differently depending on the law of each Member State"[88]

Even if that is the Commission's view, the ECJ has not settled the issue of whether national authorities are entitled to prohibit agreements that have been granted exemption by the Commission in spite of contentions by the Commission that they are not entitled to.[89]

Case allocation

14-57   Given that a national authority is generally not legally entitled to conduct investigations or enforce decisions outside its jurisdiction, the Commission usually handles those cases where the relevant activities are conducted in more than one Member State. National authorities must, on the other hand, retain sufficient capacity and be enabled by legal measures swiftly to deal with any cases covered by Community rules. There needs to be uniformity between Community and national procedures for enforcement.

In the case of any matter where the relevant geographic market is within a single Member State or the agreement or practice applies only within that State, for the purpose of case allocation, its effect will be treated as national only, even if theoretically it is capable of affecting trade between Member States. The national authority will then be expected to handle the matter, if there appears to be an infringement.[90]

14-58   Certain cases will, however, generally be dealt with by the Commission even if the matter is primarily national in effect and these are cases that raise a new point of law not already the subject of a Commission decision or judgment either of the ECJ or CFI. The scale of a matter is not itself reason enough for it to be dealt with by the Commission unless access to the relevant market by firms from other Member States is significantly impeded.

Co-operation

14-59   At the request of the Commission.   National competition authorities may deal, at the Commission's request, with matters not falling within the Commission's exclusive competence.

In the case of complaints, the Commission may reject a complaint and ask the competent authority of the relevant Member State to investigate and decide on the complaint. Before doing so, the Commission must assess whether there is a Community interest at stake. If not, the Commission is justified in not proceeding further, but it must give the complainant the reasons for its decision.[91]

14-60   In assessing whether there is a Community interest behind any complaint, a number of factors need to be balanced such as the significance of the infringement, the chances of it being proved, the extent of the investigative measures required for compliance and the availability of national remedies (including interim measures) where the

---

[88] Para. 19 of the Notice.
[89] Case C–266/93 *Bundeskartellamt v. Volkswagen and VAG Leasing* [1995] E.C.R. I-3477; [1996] 4 C.M.L.R. 478.
[90] Even agreements referred to in Art. 4(2)(i) of Reg. 17/62, to which all the parties are from the same Member State and which do not relate to imports or exports between Member States, may still be caught by Art. 85(1) because of an effect on trade between Member States.
[91] Art. 190 of the E.C. Treaty.

effects are primarily within a given territory. If national measures (including interim measures) suffice to protect the complainant's interests in cases of infringement confined to a single Member State, the Commission will expect the matter to be dealt with at national level.

In such circumstances, the Commission will ask the competent authority within the appropriate Member State to investigate the complaint and decide upon it. If that authority accepts, then the matter is referred automatically, or at the complainant's request, and the relevant documents are transferred to the relevant authority, preserving confidentiality where necessary to protect the complainant's anonymity. With regard to any investigation, the national authorities are not entitled to use as evidence unpublished information contained in replies to requests for information by the Commission under Article 11 or pursuant to the Commission's investigative powers under Article 14.

14-61   At the request of National Authority.   In those cases where a national authority deals first with a matter of Community competition law applying Article 85(1) or Article 86, whether alone or in conjunction with its own national competition rules, and whether on its own initiative or in response to a notification or complaint, the national authority should systematically inform the Commission of any proceedings which it initiates. The Commission will then pass on the information to other affected Member States. In consultation with the Commission the national authorities must determine whether there is sufficient Community interest. A Community interest may exist because the case raises a new point of law (and it is obviously important to ensure consistency with developing Community law), because the case is of utmost importance from an economic view and access to the national market is impeded for firms from other Member States, or because it involves infringement by a public undertaking entrusted with certain functions and privileges. Co-operation is especially important whenever there is a Community interest at stake.

The Notice envisages that these cases will be investigated by national competition authorities according to their own national procedures, whether they are applying national or Community competition rules. The national authorities are reminded in the Notice that they are always at liberty to seek information from the Commission on the state of any current proceedings before the Commission or if the national authority's application of Articles 85 or 86 raises particular difficulties.

14-62   The ultimate aim is to avoid divergence of decisions. If at any stage of the national procedure it appears possible that the outcome of any Commission decision could conflict with a decision of the national authority concerning the same agreement then the national authority must take appropriate measures to ensure that the measures implementing Community competition law (the Commission decision) are effective. This usually involves a stay of proceedings by the national authorities until the outcome of the Commission proceedings is known. This is obviously to give primacy to Community law and is in the interests of legal certainty. The Commission will then try to expedite its own decision. An alternative is for the national authority to consult the Commission before making its decision. This may involve exchange of documents that have been prepared in making the decision envisaged by the national authority (subject to the above limits on disclosure) so that the national decision is not delayed.

In relation to complaints, there is no reason why national competition authorities cannot handle complaints submitted initially to them even though they involve matters of Community competition law. The Commission itself cannot be forced to make a decision as to whether infringement has occurred and in any event is not bound to deal with a complaint which does not raise sufficient Community interest.

14-63   As to notifications, the Commission will not deal with "dilatory notifications".

These are applications made to the Commission under Regulation 17/62 for negative clearance, for individual exemption, or to terminate an infringement, when the applicant knows that it faces a decision from a national authority banning a restrictive practice under investigation or where it is expected that national proceedings will be initiated. The Commission will not treat a notification as dilatory until it has confirmed that the national authority's assessment matches that of the Commission. National authorities are also encouraged to inform the Commission if they themselves consider a notification to the Commission to be dilatory. The purpose of the notification to the Commission is to eclipse the jurisdiction of the national authority. If the purpose of the notification is to suspend the proceedings pending a decision by the Commission, the Commission has indicated that it will not examine the case as a matter of priority.

In such circumstances, once the national authority has initiated proceedings, it should ask the Commission for its provisional opinion on the likelihood of exemption being granted unless it is already obvious from established Community law that the agreement in question cannot be granted individual exemption. If the Commission considers on examination that the agreement is unlikely to qualify for exemption and that its effects are confined mainly to one Member State, the Commission will indicate to the national authority and the notifying parties that the matter is not a matter of Commission priority and that it is unlikely to get round to a decision before the national authority needs to make a final decision. However, immunity from fines as a matter of Community law will be preserved in the meantime.

14-64 The national authority, in response, will undertake to inform the Commission if its investigation results in a different conclusion from that of the Commission. In any event, a copy of the decision of the national authority will be sent to the Commission and copies of correspondence to other relevant Member States for information. The Commission will not initiate proceedings in the same case before the proceedings before the national authority have been completed because that would take the matter out of the hands of the national authority unless, unexpectedly, the national authority is inclined to make a finding that there is no infringement of Article 85(1) or Article 86 or of its own national competition law. The Commission may also initiate proceedings if the national proceedings are exceptionally protracted. However, before taking any such decision, the Commission will consult the national authority to discover the reasons why the national authority is proposing to reach a favourable decision when the Commission would not.

E.C. and U.S. co-operation

14-65 Co-operation is also contemplated between the E.U. and the USA[92] under supplementary provisions to the 1991 E.U.-U.S. Co-operation Agreement[93]. Its aim is to avoid duplication of investigations. It would ultimately encourage the authorities to confine investigations to one territory. If either the E.U. or USA suffers ill-effects from activities occurring in the territory of the other, it may request the other to investigate and take enforcement measures in that other's territory, provided that the activities complained of are unlawful there. In the meantime, any further action on the part of the requesting party would be suspended. This co-operation will undoubtedly result in better cohesion when attacking international cartels. The Commission annually publishes the exchanges that have occurred in each year under these co-operation arrangements.

Without international co-operation, the national laws of different States globally may

---

[92] [1998] O.J. L173/26 Council and Commission decision concerning the conclusion of the Agreement between the E.C. and U.S. on the application of positive comity principles in the enforcement of their competition laws.
[93] Agreement between European Communities and the Government of the United States of America regarding the application of their competition laws [1995] O.J. L131/38.

be in direct conflict. This was succinctly put by Lord Wilberforce in *Re: Westinghouse Electric Corporation Uranium Contract Litigation*[94]:

> "It is axiomatic that in anti-trust matters the policy of one state may be to defend what it is the policy of another state to attack."[95]

---

[94] [1978] A.C. 547.

[95] *ibid*., at 617. In spite of international co-operation, the authorities of different countries still reach different conclusions. As illustrated by Commission Dec. 97/816 *Boeing Company/McDonnell Douglas Corporation* [1997] O.J. L336/16 and Commission Dec. 97/469 *Ciba-Geigy Sandoz* [1997] O.J. L201.

CHAPTER 15

Compliance Programmes

INTRODUCTION

15-01 A compliance programme consists of a set of procedures adopted as a means of ensuring compliance with competition law. Compliance programmes may be pre-emptive (in order to avoid infringement) or corrective (to put right an infringement after the event).

There is no doubt that compliance programmes may well mitigate fines under E.C. competition law (and there is little reason to suppose that they will not equally mitigate penalties under the 1998 Act). The following Commission press release in *Parker Pen*[1] bears this out:

> "The level of fine does however reflect the co-operative behaviour of Parker during the investigation of the case and the fact that Parker has drawn up a wide-ranging competition law compliance programme for all its E.C. subsidiaries. The fine could have been significantly higher without these mitigating factors."

In view of fines of approximately 102 million ECUs in the case of *Volkswagen*,[2] and 273 million ECUs in the case of *Trans-Atlantic Conference Agreement*,[3] compliance programmes must be taken seriously and companies should as a matter of course consider implementing them at all levels. Although fines have yet to approach their maximum ceiling (and are unlikely to in the near future), the fines which the Commission is imposing are getting harsher. This is in part because the Commission considers that recent high profile competition law cases mean that companies can no longer claim ignorance or naivety. *Tippex*[4] unsuccessfully argued that they had not realised until 1982 that competition law existed.

15-02 Businesses will inevitably want agreements upon which they rely to be enforceable. Many only discover that their agreements are invalid when they come to enforce their terms and an Article 85(2) defence is raised in response. For example, *Pronuptia*[5] found that they were unable to sue a franchisee for arrears of royalties because of voidness. As has been seen, undertakings will also be liable in damages to third parties affected by infringement following the House of Lords' decision in *Garden Cottage Foods*.[6] Added to this, undertakings face enormous management disruption and expense if investigated

---

[1] Commission Dec. 92/426 *Viho/Parker Pen* [1992] O.J. L233/27 and upheld by the CFI in Case T–77/92 *Parker Pen v. Commission* [1994] E.C.R. II-549.

[2] Commission Dec. 98/208 [1998] O.J. L124/60.

[3] Commission Dec. of September 16, 1998 Commission Press Release IP/98/811.

[4] Commission Dec. 87/406 [1987] O.J. L222/1.

[5] Commission Dec. 161/84 *Pronuptia de Paris GmbH v. Pronuptia de Paris Irmgard Schillgalis* [1987] O.J. L13/39; [1986] E.C.R. 353; [1986] 1 C.M.L.R. 414.

[6] Garden Cottage Foods v. Milk Marketing Board (1984) A.C. 130; [1983] 2 All E.R. 770 HL.

and if an adverse finding is made, personal and public loss of reputation. Share prices may also suffer.

The reality is that many undertakings still do not appreciate the need for compliance either because they do not take competition law seriously, are unaware of its scope and significance, or are aware of its importance but view the risks of non-compliance as acceptable in view of the administrative inconvenience of achieving compliance.

CARRYING OUT THE COMPLIANCE PROGRAMME

15-03 A compliance programme may consist of any of the following elements:

(1) an audit;

(2) risk assessment;

(3) notification or termination of prohibited agreements and practices;

(4) staff training; and

(5) culture change.

Audit

15-04 A competition audit consists of an in-depth analysis of all the activities of a business, in particular, its position in the market relative to competitors, consumers and others in the supply chain and the effect of its arrangements on the market. The market analysis should not be approached superficially. A document analysis, though essential, is rarely sufficient.

A useful starting point is a questionnaire designed to illicit a full description from senior management of all relevant businesses practices and agreements. Obviously this will embrace practices that are neutral as well as those that are anti-competitive. A comprehensive picture is necessary of the way in which a business is conducted. Often the practices that are hardest to elicit are those that for some reason are considered to be standard and commercially justified. It is essential that those involved in the task are sufficiently devoted to achieving compliance. Some managers (hopefully few) are not appropriately motivated. In the case of *Pioneer*,[7] one distributor commented:

"I am well aware of EEC rules regarding parallel imports but quite frankly at times I am more concerned with justice than the law itself".

15-05 Businesses may be reluctant to accept that their practices are regulated by competition law, least of all from Brussels. In any event, anti-competitive practices are often referred to by names which on the surface at least seem innocuous. Advance price-sharing information might be called "market intelligence", export bans in each country of a distribution network might be referred to as "keeping your distributors happy" and out and out market-sharing referred to as "respecting each other's territory". In one case, a senior manager described various illegal practices as "orderly marketing".[8]

Compiling relevant information can be arduous. The questionnaire should be accompanied by an instruction manual or similar explanation of common anti-competitive practices or clauses which potentially restrict competition, coupled with reasons why they are

---

[7] Commission Dec. 80/256 [1980] O.J. L60/21.
[8] Examples given by John Ratliff, Stanbrook & Henderson, 2 Harcourt Buildings, E.C. Competition Compliance Seminar, February 1995.

regarded as harmful. This will serve as an essential starting point both to inform those who are required to provide the information and to provide a framework for describing the business practices. However, there is no substitute for an understanding of the dynamics of the market which cannot easily be put into questionnaire form. It is an exercise that is interpretative and analytical and requires familiarisation with competition law principles.

15-06   The questionnaire and basic instruction will hopefully result in the orderly production of historic agreements as well as dealings with customers, dealers, possibly competitors and others. All agreements that are eligible for automatic block exemption should be checked to determine whether the terms of the agreement meet the terms of the applicable block exemption Regulation. Just as important as the agreement terms are the preconditions for exemption often expressed in terms of the aggregate market share of the parties and availability of other sources of competition. Other agreements may likewise be analysed for compliance by applying the principles set out in earlier Chapters.

All contract-related documents, not simply written agreements, must be reviewed. For example, correspondence before or after execution of a contract may reveal that, in spite of its form, the agreement is intended to be operated in a manner different from the strict written terms. Often those aspects of contract implementation that are most sensitive are deliberately dealt with outside the agreement itself.

15-07   The marketing strategy of the sales team is also important to determine, for example the basis on which prices are arrived at and whether there is collusion with competitors in any marketing activities. Marketing reports will often give a subjective impression of market share and the threat posed by competitors. A provisional view may be formed of the structure of the market in which that business operates, in terms of the market power of the business when compared with competitors, suppliers and purchasers as well as the availability of potential competition and the entry barriers that exist. Sales figures may also give an indication of profitability and whether, for example there is the risk of the accusation of excessive pricing. The Finance Director (or equivalent) may be a better source of information when applying a more detailed economic analysis. In general, any provisional findings should be corroborated by other sources. Any assumptions or pre-suppositions made by anyone providing information should be checked since it is vital that established principles of competition law be applied in any analysis. Sales reports frequently give market share estimates but the calculation may have been made for a particular purpose, such as sales promotion and may have been exaggerated applying different principles from those of competition law. Members of the sales team are frequently a very good source of information concerning the market effects of particular agreements such as the likely response of customers to price increases or decreases and the activities of competitors.

Care must therefore be taken to discern the true market position of the business. If a report contains statements that suggest a dangerously high market share, the basis of the report should be examined further. Equally reports may understate market share and other indices of market power and these should not necessarily be taken at face value.

Risk assessment

15-08   Some assessment should be made of the risks of any non-compliance that is revealed. Infringement may take the form of particular restrictions in an agreement. Rather than bring this to the attention of the other party or the authorities, it may be better to keep the agreement in place for commercial reasons. The risk of a third party action may seem remote, as may the chances of the agreement being spotted by the authorities. Balanced against that, of course, would be the gravity of the infringement and the level of any fine that may result.

If, on the other hand, reliance is placed on the prohibited restrictions, then of far greater importance than the risks of third party actions or fines will be the loss of enforceability of the relevant restrictions, if not the entire agreement.

The risks of action from the authorities will increase with the scale of the business concerned (and group companies) since there is greater likelihood of detection. The effect of an infringement is also then likely to be more acutely felt. Given the disruption, cost and loss of reputation at stake it would obviously be inadvisable to leave any infringement unremedied. There is the additional cost to be considered of contesting the validity of an agreement in the national court.

Notification or termination of prohibited practices or agreements

15-09 There are no time limits for notification although for such time as parties do not notify a prohibited agreement they remain exposed to the above risks.

Where voidness favours one party to an agreement there is inevitably less incentive on that party to amend it. Care must be taken by any party relying on voidness to ensure that any payment provisions which it might be relying upon are unaffected. One party will obviously suffer commercial loss if the other party defaults and the defaulting party then raises a defence that the payment provisions are invalid, either because they are in close nexus to a prohibited restriction or because the entire agreement is void.

Whenever an agreement is notified late, there is the risk of further action by the authorities. However, given that this would be part of a compliance programme the authorities are likely to show some favour.[9]

15-10 There is little point in notifying agreements that are not likely to be granted exemption, such as export bans, price-fixing or market sharing arrangements. Obviously the agreement or practice must satisfy the criteria for exemption discussed in Chapter 6 above. If not, then it is advisable to terminate. Termination should be recorded in some way in case the matter is ever investigated subsequently but even the fact of termination should obviously be kept confidential as this discloses prior infringement.

There may be considerable room for exercising discretion in deciding whether or not to notify or terminate. If an agreement is borderline, one party may wish to continue with it without putting its validity in question since this may encourage the other party to default. It may be borderline in that it is arguable whether an agreement or clause is restrictive of competition or whether the effect on trade between Member States or within the United Kingdom (whichever is appropriate) is appreciable.

15-11 The issue of document destruction is important. Various offences are created by the 1998 Act including the destruction, disposal, falsification or concealment of documents which are required by the Director to be produced[10] whether this is done wilfully or recklessly.[11] Furthermore, the Companies Act 1985[12] prevents directors, managers and the company Secretary from destroying, mutilating or falsifying documents relating to the company's affairs unless there is no concealment. Companies in any case must maintain accounting records for three years in the case of private companies or six years in the case of public companies.[13]

There is no equivalent provision in E.C. law but the Commission is empowered by Regulation 17/62 to impose fines where companies "intentionally or negligently" supply

---

[9] Commission Dec. 92/426 *Viho/Parker Pen* [1992] O.J. L233/27 and upheld on appeal by the CFI in Case T–77/92 [1994] E.C.R. II-549; [1995] 5 C.M.L.R. 435.

[10] s. 43.

[11] See Chap. 13, *Penalties for non-compliance* above.

[12] s. 450.

[13] s. 222 of the Companies Act 1985.

incomplete or incorrect documents or information in response to a Commission request.[14]

15-12 In cartel cases, when considering whether to co-operate with the Commission, participants should obviously bear in mind the Commission's Leniency Notice discussed in Chapter 14 *Fines* above, since this may entitle them to a reduction in fine of 75 per cent or even total immunity from a fine. The consequences of co-operation should be considered extremely carefully, together with the fact that third party actions against those co-operating may nevertheless ensue and in fact be facilitated.

The process of risk assessment and the enquiry leading up to it will also serve to create awareness of the need for compliance and, better still, this may be supplemented by formalised staff training.

Staff training

15-13 Training of existing staff and induction of new staff may include regular seminars, case studies and role-playing sessions. Instruction manuals generally are not enough, no matter how informative and well-written, as they tend to remain unread. Training videos are available to make this task easier.[15]

Staff should also be made aware of what they should do in the event of a dawn raid. For further discussion of the procedure once an investigation has started, see Chapters 13 and 14 above, which also address the procedures that might usefully be adopted in order to reduce arguments concerning the privileged status of communications with legal advisers. The receptionist and security staff should know precisely whom they call in the event that officials from the European Commission or OFT arrive on the premises. The need for discretion should be emphasised even though it is obvious. There is a tendency for staff of an undertaking involved in an investigation perhaps to become caught up in the drama of the occasion. Badly suppressed whispers of "have they found anything yet?" have been heard to be uttered, which may be misunderstood by the authorities.

15-14 It goes without saying that staff involved in contract negotiations should have a thorough understanding of the requirements and risks of competition law and should commit themselves personally (possibly even in writing to evidence their willingness) to do what they can to achieve compliance.

Staff should be made aware of mechanisms to avoid common pitfalls. Infringement may be avoided merely by knowing how to conduct or participate in contractual negotiations or a trade association meeting. The Commission has in the past viewed trade association meetings as potentially collusive. Staff should therefore restrict their dialogue to limited observations such as the exchange of historic rather than current data.

15-15 Caution is particularly important in the case of collaborative ventures between competitors. For example, in the case of the formation of a joint venture company, the directors of the parent companies may need to establish Chinese walls to ensure that one parent company's pricing information does not filter through to the other's via the joint venture company. The risks of conscious parallelism remain. However, the Commission is now more likely to recognise where companies are innocently behaving in a like manner. Following criticism, it announced in its Thirteenth Report on Competition Policy in 1983 a list of factors that it would take into account. This list was extended by the Commission's 1993 Notice concerning the assessment of co-operative joint ventures.[16] Now coordinative action will be inferred if it is the only possible explanation.[17]

---

[14] See Chap. 14, *Fines* above.
[15] The OFT has made one such video in order to raise awareness. Another is "Competition Fair or Foul" made by Stanbrook & Henderson.
[16] [1993] O.J. C43/3.
[17] For further details see Chaps 2 and 8 above.

Any programme should stress that being seen not to be infringing competition law is as important as actually avoiding infringement. In the high profile cases in the 1980s, such as the Commission's *Polypropylene*[18] decisions, various petrochemical companies were found guilty of coordinative action largely because the wording of their communications with each other.[19]

Culture change

15-16 When it comes to the implementation of compliance procedures, there is real value in adopting a policy statement and guidance notes informing senior management of the need to assume responsibility for compliance and see it implemented at lower levels of the organisation. In the case Re *Supply of Ready Mixed Concrete (No. 2)*,[20] the House of Lords reaffirmed that:

> "a company . . . falls to be judged by its actions and not by its language. Any employee who acts for the company within the scope of his employment is the company".[21]

The House of Lords reversed the Court of Appeal decision that a compliance directive from senior management to employees effectively distanced the company from the actions of its employees. The case demonstrates that senior managers must not only adopt substantive compliance programmes, as opposed to paper ones, they must ensure that they are adopted in reality and furthermore are implemented throughout the fabric of the company. *Parker Pen*[22] was fined because of the conduct of a marketing director who inserted an export ban into distribution agreements when he had no authority to do so. This did not absolve Parker of responsibility.

CONCLUSION

15-17 In summary, a manual containing a list of the most obvious prohibitions is essential but employees need also to appreciate the nuance and the spirit of competition principles so that, quite apart from contract documentation, they are aware of the prohibitions. For example, procedures might be put in place concerning contact with competitors, in order to avoid any suggestion of collusion. Contact might be cleared ahead of time and followed by a report detailing what exchanges took place. The sales force should obviously not adopt any practices that might, for example act as a deterrent against exports. Even an understanding that sales are for the purchaser's "own consumption" might amount to a ban on resale. Likewise they must not try to settle any resale prices. In other words, the undertaking must understand competition principles and this should be supported by procedures. Contract vetting is another important safeguard and feedback to the contract managers will also serve to remind them of the need for compliance. Awareness is also likely to ensure that the opportunity is not missed to lodge complaints about the practices of competitors.

Even if after an investigation a company is found to have behaved in an anti-competitive

---

[18] Commission Dec. 86/398 [1986] O.J. L 230/1; [1988] 4 C.M.L.R. 347.
[19] See also Commission Dec. 85/74 *Peroxygen Products*, [1985] O.J. L35/1, where the undertakings abided by a "Red Note".
[20] *Director General of Fair Trading v. Pioneer Concrete (U.K.) Limited & Another* (on appeal from *Re Supply of Ready Mixed Concrete* (No. 2) [1994] 3 W.L.R. 1249; [1995] 1 All E.R. 135.
[21] [1994] 3 W.L.R. 1254; [1995] 1 All E.R. 141.
[22] Commission Dec. 92/426 [1992] O.J. L233/27 The Commission's decision was upheld by the CFI in Case T–77/92 *Parker Pen v. Commission* [1994] E.C.R. II-549.

manner, the implementation of an effective compliance programme before then is likely to be viewed as a mitigating factor. On the other hand, the complete absence of such a programme or the presence of one which is largely ineffectual or cosmetic could have the opposite effect.

It is worth emphasising that of overriding importance to the success of a compliance programme will be a thorough appreciation of the emerging pattern and dynamics of the commercial arrangements of an organisation, as well as its culture. Routine training for employees is an essential part of a long-term compliance programme to ensure that employees become particularly familiar with those arrangements that are of recurring importance to their business.

Training will need to be targeted at the specific business activities of the organisation and will need to be accompanied by vivid illustrations of how errors may be made in practice. A useful supplement to training would be a short guide which may be issued to employees to serve as a continual reminder of the need for compliance, with protocols and suggestions to ensure that compliance is not forgotten. Any guide must be short if it is to be of any value, otherwise it will not be used.

To succeed, the compliance programme must be supported by staff at all levels. It must not be presented to employees as a matter of duty but as something that is to be grasped enthusiastically. Ideally, compliance should become part of the work ethic of an organisation if infringement is to be avoided. This is particularly true of large organisations. A video may be made to highlight the rights and wrongs of contract formation procedures and dealings with competitors. A video may also be used to dramatise dawn raids so that employees can appreciate both the seriousness of infringement and what an investigation entails in real life.

COMPLIANCE QUESTIONNAIRE

15-18   This Chapter contains a questionnaire intended to offer a suitable framework within which to initiate a compliance programme. It is only a starting point but an extremely important one. The questionnaire is designed to emphasise the value of any compliance programme or competition audit to the business affected. It's aim is to help elicit information by means of a series of questions and commentary designed to address particular issues which have been canvassed in detail in earlier Chapters. In order to guide both the questioner and subject, the questions make cross-reference to those sections in the earlier Chapters where the significance of the issues behind the questions is explained in more detail. Reference back to those sections should be made as fully as possible to ensure that further questioning adequately covers the full significance of each issue.

When completed, the questionnaire will help an assessment to be made of the commercial activities of the business, in particular, those agreements or other trading arrangements which are of key importance, those that are commercially undesirable and may be renegotiated or challenged on the grounds of non-compliance, and those which are of critical importance but which themselves may be susceptible to challenge by others. Corrective action may be taken to remedy any shortcomings and pre-emptive measures may be taken to ensure that mistakes are not made in the future.

15-19   The compliance questionnaire serves as a springboard for initiating compliance by covering issues in a systematic way but, clearly, not all issues covered will be relevant to all organisations. For example, a research and development company will be more concerned with ensuring compliance for intellectual property agreements and will be less concerned with sales agreements. By contrast, the supplier of high turnover consumer goods will need to be more acutely attuned to issues relating to price determination, how to avoid any suggestion of price collusion and how properly to handle the exchange of information between competitors or trade association members.

15-20 The following questionnaire, though broad in its range of questions, will help establish where specific competition issues arise amid the host of activities of the organisation.

QUESTIONNAIRE

Assess the Commercial Value of Compliance

15-21 The cost of non-compliance may be measured most obviously in terms of the risk of fines, the loss of contractual restrictions imposed on others, third party claims for infringement and the cost, disruption and loss of reputation that follows from investigation. The less obvious cost of failure to address compliance may be measured in terms of the loss that stems from the unnecessary performance of void restrictions (that are unwanted) and the failure to take action against others whenever a victim of the abuse of dominant position by another or the victim of other infringing activities. Furthermore, non-compliance by an acquisition target, or a target for investment, may significantly affect the value of that target or operate as a deterrent against investment.

Fines (see Chapter 13, *Penalties for substantive infringement*, para. 13-26 and Chapter 14, *Fines*, para. 14-20, above)

15-22 What is the value of any fine that may be awarded, calculated by reference to:

    (i) 10 per cent of gross, worldwide, annual turnover in the last accounts of each of the undertakings participating in the infringement (in the case of Articles 85 (1) and 86, see para. 14-19, above);

    (ii) 10 per cent of the United Kingdom turnover in the case of the Chapter I and Chapter II prohibitions? (See para. 13-26, above)

Reliance on void restrictions (see Chapter 14, *Actions by the parties to infringement* para. 14-31 and also para. 6-09, above)

15-23 What is the commercial impact of non-compliance rendering contractual restrictions void, both when relying on them and when seeking to avoid them:

    (i) What financial and practical consequences would ensue if all restrictions which are relied upon were rendered void against the party seeking to rely on them?

    (ii) What commercial advantage could be gained by legitimately claiming unwanted restrictions to be void? For example, do agreements contain payment burdens which are onerous or undesirable and which may be challenged as unenforceable?

    (iii) What other considerations are relevant (such as the loss of good business relations that may result from contesting validity, unless it is accepted that compliance is in the interests of both parties)?

Investigation (see Chapter 13, *Investigations* and *Enforcement*, paras 13-01 to 13-22, and Chapter 14, *Article 11 Requests for Information* and *Article 14 Investigations*, paras 14-04 to 14-10, above.

15-24   Consider the impact of a Commission or OFT investigation in terms of legal costs, wastage of management time, adverse publicity, disruption and fines, both:

(i)   as an advantage when claiming infringement against another; and

(ii)   as a deterrent when at risk of an investigation.

Third party actions (see Chapter 14, *Actions by the parties to infringement* and *Actions by third parties*, paras 14-28 to 14.37, above)

15-25   Assess the level of any loss suffered by a victim of infringement (and the likely damages that may be awarded) by considering:

(i)   whether a third party may claim that it is a victim of infringement?; and

(ii)   Whether it is possible to claim to be a victim of another's infringement?

ORIENTATION CONCERNING RELEVANT AGREEMENTS/ CONCERTED PRACTICES THAT MAY AFFECT TRADE

Identify all relevant agreements/concerted practices

15-26   At the outset, it is necessary to ensure that the meaning is fully understood of each of the terms "undertakings", "agreement", "decision by association of undertakings" and "concerted practices" (see Chapter 2, *"Undertakings"* and *"Agreements, decisions by associations of undertakings and concerted practices"*, paras 2-30 to 2-37, above); otherwise, many important practices and agreements will be overlooked.
In order to characterise the manner in which business is conducted:

(i)   identify all key commercial agreements. Where standard form documents are used, the variations should also be carefully examined as these often contain provisions that are "unvetted" or unapproved by legal advisers;

(ii)   identify the way in which contracts are made. Are they always reduced to writing? If so, is the written document complete, recording all terms? Are any additional terms understood to apply outside the written contract? If so, try to isolate precisely what those additional terms are:

(iii)   identify all unwritten agreements and practices (whether or not binding) that might be described as collusive or co-ordinative, even if resulting only in "consensus" or "understanding", as well as anything that may infer commitment between parties (see Chapter 2, *"Agreements, decisions by associations of undertakings and concerted practices"*, paras 2-34 to 2-37, above); and;

(iv)   identify all decisions by trade associations of which the organisation is a member including the nature of the organisation's participation in the decision. Were any steps taken to distance the organisation from a decision or the discussion leading up to it?

15-27   The agreements to consider are all agreements for which the organisation under consideration is liable. (See Chapter 2, *"Undertakings"*, para. 2-33, above, for the range of entities liable for infringement, such as a parent for the acts of its subsidiary).

Once all agreements and practices have been identified, their status under Articles 85 and 86 and Chapters I and II should be examined to determine whether the restrictions are prohibited or exempt. (For a checklist of common forms of agreement and practice, see paras 15-30 to 15-47 below.).

Identify all restrictions on competition that may affect trade

15-28   Consider as a restriction on competition any express contractual restriction, any practice or indirect constraint (even if not embodied in a contract) which affects the freedom of any person to trade as it wishes, with everyone else, on equal terms or which places any other party or third party at a disadvantage when trading. In other words, does an undertaking in any way restrict the freedom of another to undertake any business activity it wishes? For each restriction found, consider whether steps should be taken to revise the agreement or practice to ensure that it is enforceable (if relying on it) or whether steps may be taken to terminate it (if it is unwanted).

In order to limit the range of enquiry, it is worth remembering that in general, infringement only occurs when there is an effect on trade between Member States (under Articles 85(1) and 86) or within the United Kingdom (under the Chapter I and Chapter II prohibitions). The effect must be appreciable when considering whether an agreement is caught by Article 85(1) or the Chapter I prohibition. (For guidance on the term "effect on trade", see Chapter 2 *"Trade between Member States" compared with "Trade Within The United Kingdom"*, paras 2-16 to 2-18, above and on the term "appreciable effect", see Chapter 2, *"De minimis principles"*, paras 2-19 to 2-23, above. Remember that the potential to upset trade is sufficient.)

15-29   The way in which the restrictions are categorised will help focus on whether steps should be taken to avoid unwanted agreements, to make void restrictions enforceable or to prevent any loss resulting from another's infringement. When evaluating any agreement or practice, it may be useful to categorise the restrictions in the following manner as this will help highlight the way in which non-compliance may be used to advantage:

(a) Restrictions in agreements to which the organisation is a party, differentiating those:

    (i) imposed on the organisation and unwanted;
    (ii) imposed by and relied upon only by that organisation;
    (iii) willingly accepted by all parties.

(b) Restrictions in agreements to which the organisation is not a party, differentiating those that:

    (i) adversely affect the organisation (such as a selective distribution network to which the organisation is denied access, an exclusive purchasing agreement which prevents the organisation from selling to the purchaser, an exclusive selling agreement which prevents the organisation from purchasing from certain sources or an exclusive joint venture that rules out participation by the organisation);
    (ii) benefit the organisation (such as tied maintenance services that are sub-contracted to the organisation); or
    (iii) other restrictions or market features that restrict the organisation in practice, such as difficulties in obtaining supplies of products or services or only at excessive prices or on limited terms.

PARTICULAR PRACTICES AND AGREEMENTS CAUGHT BY ARTICLE 85(1) OR THE CHAPTER I PROHIBITION

15-30   The questions in this section are directed at identifying the commercial mechanisms by which business interests are protected against the activities of competitors. These commonly take the form of non-competition or non-solicitation undertakings, territorial exclusivity for intellectual property licences or distribution agreements, tie-ins and collusion over price. This section comprises five parts. Part A concerns agreements which are generally regarded as restrictive of competition but where compliance is not necessarily apparent on the face of any document. For these purposes they are termed "background practices". Part B concerns those practices which are the subject of a block exemption Regulation and may benefit from automatic exemption if the pre-conditions for exemption are satisfied and the agreement contains no further restrictions than the relevant Regulation permits. It will be remembered that exemption may be jeopardised by the inclusion of restrictions which are not white-listed or if the market shares of the parties exceed certain levels, as expressed in certain Regulations. Thirdly, Part C directs the questions at agreements which may be caught by Article 85 (1) or the Chapter I prohibition and should be considered for individual exemption in order to avoid infringement. Part D is there to serve as a checklist of any agreements or practices that may not have been identified in previous sections (and Part E to identify certain agreements that are excluded from the Chapter I prohibition).

A   Background practices

15-31   *Price fixing* (see Chapter 2, *Directly or indirectly fix purchase or selling prices or any other trading conditions*, paras 2-40 to 2-51, above)

   (a) Do suppliers or retailers between themselves, or other businesses between themselves, discuss or exchange information concerning the prices they charge or intend to charge? (Clearly any transfer price agreed between two businesses concerning the prices charged by one when supplying to the other may be ignored for these purposes.) Are they competitors?

   (b) Are resale prices agreed (for example between a supplier and distributor, to determine the price to be charged by the distributor)?

   (c) Are maximum or minimum prices agreed for product sales?

   (d) Are resale price recommendations made by suppliers who are members of a trade association?

   (e) Does fierce price competition exist (suggesting strong competition) or are prices stable (suggesting weak competition)?

   (f) Explain the scope of any discussion that takes place concerning the prices to be charged, identifying between whom, for what purpose and the information that is exchanged?

   (g) Are records kept of meetings and other contact (formal or informal) with competitors?

15-32   *Agreements concerning production, markets, technical development or investment* (see Chapter 2, *"Limit or control production, markets, technical development or investment"*, paras 2-52 to 2-57, above.)

(a) Does any agreement exist concerning the level of production or output of any party?

(b) Is there any co-operation between competitors or suppliers concerning the standards that are to be met by them or the amount of investment to be given to development or production?

15-33   *Market Sharing* (see Chapter 2, *"Share markets or sources of supply"*, para. 2-58, above)

(a) Is there any co-operation or understanding concerning the markets that are to be serviced by one or other party, whether resulting in the allocation of territory, customers or any other matter?

15-34   *Discrimination* (see Chapter 2, *"Apply dissimilar conditions to equivalent transactions with other trading parties thereby placing them at a competitive disadvantage"*, para. 2-59, above)

(a) Is there any price discrimination between customers?

(b) On what basis are price differentials (including discounts and rebates) applied across customers?

(c) Is there discrimination concerning any other terms of supply?

15-35   *Tie-ins* (see Chapter 2, *"Make the conclusion of contracts subject to acceptance by the other parties of supplementary obligations which, by their nature, according to commercial usage, have no connection with the subject of [such] contracts"*, paras 2-60 to 2-62, above)

(a) Are sales of products "tied" in the sense that neither is available separately at a competitive price and on competitive terms?

(b) Is any pressure applied to a customer to take supplies of additional products or services?

(c) Are contracts offered that combine the supply of products or services (such as software and maintenance) without each being available separately?

15-36   *Export Bans* (See Chapter 2, *"Limit or control production, markets, technincal development or investment"*, para. 2-53, above)

(a) Does any disincentive exist against export from one Member State to another, such as a contractual ban on exports, the payment of a royalty or loss of bonus or loss of discount on export, or other deterrent against export activity?

B   Automatically exempt agreements

15-37   This section concerns particular types of agreement which are eligible for automatic exemption under a Commission Regulation or equivalent United Kingdom block exemption (for these purposes also referred to as a Regulation). If any agreement exists of a type listed below, then its terms need to be matched against the appropriate block exemption Regulation. For each agreement it is necessary to:

    (i) identify all restrictions on competition in the agreement;

   (ii) confirm that they are all permitted and none are black-listed;

 (iii) confirm that block exemption is not rendered inapplicable by the terms of the Regulation; and

 (iv) confirm that exemption has not been withdrawn under the terms of the Regulation.

Certain block exemption Regulations refer to market share criteria for which the relevant market and market share of the parties needs to be established (for example the Technology Transfer Regulation). Instead of repeating the requirements of each block exemption Regulation for each type of agreement, reference should be made (by way of check-list) to the terms of each applicable Regulation and the chapter sections at which they are discussed more fully, as identified below. The Regulations are currently under review (as discussed in Chapter 7, *E.C. and United Kingdom Policy Towards Vertical Restraints*, paras 7-10 to 7-16, above). Any compliance programme should keep abreast of developments but when challenging the validity of agreements, the key issue is whether the agreement in question complied with the terms of the applicable Regulation at the relevant date, subject to any retroactive block exemption granted by later Regulation. The types of agreement eligible for automatic exemption (if the pre-conditions for exemption are met and the terms of the agreement match appropriately) are as follows.

15-38 *Exclusive distribution agreements* (under which an exclusive distributor is appointed for the resale of products for a designated territory— see Chapter 7, *Exclusive Distribution Agreements*, para. 7-17, above). Note especially:

  (a) the type of agreement permitted (see Chapter 7, *Permitted agreements*, paras 7-17 to 7-25);

  (b) the permitted restrictions on competition such as:

    (i) the obligation on the supplier not to supply others (see Chapter 7, *Obligation on the supplier not to supply others*, para. 7-27, above);

   (ii) the obligations on the distributor not to compete, to obtain the products only from the supplier and not actively to solicit custom outside the territory (see Chapter 7, *Obligations on the distributor not to compete*, para. 7-28, above).

  (c) inapplicability of the block exemption (see Chapter 7, *Inapplicability of the block exemption*, paras 7-30 to 7-33, above);

  (d) Withdrawal of the block exemption (see Chapter 7, *Withdrawal of the block exemption*, paras 7-34 to 7-35, above).

Motor vehicle distribution and servicing agreements are dealt with in Chapter 7, *Motor vehicle distribution under Article 85(3) motor vehicle distribution and servicing agreements: the block exemption for motor vehicle distribution*, paras 7-36 to 7-58, above.

15-39 *Exclusive purchasing agreements* (under which goods for resale by a purchaser are sourced exclusively from a particular supplier—see Chapter 7, *Exclusive Purchasing Agreements*, para. 7-59, above). Note especially:

(a) the type of agreement permitted (see Chapter 7, *General provisions*, paras 7-59 to 7-67, above).

(b) the permitted restrictions on competition such as:

    (i) the obligation on the supplier not to compete (see Chapter 7, *An obligation on the supplier not to compete*, para. 7-69, above);

    (ii) the obligation on the purchaser not to compete (see Chapter 7, *An obligation on the purchaser not to compete*, para. 7-70, above).

(c) inapplicability of the block exemption (see Chapter 7, *Inapplicability of the block exemption*, paras 7-72 to 7-75, above).

(d) withdrawal of the block exemption (see Chapter 7, *Miscellaneous provisions (withdrawal of the block exemption)*, para. 7-76, above).

Beer supply agreements and service station agreements are dealt with in Chapter 7, *Beer supply agreements* and *Service station agreements*, paras 7-77 to 7-95, above.

15-40 *Specialisation agreements* (under which the parties accept reciprocal obligations to designate the other as the only manufacturer of certain products (or to manufacture products jointly)—see Chapter 7, *Specialisation Agreements*, para. 7-98, above). Note especially:

(a) the type of agreement permitted (see Chapter 7, *Permitted agreements*, paras 7-98 to 7-105, above);

(b) the permitted restrictions on competition such as:

    (i) exclusivity of specialisation;
    (ii) exclusive purchase of specialisation products;
    (iii) minimum purchase quantities;
    (iv) exclusive distribution and joint distribution.

(See Chapter 7, *Permitted restrictions on competition*, paras 7-106 to 7-111, above);

(c) inapplicability of the block exemption (see Chapter 7, *Inapplicability of the block exemption*, paras 7-113 to 7-116, above); and

(d) withdrawal of the block exemption (see Chapter 7, *Withdrawal of the block exemption*, para. 117, above).

15-41 *Franchising Agreements* (concerning distribution franchises, service franchises and master franchises—see Chapter 7, *Franchising Agreements*, para. 7-118, above). Note especially:

(a) the type of agreement permitted (see Chapter 7, *Scope of the exemption* and *Definitions*, paras 7-120 to 7-121, above);

(b) the permitted restrictions on competition (see paras 7-122 to 7-131, above) such as:

    (i) the limited territorial restrictions on the franchisor (see Chapter 7, *Restrictions on the franchisor* above);

    (ii) the obligations on the franchisee to operate only from specified premises, not actively to solicit customers outside the territory and not to deal in competing goods (see Chapter 7, *Restrictions on the franchisee* above);

(c) inapplicability of the block exemption (see Chapter 7, *Inapplicability of the block exemption*, paras 7-132 to 7-140, above);

(d) withdrawal of the block of exemption (see Chapter 7, *Withdrawal of exemption*, para. 7-141, above).

15-42 *Exclusive patent and know-how licences* (under which an exclusive licence of patents and/or know-how is granted for a given territory—see Chapter 9, *Patent and Know-How Licences (The Technology Transfer Regulation)*, para. 9-05, above). Note especially:

(a) the type of agreement permitted (see Chapter 9, *Scope of the technology transfer regulation*, paras 9-05 to 9-07, above);

(b) the permitted restrictions on competition such as:

   (i) territorial exclusivity;
   (ii) licence of improvements; or
   (iii) quantity limits.

   (See paras. 9-08 to 9-14, above);

(c) inapplicability of the block exemption;

(d) withdrawal of block exemption.

   (see paras. 9-15 to 9-21, above).

15-43 *Exclusive research and development agreements* (for the joint research and development of products or processes—see Chapter 9, *Particular R&D Agreements*, para. 9-37, above). Note especially:

(a) the type of agreement permitted (defined research and development work with all parties having access to the results);

(b) the permitted restrictions on competition such as:

   (i) ban on independent research in the same field;
   (ii) procurement of products from a designated source;
   (iii) field of use restrictions;
   (iv) exclusive distribution restrictions (where appropriate given market shares);

(c) inapplicability of exemption; and

(d) withdrawal of exemption.

   (see paras. 9-37 to 9-40, above).

C Agreements that may be eligible for individual exemption but require notification

15-44 This section is aimed at highlighting agreements which are notifiable because they are caught within the breadth of the prohibition in Article 85 (1) or the Chapter I prohibition but may not have been notified. As such, they (or the relevant restrictions) may be void. These may include any of the following:

(1) Agreements to which a block exemption Regulation would apply (as detailed above in Part B) but for the fact that not all requirements for exemption (at the relevant time) have been satisfied or exemption has been withdrawn.

(2) Joint ventures (see Chapter 8, *Joint ventures caught by Article 85(1)*, paras 8-05 to 8-35, above) which involve:

   (a) competitors and a reduction of the degree to which they would otherwise compete. Examples may include:

   (i) research & development joint ventures (see Chapter 8, *Research and development joint ventures*, para. 8-22, above);

   (ii) selling joint ventures (see Chapter 8, *Selling joint ventures*, para. 8-23, above);

   (iii) purchasing joint ventures (see Chapter 8, *Purchasing joint ventures*, para. 8-24, above);

   (iv) production joint ventures (see Chapter 8, *Production joint ventures*, para. 8-25, above);

   (v) full-function joint ventures (see Chapter 8, *Full-function joint ventures*, para. 8-26, above).

   (b) non-competitors (but where the effect is to prevent others competing, for example by precluding them from dealing on the market with the joint venture participants) (see Chapter 8, *Application of Article 85(1)*, paras 8-06 to 8-20, and *Ancillary restrictions*, paras 8-28 to 8-32, above).

For examples of common ancillary restrictions on the joint venture and its parents, their compatibility with Article 85 (1) and whether exemptible, see Chapter 8, *Ancillary restrictions*, paras 8-28 to 8-30, and *Exemption under Article 85(3)*, paras 8-31 to 8-32, above, and Chapter 9, *Joint venture licensing*, paras 9-31 to 9-35, above. Examples of common ancillary restrictions are:

   (c) limits on the business activities of the joint venture (such as limits on product range or place of business or other activities, imposed to ensure that the joint venture focuses on the purpose for which it was established);

   (d) limits on the scope of intellectual property licences granted to the joint venture by the parents (taking care especially if licences are exclusive by territory when granted to the joint venture (to support its activities) or by the joint venture to the parents (for example covering improvements).

For those joint ventures to which Article 85(1) does not apply, where they are of minor importance or intra-group, see Chapter 8, *Joint ventures not caught by Article 85(1)*, paras 8-33 to 8-35, above.

(3) Joint selling agreements (under which suppliers entrust their sales to a single entity or group of entities). Particular care should be taken where the parties are competitors or possess sizeable market shares (see Chapter 8, *Joint Selling Agreements*, para. 8-36, above).

(4) Joint purchasing agreements (under which purchasers act together in their dealings with suppliers). Particular care should be taken where this results in price uniformity or significant purchasing power (see Chapter 8, *Joint Purchasing Agreements*, paras 8-37 to 8-38, above).

(5) Selective distribution agreements (under which the profile of retail outlets is strictly prescribed—see Chapter 8, *Selective Distribution Agreements*, para. 8-39, above).

(6) Miscellaneous forms of co-operation. Chapter 8, *Miscellaneous Co-operation Between Enterprises Not Caught by Article 85(1)*, paras 8-41 to 8-49, above, sets

out the details of certain agreements to which Article 85 (1) generally does not apply, which involve co-operation. However, if the co-operation goes beyond the scope detailed, then Article 85 (1) may apply.

(7) Subcontracts. If subcontracts impose unnecessary restrictions on the use of intellectual property or on other activities of the subcontractor then Article 85 (1) and Chapter I may apply (see Chapter 8, *Sub-Contracts*, paras 8-50 to 8-52, above).

(8) Commercial Agents. Agents are often appointed on an exclusive basis. If they retain business interests of their own (whether acting for themselves or others) the appointment may infringe Article 85 (1) or the Chapter I prohibition (see Chapter 8, *Commercial Agents*, paras 8-53 to 8-55, above).

(9) Copyright and trade mark licences. All copyright and trade mark licences must be "open" in order to fall outside Article 85(1) (see Chapter 9, *Copyright Licences and Trade Mark Licences*, paras 9-22 to 9-24, above).

15-45 If individual exemption has been granted, whether under Article 85 (3) or under the 1988 Act, the terms of each exemption must be established to confirm:

(a) compliance with any pre-conditions, subject to which exemption was granted;

(b) that the time-limits applicable to any exemption have not expired. (Even agreements granted automatic exemption are subject to time-limits for expiry of exemption as set out in each applicable block exemption Regulation);

(c) whether changes have been made to the agreement which require subsequent notification (changes to agreements registered under the RTPA 1976 will need to be registered if reliance is placed on them—see Chapter 5, paras 5-15 and 5-17, above); and

(d) whether it is appropriate to seek individual exemption after the starting date under the 1998 Act for agreements for which early guidance was sought in the interim period (see Chapters 5 and 6 above).

D   Other agreements

15-46 Agreements may exist which are not referred to above but which contain restrictions on competition. Their terms, effect and compliance or otherwise with Article 85 (1) and the Chapter I prohibition should be established.

E   Exclusions

15-47 In the case of the Chapter I prohibition a number of agreements are excluded from the prohibition (see Chapter 2, *Exclusions from Chapter I (no exclusions from Article 85(1))*, paras 2-24 to 2-29, above). These include mergers and concentrations, selected business sectors, general exclusions and professional rules.

PARTICULAR PRACTICES CONSTITUTING ABUSE OF DOMINANT POSITION UNDER ARTICLE 86 OR INFRINGEMENT OF THE CHAPTER II PROHIBITION

15-48 For there to be an infringement of Article 86 or the Chapter II prohibition, there must be established both dominance and an abuse. The term "dominance" is an important one but, in essence, it refers to the ability of an undertaking to operate independently of competitive pressure and therefore able to abuse that position. See Chapter 3, *Dominant Position*, paras 3-17 to 3-21, above, for further discussion of dominance and in particular the market shares and structural features of the market that may result *prima facie* in a finding of dominance. Note especially that any market share of 40 per cent and above may result in such a finding depending on the market structure. The abuse need not necessarily stem from the dominance or take place in the same market as the one in which dominance is enjoyed. Also note the possibility of joint dominance held between different undertakings which pursue a common policy.

Dominance

15-49   Dominance needs to be established within:

    (a) the European Community or a substantial part of it under Article 86; and

    (b) the United Kingdom or any part of it under section 18 of the 1998 Act. (See Chapter 3, *"Dominant position within the common market or in a substantial part of it"* compared with *"Dominant position within the United Kingdom"*, para. 3-09, above).

Whether dominance may be established will depend on a number of factors that may give the undertaking freedom to act independently of competitive forces. These include:

    (a) high market share. See paras 15-61 to 15-65 below concerning the definition of the relevant market and calculation of market share. Can the market share be said to be in excess of 40 per cent either within the Community or a substantial part, or within the United Kingdom or any part of it?;

    (b) other indices of market power as illustration in para. 15-65, below.

Abuse

15-50   Abuse is not dependent on agreement and may be constituted *inter alia* by any of the following:

Excessive prices

15-51   Is the price excessive in relation to the economic value of the product or service provided? (See Chapter 3, *Excessive pricing*, paras 3-23 to 3-24, above.)

Predatory (low) prices

15-52   Is the price below average variable cost/average total cost (with the aim in the latter case of driving competitors out of business)? (See Chapter 3, *Predatory pricing*, paras 3-25 to 3-26, above.)

Unfair trading conditions

15-53   Are any unusual trading conditions imposed which depart from industry standard? (See Chapter 3, *Other unfair trading conditions*, para. 3-27, above.)

Refusal to supply

15-54   Has there been any refusal, whether relating to a product, service or making available intellectual property rights by way of licence or granting access to essential facilities? (See Chapter 3, *Refusal to supply* and *Withholding of intellectual property rights*, paras 3-28 to 3-34, above.)

Inefficiency

15-55 Has there been any mismanagement which results in high prices or bad service in any area protected from competitive pressure? (See Chapter 3, *Inefficient management*, para. 3-35, above.)

Discrimination

15-56 Has there been any discrimination between customers where not objectively justified (for example on the grounds of credit rating and other objective factors), whether in relation to price or other terms of business (where favourable terms are offered to some customers but not others, putting the latter at a trading disadvantage)? (See Chapter 3, *Price discrimination to Non-price related discrimination*, paras 3-36 to 3-41, above).

Tie-ins

15-57 Have any commitments been made conditional on supplementary obligations where there is insufficient connection between the primary and supplementary obligations? Examples include a software licence and maintenance contract available only together or on such terms separately that are uneconomic to the customer. Also agreements for the supply of products such as machinery sold only if service contracts are awarded in favour of the supplier. (See paras 3-42 to 3-43, above.)

Other business tactics

15-58 Does any other tactic have the effect of causing competition from other sources to be unfairly eliminated or reduced?

Effect on trade

15-59 Is there an effect on trade between Member States or within the United Kingdom? (See Chapters 2 and 3, *"Trade between Member States" compared with "Trade within the United Kingdom"*, paras 2-16 to 2-18 and 3-10 to 3-11, above).

Exclusions from Chapter II

15-60 Is the conduct excluded from infringement of the Chapter II prohibition by being a merger or under the general exclusions? (See Chapter 3, *Exclusions from Chapter II (no exclusions from Article 86)*, paras 3-12 to 3-14, above).

MARKET SHARE AND MARKET POWER

Market share

Relevance of market share calculation

15-61 The purposes for which market shares need to be established include the following:

(a) Assessment of "appreciable effect" for the purpose of:

(i) Article 85 (1) under the Commission's de minimis Notice (5 per cent for horizontal agreements and 10 per cent for vertical agreements);

(ii) the Chapter I prohibition (see Chapter 2, *"De minimis" principles*, paras
2-19 to 2-23, above).

(b) Individual exemption, to demonstrate that the agreement does not "afford the
parties the possibility of eliminating competition in respect of a substantial part
of the products in question" (as provided in Article 85 (3) (b) and section 9 (b)
(ii) of the 1998 Act). (See Chapter 6, *"Does not afford such undertakings the possibility of eliminating competition in respect of a substantial part of the products in question"*, paras 6-49 to 6-50, above).

(c) Automatic exemption, where the Regulation in question imposes maximum
market share thresholds of the parties as a pre-condition to exemption. (For
further details, see Chapter 4, *Automatic exemption*, paras 4-05 to 4-06, above).

(d) Immunity from fines (under section 39 of the 1998 Act) for certain "small agreements" (see Chapter 4, *Immunity from fines (Chapter I)*, para. 4-07, above).

(e) Assessment of dominance or joint dominance (above levels of 40 per cent of
market share) for the purposes of Article 86 and the Chapter II prohibition—(see
Chapter 3, *"Dominant position within the common market or in a substantial
part of it"* compared with *"Dominant position within the United Kingdom"*,
para. 3-09, above).

(f) Immunity from fines under section 40 of the 1998 Act for "conduct of minor significance" which infringes the Chapter II prohibition (see Chapter 4, *Immunity
from fines (Chapter II)*, para. 4-09, above).

(g) Assessment of the Fair Trading Act 1973 and whether a "monopoly situation"
exists (where a market share of 25 per cent and above is held) and whether a
merger is one that qualifies for investigation (see Chapter 11, paras 11-04 to 11-11
and 11-28 to 11-33, above).

At times, the analysis of market share will be aimed at demonstrating high values. For
example the purpose may be to claim invalidity of unnotified agreements which have an
appreciable effect, or when claiming to be the victim of another's dominance. At other
times, when defending such claims, effort will be focused on reaching lower market share
values. Similarly, when making an application for individual exemption although, in
general, there is nothing to be gained from artificially representing low market share
values since a notification is only as good as the information given in support of it.

Steps towards market share assessment

15-62   The following steps should be taken to begin the assessment of market share:

(a) Define the relevant product or service market (see paras 4-12 to 4-28 and 4-35 to
4-50, above) by identifying all products/services which are interchangeable or
substitutable by the consumer by reason of their characteristics, price and
intended use. In short, what products or services are readily substitutable?

(b) Define the geographic market by identifying the area in which the undertakings
trade and where the conditions of competition are the same for all traders. The
geographic market is not necessarily confined to the area of sales of that supplier, particularly where the market area may be expanded by the supplier, in

response to market changes. Local loyalty and high transport costs may contain the geographic market. In short, what is the area over which the products or services are readily available (especially given the geographic location of suppliers)? (See paras 4-26 and 4-43, above).

(c) Identify all sources of competitive pressure measured by:

(i) demand substitution *i.e.* the readiness of customers to switch suppliers in response to price increases of say 5 to 10 per cent. Adjust both the product/ service description and the geographical area to define the relevant market (in terms of both product/service and geography) as the one in which substitutable products/services are supplied.

Adjustments must be made to take account *inter alia* of the following factors:

i whether different conditions of competition affect the products/ services which at first sight appear substitutable. (See Chapter 4, *Exposure to competition*, para. 4-18, above);

ii whether different product usage results in different product markets. (See Chapter 4, *Single product, different uses and different markets*, para. 4-19, above).

iii whether differences in quality or price result in different markets. (See Chapter 4, *Price and quality*, para. 4-21, above); and

iv whether a distinction should be made between primary markets (for example, for the supply of goods) and secondary markets (such as the supply of spare parts for servicing those goods). (See Chapter 4, *Secondary markets*, para. 4-22, above).

(ii) Supply substitution, *i.e.* the readiness of suppliers to switch production to new products in response to price increases by existing suppliers (for example the readiness of suppliers of cat food to switch to the supply of tinned fish for human consumption). Is there the risk of others substituting manufacture and thereby competing? (See Chapter 4, *Supply substitution*, paras 4-23 and 4-41, above).

(iii) Potential competition, which is generally relevant to the issue of dominance, to highlight exposure to competition from other sources such as from overseas markets or unused capacity of other suppliers. (See Chapter 4, *Potential competition*, para. 4-25, above).

Calculation of market share

15-63 Volume of sales and value of sales may exhibit different market shares. In general, the value of sales is regarded as the better reflection of market position. (See Chapter 4, *Calculation of market share*, paras 4-28 and 4-48, above).

Consider other sources of information

15-64 Has the organisation published any statement concerning its market share, for example for sales purposes? Is there any statement that may need to be defended or which may be used to incriminate others accused of holding a high market share? (See Chapter 4, *Evidence*, paras 4-29 and 4-30, above). Does information concerning upstream or downstream markets in the supply chain add anything to the market share assessment? For example do purchasers or suppliers possess strong purchasing or selling power (either alone or in combination)?

Other indices of market power (See Chapter 11, Assessment of factors, paras 11-21 to 11-27, above)

15-65   Do any of the following evidence strong or weak market power, or strong or weak competition:

(a) market shares held by competitors. Are they large enough to rebut a suggestion of dominance? Do they suggest stability against new competition?;

(b) the number, scale and profile of competitors;

(c) the level of resources available to competitors;

(d) obstacles to market entry—is access to the market dependent on intellectual property right or access to some essential facility? Are sunk costs high? Are high levels of investment needed to join the market?;

(e) the countervailing power of purchasers against suppliers (especially if a high proportion of a supplier's output is sold to these purchasers);

(f) profitability;

(g) recent history of the market and trends such as changes in market shares held by competitors;

(h) price changes in response to the activities of competitors;

(i) threats posed by imports, new entrants to the market and surplus capacity of competitors;

(j) departure of competitors from the market; or

(k) past anti-competitive practices.

MISCELLANEOUS ISSUES

15-66   The following miscellaneous matters require examination:

Parallel imports (Articles 85 (1) and 86)

15-67   Have any steps been taken to limit parallel imports (*i.e.* exports from one Member State into another)? In particular, confirm that:

(a) The permitted territorial limits to exclusivity in any agreement that benefits from block exemption are not exceeded. (See Chapters 7 and 9 above for the terms of particular block exemption Regulations).

(b) Intellectual property rights are not used as the basis for preventing parallel imports (See Chapter 10 on the extent to which this is permissible).

(c) No deterrent to export products or services from any one Member State to another has been imposed or accepted.

United Kingdom monopoly and merger control (see Chapter 11)

15-68   A "monopoly situation" in relation to the supply of goods or services exists, broadly speaking, once a market share of 25 per cent or more is held in the United Kingdom. A merger situation qualifying for investigation is one with an asset value in excess of £70 million or in which a monopoly situation is created or enhanced. Each may result in investigation, or reference to the Competition Commission (subject to time-limits in the case of a merger reference), and ultimately a wide range of orders by the Secretary of State if it operates against the public interest.

Confirm that:

(a) A market share of more than 25 per cent is not held in the United Kingdom in relation to the supply of goods or services. If so, may it be said to operate against the public interest?

(b) A merger has not been concluded which is still within the time-limits for a reference. (See Chapter 11, *Merger references*, para. 11-34, above).

(c) No undertakings have been given to the Secretary of State in lieu of a reference (see paras 11-20 and 11-37, above).

(d) No investigation has been ordered or threatened.

E.C. merger control (See Chapter 12 above)

15-69   The Commission has exclusive jurisdiction to clear "Concentrations" with a "Community dimension". (See Chapter 12, *Scope of the Merger Regulation*, paras 12-03 to 12-08, above). Other (lesser) mergers may be caught by Article 85 (1).

Confirm that:

(a) The terms on which clearance was granted to any concentration with a Community dimension as well as any undertakings given have been met.

(b) In the case of acquisitions not constituting concentrations with a Community dimension, all restrictions in any acquisition document must be checked to verify that they are directly related to the implementation of the concentration and do not constitute additional restrictions caught by Article 85 (1). (See Chapter 12, *Ancillary Restrictions*, paras 12-33 to 12-38, above).

Restrictive Trade Practices Act 1976 (RTPA) and Resale Prices Act 1976 (RPA)

15-70   Confirm that particulars of all agreements that were registerable under the RTPA (and not rendered non-notifiable) were furnished to the OFT within time (three months) and that the agreement itself suspended the operation of relevant restrictions until that had happened (otherwise it may be possible to claim that the restrictions are void *ab initio*) (see Chapter 5, *The Restrictive Trade Practices Act 1976 ("RTPA")and Resale Prices Act 1976 ("RPA")*, paras 5-07 to 5-09, and *Agreements Entered into During the Interim Period*, paras 5-14 to 5-15, above). Sections 6 and 11 of the RTPA identify the relevant "goods agreements" or "services agreements".

Competition Act 1980

15-71   Confirm that there has been no past involvement in any "anti-competitive practice" (see Chapter 11, *The Competition Act 1980*, paras 11-02 to 11-03, above).

State aid

15-72   Confirm that the organisation has not been the recipient of any state aid caught by Articles 92 to 94 of the E.C. Treaty (see Chapter 1, *State aids*, para. 1-23, above).

Investigation and enforcement (see Chapters 13 and 14 above)

15-73   It is important to be aware of any suggestion of infringement that has been made in the past (concerning Articles 85(1) or 86, the Fair Trading Act 1973, the Restrictive Trade Practices Act 1976, the Resale Prices Act 1976, the Competition Act 1980 or the Competition Act 1988 (Chapter I or Chapter II). The enquiry should also extend to any matter falling within any foreign jurisdiction.
Confirm:

(a) Whether any third party has made any written or oral suggestion of infringement. Have there been any complaints about excessive prices, inability to enter or expand in the market or difficulties in obtaining supplies?

(b) Whether a proposal has been made by another or to another that would amount to infringement, such as an invitation to discuss commercially-sensitive information with a view to any infringing agreement or conduct.

(c) Whether a complaint or allegation has been made by the Commission or OFT and whether an investigation has been undertaken. Has any contact been made with these authorities; if so, what?

(d) Whether grounds exist for an investigation or complaint by the authorities or a third party victim.

(e) Whether complaints have been made to the authorities concerning the activities of others.

(f) Whether any action has been taken against third parties if a victim of infringement.

PROCEDURES

15-74   This section addresses the procedures that are necessary to put in place to minimise the risk of involvement in infringing activities and, should the worst happen, to serve as a reminder of some of the things to do in the event of a dawn raid.

Training

15-75   To what extent are staff at all levels trained in the importance of competition compliance, in particular:

(a) those involved in contract negotiation;

(b) the sales force and those who establish price and other contract variables;

(c) all senior staff who supervise or have responsibility for the above;

(d) lawyers to ensure that contracts, as well as all other activities of the staff referred to above, are vetted for compliance;

(e) the reception staff, so that they know what to do in the event of the unannounced arrival of officials; and

(f) all other staff, so that it is appreciated by one and all that compliance is part of the culture of the organisation.

Controlling infringement

15-76 To what extent are procedures in place to correct any infringement that comes to light, in particular to:

(a) encourage the notification of infringement or suspected infringement to the legal department or designated senior staff member;

(b) ensure that corrective action is taken to terminate any infringement or possible infringement;

(c) prevent dissemination of information concerning any infringement both within the organisation and outside;

(d) ensure that the organisation is distanced from any suggestion of infringement as much as possible;

(e) ensure that clear notes are maintained of meetings with competitors; and

(f) ensure that documents that are privileged are suitably labelled and kept separately and securely apart from other records.

Handling dawn raids

15-77 Co-operation in dawn raids should be given constructively but without prejudicing any defence. Dawn raid protocols should be readily accessible when needed, in particular to:

(a) ensure the immediate arrival of in-house or outside lawyers;

(b) ensure that the investigating authorities do not exceed their authority;

(c) determine the relevance of documents found and, where necessary to challenge questions asked, by reference to the declared subject-matter and purpose of the investigation;

(d) ensure that photocopying and other facilities can be made available for discrete use (without interruption by members of staff not assisting the investigation);

(e) prevent disclosure to the authorities of privileged documents; and

(f) keep a record of all questions asked and to keep a copy of all documents taken (maintaining a note of the files from which they came in order to provide their context).

Appendix A

APPENDIX A.1   THE COMPETITION ACT 1998

A.1-01   **Competition Act 1998**

C.41

ARRANGEMENT OF SECTIONS

PART I

COMPETITION

CHAPTER I

AGREEMENTS

Introduction

Competition Act 1998

C.41

An Act to make provision about competition and the abuse of a dominant position in the market; to confer powers in relation to investigations conducted in connection with Article 85 or 86 of the treaty establishing the European Community; to amend the Fair Trading Act 1973 in relation to information which may be required in connection with investigations under that Act; to make provision with respect to the meaning of "supply of services" in the Fair Trading Act 1973; and for connected purposes. [9th November 1998]

Be it enacted by the Queen's most Excellent Majesty, by and with the advice and consent of the Lords Spiritual and Temporal, and Commons, in this present Parliament assembled, and by the authority of the same, as follows: —

PART I

COMPETITION

CHAPTER I

AGREEMENTS

Introduction

1. The following shall cease to have effect —

    (a) the Restrictive Practices Court Act 1976 (c. 33),

    (b) the Restrictive Trade Practices Act 1976 (c. 34),

    (c) the Resale Prices Act 1976 (c. 53), and

    (d) the Restrictive Trade Practices Act 1977 (c. 19).

The prohibition

2. — (1) Subject to section 3, agreements between undertakings, decisions by associations of undertakings or concerted practices which —

(a) may affect trade within the United Kingdom, and

(b) have as their object or effect the prevention, restriction or distortion of competition within the United Kingdom

are prohibited unless they are exempt in accordance with the provisions of this Part.

(2) Subsection (1) applies, in particular, to agreements, decisions or practices which —

(a) directly or indirectly fix purchase or selling prices or any other trading conditions;

(b) limit or control production, markets, technical development or investment;

(c) share markets or sources of supply;

(d) apply dissimilar conditions to equivalent transactions with other trading parties, thereby placing them at a competitive disadvantage;

(e) make the conclusion of contracts subject to acceptance by the other parties of supplementary obligations which, by their nature or according to commercial usage, have no connection with the subject of such contracts.

(3) Subsection (1) applies only if the agreement, decision or practice is, or is intended to be, implemented in the United Kingdom.

(4) Any agreement or decision which is prohibited by subsection (1) is void.

(5) A provision of this Part which is expressed to apply to, or in relation to, an agreement is to be read as applying equally to, or in relation to, a decision by an association of undertakings or a concerted practice (but with any necessary modifications).

(6) Subsection (5) does not apply where the context otherwise requires.

(7) In this section "the United Kingdom" means, in relation to an agreement which operates or is intended to operate only in a part of the United Kingdom, that part.

(8) The prohibition imposed by subsection (1) is referred to in this Act as "the Chapter I prohibition".

Excluded agreements

3. — (1) The Chapter I prohibition does not apply in any of the cases in which it is excluded by or as a result of —

(a) Schedule 1 (mergers and concentrations);

(b) Schedule 2 (competition scrutiny under other enactments);

(c) Schedule 3 (planning obligations and other general exclusions); or

(d) Schedule 4 (professional rules).

(2) The Secretary of State may at any time by order amend Schedule 1, with respect to the Chapter I prohibition, by —

(a) providing for one or more additional exclusions; or

(b) amending or removing any provision (whether or not it has been added by an order under this subsection).

(3) The Secretary of State may at any time by order amend Schedule 3, with respect to the Chapter I prohibition, by —

(a) providing for one or more additional exclusions; or

(b) amending or removing any provision —

> (i) added by an order under this subsection; or
> (ii) included in paragraph 1, 2, 8 or 9 of Schedule 3.

(4) The power under subsection (3) to provide for an additional exclusion may be exercised only if it appears to the Secretary of State that agreements which fall within the additional exclusion —

(a) do not in general have an adverse effect on competition, or

(b) are, in general, best considered under Chapter II or the Fair Trading Act 1973.

(5) An order under subsection (2)(a) or (3)(a) may include provision (similar to that made with respect to any other exclusion provided by the relevant Schedule) for the exclusion concerned to cease to apply to a particular agreement.

(6) Schedule 3 also gives the Secretary of State power to exclude agreements from the Chapter I prohibition in certain circumstances.

Exemptions

4. — (1) The Director may grant an exemption from the Chapter I prohibition with respect to a particular agreement if —

(a) a request for an exemption has been made to him under section 14 by a party to the agreement; and

(b) the agreement is one to which section 9 applies.

(2) An exemption granted under this section is referred to in this Part as an individual exemption.

(3) The exemption —

(a) may be granted subject to such conditions or obligations as the Director considers it appropriate to impose; and

(b) has effect for such period as the Director considers appropriate.

(4) That period must be specified in the grant of the exemption.

(5) An individual exemption may be granted so as to have effect from a date earlier than that on which it is granted.

(6) On an application made in such way as may be specified by rules under section 51, the Director may extend the period for which an exemption has effect; but, if the rules so provide, he may do so only in specified circumstances.

5. — (1) If the Director has reasonable grounds for believing that there has been a material change of circumstance since he granted an individual exemption, he may by notice in writing —

(a) cancel the exemption;

(b) vary or remove any condition or obligation; or

(c) impose one or more additional conditions or obligations.

(2) If the Director has a reasonable suspicion that the information on which he based his decision to grant an individual exemption was incomplete, false or misleading in a material particular, he may by notice in writing take any of the steps mentioned in subsection (1).

(3) Breach of a condition has the effect of cancelling the exemption.

(4) Failure to comply with an obligation allows the Director, by notice in writing, to take any of the steps mentioned in subsection (1).

(5) Any step taken by the Director under subsection (1), (2) or (4) has effect from such time as may be specified in the notice.

(6) If an exemption is cancelled under subsection (2) or (4), the date specified in the notice cancelling it may be earlier than the date on which the notice is given.

(7) The Director may act under subsection (1), (2) or (4) on his own initiative or on a complaint made by any person.

6. — (1) If agreements which fall within a particular category of agreement are, in the opinion of the Director, likely to be agreements to which section 9 applies, the Director may recommend that the Secretary of State make an order specifying that category for the purposes of this section.

(2) The Secretary of State may make an order ("a block exemption order") giving effect to such a recommendation —

(a) in the form in which the recommendation is made; or

(b) subject to such modifications as he considers appropriate.

(3) An agreement which falls within a category specified in a block exemption order is exempt from the Chapter I prohibition.

(4) An exemption under this section is referred to in this Part as a block exemption.

(5) A block exemption order may impose conditions or obligations subject to which a block exemption is to have effect.

(6) A block exemption order may provide —

(a) that breach of a condition imposed by the order has the effect of cancelling the block exemption in respect of an agreement;

(b) that if there is a failure to comply with an obligation imposed by the order, the Director may, by notice in writing, cancel the block exemption in respect of the agreement;

(c) that if the Director considers that a particular agreement is not one to which section 9 applies, he may cancel the block exemption in respect of that agreement.

(7) A block exemption order may provide that the order is to cease to have effect at the end of a specified period.

(8) In this section and section 7 "specified" means specified in a block exemption order.

7. — (1) A block exemption order may provide that a party to an agreement which —

(a) does not qualify for the block exemption created by the order, but

(b) satisfies specified criteria,

may notify the Director of the agreement for the purposes of subsection (2).

(2) An agreement which is notified under any provision included in a block exemption order by virtue of subsection (1) is to be treated, as from the end of the notice period, as falling within a category specified in a block exemption order unless the Director —

(a) is opposed to its being so treated; and

(b) gives notice in writing to the party concerned of his opposition before the end of that period.

(3) If the Director gives notice of his opposition under subsection (2), the notification under subsection (1) is to be treated as both notification under section 14 and as a request for an individual exemption made under subsection (3) of that section.

(4) In this section "notice period" means such period as may be specified with a view to giving the Director sufficient time to consider whether to oppose under subsection (2).

8. — (1) Before making a recommendation under section 6(1), the Director must —

(a) publish details of his proposed recommendation in such a way as he thinks most suitable for bringing it to the attention of those likely to be affected; and

(b) consider any respresentations about it which are made to him.

(2) If the Secretary of State proposes to give effect to such a recommendation subject to modifications, he must inform the Director of the proposed modifications and take into account any comments made by the Director.

(3) If, in the opinion of the Director, it is appropriate to vary or revoke a block exemption order he may make a recommendation to that effect to the Secretary of State.

(4) Subsection (1) also applies to any proposed recommendation under subsection (3).

(5) Before exercising his power to vary or revoke a block exemption order (in a case where there has been no recommendation under subsection (3)), the Secretary of State must —

(2) inform the Director of the proposed variation or revocation; and

(3) take into account any comments made by the Director.

(6) A block exemption order may provide for a block exemption to have effect from a date earlier than that on which the order is made.

9. This section applies to any agreement which —

(a) contributes to —

(i) improving production or distribution, or
(ii) promoting technical or economic progress,

while allowing consumers a fair share of the resulting benefit; but

(b) does not —

(i) impose on the undertakings concerned restrictions which are not indispensable to the attainment of those objectives; or
(ii) afford the undertakings concerned the possibility of eliminating competition in respect of a substantial part of the products in question.

10. — (1) An agreement is exempt from the Chapter I prohibition if it is exempt from the Community prohibition —

(a) by virtue of a Regulation,

(b) because it has been given exemption by the Commission, or

(c) because it has been notified to the Commission under the appropriate opposition or objection procedure and —

    (i) the time for opposing, or objecting to, the agreement has expired and the Commission has not opposed it; or

    (ii) the Commission has opposed, or objected to, the agreement but has withdrawn its opposition or objection.

(2) An agreement is exempt from the Chapter I prohibition if it does not affect trade between Member States but otherwise falls within a category of agreement which is exempt from the Community prohibition by virtue of a Regulation.

(3) An exemption from the Chapter I prohibition under this section is referred to in this Part as parallel exemption.

(4) A parallel exemption —

(a) takes effect on the date on which the relevant exemption from the Community prohibition takes effect or, in the case of a parallel exemption under subsection (2), would take effect if the agreement in question affected trade between Member States; and

(b) ceases to have effect —

    (i) if the relevant exemption from the Community prohibition ceases to have effect; or

    (ii) on being cancelled by virtue of subsection (5) or (7).

(5) In such circumstances and manner as may be specified in rules made under section 51, the Director may —

(a) impose conditions or obligations subject to which a parallel exemption is to have effect;

(b) vary or remove any such condition or obligation;

(c) impose one or more additional conditions or obligations;

(d) cancel the exemption.

(6) In such circumstances as may be specified in rules made under section 51, the date from which cancellation of an exemption is to take effect may be earlier than the date on which notice of cancellation is given.

(7) Breach of a condition imposed by the Director has the effect of cancelling the exemption.

(8) In exercising his powers under this section, the Director may require any person who is a party to the agreement in question to give him such information as he may require.

(9) For the purpose of this section references to an agreement being exempt from the Community prohibition are to be read as including references to the prohibition being inapplicable to the agreement by virtue of a Regulation or a decision by the Commission.

(10) In this section —
"the Community prohibition" means the prohibition contained in —

(a) paragraph 1 of Article 85;

(b) any corresponding provision replacing, or otherwise derived from, that provision;

(c) such other Regulation as the Secretary of State may by order specify; and

"Regulation" means a Regulation adopted by the Commission or by the Council.

(11) This section has effect in relation to the prohibition contained in paragraph 1 of Article 53 of the EEA Agreement (and the EFTA Surveillance Authority) as it has effect in relation to the Community prohibition (and the Commission) subject to any modifications which the Secretary of State may by order prescribe.

11. — (1) The fact that a ruling may be given by virtue of Article 88 of the Treaty on the question whether or not agreements of a particular kind are prohibited by Article 85 does not prevent such agreements from being subject to the Chapter I prohibition.

(2) But the Secretary of State may by regulations make such provision as he considers appropriate for the purpose of granting an exemption from the Chapter I prohibition, in prescribed circumstances, in respect of such agreements.

(3) An exemption from the Chapter I prohibition by virtue of regulations under this section is referred to in this Part as a section 11 exemption.

Notification

12. — (1) Sections 13 and 14 provide for an agreement to be examined by the Director on the application of a party to the agreement who thinks that it may infringe the Chapter I prohibition.

(2) Schedule 5 provides for the procedure to be followed —

(a) by any person making such an application; and

(b) by the Director, in considering such an application.

(3) The Secretary of State may by regulations make provision as to the application of sections 13 to 16 and Schedule 5, with such modifications (if any) as may be prescribed, in cases where the Director —

(a) has given a direction withdrawing an exclusion; or

(b) is considering whether to give such a direction.

13. — (1) A party to an agreement who applies for the agreement to be examined under this section must —

(a) notify the Director of the agreement; and

(b) apply to him for guidance.

(2) On an application under this section, the Director may give the applicant guidance as to whether or not, in his view, the agreement is likely to infringe the Chapter I prohibition.

(3) If the Director considers that the agreement is likely to infringe the prohibition if it is not exempt, his guidance may indicate —

(a) whether the agreement is likely to be exempt from the prohibition under —

(i) a block exemption;
(ii) a parallel exemption; or
(iii) a section 11 exemption; or

(b) whether he would be likely to grant the agreement an individual exemption if asked to do so.

(4) If an agreement to which the prohibition applies has been notified to the Director under this section, no penalty is to be imposed under this Part in respect of any infringement of the prohibition by the agreement which occurs during the period —

(a) beginning with the date on which notification was given; and

(b) ending with such date as may be specified in a notice in writing given to the applicant by the Director when the application has been determined.

(5) The date specified in a notice under subsection (4)(b) may not be earlier than the date on which the notice is given.

14. — (1) A party to an agreement who applies for the agreement to be examined under this section must —

(a) notify the Director of the agreement; and

(b) apply to him for a decision.

(2) On an application under this section, the Director may make a decision as to —

(a) whether the Chapter I prohibition has been infringed; and

(b) if it has not been infringed, whether that is because of the effect of an exclusion or because the agreement is exempt from the prohibition.

(3) If an agreement is notified to the Director under this section, the application may include a request for the agreement to which it relates to be granted an individual exemption.

(4) If an agreement to which the prohibition applies has been notified to the Director under this section, no penalty is to be imposed under this Part in respect of any infringement of the prohibition by the agreement which occurs during the period —

(a) beginning with the date on which notification was given; and

(b) ending with such date as may be specified in a notice in writing given to the applicant by the Director when the application has been determined.

(5) The date specified in a notice under subsection (4)(b) may not be earlier than the date on which the notice is given.

15. — (1) This section applies to an agreement if the Director has determined an application under section 13 by giving guidance that —

(a) the agreement is unlikely to infringe the Chapter I prohibition, regardless of whether or not it is exempt;

(b) the agreement is likely to be exempt under —

   (i) a block exemption;
  (ii) a parallel exemption; or
 (iii) a section 11 exemption; or

(c) he would be likely to grant the agreement an individual exemption if asked to do so.

(2) The Director is to take no further action under this Part with respect to an agreement to which this section applies, unless —

(a) he has reasonable grounds for believing that there has been a material change of circumstance since he gave his guidance;

(b) he has a reasonable suspicion that the information on which he based his guidance was incomplete, false or misleading in a material particular;

(c) one of the parties to the agreement applies to him for a decision under section 14 with respect to the agreement; or

(d) a complaint about the agreement has been made to him by a person who is not a party to the agreement.

(3) No penalty may be imposed under this Part in respect of any infringement of the Chapter I prohibition by an agreement to which this section applies.

(4) But the Director may remove the immunity given by subsection (3) if —

(a) he takes action under this Part with respect to the agreement in one of the circumstances mentioned in subsection (2);

(b) he considers it likely that the agreement will infringe the prohibition; and

(c) he gives notice in writing to the party on whose application the guidance was given that he is removing the immunity as from the date specified in his notice.

(5) If the Director has a reasonable suspicion that information —

(a) on which he based his guidance, and

(b) which was provided to him by a party to the agreement,

was incomplete, false or misleading in a material particular, the date specified in a notice under subsection (4)(c) may be earlier than the date on which the notice is given.

16. — (1) This section applies to an agreement if the Director has determined an application under section 14 by making a decision that the agreement has not infringed the Chapter I prohibition.

(2) The Director is to take no further action under this Part with respect to the agreement unless —

(a) he has reasonable grounds for believing that there has been a material change of circumstance since he gave his decision; or

(b) he has a reasonable suspicion that the information on which he based his decision was incomplete, false or misleading in a material particular.

(3) No penalty may be imposed under this Part in respect of any infringement of the Chapter I prohibition by an agreement to which this section applies.

(4) But the Director may remove the immunity given by subsection (3) if —

(a) he takes action under this Part with respect to the agreement in one of the circumstances mentioned in subsection (2);

(b) he considers that it is likely that the agreement will infringe the prohibition; and

(c) he gives notice in writing to the party on whose application the decision was made that he is removing the immunity as from the date specified in his notice.

(5) If the Director has a reasonable suspicion that information —

(a) on which he based his decision, and

(b) which was provided to him by a party to the agreement,

was incomplete, false or misleading in a material particular, the date specified in a notice under subsection (4)(c) may be earlier than the date on which the notice is given.

CHAPTER II

ABUSE OF DOMINANT POSITION

Introduction

17. Sections 2 to 10 of the Competition Act 1980 (control of anti-competitive practices) shall cease to have effect.

The prohibition

18. — (1) Subject to section 19, any conduct on the part of one or more undertakings which amounts to the abuse of a dominant position in a market is prohibited if it may affect trade within the United Kingdom.

(2) Conduct may, in particular, constitute such an abuse if it consists in —

(a) directly or indirectly imposing unfair purchase or selling prices or other unfair trading conditions;

(b) limiting production, markets or technical development to the prejudice of consumers;

(c) applying dissimilar conditions to equivalent transactions with other trading parties, thereby placing them at a competitive disadvantage;

(d) making the conclusion of contracts subject to acceptance by the other parties of supplementary obligations which, by their nature or according to commercial usage, have no connection with the subject of the contracts.

(3) In this section —
"dominant position" means a dominant position within the United Kingdom; and
"the United Kingdom" means the United Kingdom or any part of it.

(4) The prohibition imposed by subsection (1) is referred to in this Act as "the Chapter II prohibition".

Excluded cases

19. — (1) The Chapter II prohibition does not apply in any of the cases in which it is excluded by or as a result of —

(a) Schedule 1 (mergers and concentrations); or

(b) Schedule 3 (general exclusions).

(2) The Secretary of State may at any time by order amend Schedule 1, with respect to the Chapter II prohibition, by —

(a) providing for one or more additional exclusions; or

(b) amending or removing any provision (whether or not it has been added by an order under this subsection).

(3) The Secretary of State may at any time by order amend paragraph 8 of Schedule 3 with respect to the Chapter II prohibition.

(4) Schedule 3 also gives the Secretary of State power to provide that the Chapter II prohibition is not to apply in certain circumstances.

Notification

20. — (1) Sections 21 and 22 provide for conduct of a person which that person thinks may infringe the Chapter II prohibition to be considered by the Director on the application of that person.

(2) Schedule 6 provides for the procedure to be followed —

(a) by any person making an application, and

(b) by the Director, in considering an application.

21. — (1) A person who applies for conduct to be considered under this section must —

(a) notify the Director of it; and

(b) apply to him for guidance.

(2) On an application under this section, the Director may give the applicant guidance as to whether or not, in his view, the conduct is likely to infringe the Chapter II prohibition.

22. — (1) A person who applies for conduct to be considered under this section must —

(a) notify the Director of it; and

(b) apply to him for a decision.

(2) On an application under this section, the Director may make a decision as to —

(a) whether the Chapter II prohibition has been infringed; and

(b) if it has not been infringed, whether that is because of the effect of an exclusion.

23. — (1) This section applies to conduct if the Director has determined an application under section 21 by giving guidance that the conduct is unlikely to infringe the Chapter II prohibition.

(2) The Director is to take no further action under this Part with respect to the conduct to which this section applies, unless —

(a) he has reasonable grounds for believing that there has been a material change of circumstances since he gave his guidance;

(b) he has a reasonable suspicion that the information on which he based his guidance was incomplete, false or misleading in a material particular; or

(c) a complaint about the conduct has been made to him.

(3) No penalty may be imposed under this Part in respect of any infringement of the Chapter II prohibition by conduct to which this section applies.

(4) But the Director may remove the immunity given by subsection (3) if —

(a) he takes action under this Part with respect to the conduct in one of the circumstances mentioned in subsection (2);

(b) he considers that it is likely that the conduct will infringe the prohibition; and

(c) he gives notice in writing to the undertaking on whose application the guidance was given that he is removing the immunity as from the date specified in his notice.

(5) If the Director has a reasonable suspicion that information —

(a) on which he based his guidance, and

(b) which was provided to him by an undertaking engaging in the conduct,

was incomplete, false or misleading in a material particular, the date specified in a notice under subsection (4)(c) may be earlier than the date on which the novice is given.

24. — (1) This section applies to conduct if the Director has determined an application under section 22 by making a decision that the conduct has not infringed the Chapter II prohibition.

(2) The Director is to take no further action under this Part with respect to the conduct unless —

(a) he has reasonable grounds for believing that there has been a material change of circumstance since he gave his decision; or

(b) he has a reasonable suspicion that the information on which he based his decision was incomplete, false or misleading in a material particular.

(3) No penalty may be imposed under this Part in respect of any infringement of the Chapter II prohibition by conduct to which this section applies.

(4) But the Director may remove the immunity given by subsection (3) if —

(a) he takes action under this Part with respect to the conduct in one of the circumstances mentioned in subsection (2);

(b) he considers that it is likely that the conduct will infringe the prohibition; and

(c) he gives notice in writing to the undertaking on whose application the decision was made that he is removing the immunity as from the date specified in his notice.

(5) If the Director has a reasonable suspicion that information —

(a) on which he based his decision, and

(b) which was provided to him by an undertaking engaging in the conduct,

was incomplete, false or misleading in a material particular, the date specified in a notice under subsection (4)(c) may be earlier than the date on which the notice is given.

CHAPTER III

INVESTIGATION AND ENFORCEMENT

Investigations

25. The Director may conduct an investigation if there are reasonable grounds for suspecting —

(a) that the Chapter I prohibition has been infringed; or

(b) that the Chapter II prohibition has been infringed.

26. — (1) For the purposes of an investigation under section 25, the Director may require any person to produce to him a specified document, or to provide him with specified information, which he considers relates to any matter relevant to the investigation.

(2) The power conferred by subsection (1) is to be exercised by a notice in writing.

(3) A notice under subsection (2) must indicate —

(a) the subject matter and purpose of the investigation; and

(b) the nature of the offences created by sections 42 to 44.

(4) In subsection (1) "specified" means —

(a) specified, or described, in the notice; or

(b) falling within a category which is specified, or described, in the notice.

(5) The Director may also specify in the notice —

(a) the time and place at which any document is to be produced or any information is to be provided;

(b) the manner and form in which it is to be produced or provided.

(6) The power under this section to require a person to produce a document includes power —

(a) if the document is produced —

    (i) to take copies of it or extracts from it;
    (ii) to require him, or any person who is a present or past officer of his, or is or was at any time employed by him, to provide an explanation of the document;

(b) if the document is not produced, to require him to state, to the best of his knowledge and belief, where it is.

27. — (1) Any officer of the Director who is authorised in writing by the Director to do so ("an investigating officer") may enter any premises in connection with an investigation under section 25.

(2) No investigating officer is to enter any premises in the exercise of his powers under this section unless he has given to the occupier of the premises a written notice which —

(a) gives at least two working days' notice of the intended entry;

(b) indicates the subject matter and purpose of the investigation; and

(c) indicates the nature of the offences created by sections 42 to 44.

(3) Subsection (2) does not apply —

(a) if the Director has a reasonable suspicion that the premises are, or have been, occupied by —

    (i) a party to an agreement which he is investigating under section 25(a); or
    (ii) an undertaking the conduct of which he is investigating under section 25(b); or

(b) if the investigating officer has taken all such steps as are reasonably practicable to give notice but has not been able to do so.

(4) In a case falling within subsection (3), the power of entry conferred by subsection (1) is to be exercised by the investigating officer on production of —

(a) evidence of his authorisation; and

(b) a document containing the information referred to in subsection (2)(b) and (c).

(5) An investigating officer entering any premises under this section may —

(a) take with him such equipment as appears to him to be necessary;

(b) require any person on the premises —

(i) to produce any document which he considers relates to any matter relevant to the investigation; and
(ii) if the document is produced, to provide an explanation of it;

(c) require any person to state, to the best of his knowledge and belief, where any such document is to be found;

(d) take copies of, or extracts from, any document which is produced;

(e) require any information which is held in a computer and is accessible from the premises and which the investigating officer considers relates to any matter relevant to the investigation, to be produced in a form —

(i) in which it can be taken away, and
(ii) in which it is visible and legible.

28. — (1) On an application made by the Director to the court in accordance with rules of court, a judge may issue a warrant if he is satisfied that —

(a) there are reasonable grounds for suspecting that there are on any premises documents —

(i) the production of which has been required under section 26 or 27; and
(ii) which have not been produced as required;

(b) there are reasonable grounds for suspecting that —

(i) there are on any premises documents which the Director has power under section 26 to require to be produced; and
(ii) if the documents were required to be produced, they would not be produced but would be concealed, removed, tampered with or destroyed; or

(c) an investigating officer has attempted to enter premises in the exercise of his powers under section 27 but has been unable to do so and that there are reasonable grounds for suspecting that there are on the premises documents the production of which could have been required under that section.

(2) A warrant under this section shall authorise a named officer of the Director, and any other of his officers whom he has authorised in writing to accompany the named officer —

(a) to enter the premises specified in the warrant, using such force as is reasonably necessary for the purpose;

(b) to search the premises and take copies of, or extracts from, any document appearing to be of a kind in respect of which the application under subsection (1) was granted ("the relevant kind");

(c) to take possession of any documents appearing to be of the relevant kind if —

(i) such action appears to be necessary for preserving the documents or preventing interference with them; or
(ii) it is not reasonably practicable to take copies of the documents on the premises;

(d) to take any other steps which appear to be necessary for the purpose mentioned in paragraph (c)(i);

(e) to require any person to provide an explanation of any document appearing to be of the relevant kind or to state, to the best of his knowledge and belief, where it may be found;

(f) to require any information which is held in a computer and is accessible from the premises and which the named officer considers relates to any matter relevant to the investigation, to be produced in a form —

(i) in which it can be taken away, and
(ii) in which it is visible and legible.

(3) If, in the case of a warrant under subsection (1)(b), the judge is satisfied that it is reasonable to suspect that there are also on the premises other documents relating to the investigation concerned, the warrant shall also authorise action mentioned in subsection (2) to be taken in relation to any such document.

(4) Any person entering premises by virtue of a warrant under this section may take with him such equipment as appears to him to be necessary.

(5) On leaving any premises which he has entered by virtue of a warrant under this section, the named officer must, if the premises are unoccupied or the occupier is temporarily absent, leave them as effectively secured as he found them.

(6) A warrant under this section continues in force until the end of the period of one month beginning with the day on which it is issued.

(7) Any document of which possession is taken under subsection (2)(c) may be retained for a period of three months.

29. — (1) A warrant issued under section 28 must indicate —

(a) the subject matter and purpose of the investigation;

(b) the nature of the offences created by sections 42 to 44.

(2) The powers conferred by section 28 are to be exercised on production of a warrant issued under that section.

(3) If there is no one at the premises when the named officer proposes to execute such a warrant he must, before executing it —

(a) take such steps as are reasonable in all the circumstances to inform the occupier of the intended entry; and

(b) if the occupier is informed, afford him or his legal or other representative a reasonable opportunity to be present when the warrant is executed.

(4) If the named officer is unable to inform the occupier of the intended entry he must, when executing the warrant, leave a copy of it in a prominent place on the premises.

(5) In this section —
"named officer" means the officer named in the warrant; and
"occupier", in relation to any premises, means a person whom the named officer reasonably believes is the occupier of those premises.

30. — (1) A person shall not be required, under any provision of this Part, to produce or disclose a privileged communication.

(2) "Privileged communication" means a communication —

(a) between a professional legal adviser and his client, or

(b) made in connection with, or in contemplation of, legal proceedings and for the purposes of those proceedings, which in proceedings in the High Court would be protected from disclosure on grounds of legal professional privilege.

(3) In the application of this section to Scotland —

    (a) references to the High Court are to be read as references to the Court of Session; and

    (b) the reference to legal professional privilege is to be read as a reference to confidentiality of communications.

31. — (1) Subsection (2) applies if, as the result of an investigation conducted under section 25, the Director proposes to make —

    (a) a decision that the Chapter I prohibition has been infringed, or

    (b) a decision that the Chapter II prohibition has been infringed.

(2) Before making the decision, the Director must —

    (a) give written notice to the person (or persons) likely to be affected by the proposed decision; and

    (b) give that person (or those persons) an opportunity to make representations.

Enforcement

32. — (1) If the Director has made a decision that an agreement infringes the Chapter I prohibition, he may give to such person or persons as he considers appropriate such directions as he considers appropriate to bring the infringement to an end.

(2) Subsection (1) applies whether the Director's decision is made on his own initiative or on an application made to him under this Part.

(3) A direction under this section may, in particular, include provision —

    (a) requiring the parties to the agreement to modify the agreement; or

    (b) requiring them to terminate the agreement.

(4) A direction under this section must be given in writing.

33. — (1) If the Director has made a decision that conduct infringes the Chapter II prohibition, he may give to such person or persons as he considers appropriate such directions as he considers appropriate to bring the infringement to an end.

(2) Subsection (1) applies whether the Director's decision is made on his own initiative or on an application made to him under this Part.

(3) A direction under this section may, in particular, include provision —

    (a) requiring the person concerned to modify the conduct in question; or

    (b) requiring him to cease that conduct.

(4) A direction under this section must be given in writing.

34. — (1) If a person fails, without reasonable excuse, to comply with a direction under section 32 or 33, the Director may apply to the court for an order —

(a) requiring the defaulter to make good his default within a time specified in the order; or

(b) if the direction related to anything to be done in the management or administration of an undertaking, requiring the undertaking or any of its officers to do it.

(2) An order of the court under subsection (1) may provide for all of the costs of, or incidental to, the application for the order to be borne by —

(a) the person in default; or

(b) any officer of an undertaking who is responsible for the default.

(3) In the application of subsection (2) to Scotland, the reference to "costs" is to be read as a reference to "expenses".

35. — (1) This section applies if the Director —

(a) has a reasonable suspicion that the Chapter I prohibition has been infringed, or

(b) has a reasonable suspicion that the Chapter II prohibition has been infringed,

but has not completed his investigation into the matter.

(2) If the Director considers that it is necessary for him to act under this section as a matter of urgency for the purpose —

(a) of preventing serious, irreparable damage to a particular person or category of person, or

(b) of protecting the public interest,

he may give such directions as he considers appropriate for that purpose.

(3) Before giving a direction under this section, the Director must —

(a) give written notice to the person (or persons) to whom he proposes to give the direction; and

(b) give that person (or each of them) an opportunity to make representations.

(4) A notice under subsection (3) must indicate the nature of the direction which the Director is proposing to give and his reasons for wishing to give it.

(5) A direction given under this section has effect while subsection (1) applies, but may be replaced if the circumstances permit by a direction under section 32 or (as appropriate) section 33.

(6) In the case of a suspected infringement of the Chapter I prohibition, sections 32(3) and 34 also apply to directions given under this section.

(7) In the case of a suspected infringement of the Chapter II prohibition, sections 33(3) and 34 also apply to directions given under this section.

36. — (1) On making a decision that an agreement has infringed the Chapter I prohibition, the Director may require an undertaking which is a party to the agreement to pay him a penalty in respect of the infringement.

(2) On making a decision that conduct has infringed the Chapter II prohibition, the Director may require the undertaking concerned to pay him a penalty in respect of the infringement.

(3) The Director may impose a penalty on an undertaking under subsection (1) or (2) only if he is satisfied that the infringement has been committed intentionally or negligently by the undertaking.

(4) Subsection (1) is subject to section 39 and does not apply if the Director is satisfied that the undertaking acted on the reasonable assumption that that section gave it immunity in respect of the agreement.

(5) Subsection (2) is subject to section 40 and does not apply if the Director is satisfied that the undertaking acted on the reasonable assumption that that section gave it immunity in respect of the conduct.

(6) Notice of a penalty under this section must —

(a) be in writing; and

(b) specify the date before which the penalty is required to be paid.

(7) The date specified must not be earlier than the end of the period within which an appeal against the notice may be brought under section 46.

(8) No penalty fixed by the Director under this section may exceed 10% of the turnover of the undertaking (determined in accordance with such provisions as may be specified in an order made by the Secretary of State).

(9) Any sums received by the Director under this section are to be paid into the Consolidated Fund.

37. — (1) If the specified date in a penalty notice has passed and —

(a) the period during which an appeal against the imposition, or amount, of the penalty may be made has expired without an appeal having been made, or

(b) such an appeal has been made and determined,

the Director may recover from the undertaking, as a civil debt due to him, any amount payable under the penalty notice which remains outstanding.

(2) In this section —
"penalty notice" means a notice given under section 36; and
"specified date" means the date specified in the penalty notice.

38. — (1) The Director must prepare and publish guidance as to the appropriate amount of any penalty under this Part.

(2) The Director may at any time alter the guidance.

(3) If the guidance is altered, the Director must publish it as altered.

(4) No guidance is to be published under this section without the approval of the Secretary of State.

(5) The Director may, after consulting the Secretary of State, choose how he publishes his guidance.

(6) If the Director is preparing or altering guidance under this section he must consult such persons as he considers appropriate.

(7) If the proposed guidance or alteration relates to a matter in respect of which a regulator exercises concurrent jurisdiction, those consulted must include that regulator.

(8) When setting the amount of a penalty under this Part, the Director must have regard to the guidance for the time being in force under this section.

(9) If a penalty or a fine has been imposed by the Commission, or by a court or other body in another Member State, in respect of an agreement or conduct, the Director, an appeal tribunal or the appropriate court must take that penalty or fine into account when setting the amount of a penalty under this Part in relation to that agreement or conduct.

(10) In subsection (9) "the appropriate court" means —

(a) in relation to England and Wales, the Court of Appeal;

(b) in relation to Scotland, the Court of Session;

(c) in relation to Northern Ireland, the Court of Appeal in Northern Ireland;

(d) the House of Lords.

39. — (1) In this section "small agreement" means an agreement —

(a) which falls within a category prescribed for the purposes of this section; but

(b) is not a price fixing agreement.

(2) The criteria by reference to which a category of agreement is prescribed may, in particular, include —

(a) the combined turnover of the parties to the agreement (determined in accordance with prescribed provisions);

(b) the share of the market affected by the agreement (determined in that way).

(3) A party to a small agreement is immune from the effect of section 36(1); but the Director may withdraw that immunity under subsection (4).

(4) If the Director has investigated a small agreement, he may make a decision withdrawing the immunity given by subsection (3) if, as a result of his investigation, he considered that the agreement is likely to infringe the Chapter I prohibition.

(5) The Director must give each of the parties in respect of which immunity is withdrawn written notice of his decision to withdraw the immunity.

(6) A decision under subsection (4) takes effect on such date ("the withdrawal date") as may be specified in the decision.

(7) The withdrawal date must be a date after the date on which the decision is made.

(8) In determining the withdrawal date, the Director must have regard to the amount of time which the parties are likely to require in order to secure that there is no further infringement of the Chapter I prohibition with respect to the agreement.

(9) In subsection (1) "price fixing agreement" means an agreement which has as its object or effect, or one of its objects or effects, restricting the freedom of a party to the agreement to determine the price to be charged (otherwise than as between that party and another party to the agreement) for the product, service or other matter to which the agreement relates.

40. — (1) In this section "conduct of minor significance" means conduct which falls within a category prescribed for the purposes of this section.

(2) The criteria by reference to which a category is prescribed may, in particular, include —

(a) the turnover of the person whose conduct it is (determined in accordance with prescribed provisions);

(b) the share of the market affected by the conduct (determined in that way).

(3) A person is immune from the effect of section 36(2) if his conduct is conduct of minor significance; but the Director may withdraw that immunity under subsection (4).

(4) If the Director has investigated conduct of minor significance, he may make a decision withdrawing the immunity given by subsection (3) if, as a result of his investigation, he considers that the conduct is likely to infringe the Chapter II prohibition.

(5) The Director must give the person, or persons, whose immunity has been withdrawn written notice of his decision to withdraw the immunity.

(6) A decision under subsection (4) takes effect on such date ("the withdrawal date") as may be specified in the decision.

(7) The withdrawal date must be a date after the date on which the decision is made.

(8) In determining the withdrawal date, the Director must have regard to the amount of time which the person or persons affected are likely to require in order to secure that there is no further infringement of the Chapter II prohibition.

41. — (1) This section applies if a party to an agreement which may infringe the Chapter 1 prohibition has notified the agreement to the Commission for a decision as to whether an exemption will be granted under Article 85 with respect to the agreement.

(2) A penalty may not be required to be paid under this Part in respect of any infringement of the Chapter I prohibition after notification but before the Commission determines the matter.

(3) If the Commission withdraws the benefit of provisional immunity from penalties with respect to the agreement, subsection (2) ceases to apply as from the date on which that benefit is withdrawn.

(4) The fact that an agreement has been notified to the Commission does not prevent the Director from investigating it under this Part.

(5) In this section "provisional immunity from penalties" has such meaning as may be prescribed.

Offences

42. — (1) A person is guilty of an offence if he fails to comply with a requirement imposed on him under section 26, 27 or 28.

(2) If a person is charged with an offence under subsection (1) in respect of a requirement to produce a document, it is a defence for him to prove —

(a) that the document was not in his possession or under his control; and

(b) that it was not reasonably practicable for him to comply with the requirement.

(3) If a person is charged with an offence under subsection (1) in respect of a requirement —

(a) to provide information,

(b) to provide an explanation of a document, or

(c) to state where a document is to be found,

it is a defence for him to prove that he had a reasonable excuse for failing to comply with the requirement.

(4) Failure to comply with a requirement imposed under section 26 or 27 is not an offence if the person imposing the requirement has failed to act in accordance with that section.

(5) A person is guilty of an offence if he intentionally obstructs an officer acting in the exercise of his powers under section 27.

(6) A person guilty of an offence under subsection (1) or (5) is liable —

(a) on summary conviction, to a fine not exceeding the statutory maximum;

(b) on conviction on indictment, to a fine.

(7) A person who intentionally obstructs an officer in the exercise of his powers under a warrant issued under section 28 is guilty of an offence and liable —

(a) on summary conviction, to a fine not exceeding the statutory maximum;

(b) on conviction on indictment, to imprisonment for a term not exceeding two years or to a fine or to both.

43. — (1) A person is guilty of an offence if, having been required to produce a document under section 26, 27 or 28 —

(a) he intentionally or recklessly destroys or otherwise disposes of it, falsifies it or conceals it, or

(b) he causes or permits its destruction, disposal, falsification or concealment.

(2) A person guilty of an offence under subsection (1) is liable —

(a) on summary conviction, to a fine not exceeding the statutory maximum;

(b) on conviction on indictment, to imprisonment for a term not exceeding two years or to a fine or to both.

44. — (1) If information is provided by a person to the Director in connection with any function of the Director under this Part, that person is guilty of an offence if —

(a) the information is false or misleading in a material particular, and

(b) he knows that it is or is reckless as to whether it is.

(2) A person who —

(a) provides any information to another person, knowing the information to be false or misleading in a material particular, or

(b) recklessly provides any information to another person which is false or misleading in a material particular,

knowing that the information is to be used for the purpose of providing information to the Director in connection with any of his functions under this Part, is guilty of an offence.

(3) A person guilty of an offence under this section is liable —

(a) on summary conviction, to a fine not exceeding the statutory maximum;

(b) on conviction on indictment, to imprisonment for a term not exceeding two years or to a fine or to both.

CHAPTER IV

THE COMPETITION COMMISSION AND APPEALS

The Commission

45. — (1) There is to be a body corporate known as the Competition Commission.

(2) The Commission is to have such functions as are conferred on it by or as a result of this Act.

(3) The Monopolies and Mergers Commission is dissolved and its functions are transferred to the Competition Commission.

(4) In any enactment, instrument or other document, any reference to the Monopolies and Mergers Commission which has continuing effect is to be read as a reference to the Competition Commission.

(5) The Secretary of State may by order make such consequential supplemental and incidental provision as he considers appropriate in connection with —

(a) the dissolution of the Monopolies and Mergers Commission; and

(b) the transfer of functions effected by subsection (3).

(6) An order made under subsection (5) may, in particular, include provision —

(a) for the transfer of property, rights, obligations and liabilities and the continuation of proceedings, investigations and other matters; or

(b) amending any enactment which makes provision with respect to the Monopolies and Mergers Commission or any of its functions.

(7) Schedule 7 makes further provision about the Competition Commission.

Appeals

46. — (1) Any party to an agreement in respect of which the Director has made a decision may appeal to the Competition Commission against, or with respect to, the decision.

(2) Any person in respect of whose conduct the Director has made a decision may appeal to the Competition Commission against, or with respect to, the decision.

(3) In this section "decision" means a decision of the Director —

(a) as to whether the Chapter I prohibition has been infringed,

(b) as to whether the Chapter II prohibition has been infringed,

(c) as to whether to grant an individual exemption,

(d) in respect of an individual exemption —

(i) as to whether to impose any condition or obligation under section 4(3)(a) or 5(1)(c),
(ii) where such a condition or obligation has been imposed, as to the condition or obligation,
(iii) as to the period fixed under section 4(5),

(e) as to —

    (i) whether to extend the period for which an individual exemption has effect, or

    (ii) the period of any such extension,

(f) cancelling an exemption,

(g) as to the imposition of any penalty under section 36 or as to the amount of any such penalty,

(h) withdrawing or varying any of the decisions in paragraphs (a) to (f) following an application under section 47(1),

and includes a direction given under section 32, 33 or 35 and such other decision as may be prescribed.

(4) Except in the case of an appeal against the imposition, or the amount, of a penalty, the making of an appeal under this section does not suspend the effect of the decision to which the appeal relates.

(5) Part I of Schedule 8 makes further provision about appeals.

47. — (1) A person who does not fall within section 46(1) or (2) may apply to the Director asking him to withdraw or vary a decision ("the relevant decision") falling within paragraphs (a) to (f) of section 46(3) or such other decision as may be prescribed.

(2) The application must —

(a) be made in writing, within such period as the Director may specify in rules under section 51; and

(b) give the applicant's reasons for considering that the relevant decision should be withdrawn or (as the case may be) varied.

(3) If the Director decides —

(a) that the applicant does not have a sufficient interest in the relevant decision,

(b) that, in the case of an applicant claiming to represent persons who have such an interest, the applicant does not represent such persons, or

(c) that the persons represented by the applicant do not have such an interest,

he must notify the applicant of his decision.

(4) If the Director, having considered the application, decides that it does not show sufficient reason why he should withdraw or vary the relevant decision, he must notify the applicant of his decision.

(5) Otherwise, the Director must deal with the application in accordance with such procedure as may be specified in rules under section 51.

(6) The applicant may appeal to the Competition Commission against a decision of the Director notified under subsection (3) or (4).

(7) The making of an application does not suspend the effect of the relevant decision.

48. — (1) Any appeal made to the Competition Commission under section 46 or 47 is to be determined by an appeal tribunal.

(2) The Secretary of State may, after consulting the President of the Competition Commission Appeal Tribunals and such other persons as he considers appropriate, make rules with respect to appeals and appeal tribunals.

(3) The rules may confer functions on the President.

(4) Part II of Schedule 8 makes further provision about rules made under this section but is not to be taken as restricting the Secretary of State's powers under this section.

49. — (1) An appeal lies —

(a) on a point of law arising from a decision of an appeal tribunal, or

(b) from any decision of an appeal tribunal as to the amount of a penalty.

(2) An appeal under this section may be made only —

(a) to the appropriate court;

(b) with leave; and

(c) at the instance of a party or at the instance of a person who has a sufficient interest in the matter.

(3) Rules under section 48 may make provision for regulating or prescribing any matters incidental to or consequential upon an appeal under this section.

(4) In subsection (2) —
"the appropriate court" means —

(a) in relation to proceedings before a tribunal in England and Wales, the Court of Appeal;

(b) in relation to proceedings before a tribunal in Scotland, the Court of Session;

(c) in relation to proceedings before a tribunal in Northern Ireland, the Court of Appeal in Northern Ireland;
"leave" means leave of the tribunal in question or of the appropriate court; and
"party", in relation to a decision, means a person who was a party to the proceedings in which the decision was made.

CHAPTER V

MISCELLANEOUS

Vertical agreements and land agreements

50. — (1) The Secretary of State may by order provide for any provision of this Part to apply in relation to —

(a) vertical agreements, or

(b) land agreements,

with such modifications as may be prescribed.

(2) An order may, in particular, provide for exclusions or exemptions, or otherwise provide for prescribed provisions not to apply, in relation to —

(a) vertical agreements, or land agreements, in general; or

(b) vertical agreements, or land agreements, of any prescribed description.

(3) An order may empower the Director to give directions to the effect that in prescribed circum-

stances an exclusion, exemption or modification is not to apply (or is to apply in a particular way) in relation to an individual agreement.

(4) Subsections (2) and (3) are not to be read as limiting the powers conferred by section 71.

(5) In this section —
"land agreement" and "vertical agreement" have such meaning as may be prescribed; and "prescribed" means prescribed by an order.

Director's rules, guidance and fees

51. — (1) The Director may make such rules about procedural and other matters in connection with the carrying into effect of the provisions of this Part as he considers appropriate.

(2) Schedule 9 makes further provision about rules made under this section but is not to be taken as restricting the Director's powers under this section.

(3) If the Director is preparing rules under this section he must consult such persons as he considers appropriate.

(4) If the proposed rules relate to a matter in respect of which a regulator exercises concurrent jurisdiction, those consulted must include that regulator.

(5) No rule made by the Director is to come into operation until it has been approved by an order made by the Secretary of State.

(6) The Secretary of State may approve any rule made by the Director —

(a) in the form in which it is submitted; or

(b) subject to such modifications as he considers appropriate.

(7) If the Secretary of State proposes to approve a rule subject to modifications he must inform the Director of the proposed modifications and take into account any comments made by the Director.

(8) Subsections (5) to (7) apply also to any alteration of the rules made by the Director.

(9) The Secretary of State may, after consulting the Director, by order vary or revoke any rules made under this section.

(10) If the Secretary of State considers that rules should be made under this section with respect to a particular matter he may direct the Director to exercise his powers under this section and make rules about that matter.

52. — (1) As soon as is reasonably practicable after the passing of this Act, the Director must prepare and publish general advice and information about —

(a) the application of the Chapter I prohibition and the Chapter II prohibition, and

(b) the enforcement of those prohibitions.

(2) The Director may at any time publish revised, or new, advice or information.

(3) Advice and information published under this section must be prepared with a view to —

(a) explaining provisions of this Part to persons who are likely to be affected by them; and

(b) indicating how the Director expects such provisions to operate.

(4) Advice (or information) published by virtue of subsection (3)(b) may include advice (or information) about the factors which the Director may take into account in considering whether, and if so how, to exercise a power conferred on him by Chapter I, II or III.

(5) Any advice or information published by the Director under this section is to be published in such form and in such manner as he considers appropriate.

(6) If the Director is preparing any advice or information under this section he must consult such persons as he considers appropriate.

(7) If the proposed advice or information relates to a matter in respect of which a regulator exercises concurrent jurisdiction, those consulted must include that regulator.

(8) In preparing any advice or information under this section about a matter in respect of which he may exercise functions under this Part, a regulator must consult —

(a) the Director;

(b) the other regulators; and

(c) such other persons as he considers appropriate.

53. — (1) The Director may charge fees, of specified amounts, in connection with the exercise by him of specified functions under this Part.

(2) Rules may, in particular, provide —

(a) for the amount of any fee to be calculated by reference to matters which may include —

(i) the turnover of any party to an agreement (determined in such manner as may be specified);
(ii) the turnover of a person whose conduct the Director is to consider (determined in that way);

(b) for different amounts to be specified in connection with different functions;

(c) for the repayment by the Director of the whole or part of a fee in specified circumstances;

(d) that an application or notice is not to be regarded as duly made or given unless the appropriate fee is paid.

(3) In this section —

(a) "rules" means rules made by the Director under section 51; and

(a) "specified" means specified in rules.

Regulators

54. — (1) In this Part "regulator" means any person mentioned in paragraphs (a) to (g) of paragraph 1 of Schedule 10.

(2) Parts II and III of Schedule 10 provide for functions of the Director under this Part to be exercisable concurrently by regulators.

(3) Parts IV and V of Schedule 10 make minor and consequential amendments in connection with the regulators' competition functions.

(4) The Secretary of State may make regulations for the purpose of co-ordinating the performance of functions under his Part ("Part I functions") which are exercisable concurrently by two or more competent persons as a result of any provision made by Part II or III of Schedule 10.

(5) The regulations may, in particular, make provision —

(a) as to the procedure to be followed by competent persons when determining who is to exercise Part I functions in a particular case;

(b) as to the steps which must be taken before a competent persons exercises, in a particular case, such Part I functions as may be prescribed;

(c) as to the procedure for determining, in a particular case, questions arising as to which competent person is to exercise Part I functions in respect of the case;

(d) for Part I functions in a particular case to be exercised jointly —

(i) by the Director and one or more regulators, or
(ii) by two or more regulators,

and as to the procedure to be followed in such cases;

(e) as to the circumstances in which the exercise by a competent person of such Part I functions as may be prescribed is to preclude the exercise of such functions by another such person;

(f) for cases in respect of which part I functions are being, or have been, exercised by a competent person to be transferred to another such person;

(g) for the person ("A") exercising Part I functions in a particular case —

(i) to appoint another competent person ("B") to exercise Part I functions on A's behalf in relation to the case; or
(ii) to appoint officers of B (with B's consent) to act as officers of A in relation to the case;

(h) for notification as to who is exercising Part I functions in respect of a particular case.

(6) Provision made by virtue of subsection (5)(c) may provide for questions to be referred to and determined by the Secretary of State or by such other person as may be prescribed.

(7) "Competent person" means the Director or any of the regulators.

Confidentiality and immunity from defamation

55. — (1) No information which —

(a) has been obtained under or as a result of any provision of this Part, and

(b) relates to the affairs of any individual or to any particular business of an undertaking,

is to be disclosed during the lifetime of that individual or while that business continues to be carried on, unless the condition mentioned in subsection (2) is satisfied.

(2) The condition is that consent to the disclosure has been obtained from —

(a) the person from whom the information was initially obtained under or as a result of any provision of this Part (if the identity of that person is known); and

(b) if different —

(i) the individual to whose affairs the information relates, or
(ii) the person for the time being carrying on the business to which the information relates.

(3) Subsection (1) does not apply to a disclosure of information —

(a) made for the purpose of —

(i) facilitating the performance of any relevant functions of a designated person;

   (ii) facilitating the performance of any functions of the Commission in respect of Community law about competition;

   (iii) facilitating the performance by the Comptroller and Auditor General of any of his functions;

   (iv) criminal proceedings in any part of the United Kingdom;

(b) made with a view to the institution of, or otherwise for the purposes of, civil proceedings brought under or in connection with this Part;

(c) made in connection with the investigation of any criminal offence triable in the United Kingdom or in any part of the United Kingdom; or

(d) which is required to meet a Community obligation.

(4) In subsection (3) "relevant functions" and "designated person" have the meaning given in Schedule 11.

(5) Subsection (1) also does not apply to a disclosure of information made for the purpose of facilitating the performance of specified functions of any specified person.

(6) In subsection (5) "specified" means specified in an order made by the Secretary of State.

(7) If information is disclosed to the public in circumstances in which the disclosure does not contravene subsection (1), that subsection does not prevent its further disclosure by any person.

(8) A person who contravenes this section is guilty of an offence and liable —

(a) on summary conviction, to a fine not exceeding the statutory maximum; or

(b) on conviction on indictment, to imprisonment for a term not exceeding two years or to a fine or to both.

56. — (1) This section applies if the Secretary of State or the Director is considering whether to disclose any information acquired by him under, or as a result of, any provision of this Part.

(2) He must have regard to the need for excluding, so far as is practicable, information the disclosure of which would in his opinion be contrary to the public interest.

(3) He must also have regard to —

(a) the need for excluding, so far as is practicable —

   (i) commercial information the disclosure of which would, or might, in his opinion, significantly harm the legitimate business interests of the undertaking to which it relates, or

   (ii) information relating to the private affairs of an individual the disclosure of which would, or might, in his opinion, significantly harm his interests; and

(b) the extent to which the disclosure is necessary for the purposes for which the Secretary of State or the Director is proposing to make the disclosure.

57. For the purposes of the law relating to defamation, absolute privilege attaches to any advice, guidance, notice or direction given, or decision made, by the Director in the exercise of any of his functions under this Part.

Findings of fact by Director

58. — (1) Unless the court directs otherwise or the Director has decided to take further action in accordance with section 16(2) or 24(2), a Director's finding which is relevant to an issue arising in Part I proceedings is binding on the parties if —

(a) the time for bringing an appeal in respect of the finding has expired and the relevant party has not brought such an appeal; or

(b) the decision of an appeal tribunal on such an appeal has confirmed the finding.

(2) In this section —
"a Director's finding" means a finding of fact made by the Director in the course of —

(a) determining an application for a decision under section 14 or 22, or

(b) conducting an investigation under section 25;

"Part I proceedings" means proceedings —

(a) in respect of an alleged infringement of the Chapter I prohibition or of the Chapter II prohibition; but

(b) which are brought otherwise than by the Director;
"relevant party" means —

(a) in relation to the Chapter I prohibition, a party to the agreement which is alleged to have infringed the prohibition; and

(b) in relation to the Chapter II prohibition, the undertaking whose conduct is alleged to have infringed the prohibition.

(3) Rules of court may make provision in respect of assistance to be given by the Director to the court in Part I proceedings.

Interpretation and governing principles

59 — (1) In this Part —
"appeal tribunal" means an appeal tribunal established in accordance with the provisions of Part III of Schedule 7 for the purpose of hearing an appeal under section 46 or 47;
"Article 85" means Article 85 of the Treaty;
"Article 86" means Article 86 of the Treaty;
"block exemption" has the meaning given in section 6(4);
"block exemption order" has the meaning given in section 6(2);
"the Chapter I prohibition" has the meaning given in section 2(8);
"the Chapter II prohibition" has the meaning given in section 18(4);
"the Commission" (except in relation to the Competition Commission) means the European Commission;
"the Council" means the Council of the European Union;
"the court", except in sections 58 and 60 and the expression "European Court", means —

(a) in England and Wales, the High Court;

(b) in Scotland, the Court of Session; and

(c) in Northern Ireland, the High Court;

"the Director" means the Director General of Fair Trading;
"document" includes information recorded in any form;
"the EEA Agreement" means the Agreement on the European Economic Area signed at Oporto on 2nd May 1992 as it has effect for the time being;
"the European Court" means the Court of Justice of the European Communities and includes the Court of First Instance;
"individual exemption" has the meaning given in section 4(2);
"information" includes estimates and forecasts;
"investigating officer" has the meaning given in section 27(1);
"Minister of the Crown" has the same meaning as in the Ministers of the Crown Act 1975;
"officer", in relation to a body corporate, includes a director, manager or secretary and, in relation to a partnership in Scotland, includes a partner;

"parallel exemption" has the meaning given in section 10(3);

"person", in addition to the meaning given by the Interpretation Act 1978, includes any undertaking;

"premises" does not include domestic premises unless —

(a) they are also used in connection with the affairs of an undertaking, or

(b) documents relating to the affairs of an undertaking are kept there,

but does include any vehicle;

"prescribed" means prescribed by regulations made by the Secretary of State;

"regulator" has the meaning given by section 54;

"section 11 exemption" has the meaning given in section 11(3); and

"the Treaty" means the treaty establishing the European Community.

(2) The fact that to a limited extent the Chapter I prohibition does not apply to an agreement, because of an exclusion provided by or under this Part or any other enactment, does not require those provisions of the agreement to which the exclusion relates to be disregarded when considering whether the agreement infringes the prohibition for other reasons.

(3) For the purposes of this Part, the power to require information, in relation to information recorded otherwise than in a legible form, includes power to require a copy of it in a legible form.

(4) Any power conferred on the Director by this Part to require information includes power to require any document which he believes may contain that information.

60. — (1) The purpose of this section is to ensure that so far as is possible (having regard to any relevant differences between the provisions concerned), questions arising under this Part in relation to competition within the United Kingdom are dealt with in a manner which is consistent with the treatment of corresponding questions arising in Community law in relation to competition within the Community.

(2) At any time when the court determines a question arising under this Part, it must act (so far as is compatible with the provisions of this Part and whether or not it would otherwise be required to do so) with a view to securing that there is no inconsistency between —

(a) the principles applied, and decision reached, by the court in determining that question; and

(b) the principles laid down by the Treaty and the European Court, and any relevant decision of that Court, as applicable at that time in determining any corresponding question arising in Community law.

(3) The court must, in addition, have regard to any relevant decision or statement of the Commission.

(4) Subsections (2) and (3) also apply to —

(a) the Director; and

(b) any person acting on behalf of the Director, in connection with any matter arising under this Part.

(5) In subsections (2) and (3), "court" means any court or tribunal.

(6) In subsections (2)(b) and (3), "decision" includes a decision as to —

(a) the interpretation of any provision of Community law;

(b) the civil liability of an undertaking for harm caused by its infringement of Community law.

PART II

INVESTIGATIONS IN RELATION TO ARTICLES 85 AND 86

61. — (1) In this Part —

"Article 85" and "Article 86" have the same meaning as in Part I;

"authorised officer", in relation to the Director, means an officer to whom an authorisation has been given under subsection (2);

"the Commission" means the European Commission;

"the Director" means the Director General of Fair Trading;

"Commission investigation" means an investigation ordered by a decision of the Commission under a prescribed provision of Community law relating to Article 85 or 86;

"Director's investigation" means an investigation conducted by the Director at the request of the Commission under a prescribed provision of Community law relating to Article 85 or 86;

"Director's special investigation" means a Director's investigation conducted at the request of the Commission in connection with a Commission investigation;

"prescribed" means prescribed by order made by the Secretary of State;

"premises" means —

(a) in relation to a Commission investigation, any premises, land or means of transport which an official of the Commission has power to enter in the course of the investigation; and

(b) in relation to a Director's investigation, any premises, land or means of transport which an official of the Commission would have power to enter if the investigation were being conducted by the Commission.

(2) For the purposes of a Director's investigation, an officer of the Director to whom an authorisation has been given has the powers of an official authorised by the Commission in connection with a Commission investigation under the relevant provision.

(3) "Authorisation" means an authorisation given in writing by the Director which —

(a) identifies the officer;

(b) specifies the subject matter and purpose of the investigation; and

(c) draws attention to any penalties which a person may incur in connection with the investigation under the relevant provision of Community law.

62. — (1) A judge of the High Court may issue a warrant if satisfied, on an application made to the High Court in accordance with rules of court by the Director, that a Commission investigation is being, or is likely to be, obstructed.

(2) A Commission investigation is being obstructed if —

(a) an official of the Commission ("the Commission official"), exercising his power in accordance with the provision under which the investigation is being conducted, has attempted to enter premises but has been unable to do so; and

(b) there are reasonable grounds for suspecting that there are books or records on the premises which the Commission official has power to examine.

(3) A Commission investigation is also being obstructed if there are reasonable grounds for suspecting that there are books or records on the premises —

(a) the production of which has been required by an official of the Commission exercising his power in accordance with the provision under which the investigation is being conducted; and

(b) which have not been produced as required.

(4) A Commission investigation is likely to be obstructed if —

    (a) an official of the Commission ("the Commission official") is authorised for the purpose of the investigation;

    (b) there are reasonable grounds for suspecting that there are books or records on the premises which the Commission official has power to examine; and

    (c) there are also reasonable grounds for suspecting that, if the Commission official attempted to exercise his power to examine any of the books or records, they would not be produced but would be concealed, removed, tampered with or destroyed.

(5) A warrant under this section shall authorise —

    (a) a named officer of the Director,

    (b) any other of his officers whom he has authorised in writing to accompany the named officer, and

    (c) any official of the Commission authorised for the purpose of the Commission investigation,

to enter the premises specified in the warrant, and search for books and records which the official has power to examine, using such force as is reasonably necessary for the purpose.

(6) Any person entering any premises by virtue of a warrant under this section may take with him such equipment as appears to him to be necessary.

(7) On leaving any premises entered by virtue of the warrant the named officer must, if the premises are unoccupied or the occupier is temporarily absent, leave them as effectively secured as he found them.

(8) A warrant under this section continues in force until the end of the period of one month beginning with the day on which it is issued.

(9) In the application of this section to Scotland, references to the High Court are to be read as references to the Court of Session.

63. — (1) A judge of the High Court may issue a warrant if satisfied, on an application made to the High Court in accordance with rules of court by the Director, that a Director's special investigation is being, or is likely to be, obstructed.

(2) A Director's special investigation is being obstructed if —

    (a) an authorised officer of the Director has attempted to enter premises but has been unable to do so;

    (b) the officer has produced his authorisation to the undertaking, or association of undertakings, concerned; and

    (c) there are reasonable grounds for suspecting that there are books or records on the premises which the officer has power to examine.

(3) A Director's special investigation is also being obstructed if —

    (a) there are reasonable grounds for suspecting that there are books or records on the premises which an authorised officer of the Director has power to examine;

    (b) the officer has produced his authorisation to the undertaking, or association of undertakings, and has required production of the books or records; and

    (c) the books and records have not been produced as required.

(4) A Director's special investigation is likely to be obstructed if —

(a) there are reasonable grounds for suspecting that there are books or records on the premises which an authorised officer of the Director has power to examine; and

(b) there are also reasonable grounds for suspecting that, if the officer attempted to exercise his power to examine any of the books or records, they would not be produced but would be concealed, removed, tampered with or destroyed.

(5) A warrant under this section shall authorise —

(a) a named authorised officer of the Director,

(b) any other authorised officer accompanying the named officer, and

(c) any named official of the Commission,

to enter the premises specified in the warrant, and search for books and records which the authorised officer has power to examine, using such force as is reasonably necessary for the purpose.

(6) Any person entering any premises by virtue of a warrant under this section may take with him such equipment as appears to him to be necessary.

(7) On leaving any premises which he has entered by virtue of the warrant the named officer must, if the premises are unoccupied or the occupier is temporarily absent, leave them as effectively secured as he found them.

(8) A warrant under this section continues in force until the end of the period of one month beginning with the day on which it issued.

(9) In the application of this section to Scotland, references to the High Court are to be read as references to the Court of Session.

64. — (1) A warrant issued under section 62 or 63 must indicate —

(a) the subject matter and purpose of the investigation;

(b) the nature of the offence created by section 65.

(2) The powers conferred by section 62 or 63 are to be exercised on production of a warrant issued under that section.

(3) If there is no one at the premises when the named officer proposes to execute such a warrant he must, before executing it —

(a) take such steps as are reasonable in all the circumstances to inform the occupier of the intended entry; and

(b) if the occupier is informed, afford him or his legal or other representative a reasonable opportunity to be present when the warrant is executed.

(4) If the named officer is unable to inform the occupier of the intended entry he must, when executing the warrant, leave a copy of it in a prominent place on the premises.

(5) In this section —
"named officer" means the officer named in the warrant; and
"occupier", in relation to any premises, means a person whom the named officer reasonably believes is the occupier of those premises.

65. — (1) A person is guilty of an offence if he intentionally obstructs any person in the exercise of his powers under a warrant issued under section 62 or 63.

(2) A person guilty of an offence under subsection (1) is liable —

(a) on summary conviction, to a fine not exceeding the statutory maximum;

(b) on conviction on indictment, to imprisonment for a term not exceeding two years or to a fine or to both.

PART III

MONOPOLIES

66. (1) Section 44 of the Fair Trading Act 1973 (power of the Director to require information about monopoly situations) is amended as follows.

(2) In subsection (1), for the words after paragraph (b) substitute —
"the Director may exercise the powers conferred by subsection (2) below for the purpose of assisting him in determining whether to take either of the following decisions with regard to that situation."

(3) After subsection (1) insert —
"(1A) Those decisions are —

(a) whether to make a monopoly reference with respect to the existence or possible existence of the situation;

(b) whether, instead, to make a proposal under section 56A below for the Secretary of State to accept undertakings."

(4) For subsection (2) substitute —
"(2) In the circumstances and for the purpose mentioned in subsection (1) above, the Director may —

(a) require any person within subsection (3) below to produce to the Director, at a specified time and place —

    (i) any specified documents, or
    (ii) any document which falls within a specified category,

which are in his custody or under his control and which are relevant;

(b) require any person within subsection (3) below who is carrying on a business to give the Director specified estimates, forecasts, returns, or other information, and specify the time at which and the form and manner in which the estimates, forecasts, returns or information are to be given;

(c) enter any premises used by a person within subsection (3) below for business purposes, and —

    (i) require any person on the premises to produce any documents on the premises which are in his custody or under his control and which are relevant;
    (ii) require any person on the premises to give the Director such explanation of the documents as he may require.

(3) A person is within this subsection if —

(a) he produces goods of the description in question in the United Kingdom;

(b) he supplies goods or (as the case may be) services of the description in question in the United Kingdom; or

(c) such goods (or services) are supplied to him in the United Kingdom.

(4) The power to impose a requirement under subsection (2)(a) or (b) above is to be exercised by notice in writing served on the person on whom the requirement is imposed; and "specified" in those

provisions means specified or otherwise described in the notice, and "specify" is to be read accordingly.

(5) The power under subsection (2)(a) above to require a person ("the person notified") to produce a document includes power —

(a) if the document is produced —

(i) to take copies of it or extracts from it;
(ii) to require the person notified, or any person who is a present or past officer of his, or is or was at any time employed by him, to provide an explanation of the document;

(b) if the document is not produced, to require the person notified to state, to the best of his knowledge and belief, where it is.

(6) Nothing in this section confers power to compel any person —

(a) to produce any document which he could not be compelled to produce in civil proceedings before the High Court or, in Scotland, the Court of Session; or

(b) in complying with any requirement for the giving of information, to give any information which he could not be compelled to give in evidence in such proceedings.

(7) No person has to comply with a requirement imposed under subsection (2) above by a person acting under an authorisation under paragraph 7 of Schedule 1 to this Act unless evidence of the authorisation has, if required, been produced.

(8) For the purposes of subsection (2) above —

(a) a document is relevant if —

(i) it is relevant to a decision mentioned in subsection (1A) above; and
(ii) the powers conferred by this section are exercised in relation to the document for the purpose of assisting the Director in determining whether to take that decision;

(b) "document" includes information recorded in any form; and

(c) in relation to information recorded otherwise than in legible form, the power to require its production includes power to require production of it in legible form, so far as the means to do so are within the custody or under the control of the person on whom the requirement is imposed."

(5) The amendments made by this section and section 67 have effect in relation to sectoral regulators in accordance with paragraph 1 of Schedule 10.

67. — (1) Section 46 of the Fair Trading Act 1973 is amended as follows.

(2) Omit subsections (1) and (2).

(3) At the end insert —
"(4) Any person who refuses or wilfully neglects to comply with a requirement imposed under section 44(2) above is guilty of an offence and liable —

(a) on summary conviction, to a fine not exceeding the prescribed sum, or

(b) on conviction on indictment, to imprisonment for a term not exceeding two years or to a fine or to both.

(5) If a person is charged with an offence under subsection (4) in respect of a requirement to produce a document, it is a defence for him to prove —

(a) that the document was not in his possession or under his control; and

(b) that it was not reasonably practicable for him to comply with the requirement.

(6) If a person is charged with an offence under subsection (4) in respect of a requirement —

(a) to provide an explanation of a document, or

(b) to state where a document is to be found,

it is a defence for him to prove that he had a reasonable excuse for failing to comply with the requirement.

(7) A person who intentionally obstructs the Director in the exercise of his powers under section 44 is guilty of an offence and liable —

(a) on summary conviction, to a fine not exceeding the prescribed sum;

(b) on conviction on indictment, to a fine.

(8) A person who wilfully alters, suppresses or destroys any document which he has been required to produce under section 44(2) is guilty of an offence and liable —

(a) on summary conviction, to a fine not exceeding the prescribed sum;

(b) on conviction on indictment, to imprisonment for a term not exceeding two years or to a fine or to both."

68. In section 137 of the Fair Trading Act 1973, after subsection (3) insert —
"(3A) The Secretary of State may by order made by statutory instrument —

(a) provide that "the supply of services" in the provisions of this Act is to include, or to cease to include, any activity specified in the order which consists in, or in making arrangements in connection with, permitting the use of land; and

(b) for that purpose, amend or repeal any of paragraphs (c), (d), (e) or (g) of subsection (3) above.

(3B) No order under subsection (3A) above is to be made unless a draft of the order has been laid before Parliament and approved by a resolution of each House of Parliament.

(3C) The provisions of Schedule 9 to this Act apply in the case of a draft of any such order as they imply in the case of a draft of an order to which section 91(1) above applies."

69. In section 83 of the Fair Trading Act 1973 —

(a) in subsection (1), omit "Subject to subsection (1A) below"; and

(b) omit subsection (1A) (reports on monopoly references to be transmitted to certain persons at least twenty-four hours before laying before Parliament).

PART IV

SUPPLEMENTAL AND TRANSITIONAL

70. Sections 44 and 45 of the Patents Act 1977 shall cease to have effect.

71. — (1) Any power to make regulations or orders which is conferred by this Act is exercisable by statutory instrument.

(2) The power to make rules which is conferred by section 48 is exercisable by statutory instrument.

(3) Any statutory instrument made under this Act may —

(a) contain such incidental, supplemental, consequential and transitional provision as the Secretary of State considers appropriate; and

(b) make different provision for different cases.

(4) No order is to be made under —

(a) section 3,

(b) section 19,

(c) section 36(8),

(d) section 50, or

(e) paragraph 6(3) of Schedule 4,

unless a draft of the order has been laid before Parliament and approved by a resolution of each House.

(5) Any statutory instrument made under this Act, apart from one made —

(a) under any of the provisions mentioned in subsection (4), or

(b) under section 76(3),

shall be subject to annulment by a resolution of either House of Parliament.

72. — (1) This section applies to an offence under any of sections 42 to 44, 55(8) or 65.

(2) If an offence committed by a body corporate is proved —

(a) to have been committed with the consent or connivance of an officer, or

(b) to be attributable to any neglect on his part,

the officer as well as the body corporate is guilty of the offence and liable to be proceeded against and punished accordingly.

(3) In subsection (2) "officer", in relation to a body corporate, means a director, manager, secretary or other similar officer of the body, or a person purporting to act in any such capacity.

(4) If the affairs of a body corporate are managed by its members, subsection (2) applies in relation to the acts and defaults of a member in connection with his functions of management as if he were a director of the body corporate.

(5) If an offence committed by a partnership in Scotland is proved —

(a) to have been committed with the consent or connivance of a partner, or

(b) to be attributable to any neglect on his part,

the partner as well as the partnership is guilty of the offence and liable to be proceeded against and punished accordingly.

(6) In subsection (5) "partner" includes a person purporting to act as a partner.

73. — (1) Any provision made by or under this Act binds the Crown except that —

(a) the Crown is not criminally liable as a result of any such provision;

(b) the Crown is not liable for any penalty under any such provision; and

(c) nothing in this Act affects Her Majesty in her private capacity.

(2) Subsection (1)(a) does not affect the application of any provision of this Act in relation to persons in the public service of the Crown.

(3) Subsection (1)(c) is to be interpreted as if section 38(3) of the Crown Proceedings Act 1947 (interpretation of references in that Act to Her Majesty in her private capacity) were contained in this Act.

(4) If, in respect of a suspected infringement of the Chapter I prohibition or of the Chapter II prohibition otherwise than by the Crown or a person in the public service of the Crown, an investigation is conducted under section 25 —

(a) the power conferred by section 27 may not be exercised in relation to land which is occupied by a government department, or otherwise for purposes of the Crown, without the written consent of the appropriate person; and

(b) section 28 does not apply in relation to land so occupied.

(5) In any case in which consent is required under subsection (4), the person who is the appropriate person in relation to that case is to be determined in accordance with regulations made by the Secretary of State.

(6) Sections 62 and 63 do not apply in relation to land which is occupied by a government department, or otherwise for purposes of the Crown, unless the matter being investigated is a suspected infringement by the Crown or by a person in the public service of the Crown.

(7) In subsection (6) "infringement" means an infringement of Community law relating to Article 85 or 86 of the Treaty establishing the European Community.

(8) If the Secretary of State certifies that it appears to him to be in the interests of national security that the powers of entry —

(a) conferred by section 27, or

(b) that may be conferred by a warrant under section 28, 62 or 63,

should not be exercisable in relation to premises held or used by or on behalf of the Crown and which are specified in the certificate, those powers are not exercisable in relation to those premises.

(9) Any amendment, repeal or revocation made by this Act binds the Crown to the extent that the enactment amended, repealed or revoked binds the Crown.

74. — (1) The minor and consequential amendments set out in Schedule 12 are to have effect.

(2) The transitional provisions and savings set out in Schedule 13 are to have effect.

(3) The enactments set out in Schedule 14 are repealed.

75. — (1) The Secretary of State may by order make such incidental, consequential, transitional or supplemental provision as he thinks necessary or expedient for the general purposes, or any particular purpose, of this Act or in consequence of any of its provisions or for giving full effect to it.

(2) An order under subsection (1) may, in particular, make provisions —

(a) for enabling any person by whom any powers will become exercisable, on a date specified by or under this Act, by virtue of any provision made by or under this Act to take before that date any steps which are necessary as a preliminary to the exercise of those powers;

(b) for making savings, or additional savings, from the effect of any repeal made by or under this Act.

(3) Amendments made under this section shall be in addition, and without prejudice, to those made by or under any other provision of this Act.

(4) No other provision of this Act restricts the powers conferred by this section.

76. — (1) This Act may be cited as the Competition Act 1998.

(2) Sections 71 and 75 and this section and paragraphs 1 to 7 and 35 of Schedule 13 come into force on the passing of this Act.

(3) The other provisions of this Act come into force on such day as the Secretary of State may by order appoint; and different days may be appointed for different purposes.

(4) This Act extends to Northern Ireland.

SCHEDULES

Sections 3(1)(1) and 19(1)(a)   SCHEDULE 1

EXCLUSIONS: MERGERS AND CONCENTRATIONS

PART I

MERGERS

Enterprises ceasing to be distinct: the Chapter I prohibition

1. — (1) To the extent to which an agreement (either on its own or when taken together with another agreement) results, or if carried out would result, in any two enterprises ceasing to be distinct enterprises for the purposes of Part V of the Fair Trading Act 1973 ("the 1973 Act"), the Chapter I prohibition does not apply to the agreement.

(2) The exclusion provided by sub-paragraph (1) extends to any provision directly related and necessary to the implementation of the merger provisions.

(3) In sub-paragraph (2) "merger provisions" means the provisions of the agreement which cause, or if carried out would cause, the agreement which cause, or if carried out would cause, the agreement to have the result mentioned in sub-paragraph (1).

(4) Section 65 of the 1973 Act applies for the purposes of this paragraph as if —

(a) in subsection (3) (circumstances in which a person or group of persons may be treated as having control of an enterprise), and

(b) in subsection (4) (circumstances in which a person or group of persons may be treated as bringing an enterprise under their control),

for "may" there were substituted "must".

Enterprises ceasing to be distinct: the Chapter II prohibition

2. — (1) to the extent to which conduct (either on its own or when taken together with other conduct) —

(a) results in any two enterprises ceasing to be distinct enterprises for the purposes of Part V of the 1973 Act), or

(b) is directly related and necessary to the attainment of the result mentioned in paragraph (a),

(2) Section 65 of the 1973 Act applies for the purposes of this paragraph as it applies for the purposes of paragraph 1.

Transfer of a newspaper or of newspaper assets

3. — (1) The Chapter I prohibition does not apply to an agreement to the extent to which it constitutes, or would if carried out constitute, a transfer of a newspaper or of newspaper assets for the purposes of section 57 of the 1973 Act.

(2) The Chapter II prohibition does not apply to conduct (either on its own or when taken together with other conduct) to the extent to which —

(a) it constitutes such a transfer, or

(b) it is directly related and necessary to the implementation of the transfer.

(3) The exclusion provided by sub-paragraph (1) extends to any provision directly related and necessary to the implementation of the transfer.

Withdrawal of the paragraph 1 exclusion

4. — (1) The exclusion provided by paragraph 1 does not apply to a particular agreement if the Director gives a direction under this paragraph to that effect.

(2) If the Director is considering whether to give a direction under this paragraph, he may by notice in writing require any party to the agreement in question to give him such information in connection with the agreement as he may require.

(3) The Director may give a direction under this paragraph only as provided in sub-paragraph (4) or (5).

(4) If at the end of such period as may be specified in rules under section 51 a person has failed, without reasonable excuse, to comply with a requirement imposed under sub-paragraph (2), the Director may give a direction under this paragraph.

(5) The Director may also give a direction under this paragraph if —

(a) he considers —

(i)   that the agreement will, if not excluded, infringe the Chapter I prohibition; and
(ii) that he is not likely to grant it an unconditional individual exemption; and

(b) the agreement is not a protected agreement.

(6) For the purposes of sub-paragraph (5), an individual exemption is unconditional if no conditions or obligations are imposed in respect of it under section 4(3)(a).

(7) A direction under this paragraph —

(a) must be in writing;

(b) may be made so as to have effect from a date specified in the direction (which may not be earlier than the date on which it is given).

Protected agreements

5. An agreement is a protected agreement for the purposes of paragraph 4 if —

(a) the Secretary of State has announced his decision not to make a merger reference to the Competition Commission under section 64 of the 1973 Act in connection with the agreement;

(b) the Secretary of State has made a merger reference to the Competition Commission under section 64 of the 1973 Act in connection with the agreement and the Commission has found that the agreement has given rise to, or would if carried out give rise to, a merger situation qualifying for investigation;

(c) the agreement does not fall within sub-paragraph (a) or (b) but has given rise to, or would if carried out give rise to, enterprises to which it relates being regarded under section 65 of the 1973 Act as ceasing to be distinct enterprises (otherwise than as the result of subsection (3) or (4)(b) of that section); or

(d) the Secretary of State has made a merger reference to the Competition Commission under section 32 of the Water Industry Act 1991 in connection with the agreement and the Commission has found that the agreement has given rise to, or would if carried out give rise to, a merger of the kind to which that section applies.

Part II

Concentrations subject to EC controls

6. — (1) To the extent to which an agreement (either on its own or when taken together with another agreement) gives rise to, or would if carried out give rise to, a concentration, the Chapter I prohibition does not apply to the agreement if the Merger Regulation gives the Commission exclusive jurisdiction in the matter.

(2) To the extent to which conduct (either on its own or when taken together with other conduct) gives rise to, or would if pursued give rise to, a concentration, the Chapter II prohibition does not apply to the conduct if the Merger Regulation gives the Commission exclusive jurisdiction in the matter.

(3) In this paragraph —
"concentration" means a concentration with a Community dimension within the meaning of Articles 1 and 3 of the Merger Regulation; and
"Merger Regulation" means Council Regulation (EEC) No. 4064/89 of 21st December 1989 on the control of concentrations between undertakings as amended by Council Regulation (EC) No. 1310/97 of 30th June 1997.

Section 3(1)(b)   SCHEDULE 2

Exclusions: Other Competition Scrutiny

Part I

Financial Services

The Financial Services Act 1986 (c.60)

1. — (1) The Financial Services Act 1986 is amended as follows.

(2) For section 125 (effect of the Restrictive Trade Practices Act 1976), substitute —

125. — (1) The Chapter I prohibition does not apply to an agreement for the constitution of —

(a) a recognised self-regulating organisation,

(b) a recognised investment exchange, or

(c) a recognised clearing house,

to the extent to which the agreement relates to the regulating provisions of the body concerned.

(2) Subject to subsection (3) below, the Chapter I prohibition does not imply to an agreement for the constitution of —

(a) a self-regulating organisation,

(b) an investment exchange, or

(c) a clearing house,

to the extent to which the agreement relates to the regulating provisions of the body concerned.

(3) The exclusion provided by subsection (2) above applies only if —

(a) the body has applied for a recognition order in accordance with the provisions of this Act; and

(b) the application has not been determined.

(4) The Chapter I prohibition does not apply to a decision made by —

(a) a recognised self-regulating organisation,

(b) a recognised investment exchange, or

(c) a recognised clearing house,

to the extent to which the decision relates to any of that body's regulating provisions or specified practices.

(5) The Chapter I prohibition does not apply to the specified practices of —

(a) a recognised self-regulating organisation, a recognised investment exchange or a recognised clearing house; or

(b) a person who is subject to —

    (i) the rules of one of those bodies, or

    (ii) the statements of principle, rules, regulations or codes of practice made by a designated agency in the exercise of functions transferred to it by a delegation order.

(6) The Chapter I prohibition does not apply to any agreement the parties to which consist of or include

(a) a recognised self-regulating organisation, a recognised investment exchange or a recognised clearing house; or

(b) a person who is subject to —

    (i) the rules of one of those bodies, or

    (ii) the statements of principle, rules, regulations or codes of practice made by a designated agency in the exercise of functions transferred to it by a delegation order,

to the extent to which the agreement consists of provisions the inclusion of which is required or contemplated by any of the body's regulating provisions or specified practices or by the statements of principle, rules, regulations or codes of practice of the agency.

(7) The Chapter I prohibition does not apply to —

(a) any clearing arrangements; or

(b) any agreement between a recognised investment exchange and a recognised clearing house, to the extent to which the agreement consists of provisions the inclusion of which in the agreement is required or contemplated by any clearing arrangements.

(8) If the recognition order in respect of a body of the kind mentioned in subsection (1)(a), (b) or (c) above is revoked, subsections (1) and (4) to (7) above are to have effect as if that body had continued to be recognised until the end of the period of six months beginning with the day on which the revocation took effect.

(9) In this section —
"the Chapter I prohibition" means the prohibition imposed by section 2(1) of the Competition Act 1998;
"regulating provisions" means —

(a) in relation to a self-regulating organisation, any rules made, or guidance issued, by the organisation;

(b) in relation to an investment exchange, any rules made, or guidance issued, by the exchange;

(c) in relation to a clearing house, any rules made, or guidance issued, by the clearing house;
"specified practices" means —

(a) in the case of a recognised self-regulating organisation, the practices mentioned in section 119(2)(a)(ii) and (iii) above (read with section 119(5) and (6)(a));

(b) in the case of a recognised investment exchange, the practices mentioned in section 119(2)(b)(ii) and (iii) above (read with section 119(5) and (6)(b));

(c) in the case of a recognised clearing house, the practices mentioned in section 119(2)(c)(ii) and (iii) above (read with section 119(5) and (6)(b));

(d) in the case of a person who is subject to the statements of principle, rules, regulations or codes of practice issued or made by a designated agency in the exercise of functions transferred to it by a delegation order, the practices mentioned in section 121(2)(c) above (read with section 121(4));

and expressions used in this section which are also used in Part I of the Competition Act 1998 are to be interpreted in the same way as for the purposes of that Part of that Act."

(3) Omit section 126 (certain practices not to constitute anti-competitive practices for the purposes of the Competition Act 1980).

(4) For section 127 (modification of statutory provisions in relation to recognised professional bodies), substitute —

127. — (1) This section applies to —

    (a) any agreement for the constitution of a recognised professional body to the extent to which it relates to the rules or guidance of that body relating to the carrying on of investment business by persons certified by it ("investment business rules"); and

    (b) any other agreement, the parties to which consist of or include —

        (i) a recognised professional body,
        (ii) a person certified by such a body, or
        (iii) a member of such a body,

and which contains a provision required or contemplated by that body's investment business rules.

(2) If it appears to the Treasury, in relation to some or all of the provisions of an agreement to which this section applies —

    (a) that the provisions in question do not have, and are not intended or likely to have, to any significant extent the effect of restricting, distorting or preventing competition; or

    (b) that the effect of restricting, distorting or preventing competition which the provisions in question do have, or are intended or are likely to have, is not greater than is necessary for the protection of investors,

the Treasury may make a declaration to that effect.

(3) If the Treasury make a declaration under this section, the Chapter I prohibition does not apply to the agreement to the extent to which the agreement consists of provisions to which the declaration relates.

(4) If the Treasury are satisfied that there has been a material change of circumstances, they may —

    (a) revoke a declaration made under this section, if they consider that the grounds on which it was made no longer exist;

    (b) vary such a declaration, if they consider that there are grounds for making a different declaration; or

    (c) make a declaration even though they have notified the Director of their intention not to do so.

(5) If the Treasury make, vary or revoke a declaration under this section they must notify the Director of their decision.

(6) If the Director proposes to exercise any Chapter III powers in respect of any provisions of an agreement to which this section applies, he must —

    (a) notify the Treasury of his intention to do so; and

    (b) give the Treasury particulars of the agreement and such other information —

        (i) as he considers will assist the Treasury to decide whether to exercise their powers under this section; or
        (ii) as the Treasury may request.

(7) The Director may not exercise his Chapter III powers in respect of any provisions of an agreement to which this section applies, unless the Treasury —

    (a) have notified him that they have not made a declaration in respect of those provisions under this section and that they do not intend to make such a declaration; or

    (b) have revoked a declaration under this section and a period of six months beginning with the date on which the revocation took effect has expired.

(8) A declaration under this section ceases to have effect if the agreement to which it relates ceases to be one to which this section applies.

(9) In this section —
"the Chapter I prohibition" means the prohibition imposed by section 2(1) of the Competition Act 1998.
"Chapter III powers" means the powers given to the Director by Chapter III of Part I of that Act so far as they relate to the Chapter I prohibition, and

expressions used in this section which are also used in Part I of the Competition Act 1998 are to be interpreted in the same way as for the purposes of that Part of that Act.

(10) In this section references to an agreement are to be read as applying equally to, or in relation to, a decision or concerted practice.

(11) In the application of this section to decisions and concerted practices, references to provisions of an agreement are to be read as references to elements of a decision or concerted practice."

PART II

COMPANIES

The Companies Act 1989 (c.40)

2. — (1) The Companies Act 1989 is amended as follows.

(2) In Schedule 14, for paragraph 9 (exclusion of certain agreements from the Restrictive Trade Practices Act 1976), substitute —

"The Competition Act 1998

9. — (1) The Chapter I prohibition does not apply to an agreement for the constitution of a recognised supervisory or qualifying body to the extent to which it relates to —

(a) rules of, or guidance issued by, the body; and

(b) incidental matters connected with the rules or guidance.

(2) The Chapter I prohibition does not apply to an agreement the parties to which consist of or include —

(a) a recognised supervisory or qualifying body, or

(b) any person mentioned in paragraph 3(5) or (6) above,

to the extent to which the agreement consists of provisions the inclusion of which in the agreement is required or contemplated by the rules or guidance of that body.

(3) The Chapter I prohibition does not apply to the practices mentioned in paragraph 3(4)(a) and (b) above.

(4) Where a recognition order is revoked, sub-paragraphs (1) to (3) above are to continue to apply for a period of six months beginning with the day on which the revocation takes effect, as if the order were still in force.

(5) In this paragraph —

(a) "the Chapter I prohibition" means the prohibition imposed by section 2(1) of the Competition Act 1998,

(b) references to an agreement are to be read as applying equally to, or in relation to, a decision or concerted practice,

and expressions used in this paragraph which are also used in Part I of the Competition Act 1998 are to be interpreted in the same way as for the purposes of that Part of that Act.

(6) In the application of this paragraph to decisions and concerted practices, references to provisions of an agreement are to be read as references to elements of a decision or concerted practice."

The Companies (Northern Ireland) Order 1990 (S.I. 1990/593 (N.I.5))

3. — (1) The Companies (Northern Ireland) Order 1990 is amended as follows.

(2) In Schedule 14, for paragraph 9 (exclusion of certain agreements from the Restrictive Trade Practices Act 1976), substitute —

"The Competition Act 1998

9. — (1) The Chapter I prohibition does not apply to an agreement for the constitution of a recognised supervisory or qualifying body to the extent to which it relates to —

(a) rules of, or guidance issued by, the body; and

(b) incidental matters connected with the rules or guidance.

(2) The Chapter I prohibition does not apply to an agreement the parties to which consist of or include —

    (a) a recognised supervisory or qualifying body, or

    (b) any person mentioned in paragraph 3(5) or (6),

to the extent to which the agreement consists of provisions the inclusion of which in the agreement is required or contemplated by the rules or guidance of that body.

(3) The Chapter I prohibition does not apply to the practices mentioned in paragraph 3(4)(a) and (b).

(4) Where a recognition order is revoked, sub-paragraphs (1) to (3) are to continue to apply for a period of 6 months beginning with the day on which the revocation takes effect, as if the order were still in force.

(5) In this paragraph —

    (a) "the Chapter I prohibition" means the prohibition imposed by section 2(1) of the Competition Act 1998,

    (b) references to an agreement are to be read as applying equally to, or in relation to, a decision or concerted practice,

and expressions used in this paragraph which are also used in Part I of the Competition Act 1998 are to be interpreted in the same way as for the purposes of that Part of that Act.

(6) In the application of this paragraph to decisions and concerted practices, references to provisions of an agreement are to be read as references to elements of a decision or concerted practice."

PART III

BROADCASTING

The Broadcasting Act 1990 (c.42)

4. — (1) The Broadcasting Act 1990 is amended as follows.

(2) In section 194A (which modifies the Restrictive Trade Practices Act 1976 in its application to agreements relating to Channel 3 news provision), for subsections (2) to (6), substitute —

"(2) If, having sought the advice of the Director, it appears to the Secretary of State, in relation to some or all of the provisions of a relevant agreement, that the conditions mentioned in subsection (3) are satisfied, he may make a declaration to that effect.

(3) The conditions are that —

    (a) the provisions in question do not have, and are not intended or likely to have, to any significant extent the effect of restricting, distorting or preventing competition; or

    (b) the effect of restricting, distorting or preventing competition which the provisions in question do have or are intended or are likely to have, is not greater than is necessary —

        (i) in the case of a relevant agreement falling within subsection (1)(a), for securing the appointment by holders of regional Channel 3 licences of a single body corporate to be the appointed news provider for the purposes of section 31(2), or

        (ii) in the case of a relevant agreement falling within subsection (1)(b), for compliance by them with conditions included in their licences by virtue of section 31(1) and (2).

(4) If the Secretary of State makes a declaration under this section, the Chapter I prohibition does not apply to the agreement to the extent to which the agreement consists of provisions to which the declaration relates.

(5) If the Secretary of State is satisfied that there has been a material change of circumstances, he may —

    (a) revoke a declaration made under this section, if he considers that the grounds on which it was made no longer exist;

    (b) vary such a declaration, if he considers that there are grounds for making a different declaration; or

    (c) make a declaration, even though he has notified the Director of his intention not to do so.

(6) If the Secretary of State makes, varies or revokes a declaration under this section, he must notify the Director of his decision.

(7) The Director may not exercise any Chapter III powers in respect of a relevant agreement, unless —

    (a) he has notified the Secretary of State of his intention to do so; and

    (b) the Secretary of State —

        (i) has notified the Director that he has not made a declaration in respect of the agreement, or provisions of the agreement, under this section and that he does not intend to make such a declaration; or

        (ii) has revoked a declaration under this section and a period of six months beginning with the date on which the revocation took effect has expired.

(8) If the Director proposes to exercise any Chapter III powers in respect of a relevant agreement, he must give the Secretary of State particulars of the agreement and such other information —

    (a) as he considers will assist the Secretary of State to decide whether to exercise his powers under this section; or

    (b) as the Secretary of State may request.

(9) In this section —
"the Chapter I prohibition" means the prohibition imposed by section 2(1) of the Competition Act 1998;
"Chapter III powers" means the powers given to the Director by Chapter III of Part I of that Act so far as they relate to the Chapter I prohibition;
"Director" means the Director General of Fair Trading;
"regional Channel 3 licence" has the same meaning as in Part I;

and expressions used in this section which are also used in Part I of the Competition Act 1998 are to be interpreted in the same way as for the purposes of that Part of that Act.

(10) In this section references to an agreement are to be read as applying equally to, or in relation to, a decision or concerted practice.

(11) In the application of this section to decisions and concerted practices, references to provisions of an agreement are to be read as references to elements of a decision or concerted practice."

Networking arrangements under the Broadcasting Act 1990 (c.42)

5. — (1) The Chapter I prohibition does not apply in respect of any networking arrangements to the extent to which they —

    (a) are subject to Schedule 4 to the Broadcasting Act 1990 (competition references with respect to networking arrangements); or

    (b) contain provisions which have been considered under that Schedule.

(2) The Independent Television Commission ("ITC") must publish a list of the networking arrangements which in their opinion are excluded from the Chapter I prohibition by virtue of sub-paragraph (1).

(3) The ITC must —

    (a) consult the Director before publishing the list, and

    (b) publish the list in such a way as they think most suitable for bringing it to the attention of persons who, in their opinion, would be affected by, or likely to have an interest in, it.

(4) In this paragraph "networking arrangements" means —

    (a) any arrangements entered into as mentioned in section 39(4) or (7)(b) of the Broadcasting Act 1990, or

    (b) any agreements —

        (i) which do not constitute arrangements of the kind mentioned in paragraph (a), but

        (ii) which are made for the purpose mentioned in section 39(1) of that Act, or

    (c) any modification of the arrangements or agreements mentioned in paragraph (a) or (b).

PART IV

ENVIRONMENTAL PROTECTION

Producer responsibility obligations

6. — (1) The Environment Act 1995 is amended as follows.

(2) In section 94(1) (supplementary provisions about regulations imposing producer responsibility obligations on prescribed persons), after paragraph (o), insert —

"(oa) the exclusion or modification of any provision of Part I of the Competition Act 1998 in relation to exemption schemes or in relation to any agreement, decision or concerted practice at least one of the parties to which is an operator of an exemption scheme;".

(3) After section 94(6), insert —

"(6A) Expressions used in paragraph (oa) of subsection (1) above which are also used in Part I of the Competition Act 1998 are to be interpreted in the same way as for the purposes of that Part of that Act."

(4) After section 94, insert —

94A. — (1) For the purposes of this section, the relevant paragraphs are paragraphs (n), (o), (oa) and (ya) of section 94(1) above.

(2) Regulations made by virtue of any of the relevant paragraphs may include transitional provision in respect of agreements or exemption schemes —

(a) in respect of which information has been required for the purposes of competition scrutiny under any regulation made by virtue of paragraph (ya);

(b) which are being, or have been, considered for the purposes of competition scrutiny under any regulation made by virtue of paragraph (n) or (ya); or

(c) in respect of which provisions of the Restrictive Trade Practices Acts 1976 and 1977 have been modified or excluded in accordance with any regulation made by virtue of paragraph (o).

(3) Subsections (2), (3), (5) to (7) and (10) of section 93 above do not apply to a statutory instrument which contains only regulations made by virtue of any of the relevant paragraphs or subsection (2) above.

(4) Such a statutory instrument shall be subject to annulment in pursuance of a resolution of either House of Parliament."

Sections 3(1)(c) and 19(1)(b).   SCHEDULE 3

GENERAL EXCLUSIONS

Planning obligations

1. — (1) The Chapter I prohibition does not apply to an agreement —

(a) to the extent to which it is a planning obligation;

(b) which is made under section 75 (agreements regulating development or use of land) or 246 (agreements relating to Crown land) of the Town and Country Planning (Scotland) Act 1997; or

(c) which is made under Article 40 of the Planning (Northern Ireland) Order 1991.

(2) In sub-paragraph (1)(a), "planning obligation" means —

(a) a planning obligation for the purposes of section 106 of the Town and Country Planning Act 1990; or

(b) a planning obligation for the purposes of section 299A of that Act.

Section 21(2) agreements

2. — (1) The Chapter I prohibition does not apply to an agreement in respect of which a direction under section 21(2) of the Restrictive Trade Practices Act 1976 is in force immediately before the coming into force of section 2 ("a section 21(2) agreement").

(2) If a material variation is made to a section 21(2) agreement, sub-paragraph (1) ceases to apply to the agreement on the coming into force of the variation.

(3) Sub-paragraph (1) does not apply to a particular section 21(2) agreement if the Director gives a direction under this paragraph to that effect.

(4) If the Director is considering whether to give a direction under this paragraph, he may by notice in writing require any party to the agreement in question to give him such information in connection with the agreement as he may require.

(5) The Director may give a direction under this paragraph only as provided in sub-paragraph (6) or (7).

(6) If at the end of such period as may be specified in rules under section 51 a person had failed, without reasonable excuse, to comply with a requirement imposed under sub-paragraph (4), the Director may give a direction under this paragraph.

(7) The Director may also give a direction under this paragraph if he considers —

(a) that the agreement will, if not excluded, infringe the Chapter I prohibition; and

(b) that he is not likely to grant it an unconditional individual exemption.

(8) For the purposes of sub-paragraph (7) an individual exemption is unconditional if no conditions or obligations are imposed in respect of it under section 4(3)(a).

(9) A direction under this paragraph —

(a) must be in writing;

(b) may be made so as to have effect from a date specified in the direction (which may not be earlier than the date on which it is given).

EEA Regulated Markets

3. — (1) The Chapter I prohibition does not apply to an agreement for the constitution of an EEA regulated market to the extent to which the agreement relates to any of the rules made, or guidance issued, by that market.

(2) The Chapter I prohibition does not apply to a decision made by an EEA regulated market, to the extent to which the decision relates to any of the market's regulating provisions.

(3) The Chapter I prohibition does not apply to —

(a) any practices of an EEA regulated market; or

(b) any practices which are trading practices in relation to an EEA regulated market.

(4) The Chapter I prohibition does not apply to an agreement the parties to which are or include —

(a) an EEA regulated market, or

(b) a person who is subject to the rules of that market,

to the extent to which the agreement consists of provisions the inclusion of which is required or contemplated by the regulating provisions of that market.

(5) In this paragraph —
"EEA regulated market" is a market which —

(a) is listed by EEA State other than the United Kingdom pursuant to article 16 of Council Directive No. 93/22/EEC of 10th May 1993 on investment services in the securities field; and

(b) operates without any requirement that a person dealing on the market should have a physical presence in the EEA State from which any trading facilities are provided or on any trading floor that the market may have;

"EEA State" means a State which is a contracting party to the EEA Agreement;
"regulating provisions", in relation to an EEA regulated market, means —

(a) rules made, or guidance issued, by that market,

(b) practices of that market, or

(c) practices which, in relation to that market, are trading practices;

"trading practices", in relation to an EEA regulated market, means practices of persons who are subject to the rules made by that market, and —

(a) which relate to business in respect of which those persons are subject to the rules of that market, and which are required or contemplated by those rules or by guidance issued by that market; or

(b) which are otherwise attributable to the conduct of that market as such.

Services of general economic interest etc.

4. Neither the Chapter I prohibition nor the Chapter II prohibition applies to an undertaking entrusted with the operation of services of general economic interest or having the character of a revenue-producing monopoly in so far as the prohibition would obstruct the performance, in law or in fact, of the particular tasks assigned to that understanding.

Compliance with legal requirements

5. — (1) The Chapter I prohibition does not apply to an agreement to the extent to which it is made in order to comply with a legal requirement.

(2) The Chapter II prohibition does not apply to an agreement to the extent to which it is made in order to comply with a legal requirement.

(3) In this paragraph "legal requirement" means a requirement —

(a) imposed by or under any enactment in force in the United Kingdom;

(b) imposed by or under the Treaty or the EEA Agreement and having legal effect in the United Kingdom without further enactment; or

(c) imposed by or under the law in force in another Member State and having legal effect in the United Kingdom.

Avoidance of conflict with international obligations

6. — (1) If the Secretary of State is satisfied that, in order to avoid a conflict between provisions of this Part and an international obligation of the United Kingdom, it would be appropriate for the Chpater I prohibition not to apply to —

(a) a particular agreement, or

(b) any agreement of a particular description,

he may by order exclude the agreement, or agreements of that description, from the Chapter I prohibition.

(2) An order under sub-paragraph (1) may make provision for the exclusion of the agreement or agreements to which the order applies, or of such of them as may be specified, only in specified circumstances.

(3) An order under sub-paragraph (1) may also provide that the Chapter I prohibition is to be deemed never to have applied in relation to the agreement or agreements, or in relation to such of them as may be specified.

(4) If the Secretary of State is satisfied that, in order to avoid a conflict between provisions of this Part and an international obligation of the United Kingdom, it would be appropriate for the Chapter II prohibition not to apply in particular circumstances, he may by order provide for it not to apply in such circumstances as may be specified.

(5) An order under sub-paragraph (4) may provide that the Chapter II prohibition is to be deemed never to have applied in relation to specified conduct.

(6) An international arrangement relating to civil aviation and designated by an order made by the Secretary of State is to be treated as an international obligation for the purposes of this paragraph.

(7) In this paragraph and paragraph 7 "specified" means specified in the order.

Public policy

7. — (1) If the Secretary of State is satisfied that there are exceptional and compelling reasons of public policy why the Chapter I prohibition ought not to apply to —

(a) a particular agreement, or

(b) any agreement of a particular description,

he may by order exclude the agreement, or agreements of that description, from the Chapter I prohibition.

(2) An order under sub-paragraph (1) may make provision for the exclusion of the agreement or agreements to which the order applies, or of such of them as may be specified, only in specified circumstances.

(3) An order under sub-paragraph (1) may also provide that the Chapter I prohibition is to be deemed never to have applied in relation to the agreement or agreements, or in relation to such of them as may be specified.

(4) If the Secretary of State is satisfied that there are exceptional and compelling reasons of public policy why the Chapter II prohibition ought not to apply in particular circumstances, he may by order provide for it not to apply in such circumstances as may be specified.

(5) An order under sub-paragraph (4) may provide that the Chapter II prohibition is to be deemed never to have applied in relation to specified conduct.

Coal and steel

8. — (1) The Chapter I prohibition does not apply to an agreement which relates to a coal or steel product to the extent to which the ECSC Treaty gives the Commission exclusive jurisdiction in the matter.

(2) Sub-paragraph (1) ceases to have effect on the date on which the ECSC Treaty expires ("the expiry date").

(3) The Chapter II prohibition does not apply to conduct which relates to a coal or steel product to the extent to which the ECSC Treaty gives the Commission exclusive jurisdiction in the matter.

(4) Sub-paragraph (3) ceases to have effect on the expiry date.

(5) In this paragraph —
"coal or steel product" means any product of a kind listed in Annex I to the ECSC Treaty; and
"ECSC Treaty" means the Treaty establishing the European Coal and Steel Community.

Agricultural products

9. — (1) The Chapter I prohibition does not apply to an agreement to the extent to which it relates to production of or trade in an agricultural product and —

(a) forms an integral part of a national market organisation;

(b) is necessary for the attainment of the objectives set out in Article 39 of the Treaty; or

(c) is an agreement of farmers or farmers' associations (or associations of such association) belonging to a single member State which concerns —

(i) the production or sale of agricultural products, or
(ii) the use of joint facilities for the storage, treatment or processing of agricultural products,

and under which there is no obligation to charge identical prices.

(2) If the Commission determines that an agreement does not fulfil the conditions specified by the provision for agricultural products for exclusion from Article 85(1), the exclusion provided by this paragraph ("the agriculture exclusion") is to be treated as ceasing to apply to the agreement on the date of the decision.

(3) The agriculture exclusion does not apply to a particular agreement if the Director gives a direction under this paragraph to that effect.

(4) If the Director is considering whether to give a direction under this paragraph, he may by notice in writing require any party to the agreement in question to give him such information in connection with the agreement as he may require.

(5) The Director may give a direction under this paragraph only as provided in sub-paragraph (6) or (7).

(6) If at the end of such period as may be specified in rules under section 51 a person has failed, without reasonable excuse, to comply with a requirement imposed under sub-paragraph (4), the Director may give a direction under this paragraph.

(7) The Director may also give a direction under this paragraph if he considers that an agreement (whether or not he considers that it infringes the Chapter I prohibition) is likely, or is intended, substantially and unjustifiably to prevent, restrict or distort competition in relation to an agricultural product.

(8) A direction under this paragraph —

(a) must be in writing;

(b) may be made so as to have effect from a date specified in the direction (which may not be earlier than the date on which it is given).

(9) In this paragraph —
"agricultural product" means any product of a kind listed in Annex II to the Treaty; and
"provision for agricultural products" means Council Regulation (EEC) No. 26/62 of 4th April 1962 applying certain rules of competition to production of and trade in agricultural products.

Section 3(1)(d).

SCHEDULE 4

PROFESSIONAL RULES

PART I

EXCLUSION

General

1. — (1) To the extent to which an agreement (either on its own or when taken together with another agreement) —

(a) constitutes a designated professional rule,

(b) imposes obligations arising from designated professional rules, or

(c) constitutes an agreement to act in accordance with such rules, the Chapter I prohibition does not apply to the agreement.

(2) In this Schedule —
"designated" means designated by the Secretary of State under paragraph 2;
"professional rules" means rules regulating a professional service or the persons providing, or wishing to provide, that service;
"professional service" means any of the services described in Part II of this Schedule; and
"rules" includes regulations, codes of practice and statements of principle.

Designated rules

2. — (1) The Secretary of State must establish and maintain a list designating, for the purposes of this Schedule, rules —

(a) which are notified to him under paragraph 3; and

(b) which, in his opinion, are professional rules.

(2) The list is to be established, and any alteration in the list is to be effected, by an order made by the Secretary of State.

(3) The designation of any rule is to have effect from such date (which may be earlier than the date on which the order listing it is made) as may be specified in that order.

Application for designation

3. — (1) Any body regulating a professional service or the persons who provide, or wish to provide, that service may apply to the Secretary of State for rules of that body to be designated.

(2) An application under this paragraph must —

(a) be accompanied by a copy of the rules to which it relates; and

(b) be made in the prescribed manner.

Alterations

4. — (1)A rule does not cease to be a designated professional rule merely because it is altered.

(2) If such a rule is altered (whether by being modified, revoked or replaced), the body concerned must notify the Secretary of State and the Director of the alteration as soon as is reasonably practicable.

Reviewing the list

5. — (1) The Secretary of State must send to the Director —

(a) a copy of any order made under paragraph 2; and

(b) a copy of the professional rules to which the order relates.

(2) The Director must —

(a) retain any copy of a professional rule which is sent to him under subparagraph (1)(b) so long as the rule remains in force;

(b) maintain a copy of the list, as altered from time to time; and

(c) keep the list under review.

(3) If the Director considers —

(a) that, with a view to restricting the exclusion provided by this Schedule, some or all of the rules of a particular body should no longer be designated, or

(b) that rules which are not designated should be designated,

he must advise the Secretary of State accordingly.

Removal from the list

6. — (1) This paragraph applies if the Secretary of State receives advice under paragraph 5(3)(a).

(2) If it appears to the Secretary of State that another Minister of the Crown has functions in relation to the professional service concerned, he must consult that Minister.

(3) If it appears to the Secretary of State, having considered the Director's advice and the advice of any other Minister resulting from consultation under sub-paragraph (2), that the rules in question should no longer be designated, he may by order revoke their designation.

(4) Revocation of a designation is to have effect from such date as the order revoking it may specify.

Inspection

7. — (1) Any person may inspect, and take a copy of —

(a) any entry in the list of designated professional rules as kept by the Director under paragraph 5(2); or

(b) any copy of professional rules retained by him under paragraph 5(1).

(2) The right conferred by sub-paragraph (1) is to be exercised only —

(a) at a time which is reasonable;

(b) on payment of such fee as the Director may determine; and

(c) at such offices of his as the Director may direct.

PART II

PROFESSIONAL SERVICES

Legal

8. The services of barristers, advocates or solicitors.

Medical

9. The provision of medical or surgical advice or attendance and the performance of surgical operations.

Dental

10. Any services falling within the practice of dentistry within the meaning of the Dentists Act 1984.

Ophthalmic

11. The testing of sight.

Veterinary

12. Any services which constitute veterinary surgery within the meaning of the Veterinary Surgeons Act 1966.

Nursing

13. The services of nurses.

Midwifery

14. The services of midwives.

Physiotherapy

15. The services of physiotherapists.

Chiropody

16. The services of chiropodists.

Architectural

17. The services of architects.

Accounting and auditing

18. The making or preparation of accounts or accounting records and the examination, verification and auditing of financial statements.

Insolvency

19. Insolvency services within the meaning of section 428 of the Insolvency Act 1986.

Patent agency

20. The services of registered patent agents (within the meaning of Part V of the Copyright, Designs and Patents Act 1988).

21. The services of persons carrying on for gain in the United Kingdom the business of acting as agents or other representatives for or obtaining European patents or for the purpose of conducting proceedings in relation to applications for or otherwise in connection with such patents before the European Patent Office or the comptroller and whose names appear on the European list (within the meaning of Part V of the Copyright, Designs and Patents Act 1988).

Parliamentary agency

22. The services of parliamentary agents entered in the register in either House of Parliament as agents entitled to practise both in promoting and in opposing Bills.

Surveying

23. The services of surveyors of land, of quantity surveyors, of surveyors of buildings or other structures and of surveyors of ships.

Engineering and technology etc.

24. The services of persons practising or employed as consultants in the field of —

   (a) civil engineering;

   (b) mechanical, aeronautical, marine, electrical or electronic engineering;

   (c) mining, quarrying, soil analysis or other forms of mineralogy or geology;

   (d) agronomy, forestry, livestock rearing or ecology;

   (e) metallurgy, chemistry, biochemistry or physics; or

   (f) any other form of engineering or technology analogous to those mentioned in sub-paragraphs (a) to (e).

Educational

25. The provision of education or training.

Religious

26. The services of ministers of religion.

SCHEDULE 5   **Section 12(2).**

NOTIFICATION UNDER CHAPTER I: PROCEDURE

Terms used

1. In this Schedule —
"applicant" means the person making an application to which this Schedule applies;
"application" means an application under section 13 or an application under section 14;
"application for guidance" means an application under section 13;
"application for a decision" means an application under section 14;
"rules" means rules made by the Director under section 51; and
"specified" means specified in the rules.

General rules about applications

2. — (1) An application must be made in accordance with rules.

(2) A party to an agreement who makes an application must take all reasonable steps to notify all other parties to the agreement of whom he is aware —

(a) that the application has been made; and

(b) as to whether it is for guidance or a decision.

(3) Notification under sub-paragraph (2) must be in the specified manner.

Preliminary investigation

3. — (1) If, after a preliminary investigation of an application, the Director considers that it is likely —

(a) that the agreement concerned will infringe the Chapter I prohibition, and

(b) that it would not be appropriate to grant the agreement an individual exemption,

he may make a decision ("a provisional decision") under this paragraph.

(2) If the Director makes a provisional decision —

(a) the Director must notify the applicant in writing of his provisional decision; and

(b) section 13(4) or (as the case may be) section 14(4) is to be taken as never having applied.

(3) When making a provisional decision, the Director must follow such procedure as may be specified.

(4) A provisional decision does not affect the final determination of an application.

(5) If the Director has given notice to the applicant under sub-paragraph (2) in respect of an application for a decision, he may continue with the application under section 14.

Procedure on application for guidance

4. When determining an application for guidance, the Director must follow such procedure as may be specified.

Procedure on application for a decision

5. — (1) When determining an application for a decision, the Director must follow such procedure as may be specified.
(2) The Director must arrange for the application to be published in such a way as he thinks most suitable for bringing it to the attention of those likely to be affected by it, unless he is satisfied that it will be sufficient for him to seek information from one or more particular persons other than the applicant.
(3) In determining the application, the Director must take into account any representations made to him by persons other than the applicant.

Publication of decisions

6. If the Director determines an application for a decision he must publish his decision, together with his reasons for making it, in such manner as may be specified.

Delay by the Director

7. — (1) This paragraph applies if the court is satisfied, on the application of a person aggrieved by the failure of the Director to determine an application for a decision in accordance with the specified procedure, that there has been undue delay on the part of the Director in determining the application.

(2) The court may give such directions to the Director as it considers appropriate for securing that the application is determined without unnecessary further delay.

Section 20(2)   SCHEDULE 6

NOTIFICATION UNDER CHAPTER II: PROCEDURE

Terms used

1. In this Schedule —
"applicant" means the person making an application to which this Schedule applies;
"application" means an application under section 21 or an application under section 22;
"application for guidance" means an application under section 21;
"application for a decision" means an application under section 22;
"other party", in relation to conduct of two or more persons, means one of those persons other than the applicant;
"rules" means rules made by the Director under sections 51; and
"specified" means specified in the rules.

General rules about applications

2. — (1) An application must be made in accordance with rules.

(2) If the conduct to which an application relates is conduct of two or more persons, the applicant must take all reasonable steps to notify all of the other parties of whom he is aware —

(a) that the application has been made; and

(b) as to whether it is for guidance or a decision.

(3) Notification under sub-paragraph (2) must be in the specified manner.

Preliminary investigation

3. — (1) If, after a preliminary investigation of an application, the Director considers that it is likely that the conduct concerned will infringe the Chapter II prohibition, he may make a decision ("a provisional decision") under this paragraph.

(2) If the Director makes a provisional decision, he must notify the applicant in writing of that decision.

(3) When making a provisional decision, the Director must follow such procedure as may be specified.

(4) A provisional decision does not affect the final determination of an application.

(5) If the Director has given notice to the applicant under sub-paragraph (2) in respect of an application for a decision, he may continue with the application under section 22.

Procedure on application for guidance

4. When determining an application for guidance, the Director must follow such procedure as may be specified.

Procedure on application for a decision

5. — (1) When determining an application for a decision, the Director must follow such procedure as may be specified.

(2) The Director must arrange for the application to be published in such a way as he thinks most suitable for bringing it to the attention of those likely to be affected by it, unless he is satisfied that it will be sufficient for him to seek information from one or more particular persons other than the applicant.

(3) In determining the application, the Director must take into account any representations made to him by persons other than the applicant.

Publication of decisions

6. If the Director determines an application for a decision he must publish his decision, together with his reasons for making it, in such manner as may be specified.

Delay by the Director

7. — (1) This paragraph applies if the court is satisfied, on the application of a person aggrieved by the failure of the Director to determine an application for a decision in accordance with the specified procedure, that there has been undue delay on the part of the Director in determining the application.

(2) The court may give such directions to the Director as it considers appropriate for securing that the application is determined without unnecessary further delay.

SECTION 45(7). Schedule 7

THE COMPETITION COMMISSION

PART I

GENERAL

Interpretation

1. In this Schedule —
"the 1973 Act" means the Fair Trading Act 1973;
"appeal panel member" means a member appointed under paragraph 2(1)(a);
"Chairman" means the chairman of the Commission;
"the Commission" means the Competition Commission;
"Council" has the meaning given in paragraph 5;
"general functions" means any functions of the Commission other than functions —

(a) in connection with appeals under this Act; or

(b) which are to be discharged by the Council;
"member" means a member of the Commission;
"newspaper merger reference" means a newspaper merger reference under section 59 of the 1973 Act;
"President" has the meaning given by paragraph 4(2);
"reporting panel member" means a member appointed under paragraph 2(1)(b);
"secretary" means the secretary of the Commission appointed under paragraph 9; and
"specialist panel member" means a member appointed under any of the provisions mentioned in paragraph 2(1)(d).

Membership of the Commission

2. — (1) The Commission is to consist of —

(a) members appointed by the Secretary of State to form a panel for the purposes of the Commission's functions in relation to appeals;

(b) members appointed by the Secretary of State to form a panel for the purposes of the Commission's general functions;

(c) members appointed (in accordance with paragraph 15(5)) from the panel maintained under paragraph 22;

(d) members appointed by the Secretary of State under or by virtue of —

(i) section 12(4) or 14(8) of the Water Industry Act 1991;
(ii) section 12(9) of the Electricity Act 1989;
(iii) section 13(1) of the Telecommunications Act 1984;
(iv) Article 15(9) of the Electricity (Northern Ireland) Order 1992.

(2) A person who is appointed as a member of a kind mentioned in one of paragraphs (a) to (c) of sub-paragraph (3) may also be appointed as a member of either or both of the other kinds mentioned in those paragraphs.

(3) The kinds of member are —

(a) an appeal panel member;

(b) a reporting panel member;

(c) a specialist panel member.

(4) Before appointing a person who is qualified for appointment to the panel of chairmen (see paragraph 26(2)), the Secretary of State must consult the Lord Chancellor or Lord Advocate, as he considers appropriate.

(5) The validity of the Commission's proceedings is not affected by a defect in the appointment of a member.

Chairman and deputy chairmen

3. — (1) The Commission is to have a chairman appointed by the Secretary of State from among the reporting panel members.

(2) The Secretary of State may appoint one or more of the reporting panel members to act as deputy chairman.

(3) The Chairman, and any deputy chairman, may resign that office at any time by notice in writing addressed to the Secretary of State.

(4) If the Chairman (or a deputy chairman) ceases to be a member he also ceases to be Chairman (or a deputy chairman).

(5) If the Chairman is absent or otherwise unable to act, or there is no chairman, any of his functions may be performed —

    (a) if there is one deputy chairman, by him;

    (b) if there is more than one —

        (i) by the deputy chairman designated by the Secretary of State; or
        (ii) if no such designation has been made, by the deputy chairman designated by the deputy chairmen;

    (c) if there is no deputy chairman able to act —

        (i) by the member designated by the Secretary of State; or
        (ii) if no such designation has been made, by the member designated by the Commission.

President

4. — (1) The Secretary of State must appoint one of the appeal panel members to preside over the discharge of the Commission's functions in relation to appeals.

(2) The member so appointed is to be known as the President of the Competition Commission Appeal Tribunals (but is referred to in this Schedule as "the President").

(3) The Secretary of State may not appoint a person to be the President unless that person —

    (a) has a ten year general qualification within the meaning of section 71 of the Courts and Legal Services Act 1990,

    (b) is an advocate or solicitor in Scotland of at least ten years' standing, or

    (c) is —

        (i) a member of the Bar of Northern Ireland of at least ten years standing, or
        (ii) a solicitor of the Supreme Court of Northern Ireland of at least ten years' standing,

and appears to the Secretary of State to have appropriate experience and knowledge of competition law and practice.

(4) Before appointing the President, the Secretary of State must consult the Lord Chancellor or Lord Advocate, as he considers appropriate.

(5) If the President ceases to be a member he also ceases to be President.

The Council

5. — (1) The Commission is to have a management board to be known as the Competition Commission Council (but referred to in this Schedule as "the Council").

(2) The Council is to consist of —

    (a) the Chairman;

    (b) the President;

(c) such other members as the Secretary of State may appoint; and

(d) the secretary.

(3) In exercising its functions under paragraphs 3 and 7 to 12 and paragraph 5 of Schedule 8, the Commission is to act through the Council.

(4) The Council may determine its own procedure including, in particular, its quorum.

(5) The Chairman (and any person acting as Chairman) is to have a casting vote on any question being decided by the Council.

Term of office

6. — (1) Subject to the provisions of this Schedule, each member is to hold and vacate office in accordance with the terms of his appointment.

(2) A person is not to be appointed as a member for more than five years at a time.

(3) Any member may at any time resign by notice in writing addressed to the Secretary of State.

(4) The Secretary of State may remove a member on the ground of incapacity or misbehaviour.

(5) No person is to be prevented from being appointed as a member merely because he has previously been a member.

Expenses, remuneration and pensions

7. — (1) The Secretary of State shall pay to the Commission such sums as he considers appropriate to enable it to perform its functions.

(2) The Commission may pay, or make provision for paying, to or in respect of each member such salaries or other remuneration and such pensions, allowances, fees, expenses or gratuities as the Secretary of State may determine.

(3) If a person ceases to be a member otherwise than on the expiry of his term of office and it appears to the Secretary of State that there are special circumstances which make it right for him to receive compensation, the Commission may make a payment to him of such amount as the Secretary of State may determine.

(4) The approval of the Treasury is required for —

(a) any payment under sub-paragraph (1);

(b) any determination of the Secretary of State under sub-paragraph (2) or (3).

The Commission's powers

8. Subject to the provisions of this Schedule, the Commission has power to do anything (except borrow money) —

(a) calculated to facilitate the discharge of its functions; or

(b) incidental or conducive to the discharge of its functions.

Staff

9. — (1) The Commission is to have a secretary appointed by the Secretary of State on such terms and conditions of service as he considers appropriate.

(2) The approval of the Treasury is required as to those terms and conditions.

(3) Before appointing a person to be secretary, the Secretary of State must consult the Chairman and the President.

(4) Subject to obtaining the approval of —

(a) the Secretary of State, as to numbers, and

(b) the Secretary of State and Treasury, as to terms and conditions of service,

the Commission may appoint such staff as it thinks appropriate.

Procedure

10. Subject to any provision made by or under this Act, the Commission may regulate its own procedure.

Application of seal and proof of instruments

11. — (1) The application of the seal of the Commission must be authenticated by the signature of the secretary or of some other person authorised for the purpose.

(2) Sub-paragraph (1) does not apply in relation to any document which is or is to be signed in accordance with the law of Scotland.

(3) A document purporting to be duly executed under the seal of the Commission —

(a) is to be received in evidence; and

(b) is to be taken to have been so executed unless the contrary is proved.

Accounts

12. — (1) The Commission must —

(a) keep proper accounts and proper records in relation to its accounts;

(b) prepare a statement of accounts in respect of each of its financial years; and

(c) send copies of the statement to the Secretary of State and to the Comptroller and Auditor General before the end of the month of August next following the financial year to which the statement relates.

(2) The statement of accounts must comply with any directions given by the Secretary of State with the approval of the Treasury as to —

(a) the information to be contained in it,

(b) the manner in which the information contained in it is to be presented, or

(c) the methods and principles according to which the statement is to be prepared,

and must contain such additional information as the Secretary of State may with the approval of the Treasury require to be provided for informing Parliament.

(3) The Comptroller and Auditor General must —

(a) examine, certify and report on each statement received by him as a result of this paragraph; and

(b) lay copies of each statement and of his report before each House of Parliament.

(4) In this paragraph "financial year" means the period beginning with the date on which the Commission is established and ending with March 31st next, and each successive period of twelve months.

Status

13. — (1) The Commission is not to be regarded as the servant or agent of the Crown or as enjoying any status, privilege or immunity of the Crown.

(2) The Commission's property is not to be regarded as property of, or held on behalf of, the Crown.

PART II

PERFORMANCE OF THE COMMISSION'S GENERAL FUNCTIONS

Interpretation

14. In this Part of this Schedule "group" means a group selected under paragraph 15.

Discharge of certain functions by groups

15. — (1) Except where sub-paragraph (7) gives the Chairman power to act on his own, any general function of the Commission must be performed through a group selected for the purpose by the Chairman.

(2) The group must consist of at least three persons one of whom may be the Chairman.

(3) In selecting the members of the group, the Chairman must comply with any requirement as to its constitution imposed by any enactment applying to specialist panel members.

(4) If the functions to be performed through the group relate to a newspaper merger reference, the group must, subject to sub-paragraph (5), consist of such reporting panel members as the Chairman may select.

(5) The Secretary of State may appoint one, two or three persons from the panel maintained under paragraph 22 to be members and, if he does so, the group —

(a) must include that member or those members; and

(b) if there are three such members, may (if the Chairman so decides) consist entirely of those members.

(6) Subject to sub-paragraphs (2) to (5), a group must consist of reporting panel members or specialist panel members selected by the Chairman.

(7) While a group is being constituted to perform a particular general function of the Commission, the Chairman may —

(a) take such steps (falling within that general function) as he considers appropriate to facilitate the work of the group when it has been constituted; or

(b) exercise the power conferred by section 75(5) of the 1973 Act (setting aside references).

Chairmen of groups

16. The Chairman must appoint one of the members of a group to act as the chairman of the group.

Replacement of member of group

17. — (1) If, during the proceedings of a group —

(a) a member of the group ceases to be a member of the Commission,

(b) the Chairman is satisfied that a member of the group will be unable for a substantial period to perform his duties as a member of the group, or

(c) it appears to the Chairman that because of a particular interest of a member of the group it is inappropriate for him to remain in the group,

the Chairman may appoint a replacement.

(2) The Chairman may also at any time appoint any reporting panel member to be an additional member of a group.

Attendance of other members

18. — (1) At the invitation of the chairman of a group, any reporting panel member who is not a member of the group may attend meetings or otherwise take part in the proceedings of the group.

(2) But any person attending in response to such an invitation may not —

(a) vote in any proceedings of the group; or

(b) have a statement of his dissent from a conclusion of the group included in a report made by them.

(3) Nothing in sub-paragraph (1) is to be taken to prevent a group, or a member of a group, from consulting any member of the Commission with respect to any matter or question with which the group is concerned.

Procedure

19. — (1) Subject to any special or general directions given by the Secretary of State, each group may determine its own procedure.

(2) Each group may, in particular, determine its quorum and determine —

(a) the extent, if any, to which persons interested or claiming to be interested in the subject-matter of the reference are allowed —

(i) to be present or to be heard, either by themselves or by their representatives;
(ii) to cross-examine witnesses; or
(iii) otherwise to take part; and

(b) the extent, if any, to which sittings of the group are to be held in public.

(3) In determining its procedure a group must have regard to any guidance issued by the Chairman.

(4) Before issuing any guidance for the purposes of this paragraph the Chairman must consult the members of the Commission.

Effect of exercise of functions by group

20. — (1) Subject to sub-paragraph (2), anything done by or in relation to a group in, or in connection with, the performance of functions to be performed by the group is to have the same effect as if done by or in relation to the Commission.

(2) For the purposes of —

    (a) sections 56 and 73 of the 1973 Act,

    (b) section 19A of the Agricultural Marketing Act 1958,

    (c) Articles 23 and 42 of the Agricultural Marketing (Northern Ireland) Order 1982,

a conclusion contained in a report of a group is to be disregarded if the conclusion is not that of at least two-thirds of the members of the group.

Casting votes

21. The chairman of a group is to have a casting vote on any question to be decided by the group.

Newspaper merger references

22. The Secretary of State must maintain a panel of persons whom he regards as suitable for selection as members of a group constituted in connection with a newspaper merger reference.

Part III

Appeals

Interpretation

23. In this Part of this Schedule —
"panel of chairmen" means the panel appointed under paragraph 26; and
"tribunal" means an appeal tribunal constituted in accordance with paragraph 27.

Training of appeal panel members

24. The President must arrange such training for appeal panel members as he considers appropriate.

Acting President

25. If the President is absent or otherwise unable to act, the Secretary of State may appoint as acting president an appeal panel member who is qualified to act as chairman of a tribunal.

Panel of tribunal chairmen

26. — (1) There is to be a panel of appeal panel members appointed by the Secretary of State for the purposes of providing chairmen of appeal tribunals established under this Part of this Schedule.

(2) A person is qualified for appointment to the panel of chairmen only if —

    (a) he has a seven year general qualification within the meaning of section 71 of the Courts and Legal Services Act 1990,

    (b) he is an advocate or solicitor in Scotland of at least seven years' standing, or

    (c) he is —

        (i) a member of the Bar of Northern Ireland of at least seven years' standing, or
        (ii) a solicitor of the Supreme Court of Northern Ireland of at least seven years' standing,

and appears to the Secretary of State to have appropriate experience and knowledge of competition law and practice.

Constitution of tribunals

27. — (1) On receipt of a notice of appeal, the President must constitute an appeal tribunal to deal with the appeal.

(2) An appeal tribunal is to consist of —

(a) a chairman, who must be either the President or a person appointed by him to be chairman from the panel of chairmen; and

(b) two other appeal panel members appointed by the President.

PART IV

MISCELLANEOUS

Disqualification of members for House of Commons

28. In Part II of Schedule 1 to the House of Commons Disqualification Act 1975 (bodies of which all members are disqualified) insert at the appropriate place —
"The Competition Commission".

Disqualification of members for Northern Ireland Assembly

29. In Part II of Schedule 1 to the Northern Ireland Assembly Disqualification Act 1975 (bodies of which all members are disqualified) insert at the appropriate place —
"The Competition Commission".

PART V

TRANSITIONAL

Interpretation

30. In this Part of this Schedule —
"commencement date" means the date on which section 45 comes into force; and
"MMC" means the Monopolies and Mergers Commission.

Chairman

31. — (1) The person who is Chairman of the MMC immediately before the commencement date is on that date to become both a member of the Commission and its chairman as if he had been duly appointed under paragraphs 2(1)(b) and 3.

(2) He is to hold office as Chairman of the Commission for the remainder of the period for which he was appointed as Chairman of the MMC and on the terms on which he was so appointed.

Deputy chairmen

32. The persons who are deputy chairmen of the MMC immediately before the commencement date are on that date to become deputy chairmen of the Commission as if they had been duly appointed under paragraph 3(2).

Reporting panel members

33. — (1) The persons who are members of the MMC immediately before the commencement date are on that date to become members of the Commission as if they had been duly appointed under paragraph 2(1)(b).

(2) Each of them is to hold office as a member for the remainder of the period for which he was appointed as a member of the MMC and on the terms on which he was so appointed.

Specialist panel members

34. — (1) The persons who are members of the MMC immediately before the commencement date by virtue of appointments made under any of the enactment's mentioned in paragraph 2(1)(d) are on that date to become members of the Commission as if they had been duly appointed to the Commission under the enactment in question.

(2) Each of them is to hold office as a member for such period and on such terms as the Secretary of State may determine.

Secretary

35. The person who is the secretary of the MMC immediately before the commencement date is on that date to become the secretary of the Commission as if duly appointed under paragraph 9, on the same terms and conditions.

Council

36. — (1) The members who became deputy chairmen of the Commission under paragraph 32 are also to become members of the Council as if they had been duly appointed under paragraph 5(2)(c).

(2) Each of them is to hold office as a member of the Council for such period as the Secretary of State determines.

Sections 46(5) and 48(4).   SCHEDULE 8

APPEALS

PART I

GENERAL

Interpretation

1. In this Schedule —
"the chairman" means a person appointed as chairman of a tribunal in accordance with paragraph 27(2)(a)
   of Schedule 7;
"the President" means the President of the Competition Commission Appeal Tribunals appointed under paragraph 4 of Schedule 7;
"rules" means rules made by the Secretary of State under section 48;
"specified" means specified in rules;
"tribunal" means an appeal tribunal constituted in accordance with paragraph 27 of Schedule 7.

General procedure

2. — (1) An appeal to the Competition Commission must be made by sending a notice of appeal to the Commission within the specified period.

(2) The notice of appeal must set out the grounds of appeal in sufficient detail to indicate —

   (a) under which provision of this Act the appeal is brought;

   (b) to what extent (if any) the appellant contends that the decision against, or with respect to which, the appeal is brought was based on an error of fact or was wrong in law; and

   (c) to what extent (if any) the appellant is appealing against the Director's exercise of his discretion in making the disputed decision.

(3) The tribunal may give an appellant leave to amend the grounds of appeal identified in the notice of appeal.

Decisions of the tribunal

3. — (1) The tribunal must determine the appeal on the merits by reference to the grounds of appeal set out in the notice of appeal.

(2) The tribunal may confirm or set aside the decision which is the subject of the appeal, or any part of it, and may —

   (a) remit the matter to the Director,

   (b) impose or revoke, or vary the amount of, a penalty,

   (c) grant or cancel an individual exemption or vary any conditions or obligations imposed in relation to the exemption by the Director,

   (d) give such directions, or take such other steps, as the Director could himself have given or taken, or

   (e) make any other decision which the Director could himself have made.

(3) Any decision of the tribunal on an appeal has the same effect, and may be enforced in the same manner, as a decision of the Director.

(4) If the tribunal confirms the decision which is the subject of the appeal it may nevertheless set aside any finding of fact on which the decision was based.

4. — (1) A decision of the tribunal may be taken by a majority.

(2) The decision must —

(a) state whether it was unanimous or taken by a majority; and

(b) be recorded in a document which —

    (i) contains a statement of the reasons for the decision; and
    (ii) is signed and dated by the chairman of the tribunal.

(3) When the tribunal is preparing the document mentioned in sub-paragraph (2)(b), section 56 is to apply to the tribunal as it applies to the Director.

(4) The President must make such arrangements for the publication of the tribunal's decision as he considers appropriate.

PART II

RULES

Registrar of Appeal Tribunals

5. — (1) Rules may provide for the appointment by the Competition Commission, with the approval of the Secretary of State, of a Registrar of Appeal Tribunals.

(2) The rules may, in particular —

(a) specify the qualifications for appointment as Registrar; and

(b) provide for specified functions relating to appeals to be exercised by the Registrar in specified circumstances.

Notice of appeal

6. Rules may make provision —

(a) as to the period within which appeals must be brought;

(b) as to the form of the notice of appeal and as to the information which must be given in the notice;

(c) with respect to amendment of a notice of appeal;

(d) with respect to acknowledgement of a notice of appeal.

Response to the appeal

7. Rules may provide for the tribunal to reject an appeal if —

(a) it considers that the notice of appeal reveals no valid ground of appeal; or

(b) it is satisfied that the appellant has habitually and persistently and without any reasonable ground —

    (i) instituted vexatious proceedings, whether against the same person or against different persons; or
    (ii) made vexatious applications in any proceedings.

Pre-hearing reviews and preliminary matters

8. — (1) Rules may make provision —

(a) for the carrying-out by the tribunal of a preliminary consideration of proceedings (a "pre-hearing review"); and

(b) for enabling such powers to be exercised in connection with a pre-hearing review as may be specified.

(2) If rules make provision of the kind mentioned in sub-paragraph (1), they may also include —

(a) provision for security; and

(b) supplemental provision.

(3) In sub-paragraph (2) "provision for security" means provision authorising a tribunal carrying out a pre-hearing review under the rules, in specified circumstances, to make an order requiring a party to the proceedings, if he wishes to continue to participate in them, to pay a deposit of an amount not exceeding such sum

(a) as may be specified; or

(b) as may be calculated in accordance with specified provisions.

(4) In sub-paragraph (2) "supplemental provision" means any provision as to —

(a) the manner in which the amount of such a deposit is to be determined;

(b) the consequences of non-payment of such a deposit; and

(c) the circumstances in which any such deposit, or any part of it, may be —

    (i) refunded to the person who paid it; or
    (ii) paid to another party to the proceedings.

Conduct of the hearing

9. — (1) Rules may make provision —

(a) as to the manner in which appeals are to be conducted, including provision for any hearing to be held in private if the tribunal considers it appropriate because it may be considering information of a kind to which section 56 applies;

(b) as to the persons entitled to appear on behalf of the parties;

(c) for requiring persons to attend to give evidence and produce documents and for authorising the administration of oaths to witnesses;

(d) as to the evidence which may be required or admitted in proceedings before the tribunal and the extent to which it should be oral or written;

(e) allowing the tribunal to fix time limits with respect to any aspect of the proceedings before it and to extend any time limit (whether or not it has expired);

(f) for enabling the tribunal to refer a matter back to the Director if it appears to the tribunal that the matter has not been adequately investigated;

(g) for enabling the tribunal, on the application of any party to the proceedings before it or on its own initiative —

    (i) in England and Wales or Northern Ireland, to order the disclosure between, or the production by, the parties of documents or classes of documents;
    (ii) in Scotland, to order such recovery or inspection of documents as might be ordered by a sheriff;

(h) for the appointment of experts for the purposes of any proceedings before the tribunal;

(i) for the award of costs or expenses, including any allowances payable to persons in connection with their attendance before the tribunal;

(j) for taxing or otherwise settling any costs or expenses directed to be paid by the tribunal and for the enforcement of any such direction.

(2) A person who without reasonable excuse fails to comply with —

(a) any requirement imposed by virtue of sub-paragraph (1)(c), or

(b) any requirement with respect to the disclosure, production, recovery or inspection of documents which is imposed by virtue of sub-paragraph (1)(g),

is guilty of an offence and liable on summary conviction to a fine not exceeding level 3 on the standard scale.

Interest

10. — (1) Rules may make provision —

(a) as to the circumstances in which the tribunal may order that interest is payable;

(b) for the manner in which and the periods by reference to which interest is to be calculated and paid.

(2) The rules may, in particular, provide that compound interest is to be payable if the tribunal —

(a) upholds a decision of the Director to impose a penalty, or

(b) does not reduce a penalty so imposed by more than a specified percentage,

but in such a case the rules may not provide that interest is to be payable in respect of any period before the date on which the appeal was brought.

Fees

11. — (1) Rules may provide —

    (a) for fees to be chargeable in respect of specified costs of proceedings before the tribunal;

    (b) for the amount of such costs to be determined by the tribunal.

(2) Any sums received in consequence of rules under this paragraph are to be paid into the Consolidated Fund.

Withdrawing an appeal

12. Rules may make provision —

    (a) that a party who has brought an appeal may not withdraw it without the leave of —

        (i) the tribunal, or
        (ii) in specified circumstances, the President or the Registrar;

    (b) for the tribunal to grant leave to withdraw the appeal on such conditions as it considers appropriate;

    (c) enabling the tribunal to publish any decision which it could have made had the appeal not been withdrawn;

    (d) as to the effect of withdrawal of an appeal;

    (e) as to any procedure to be followed if parties to proceedings on an appeal agree to settle.

Interim orders

13. — (1) Rules may provide for the tribunal to make an order ("an interim order") granting, on an interim basis, any remedy which the tribunal would have power to grant in its final decision.

(2) An interim order may, in particular, suspend the effect of a decision made by the Director or vary the conditions or obligations attached to an exemption.

(3) Rules may also make provision giving the tribunal powers similar to those given to the Director by section 35.

Miscellaneous

14. Rules may make provision —

    (a) for a person who is not a party to proceedings on an appeal to be joined in those proceedings;

    (b) for appeals to be consolidated on such terms as the tribunal thinks appropriate in such circumstances as may be specified.

SCHEDULE 9   **Section 51(2).**

DIRECTOR'S RULES

General

1. In this Schedule —
"application for guidance" means an application for guidance under section 13 or 21;
"application for a decision" means an application for a decision under section 14 or 22;
"guidance" means guidance given under section 13 or 21;
"rules" means rules made by the Director under section 51; and
"specified" means specified in rules.

Applications

2. Rules may make provision —

    (a) as to the form and manner in which an application for guidance or an application for a decision must be made;

    (b) for the procedure to be followed in dealing with the application;

    (c) for the application to be dealt with in accordance with a timetable;

    (d) as to the documents and information which must be given to the Director in connection with the application;

(e) requiring the applicant to give such notice of the application, to such other persons, as may be specified;

(f) as to the consequences of a failure to comply with any rule made by virtue of sub-paragraph (e);

(g) as to the procedure to be followed when the application is subject to the concurrent jurisdiction of the Director and a regulator.

Provisional decisions

3. Rules may make provision as to the procedure to be followed by the Director when making a provisional decision under paragraph 3 of Schedule 5 or paragraph 3 of Schedule 6.

Guidance

4. Rules may make provision as to —

(a) the form and manner in which guidance is to be given;

(b) the procedure to be followed if —

    (i) the Director takes further action with respect to an agreement after giving guidance that it is not likely to infringe the Chapter I prohibition; or

    (ii) the Director takes further action with respect to conduct after giving guidance that it is not likely to infringe the Chapter II prohibition.

Decisions

5. — (1) Rules may make provision as to —

(a) the form and manner in which notice of any decision is to be given;

(b) the person or persons to whom the notice is to be given;

(c) the manner in which the Director is to publish a decision;

(d) the procedure to be followed if —

    (i) the Director takes further action with respect to an agreement after having decided that it does not infringe the Chapter I prohibition; or

    (ii) the Director takes further action with respect to conduct after having decided that it does not infringe the Chapter II prohibition.

(2) In this paragraph "decision" means a decision of the Director (whether or not made on an application) —

(a) as to whether or not an agreement has infringed the Chapter I prohibition, or

(b) as to whether or not conduct has infringed the Chapter II prohibition, and, in the case of an application for a decision under section 14 which includes a request for an individual exemption, includes a decision as to whether or not to grant the exemption.

Individual exemptions

6. Rules may make provision as to —

(a) the procedure to be followed by the Director when deciding whether, in accordance with section 5 —

    (i) to cancel an individual exemption that he has granted,

    (ii) to vary or remove any of its conditions or obligations, or

    (iii) to impose additional conditions or obligations;

(b) the form and manner in which notice of such a decision is to be given.

7. Rules may make provision as to —

(a) the form and manner in which an application under section 4(6) for the extension of an individual exemption is to be made;

(b) the circumstances in which the Director will consider such an application;

(c) the procedure to be followed by the Director when deciding whether to grant such an application;

(d) the form and manner in which notice of such a decision is to be given.

Block exemptions

8. Rules may make provision as to —

(a) the form and manner in which notice of an agreement is to be given to the Director under subsection (1) of section 7;

(b) the procedure to be followed by the Director if he is acting under subsection (2) of that section;

(c) as to the procedure to be followed by the Director if he cancels a block exemption.

Parallel exemptions

9. Rules may make provision as to —

(a) the circumstances in which the Director may —

    (i) impose conditions or obligations in relation to a parallel exemption,
    (ii) vary or remove any such conditions or obligations,
    (iii) impose additional conditions or obligations, or
    (iv) cancel the exemption;

(b) as to the procedure to be followed by the Director if he is acting under section 10(5);

(c) the form and manner in which notice of a decision to take any of the steps in sub-paragraph (a) is to be given;

(d) the circumstances in which an exemption may be cancelled with retrospective effect.

Section 11 exemptions

10. Rules may, with respect to any exemption provided by regulations made under section 11, make provision similar to that made with respect to parallel exemptions by section 10 or by rules under paragraph 9.

Directions withdrawing exclusions

11. Rules may make provision as to the factors which the Director may take into account when he is determining the date on which a direction given under paragraph 4(1) of Schedule 1 or paragraph 2(3) or 9(3) of Schedule 3 is to have effect.

Disclosure of information

12. — (1) Rules may make provision as to the circumstances in which the Director is to be required, before disclosing information given to him by a third party in connection with the exercise of any of the Director's functions under Part I, to give notice, and an opportunity to make representations, to the third party.

(2) In relation to the agreement (or conduct) concerned, "third party" means a person who is not a party to the agreement (or who has not engaged in the conduct).

Applications under section 47

13. Rules may make provision as to —

(a) the period within which an application under section 47(1) must be made;

(b) the procedure to be followed by the Director in dealing with the application;

(c) the person or persons to whom notice of the Director's response to the application is to be given.

Enforcement

14. Rules may make provision as to the procedure to be followed when the Director takes action under any of sections 32 to 41 with respect to the enforcement of the provisions of this Part.

SCHEDULE 10   Sections 54 and 66(5).

REGULATORS

PART I

Monopolies

1. The amendments of the Fair Trading Act 1973 made by sections 66 and 67 of this Act are to have effect, not only in relation to the jurisdiction of the Director under the provisions amended, but also in relation to the jurisdiction under those provisions of each of the following —

(a) the Director General of Telecommunications;

(b) the Director General of Electricity Supply;

(c) the Director General of Electricity Supply for Northern Ireland;

(d) the Director General of Water Services;

(e) the Rail Regulator;

(f) the Director General of Gas Supply; and

(g) the Director General of Gas for Northern Ireland.

PART II

THE PROHIBITIONS

Telecommunications

2. — (1) In consequence of the repeal by this Act of provisions of the Competition Act 1980, the functions transferred by subsection (3) of section 50 of the Telecommunications Act 1984 (functions under 1973 and 1980 Acts) are no longer exercisable by the Director General of Telecommunications.

(2) Accordingly, that Act is amended as follows.

(3) In section 3 (general duties of Secretary of State and Director), in subsection (3)(b), for "section 50" substitute "section 50(1) or (2)".

(4) In section 3, after subsection (3A), insert —

"(3B) Subsections (1) and (2) above do not apply in relation to anything done by the Director in the exercise of functions assigned to him by section 50(3) below ("Competition Act functions").

(3C) The Director may nevertheless, when exercising any Competition Act function, have regard to any matter in respect of which a duty is imposed by subsection (1) or (2) above ("a general matter"), if it is a matter to which the Director General of Fair Trading could have regard when exercising that function; but that is not to be taken as implying that, in relation to any of the matters mentioned in subsection (3) or (3A) above, regard may not be had to any general matter."

(5) Section 50 is amended as follows.

(6) For subsection (3) substitute —

"(3) The Director shall be entitled to exercise, concurrently with the Director General of Fair Trading, the functions of that Director under the provisions of Part I of the Competition Act 1998 (other than sections 38(1) to (6) and 51), so far as relating to —

(a) agreements, decisions or concerted practices of the kind mentioned in section 2(1) of that Act, or

(b) conduct of the kind mentioned in section 18(1) of that Act,

which relate to commercial activities connected with telecommunications.

(3A) So far as necessary for the purposes of, or in connection with, the provisions of subsection (3) above, references in Part I of the Competition Act 1998 to the Director General of Fair Trading are to be read as including a reference to the Director (except in sections 38(1) to (6), 51, 52(6) and (8) and 54 of that Act and in any other provision of that Act where the context otherwise requires)."

(7) In subsection (4), omit paragraph (c) and the "and" immediately after it.

(8) In subsection (5), omit "or (3)".

(9) In subsection (6), for paragraph (b) substitute —
"(b) Part I of the Competition Act 1998 (other than sections 38(1) to (6) and 51),".

(10) In subsection (7), omit "or the 1980 Act".

Gas

3. — (1) In consequence of the repeal by this Act of provisions of the Competition Act 1980, the functions transferred by subsection (3) of section 36A of the Gas Act 1986 (functions with respect to competition) are no longer exercisable by the Director General of Gas Supply.

(2) Accordingly, that Act is amended as follows.

(3) In section 4 (general duties of Secretary of State and Director), after subsection (3), insert —

"(3A) Subsections (1) to (3) above and section 4A below do not apply in relation to anything done by the Director in the exercise of functions assigned to him by section 36A below ("Competition Act functions").

(3B) The Director may nevertheless, when exercising any Competition Act function, have regard to any matter in respect of which a duty is imposed by any of subsections (1) to (3) above or section 4A below, if it is a matter to which the Director General of Fair Trading could have regard when exercising that function."

(4) Section 36A is amended as follows.

(5) For subsection (3) substitute —

"(3) The Director shall be entitled to exercise, concurrently with the Director General of Fair Trading, the functions of that Director under the provisions of Part I of the Competition Act 1998 (other than sections 38(1) to (6) and 51), so far as relating to —

(a) agreements, decisions or concerted practices of the kind mentioned in section 2(1) of that act, or

(b) conduct of the kind mentioned in section 18(1) of that Act,

which relate to the carrying on of activities to which this subsection applies.

(3A) So far as necessary for the purposes of, or in connection with, the provisions of subsection (3) above, references in Part I of the Competition Act 1998 to the Director General of Fair Trading are to be read as including a reference to the Director (except in sections 38(1) to (6), 51, 52(6) and (8) and 54 of that Act and in any other provision of that Act where the context otherwise requires)."

(6) In subsection (5) —

(a) for "transferred by", in each place, substitute "mentioned in";

(b) after paragraph (b), insert "and";

(c) omit paragraph (d) and the "and" immediately before it.

(7) In subsection (6), omit "or (3)".

(8) In subsection (7), for paragraph (b) substitute —
"(b) Part I of the Competition Act 1998 (other than sections 38(1) to (6) and 51),".

(9) In subsection (8) —

(a) omit "or under the 1980 Act";

(b) for "or (3) above" substitute "above and paragraph 1 of Schedule 10 to the Competition Act 1998".

(10) In subsection (9), omit "or the 1980 Act".

(11) In subsection (10), for the words from "transferred" to the end substitute "mentioned in subsection (2) or (3) above."

Electricity

4. — (1) In consequence of the repeal by this Act of provisions of the Competition Act 1980, the functions transferred by subsection (3) of section 43 of the Electricity Act 1989 (functions with respect to competition) are no longer exercisable by the Director General of Electricity Supply.

(2) Accordingly, that Act is amended as follows.

(3) In section 3 (general duties of Secretary of State and Director), after subsection (6), insert —

"(6A) Subsections (1) to (5) above do not apply in relation to anything done by the Director in the exercise of functions assigned to him by section 43(3) below ("Competition Act functions").

(6B) The Director may nevertheless, when exercising any Competition Act function, have regard to any matter in respect of which a duty is imposed by any of subsections (1) to (5) above ("a general matter"), if it is a matter to which the Director General of Fair Trading could have regard when exercising that function; but that is not to be taken as implying that, in the exercise of any function mentioned in subsection (6) above, regard may not be had to any general matter."

(4) Section 43 is amended as follows.

(5) For subsection (3) substitute —

"(3) The Director shall be entitled to exercise, concurrently with the Director General of Fair Trading, the functions of that Director under the provisions of Part I of the Competition Act 1998 (other than sections 38(1) to (6) and 51), so far as relating to —

(a) agreements, decisions, or concerted practices of the kind mentioned in section 2(1) of that Act, or

(b) conduct of the kind mentioned in section 18(1) of that Act,

which relate to commercial activities connected with the generation, transmission or supply of electricity.

(3A) So far as necessary for the purposes of, or in connection with, the provisions of subsection (3) above, references in Part I of the Competition Act 1998 to the Director General of Fair Trading are to be read as including a reference to the Director (except in sections 38(1) to (6), 51, 52(6) and (8) and 54 of that Act and in any other provision of that Act where the context otherwise requires)."

(6) In subsection (4), omit paragraph (c) and the "and" immediately after it.

(7) In subsection (5), omit "or (3)".

(8) In subsection (6), for paragraph (b) substitute —
"(b) Part I of the Competition Act 1998 (other than sections 38(1) to (6) and 51),".

(9) In subsection (7), omit "or the 1980 Act".

Water

5. — (1) In consequence of the repeal by this Act of provisions of the Competition Act 1980, the functions exercisable by virtue of subsection (3) of section 31 of the Water Industry Act 1991 (functions of Director with respect to competition) are no longer exercisable by the Director General of Water Services.

(2) Accordingly, that Act is amended as follows.

(3) In section 2 (general duties with respect to water industry), in subsection (6)(a), at the beginning, insert "subject to subsection (6A) below".

(4) In section 2, after subsection (6), insert —

"(6A) Subsections (2) to (4) above do not apply in relation to anything done by the Director in the exercise of functions assigned to him by section 31(3) below ("Competition Act functions").

(6B) The Director may nevertheless, when exercising any Competition Act function, have regard to any matter in respect of which a duty is imposed by any of subsections (2) to (4) above, it is a matter to which the Director General of Fair Trading could have regard when exercising that function."

(5) Section 31 is amended as follows.

(6) For subsection (3) substitute —

"(3) The Director shall be entitled to exercise, concurrently with the Director General of Fair Trading, the functions of that Director under the provisions of Part I of the Competition Act 1998 (other than sections 38(1) to (6) and 51), so far as relating to —

(a) agreements, decisions or concerted practices of the kind mentioned in section 2(1) of that Act, or

(b) conduct of the kind mentioned in section 18(1) of that Act,

which relate to commercial activities connected with the supply of water or securing a supply of water or with the provision of securing of sewerage services."

(7) In subsection (4) —

(a) for "to (3)" substitute "and (2)";

(b) omit paragraph (c) and the "and" immediately before it.

(8) After subsection (4), insert —

"(4A) So far as necessary for the purposes of, or in connection with, the provisions of subsection (3) above, references in Part I of the Competition Act 1998 to the Director General of Fair Trading are to be read as including a reference to the Director (except in sections 38(1) to (6), 51, 52(6) and (8) and 54 of that Act and in any other provision of that Act where the context otherwise requires)."

(9) In subsection (5), omit "or in subsection (3) above".

(10) In subsection (6), omit "or in subsection (3) above".

(11) In subsection (7), omit "or (3)".

(12) In subsection (8), for paragraph (b) substitute —
"(b) Part I of the Competition Act 1998 (other than sections 38(1) to (6) and 51),".

(13) In subsection (9), omit "or the 1980 Act".

Railways

6. — (1) In consequence of the repeal by this Act of provisions of the Competition Act 1980, the functions transferred by subsection (3) of section 67 of the Railways Act 1993 (respective functions of the Regulator and the Director etc) are no longer exercisable by the Rail Regulator.

(2) Accordingly, that Act is amended as follows.

(3) In section 4 (general duties of the Secretary of State and the Regulator), after subsection (7), insert —

"(7A) Subsections (1) to (6) above do not apply in relation to anything done by the Regulator in the exercise of functions assigned to him by section 67(3) below ("Competition Act functions").

(7B) The Regulator may nevertheless, when exercising any Competition Act function, have regard to any matter in respect of which a duty is imposed by any of subsections (1) to (6) above, if it is a matter to which the Director General of Fair Trading could have regard when exercising that function."

(4) Section 67 is amended as follows.

(5) For subsection (3) substitute —

"(3) The Regulator shall be entitled to exercise, concurrently with the Director, the functions of the Director under the provisions of Part I of the Competition Act 1998 (other than sections 38(1) to (6) and 51), so far as relating to —

(a) agreements, decisions or concerted practices of the kind mentioned in section 2(1) of that Act, or

(b) conduct of the kind mentioned in section 18(1) of that Act,

which relate to the supply of railway services.

(3A) So far as necessary for the purposes of, or in connection with, the provisions of subsection (3) above, references in Part I of the Competition Act 1998 to the Director are to be read as including a reference to the Regulator (except in sections 38(1) to (6), 51, 52(6) and (8) and 54 of that Act and in any other provision of that Act where the context otherwise requires)."

(6) In subsection (4), omit paragraph (c) and the "and" immediately after it.

(7) In subsection (6)(a), omit "or (3)".

(8) In subsection (8), for paragraph (b) substitute —

"(b) Part I of the Competition act 1998 (other than sections 38(1) to (6) and 51),".

(9) In subsection (9) —

(a) omit "or under the 1980 Act";

(b) for "or (3) above" substitute "above and paragraph 1 of Schedule 10 to the Competition Act 1998".

PART III

THE PROHIBITIONS: NORTHERN IRELAND

Electricity

7. — (1) In consequence of the repeal by this Act of provisions of the Competition Act 1980, the functions transferred by paragraph (3) of Article 46 of the Electricity (Northern Ireland) Order 1992 (functions with respect to competition) are no longer exercisable by the Director General of Electricity Supply for Nothern Ireland.

(2) Accordingly, that Order is amended as follows.

(3) In Article 6 (general duties of the Director), after paragraph (2), add —

"(3) Paragraph (1) does not apply in relation to anything done by the Director in the exercise of functions assigned to him by Article 46(3) ("Competiton Act functions").

(4) The Director may nevertheless, when exercising any Competition Act function, have regard to any matter in respect of which a duty is imposed by paragraph (1) ("a general matter"), if it is a matter to which the Director General of Fair Trading could have regard when exercising that function; but that is not to be taken as implying that, in the exercise of any function mentioned in Article 4(7) or paragraph (2), regard may not be had to any general matter."

(4) Article 46 is amended as follows.

(5) For paragraph (3) substitute —

"(3) The Director shall be entitled to exercise, concurrently with the Director General of Fair Trading, the functions of that Director under the provisions of Part I of the Competition Act 1998 (other than sections 38(1) to (6) and 51), so far as relating to —

(a) agreements, decisions or concerted practices of the kind mentioned in section 2(1) of that Act, or

(b) conduct of the kind mentioned in section 18(1) of that Act,

which relate to commercial activities connected with the generation, transmission or supply of electricity.

(3A) So far as necessary for the purposes of, or in connection with, the provisions of paragraph (3), references in Part I of the Competition Act 1998 to the Director General of Fair Trading are to be read as including a reference to the Director (except in sections 38(1) to (6), 51, 52(6) and (8) and 54 of that Act and in any other provision of that Act where the context otherwise requires)."

(6) In Paragraph (4), omit sub-paragraph (c) and the "and" immediately after it.

(7) In paragraph (5), omit "or (3)".

(8) In paragraph (6), for sub-paragraph (b) substitute —
"(b) Part I of the Competition Act 1998 (other than sections 38(1) to (6) and 51),".

(9) In paragraph (7), omit "or the 1980 Act"'.

Gas

8. — (1) In consequence of the repeal by this Act of provisions of the Competition Act 1980, the functions transferred by paragraph (3) of Article 23 of the Gas (Northern Ireland) Order 1996 (functions with respect to competition) are no longer exercisable by the Director General of Gas for Northern Ireland.

(2) Accordingly, that Order is amended as follows.

(3) In Article 5 (general duties of the Department and Director), after paragraph (4), insert —

"(4A) Paragraphs (2) to (4) do not apply in relation to anything done by the Director in the exercise of functions assigned to him by Article 23(3) ("Competiton Act functions").

(4B) The Director may nevertheless, when exercising any Competition Act function, have regard to any matter in respect of which a duty is imposed by any of paragraphs (2) to (4), if it is a matter to which the Director General of Fair Trading could have regard when exercising that function."

(4) Article 23 is amended as follows.

(5) For paragraph (3) substitute —

"(3) The Director shall be entitled to exercise, concurrently with the Director General of Fair Trading, the functions of that Director under the provisions of Part I of the Competition Act 1998 (other than sections 38(1) to (6) and 51), so far as relating to —

    (a) agreements, decisions or concerted practices of the kind mentioned in section 2(1) of that Act, or

    (b) conduct of the kind mentioned in section 18(1) of that Act, connected with the conveyance, storage or supply of gas.

(3A) So far as necessary for the purposes of, or in connection with, the provisions of paragraph (3), references in Part I of the Competition Act 1998 to the Director General of Fair Trading are to be read as including a reference to the Director (except in sections 38(1) to (6), 51, 52(6) and (8) and 54 of that Act and in any other provision of that Act where the context otherwise requires)."

(6) In paragraph (4) —

    (a) for "transferred by", in each place, substitute "mentioned in";

    (b) after sub-paragraph (b), insert "and";

    (c) omit sub-paragraph (d) and the "and" immediately before it.

(7) In paragraph (5), omit "or (3)".

(8) In paragraph (6), for sub-paragraph (b) substitute —
    "(b) Part I of the Competition Act 1998 (other than sections 38(1) to (6) and 51),".

    (9) In paragraph (7) —

    (a) omit "or under the 1980 Act";

    (b) for "or (3)" substitute "and paragraph 1 of Schedule 10 to the Competition Act 1998".

(10) In paragraph (8), omit "or the 1980 Act".

(11) In paragraph (9), for the words from "transferred" to the end substitute "mentioned in paragraph (2) or (3)."

PART IV

UTILITIES: MINOR AND CONSEQUENTIAL AMENDMENTS

The Telecommunications Act 1984 (c.12)

9. — (1) The Telecommunications Act 1984 is amended as follows.

(2) In section 13 (licence modification references to Competition Commission), for subsections (9) and (10) substitute —

"(9) The provisions mentioned in subsection (9A) are to apply in relation to references under this section as if —

    (a) the functions of the Competition Commission in relation to those references were functions under the Fair Trading Act 1973 (in this Act referred to as "the 1973 Act");

    (b) the expression "merger reference" included a reference under this section;

    (c) in section 70 of the 1973 Act —

        (i) references to the Secretary of State were references to the Director, and
        (ii) the reference to three months were a reference to six months.

(9A) The provisions are —

    (a) sections 70 (time limit for report on merger) and 85 (attendance of witnesses and production of documents) of the 1973 Act;

(b) Part II of Schedule 7 to the Competition Act 1998 (performance of the Competition Commission's general functions); and

(c) section 24 of the Competition Act 1980 (modification of provisions about performance of such functions).

(10) For the purposes of references under this section, the Secretary of State is to appoint not less than three members of the Competition Commission.

(10A) In selecting a group to perform the Commission's functions in relation to any such reference, the chairman of the Commission must select up to three of the members appointed under subsection (10) to be members of the group."

(3) In section 14, omit subsection (2) (which falls with the repeal of the Restrictive Trade Practices Act 1976).

(4) In section 16 (securing compliance with licence conditions), in subsection (5), after paragraph (a), omit "or" and after paragraph (b), insert "or

(c) that the most appropriate way of proceeding is under the Competition Act 1998."

(5) In section 50 (functions under 1973 and 1980 Acts), after subsection (6), insert —

"(6A) Section 93B of the 1973 Act (offences of supplying false or misleading information) is to have effect so far as relating to functions exercisable by the Director by virtue of —

(a) subsection (2) above and paragraph 1 of Schedule 10 to the Competition Act 1998, or

(b) paragraph 1 of Schedule 2 to the Deregulation and Contracting Out Act 1994,

as if the reference in section 93B(1)(a) to the Director General of Fair Trading included a reference to the Director."

(6) In section 95 (modification by orders under other enactments) —

(a) in subsection (1), omit "or section 10(2)(a) of the 1980 Act";

(b) in subsection (2) —

(i) after paragraph (a), insert "or";
(ii) omit paragraph (c) and the "or" immediately before it;

(c) in subsection (3), omit "or the 1980 Act".

(7) In section 101(3) (general restrictions on disclosure of information) —

(a) omit paragraphs (d) and (e) (which refer to the Restrictive Trade Practices Act 1976 and the Resale Prices Act 1976);

(b) after paragraph (m), insert —

"(n) the Competition Act 1998".

(8) At end of section 101, insert —

"(6) Information obtained by the Director in the exercise of functions which are exercisable concurrently with the Director General of Fair Trading under Part I of the Competition Act 1998 is subject to sections 55 and 56 of that Act (disclosure) and not to subsections (1) to (5) of this section."

The Gas Act 1986 (c.44)

10. — (1) The Gas Act 1986 is amended as follows.

(2) In section 24 (modification references to the Competition Commission), for subsection (7) substitute —

"(7) The provisions mentioned in subsection (7A) are to apply in relation to references under this section as if —

(a) the functions of the Competition Commission in relation to those references were functions under the Fair Trading Act 1973;

(b) the expression "merger reference" included a reference under this section;

(c) in section 70 of the Fair Trading Act 1973 —

    (i) references to the Secretary of State were references to the Director, and

    (ii) the reference to three months were a reference to six months.

(7A) The provisions are —

(a) sections 70 (time limit for report on merger) and 85 (attendance of witnesses and production of documents) of the Fair Trading Act 1973;

(b) Part II of Schedule 7 to the Competition Act 1998 (performance of the Competition Commission's general functions); and

(c) section 24 of the Competition Act 1980 (modification of provisions about performance of such functions)."

(3) In section 25, omit subsection (2) (which falls with the repeal of the Restrictive Trade Practices Act 1976).

(4) In section 27 (modification by order under other enactments) —

(a) in subsection (1), omit "or section 10(2)(a) of the Competition Act 1980";

(b) in subsection (3)(a), omit from "or" to "competition reference";

(c) in subsection (6), omit "or the said Act of 1980".

(5) In section 28 (orders for securing compliance with certain provisions), in subsection (5), after paragraph (aa), omit "or" and after paragraph (b), insert "or

(c) that the most appropriate way of proceeding is under the Competition Act 1998."

(6) In section 42(3) (general restrictions on disclosure of information) —

(a) omit paragraphs (e) and (f) (which refer to the Restrictive Trade Practices Act 1976 and the Resale Prices Act 1976);

(b) after paragraph ((n), insert —

"(o) the Competition Act 1998".

(7) At the end of section 42, insert —

"(7) Information obtained by the Director in the exercise of functions which are exercisable concurrently with the Director General of Fair Trading under Part I of the Competition Act 1998 is subject to sections 55 and 56 of that Act (disclosure) and not to subsections (1) to (6) of this section."

The Water Act 1989 (c.15)

11. In section 174(3) of the Water Act 1989 (general restrictions on disclosure of information) —

(a) omit paragraphs (d) and (e) (which refer to the Restrictive Trade Practices Act 1976 and the Resale Prices Act 1976);

(b) after paragraph (l), insert —

"(ll) the Competition Act 1998".

The Electricity Act 1989 (c.29)

12. — (1) The Electricity Act 1989 is amended as follows.

(2) In section 12 (modification references to Competition Commission), for subsections (8) and (9) substitute —

"(8) The provisions mentioned in subsection (8A) are to apply in relation to references under this section as if —

(a) the functions of the Competition Commission in relation to those references were functions under the 1973 Act;

(b) the expression "merger reference" included a reference under this section;

(c) in section 70 of the 1973 Act —

(i) references to the Secretary of State were references to the Director, and

(ii) the reference to three months were a reference to six months.

(8A) The provisions are —

(a) sections 70 (time limit for report on merger) and 85 (attendance of witnesses and production of documents) of the 1973 Act;

(b) Part II of Schedule 7 to the Competition Act 1998 (performance of the Competition Commission's general functions); and

(c) section 24 of the 1980 Act (modification of provisions about performance of such functions).

(9) For the purposes of references under this section, the Secretary of State is to appoint not less than eight members of the Competition Commission.

(9A) In selecting a group to perform the Commission's functions in relation to any such reference, the chairman of the Commission must select up to three of the members appointed under subsection (9) to be members of the group."

(3) In section1 3, omit subsection (2) (which falls with the repeal of the Restrictive Trade Practices Act 1976).

(4) In section 15 (modification by order under other enactments) —

(a) in subsection (1), omit paragraph (b) and the "or" immediately before it;

(b) in subsection (2) —

(i) after paragraph (a), insert "or";

(ii) omit paragraph (c) and the "or" immediately before it;

(c) in subsection (3), omit "or the 1980 Act".

(5) In section 25 (orders for securing compliance), in subsection (5), after paragraph (b), omit "or" and after paragraph (c), insert "or

(d) that the most appropriate way of proceeding is under the Competition Act 1998."

(6) In section 43 (functions with respect to competition), after subsection (6), insert —

"(6A) Section 93B of the 1973 Act (offences of supplying false or misleading information) is to have effect so far as relating to functions exercisable by the Director by virtue of —

(a) subsection (2) above and paragraph 1 of Schedule 10 to the Competition act 1998, or

(b) paragraph 4 of Schedule 2 to the Deregulation and Contracting Out Act 1994,

as if the reference in section 93B(1)(a) to the Director General of Fair Trading included a reference to the Director."

(7) In section 57(3) (general restrictions on disclosure of information) —

(a) omit paragraphs (d) and (e) (which refer to the Restrictive Trade Practices Act 1976 and the Resale Prices Act 1976);

(b) after paragraph (no), insert —

"(nop) the Competition Act 1998".

(8) At the end of section 57, insert —

"(7) Information obtained by the Director in the exercise of functions which are exercisable concurrently with the Director General of Fair Trading under Part I of the Competition Act 1998 is subject to sections 55 and 56 of that Act (disclosure) and not to subsections (1) to (6) of this section."

The Water Industry Act 1991 (c.56)

13. — (1) The Water Industry Act 1991 is amended as follows.

(2) In section 12(5) (determinations under conditions of appointment) —

(a) after "this Act", insert "or";

(b) omit "or the 1980 act".

(3) In section 14 (modification references to Competition Commission), for subsections (7) and (8) substitute —

"(7) The provisions mentioned in subsection (7A) are to apply in relation to references under this section as if —

(a) the functions of the Competition Commission in relation to those references were functions under the 1973 Act;

(b) the expression "merger reference" included a reference under this section;

(c) in section 70 of the 1973 Act —

(i) references to the Secretary of State were references to the Director, and
(ii) the reference to three months were a reference to six months.

(7A) The provisions are —

(a) sections 70 (time limit for report on merger) and 85 (attendance of witnesses and production of documents) of the 1973 Act;

(b) Part II of Schedule 7 to the Competition Act 1998 (performance of the Competition Commission's general functions); and

(c) section 24 of the 1980 Act (modification of provisions about performance of such functions).

(8) For the purposes of references under this section, the Secretary of State is to appoint not less than eight members of the Competition Commission.

(8A) In selecting a group to perform the Commission's functions in relation to any such reference, the chairman of the Commission must select one or more of the members appointed under subsection (8) to be members of the group."

(4) In section 15, omit subsection (2) (which falls with the repeal of the Restrictive Trade Practices Act 1976).

(5) In section 17 (modification by order under other enactments) —

(a) in subsection (1), omit paragraph (b) and the "or" immediately before it;

(b) in subsection (2) —

(i) after paragraph (a), insert "or";
(ii) omit paragraph (c) and the "or" immediately before it;

(c) in subsection (4), omit "or the 1980 Act".

(6) In section 19 (exceptions to duty to enforce), after subsection (1), insert —

"(1A) The Director shall not be required to make an enforcement order, or to confirm a provisional enforcement order, if he is satisfied that the most appropriate way of proceeding is under the Competition Act 1998."

(7) In section 19(3), after "subsection (1) above", insert "or, in the case of the Director, is satisfied as mentioned in subsection (1A) above,".

(8) In section 31 (functions of Director with respect to competition), after subsection (8), insert —

"(8A) Section 93B of the 1973 Act (offences of supplying false or misleading information) is to have effect so far as relating to functions exercisable by the Director by virtue of —

(a) subsection (2) above and paragraph 1 of Schedule 10 to the Competition Act 1998, or

(b) paragraph 8 of Schedule 2 to the Deregulation and Contracting Out Act 1994,

as if the reference in section 93B(1)(a) to the Director General of Fair Trading included a reference to the Director."

(9) After section 206(9) (restriction on disclosure of information), insert —

"(9A) Information obtained by the Director in the exercise of functions which are exercisable concurrently with the Director General of Fair Trading under Part I of the Competition Act 1998 is subject to sections 55 and 56 of that Act (disclosure) and not to subsections (1) to (9) of this section."

(10) In Schedule 15 (disclosure of information), in Part II (enactments in respect of which disclosure may be made) —

(a) omit the entries relating to the Restrictive Trade Practices Act 1976 and the Resale Prices Act 1976;

(b) after the entry relating to the Railways Act 1993, insert the entry —

"The Competition Act 1998".

The Water Resources Act 1991 (c.57)

14. In Schedule 24 to the Water Resources Act 1991 (disclosure of information), in Part II (enactments in respect of which disclosure may be made) —

(a) omit the entries relating to the Restrictive Trade Practices Act 1976 and the Resale Prices act 1976;

(b) after the entry relating to the Coal Industry Act 1994, insert the entry —

"The Competition Act 1998".

The Railways Act 1993 (c.43)

15. — (1) The Railways Act 1993 is amended as follows.

(2) In section 13 (modification references to the Competition Commission), for subsection (8) substitute —

"(8) The provisions mentioned in subsection (8A) are to apply in relation to references under this section as if —

(a) the functions of the Competition Commission in relation to those references were functions under the 1973 Act;

(b) the expression "merger reference" included a reference under this section;

(c) in section 70 of the 1973 Act —

(i) references to the Secretary of State were references to the Director, and
(ii) the reference to three months were a reference to six months.

(8A) The provisions are —

(a) sections 70 (time limit for report on merger) and 85 (attendance of witnesses and production of documents) of the 1973 Act;

(b) Part II of Schedule 7 to the Competition Act 1998 (performance of the Competition Commission's general functions); and

(c) section 24 of the Competition Act 1980 (in this Part referred to as "the 1980 Act") (modification of provisions about performance of such functions).

(3) In section 14, omit subsection (2) (which falls with the repeal of the Restrictive Trade Practices Act 1976).

(4) In section 16 (modification by order under other enactments) —

(a) in subsection (1), omit paragraph (b) and the "or" immediately before it;

(b) in subsection (2) —

(i) after paragraph (a), insert "or";
(ii) omit paragraph (c) and the "or" immediately before it;

(c) in subsection (5), omit "or the 1980 Act".

(5) In section 22, after subsection (6), insert —

"(6A) Neither the Director General of Fair Trading nor the Regulator may exercise, in respect of an access agreement, the powers given by section 32 (enforcement directions) or section 35(2) (interim directions) of the Competition Act 1998.

(6B) Subsection (6A) does not apply to the exercise of the powers given by section 35(2) in respect of conduct —

(a) which is connected with an access agreement; and

(b) in respect of which section 35(1)(b) of that Act applies."

(6) In section 55 (orders for securing compliance), after subsection (5), insert —

"(5A) The Regulator shall not make a final order, or make or confirm a provisional order, in relation to a licence holder or person under closure restrictions if he is satisfied that the most appropriate way of proceeding is under the Competition Act 1998."

(7) In section 55 —

(a) in subsection (6), after "subsection (5)", insert "or (5A)";

(b) in subsection (11), for "subsection (10)" substitute "subsections (5A) and (10)".

(8) Omit section 131 (modification of Restrictive Trade Practices Act 1976).

(9) In section 145(3) (general restrictions on disclosure of information) —

(a) omit paragraphs (d) and (e) (which refer to the Restrictive Trade Practices Act 1976 and the Resale Prices Act 1976);

(b) after paragraph (q), insert —

"(qq) the Competition Act 1998."

(10) After section 145(6), insert —

"(6A) Information obtained by the Regulator in the exercise of functions which are exercisable concurrently with the Director General of Fair Trading under Part I of the Competition Act 1998 is subject to sections 55 and 56 of that Act (disclosure) and not to subsections (1) to (6) of this section."

The Channel Tunnel Rail Link Act 1996 (c.61)

16. — (1) The Channel Tunnel Rail Link Act 1996 is amended as follows.

(2) In section 21 (duties as to exercise of regulatory functions), in subsection (6), at the end of the paragraph about regulatory functions, insert "other than any functions assigned to him by virtue of section 67(3) of that Act ("Competition Act functions").

(7) The Regulator may, when exercising any Competition Act function, have regard to any matter to which he would have regard if —

(a) he were under the duty imposed by subsection (1) or (2) above in relation to that function; and

(b) the matter is one to which the Director General of Fair Trading could have regard if he were exercising that function."

(3) In section 22 (restriction of functions in relation to competition etc.), for subsection (3) substitute —

"(3) The Rail Regulator shall not be entitled to exercise any functions assigned to him by section 67(3) of the Railways Act 1993 (by virtue of which he exercises concurrently with the Director General of Fair Trading certain functions under Part I of the Competition Act 1998 so far as relating to matters connected with the supply of railway services) in relation to —

(a) any agreements, decisions or concerted practices of the kind mentioned in section 2(1) of that Act that have been entered into or taken by, or

(b) any conduct of the kind mentioned in section 18(1) of that Act that has been engaged in by,

a rail link undertaker in connection with the supply of railway services, so far as relating to the rail link."

PART V

MINOR AND CONSEQUENTIAL AMENDMENTS: NORTHERN IRELAND

The Electricity (Northern Ireland) Order 1992

17. — (1) The Electricity (Northern Ireland) Order 1992 is amended as follows.

(2) In Article 15 (modification references to Competition Commission), for paragraphs (8) and (9) substitute —

"(8) The provisions mentioned in paragraph (8A) are to apply in relation to references under this Article as if —

   (a) the functions of the Competition Commission in relation to those references were functions under the 1973 Act;

   (b) "merger reference" included a reference under this Article;

   (c) in section 70 of the 1973 Act —

      (i) references to the Secretary of State were references to the Director, and
      (ii) the reference to three months were a reference to six months.

(8A) The provisions are —

   (a) sections 70 (time limit for report on merger) and 85 (attendance of witnesses and production of documents) of the 1973 Act;

   (b) Part II of Schedule 7 to the Competition Act 1998 (performance of the Competition Commission's general functions); and

   (c) section 24 of the 1980 Act (modification of provisions about performance of such functions).

(9) The Secretary of State may appoint members of the Competition Commission for the purposes of references under this Article.

(9A) In selecting a group to perform the Commission's functions in relation to any such reference, the chairman of the Commission must select up to three of the members appointed under paragraph (9) to be members of the group."

(3) In Article 16, omit paragraph (2) (which falls with the repeal of the Restrictive Trade Practices Act 1976).

(4) In Article 18 (modification by order under other statutory provisions) —

   (a) in paragraph (1), omit sub-paragraph (b) and the "or" immediately before it;

   (b) in paragraph (2) —

      (i) after sub-paragraph (a), insert "or";
      (ii) omit sub-paragraph (c) and the "or" immediately before it;

   (c) in paragraph (3), omit "or the 1980 Act".

(5) In Article 28 (orders for securing compliance), in paragraph (5), after sub-paragraph (b), omit "or" and after sub-paragraph (c), insert"or

   (d) that the most appropriate way of proceeding is under the Competition Act 1998."

(6) In Article 46 (functions with respect to competition), after paragraph (6), insert —

"(6A) Section 93B of the 1973 Act (offences of supplying false or misleading information) is to have effect so far as relating to functions exercisable by the Director by virtue of —

   (a) paragraph (2) and paragraph 1 of Schedule 10 to the Competition Act 1998, or

   (b) paragraph 5 of Schedule 2 to the Deregulation and Contracting Out Act 1994,

as if the reference in section 93B(1)(a) to the Director General of Fair Trading included a reference to the Director."

(7) In Article 61(3) (general restrictions on disclosure of information) —

(a) omit sub-paragraphs (f) and (g) (which refer to the Restrictive Trade Practices Act 1976 and the Resale Prices Act 1976);

(b) after sub-paragraph (t), add —

"(u) the Competition Act 1998".

(8) At the end of Article 61, insert —

"(7) Information obtained by the Director in the exercise of functions which are exercisable concurrently with the Director General of Fair Trading under Part I of the Competition Act 1998 is subject to sections 55 and 56 of that Act (disclosure) and not to paragraphs (1) to (6)."

(9) In Schedule 12, omit paragraph 16 (which amends the Restrictive Trade Practices Act 1976).

The Gas (Northern Ireland) Order 1996

18. — (1) The Gas (Northern Ireland) Order 1996 is amended as follows.

(2) In Article 15 (modification references to the Competition Commission), for paragraph (9) substitute —

"(9) The provisions mentioned in paragraph (9A) are to apply in relation to references under this Article as if —

(a) the functions of the Competition Commission in relation to those references were functions under the 1973 Act;

(b) "merger reference" included a reference under this Article;

(c) in section 70 of the 1973 Act —

(i) references to the Secretary of State were references to the Director, and
(ii) the reference to three months were a reference to six months.

(9A) The provisions are —

(a) sections 70 (time limit for report on merger) and 85 (attendance of witnesses and production of documents) of the 1973 Act;

(b) Part II of Schedule 7 to the Competition Act 1998 (performance of the Competition Commission's general functions); and

(c) section 24 of the 1980 Act (modification of provisions about performance of such functions)."

(3) In Article 16, omit paragraph (2) (which falls with the repeal of the Restrictive Trade Practices Act 1976).

(4) In Article 18 (modification by order under other statutory provisions) —

(a) in paragraph (1), omit sub-paragraph (b) and the "or" immediately before it;

(b) in paragraph (3) —

(i) after sub-paragraph (a), insert "or";
(ii) omit sub-paragraph (c) and the "or" immediately before it;

(c) in paragraph (5), omit "or the 1980 Act".

(5) In Article 19 (orders for securing compliance), in paragraph (5), after sub-paragraph (b), omit "or" and after sub-paragraph (c), insert "or

(d) that the most appropriate way of proceeding is under the Competition Act 1998."

(6) In Article 44(4) (general restrictions on disclosure of information) —

(a) omit sub-paragraphs (f) and (g) (which refer to the Restrictive Trade Practices Act 1976 and the Resale Prices Act 1976);

(b) after sub-paragraph (u), add —

"(v) the Competition Act 1998".

(7) At the end of Article 44, insert —

"(8) Information obtained by the Director in the exercise of functions which are exercisable concurrently with the Director General of Fair Trading under Part I of the Competition Act 1988 is subject to sections 55 and 56 of that Act (disclosure) and not to paragraphs (1) to (7)."

Section 55(4).   SCHEDULE 11

INTERPRETATION OF SECTION 55

Relevant functions

1. In section 55(3) "relevant functions" means any function under —

(a) Part I or any enactment repealed in consequence of Part I;

(b) the Fair Trading Act 1973 (c. 41) or the Competition Act 1980 (c. 21);

(c) the Estate Agents Act 1979 (c. 38);

(d) the Telecommunications Act 1984 (c. 12);

(e) the Gas Act 1986 (c. 44) or the Gas Act 1995 (c. 45);

(f) the Gas (Northern Ireland) Order 1996;

(g) the Airports Act 1986 (c. 31) or Part IV of the Airports (Northern Ireland) Order 1994;

(h) the Financial Services Act 1986 (c. 60);

(i) the Electricity Act 1989 (c. 29) or the Electricity (Northern Ireland) Order 1992;

(j) the Broadcasting Act 1990 (c. 42) or the Broadcasting Act 1996 (c. 55);

(k) the Courts and Legal Services Act 1990 (c. 41);

(l) the Water Industry Act 1991 (c. 56), the Water Resources Act 1991 (c. 57), the Statutory Water Companies Act 1991 (c. 58), the Land Drainage Act 1991 (c. 59) and the Water Consolidation (Consequential Provisions) Act 1991 (c. 60);

(m) the Railways Act 1993 (c. 43);

(n) the Coal Industry Act 1994 (c. 21);

(o) the EC Competition Law (Articles 88 and 89) Enforcement Regulations 1996;

(p) any subordinate legislation made (whether before or after the passing of this Act) for the purpose of implementing Council Directive No. 91/440/EEC of 29th July 1991 on the development of the Community's railways, Council Directive No. 95/18/EC of 19th June 1995 on the licensing of railway undertakings or Council Directive No. 95/19/EC of 19th June 1995 on the allocation of railway infrastructure capacity and the charging of infrastructure fees.

Designated persons

2. In section 55(3) "designated person" means any of the following —

(a) the Director;

(b) the Director General of Telecommunications;

(c) the Independent Television Commission;

(d) the Director General of Gas Supply;

(e) the Director General of Gas for Northern Ireland;

(f) the Civil Aviation Authority;

(g) the Director General of Water Services;

(h) the Director General of Electricity Supply;

(i) the Director General of Electricity Supply for Northern Ireland;

(j) the Rail Regulator;

(k) the Director of Passenger Rail Franchising;

(l) the International Rail Regulator;

(m) the Authorised Conveyancing Practitioners Board;

(n) the Scottish Conveyancing and Executry Services Board;

(o) the Coal Authority;

(p) the Monopolies and Mergers Commission;

(q) the Competition Commission;

(r) the Securities and Investments Board;

(s) any Minister of the Crown or any Northern Ireland department.

SCHEDULE 12   Section 74(1).

MINOR AND CONSEQUENTIAL AMENDMENTS

The Fair Trading Act 1973 (c.41)

1. — (1) The Fair Trading Act 1973 is amended as follows.

(2) Omit section 4 and Schedule 3 (which make provisions in respect of the Monopolies and Mergers Commission).

(3) Omit —

(a) section 10(2),

(b) section 54(5),

(c) section 78(3),

(d) paragraph 3(1) and (2) of Schedule 8,

(which fall with the repeal of the Restrictive Trade Practices Act 1976).

(4) In section 10 (supplementary provisions about monopoly situations), in subsection (8), for "to (7)" substitute "and (3) to (7)".

(5) In sections 35 and 37 to 41, for "the Restrictive Practices Court", in each place, substitute "a relevant Court".

(6) After section 41, insert —

41A. In this Part of this Act, "relevant Court", in relation to proceedings in respect of a course of conduct maintained in the course of a business, means any of the following courts in whose jurisdiction that business is carried on —

(a) in England and Wales or Northern Ireland, the High Court;

(b) in Scotland, the Court of Session."

(7) In section 42 (appeals from decisions or orders of courts under Part III) —

(a) in subsection (1), at the end, add "; but this subsection is subject to subsection (3) of this section";

(b) in subsection (2)(b), after "Scotland," insert "from the sheriff court"; and

(c) after subsection (2), add —

"(3) A decision or order of the Court of Session as the relevant Court may be reviewed, whether on a question of fact or on a question of law, by reclaiming to the Inner House."

(8) Omit section 45 (power of the Director to require information about complex monopoly situations).

(9) In section 81 (procedure in carrying out investigations) —

(a) in subsection (1) —

(i) in the words before paragraph (a), omit from "and the Commission" to "of this Act)";

(ii) in paragraph (b), omit "or the Commission, as the case may be," and "or of the Commission";

(b) in subsection (2), omit "or the Commission" and "or of the Commission"; and

(c) in subsection (3), omit from "and, in the case," to "85 of this Act" and "or the Commission, as the case may be,".

(10) In section 85 (attendance of witnesses and production of documents on investigations by Competition Commission of references under the Fair Trading Act 1973), in subsection (1)(b) —

(a) after "purpose", insert "(i)";

(b) after the second "notice", insert "or

(ii) any document which falls within a category of document which is specified, or described, in the notice,".

(11) In section 85, in subsection (1)(c), after "estimates" (in both places), insert "forecasts".

(12) In section 85, after subsection (1), insert —

"(1A) For the purposes of subsection (1) above —

(a) "document" includes information recorded in any form;

(b) the power to require the production of documents includes power to take copies of, or extracts from, any document produced; and

(c) in relation to information recorded otherwise than in legible form, the power to require it to be produced includes power to require it to be produced in legible form, so far as the means to do so are within the custody or under the control of the person on whom the requirement is imposed."

(13) In section 85(2), for "any such investigation" substitute "an investigation of the kind mentioned in subsection (1)".

(14) In section 133 (general restrictions on disclosure of information), in subsection (2)(a), after "the Coal Industry Act 1994" insert "or the Competition Act 1998".

(15) In section 135(1) (financial provisions) —

(a) in the words before paragraph (a) and in paragraph (b), omit "or the Commission"; and

(b) omit paragraph (a).

The Energy Act 1976 (c.76)

2. In the Energy Act 1976, omit section 5 (temporary relief from restrictive practices law in relation to certain agreements connected with petroleum).

The Estate Agents Act 1979 (c.38)

3. In section 10(3) of the Estate Agents act 1979 (restriction on disclosure of information), in paragraph (a) —

(a) omit "or the Restrictive Trade Practices Act 1976"; and

(b) after "the Coal Industry Act 1994", insert "or the Competition Act 1998".

The Competition Act 1980 (c.21)

4. — (1) The Competition Act 1980 is amended as follows.

(2) In section 11(8) (public bodies and other persons referred to the Commission), omit paragraph (b) and the "and" immediately before it.

(3) For section 11(9) (which makes provision for certain functions of the Competition Commission under the Fair Trading Act 1973 to apply in relation to references under the Competition Act 1980) substitute —

"(9) The provisions mentioned in subsection (9A) are to apply in relation to a reference under this section as if —

(a) the functions of the Competition Commission under this section were functions under the Fair Trading Act 1973;

(b) the expression "merger reference" included a reference to the Commission under this section; and

(c) in paragraph 20(2)(a) of Schedule 7 to the Competition Act 1998, the reference to section 56 of the Fair Trading Act 1973 were a reference to section 12 below.

(9A) The provisions are —

(a) sections 70 (time limit for report on merger), 84 (public interest) and 85 (attendance of witnesses and production of documents) of the Fair Trading Act 1973; and

(b) Part II of Schedule 7 to the Competition Act 1998 (performance of the Competition Commission's general functions)."

(4) In section 13 (investigation of prices directed by Secretary of State) —

(a) in subsection (1), omit from "but the giving" to the end;

(b) for subsection (6) substitute —

"(6) For the purposes of an investigation under this section the Director may, by notice in writing signed by him —

(a) require any person to produce —

    (i) at a time and a place specified in the notice,
    (ii) to the Director or to any person appointed by him for the purpose,

any documents which are specified or described in the notice and which are documents in his custody or under his control and relating to any matter relevant to the investigation; or

(b) require any person carrying on any business to —

    (i) furnish to the Director such estimates, forecasts, returns or other information as may be specified or described in the notice; and
    (ii) specify the time, manner and form in which any such estimates, forecasts, returns or information are to be furnished.

(7) No person shall be compelled, for the purpose of any investigation under this section —

(a) to produce any document which he could not be compelled to produce in civil proceedings before the High Court or, in Scotland, the Court of Session; or

(b) in complying with any requirement for the furnishing of information, to give any information which he could not be compelled to give in evidence in such proceedings.

(8) Subsections (6) to (8) of section 85 of the Fair Trading Act 1973 (enforcement provisions relating to notices requiring production of documents etc.) shall apply in relation to a notice under subsection (6) above as they apply in relation to a notice under section 85(1) but as if, in section 85(7), for the words from "any one" to "the Commission" there were substituted "the Director.""

(5) In section 15 (special provisions for agricultural schemes) omit subsections (2)(b), (3) and (4).

(6) In section 16 (reports), omit subsection (3).

(7) In section 17 (publication etc. of reports) —

(a) in subsections (1) and (3) to (5), omit "8(1)";

(b) in subsection (2), omit "8(1) or"; and

(c) in subsection (6), for "sections 9, 10 or" substitute "section".

(8) In section 19(3) (restriction on disclosure of information), omit paragraphs (d) and (e).

(9) In section 19(3), after paragraph (q), insert —

"(r) the Competition Act 1998".

(10) In section 19(5)(a), omit "or in anything published under section 4(2)(a) above".

(11) Omit section 22 (which amends the Fair Trading Act 1973).

(12) In section 24(1) (modifications of provisions about performance of Commission's functions), for from "Part II" to the first "Commission" substitute "Part II of Schedule 7 to the Competition Act 1998 (performance of the Competition Commission's general functions)".

(13) Omit sections 25 to 30 (amendments of the Restrictive Trade Practices Act 1976).

(14) In section 31 (orders and regulations) —

(a) omit subsection (2); and

(b) in subsection (3), omit "10".

(15) In section 33 (short title etc) —

(a) in subsection (2), for "sections 2 to 24" substitute "sections 11 to 13 and sections 15 to 24";

(b) omit subsections (3) and (4).

Magistrates' Courts (Northern Ireland) Order 1981 (S.I. 1981/1675 (N.I. 26))

5. In Schedule 6 to the Magistrates' Courts (Northern Ireland) Order 1981, omit paragraphs 42 and 43 (which amend the Restrictive Trade Practices Act 1976).

Agricultural Marketing (Northern Ireland) Order 1982 (S.I. 1982/1080 (N.I. 12))

6. In Schedule 8 to the Agricultural Marketing (Northern Ireland) Order 1982 —

(a) omit the entry relating to paragraph 16(2) of Schedule 3 to the Fair Trading Act 1973; and

(b) in the entry relating to the Competition Act 1980 —

(i) for "sections" substitute "section";
(ii) omit "and 15(3)".

The Airports Act 1986 (c.31)

7. — (1) The Airports Act 1986 is amended as follows.

(2) In section 44 (which makes provision about references by the CAA to the Competition Commission), for subsection (3) substitute —

"(3) The provisions mentioned in subsection (3A) are to apply in relation to references under this section as if —

(a) the functions of the Competition Commission in relation to those references were functions under the 1973 Act;

(b) the expression "merger reference" included a reference under this section;

(c) in section 70 of the 1973 Act —

(i) references to the Secretary of State were references to the CAA, and
(ii) the reference to three months were a reference to six months.

(3A) The provisions are —

(a) sections 70 (time limit for report on merger) and 85 (attendance of witnesses and production of documents) of the 1973 Act;

(b) Part II of Schedule 7 to the Competition Act 1998 (performance of the Competition Commission's general functions); and

(c) section 24 of the 1980 Act (modification of provisions about performance of such functions)."

(3) In section 45, omit subsection (3) (which falls with the repeal of the Restrictive Trade Practices Act 1976).

(4) In section 54 (orders under the 1973 Act or 1980 Act modifying or revoking conditions) —

(a) in subsection (1), omit "or section 10(2)(a) of the 1980 Act";

(b) in subsection (3), omit paragraph (c) and the "or" immediately before it;

(c) in subsection (4), omit "or the 1980 Act".

(5) In section 56 (co-ordination of exercise of functions by CAA and Director General of Fair Trading), in paragraph (a)(ii), omit "or the 1980 Act".

The Financial Services Act 1986 (c.60)

8. In Schedule 11 to the Financial Services Act 1986, in paragraph 12 —

(a) in sub-paragraph (1), omit "126";

(b) omit sub-paragraph (2).

The Companies Consolidation (Consequential Provisions) (Northern Ireland) Order 1986 (S.I. 1986/1035 (N.I.9))

9. In Part II of Schedule 1 to the Companies Consolidation (Consequential Provisions) (Northern Ireland) Order 1986, omit the entries relating to the Restrictive Trade Practices Act 1976 and the Resale Prices Act 1976.

The Consumer Protection Act 1987 (c.43)

10. In section 38(3) of the Consumer Protection Act 1987 (restrictions on disclosure of information) —

(a) omit paragraphs (e) and (f); and

(b) after paragraph (o), insert —

   "(p) the Competition Act 1998."

The Channel Tunnel Act 1987 (c.53)

11. In section 33 of the Channel Tunnel Act 1987 —

(a) in subsection (2), omit paragraph (c) and the "and" immediately before it;

(b) in subsection (5), omit paragraphs (b) and (c).

The Road Traffic (Consequential Provisions) Act 1998 (c.54)

12. In Schedule 3 to the Road Traffic (Consequential Provisions) Act 1988 (consequential amendments), omit paragraph 19.

The Companies Act 1989 (c.40)

13. In Schedule 20 to the Companies Act 1989 (amendments about mergers and related matters), omit paragraphs 21 to 24.

The Broadcasting Act 1990 (c.42)

14. — (1) The Broadcasting Act 1990 is amended as follows.

(2) In section 193 (modification of networking arrangements in consequence of reports under competition legislation) —

(a) in subsection (2), omit paragraph (c) and the "and" immediately before it;

(b) in subsection (4), omit "or the Competition Act 1980".

(3) In Schedule 4 (which makes provision for references to the Director or the Competition Commission in respect of networking arrangements), in paragraph 4, for sub-paragraph (7) substitute —

   "(7) The provisions mentioned in sub-paragraph (7A) are to apply in relation to references under this paragraph as if —

   (a) the functions of the Competition Commission in relation to those references were functions under the Fair Trading Act 1973;

   (b) the expression "merger reference" included a reference under this paragraph.

   (7A) The provisions are —

   (a) section 85 of the Fair Trading Act 1973 (attendance of witnesses and production of documents);

   (b) Part II of Schedule 7 to the Competition Act 1998 (performance of the Competition Commission's general functions); and

   (c) section 24 of the Competition Act 1980 (modification of provisions about performance of such functions)."

The Tribunals and Inquiries Act 1992 (c.53)

15. In Schedule 1 to the Tribunals and Inquiries Act 1992 (tribunals under the supervision of the Council on Tribunals), after paragraph 9, insert —

"Competition 9A. An appeal tribunal established under section 48 of the Competition Act 1998."

The Osteopaths Act 1993 (c.21)

16. Section 33 of the Osteopaths Act 1993 (competition and anti-competitive practices) is amended as follows —

(a) in subsection (4), omit paragraph (b) and the "or" immediately before it;

(b) in subsection (5), omit "or section 10 of the Act of 1980".

The Chiropractors Act 1994 (c.17)

17. Section 33 of the Chiropractors Act 1994 (competition and anti-competitive practices) is amended as follows —

(a) in subsection (4), omit paragraph (b) and the "or" immediately before it;

(b) in subsection (5), omit "or section 10 of the Act of 1980".

The Coal Industry Act 1994 (c.21)

18. In section 59(4) of the Coal Industry Act 1994 (information to be kept confidential by the Coal Authority) —

(a) omit paragraphs (e) and (f); and

(b) after paragraph (m), insert —

"(n) the Competition Act 1998."

The Deregulation and Contracting Out Act 1994 (c.40)

19. — (1) The Deregulation and Contracting Out Act 1994 is amended as follows.

(2) Omit —

(a) section 10 (restrictive trade practices: non-notifiable agreements); and

(b) section 11 (registration of commercially sensitive information).

(3) In section 12 (anti-competitive practices: competition references), omit subsections (1) to (6).

(4) In Schedule 4, omit paragraph 1.

(5) In Schedule 11 (miscellaneous deregulatory provisions: consequential amendments), in paragraph 4, omit sub-paragraphs (3) to (7).

The Airports (Northern Ireland) Order 1994 (S.I. 1994/426 (N.I.))

20. — (1) The Airports (Northern Ireland) Order 1994 is amended as follows.

(2) In Article 35 (which makes provision about references by the CAA to the Competition Commission), for paragraph (3) substitute —

"(3) The provisions mentioned in paragraph (3A) are to apply in relation to references under Article 34 as if —

(a) the functions of the Competition Commission in relation to those references were functions under the 1973 Act;

(b) the expression "merger reference" included a reference under that Article;

(c) in section 70 of the 1973 Act —

(i) references to the Secretary of State were references to the Director, and
(ii) the reference to three months were a reference to six months.

(3A) The provisions are —

(a) sections 70 (time limit for report on merger) and 85 (attendance of witnesses and production of documents) of the 1973 Act;

(b) Part II of Schedule 7 to the Competition Act 1998 (performance of the Competition Commission's general functions); and

(c) section 24 of the 1980 Act (modification of provisions about performance of such functions)."

(3) In Article 36, omit paragraph (3) (which falls with the repeal of the Restrictive Trade Practices Act 1976).

(4) In Article 45 (orders under the 1973 Act or 1980 Act modifying or revoking conditions) —

(a) in paragraph (1), omit "or section 10(2)(a) of the 1980 Act";

(b) in paragraph (3), omit sub-paragraph (c) and the "or" immediately before it;

(c) in paragraph (4), omit "or the 1980 Act".

(5) In Article 47 (co-ordination of exercise of functions by CAA and Director of Fair Trading), in paragraph (a)(ii), omit "or the 1980 Act".

(6) In Schedule 9, omit paragraph 5 (which amends the Restrictive Trade Practices Act 1976).

The Broadcasting Act 1996 (c.55)

21. In section 77 of the Broadcasting Act 1996 (which modifies the Restrictive Trade Practices Act 1976 in its application to agreements relating to Channel 3 new provision), omit subsection (2).

SCHEDULE 13   Section 74(2).

TRANSITIONAL PROVISIONS AND SAVINGS

PART I

GENERAL

Interpretation

1. — (1) In this Schedule —
"RPA" means the Resale Prices Act 1976;
"RTPA" means the Restrictive Trade Practices Act 1976;
"continuing proceedings" has the meaning given by paragraph 15;
"the Court" means the Restrictive Practices Court;
"Director" means the Director General of Fair Trading;
"document" includes information recorded in any form;
"enactment date" means the date on which this Act is passed;
"information" includes estimates and forecasts;
"interim period" means the period beginning on the enactment date and ending immediately before the starting date;
"prescribed" means prescribed by an order made by the Secretary of State;
"regulator" means any person mentioned in paragraphs (a) to (g) of paragraph 1 of Schedule 10;
"starting date" means the date on which section 2 comes into force;
"transitional period" means the transitional period provided for in Chapters III and IV of Part IV of this Schedule.

(2) Sections 30, 44, 51, 53, 55, 56, 57 and 59(3) and (4) and paragraph 12 of Schedule 9 ("the applied provisions") apply for the purposes of this Schedule as they apply for the purposes of Part I of this Act.

(3) Section 2(5) applies for the purposes of any provisions of this Schedule which are concerned with the operation of the Chapter I prohibition as it applies for the purposes of Part I of this Act.

(4) In relation to any of the matters in respect of which a regulator may exercise powers as a result of paragraph 35(1), the applied provisions are to have effect as if references to the Director included references to the regulator.

(5) The fact that to a limited extent the Chapter I prohibition does not apply to an agreement, because a transitional period is provided by virtue of this Schedule, does not require those provisions of the agreement in respect of which there is a transitional period to be disregarded when considering whether the agreement infringes the prohibition for other reasons.

General power to make transitional provision and savings

2. — (1) Nothing in this Schedule affects the power of the Secretary of State under section 75 to make transitional provisions or savings.

(2) An order under that section may modify any provision made by this Schedule.

Advice and information

3. — (1) The Director may publish advice and information explaining provisions of this Schedule to persons who are likely to be affected by them.

(2) Any advice or information published by the Director under this paragraph is to be published in such form and manner as he considers appropriate.

Part II

During the Interim Period

Block exemptions

4. — (1) The Secretary of State may, at any time during the interim period, make one or more orders for the purpose of providing block exemptions which are effective on the starting date.

(2) An order under this paragraph has effect as if properly made under section 6.

Certain agreements to be non-notifiable agreements

5. An agreement which —

(a) is made during the interim period, and

(b) satisfies the conditions set out in paragraphs (a), (c) and (d) of section 27A(1) of the RTPA,

is to be treated as a non-notifiable agreement for the purposes of the RTPA.

Application of RTPA during the interim period

6. In relation to agreements made during the interim period —

(a) the Director is no longer under the duty to take proceedings imposed by section 1(2)(c) of the RTPA but may continue to do so;

(b) section 21 of that Act has effect as if subsections (1) and (2) were omitted; and

(c) section 35(1) of that Act has effect as if the words "or within such further time as the Director may, upon application made within that time, allow" were omitted.

Guidance

7. — (1) Sub-paragraphs (2) to (4) apply in relation to agreements made during the interim period.

(2) An application may be made to the Director in anticipation of the coming into force of section 13 in accordance with directions given by the Director and such an application is to have effect on and after the starting date as if properly made under section 13.

(3) The Director may, in response to such an application —

(a) give guidance in anticipation of the coming into force of section 2; or

(b) on and after the starting date, give guidance under section 15 as if the application had been properly made under section 13.

(4) Any guidance so given is to have effect on and after the starting date as if properly given under section 15.

Part III

On the Starting Date

Applications which fall

8. — (1) Proceedings in respect of an application which is made to the Court under any of the provisions mentioned in sub-paragraph (2), but which is not determined before the starting date, cease on that date.

(2) The provisions are —

(a) sections 2(2), 35(3), 37(1) and 40(1) of the RTPA and paragraph 5 of Schedule 4 to that Act;

(b) section 4(1) of the RTPA so far as the application relates to an order under section 2(2) of that Act; and

(c) section 25(2) of the RPA.

(3) The power of the Court to make an order for costs in relation to any proceedings is not affected by anything in this paragraph or by the repeals made by section 1.

Orders and approvals which fall

9. — (1) An order in force immediately before the starting date under —

(a) section 2(2), 29(1), 30(1), 33(4), 35(3) or 37(1) of the RTPA; or

(b) section 25(2) of the RPA,

ceases to have effect on that date.

(2) An approval in force immediately before the starting date under section 32 of the RTPA ceases to have effect on that date.

PART IV

ON AND AFTER THE STARTING DATE

CHAPTER I

GENERAL

Duty of Director to maintain register etc.

10.(1) This paragraph applies even though the relevant provisions of the RTPA are repealed by this Act.

(2) The Director is to continue on and after the starting date to be under the duty imposed by section 1(2)(a) of the RTPA to maintain a register in respect of agreements —

(a) particulars of which are, on the starting date, entered or filed on the register;

(b) which fall within sub-paragraph (4);

(c) which immediately before the starting date are the subject of proceedings under the RTPA which do not cease on that date by virtue of this Schedule; or

(d) in relation to which a court gives directions to the Director after the starting date in the course of proceedings in which a question arises as to whether an agreement was, before that date —

(i) one to which the RTPA applied;
(ii) subject to registration under that Act;
(iii) a non-notifiable agreement for the purposes of that Act.

(3) The Director is to continue on and after the starting date to be under the duties imposed by section 1(2)(a) and (b) of the RTPA of compiling a register of agreements and entering or filing certain particulars in the register, but only in respect of agreements of a kind referred to in paragraph (b), (c) or (d) of subparagraph (2).

(4) An agreement falls within this sub-paragraph if —

(a) it is subject to registration under the RTPA but —

(i) is not a non-notifiable agreement within the meaning of section 27A of the RTPA, or
(ii) is not one to which paragraph 5 applies;

(b) particulars of the agreement have been provided to the Director before the starting date; and

(c) as at the starting date no entry or filing has been made in the register in respect of the agreement.

(5) Sections 23 and 27 of the RTPA are to apply after the starting date in respect of the register subject to such modifications, if any, as may be prescribed.

(6) In sub-paragraph (2)(d) "court" means —

(a) the High Court;

(b) the Court of Appeal;

(c) the Court of Session;

(d) the High Court or Court of Appeal in Northern Ireland; or

(e) the House of Lords.

RTPA section 3 applications

11. — (1) Even though section 3 of the RTPA is repealed by this Act, its provisions (and so far as necessary that Act) are to continue to apply, with such modifications (if any) as may be prescribed —

(a) in relation to a continuing application under that section; or

(b) so as to allow an application to be made under that section on or after the starting date in respect of a continuing application under section 1(3) of the RTPA.

(2) "Continuing application" means an application made, but not determined, before the starting date.

RTPA section 26 applications

12. — (1) Even though section 26 of the RTPA is repealed by this Act, its provisions (and so far as necessary that Act) are to continue to apply, with such modifications (if any) as may be prescribed, in relation to an application which is made under that section, but not determined, before the starting date.

(2) If an application under section 26 is determined on or after the starting date, this Schedule has effect in relation to the agreement concerned as if the application had been determined immediately before that date.

Right to bring civil proceedings

13. — (1) Even though section 35 of the RTPA is repealed by this Act, its provisions (and so far as necessary that Act) are to continue to apply in respect of a person who, immediately before the starting date, has a right by virtue of section 27ZA or 35(2) of that Act to bring civil proceedings in respect of an agreement (but only so far as that right relates to any period before the starting date or, where there are continuing proceedings, the determination of the proceedings).

(2) Even though section 25 of the RPA is repealed by this Act, the provision of that section (and so far as necessary that Act) are to continue to apply in respect of a person who, immediately before the starting date, has a right by virtue of subsection (3) of that section to bring civil proceedings (but only so far as that right relates to any period before the starting date or, where there are continuing proceedings, the determination of the proceedings).

CHAPTER II

CONTINUING PROCEEDINGS

The general rule

14. — (1) The Chapter I prohibition does not apply to an agreement at any time when the agreement is the subject of continuing proceedings under the RTPA.

(2) The chapter I prohibition does not apply to an agreement relating to goods which are the subject of continuing proceedings under section 16 or 17 of the RPA to the extent to which the agreement consists of exempt provisions.

(3) In sub-paragraph (2) "exempt provisions" means those provisions of the agreement which would, disregarding section 14 of the RPA, be —

(a) void as a result of section 9(1) of the RPA; or

(b) unlawful as a result of section 9(2) or 11 of the RPA.

(4) If the Chapter I prohibition does not apply to an agreement because of this paragraph, the provisions of, or made under, the RTPA or the RPA are to continue to have effect in relation to the agreement.

(5) The repeals made by section 1 do not affect —

(a) continuing proceedings; or

(b) proceedings of the kind referred to in paragraph 11 or 12 of this Schedule which are continuing after the starting date.

Meaning of "continuing proceedings"

15. — (1) For the purposes of this Schedule "continuing proceedings" means proceedings in respect of an application made to the Court under the RTPA or the RPA, but not determined, before the starting date.

(2) But proceedings under section 3 or 26 of the RTPA to which paragraph 11 or 12 applies are not continuing proceedings.

(3) The question whether (for the purposes of Part III, or this Part, of this Schedule) an application has been determined is to be decided in accordance with sub-paragraphs (4) and (5).

(4) If an appeal against the decision on the application is brought, the application is not determined until —

(a) the appeal is disposed of or withdrawn; or

(b) if as a result of the appeal the case is referred back to the Court —

(i) the expiry of the period within which an appeal ("the further appeal") in respect of the Court's decision on that reference could have been brought had this Act not been passed; or

(ii) if later, the date on which the further appeal is disposed of or withdrawn.

(5) Otherwise, the application is not determined until the expiry of the period within which any party to the application would have been able to bring an appeal against the decision on the application had this Act not been passed.

RTPA section 4 proceedings

16. Proceedings on an application for an order under section 4 of the RTPA are also continuing proceedings if —

(a) leave to make the application is applied for before the starting date but the proceedings in respect of that application for leave are not determined before that date; or

(b) leave to make an application for an order under that section is granted before the starting date but the application itself is not made before that date.

RPA section 16 or 17 proceedings

17. Proceedings on an application for an order under section 16 or 17 of the RPA are also continuing proceedings if —

(a) leave to make the application is applied for before the starting date but the proceedings in respect of that application for leave are not determined before that date; or

(b) leave to make an application for an order under section 16 or 17 of the RPA is granted before the starting date, but the application itself is not made before that date.

Continuing proceedings which are discontinued

18. — (1) On an application made jointly to the Court by all the parties to any continuing proceedings, the Court must, if it is satisfied that the parties wish it to do so, discontinue the proceedings.

(2) If, on an application under sub-paragraph (1) or for any other reason, the Court orders the proceedings to be discontinued, this Schedule has effect (subject to paragraphs 21 and 22) from the date on which the proceedings are discontinued as if they had never been instituted.

CHAPTER III

THE TRANSITIONAL PERIOD

The general rule

19. — (1) Except where this Chapter or Chapter IV provides otherwise, there is a transitional period, beginning on the starting date and lasting for one year, for any agreement made before the starting date.

(2) The Chapter I prohibition does not apply to an agreement to the extent to which there is a transitional period for the agreement.

(3) The Secretary of State may by regulations provide for sections 13 to 16 and Schedule 5 to apply with such modifications (if any) as may be specified in the regulations, in respect of applications to the Director about agreements for which there is a transitional period.

Cases for which there is no transitional period

20. — (1) There is no transitional period for an agreement to the extent to which, immediately before the starting date, it is —

(a) void under section 2(1) or 35(1)(a) of the RTPA;

(b) the subject of an order under section 2(2) or 35(3) of the RTPA; or

(c) unlawful under section 1, 2 or 11 of the RPA or void under section 9 of that Act.

(2) There is no transitional period for an agreement to the extent to which, before the starting date, a person has acted unlawfully for the purposes of section 27ZA(2) or (3) of the RTPA in respect of the agreement.

(3) There is no transitional period for an agreement to which paragraph 25(4) applies.

(4) There is no transitional period for —

   (a) an agreement in respect of which there are continuing proceedings, or

   (b) an agreement relating to goods in respect of which there are continuing proceedings,

to the extent to which the agreement is, when the proceedings are determined, void or unlawful.

Continuing proceedings under the RTPA

21. In the case of an agreement which is the subject of continuing proceedings under the RTPA, the transitional period begins —

   (a) if the proceedings are discontinued, on the date of discontinuance;

   (b) otherwise, when the proceedings are determined.

Continuing proceedings under the RPA

22. — (1) In the case of an agreement relating to goods which are the subject of continuing proceedings under the RPA, the transitional period for the exempt provisions of the agreement begins —

   (a) if the proceedings are discontinued, on the date of discontinuance;

   (b) otherwise, when the proceedings are determined.

(2) In sub-paragraph (1) "exempt provisions" has the meaning given by paragraph 14(3).

Provisions not contrary to public interest

23. — (1) To the extent to which an agreement contains provisions which, immediately before the starting date, are provisions which the Court has found not to be contrary to the public interest, the transitional period lasts for five years.

(2) Sub-paragraph (1) is subject to paragraph 20(4).

(3) To the extent to which an agreement which on the starting date is the subject of continuing proceedings is, when the proceedings are determined, found by the Court not to be contrary to the public interest, the transitional period lasts for five years.

Goods

24. — (1) In the case of an agreement relating to goods which, immediately before the starting date, are exempt under section 14 of the RPA, there is a transitional period for the agreement to the extent to which it consists of exempt provisions.

(2) Sub-paragraph (1) is subject to paragraph 20(4).

(3) In the case of an agreement relating to goods —

   (a) which on the starting date are the subject of continuing proceedings, and

   (b) which, when the proceedings are determined, are found to be exempt under section 14 of the RPA,

there is a transitional period for the agreement, to the extent to which it consists of exempt provisions.

(4) In each case, the transitional period lasts for five years.

(5) In sub-paragraphs (1) and (3) "exempt provisions" means those provisions of the agreement which would, disregarding section 14 of the RPA, be —

   (a) void as a result of section 9(1) of the RPA; or

   (b) unlawful as a result of section 9(2) or 11 of the RPA.

Transitional period for certain agreements

25. — (1) This paragraph applies to agreements —

(a) which are subject to registration under the RTPA but which —

    (i) are not non-notifiable agreements within the meaning of section 27A of the RTPA, or

    (ii) are not agreements to which paragraph 5 applies; and

(b) in respect of which the time for furnishing relevant particulars as required by or under the RTPA expires on or after the starting date.

(2) "Relevant particulars" means —

(a) particulars which are required to be furnished by virtue of section 24 of the RTPA; or

(b) particulars of any variation of an agreement which are required to be furnished by virtue of sections 24 and 27 of the RTPA.

(3) There is a transitional period of one year for an agreement to which this paragraph applies if —

(a) relevant particulars are furnished before the starting date; and

(b) no person has acted unlawfully (for the purposes of section 27ZA(2) or (3) of the RTPA) in respect of the agreement.

(4) If relevant particulars are not furnished by the starting date, section 35(1)(a) of the RTPA does not apply in relation to the agreement (unless sub-paragraph (5) applies).

(5) This sub-paragraph applies if a person falling within section 27ZA(2) or (3) of the RTPA has acted unlawfully for the purposes of those subsections in respect of the agreement.

Special cases

26. — (1) In the case of an agreement in respect of which —

(a) a direction under section 127(2) of the Financial Services act 1986 ("the 1986 Act") is in force immediately before the starting date, or

(b) a direction under section 194A(3) of the Broadcasting Act 1990 ("the 1990 Act") is in force immediately before the starting date,

the transitional period lasts for five years.

(2) To the extent to which an agreement is the subject of a declaration —

(a) made by the Treasury under section 127(3) of the 1986 Act, and

(b) in force immediately before the starting date,

the transitional period lasts for five years.

(3) Sub-paragraphs (1) and (2) do not affect the power of —

(a) the Treasury to make a declaration under section 127(2) of the 1986 Act (as amended by Schedule 2 to this Act),

(b) the Secretary of State to make a declaration under section 194A of the 1990 Act (as amended by Schedule 2 to this Act),

in respect of an agreement for which there is a transitional period.

CHAPTER IV

THE UTILITIES

General

27. In this Chapter "the relevant period" means the period beginning with the starting date and ending immediately before the fifth anniversary of that date.

Electricity

28. — (1) For an agreement to which, immediately before the starting date, the RTPA does not apply by virtue of a section 100 order, there is a transitional period —

(a) beginning on the starting date; and

(b) ending at the end of the relevant period.

(2) For an agreement which is made at any time after the starting date and to which, had the RTPA not been repealed, that Act would not at the time at which the agreement is made have applied by virtue of a section 100 order, there is a transitional period —

(a) beginning on the date on which the agreement is made; and

(b) ending at the end of the relevant period.

(3) For an agreement (whether made before or after the starting date) which, during the relevant period, is varied at any time in such a way that it becomes an agreement which, had the RTPA not been repealed, would at that time have been one to which that Act did not apply by virtue of a section 100 order, there is a transitional period —

(a) beginning on the date on which the variation is made; and

(b) ending at the end of the relevant period.

(4) If an agreement for which there is a transitional period as a result of sub-paragraph (1), (2) or (3) is varied during the relevant period, the transitional period for the agreement continues if, had the RTPA not been repealed, the agreement would have continued to be one to which that Act did not apply by virtue of a section 100 order.

(5) But if an agreement for which there is a transitional period as a result of sub-paragraph (1), (2) or (3) ceases to be one to which, had it not been repealed, the RTPA would not have applied by virtue of a section 100 order, the transitional period ends on the date on which the agreement so ceases.

(6) Sub-paragraph (3) is subject to paragraph 20.

(7) In this paragraph and paragraph 29 —
"section 100 order" means an order made under section 100 of the Electricity Act 1989; and
expressions which are also used in Part I of the Electricity Act 1989 have the same meaning as in that Part.

Electricity: power to make transitional orders

29. — (1) There is a transitional period for an agreement (whether made before or after the starting date) relating to the generation, transmission or supply of electricity which —

(a) is specified, or is of a description specified, in an order ("a transitional order") made by the Secretary of State (whether before or after the making of the agreement but before the end of the relevant period); and

(b) satisfies such conditions as may be specified in the order.

(2) A transitional order may make provision as to when the transitional period is respect of such an agreement is to start or to be deemed to have started.

(3) The transitional period for such an agreement ends at the end of the relevant period.

(4) But if the agreement —

(a) ceases to be one to which a transitional order applies, or

(b) ceases to satisfy one or more of the conditions specified in the transitional order,

the transitional period ends on the date on which the agreement so ceases.

(5) Before making a transitional order, the Secretary of State must consult the Director General of Electricity Supply and the Director.

(6) The conditions specified in a transitional order may include conditions which refer any matter to the Secretary of State for determination after such consultation as may be so specified.

(7) In the application of this paragraph to Northern Ireland, the reference in sub-paragraph (5) to the Director General of Electricity Supply is to be read as a reference to the Director General of Electricity Supply for Northern Ireland.

Gas

30. — (1) For an agreement to which, immediately before the starting date, the RTPA does not apply by virtue of section 62 or a section 62 order, there is a transitional period —

(a) beginning on the starting date; and

(b) ending at the end of the relevant period.

(2) For an agreement which is made at any time after the starting date and to which, had the RTPA not been repealed, that Act would not at the time at which the agreement is made have applied by virtue of section 62 or a section 62 order, there is a transitional period —

(a) beginning on the date on which the agreement is made; and

(b) ending at the end of the relevant period.

(3) For an agreement (whether made before or after the starting date) which, during the relevant period, is varied at any time in such a way that it becomes an agreement which, had the RTPA not been repealed, would at that time have been one to which that Act did not apply by virtue of section 62 or a section 62 order, there is a transitional period —

(a) beginning on the date on which the variation is made; and

(b) ending at the end of the relevant period.

(4) If an agreement for which there is a transitional period as a result of subparagraph (1), (2) or (3) is varied during the relevant period, the transitional period for the agreement continues if, had the RTPA not been repealed, the agreement would have continued to be one to which that Act did not apply by virtue of section 62 or a section 62 order.

(5) But if an agreement for which there is a transitional period as a result of sub-paragraph (1), (2) or (3) ceases to be one to which, had it not been repealed, the RTPA would not have applied by virtue of section 62 or a section 62 order, the transitional period ends on the date on which the agreement so ceases.

(6) Sub-paragraph (3) also applies in relation to a modification which is treated as an agreement made on or after 28th November 1985 by virtue of section 62(4).

(7) Sub-paragraph (3) is subject to paragraph 20.

(8) In this paragraph and paragraph 31 —
"section 62" means section 62 of the Gas Act 1986;
"section 62 order" means an order made under section 62.

Gas: power to make transitional orders

31. — (1) There is a transitional period for an agreement of a description falling within section 62(2)(a) and (b) or section 62(2A)(a) and (b) which —

(a) is specified, or is of a description specified, in an order ("a transitional order") made by the Secretary of State (whether before or after the making of the agreement but before the end of the relevant period); and

(b) satisfies such conditions as may be specified in the order.

(2) A transitional order may make provision as to when the transitional period in respect of such an agreement is to start or to be deemed to have started.

(3) The transitional period for such an agreement ends at the end of the relevant period.

(4) But if the agreement —

(a) ceases to be one to which a transitional order applies, or

(b) ceases to satisfy one or more of the conditions specified in the transitional order,

the transitional period ends on the date when the agreement so ceases.

(5) Before making a transitional order, the Secretary of State must consult the Director General of Gas Supply and the Director.

(6) The conditions specified in a transitional order may include —

    (a) conditions which are to be satisfied in relation to a time before the coming into force of this paragraph;

    (b) conditions which refer any matter (which may be the general question whether the Chapter I prohibition should apply to a particular agreement) to the Secretary of State, the Director or the Director General of Gas Supply for determination after such consultation as may be so specified.

Gas: Northern Ireland

32. — (1) For an agreement to which, immediately before the starting date, the RTPA does not apply by virtue of an Article 41 order, there is a transitional period —

    (a) beginning on the starting date; and

    (b) ending at the end of the relevant period.

(2) For an agreement which is made at any time after the starting date and to which, had the RTPA not been repealed, that Act would not at the time at which the agreement is made have applied by virtue of an article 41 order, there is a transitional period —

    (a) beginning on the date on which the agreement is made; and

    (b) ending at the end of the relevant period.

(3) For an agreement (whether made before or after the starting date) which, during the relevant period, is varied at any time in such a way that it becomes an agreement which, had the RTPA not been repealed, would at that time have been one to which that Act did not apply by virtue of an Article 41 order, there is a transitional period —

    (a) beginning on the date on which the variation is made; and

    (b) ending at the end of the relevant period.

(4) If an agreement for which there is a transitional period as a result of sub-paragraph (1), (2) or (3) is varied during the relevant period, the transitional period for the agreement continues if, had the RTPA not been repealed, the agreement would have continued to be one to which that Act did not apply by virtue of an Article 41 order.

(5) But if an agreement for which there is a transitional period as a result of sub-paragraph (1), (2) or (3) ceases to be one to which, had it not been repealed, the RTPA would not have applied by virtue of an Article 41 order, the transitional period ends on the date on which the agreement so ceases.

(6) Sub-paragraph (3) is subject to paragraph 20.

(7) In this paragraph and paragraph 33 —
"Article 41 order" means an order under Article 41 of the Gas (Northern Ireland) Order 1996;
"Department" means the Department of Economic Development.

Gas: Northern Ireland — power to make transitional orders

33. — (1) There is a transitional period for an agreement of a description falling within Article 41(1) which —

    (a) is specified, or is of a description specified, in an order ("a transitional order") made by the Department (whether before or after the making of the agreement but before the end of the relevant period); and

    (b) satisfies such conditions as may be specified in the order.

(2) A transitional order may make provision as to when the transitional period in respect of such an agreement is to start or to be deemed to have started.

(3) The transitional period for such an agreement ends at the end of the relevant period.

(4) But if the agreement —

    (a) ceases to be one to which a transitional order applies, or

    (b) ceases to satisfy one or more of the conditions specified in the transitional order,

the transitional period ends on the date when the agreement so ceases.

(5) Before making a transitional order, the Department must consult the Director General of Gas for Northern Ireland and the Director.

(6) The conditions specified in a transitional order may include conditions which refer any matter (which may be the general question whether the Chapter I prohibition should apply to a particular agreement) to the Department for determination after such consultation as may be so specified.

Railways

34. — (1) In this paragraph —
"section 131" means section 131 of the Railways Act 1993 ("the 1993 Act");
"section 131 agreement" means an agreement —

(a) to which the RTPA does not apply immediately before the starting date by virtue of section 131(1); or

(b) in respect of which a direction under section 131(3) is in force immediately before that date;
"non-exempt agreement" means an agreement relating to the provision of railway services (whether made before or after the starting date) which is not a section 131 agreement; and
"railway services" has the meaning given by section 82 of the 1993 Act.

(2) For a section 131 agreement there is a transitional period of five years.

(3) There is a transitional period for a non-exempt agreement to the extent to which the agreement is at any time before the end of the relevant period required or approved —

(a) by the Secretary of State or the Rail Regulator in pursuance of any function assigned or transferred to him under or by virtue of any provision of the 1993 Act;

(b) by or under any agreement the making of which is required or approved by the Secretary of State or the Rail Regulator in the exercise of any such function; or

(c) by or under a licence granted under Part I of the 1993 Act.

(4) The transitional period conferred by sub-paragraph (3) —

(a) is to be taken to have begun on the starting date; and

(b) ends at the end of the relevant period.

(5) Sub-paragraph (3) is subject to paragraph 20.

(6) Any variation of a section 131 agreement on or after the starting date is to be treated, for the purposes of this paragraph, as a separate non-exempt agreement.

The regulators

35. — (1) Subject to sub-paragraph (3), each of the regulators may exercise, in respect of sectoral matters and concurrently with the Director, the functions of the Director under paragraph 3, 7, 19(3), 36, 37, 38 or 39.

(2) In sub-paragraph (1) "sectoral matters" means —

(a) in the case of the Director General of Telecommunications, the matters referred to in section 50(3) of the Telecommunications Act 1984;

(b) in the case of the Director General of Gas supply, the matters referred to in section 36A(3) and (4) of the Gas Act 1986;

(c) in the case of the Director General of Electricity Supply, the matters referred to in section 43(3) of the Electricity Act 1989;

(d) in the case of the Director General of Electricity Supply for Northern Ireland, the matters referred to in Article 46(3) of the Electricity (Northern Ireland) Order 1992;

(e) in the case of the Director General of Water Services, the matters referred to in section 31(3) of the Water Industry Act 1991;

(f) in the case of the Rail Regulator, the matters referred to in section 67(3) of the Railways Act 1993;

(g) in the case of the Director General of Gas for Northern Ireland, the matters referred to in Article 23(3) of the Gas (Northern Ireland) Order 1996.

(3) The power to give directions in paragraph 7(2) is exercisable by the Director only but if the Director is preparing directions which relate to a matter in respect of which a regulator exercises concurrent jurisdiction, he must consult that regulator.

(4) Consultations conducted by the Director before the enactment date, with a view to preparing directions which have effect on or after that date, are to be taken to satisfy sub-paragraph (3).

(5) References to enactments in sub-paragraph (2) are to the enactments as amended by or under this Act.

CHAPTER V

EXTENDING THE TRANSITIONAL PERIOD

36. — (1) A party to an agreement for which there is a transitional period may apply to the Director, not less than three months before the end of the period, for the period to be extended.

(2) The Director may (on his own initiative or on an application under sub-paragraph (1)) —

    (a) extend a one-year transitional period by not more than twelve months;

    (b) extend a transitional period of any period other than one year by not more than six months.

(3) An application under sub-paragraph (1) must —

    (a) be in such form as may be specified; and

    (b) include such documents and information as may be specified.

(4) If the Director extends the transitional period under this paragraph, he must give notice in such form, and to such persons, as may be specified.

(5) The Director may not extend a transitional period more than once.

(6) In this paragraph —
"person" has the same meaning as in Part I; and
"specified" means specified in rules made by the Director under section 51.

CHAPTER VI

TERMINATING THE TRANSITIONAL PERIOD

General

37. — (1) Subject to sub-paragraph (2), the Director may by a direction in writing terminate the transitional period for an agreement, but only in accordance with paragraph 38.

(2) The Director may not terminate the transitional period, nor exercise any of the powers in paragraph 38, in respect of an agreement which is excluded from the Chapter I prohibition by virtue of any of the provisions of Part I of this Act other than paragraph 1 of Schedule 1 or paragraph 2 or 9 of Schedule 3.

Circumstances in which the Director may terminate the transitional period

38. — (1) If the Director is considering whether to give a direction under paragraph 37 ("a direction"), he may in writing require any party to the agreement concerned to give him such information in connection with that agreement as he may require.

(2) If at the end of such period as may be specified in rules made under section 51, a person has failed, without reasonable excuse, to comply with a requirement imposed under sub-paragraph (1), the Director may give a direction.

(3) The Director may also give a direction if he considers —

    (a) that the agreement would, but for the transitional period or a relevant exclusion, infringe the Chapter I prohibition; and

    (b) that he would not be likely to grant the agreement an unconditional individual exemption.

(4) For the purposes of sub-paragraph (3) an individual exemption is unconditional if no conditions or obligations are imposed in respect of it under section 4(3)(a).

(5) In this paragraph —
"person" has the same meaning as in Part I;
"relevant exclusion" means an exclusion under paragraph 1 of Schedule 1 or paragraph 2 or 9 of Schedule 3.

Procedural requirements on giving a paragraph 37 direction

39. — (1) The Director must specify in a direction under paragraph 37 ("a direction") the date on which it is to have effect (which must not be less than 28 days after the direction is given).

(2) Copies of the direction must be given to —

(a) each of the parties concerned, and

(b) the Secretary of State,

not less than 28 days before the date on which the direction is to have effect.

(3) In relation to an agreement to which a direction applies, the transitional period (if it has not already ended) ends on the date specified in the direction unless, before that date, the direction is revoked by the Director or the Secretary of State.

(4) If a direction is revoked, the Director may give a further direction in respect of the same agreement only if he is satisfied that there has been a material change of circumstance since the revocation.

(5) If, as a result of paragraph 24(1) or (3), there is a transitional period in respect of provisions of an agreement relating to goods —

(a) which immediately before the starting date are exempt under section 14 of the RPA, or

(b) which, when continuing proceedings are determined, are found to be exempt under section 14 of the RPA,

the period is not affected by paragraph 37 or 38.

PART V

THE FAIR TRADING ACT 1973

References to the Monopolies and Mergers Commission

40. — (1) If, on the date on which the repeal by this Act of a provision mentioned in sub-paragraph (2) comes into force, the Monopolies and Mergers Commission has not completed a reference which was made to it before that date, continued consideration of the reference may include consideration of a question which could not have been considered if the provision had not been repealed.

(2) The provisions are —

(a) sections 10(2), 54(5) and 78(3) and paragraph 3(1) and (2) of Schedule 8 to the Fair Trading Act 1973 (c. 41);

(b) section 11(8)(b) of the Competition Act 1980 (c. 21);

(c) section 14(2) of the Telecommunications Act 1984 (c. 12);

(d) section 45(3) of the Airports Act 1986 (c. 31);

(e) section 25(2) of the Gas Act 1986 (c. 44);

(f) section 13(2) of the Electricity Act 1989 (c. 29);

(g) section 15(2) of the Water Industry Act 1991 (c. 56);

(h) article 16(2) of the Electricity (Northern Ireland) Order 1992;

(i) section 14(2) of the Railways Act 1993 (c. 43);

(j) article 36(3) of the Airports (Northern Ireland) Order 1994;

(k) article 16(2) of the Gas (Northern Ireland) Order 1996.

Orders under Schedule 8

41. — (1) In this paragraph —
"the 1973 Act" means the Fair Trading Act 1973;

"agreement" means an agreement entered into before the date on which the repeal of the limiting provisions comes into force;

"the order" means an order under section 56 or 73 of the 1973 Act;

"the limiting provisions" means sub-paragraph (1) or (2) of paragraph 3 of Schedule 8 to the 1973 Act (limit on power to make orders under paragraph 1 or 2 of that Schedule) and includes any provision of the order included because of either of those sub-paragraphs; and

"transitional period" means the period which —

(a) begins on the day on which the repeal of the limiting provisions comes into force; and

(b) ends on the first anniversary of the starting date.

(2) Sub-paragraph (3) applies to any agreement to the extent to which it would have been unlawful (in accordance with the provisions of the order) but for the limiting provisions.

(3) As from the end of the transitional period, the order is to have effect in relation to the agreement as if the limiting provisions had never had effect.

Part III of the Act

42. — (1) The repeals made by section 1 do not affect any proceedings in respect of an application which is made to the Court under Part III of the Fair Trading Act 1973, but is not determined, before the starting date.

(2) The question whether (for the purposes of sub-paragraph (1)) an application has been determined is to be decided in accordance with sub-paragraphs (3) and (4).

(3) If an appeal against the decision on the application is brought, the application is not determined until —

(a) the appeal is disposed of or withdrawn; or

(b) if as a result of the appeal the case is referred back to the Court —

(i) the expiry of the period within which an appeal ("the further appeal") in respect of the Court's decision on that reference could have been brought had this Act not been passed; or

(ii) if later, the date on which the further appeal is disposed of or withdrawn.

(4) Otherwise, the application is not determined until the expiry of the period within which any party to the application would have been able to bring an appeal against the decision on the application had this Act not been passed.

(5) Any amendment made by Schedule 12 to this Act which substitutes references to a relevant Court for references to the Court is not to affect proceedings of the kind referred to in sub-paragraph (l).

Part VI

The Competition Act 1980

Undertakings

43. — (1) Subject to sub-paragraph (2), an undertaking accepted by the Director under section 4 or 9 of the Competition Act 1980 ceases to have effect on the coming into force of the repeal by this Act of that section.

(2) If the undertaking relates to an agreement which on the starting date is the subject of continuing proceedings, the undertaking continues to have effect for the purposes of section 29 of the Competition act 1980 until the proceedings are determined.

Application of sections 25 and 26

44. The repeals made by section 1 do not affect —

(a) the operation of section 25 of the Competition Act 1980 in relation to an application under section 1(3) of the RTPA which is made before the starting date;

(b) an application under section 26 of the Competition Act 1980 which is made before the starting date.

Part VII

Miscellaneous

Disclosure of information

45. — (1) Section 55 of this Act applies in relation to information which, immediately before the starting date, is subject to section 41 of the RTPA as it applies in relation to information obtained under or as a result of Part I.

(2) But section 55 does not apply to any disclosure of information of the kind referred to in sub-paragraph (1) if the disclosure is made —

    (a) for the purpose of facilitating the performance of functions of a designated person under the Control of Misleading Advertisements Regulations 1988; or

    (b) for the purposes of any proceedings before the Court or of any other legal proceedings under the RTPA or the Fair Trading Act 1973 or the Control of Misleading Advertisements Regulations 1988.

(3) Section 56 applies in relation to information of the kind referred to in sub-paragraph (1) if particulars containing the information have been entered or filed on the special section of the register maintained by the Director under, or as a result of, section 27 of the RTPA or paragraph 10 of this Schedule.

(4) Section 55 has effect, in relation to the matters as to which section 41(2) of the RTPA had effect, as if it contained a provision similar to section 41(2).

The Court

46. If it appears to the Lord Chancellor that a person who ceases to be a non-judicial member of the Court as a result of this Act should receive compensation for loss of office, he may pay to him out of moneys provided by Parliament such sum as he may with the approval of the Treasury determine.

SCHEDULE 14   Section 74(3).

REPEALS AND REVOCATIONS

PART I

REPEALS

Chapter	Short title	Extent of repeal
1973 c. 41.	The Fair Trading Act 1973.	Section 4. Section 10(2). Section 45. Section 54(5). Section 78(3). In section 81(1), in the words before paragraph (1), from "and the Commission" to "of this Act)"; in paragraph (b), "or the Commission, as the case may be" and "or of the Commission"; in subsection (2), "or the Commission" and "or of the Commission" and in subsection (3), from "and, in the case," to "85 of this Act", and "or the Commission, as the case may be,". In section 83, in subsection (1) "Subject to subsection (1A) below" and subsection (1A). In section 135(1), in the words before paragraph (a) and in paragraph (b), "or the Commission", and paragraph (a). Schedule 3. In Schedule 8, paragraph 3(1) and (2).
1976 c. 33.	The Restrictive Practices Court Act 1976.	The whole Act.
1976 c. 34.	The Restrictive Trade Practices Act 1976.	The whole Act.
1976 c. 53.	The Resale Prices Act 1976.	The whole Act.
1976 c. 76.	The Energy Act 1976.	Section 5.
1977 c. 19.	The Restrictive Trade Practices Act 1977.	The whole Act.

Chapter	Short title	Extent of repeal
1977 c. 37.	The Patents Act 1977.	Sections 44 and 45.
1979 c. 38.	The Estate Agents Act 1979.	In section 10(3), "or the Restrictive Trade Practices Act 1976."
1980 c. 21.	The Competition Act 1980.	Sections 2 to 10.
		In section 11(8), paragraph (b) and the "and" immediately before it.
		In section 13(1), from "but the giving" to the end.
		In section 15, subsections (2)(b), (3) and (4).
		Section 16(3).
		In section 17, "8(1)" in subsections (1) and (3) to (5) and in subection (2) "8(1) or".
		In section 19(3), paragraph (d).
		In section 19(5)(a), "or in anything published under section 4(2)(a) above".
		Section 22.
		Sections 25 to 30.
		In section 31, subsection (2) and "10" in subsection (3).
		Section 33(3) and (4).
1984 c. 12.	The Telecommunications Act 1984.	Section 14(2).
		In section 16(5), the "or" immediately after paragraph (a).
		In section 50(4), paragraph (c) and the "and" immediately after it.
		In section 50(5), "or (3)".
		In section 50(7), "or the 1980 Act".
		In section 95(1), "or section 10(2)(a) of the 1980 Act".
		In section 95(2), paragraph (c) and the "or" immediately before it.
		In section 95(3), "or the 1980 Act".
		In section 101(3), paragraphs (d) and (e).
1986 c. 31.	The Airports Act 1986.	Section 45(3).
		In section 54(1), "or section 10(2)(a) of the 1980 Act".
		In section 54(3), paragraph (c) and the "or" immediately before it.
		In section 54(4), "or the 1980 Act".
		In section 56(a)(ii), "or the 1980 Act".
1986 c. 44.	The Gas Act 1986.	Section 25(2).
		In section 27(1), "or section 10(2)(a) of the Competition Act 1980".
		In section 27(3)(a), from "or" to "completion reference".
		In section 27(6), "or the said Act of 1980".
		In section 28(5), the "or" immediately after paragraph (aa).
		In section 36A(5), paragraph (d) and the "and" immediately before it.

Chapter	Short title	Extent of repeal
		In section 36A(6), "or (3)".
		In section 36A(8), "or under the 1980 Act".
		In section 36A(9), "or the 1980 Act".
		In section 42(3), paragraphs (e) and (f).
1986 c. 60.	The Financial Services Act 1986.	Section 126.
1987 c. 43.	The Consumer Protection Act 1987.	In section 38(3), paragraphs (e) and (f).
1987 c. 53.	The Channel Tunnel Act 1987.	In section 33(2), paragraph (c) and the "and" immediately before it.
		In section 33(5), paragraphs (b) and (c).
1988 c. 54.	The Road Traffic (Consequential Provisions) Act 1988.	In Schedule 3, paragraph 19.
1989 c. 15.	The Water Act 1989.	In section 174(3), paragraphs (d) and (e).
1989 c. 29.	The Electricity Act 1989.	Section 13(2).
		In section 15(1), paragraph (b) and the "or" immediately before it.
		In section 15(2), paragraph (c) and the "or" immediately before it.
		In section 15(3), "or the 1980 Act".
		In section 25(5), the "or" immediately after paragraph (b).
		In section 43(4), paragraph (c) and the "and" immediately after it.
		In section 43(5), "or (3)".
		In section 43(7), "or the 1980 Act".
		In section 57(3), paragraphs (d) and (e).
1989 c. 40.	The Companies Act 1989.	In Schedule 20, paragraphs 21 to 24.
1990 c. 42.	The Broadcasting Act 1990.	In section 193(2), paragraph (c) and the "and" immediately before it.
		In section 193(4), "or the Competition Act 1980".
1991 c. 56.	The Water Industry Act 1991.	In section 12(5), "or the 1980 Act".
		Section 15(2).
		In section 17(1), paragraph (b) and the "or" immediately before it.
		In section 17(2), paragraph (c) and the "or" immediately before it.
		In section 17(4), "or the 1980 Act".
		In section 31(4), paragraph (c) and the "and" immediately before it.
		In section 31(5), "or in subsection (3) above".
		In section 31(6), "or in subsection (3) above".
		In section 31(7), "or (3)".
		In section 31(9), "or the 1980 Act".

Chapter	Short title	Extent of repeal
		In Part II of Schedule 15, the entries relating to the Restrictive Trade Practices Act 1976 and the Resale Prices Act 1976.
1991 c. 57.	The Water Resources Act 1991.	In Part II of Schedule 24, the entries relating to the Restrictive Trade Practices Act 1976 and the Resale Prices Act 1976.
1993 c. 21.	The Osteopaths Act 1993.	In section 33(4), paragraph (b) and the "or" immediately before it. In section 33(5), "or section 10 of the Act of 1980".
1993 c. 43.	The Railways Act 1993.	Section 14(2). In section 16(1), paragraph (b) and the "or" immediately before it. In section 16(2), paragraph (c) and the "or" immediately before it. In section 16(5), "or the 1980 Act". In section 67(4), paragraph (c) and the "and" immediately after it.
1993 c. 43. — contd.	The Railways Act 1993. — contd.	In section 67(6)(a), "or (3)". In section 67(9), "or under the 1980 Act". Section 131. In section 145(3), paragraphs (d) and (e).
1994 c. 17.	The Chiropractors Act 1994.	In section 33(4), paragraph (b) and the "or" immediately before it. In section 33(5), "or section 10 of the Act of 1980".
1994 c. 21.	The Coal Industry Act 1994.	In section 59(4), paragraphs (e) and (f).
1994 c. 40.	The Deregulation and Contracting Out Act 1994.	Sections 10 and 11. In section 12, subsections (1) to (6). In schedule 4, paragraph 1. In Schedule 11, in paragraph 4, sub-paragraphs (3) to (6).
1996 c. 55.	The Broadcasting Act 1996.	Section 77(2).

PART II

REVOCATIONS

Reference	Title	Extent of revocation
S.I. 1981/1675 (N.I.26).	The Magistrates' Courts (Northern Ireland) Order 1981.	In Schedule 6, paragraphs 42 and 43.
S.I. 1982/1080 (N.I.12)	The Agricultural Marketing (Northern Ireland) Order 1982.	In Schedule 8, the entry relating to paragraph 16(2) of Schedule 3 to the Fair Trading Act 1973 and in the entry relating to the Competition Act 1980, "and 15(3)".
S.I. 1986/1035 (N.I.9).	The Companies Consolidation (Consequential Provisions) (Northern Ireland) Order 1986.	In Part II of Schedule 1, the entries relating to the Restrictive Trade Practices Act 1976 and the Resale Prices Act 1976.

Chapter	Short title	Extent of repeal
S.I. 1992/231 (N.I.1).	The Electricity (Northern Ireland) Order 1992.	Article 16(2). In Article 18 — (a) in paragraph (1), sub-paragraph (b) and the "or" immediately before it; (b) in paragraph (2), subparagraph (c) and the "or" immediately before it; (c) in paragraph (3) "or the 1980 Act". In Article 28(5), the "or" immediately after sub-paragraph (b). In Article 46 — (a) in paragraph (4), sub-paragraph (c) and the "and" immediately after it; (b) in paragraph (5), "or (3)"; (c) in paragraph (7), "or the 1980 Act". Article 61(3)(f) and (g). In Schedule 12, paragraph 16.
S.I. 1994/426 (N.I.1)	The Airports (Northern Ireland) Order 1994.	Article 36(3). In Article 45 — (a) in paragraph (1), "or section 10(2)(a) of the 1980 Act"; (b) in paragraph (3), sub-paragraph (c) and the "or" immediately before it; (c) in paragraph (4), "or the 1980 Act". In Article 47(a)(ii), "or the 1980 Act". In Schedule 9, paragraph 5.
S.I. 1996/275 (N.I.2).	The Gas (Northern Ireland) Order 1996.	Article 16(2). In Article 18 — (a) in paragraph (1), sub-paragraph (b) and the "or" immediately before it; (b) in paragraph (3), sub-paragraph (c) and the "or" immediately before it; (c) in paragraph (5), "or the 1980 Act". In Article 19(5), the "or" immediately after sub-paragraph (b) In Article 23 — (a) in paragraph (4), sub-paragraph (d) and the "and" immediately before it; (b) in paragraph (5), "or (3)"; (c) in paragraph (7), "or under the 1980 Act"; (d) in paragraph (8), "or the 1980 Act". Article 44(4)(f) and (g).

APPENDIX A.2   EXTRACTS FROM THE TREATY OF ROME

Articles 1–6

Article 1

A.2-01   By this Treaty, the High Contracting Parties establish among themselves a EUROPEAN COMMUNITY.

Article 2

The Community shall have as its task, by establishing a common market [and an economic and monetary union and by implementing the common policies or activities referred to in Articles 3 and 3a,] to promote throughout the Community a harmonious [and balanced] development of economic activities, [sustainable and non-inflationary growth respecting the environment, a high degree of convergence of economic performance, a high level of employment and of social protection, the] raising of the standard of living [and quality of life, and economic and social cohesion and solidarity among Member States].

Article 3

For the purposes set out in Article 2, the activities of the Community shall include, as provided in this Treaty and in accordance with the timetable set out therein:

[(a) the elimination, as between Member States, of customs duties and quantitative restrictions on the import and export of goods, and of all other measures having equivalent effect;

(b) a common commercial policy;

(c) an internal market characterized by the abolition, as between Member States, of obstacles to the free movement of goods, persons, services and capital;

(d) measures concerning the entry and movement of persons in the internal market as provided for in Article 100c;

(e) a common policy in the sphere of agriculture and fisheries;

(f) a common policy in the sphere of transport;

(g) a system ensuring that competition in the internal market is not distorted;

(h) the approximation of the laws of Member States to the extent required for the functioning of the common market;

(i) a policy in the social sphere comprising a European Social Fund;

(j) the strengthening of economic and social cohesion;

(k) a policy in the sphere of the environment;

(l) the strengthening of the competitiveness of Community industry;

(m) the promotion of research and technological development;

(n) encouragement for the establishment and development of trans-European networks;

(o) a contribution to the attainment of a high level of health protection;

(p) a contribution to education and training of quality and to the flowering of the cultures of the Member States;

(q) a policy in the sphere of development cooperation;

(r) the association of the overseas countries and territories in order to increase trade and promote jointly economic and social development;

(s) a contribution to the strengthening of consumer protection;

(t) measures in the spheres of energy, civil protection and tourism.]

[Article 3a

1. For the purposes set out in Article 2, the activities of the Member States and the Community shall include, as provided in this Treaty and in accordance with the timetable set out therein, the adoption of an economic policy which is based on the close coordination of Member States' economic policies, on the internal market and on the definition of common objectives, and conducted in accordance with the principle of an open market economy with free competition.

2. Concurrently with the foregoing, and as provided in this Treaty and in accordance with the timetable and the procedures set out therein, these activities shall include the irrevocable fixing of exchange rates leading to the introduction of a single currency, the ecu, and the definition and conduct of a single monetary policy and exchange-rate policy the primary objective of both of which shall be to maintain price stability and, without prejudice to this objective, to support the general economic policies in the Community, in accordance with the principle of an open market economy with free competition.

3. These activities of the Member States and the Community shall entail compliance with the following guiding principles: stable prices, sound public finances and monetary conditions and a sustainable balance of payments.]

[Article 3b

The Community shall act within the limits of the powers conferred upon it by this Treaty and of the objectives assigned to it therein.

In areas which do not fall within its exclusive competence, the Community shall take action, in accordance with the principle of subsidiarity, only if and in so far as the objectives of the proposed action cannot be sufficiently achieved by the Member States and can therefore, by reason of the scale or effects of the proposed action, be better achieved by the Community.

Any action by the Community shall not go beyond what is necessary to achieve the objectives of this Treaty.]

Article 4

1. The tasks entrusted to the Community shall be carried out by the following institutions:

a EUROPEAN PARLIAMENT,

a COUNCIL,

a COMMISION,

a COURT OF JUSTICE,

a COURT OF AUDITORS

Each institution shall act within the limits of the powers conferred upon it by this Treaty.

2. The Council and the Commission shall be assisted by an Economic and Social Committee and a Committee of the Regions acting in an advisory capacity.

Article 5

Member States shall take all appropriate measures, whether general or particular, to ensure fulfilment of the obligations arising out of this Treaty or resulting from action taken by the institutions of the Community. They shall facilitate the achievement of the Community's tasks.

They shall abstain from any measure which could jeopardise the attainment of the objectives of this Treaty.

Article [6]

Within the scope of application of this Treaty, and without prejudice to any special provisions contained therein, any discrimination on grounds of nationality shall be prohibited.

The Council, acting in accordance with the procedure referred to in Article 189c, may adopt rules designed to prohibit such discrimination.

Articles 30–36

Article 30

A.2-02   Quantitative restrictions on imports and all measures having equivalent effect shall, without prejudice to the following provisions, be prohibited between Member States.

Article 31

Member States shall refrain from introducing between themselves any new quantitative restrictions or measures having equivalent effect.

This obligation shall, however, relate only to the degree of liberalisation attained in pursuance of the decisions of the Council of the Organisation for European Economic Co-operation of 14 January 1955. Member States shall supply the Commission, not later than six months after the entry into force of this Treaty, with lists of the products liberalised by them in pursuance of these decisions. These lists shall be consolidated between Member States.

Article 32

In their trade with one another Member States shall refrain from making more restrictive the quotas and measures having equivalent effect existing at the date of the entry into force of this Treaty.

These quotas shall be abolished by the end of the transitional period at the latest. During that period, they shall be progressively abolished in accordance with the following provisions.

Article 33

1. One year after the entry into force of this Treaty, each Member State shall convert any bilateral quotas open to any other Member States into global quotas open without discrimination to all other Member States.

On the same date, Member States shall increase the aggregate of the global quotas so established in such a manner as to bring about an increase of not less than 20 per cent. in their total value as compared with the preceding year. The global quota for each product, however, shall be increased by not less than 10 per cent.

The quota shall be increased annually in accordance with the same rules and in the same proportions in relation to the preceding year.

The fourth increase shall take place at the end of the fourth year after the entry into force of this Treaty; the fifth, one year after the beginning of the second stage.

2. Where, in the case of a product which has not been liberalised, the global quota does not amount to 3 per cent. of the national production of the State concerned, a quota equal to not less than 3 per cent. of such national production shall be introduced not later than one year after the entry into force of this Treaty. This quota shall be raised to 4 per cent. at the end of the second year, and to 5 per cent. at the end of the third. Thereafter, the Member State concerned shall increase the quota by not less than 15 per cent. annually.

Where there is no such national production, the Commission shall take a decision establishing an appropriate quota.

3. At the end of the tenth year, each quota shall be equal to not less than 20 per cent. of the national production.

4. If the Commission finds by means of a decision that during two successive years the imports of any products have been below the level of the quota opened, this global quota shall not be taken into account in calculating the total value of the global quotas. In such case, the Member State shall abolish quota restrictions on the product concerned.

5. In the case of quotas representing more than 20 per cent. of the national production of the product concerned, the Council may, acting by a qualified majority on a proposal from the Commission, reduce the minimum percentage of 10 per cent. laid down in paragraph 1. This alteration shall not, however, affect the obligation to increase the total value of global quotas by 20 per cent. annually.

6. Member States which have exceeded their obligations as regards the degree of liberalisation attained in pursuance of the decisions of the Council of the Organisation for European Economic Co-operation of 14 January 1955 shall be entitled, when calculating the annual total increase of 20 per cent. provided for in paragraph 1, to take into account the amount of imports liberalised by autonomous action. Such calculation shall be submitted to the Commission for its prior approval.

7. The Commission shall issue directives establishing the procedure and timetable in accordance with which Member States shall abolish, as between themselves, any measures in existence when this Treaty enters into force which have an effect equivalent to quotas.

8. If the Commission finds that the application of the provisions of this Article, and in particular of the provisions concerning percentages, makes it impossible to ensure that the abolition of quotas provided for in the second paragraph of Article 32 is carried out progressively, the Council may, on a proposal from the Commission, acting unanimously during the first stage and by a qualified majority thereafter, amend the procedure laid down in this Article and may, in particular, increase the percentages fixed.

Article 34

1. Quantitative restrictions on exports, and all members having equivalent effect shall be prohibited between Member States.

2. Member States shall, by the end of the first stage at the latest, abolish all quantitative restrictions on exports and any measures having equivalent effect which are in existence when this Treaty enters into force.

Article 35

The Member States declare their readiness to abolish quantitative restrictions on imports from and exports to other Member States more rapidly than is provided for in the preceding Articles, if their general economic situation of the economic sector concerned so permits.

To this end, the Commission shall make recommendations to the States concerned.

Article 36

The provisions of Articles 30 to 34 shall not preclude prohibitions or restrictions on imports, exports or goods in transit justified on grounds of public morality, public policy or public security;

the protection of health and life of humans, animals or plants; the protection of national treasures possessing artistic, historic or archaeological value; or the protection of industrial and commercial property. Such prohibitions or restrictions shall not, however, constitute a means of arbitrary discrimination or a disguised restriction on trade between Member States.

Articles 85–86

Article 85

A.2-03   1. The following shall be prohibited as incompatible with the common market: all agreements between undertakings, decisions by associations of undertakings and concerted practices which may affect trade between Member States and which have as their object or effect the prevention, restriction or distortion of competition within the common market, and in particular those which:

(a) directly or indirectly fix purchase or selling prices or any other trading conditions;

(b) limit or control production, markets, technical development, or investment;

(c) share markets or sources of supply;

(d) apply dissimilar conditions to equivalent transactions with other trading parties, thereby placing them at a competitive disadvantage;

(e) make the conclusion of contracts subject to acceptance by the other parties of supplementary obligations which, by their nature or according to commercial usage, have no connection with the subject of such contracts.

2. Any agreements or decisions prohibited pursuant to this Article shall be automatically void.

3. The provisions of paragraph 1 may, however, be declared inapplicable in the case of:
— any agreement or category of agreements between undertakings;
— any decision or category of decisions by associations of undertakings;
— any concerted practice or category of concerted practices;
which contributes to improving the production or distribution of goods or to promoting technical or economic progress, while allowing consumers a fair share of the resulting benefit, and which does not:

(a) impose on the undertakings concerned restrictions which are not indispensable to the attainment of these objectives;

(b) afford such undertakings the possibility of eliminating competition in respect of a substantial part of the products in question.

Article 86

Any abuse by one or more undertakings of a dominant position within the common market or in a substantial part of it shall be prohibited as incompatible with the common market in so far as it may affect trade between Member States. Such abuse may, in particular, consist in:

(a) directly or indirectly imposing unfair purchase or selling prices or other unfair trading conditions;

(b) limiting production, markets or technical development to the prejudice of consumers;

(c) applying dissimilar conditions to equivalent transactions with other trading parties, thereby placing them at a competitive disadvantage;

(d) making the conclusion of contracts subject to acceptance by the other parties of supplementary obligations which, by their nature or according to commercial usage, have no connection with the subject of such contracts.

Articles 172–177

[Article 172

A.2-04 Regulations adopted jointly by the European Parliament and the Council, and by the Council, pursuant to the provisions of this Treaty, may give the Court of Justice unlimited jurisdiction with regard to the penalties provided for in such regulations.]

[Article 173

The Court of Justice shall review the legality of acts adopted jointly by the European Parliament and the Council, of acts of the Council, of the Commission and of the ECB, other than recommendations and opinions, and of acts of the European Parliament intended to produce legal effects *vis-à-vis* third parties.

It shall for this purpose have jurisdiction in actions brought by a Member State, the Council or the Commission on grounds of lack of competence, infringement of an essential procedural requirement, infringement of this Treaty or of any rule of law relating to its application, or misuse of powers.

The Court shall have jurisdiction under the same conditions in actions brought by the European Parliament and by the ECB for the purpose of protecting their prerogatives.

Any natural or legal person may, under the same conditions, institute proceedings against a decision addressed to that person or against a decision which, although in the form of a regulation or a decision addressed to another person, is of direct and individual concern to the former.

The proceedings provided for in this Article shall be instituted within two months of the publication of the measure, or of its notification to the plaintiff, or, in the absence thereof, of the day on which it came to the knowledge of the latter, as the case may be.]

Article 174

If the action is well founded, the Court of Justice shall declare the act concerned to be void.

In the case of a regulation, however, the Court of Justice shall, if it considers this necessary, state which of the effects of the regulation which it has declared void shall be considered as definitive.

[Article 175

Should the European Parliament, the Council or the Commission, in infringement of this Treaty, fail to act, the Member States and the other institutions of the Community may bring an action before the Court of Justice to have the infringement established.

The action shall be admissible only if the institution concerned has first been called upon to act. If, within two months of being so called upon, the institution concerned has not defined its position, the action may be brought within a further period of two months.

Any natural or legal person may, under the conditions laid down in the preceding paragraphs, complain to the Court of Justice that an institution of the Community has failed to address to that person any act other than a recommendation or an opinion.

The Court of Justice shall have jurisdiction, under the same conditions, in actions or proceedings brought by the ECB in the areas falling within the latter's field of competence and in actions or proceedings brought against the latter.]

[Article 176

The institution or institutions whose act has been declared void or whose failure to act has been declared contrary to this Treaty shall be required to take the necessary measures to comply with the judgment of the Court of Justice.

This obligation shall not affect any obligation which may result from the application of the second paragraph of Article 215.

This Article shall also apply to the ECB.]

[*Article 177*

The Court of Justice shall have jurisdiction to give preliminary rulings concerning:

(a) the interpretation of this Treaty;

(b) the validity and interpretation of acts of the institutions of the Community and of the ECB;

(c) the interpretation of the statutes of bodies established by an act of the Council, where those statutes so provide.

Where such a question is raised before any court or tribunal of a Member State, that court or tribunal may, if it considers that a decision on the question is necessary to enable it to give judgment, request the Court of Justice to give a ruling thereon.

Where any such question is raised in a case pending before a court or tribunal of a Member State against whose decisions there is no judicial remedy under national law, that court or tribunal shall bring the matter before the Court of Justice.]

APPENDIX A.3   ARTICLE CHANGES FOLLOWING THE AMSTERDAM TREATY

A.3-01   Here is a list of changes to the numbering of the E.C. Treaty Articles as effected by the Treaty of Amsterdam:

Before ratification	After ratification	Before ratification	After ratification
Article 1	Article 1	Article 15 (repealed)	—
Article 2	Article 2	Article 16 (repealed)	—
Article 3	Article 3	Article 17 (repealed)	—
Article 3a	Article 4	Section 2 (deleted)	—
Article 3b	Article 5	Article 18 (repealed)	—
Article 3c (*)	Article 6	Article 19 (repealed)	—
Article 4	Article 7	Article 20 (repealed)	—
Article 4a	Article 8	Article 21 (repealed)	—
Article 4b	Article 9	Article 22 (repealed)	—
Article 5	Article 10	Article 23 (repealed)	—
Article 5a (*)	Article 11	Article 24 (repealed)	—
Article 6	Article 12	Article 25 (repealed)	—
Article 6a (*)	Article 13	Article 26 (repealed)	—
Article 7 (repealed)*	—	Article 27 (repealed)	—
Article 7a	Article 14	Article 28 (repealed)	—
Article 7b (repealed)	—	Article 29 (repealed)	—
Article 7c	Article 15	Chapter 2	Chapter 2
Article 7d (*)	Article 16	Article 30	Article 28
Part Two	**Part Two**	Article 31 (repealed)	—
Article 8	Article 17	Article 32 (repealed)	—
Article 8a	Article 18	Article 33 (repealed)	—
Article 8b	Article 19	Article 34	Article 29
Article 8c	Article 20	Article 35 (repealed)	—
Article 8d	Article 21	Article 36	Article 30
Article 83	Article 22	Article 37	Article 31
Part Three	**Part Three**	Title II	Title II
Title I	Title I	Article 38	Article 32
Article 9	Article 23	Article 39	Article 33
Article 10	Article 24	Article 40	Article 34
Article 11 (repealed)	—	Article 41	Article 35
Chapter 1	Chapter 1	Article 42	Article 36
Section 1 (deleted)	—	Article 43	Article 37
Article 12	Article 25	Article 44 (repealed)	—
Article 13 (repealed)	—	Article 45 (repealed)	—
Article 14 (repealed)	—	Article 46	Article 38

Before ratification	After ratification	Before ratification	After ratification
Article 47 (repealed)	—	Article 84	Article 80
Title III	Title III	Title V	Title VI
Chapter 1	Chapter 1	Chapter 1	Chapter 1
Article 48	Article 39	Section 1	Section 1
Article 49	Article 40	Article 85	Article 81
Article 50	Article 41	Article 86	Article 82
Article 51	Article 42	Article 87	Article 83
Chapter 2	Chapter 2	Article 88	Article 84
Article 52	Article 43	Article 89	Article 85
Article 53 (repealed)	—	Article 90	Article 86
Article 54	Article 44	Section 2 (deleted)	—
Article 55	Article 45	Article 91 (repealed)	—
Article 56	Article 46	Section 3	Section 2
Article 57	Article 47	Article 92	Article 87
Article 58	Article 48	Article 93	Article 88
Chapter 3	Chapter 3	Article 94	Article 89
Article 59	Article 49	Chapter 2	Chapter 2
Article 60	Article 50	Article 95	Article 90
Article 61	Article 51	Article 96	Article 91
Article 62 (repealed)	—	Article 97 (repealed)	—
Article 63	Article 52	Article 98	Article 92
Article 64	Article 53	Article 99	Article 93
Article 65	Article 54	Chapter 3	Chapter 3
Article 66	Article 55	Article 100	Article 94
Chapter 4	Chapter 4	Article 100a	Article 95
Article 67 (repealed)	—	Article 100b (repealed)	—
Article 68 (repealed)	—	Article 100c (repealed)	—
Article 69 (repealed)	—	Article 100d (repealed)	—
Article 70 (repealed)	—	Article 101	Article 96
Article 71 (repealed)	—	Article 102	Article 97
Article 72 (repealed)	—	Title VI	Title VII
Article 73 (repealed)	—	Chapter 1	Chapter 1
Article 73a (repealed)	—	Article 102a	Article 98
Article 73b	Article 56	Article 103	Article 99
Article 73c	Article 57	Article 103a	Article 100
Article 73d	Article 58	Article 104	Article 101
Article 73e (repealed)	—	Article 104a	Article 102
Article 73f	Article 59	Article 104b	Article 103
Article 73g	Article 60	Article 104c	Article 104
Article 73h (repealed)	—	Chapter 2	Chapter 2
Title IIIa (**)	Title IV	Article 105	Article 105
Article 73i (*)	Article 61	Article 105a	Article 106
Article 73j (*)	Article 62	Article 106	Article 107
Article 73k (*)	Article 63	Article 107	Article 108
Article 73l (*)	Article 64	Article 108	Article 109
Article 73m (*)	Article 65	Article 108a	Article 110
Article 73n (*)	Article 66	Article 109	Article 111
Article 73o (*)	Article 67	Chapter 3	Chapter 3
Article 73p (*)	Article 68	Article 109a	Article 112
Article 73q (*)	Article 69	Article 109b	Article 113
Title IV	Title V	Article 109c	Article 114
Article 74	Article 70	Article 109d	Article 115
Article 75	Article 71	Chapter 4	Chapter 4
Article 76	Article 72	Article 109e	Article 116
Article 77	Article 73	Article 109f	Article 117
Article 78	Article 74	Article 109g	Article 118
Article 79	Article 75	Article 109h	Article 119
Article 80	Article 76	Article 109i	Article 120
Article 81	Article 77	Article 109j	Article 121
Article 82	Article 78	Article 109k	Article 122
Article 83	Article 79	Article 109l	Article 123

Before ratification	*After ratification*	*Before ratification*	*After ratification*
Article 109m	Article 124	Article 130l	Article 169
Title VIa (**)	Title VIII	Article 130m	Article 170
Article 109n (*)	Article 125	Article 130n	Article 171
Article 109o (*)	Article 126	Article 130o	Article 172
Article 109p (*)	Article 127	Article 130p	Article 173
Article 109q (*)	Article 128	Article 130q (repealed)	—
Article 109r (*)	Article 129	Title XVI	Title XIX
Article 109s (*)	Article 130	Article 130r	Article 174
Title VII	Title IX	Article 130s	Article 175
Article 110	Article 131	Article 130t	Article 176
Article 111 (repealed)	—	Title XCII	Title XX
Article 112	Article 132	Article 130u	Article 177
Article 113	Article 133	Article 130v	Article 178
Article 114 (repealed)	—	Article 130w	Article 179
Article 115	Article 134	Article 130x	Article 180
Title VIIa (**)	Title X	Article 130y	Article 181
Article 116 (*)	Article 135	**Part Four**	**Part Four**
Title VIII	Title XI	Article 131	Article 182
Chapter 1 (***)	Chapter 1	Article 132	Article 183
Article 117	Article 136	Article 133	Article 184
Article 118	Article 137	Article 134	Article 185
Article 118a	Article 138	Article 135	Article 186
Article 118b	Article 139	Article 136	Article 187
Article 118c	Article 140	Article 136a	Article 188
Article 119	Article 141	**Part Five**	**Part Five**
Article 119a	Article 142	Title I	Title I
Article 120	Article 143	Chapter 1	Chapter 1
Article 121	Article 144	Section 1	Section 1
Article 122	Article 145	Article 137	Article 189
Chapter 2	Chapter 2	Article 138	Article 190
Article 123	Article 146	Article 138a	Article 191
Article 124	Article 147	Article 138b	Article 192
Article 125	Article 148	Article 138c	Article 193
Chapter 3	Chapter 3	Article 138d	Article 194
Article 126	Article 149	Article 138e	Article 195
Article 127	Article 150	Article 139	Article 196
Title IX	Title XII	Article 140	Article 197
Article 128	Article 151	Article 141	Article 198
Title X	Title XIII	Article 142	Article 199
Article 129	Article 152	Article 143	Article 200
Title XI	Title XIV	Article 144	Article 201
Article 129a	Article 153	Section 2	Section 2
Title XII	Title XV	Article 145	Article 202
Article 129b	Article 154	Article 146	Article 203
Article 129c	Article 155	Article 147	Article 204
Article 129d	Article 156	Article 148	Article 205
Title XIII	Title XVI	Article 149 (repealed)	—
Article 130	Article 157	Article 150	Article 206
Title XIV	Title XVII	Article 151	Article 207
Article 130a	Article 158	Article 152	Article 208
Article 130b	Article 159	Article 153	Article 209
Article 130c	Article 160	Article 154	Article 210
Article 130d	Article 161	Section 3	Section 3
Article 130e	Article 161	Article 155	Article 211
Title XV	Title XVIII	Article 156	Article 212
Article 130f	Article 163	Article 157	Article 213
Article 130g	Article 164	Article 158	Article 214
Article 130h	Article 165	Article 159	Article 215
Article 130i	Article 166	Article 160	Article 216
Article 130j	Article 167	Article 161	Article 217
Article 130k	Article 168	Article 162	Article 218

Before ratification	After ratification	Before ratification	After ratification
Article 163	Article 219	Article 200 (repealed)	—
Section 4	Section 4	Article 201	Article 269
Article 164	Article 220	Article 201a	Article 270
Article 165	Article 221	Article 202	Article 271
Article 166	Article 222	Article 203	Article 272
Article 167	Article 223	Article 204	Article 273
Article 168	Article 224	Article 205	Article 274
Article 168a	Article 225	Article 205a	Article 275
Article 169	Article 226	Article 206	Article 276
Article 170	Article 227	Article 206a (repealed)	—
Article 171	Article 228	Article 207	Article 277
Article 172	Article 229	Article 208	Article 278
Article 173	Article 230	Article 209	Article 279
Article 174	Article 231	Article 209a	Article 280
Article 175	Article 232	**Part Six**	**Part Six**
Article 176	Article 233	Article 210	Article 281
Article 177	Article 234	Article 211	Article 282
Article 178	Article 235	Article 212 (*)	Article 283
Article 179	Article 236	Article 213	Article 284
Article 180	Article 237	Article 213a (*)	Article 285
Article 181	Article 238	Article 213b (*)	Article 286
Article 182	Article 239	Article 214	Article 287
Article 183	Article 239	Article 215	Article 288
Article 183	Article 240	Article 216	Article 289
Article 184	Article 241	Article 217	Article 290
Article 185	Article 242	Article 218 (*)	Article 291
Article 186	Article 243	Article 219	Article 292
Article 187	Article 244	Article 220	Article 293
Article 188	Article 245	Article 221	Article 294
Section 5	Section 5	Article 222	Article 293
Article 188a	Article 246	Article 223	Article 296
Article 188b	Article 247	Article 224	Article 297
Article 188c	Article 248	Article 225	Article 298
Chapter 2	Chapter 2	Article 226 (repealed)*	—
Article 189	Article 249	Article 227	Article 299
Article 189a	Article 250	Article 228	Article 300
Article 189b	Article 251	Article 228a	Article 301
Article 189c	Article 252	Article 229	Article 302
Article 190	Article 253	Article 230	Article 303
Article 191	Article 254	Article 231	Article 304
Article 191a (*)	Article 255	Article 232	Article 305
Article 192	Article 256	Article 233	Article 306
Chapter 3	Chapter 3	Article 234	Article 307
Article 193	Article 257	Article 235	Article 308
Article 194	Article 258	Article 236 (*)	Article 309
Article 195	Article 259	Article 237 (repealed)	—
Article 196	Article 260	Article 238	Article 310
Article 197	Article 261	Article 239	Article 311
Article 198	Article 262	Article 240	Article 312
Chapter 4	Chapter 4	Article 241 (repealed)	—
Article 198a	Article 263	Article 242 (repealed)	—
Article 198b	Article 264	Article 243 (repealed)	—
Article 198c	Article 265	Article 244 (repealed)	—
Chapter 5	Chapter 5	Article 245 (repealed)	—
Article 198d	Article 266	Article 246 (repealed)	—
Article 198e	Article 267	Final Provisions	Final Provisions
Title II	Title II	Article 247	Article 313
Article 199	Article 268	Article 248	Article 314 (*)

(*) New Article introduced by the Treaty of Amsterdam
(**) New Title introduced by the Treaty of Amsterdam
(***) Chapter 1 restructured by the Treaty of Amsterdam

Appendix B

APPENDIX B.1 — FORM A/B, COMMISSION REGULATION 3385/94 OF DECEMBER 21 1994

([1994] O.J. L377/28)

B.1-01   On the form, content and other details of application and notifications provided for in Council Regulation No. 17

THE COMMISSION OF THE EUROPEAN COMMUNITIES,
Having regard to the Treaty establishing the European Community,
Having regard to the Agreement on the European Economic Area,
Having regard to Council Regulation No. 17 of Febrary 6, 1962, First Regulation implementing Articles 85 and 86 of the Treaty, at last amended by the Act of Accession of Spain and Portugal, and in particular Article 24 thereof,

Whereas Commission Regulation No. 27 of May 3, 1962, First Regulation implementing Council Regulation No. 17, as last amended by Regulation (EC) No. 3666/93, no longer meets the requirements of efficient administration procedure; whereas it should therefore be replaced by a new regulation;

Whereas, on the one hand, applications for negative clearance under Article 2 and notifications under Articles 4, 5 and 25 of Regulation No. 17 have important legal consequences, which are favourable to the parties to an agreement, a decision or a practice, while, on the other hand, incorrect or misleading information in such applications or notifications may lead to the imposition of fines and may also entail civil law disadvantages for the parties; whereas it is therefore necessary in the interests of legal certainty to define precisely the persons entitled to submit applications and notifications, the subject matter and content of the information which such applications and notifications must contain, and the time when they become effective;

Whereas each of the parties should have the right to submit the application or the notification to the Commission; whereas, furthermore, a party exercising the right should inform the other parties in order to enable them to protect their interests; whereas applications and notification relating to agreements, decisions or practices of association of undertakings should be submitted only by such association;

Whereas it is for the applicants and the notifying parties to make full and honest disclosure to the Commission of the facts and circumstances which are relevant for coming to a decision on the agreements, decisions or practices concerned;

Whereas, in order to simplify and expedite their examination, it is desirable to prescribe that a form be used for applications for negative clearance relating to Article 85(1) and for notifications for negative clearance relating to Article 85(1) and for notifications relating to Article 85(3); whereas the use of this form should also be possible in the case of applications for negative clearance relating to Article 86;

Whereas the Commission, in appropriate cases, will give the parties, if they so request, an opportunity before the application or the notification to discuss the intended agreement, decision or practice informally and in strict confidence; whereas, in addition, it will, after the application or notification, maintain close contact with the parties to the extent necessary to discuss with them any practical or legal problems which it discovers on a first examination of the case and if possible to remove such problems by mutual agreement;

Whereas the provisions of this Regulation must also cover cases in which applications for negative clearance relating to Article 53(1) or Article 54 of the EEA Agreement, or notifications, relating to Article 53(3) of the EEA Agreement are submitted to the Commission,

HAS ADOPTED THIS REGULATION:

Article 1

Persons entitled to submit applications and notifications

1. The following may submit an application under Article 2 of Regulation No. 17 relating to Article 85 (1) of the Treaty or a notification under Articles 4, 5 and 25 of Regulation No. 17:

(a) any undertaking and any association of undertakings being a party to agreements to or concerted practices; and

(b) any association of undertakings adopting decisions or engaging in practices;

which may fall within the scope of Article 85(1).

Where the application or notification is submitted by some, but not all, of the parties, referred to in point (a) of the first subparagraph, they shall give notice to the other parties.

2. Any undertakings which may hold, alone or with other undertakings, a dominant position within the common market or in a substantial part of it, may submit an application under Article 2 of Regulation No. 17 relating to Article 86 of the Treaty.

3. Where the application or notification is signed by representatives of persons, undertakings or associations of undertakings, such representatives shall produce written proof that they are authorized to act.

4. Where a joint application or notification is made, a joint representative should be appointed who is authorized to transmit and receive documents on behalf of all the applicants or notifying parties.

Article 2

Submission of applications and notifications

1. Applications under Article 2 of Regulation No. 17 relating to Article 85(1) of the Treaty and notifications under Articles 4, 5 and 25 of Regulation No. 17 shall be submitted in the manner prescribed by Form A/B as showing the Annex to this Regulation. Form A/B may also be used for applications under Article 2 of Regulation No. 17 relating to Article 86 of the Treaty. Joint applications and joint notifications shall be submitted, on a single form.

2. Seventeen copies of each application and notification and three copies of the Annexes thereto shall be submitted to the Commission at the address indicated in Form A/B.

3. The documents annexed to the application or notification shall be either originals or copies of the originals; in the latter case the applicant or notifying party shall confirm that they are true copies of the originals and complete.

4. Applications and notifications shall be in one of the official languages of the Community. This language shall also be the language of the proceeding for the applicant or notifying party. Documents shall be submitted in their original language. Where the original language is not one of the official languages, a translation into the language of the proceeding shall be attached.

5. Where applications for negative clearance relating to Article 53(1) or Article 54 of the EEA Agreement or notifications relating to Article 53(3) of the EEA Agreement are submitted, they may

also be in one of the official languages of the EFTA States or the working language of the EFTA Surveillance Authority. If the language chosen for the application or notification is not an official language of the Community, the applicant or notifying party shall supplement all documentation with a translation into an official language of the Community. The language which is chosen for the translation shall be the language of the proceeding for the applicant or notifying party.

Article 3

Content of applications and notifications

1. Applications and notifications shall contain the information, including documents, required by Form A/B. The information must be correct and complete.

2. Applications under Article 2 of Regulation No. 17 relating to Article 86 of the Treaty shall contain a full statement of the facts, specifying, in particular, the practice concerned and the position of the undertaking or undertakings within the common market or a substantial part thereof in regard to the products or services to which the practice relates.

3. The Commission may dispense with the obligation to provide any particular information, including documents, required by Form A/B where the Commission considers that such information is not necessary for the examination of the case.

4. The Commission shall, without delay; acknowledge in writing to the applicant or notifying party receipt of the application or notification, and of any reply to a letter sent by the Commission pursuant to Article 4(2).

Article 4

Effective date of submission of applications and notifications

1. Without prejudice to paragraphs 2 to 5, applications and notifications shall become effective on the date on which they are received by the Commission. Where, however, the application or notification is sent by registered post, it shall become effective on the date shown on the postmark of the place of posting.

2. Where the Commission finds that the information, including documents, contained in the application or notification is incomplete in a material respect, it shall, without delay, inform the applicant or notifying party in writing of this fact and shall fix an appropriate time limit for the completion of the information. In such cases, the application or notification shall become effective on the date on which the complete information is received by the Commission.

3. Material changes in the facts contained in the application or notification which the applicant or notifying party knows or ought to know must be communicated to the Commission voluntarily and without delay.

4. Incorrect or misleading information shall be considered to be incomplete information.

5. Where, at the expiry of a period of one month following the date on which the application or notification has been received, the Commission has not provided the applicant or notifying party with the information referred to in paragraph 2, the application or notification shall be deemed to have become effective on the date of its receipt by the Commission.

Article 5

Repeal

Regulation No. 27 is repealed.

Article 6

Entry into force

This Regulation shall enter into force on March 1, 1995.

FORM A/B

INTRODUCTION

Form A/B, as its Annex, is an integral part of the Commission Regulation (E.C.) No. 3385/94 of December 21, 994 on the form, content and other details of applications and notifications provided for in Council Regulation No. 17 (hereinafter referred to as 'the Regulation'). It allows undertakings and associations of undertakings to apply to the Commission for negative clearance agreements or practices which may fall within the prohibitions of Article 85(1) and Article 86 of the E.C. Treaty, or within Articles 53 1) and 54 of the EEA Agreement or to notify such agreement and apply to have it exempted from the prohibition set out in Article 85(1) by virtue of the provisions of Article 58(3) of the E.C. Treaty or from the prohibition of Article 53(1) by virtue of the provisions of Article 53(3) of the EEA Agreement.

To facilitation the use of the Form A/B the following pages set out:

— in which situations it is necessary to make an application or a notification (Point A),

— to which authority (the Commission or the EFTA Surveillance Authority) the application or notification should be made (Point B),

— for which purposes the application or notification can be used (Point C);

— what information must be given in the application or notification (Points D, E and F),

— who can make an application or notification (Point G),

— how to make an application or notification (Point H),

— how the business secrets of the undertakings can be protected (Point I),

— how certain technical terms used in the operational part of the Form A/B should be interpreted (Point J), and

— the subsequent procedure after the application or notification has been made (Point K).

A. In which situations is it necessary to make an application or a notification?

I Purpose of the competition rules of the E.C. Treaty and the EEA Agreement

1. Purpose of the E.C. Competition Rules
    The purpose of the competition rules is to prevent the distortion of competition in the common market by restrictive practices or the abuse of dominant positions. They apply to any enterprise trading directly or indirectly in the common market, wherever established.

Article 85(1) of the E.C. Treaty (the text of Articles 85 and 86 is reproduced in Annex I to this form) prohibits restrictive agreements, decisions or concerted practices (arrangements) which may affect trade between Member States, and Article 85(2) declares agreements and decisions containing such restrictions void (although the Court of Justice has held that if restrictive terms of agreements are severable, only those terms are void); Article 85(3), however, provides for exemption of arrangements with beneficial effects, if its conditions are met, Article 86 prohibits the abuse of a dominant position which may affect trade between Member States. The original procedures for implementing these articles, which provide for 'negative clearance' and exemption pursuant to Article 85(3), were laid down in Regulation No. 17.

2. Purpose of the EEA Competition Rules
    The competition rules of the Agreement on the European Economic Area (concluded between the Community, the Member States and the EFTA States are based on the same principles as those contained in the Community competition rules and have the same purpose, i.e. to prevent the distortion of competition in the EEA territory by cartels or the abuse of dominant position. They apply to any enterprise trading directly or indirectly in the EEA territory, wherever established.

Article 53(1) of the EEA Agreement (the text of Articles 53, 54 and 56 of the EEA Agreement is reproduced in Annex I) prohibits restrictive agreements, decisions or concerted practices (arrangements) which may affect trade between the Community and one or more EFTA States (or between EFTA States), and Article 53(2) declares agreements or decisions containing such restrictions void; Article 53(3), however, provides for exemption of arrangements with beneficial effects, if its conditions are met. Article 54 prohibits the abuse of a dominant position which may affect trade between the Community and one or more EFTA States (or between EFTA States). The procedures for implementing these Articles, which provide for "negative clearance" and exemption pursuant to Article 53(3), are laid down in Regulation No. 17, supplemented for EEA purposes, by Protocols 21, 22 and 23 to the EEA Agreement.

II. The scope of the competition rules of the E.C. Treaty and EEA Agreement

The applicability of Articles 85 and 86 of the E.C. Treaty and Articles 53 and 54 of the EEA Agreement depends on the circumstances of each individual case. It presupposes that the arrangement or behaviour satisfies all the conditions set out in the relevant provisions. This question must consequently be examined before any application for negative clearance or any notification is made.

1. Negative clearance

The negative clearance procedure allows undertakings to ascertain whether the Commission considers that their arrangement or their behaviour is or is not prohibited by Article 85(1), or Article 86 of the E.C. Treaty or by Article 53(1) or Article 54 of the EEA Agreement. This procedure is governed by Article 2 of Regulation No. 17. The negative clearance takes the form of a decision by which the Commission certifies that, on the basis of the facts in its possession, there are no grounds pursuant to Article 85(1) or Article 86 of the E.C. Treaty or under Article 53(1) or Article 54 of the EEA Agreement for action on its part in respect of the arrangement or behaviour.

There is, however, no point in making an application when the arrangements or the behaviour are manifestly not prohibited by the abovementioned provisions. Nor is the Commission obliged to give negative clearance. Article 2 of Regulation No. 17 states that ". . . the Commission may certify . . .". The Commission issues negative clearance decisions only where an important problem of interpretation has to be solved. In the other cases it reacts to the application by sending a comfort letter.

The Commission has published several notices relating the interpretation of Article 85(1) of the E.C. Treaty. They define certain categories of agreements which, by their nature or because of their minor importance, are not caught by the prohibition.

2. Exemption

The procedure for exemption pursuant to Article 85(3) of the E.C. Treaty and Article 53(3) of the EEA Agreement allows companies to enter into arrangements which, in fact, offer economic advantages but which, without exemption, would be prohibited by Article 85(1) of the E.C. Treaty or by Article 53(1) of the EEA Agreement. This procedure is governed by Articles 4, 6 and 8 and, for the new Member States, also by Articles 5, 7 and 25 of Regulation No. 17. The exemption takes the form of a decision by the Commission declaring Article 85(1) of the E.C. Treaty or Article 53(1) of the EEA Agreement to be inapplicable to the arrangements described in the decision. Article 8 requires the Commissioner to specify the period of validity of any such decision, allows the Commission to attach conditions and obligations and provides for decisions to be amended or revoked or specified acts by the parties to be prohibited in certain circumstances, notably if the decisions were based on incorrect information or if there is any material change in the facts.

The Commission has adopted a number of regulations granting exemptions to categories of agreements. Some of these regulations provide that some agreements may benefit from exemption only if they are notified to the Commission pursuant to Article 4 or 5 of Regulation No. 17 with a view to obtaining exemption, and the benefit of the opposition procedure is claimed in the notification.

A decision granting exemption may have retroactive effect, but, with certain exceptions, cannot be made effective earlier than the date of notification (Article 6 of Regulation No. 17). Should the Commission find that notified arrangements are indeed prohibited and cannot be exempted and, therefore, take a decision condemning them, the participants are nevertheless protected, between the date of the notification and the date of the decision, against fines for any infringement described in the notification (Article 3 and Article 15(5) and (6) of Regulation No. 17).

Normally the Commission issues exemption decisions only in cases of particular legal, economic or political importance. In the other cases it terminates the procedure by sending a comfort letter.

B. To which authority should application or notification be made?

The applications and notifications must be made to the authority which has competence for the matter. The Commission is responsible for the application of the competition rules of the E.C. Treaty. However there is shared competence in relation to the application of the competition rules of the EEA agreement.

The competence of the Commission and of the EFTA Surveillance Authority to apply the EEA competition rules follows from Article 56 of the EEA Agreement. Applications and notifications relating to agreements, decisions or concerted practices liable to affect trade between Member States should be addressed to the Commission unless their effects on trade between Member States or on competition within the Community are not appreciable within the meaning of the Commission notice of 1986 on agreements of minor importance. Furthermore, all restrictive agreements, decisions or concerted practices affecting trade between one Member State and one or more EFTA States fall within the competence of the Commission, provided that the undertakings concerned achieve more than 67% of their combined EEA-wide turnover within the Community. However, if the effects of such agreements, decisions or concerted practices on trade between Member States or on competition within the Community are not appreciable, the notification should, where necessary, be addressed to the EFTA Surveillance Authority. All other agreements, decisions and concerned practices falling under Article 53 of the EEA Agreement should be notified to the EFTA Surveillance Authority (the address of which is given in Annex III).

Applications for negative clearance regarding Article 54 of the EEA Agreement should be lodged with the Commission if the Dominant position exists only in the Community, or with the EFTA Surveillance Authority, if the dominant position exists only in the whole of the territory of the EFTA States, or a substantial part of it. Only where the dominant position exists within both territories should be rules outlined above with respect to Article 53 be applied.

The Commission will apply, as a basis for appraisal, the competition rules of the E.C. Treaty. Where the case falls under the EEA Agreement and is attributed to the Commission pursuant to Article 56 of that Agreement, it will simultaneously apply the EEA rules.

C. The Purpose of this Form

Form A/B lists the questions that must be answered and the information and documents that must be provided when applying for the following:

— a negative clearance with regard to Article 58(1) of the E.C. Treaty and/or Article 53(1) of the EEA Agreement, pursuant to Article 2 of Regulation No. 17, with respect to agreements between undertakings, decisions by associations of undertakings and concerted practices,

— an exemption pursuant to Article 85(3) of the E.C. Treaty and/or Article 53(3) of the EEA Agreement with respect to agreements between undertakings, decisions by associations of undertakings and concerted practices,

— the benefit of the opposition procedure contained in certain Commission regulations granting exemption by category.

This form allows undertakings applying for negative clearance to notify, at the same time, in order to obtain an exemption in the event that the Commission reaches the conclusion that no negative clearance can be granted.

Applications for negative clearance and notifications relating to Article 85 of the E.C. Treaty shall be submitted in the manner prescribed by form A/B (see Article 2(1), first sentence of the Regulation).

This form can also be used by undertakings that wish to apply for a negative clearance from Article 86 of the E.C. Treaty or Article 53 of the EEA Agreement, pursuant to Article 2 of Regulation No. 17. Applicants requesting negative clearance from Article 86 are not required to use form A/B. They are nonetheless strongly recommended to give all the information requested below to ensure that their application gives a full statement of the facts (see Article 2(1), second sentence of the Regulation).

The applications or notifications made on the form A/B issued by the EFTA side are equally valid. However, if the agreements, decisions or practices concerned fall solely within Articles 85 or 86 of the E.C. Treaty, i.e. have no EEA relevance whatsoever, it is advisable to use the present form established by the Commission.

D. Which chapters of the form should be completed?

The operational part of this form is sub-divided into four chapters. Undertakings wishing to make an application for a negative clearance or a notification must complete Chapters I, II and IV. An exemption to this rule is provided for in the case where the application or notification concerns an agreement concerning the creation of a cooperative joint venture of a structural character if the parties wish to benefit from an accelerated procedure. In this situation Chapters I, III and IV should be completed.

In 1992, the Commission announced that it had adopted new internal administrative rules that provided that certain applications and notifications — those of cooperative joint ventures which are structural in nature — would be dealt with within fixed deadlines. In such cases the services of the Commission will, within two months of receipt of the complete notification of the agreement, inform the parties in writing of the results of the initial analysis of the case and, as appropriate, the nature and probable length of the administrative procedure they intend to engage.

The contents of this letter may vary according to the characteristics of the case under investigation:

— in cases not posing any problems, the Commission will send a comfort letter confirming the compatibility of the agreement with Article 85(1) or (3),

— if a comfort letter cannot be sent because of the need to settle the case by formal decision, the Commission will inform the undertakings concerned of its intention to adopt a decision either granting or rejecting exemption,

— if the Commission has serious doubts as to the compatibility of the agreement with the competition rules, it will send a letter to the parties giving notice of an in-depth examination which may, depending on the case, result in a decision either prohibiting, exempting subject to conditions and obligations, or simply exempting the agreement in question.

This new accelerated procedure, applicable since 1 January 1993, is based entirely on the principle of self-discipline. The deadline of two months from the complete notification — intended for the initial examination of the case — does not constitute a statutory term and is therefore in no way legally binding. However, the Commission will do its best to abide by it. The Commission reserves the right, moreover, to extend this accelerated procedure to other forms of cooperation between undertakings.

A cooperative joint venture of a structural nature is one that involves an important change in the structure and organization of the business assets of the parties to the agreement. This may occur because the joint venture takes over or extends existing activities of the parent companies or because it undertakes new activities on their behalf. Such operations are characterized by the commitment of significant financial, material and/or non-tangible assets such as intellectual property rights and know how. Structural joint ventures are therefore normally intended to operate on a medium- or long-term basis.

This concept includes certain "partial function" joint ventures which take over one or several specific functions within the parents' business activity without access to the market, in particular research and development and/or production. It also covers those "full function" joint ventures which give rise to coordination of the competitive behaviour of independent undertakings, in particular between the parties to the joint venture or between them and the joint venture.

In order to respect the internal deadline, it is important that the Commission has available on notification all the relevant information reasonably available to the notifying parties that is necessary for it to assess the impact of the operation in question on competition. Form A/B therefore contains a special section (Chapter III) that must be completed only by persons notifying cooperative joint venture of a structural character that wish to benefit from the accelerated procedure.

Persons notifying joint ventures of a structural character that wish to claim the benefit of the aforementioned accelerated procedure should therefore complete Chapters I, III and IV of this form. Chapter III contains a series of detailed questions necessary for the Commission to assess the relevant market(s) and the position of the parties to the joint venture on that (those) market(s).

Where the parties do not wish to claim the benefit of an accelerated procedure for their joint ventures of a structural character they should complete Chapters I, II and IV of this form. Chapter II contains a far more limited range of questions on the relevant market(s) and the position of the parties to the operation in question on that (those) market(s), but sufficient to enable the Commission to commence its examination and investigation.

E. The need for complete information

The receipt of a valid notification by the Commission has two main consequences. First, it affords immunity from fines from the date that the valid notification is received by the Commission with respect to applications made in order to obtain exemption (see Article 15(5) of Regulation No 17). Second, until a valid notification is received, the Commission cannot grant an exemption pursuant to Article 85(3) of the E.C. Treaty and/or Article 53(3) of the EEA Agreement, and any exemption that is granted can be effective only from the date of receipt of a valid notification. Thus, whilst there is no legal obligation to notify as such, unless and until an arrangement that falls within the scope of Article 85(1) and/or Article 53(1) has not been notified and is, therefore, not capable of being exempted, it may be declared void by a national court pursuant to Article 85(2) and/or Article 53(2).

Where an undertaking is claiming the benefit of a group exemption by recourse to an opposition procedure, the period within which the Commission must oppose the exemption by category only applies from the date that a valid notification is received. This is also true of the two months period imposed on the Commission services for an initial analysis of applications for negative clearance and notifications relating to cooperative joint ventures of a structural character which benefit from the accelerated procedure.

A valid application or notification for this purpose means one that is not incomplete (see Article 3(1) of the Regulation). This is subject to two qualifications. First, if the information or documents required by this form are not reasonably available to you in part or in whole, the Commission will accept that a notification is complete and thus valid notwithstanding the failure to provide such information, providing that you give reasons for the unavailability of the information, and provide your best estimates for missing data together with the sources for the estimates. Indications as to where any of the requested information or documents that are unavailable to you could be obtained by the Commission must also be provided. Second, the Commission only requires the submission of information relevant and necessary to its inquiry into the notified operation. In some cases not all the information required by this form will be necessary for this purpose. The Commission may therefore dispense with the obligation to provide certain information required by this form (see Article 3 (3) of the Regulation. This provision enables, where appropriate, each application or notification to be tailored to each case so that only the information strictly necessary for the Commission's examination is provided. This avoids unnecessary administrative burdens being imposed on undertakings, in particular on small and medium-sized ones. Where the information or documents required by this form are not provided for this reason, the application or notification should indicate the reasons why the information is considered to be unnecessary to the Commission's investigation.

Where the Commission finds that the information contained in the application or notification is incomplete in a material respect, it will, within one month from receipt, inform the applicant or the notifying party in writing of this fact and the nature of the missing information. In such cases, the application or notification shall become effective on the date on which the complete information is received by the Commission. If the Commission has not informed the applicant or the notifying party within the one month period that the application or notification is incomplete in a material respect, the application or notification will be deemed to be complete and valid (see Article 4 of the Regulation).

It is also important that undertakings inform the Commission of important changes in the factual situation including those of which they become aware after the application or notification has been submitted. The Commission must, therefore, be informed immediately of any changes to an agreement, decision or practice which is the subject of an application or notification (see Article 4(3) of the Regulation). Failure to inform the Commission of such relevant changes could result in any negative clearance decision being without effect or in the withdrawal of any exemption decision adopted by the Commission on the basis of the notification.

F. The need for accurate information

In addition to the requirement that the application or notification be complete, it is important that you ensure that the information provided is accurate (see Article 3(1) of the Regulation). Article 15(1)(a) of Regulation No. 17 states that the Commission may, by decision, impose on undertakings or associations of undertakings fines of up to ECU 5,000 where, intentionally or negligently, they supply incorrect or misleading information in an application for negative clearance or notification. Such information is, moreover, considered to be incomplete (see Article 4(4) of the Regulation), so that the parties cannot benefit from the advantages of the opposition procedure or accelerated procedure (see above, Point E).

G. Who can lodge an application or a notification?

Any of the undertakings party to an agreement, decision or practice of the kind described in Articles 85 or 86 of the E.C. Treaty and Articles 53 or 54 of the EEA Agreement may submit an application for negative clearance, in relation to Article 85 and Article 53, or a notification requesting an exemption. An association of undertakings may submit an application or a notification in relation to decisions taken or practices pursued into in the operation of the association.

In relation to agreements and concerted practices between undertakings it is common practice for all the parties involved to submit a joint application or notification. Although the Commission strongly recommends this approach, because it is helpful to have the views of all the parties directly concerned at the same time, it is not obligatory. Any of the parties to an agreement may submit an application or notification in their individual capacities, but in such circumstances the notifying party should inform all the other parties to the agreement, decision or practice of that fact (see Article 1(3) of the Regulation). They may also provide them with a copy of the completed form, where relevant once confidential information and business secrets have been deleted (see below, operational part, question 1.2).

Where a joint application or notification is submitted, it has also become common practice to appoint a joint representative to act on behalf of all the undertakings involved, both in making the application or notification, and in dealing with any subsequent contacts with the Commission (see Article 1 (4) of the Regulation). Again, whilst this is helpful, it is not obligatory, and all the undertakings jointly submitting an application or a notification may sign it in their individual capacities.

H. How to submit an application or notification

Applications and notifications may be submitted in any of the official languages of the European Community or of an EFTA State (see Article 2 (4) and (5) of the Regulation). In order to ensure rapid proceedings, it is, however, recommended to use, in case of an application or notification to the EFTA Surveillance Authority one of the official languages of an EFTA State or the working language of the EFTA Surveillance Authority, which is English, or, in case of an application or notification to the Commission, one of the official languages of the Community or the working language of the EFTA Surveillance Authority. This language will thereafter be the language of the proceeding for the applicant or notifying party.

Form A/B is not a form to be filled in. Undertakings should simply provide the information requested by this form, using its sections and paragraph numbers, signing a declaration as stated in Section 19 below, and annexing the required supporting documentation.

Supporting documents shall be submitted in their original language; where this is not an official language of the Community they must be translated into the language of the proceeding. The supporting documents may be originals or copies of the originals (see (Article 2(4) of the Regulation).

All information requested in this form shall, unless otherwise stated, relate to the calendar year preceding that of the application or notification. Where information is not reasonably available on this basis (for example if accounting periods are used that are not based on the calendar year, or the previous year's figures are not yet available) the most recently available information should be provided and reasons given why figures on the basis of the calendar year preceding that of the application or notification cannot be provided.

Financial data may be provided in the currency in which the official audited accounts of the undertaking(s) concerned are prepared or in Ecus. In the latter case the exchange rate used for the conversion must be stated.

Seventeen copies of each application or notification, but only three copies of all supporting documents must be provided (see Article 2(2) of the Regulation).

The application or notification is to be sent to:
    Commission of the European Communities,
    Directorate-General for Competition (DG IV),
    The Registrar,
    200, Rue de la Loi,
    B–1049 Brussels.

or be delivered by hand during Commission working days and official working hours at the following address:

    Commission of the European Communities,
    Directorate-General for Competition (DG IV),
    The Registrar,
    158, Avenue de Cortenberg,
    B–1040 Brussels.

I. Confidentiality
Article 214 of the E.C. Treaty, Article 20 of Regulation No. 17, Article 9 of Protocol 23 to the EEA Agreement, Article 122 of the EEA Agreement and Articles 20 and 21 of Chapter II of Protocol 4 to the Agreement between the EFTA States on the establishment of a Surveillance Authority and of a Court of Justice require the Commission, the Member States, the EEA Surveillance Authority and EFTA States not to disclose information of the kind covered by the obligation of professional secrecy. On the other hand, Regulation No. 17 requires the Commission to publish a summary of the application or notification, should it intend to take a favourable decision. In this publication, the Commission " . . . shall have regard to the legitimate interest of undertakings in the protection of their business secrets" (Article 19(3) of Regulation No. 17; see also Article 21(2) in relation to the publication of decisions). In this connection, if an undertaking believes that its interests would be harmed if any of the information it is asked to supply were to be published or otherwise divulged to other undertakings, it should put all such information in a separate annex with each page clearly marked "Business Secrets". It should also give reasons why any information identified as confidential or secret should not be divulged or published. (See below, Section 5 of the operational part that requests a non-confidential summary of the notification).

J. Subsequent Procedure
The application or notification is registered in the Registry of the Directorate-General for Competition (DG IV). The date of receipt by the Commission (or the date of posting if sent by registered post) is the effective date of the submission (see Article 4(1) of the Regulation). However, special rules apply to incomplete applications and notifications (see above under Point E).

The Commission will acknowledge receipt of all applications and notifications in writing, indicating the case number attributed to the file. This number must be used in all future correspondence regarding the notification. The receipt of acknowledgement does not prejudge the question whether the application or notification is valid.

Further information may be sought from the third parties (Articles 11 to 14 of Regulation No. 17) and suggestions might be made as to amendments to the arrangements that might make them acceptable. Equally, a short preliminary notice may be published in the C series of the *Official Journal of the European Communities*, stating the names of the interested undertakings, the groups to which they belong, the economic sectors involved and the nature of the arrangements, and inviting third party comments (see below, operational part, Section 5).

Where a notification is made together for the purpose of the application of the opposition procedure, the Commission may oppose the grant of the benefit of the group exemption with respect to the notified agreement. If the Commission opposes the claim, and unless it subsequently withdraws its opposition, that notification will then be treated as an application for an individual exemption.

If, after examination, the Commission intends to grant the application for negative clearance or exemption, it is obliged (by Article 19(3) of Regulation No. 17) to publish a summary and invite comments from third parties. Subsequently, a preliminary draft decision has to be submitted to and discussed with the Advisory Committee on Restrictive Practices and Dominant Positions composed of officials of the competent authorities of the Member States in the matter of restrictive practices and monopolies (Article 10 of Regulation No. 17) and attended, where the case falls within the EEA Agreement, by representatives of the EFTA Surveillance Authority and the EFTA States which will already have received a copy of the application or notification. Only then, and providing nothing has happened to change the Commission's intention, can it adopt the envisaged decision.

Files are often closed without any formal decision being taken, for example, because it is found that the arrangements are already covered by a block exemption, or because they do not call for any action by the Commission, at least in circumstances at that time. In such cases comfort letters are sent. Although not a Commission decision, a comfort letter indicates how the Commission's departments view the case on the facts currently in their possession which means that the Commission could where necessary — for example, if it were to be asserted that a contract was void under Article 85(2) of the EC Treaty and/or Article 53(2) of the EEA Agrement — take an appropriate decision to clarify the legal situation.

K. Definitions used in the operational part of this form

Agreement: The word "agreement" is used to refer to all categories of arrangements, *i.e.* agreements between undertakings, decisions by associations of undertakings and concerted practices.

Year: All references to the word "year" in this form shall be read as meaning calendar year, unless otherwise stated.

Group: A group relationship exists for the purpose of this form where one undertaking:

— owns more than half the capital or business assets of another undertaking, or

— has the power to exercise more than half the voting rights in another undertaking, or

— has the power to appoint more than half the members of the supervisory board, board of directors or bodies legally representing the undertaking, or

— has the right to manage the affairs of another undertaking.

An undertaking which is jointly controlled by several other undertakings (joint venture) forms part of the group of each of these undertakings.

Relevant product marked: questions 6.1 and 11.1 of this form require the undertaking or individual submitting the notification to define the relevant product and/or service market(s) that are likely to be affected by the agreement in question. That definition(s) is then used as the basis for a number of other questions contained in this form. The definition(s) thus submitted by the notifying parties are referred to in this form as the relevant product market(s). These words can refer to a market made up either of products or of services.

Relevant geographic market: questions 62. and 11.2 of this form require the undertaking or individual submitting the notification to define the relevant geographic market(s) that are likely to be affected by the agreement in question. That definition(s) is then used as the basis for a number of other questions contained in this form. The definition(s) thus submitted by the notifying parties are referred to in this form as the relevant geographic market(s).

Relevant product and geographic market: by virtue of the combination of their replies to questions 6 and 11 the parties provide their definition of the relevant market(s) affected by the notified agreement(s). That (those) definition(s) is (are) then used as the basis for a number of other questions contained in this form. The definition(s) thus submitted by the notifying parties is referred to in this form as the relevant geographic and product market(s).

Notification: this form can be used to make an application for negative clearance and/or a notification requesting an exemption. The word "notification" is used to refer to either an application or a notification.

Parties and notifying parties: the word "party" is used to refer to all the undertakings which are party to the agreement being notified. As a notification may be submitted by only one of the undertakings which are party to an agreement, "notifying party" is used to refer only to the undertaking or undertakings actually submitting the notification.

PLEASE MAKE SURE THAT THE FIRST PAGE OF YOUR APPLICATION OR NOTIFICATION CONTAINS THE WORDS "APPLICATION FOR NEGATIVE CLEARANCE/NOTIFICATION IN ACCORDANCE WITH FORM A/B"

CHAPTER 1

Section concerning the parties, their groups and the agreement (to be completed for all notifications)

Section 1

IDENTITY OF THE UNDERTAKINGS OR PERSONS SUBMITTING THE NOTIFICATION

1.1. Please list the undertakings on behalf of which the notification is being submitted and indicate their legal denomination or commercial name, shortened or commonly used as appropriate (if it differs from the legal denomination).

1.2. If the notification is being submitted on behalf of only one or some of the undertakings party to the agreement being notified, please confirm that the remaining undertakings have been informed of that fact and indicate whether they have received a copy of the notification, with relevant confidential information and business secrets deleted. (In such circumstances a copy of the edited copy of the notification which has been provided to such other undertakings should be annexed to this notification.)

1.3. If a joint notification is being submitted, has a joint representative been appointed?

If yes, please give details requested in 1.3.1 to 1.3.3 below.

If no, please give details of any representatives who have been authorized to act for each or either of the parties to the agreement indicating who they represent.

1.3.1. Name of representative.

1.3.2. Address of representative.

1.3.3. Telephone and fax number of representative.

1.4. In cases where one or more representatives have been appointed, an authority to act on behalf of the undertaking(s) submitting the notification must accompany the notification.

Section 2

INFORMATION ON THE PARTIES TO THE AGREEMENT AND THE GROUPS TO WHICH THEY BELONG

2.1. State the name and address of the parties to the agreement being notified, and the country of their incorporation.

2.2. State the nature of the business of each of the parties to the agreement being notified.

2.3 For each of the parties to the agreement, give the name of a person that can be contacted, together with his or her name, address, telephone number, fax number and position held in the undertaking.

2.4. Identify the corporate groups to which the parties to the agreement being notified belong. State the sectors in which these groups are active, and the world-wide turnover of each group.

Section 3

PROCEDURAL MATTERS

3.1. Please state whether you have made any formal submission to any other competition authorities in relation to the agreement in question. If yes, state which authorities, the individual or department in question, and the nature of the contact. In addition to this, mention any earlier proceedings or informal contacts, of which you are aware, with the Commission and/or the EFTA Surveillance Authority and any earlier proceedings with any national authorities or courts in the Community or in EFTA concerning these or any related agreements.

3.2. Please summarize any reasons for any claim that the case involves an issue of exceptional urgency.

3.3. The Commission has stated that where notifications do not have particular political, economic or legal significance for the Community they will normally be dealt with by means of comfort letter. Would you be satisfied with a comfort letter? If you consider that it would be inappropriate to deal with the notified agreement in this manner, please explain the reasons for this view.

3.4. State whether you intend to produce further supporting facts or arguments not yet available and, if so, on which points.

Section 4

FULL DETAILS OF THE ARRANGEMENTS

4.1. Please summarize the nature, content and objectives pursued by the agreement being notified.

4.2. Detail any provisions contained in the agreements which may restrict the parties in their freedom to take independent commercial decisions, for example regarding:

— buying or selling prices, discounts or other trading conditions,

— the quantities of goods to be manufactured or distributed or services to be offered,

— technical development or investment,

— the choice of markets or sources of supply,

— purchases from or sales to third parties,

— whether to apply similar terms for the supply of equivalent goods or services,

— whether to offer different services separately or together.

If you are claiming the benefit of the opposition procedure, identify in this list the restrictions that exceed those automatically exempted by the relevant regulation.

4.3. State between which Member States of the Community and/or EFTA States trade may be affected by the arrangements. Please give reasons for your reply to this question, giving data on trade flows where relevant. Furthermore please state whether trade between the Community or the EEA territory and any third countries is affected, again giving reasons for your reply.

Section 5

NON-CONFIDENTIAL SUMMARY

Shortly following receipt of a notification, the Commission may publish a short notice inviting third party comments on the agreement in question. As the objective pursued by the Commission in publishing an informal preliminary notice is to receive third party comments as soon as possible after the notification has been received, such a notice is usually published without first providing it to the notifying parties for their comments. This section requests the information to be used in an informal preliminary notice in the event that the Commission decides to issue one. It is important, therefore, that your replies to these questions do not contain any business secrets or other confidential information.

1. State the names of the parties to the agreement notified and the groups of undertakings to which they belong.

2. Give a short summary of the nature and objectives of the agreement. As a guide-lines this summary should not exceed 100 words.

3. Identify the product sectors affected by the agreement in question.

CHAPTER II

Section concerning the relevant market (to be completed for all notifications except those relating to structural joint ventures for which accelerated treatment is claimed)

Section 6

THE RELEVANT MARKET

A relevant product market comprises all those products and/or services which are regarded as interchangeable or substitutable by the consumer, by reason of the products' characteristics, their prices and their intended use.

The following factors are normally considered to be relevant to the determination of the relevant product market and should be taken into account in this analysis:

— the degree of physical similarity between the products/services in question,

— any differences in the end use to which the goods are put,

— differences in price between two products,

— the cost of switching between two potentially competing products,

— established or entrenched consumer preferences for one type or category of product over another,

— industry-wide product classifications (*e.g.* classifications maintained by trade associations).

The relevant geographic market comprises the area in which the undertakings concerned are involved in the supply of products or services, in which the conditions of competition are sufficiently homogeneous and which can be distinguished from neighbouring areas because, in particular, conditions of competition are appreciably different in those areas.

Factors relevant to the assessment of the relevant geographic market include the nature and characteristics of the products or services concerned, the existence of entry barriers or consumer preferences, appreciable differences of the undertakings' market share or substantial price differences between neighbouring areas, and transport costs.

6.1. In the light of the above please explain the definition of the relevant product market or markets that in your opinion should form the basis of the Commission's analysis of the notification.

In your answer, please give reasons for assumptions or findings, and explain how the factors outlined above have been taken into account. In particular, please state the specific products or services directly or indirectly affected by the agreement being notified and identify the categories of goods viewed as substitutable in your market definition.

In the questions figuring below, this (or these) definition(s) will be referred to as "the relevant product market(s)".

6.2. Please explain the definition of the relevant geographic market or markets that in your opinion should form the basis of the Commission's analysis of the notification. In your answer, please give reasons for assumptions or findings, and explain how the factors outlined above have been taken into account. In particular, please identify the countries in which the parties are active in the relevant product market(s), and in the event that you consider the relevant geographic market to be wider than the individual Member States of the Community or EFTA on which the parties to the agreement are active, give the reasons for this.

In the questions below, this (or these) definition(s) will be referred to as "the relevant geographic market(s".

Section 7

GROUP MEMBERS OPERATING ON THE SAME MARKETS AS THE PARTIES

7.1. For each of the parties to the agreement being notified, provide a list of all undertakings belonging to the same group which are:

7.1.1. active in the relevant product market(s);

7.1.2. active in markets neighbouring the *relevant product market(s)* (*i.e.* active in products and/or services that represent imperfect and partial substitutes for those included in your definition of the relevant product market(s)).

Such undertakings must be identified even if they sell the product or service in question in other geographic areas than those in which the parties to the notified agreement operate. Please list the name, place of incorporation, exact product manufactured and the geographic scope of operation of each group member.

Section 8

THE POSITION OF THE PARTIES ON THE AFFECTED RELEVANT PRODUCT MARKETS

Information requested in this section must be provided for the groups of the parties as a whole. It is not sufficient to provide such information only in relation to the individual undertakings directly concerned by the agreement.

8.1. In relation to each relevant product market(s) identified in your reply to question 6.1 please provide the following information:

8.1.1. the market shares of the parties on the *relevant geographic market* during the previous three years;

8.1.2 where different, the market shares of the parties in (a) the EEA territory as a whole, (b) the Community, (c) the territory of the EFTA States and (d) each E.C. Member State and EFTA State during the previous three years. For this section, where market shares are less than 20%, please state simply which of the following bands are relevant: 0 to 5%, 5 to 10%, 10 to 15%, 15 to 20%.

For the purpose of answering these questions, market share may be calculated either on the basis of value or volume. Justification for the figures provided must be given. Thus, for each answer, total market value/volume must be stated, together with the sales/turnover of each of the parties in question. The source or sources of the information should also be given (*e.g.* official statistics, estimates, etc.), and where possible, copies should be provided of documents from which information has been taken.

Section 9

THE POSITION OF COMPETITORS AND CUSTOMERS ON THE RELEVANT PRODUCT MARKET(S)

Information requested in this section must be provided for the group of the parties as a whole and not in relation to the individual companies directly concerned by the agreement notified.

For the (all) relevant product and geographic market(s) in which the parties have a combined market share exceeding 15%, the following questions must be answered.

9.1. Please identify the five main competitors of the parties. Please identify the company and give your best estimate as to their market share in the relevant geographic market(s). Please also provide address, telephone and fax number, and, where possible, the name of a contact person at each company identified.

9.2. Please identify the five main customers of each of the parties. State company name, address, telephone and fax numbers, together with the name of a contact person.

Section 10

MARKET ENTRY AND POTENTIAL COMPETITION IN PRODUCT AND GEOGRAPHIC TERMS

For the (all) relevant product and geographic market(s) in which the parties have a combined market share exceeding 15%, the following questions must be answered.

10.1. Describe the various factors influencing entry in product terms into the *relevant product market(s)* that exist in the present case (*i.e.* what barriers exist to prevent undertakings that do not presently manufacture goods within the relevant product market(s) entering this market(s)). In so doing take account of the following where appropriate:

— to what extent is entry to the markets influenced by the requirement of government authorization or standard setting in any form? Are there any legal or regulatory controls on entry to these markets?

— to what extent is entry to the markets influenced by the availability of raw materials?

— to what extent is entry to the markets influenced by the length of contracts between an undertaking and its suppliers and/or customers?

— describe the importance of research and development and in particular the importance of licensing patents, know-how and other rights in these markets.

10.2. Describe the various factors influencing entry in geographic terms into the relevant geographic market(s) that exist in the present case (i.e. what barriers exist to prevent undertakings already producing and/or marketing products within the relevant product markets(s) but in areas outside the relevant geographic market(s) extending the scope of their sales into the relevant geographic market(s)?). Please give reasons for your answer, explaining, where relevant, the importance of the following factors:

— trade barriers imposed by law, such as tariffs, quotas etc.,

— local specification or technical requirements,

— procurement policies,

— the existence of adequate and available local distribution and retailing facilities,

— transport costs,

— entrenched consumer preferences for local brands or products,

— language.

10.3. Have any new undertakings entered the relevant product market(s) in geographic areas where the parties sell during the last three years? Please provide this information with respect to both new entrants in product terms and new entrants in geographic terms. If such entry has occurred, please identify the undertaking(s) concerned (name, address, telephone and fax numbers, and, where possible, contact person), and provide your best estimate of their market share in the relevant product and geographic market(s).

CHAPTER III

Section concerning the relevant market only for structural joint ventures for which accelerated treatment is claimed

Section 11

THE RELEVANT MARKET

A relevant product market comprises all those products and/or services which are regarded as interchangeable or substitutable by the consumer, by reason of the products' characteristics, their prices and their intended use.

The following factors are normally considered to be relevant to the determination of the relevant product market and should be taken into account in this analysis:

— the degree of physical similarity between the products/services in question,

— any differences in the end use to which the goods are put,

— differences in price between two products,

— the cost of switching between two potentially competing products,

— established or entrenched consumer preferences for one type or category of product over another,

— different or similar industry-wide product classifications (*e.g.* classifications maintained by trade associations)

The relevant geographic market comprises the area in which the undertakings concerned are involved in the supply to products or services, in which the conditions of competition are sufficiently homogeneous and which can be distinguished from neighbouring areas because, in particular, conditions of competition are appreciably different in those areas.

Factors relevant to the assessment of the relevant geographic market include the nature and characteristics of the products or services concerned, the existence of entry barriers or consumer preferences, appreciable differences of the undertakings' market share or substantial price differences between neighbouring areas, and transport costs.

Part 11.1

THE NOTIFYING PARTIES' ANALYSIS OF THE RELEVANT MARKET

11.1.1. In the light of the above please explain the definition of the relevant product market or markets that in the opinion of the parties should form the basis of the Commission's analysis of the notification.

In your answer, please give reasons for assumptions or findings, and explain how the factors outlined above have been taken into account.

In the questions figuring below, this (or these) definition(s) will be referred to as "the relevant product market(s)".

11.1.2. Please explain the definition of the relevant geographic market or markets that in the opinion of the parties should form the basis of the Commission's analysis of the notification.

In your answer, please give reasons for assumptions or findings, and explain how the factors outlined above have been taken into account.

Part 11.2

QUESTIONS ON THE RELEVANT PRODUCT AND GEOGRAPHIC MARKET(S)

Answers to the following questions will enable the Commission to verify whether the product and geographic market definitions put forward by you in Section 11.1 are compatible with definitions figuring above.
Product market definition
11.2.1. List the specific products or services directly or indirectly affected by the agreement being notified.

11.2.2. List the categories of products and/or services that are, in the opinion of the notifying parties, close economic substitutes for those identified in the reply to question 11.2.1.Where more than one product or service has been identified in the reply to question 11.2.1, a list for each product must be provided for this question.

The products identified in this list should be ordered in their degree of substitutability, first listing the most perfect substitute for the products of the parties, finishing with the least perfect substitute.

Please explain how the factors relevant to the definition of the relevant product market have been taken into account in drawing up this list and in placing the products/services in their correct order.

Geographic market definition
11.2.3. List all the countries in which the parties are active in the relevant product market(s). Where they are active in all countries within any given groups of countries or trading area (*e.g.* the whole Community or EFTA, the EEA countries, world-wide) it is sufficient to indicate the area in question.

11.2.4. Explain the manner in which the parties produce and sell the goods and/or services in each of these various countries or areas. For example, do they manufacture locally, do they sell through local distribution facilities, or do they distribute through exclusive, or non-exclusive, importers and distributors?

11.2.5. Are there significant trade flows in the goods/services that make up the relevant product market(s) (i) between the E.C. Member States (please specify which and estimate the percentage of total sales made up by imports in each Member State in which the parties are active), (ii) between all or part of the E.C. Member States and all or part of the EFTA States (again, please specify and estimate the percentage of total sales made up by imports), (iii) between EFTA States (please specify which and estimate the percentage of total sales made up by imports in each such State in which the parties are active), and (iv) between all or part of the EEA territory and other countries? (again, please specify and estimate the percentage of total sales made up by imports.)

11.2.6. Which producer undertakings based outside the Community or the EEA territory sell within the EEA territory in countries in which the parties are active in the affected products? How do these undertakings market their products? Does this differ between different E.C. Member States and/or EFTA States?

Section 12

GROUP MEMBERS OPERATING ON THE SAME MARKETS AS THE PARTIES TO THE NOTIFIED AGREEMENT

12.1. For each of the parties to the agreement being notified, provide a list of all undertakings belonging to the same group which are:

12.1.1. active in the relevant product market(s);

12.1.2. active in markets neighbouring the relevant product market(s) (*i.e.* active in products/services that represent imperfect and partial substitutes for those included in your definition of the relevant product market(s);

12.1.3. active in markets upstream and/or downstream from those included in the relevant product market(s).

Such undertakings must be identified even if they sell the product or service in question in other geographic areas than those in which the parties to the notified agreement operate. Please list the name, place of incorporation, exact product manufactured and the geographic scope of operation of each group member.

Section 13

THE POSITION OF THE PARTIES ON THE RELEVANT PRODUCT MARKET(S)

Information requested in this section must be provided for the group of the parties as a whole and not in relation to the individual companies directly concerned by the agreement notified.

13.1. In relation to each relevant product market(s), as defined in your reply to question 11.1.2, please provide the following information:

13.1.1. the market shares of the parties on the relevant geographic market during the previous three years;

13.1.2. where different, the market shares of the parties in (a) the EEA territory as a whole, (b) the Community, (c) the territory of the EFTA States and (d) each E.C. Member State and EFTA State during the previous three years. For this section, where market shares are less than 20%, please state simply which of the following bands are relevant: 0 to 5%, 5 to 10%, 10 to 15%, 15 to 20% in terms of value or volume.

For the purpose of answering these questions, market share may be calculated either on the basis of value or volume. Justification for the figures provided must be given. Thus, for each answer, total market value/volume must be stated, together with the sales/turnover of each of the parties in question. The source or sources of the information should also be given, and where possible, copies should be provided of documents from which information has been taken.

13.2. If the market shares in question 13.1 were to be calculated on a basis other than that used by the parties, would the resultant market shares differ by more than 5% in any market (*i.e.* if the parties have calculated market shares on the basis of volume, what would be the relevant figure if it was calculated on the basis of value?) If the figure were to differ by more than 5% please provide the information requested in question 13.1 on the basis of both value and volume.

13.3. Give your best estimate of the current rate of capacity utilization of the parties and in the industry in general in the relevant product and geographic market(s).

Section 14

THE POSITION OF COMPETITORS AND CUSTOMERS ON THE RELEVANT PRODUCT MARKET(S)

Information requested in this section must be provided for the group of the parties as a whole and not in relation to the individual companies directly concerned by the agreement notified.

For the (all) relevant product market(s) in which the parties have a combined market share exceeding 10% in the EEA as a whole, the Community, the EFTA territory or in any E.C. Member State or EFTA Member State, the following questions must be answered.

14.1. Please identify the competitors of the parties on the relevant product market(s) that have a market share exceeding 10% in any E.C. Member State, EFTA State, in the territory of the EFTA States, in the EEA, or worldwide. Please identify the company and give your best estimate as to their market share in these geographic areas. Please also provide the address, telephone and fax numbers, and, where possible, the name of a contact person at each company identified.

14.2. Please describe the nature of demand on the relevant product market(s). For example, are there few or many purchasers, are there different categories of purchasers, are government agencies or departments important purchasers?

14.3. Please identify the five largest customers of each of the parties for each *relevant product market(s)*. State company name, address, telephone and fax numbers, together with the name of a contact person.

Section 15

MARKET ENTRY AND POTENTIAL COMPETITION

For the (all) relevant product market(s) in which the parties have a combined market share exceeding 10% in the EEA as a whole, the Community, the EFTA territory or in any E.C. Member State or EFTA State, the following questions must be answered.

15.1. Describe the various factors influencing entry into the relevant product market(s) that exist in the present case. In so doing take account of the following where appropriate:

— to what extent is entry to the markets influenced by the requirement of government authorization or standard setting in any form? Are there any legal or regulatory controls on entry to these markets?

— to what extent is entry to the markets influenced by the availability of raw materials?

— to what extent is entry to the markets influenced by the length of contracts between an undertaking and its suppliers and/or customers?

— what is the importance of research and development and in particular the importance of licensing patents, know-how and other rights in these markets.

15.2. Have any new undertakings entered the relevant product market(s) in geographic areas where the parties sell during the last three years? If so, please identify the undertaking(s) concerned (name, address, telephone and fax numbers, and, where possible, contact person), and provide your best estimate of their market share in each E.C. Member State and EFTA State that they are active and in the Community, the territory of the EFTA States and the EEA territory as a whole.

15.3. Give your best estimate of the minimum viable scale for the entry into the relevant product market(s) in terms of appropriate market share necessary to operate profitably.

15.4. Are there significant barriers to entry preventing companies active on the relevant product market(s):

15.4.1. in one E.C. Member State or EFTA State selling in other areas of the EEA territory;

15.4.2 outside the EEA territory selling into all or parts of the EEA territory.

Please give reasons for your answers, explaining, where relevant, the importance of the following factors:

— trade barriers imposed by law, such as tariffs, quotas etc.,

— local specification or technical requirements,

— procurement policies,

— the existence of adequate and available local distribution and retailing facilities,

— transport costs,

— entrenched consumer preferences for local brands or products,

— language.

CHAPTER IV

Final sections

To be completed for all notifications

Section 16

REASONS FOR THE APPLICATION FOR NEGATIVE CLEARANCE

If you are applying for negative clearance state:

16.1. why, *i.e.* state which provision or effects of the agreement or behaviour might, in your view, raise questions of compatibility with the Community's and/or the EEA rules of competition. The object of this subheading is to give the Commission the clearest possible idea of the doubts you have about your agreement or behaviour that you wish to have resolved by a negative clearance.

Then, under the following three references, give a statement of the relevant facts and reasons as to why you consider Article 85(1) or 86 of the E.C. Treaty and/or Article 53(1) or 54 of the EEA Agreement to be inapplicable, *i.e.*:

16.2. why the agreements or behaviour do not have the object or effect of preventing, restricting or distorting competition within the common market or within the territory of the EFTA States to any appreciable extent, or why your undertaking does not have or its behaviour does not abuse a dominant position; and/or

16.3. why the agreements or behaviour do not have the object or effect of preventing, restricting or distorting competition within the EEA territory to any appreciable extent, or why your undertaking does not have or its behaviour does not abuse a dominant position; and/or

16.4. why the agreements or behaviour are not such as may affect trade between Member States or between the Community and one or more EFTA States, or between EFTA States to any appreciable extent.

Section 17

REASONS FOR THE APPLICATION FOR EXEMPTION

If you are notifying the agreement, even if only as a precaution, in order to obtain an exemption under Article 85(3) of the E.C. Treaty and/or Article 53(3) of the EEA Agreement, explain how:

17.1. the agreement contributes to improving production or distribution, and/or promoting technical or economic progress. In particular, please explain the reasons why these benefits are expected to result from the collaboration; for example, do the parties to the agreement possess complementary technologies or distribution systems that will product important synergies? (if, so, please state which). Also please state whether any documents or studies were drawn up by the notifying parties when assessing the feasibility of the operation and the benefits likely to result therefrom, and whether any such documents or studies provided estimates of the savings or efficiencies likely to result. Please provide copies of any such documents or studies;

17.2. a proper share of the benefits arising from such improvement or progress accrues to consumers;

17.3. all restrictive provisions of the agreement are indispensable to the attainment of the aims set out under 17.1 (if you are claiming the benefit of the opposition procedure, it is particularly important that you should identify and justify restrictions that exceed those automatically exempted by the relevant Regulations). In this respect please explain how the benefits resulting from the agreements identified in your reply to question 17.1 could not be achieved, or could not be achieved so quickly or efficiently or only at higher cost or with less certainty of success (i) without the conclusion of the agreement as a whole and (ii) without those particular classes and provisions of the agreement identified in your reply to question 4.2;

17.4. the agreement does not eliminate competition in respect of a substantial part of the goods or services concerned.

Section 18

SUPPORTING DOCUMENTATION

The completed notification must be drawn up and submitted in one original. It shall contain the last versions of all agreements which are the subject of the notification and be accompanied by the following:

(a) sixteen copies of the notification itself;

(b) three copies of the annual reports and accounts of all the parties to be notified agreement, decision or practice for the last three years;

(c) three copies of the most recent in-house or external long-term market studies or planning documents for the purpose of assessing or analysing the affected markets) with respect to competitive conditions, competitors (actual and potential), and market conditions. Each document should indicate the name and position of the author;

(d) three copies of reports and analyses which have been prepared by or for any officers(s) or director(s) for the purposes of evaluating or analysing the notified agreement.

Section 19

DECLARATION

The notification must conclude with the following declaration which is to be signed by or on behalf of all the applicants or notifying parties.

"The undersigned declare that the information given in this notification is correct to the best of their knowledge and belief, that complete copies of all documents requested by form A/B have been supplied to the extent that they are in the possession of the group of undertakings to which the applicant(s) or notifying party(ies) belong(s) and are accessible to the latter, that all estimates are identified as such and are their best estimates of the underlying facts and that all the opinions expressed are sincere.
They are aware of the provisions of Article 15(1)(a) of Regulation No. 17.
Place and date:
Signatures:"

Please add the name(s) of the person(s) signing the application or notification and their function(s).

ANNEX I

Text of articles 85 and 86 of the E.C. Treaty, Articles 53, 54 and 56 of the EEA Agreement, and of Articles 2, 3 and 4 of protocol 22 to that Agreement

ARTICLES 85 OF THE E.C. TREATY

1. The following shall be prohibited as incompatible with the common market: all agreements between undertakings, decisions by associations of undertakings and concerted practices which may affect trade between Member States and which have as their object or effect the prevention, restriction or distortion of competition within the common market, and in particular those which:

   (a) directly or indirectly fix purchase or selling prices or any other trading conditions;

   (b) limit or control production, markets, technical development, or investment;

   (c) share markets or sources of supply;

   (d) apply dissimilar conditions to equivalent transactions with other trading parties, thereby placing them at a competitive disadvantage;

   (e) make the conclusion of contracts subject to acceptance by the other parties of supplementary obligations which, by their nature or according to commercial usage, have no connection with the subject of such contracts.

2. Any agreements or decisions prohibited pursuant to this Article shall be automatically void.

3. The provisions of paragraph 1, may, however, be declared inapplicable in the case of:

   — any agreement or category of agreements between undertakings,

   — any decision or category of decisions by associations or undertakings,

   — any concerted parties or category of concerted practices,

where contributes to improving the production or distribution of goods or to promoting technical or economic progress, while allowing consumers a fair share of the resulting benefit, and which does not:

   (a) impose on the undertakings concerned restrictions which are not indispensable to the attainment of these objectives;

   (b) afford such undertakings the possibility of eliminating competition in respect of a substantial part of the products in question.

ARTICLE 86 OF THE E.C. TREATY

Any abuse by one or more undertakings of a dominant position within the common market or in a substantial part of it shall be prohibited as incompatible with the common market in so far as it may affect trade between Member States.

Such abuse may, in particular, consist in:

(a) directly or indirectly imposing unfair purchase or selling prices or other unfair trading conditions;

(b) limiting production, markets or technical development to the prejudice of consumers;

(c) applying dissimilar conditions to equivalent transations with other trading parties, thereby placing them at a competitive disadvantage;

(d) making the conclusion of contracts subject to acceptance by the other parties of supplementary obligations which, by their nature or according to commercial usage, have no connection with the subject of such contracts.

ARTICLE 53 OF THE EEA AGREEMENT

1. The following shall be prohibited as incompatible with the functioning of this Agreement: all agreements between undertakings, decisions by associations of undertakings and concerted practices which may affect trade between Contracting Parties and which have as their object or effect the prevention, restriction or distortion of competition within the territory covered by this Agreement, and in particular those which:

(a) directly or indirectly fix purchase or selling prices or any other trading conditions;

(b) limit or control production, markets, technical development, or investment;

(c) share markets or sources of supply;

(d) apply dissimilar conditions to equivalent transactions with other trading parties, thereby placing them at a competitive disadvantage;

(e) make the conclusion of contracts subject to acceptance by the other parties of supplementary obligations which, by their nature or according to commercial usage, have no connection with the subject of such contracts.

2. Any agreements or decisions prohibited pursuant to this Article shall be automatically void.

3. The provisions of paragraph 1 may, however, be declared inapplicable in the case of:

— any agreement or category of agreements between undertakings,

— any decision or category of decisions by associations of undertakings,

— any concerted practice or category of concerted practices,

which contributes to improving the production of distribution of goods or to promoting technical or economic progress, while allowing consumers a fair share of the resulting benefit, and which does not:

(a) impose on the undertakings concerned restrictions which are not indispensable to the attainment of these objectives;

(b) afford such undertakings the possibility of eliminating competition in respect of a substantial part of the products in question.

ARTICLE 54 OF THE EEA AGREEMENT

Any abuse by one or more undertakings of a dominant position within the territory covered by this agreement or in a substantial part of it shall be prohibited as incompatible with the functioning of this Agreement in so far as it may affect trade between Contracting Parties.

Such abuse may, in particular, consist in:

(a) directly or indirectly imposing unfair purchase or selling prices or other unfair trading conditions;

(b) limiting production, markets, technical development to the prejudice of consumers;

(c) applying dissimilar conditions to equivalent transactions with other trading parties, thereby placing them at a competitive disadvantage;

(d) making the conclusion of contracts subject to acceptance by the other parties of supplementary obligations which, by their nature or according to commercial usage, have no connection with the subject of such contracts.

ARTICLE 56 OF THE EEA AGREEMENT

1. Individual cases falling under Article 53 shall be decided upon by the surveillance authorities in accordance with the following provisions:

(a) individual cases where only trade between EFTA States is affected shall be decided upon by the EFTA Surveillance Authority;

(b) without prejudice to subparagraph (c), the EFTA Surveillance Authority decides, as provided for in the provisions set out in Article 58, Protocol 21 and the rules adopted for its implementation, Protocol 23 and Annex XIV, on cases where the turnover of the undertakings concerned in the territory of the EFTA States equals 33% or more of their turnover in the territory covered by this Agreement;

(c) the E.C. Commission decides on the other cases as well as on cases under (b) where trade between E.C. Member States is affected, taking into account the provisions set out in Article 58, Protocol 21, Protocol 23 and Annex XIV.

2. Individual cases falling under Article 54 shall be decided upon by the surveillance authority in the territory of which a dominant position is found to exist. The rules set out in paragraph 1(b) and (c) shall apply only if dominance exists within the territories of both surveillance authorities.

3. Individual cases falling under paragraph 1(c), whose effects on trade E.C. Member States or on competition within the Community are not appreciable, shall be decided upon by the EFTA Surveillance Authority.

4. The terms "undertaking" and "turnover" are, for the purpose of this Article, defined in Protocol 22.

ARTICLES 2, 3 AND 4 OF PROTOCOL 22 TO THE EEA AGREEMENT

Article 2

"Turnover" within the meaning of Article 56 of the Agreement shall comprise the amounts derived by the undertaking concerned, in the territory covered by this Agreement, in the preceding financial year from the sale of products and the provision of services falling within the undertaking's ordinary scope of activities after deduction of sales rebates and of value added tax and other taxes directly related to turnover.

Article 3

In place of turnover the following shall be used:

(a) for credit institutions and other financial institutions, their total assets multiplied by the ratio between loans and advances to credit institutions and customers in transactions with residents in the territory covered by this Agreement and the total sum of those loans and advances;

(b) for insurance undertakings, the value of gross premiums received from residents in the territory covered by this Agreement, which shall comprise all amounts received and receivable in respect of insurance contracts issued by or on behalf of the insurance undertakings, including also outgoing reinsurance premiums, and after deduction of taxes and parafiscal contributions or levies charged by reference to the amounts of individual premiums or the total value of premiums.

Article 4

1. In derogation of the definition of the turnover relevant for the application of Article 56 of the Agreement, as contained in Article 2 of this Protocol, the relevant turnover shall be constituted:

(a) as regards agreements, decisions of associations of undertakings and concerted practices related to distribution and supply arrangements between non-competing undertakings, of the amounts derived from the sale of goods or the provision of services which are the subject matter of the agreements, decisions or concerted practices, and from the other goods or services which are considered by users to be equivalent in view of their characteristics, price and intended use;

(b) as regards agreements, decisions of associations of undertakings and concerted practices related to arrangements on transfer of technology between non-competing undertakings, of the amounts derived from the sale of goods or the provision of services which result from the technology which is the subject matter of the agreements, decisions or concerted practices, and of the amounts derived from the sale of those goods or the provisions of those services which that technology is designed to improve or replace.

2. However, where at the time of the coming to existence of arrangements as described in paragraph 1(a) and (b) turnover as regards the sale of products or the provision of services is not in evidence, the general provision as contained in Article 2 shall apply.

ANNEX II

List of relevant Acts

(as of 1 March 1995)

If you think it possible that your arrangements do not need to be notified by virtue of any of these regulations or notices it may be worth your while to obtain a copy.

IMPLEMENTING REGULATIONS

Council Regulation No. of 6 February 1992: First Regulation implementing Articles 85 and 86 of the Treaty (OJ No. 13, 21.2.1962, p. 204/62, English Special Edition 1959–1962, November 1972, p. 87) as amended (OJ No. 58, 10.7.1962, p. 1655/62; OJ No. 162, 7.11.1963, p. 269/63; OJ No. L 285, 29.12.1971, p. 49; OJ No. L 73, 27.3.1972, p. 92; OJ No. L 291, 19.11.1979, p. 94 and OJ No. L 302, 15. 11. 1985, p. 165).

Commission Regulation (E.C.) No. 3385/94 of 21 December 1994 on the form, content and other details of applications and notifications provided for in Council Regulation No. 17.

REGULATIONS GRANTING BLOCK EXEMPTION IN RESPECT OF A WIDE RANGE OF AGREEMENTS

Commission Regulation E.C.) No. 1983/83 of 22 June 1983 on the application of Article 85(3) of the Treaty to categories of exclusive distribution agreements (OJ No. L 173, 30.6.1983, p. 1, as corrected in OJ No. L 281, 13.10.1983, p. 24), as well as this Regulation as adapted for EEA purposes (see point 2 of Annex XIV to the EEA Agreement).

Commission Regulation (EEC) No. 1984/83 of 22 June 1983 on the application of Article 85(3) of the Treaty to categories of exclusive purchasing agreements (OJ No. L 173, 30.6.1983, p. 5, as corrected in OJ No. L 281, 13.10.1983, p. 24), as well as this Regulation as adapted for EEA purposes (see point 3 of Annex XIV to the EEA Agreement).

See also the Commission notices concerning Regulations (EEC) No. 1983/93 and (EEC) No. 1984/93 and (EEC) No. 1984/83 (OJ No. C 101, 13.4.1984, p. 2 and OJ No. C 121, 13.5.1992, p. 2).

Commission Regulation (EEC) No. 2349/84 of 23 July 1984 on the application of Article 85(3) of the Treaty to certain categories of patent licensing agreements (OJ No. L 219, 16.8.1984, p. 15, as corrected in OJ No. L 113, 26.4.1985, p. 34), as amended (OJ No. L 12, 18.1.1995, p. 13), as well as this Regulation as adapted for EEA purposes (see point 5 of Annex XIV to the EEA Agreement). Article 4 of this Regulation provides for an opposition procedure.

Commission Regulation (EEC) No. 123/85 of 12 December 1984 on the application of Article 85(3) of the Treaty to certain categories of motor vehicle distributing and servicing agreements (OJ No. L 15, 18.1.1985, p. 16); as well as this Regulation as adapted for EEA purposes (see point 4 of Annex XIV to the EEA Agreement). See also the Commission notices concerning this Regulation (OJ No. C 17, 18.1.1985 p. 4 and OJ No. C 329, 18.12.1991, p. 20).

Commission Regulation (EEC) No. 417/85 of 19 December 1984 on the application of Article 85(3) of the Treaty to categories of specialization agreements (OJ No. L 53, 22.2.1985, p. 1), as amended (OJ No. L 21, 29.1.1993, p. 8), as well as this Regulation as adapted for EEA purposes (see point 6 of Annex XIV to the EEA Agreement). Article 4 of this Regulation provides for an opposition procedure.

Commission Regulation (EEC) No. 418/85 of 19 December 1984 on the application of Article 85(3) of the Treaty to categories of research and development cooperation agreements (OJ No. L 53, 22.2.1985, p. 5), as amended (OJ No. L 21, 29.1.1993, p. 8), as well as this Regulation as adapted for EEA purposes (see point 7 of Annex XIV to the EEA Agreement). Article 7 of this Regulation provides for an opposition procedure.

Commission Regulation (EEC) No. 4087/88 of 30 November 1988 on the application of Article 85(3) of the Treaty to categories of franchise agreements (OJ No. L 359, 28.12.1988, p. 46), as well as this Regulation as adapted for EEA purposes (see point 8 of Annex XIV to the EEA Agreement). Article 6 of this Regulation provides for an opposition procedure.

Commission Regulation (EEC) No. 556/89 of 30 November 1988 on the application of Article 85(3) of the Treaty to certain categories of know-how licensing agreements (OJ No. L 61, 4.3.1989, p. 1), as amended (OJ No. L 21, 29.1.1993, p. 8), as well as this Regulation as adapted for EEA purposes (see point 9 of Annex XIV to the EEA Agreement). Article 4 of this Regulation provides for an opposition procedure.

Commission Regulation (EEC) No. 3932/92 of 21 December 1992 on the application of Article 85(3) of the Treaty to certain categories of agreements, decisions and concerted practices in the insurance sector (OJ No. L 398, 31.12.1992, p. 7). This Regulation will be adapted for EEA purposes.

Notices of a general nature

Commission notice on exclusive dealing contracts with commercial agents (OJ No. 139, 24.12.1962, p. 2921/62). This states that the Commission does not consider most such agreements to fall under the prohibition of Article 85(1).

Commission notice concerning agreements, decisions and concerted practices in the field of cooperation between enterprises (OJ No. C 75, 29.7.1968, p. 3, as corrected in OJ No. C 84, 28.8.1968, p. 14). This defines the sorts of cooperation on market studies, accounting, R & D, joint use of production, storage or transport, ad hoc consortia, selling or after-sales service, advertising or quality labelling that the Commission considers not to fall under the prohibition of Article 85(1).

Commission notice concerning its assessment of certain subcontracting agreements in relation to Article 85(1) of the Treaty (OJ No. C 1, 3.1.1979, p. 2).

Commission notice on agreements, decisions and concerted practices of minor importance which do not fall under Article 85(1) of the Treaty (OJ No. C 231, 12.9.1986, p. 2) as amended by Commission notice (OJ No. C 368, 23.12.1994, p. 20) — in the main, those where the parties have less than 5% of the market between them, and a combined annual turnover of less than ECU 300 million.

Commission guidelines on the application of EEC competition rules in the telecommunications sector (OJ No. C 233, 6.9.1991, p. 2). These guidelines aim at clarifying the application of Community competition rules to the market participants in the telecommunications sector.

Commission notice on cooperation between national courts and the Commission in applying Articles 85 and 86 (OJ No. C 39, 13.2.1993, p. 6). This notice sets out the principles on the basis of which such cooperation takes place.

Commission notice concerning the assessment of cooperative joint ventures pursuant to Article 85 of the EC Treaty (OJ No. C 43, 16.2.1993, p. 2). This notice sets out the principles on the assessment of joint ventures.

A collection of these texts (as at 31 December 1989) was published by the Office for Official Publications of the European Communities (references Vol I: ISBN 92–826–1307–0, catalogue No: CV–42–90–001–EN–C). An updated collection is in preparation.

Pursuant to the Agreement, these texts will also cover the European Economic Area.

ANNEX III

List of Member States and EFTA States, address of the Commission and of the EFTA Surveillance Authority, list of Commission Information Offices within the community and in EFTA States and addresses of competent authorities in EFTA States
The Member States as at the date of this Annex are: Austria, Belgium, Denmark, Finland, France, Germany, Greece, Ireland, Italy, Luxembourg, the Netherlands, Portugal, Spain, Sweden and the United Kingdom.

The EFTA States which will be Contracting Parties of the EEA Agreement, as at the date of this Annex, are: Iceland, Liechtenstein and Norway.

The address of the Commission's Directorate-General for Competition is:
Commission of the European Communities
Directorate-General for Competition
200 rue de la Loi
B-1049 Brussels

The address of the EFTA Surveillance Authority's Competition Directorate is:

EFTA Surveillance Authority
Competition Directorate
1–3 rue Marie-Thérèse
B-1040 Brussels
Tel. (322) 286 17 11

The addresses of the Commission's Information Offices in the Community are:

BELGIUM
73 Rue Archimède
B-1040 Bruxelles
Te. (322) 299 11 11

DENMARK
Højbrohus
Østergade 61
Postboks 144
DK-1004 København K
Tel. (4533) 14 41 40

FEDERAL REPUBLIC OF GERMANY
Zitelmannstraße 22
D-53113 Bonn
Tel. (49228) 53 00 90

Kurfürstendamm 102
D-10711 Berlin 31
Tel. (4930) 896 09 30

Erhardstraße 27
D-80331 München
Tel. (4989) 202 10 11

GREECE
2 Vassilissis Sofias
Case Postale 11002
GR-Athina 10674
Tel. (301) 724 39 82/83/84

SPAIN
Calle De Serrano 41
5a Planta
E-28001 Madrid
Tel. (341) 435 17 00

Av. Diagonal, 407 bis
18 Planta
E-08008 Barcelona
Tel. (343) 415 81 77

FRANCE
288, boulevard Saint-Germain
F-75007 Paris
Tel. (331) 40 63 38 00

CMCI
2, rue Henri Barbusse
F-13241 Marseille, Cedex 01
Tel. (3391) 91 46 00

IRELAND
39 Molesworth Street
IRL-Dublin 2
Tel. (3531) 71 22 44

ITALY
Via Poli 29
I-00187 Roma
Tel. (396) 699 11 60

Corso Magenta 61
I-20123 Milano
Tel. (392) 480 15 05

LUXEMBOURG
Bâtiment Jean Monnet
Rue Alcide de Gasperi
L-2920 Luxembourg
Tel. (352) 430 11

NETHERLANDS
Postbus 30465
NL-2500 GL Den Haag
Tel. (3170) 346 93 26

AUSTRIA
Hoyosgasse 5
A-1040 Wien
Tel. (431) 505 33 79

PORTUGAL
Centro Europeu Jean Monnet
Largo Jean Monnet, 1–10°
P-1200 Lisboa
Tel. (3511) 54 11 44

FINLAND
31 Pohjoisesplanadi
00100 Helsinki
Tel. (3580) 65 64 20

SWEDEN
PO Box 16396
Hamngatan 6
11147 Stockholm
Tel. (468) 611 11 72

UNITED KINGDOM
8 Storey's Gate
UK-London SW1P 3AT
Tel. (44171) 973 19 92

Windsor House
9/15 Bedford Street
UK-Belfast BT2 7EG
Tel. (441232) 24 07 08

4 Cathedral Road
UK-Cardiff CF1 9SG
Tel. (441222) 37 16 31

9 Alva Street
UK-Edinburgh EH2 4PH
Tel. (44131) 225 20 58

The addresses of the Commission's Information Offices in the EFTA States are:

NORWAY
Postboks 1643 Vika 0119 Oslo 1
Haakon's VII Gate No. 6
0161 Oslo 1
Tel. (472) 83 35 83

Forms for notifications and applications, as well as more detailed information on the EEA competition rules, can also be obtained from the following offices:

AUSTRIA
Federal Ministry for Economic Affairs
Tel. (431) 71 100

NORWAY
Price Directorate
Tel. (4722) 40 09 00

FINLAND
Office of Free Competition
Tel. (3580) 731 41

SWEDEN

Competitive Authority
Tel. (468) 700 16 00

ICELAND
Directorate of Competition and Fair Trade
Tel. (3541) 27 422

LIECHTENSTEIN
Office of National Economy
Division of Economy and Statistics
Tel. (4175) 61 11

APPENDIX B.2   FORM N

Formal Consultation Draft

FORM FOR NOTIFICATIONS FOR GUIDANCE OR DECISION UNDER CHAPTERS I AND II OF THE COMPETITION ACT 1998

PART 1:   NOTES

B.2-01   *1.1 Although this document is described as "a Form", it is essentially a check-list of information which must be supplied to the Director General of Fair Trading to enable him to determine a notification. Before completing the Form, reference should be made to the Procedural Rules of the Director General of Fair Trading.*

1.2 The information must be correct and complete for the notification to be effective.

1.3 The Form must be supplied in original version plus two copies, together with either an original or a certified copy, plus two further copies, of any relevant agreement and Annexes.

1.4 All notifications for guidance or a decision under Chapter I or Chapter II of the Act should be sent to the Director General of Fair Trading. He will place details of all notifications for decision (although not for guidance) on the public register maintained by him at the Office of Fair Trading and on the Office's Internet website. Details of the notification for decision may subsequently be published in suitable trade and/or national press, where it is considered appropriate to do so.

1.5 The Act is enforced by the Director General of Fair Trading and, in relation to the regulated utility sectors shown in question 3.5 below, concurrently with the sector regulators; if any positive answer is given to that question, provide one further copy of the Form and attachments for each relevant regulator who may have concurrent jurisdiction. A copy of the Form (together with its Annexes and copies of agreements) should also be sent to the relevant regulator(s), if the agreement or conduct being notified may fall within their sector(s). In general, the relevant regulator will deal with the notification. If the Director General considers that a regulator has, or may have, concurrent jurisdiction in relation to an agreement or conduct in respect of which a notification has been submitted, he will send a copy of the Form N to the regulator(s) and inform the notifying party that he has done so.

1.6 *Indicate clearly to which section of the Form any additional pages relate. The notification* **must** *include the form of receipt at Part 3.* **Information which is regarded by the under-taking or undertakings as confidential should be clearly identified as such and placed in a separate identified annex, explaining why the information should be regarded as confidential.** *Notifications may also be made on disk or using other electronic format: please telephone the enquiry point at the Office of Fair Trading on 0171 211 xxxx before using this facility.*

1.7 **The Director General must be informed of any changes which occur after notifica-tion has been made and which may affect any information given in this Form.**

COMPLAINTS

1.8 *Complaints may be sent either to the Director General of Fair Trading or direct to the rel-evant regulator. There is no form to complete to make a complaint; further information on making complaints is contained in the guideline* **The Competition Act 1998: the Major Provisions.**

PART 2: INFORMATION TO THE PROVIDED BY THE UNDERTAKING NOTIFYING THE AGREEMENT OR CONDUCT

Number sections as below. In some cases, it may be possible to dispense with the requirement to provide information in all categories. This should be discussed with officials before making the noti-fication. **Information which is regarded by the undertaking(s) as confidential should be clearly identified as such and placed in a separate identified annex.**

1. THE UNDERTAKING(S) SUBMITTING THE NOTIFICATION

1.1 The identity of the undertaking submitting the notification (full name and address, name of representative, telephone and fax numbers, and brief description of the undertaking or association of undertakings). For a partnership, sole trader or other unincorporated body trading under a business name, give the name(s) and address(es) of the proprietor(s) or partners. Please quote any reference which should be used;

1.2 if acting on behalf of another undertaking, state in what capacity, eg solicitor;

Where the Form is signed by a solicitor or other representative, proof of authority to act on behalf of the undertaking submitting notification must be provided.

1.3 if the notification is submitted by or on behalf of more than one undertaking, give the details of the representative(s) as requested in 1.1 above. Indicate whether the representa-tive has been appointed on a joint basis. If not, give the details in respect of representatives who have been authorised to act on behalf of each or either of the parties to the agree-ment, indicating who they represent;

1.4 the Standard Industrial Classification code for the relevant good(s) or service(s), if known. If the code is not known, describe the goods or services involved as fully and accurately as possible;

Schedules 5 and 6 to the Act require a party to an agreement or conduct who makes a notification for guidance or a decision in respect of that agreement or conduct to take all reasonable steps to notify all other parties to the agreement or conduct of whom he is aware that the notification has been made and whether it is for guidance or a decision. In exceptional cases, it may not be practicable to inform all non-notifying parties to the notified agreement or conduct that it has been notified, if, for example, an agreement is concluded with a large number of undertakings. The notification to such other undertakings must be made (a) in writing; and (b) within seven working days of the notifying undertaking receiving the Director General's acknowledgment of receipt.

1.5 the full names, addresses (by registered office, where appropriate, and principal place of business, if different), telephone and fax numbers, nature of business, and brief description of any other parties to the agreement, decision or concerted practice ("the arrangement") or conduct being notified;

1.6 details of the steps to be taken to inform any other such parties that the notification has been made and indicate whether the remaining parties have received a copy of the notification with confidential information and business secrets deleted. State the reasons, if it is not practicable to inform other parties of the notification in accordance with the requirements outlined above.

2.   PURPOSE OF THE NOTIFICATION

The Chapter I prohibition does not apply unless the arrangement has an "appreciable effect" on competition, and notification will not normally be appropriate when that is not the case. Further information is given in the guideline **The Competition Act 1998: the Chapter I prohibition.** *The concept of appreciability does not apply to the Chapter II prohibition.*

2.1 whether the notification is being made under Chapter I, Chapter II or both;

2.2 whether it is for guidance or a decision;

2.3 if for guidance as to whether the Chapter I prohibition has been infringed: specify why it is considered that the Chapter I prohibition has been infringed and whether the arrangement qualifies (or in the case of an individual exemption, would qualify if notified) for an exemption (individual, UK block exemption, parallel, or under section 11 of the Act); or

2.4 if for a decision as to whether the Chapter I prohibition has been infringed: whether an individual exemption is requested, and, if so, the date from which it is required to have effect, if different from the date of notification, giving reasons;

2.5 if the notification is for an extension of an individual exemption, state the date of expiry of the existing exemption and the reason why an extension is sought. Enclose a copy of the decision letter granting the exemption;

2.6 whether the arrangement or conduct that is the subject of the notification is considered to benefit from any exclusion from the Chapter I or Chapter II prohibitions. Specify the exclusion: give reasons why you are unsure whether the arrangement or conduct is covered by the exclusion and why notification is considered appropriate;

3.   JURISDICTION

In general when an arrangement is also caught by Article 85 of the EC Treaty, the Director General considers that the EC Commission is the more appropriate authority to whom notification should be made (see the guideline **The Competition Act 1998: the Chapter I prohibition**).

3.1 why the arrangement is considered to be not caught by Article 85(1);

3.2 whether the arrangement or conduct is the subject of a notification to the European Commission. If so, it would assist consideration of the notification if three copies of the completed Form A/B and supporting documents, and one further copy if information has been given in response to question 3.5 below, were attached. It is unnecessary to repeat information given on Form A/B, but information specific to the UK market will be necessary (following the format in question 7.1) to the extent that it has not been given on Form A/B, and should be provided separately. Supply three copies of any "comfort" letter received from the European Commission;

3.3 whether the arrangement or conduct is the subject of a notification to any other national competition authority;

3.4 if the arrangement relates to transport by rail, road, inland waterway or to services ancillary to transport and is the subject of a notification to the European Commission under Regulation 1017/68, it would similarly assist consideration of the notification if three copies of the completed Form II and any supporting documents and one further copy if information has been given in response to question 3.5 below were attached;

3.5 whether the arrangement or conduct being notified relates to any one or more of:

    a commercial activities connected with telecommunications;
    b the shipping, conveyance or supply of gas and activities ancillary thereto;
    c commercial activities connected with the generation, transmission or supply of electricity;
    d commercial activities connected with the supply of water or securing a supply of water or with the provision or securing of sewerage services;
    e commercial activities connected with the generation, transmission or supply of electricity in Northern Ireland;
    f the conveyance, storage or supply of gas in Northern Ireland;
    g the supply of railway services.

Identify the sector regulator or regulators who may have concurrent jurisdiction with the Director General of Fair Trading to deal with the notification;

3.6 names and addresses, telephone and fax numbers, date, details and case references of any previous contacts with the Office of Fair Trading, a regulator, any other national competition authority, or the EC Commission, and of any proceedings in any national court in the European Community, relating to the arrangement or conduct being notified and of any relevant previous arrangements or conduct.

4. DETAILS OF THE ARRANGEMENT OR CONDUCT

4.1 a brief description of the arrangement or conduct being notified (nature, content purpose, date(s) and duration);

4.2 if written, attach either an original or a certified copy, together with two further copies, of the most recent version of the text of the arrangement being notified (technical details contained in know-how agreements, for example, may be omitted but omissions should be indicated); if not written, provide a full description;

4.3 identify any provisions in the arrangement which may restrict the parties in their freedom to take independent commercial decisions or to act on those decisions;

4.4 if the notification relates to a standard contract, the number expected to be concluded.

5. CHAPTER I NOTIFICATIONS: INFORMATION ON THE PARTIES TO THE ARRANGEMENT AND THE GROUPS TO WHICH THEY BELONG

5.1 for each undertaking identified in 1.5 above, the name of a contact, together with his or her address, telephone and fax numbers, and position held in the undertaking;

5.2 the corporate groups to which each undertaking belongs and the product and/or services market(s) in which the groups are active (hereafter called "the relevant product market"); include one copy of the most recent consolidated annual report and accounts (or equivalent for unincorporated bodies) for each undertaking;

5.3 for each of the parties to the arrangement, provide a list of all undertakings belonging to the same group which are active in the same relevant product market(s), and those active in markets neighbouring the relevant product markets — that is, those which are not regarded by the consumer as fully interchangeable or substitutable for products in the defined relevant product market, as defined in question 6.1 below.

6. THE RELEVANT PRODUCT AND GEOGRAPHIC MARKETS

A relevant product market comprises all those products and/or services regarded by the consumer of the product or service as interchangeable or substitutable by reason of their characteristics, prices or intended use. The following factors are among those normally considered when determin-

ing the relevant product market and should be taken into account, together with any others considered relevant:

(i)   the degree of physical similarity between the products/services in question;

(ii) any differences in end-use to which the goods are or may be put;

(iii) differences in price between the products/services;

(iv) the cost of switching between two potentially competing products/services; and

(v)   established consumer preferences for one type or category or product/service.

The relevant geographic market is the area in which the undertakings concerned are involved in the supply of products or services in which the conditions of competition are appreciably different from neighbouring areas. The following factors are among those normally considered when determining the relevant geographic market and should be taken into account, together with any others considered relevant:

(i)   the nature and characteristics of the products or services concerned;

(ii) the existence of entry barriers or consumer preferences;

(iii) appreciable differences of the undertakings' market share or substantial price differences between neighbouring areas; and

(iv) transport costs.

6.1   In the light of the relevant factors given above (which are not exhaustive), explain the definitions of the relevant product and geographic markets which should be considered, with full reasons, in particular stating the specific products or services directly or indirectly affected by the notification and other goods or services that may be viewed as substitutable, with reasons. If the relevant geographic market is considered to be an area smaller, or larger, than the whole of the United Kingdom, the boundaries considered applicable, with reasons. Give reasons for all assumptions or findings, and explain how the factors outlined above have been taken into account. Further details are in the guideline *The Competition Act 1998: Market Definition*.

6.2   provide a copy of the most recent in-house long-term market studies assessing or analysing the relevant markets (including any commissioned by the undertakings from outside consultants), and give references of any external studies of the relevant product market, and, where possible, include a copy of any such studies.

7.   THE POSITION OF THE UNDERTAKINGS IN THE RELEVANT PRODUCT MARKETS

The information required under this section relates to both the relevant geographic market and the relevant product market, for the groups of the parties as a whole. Market shares may be calculated either on the basis of value or volume. Justification for the figures provided must be given by reference to the sales or turnover of each of the undertakings in question. The source or sources of information should be given, and, where possible, a copy of the document from which information has been taken.

7.1   for each of the previous three calendar or financial years, as available, give:

a   details of the market shares of each undertaking in the goods or services in the relevant product and geographic markets, as identified in 6.1 above, and, if different, in the UK, and in the European Community;

b   estimates of market shares in the relevant product and geographic markets for each of the five main competitors of each of the undertakings, giving the undertaking's name, address, telephone and fax number, and, where possible, a contact name;

c   identify the five main customers of each of the undertakings in the relevant product and geographic markets, giving the undertaking's name, address, telephone and fax number, and, where possible, a contact name;

d   details of the undertakings' interests in, and arrangements with, any other companies competing in the relevant product and geographic market, together with details of their market shares, if known.

8.   *MARKET ENTRY AND POTENTIAL COMPETITION COMPETITION IN THE RELEVANT PRODUCT AND GEOGRAPHIC MARKETS*

8.1 For all relevant product and geographic markets:

   a describe the factors influencing entry into the relevant product market(s): that is, the barriers which exist to prevent undertakings not presently manufacturing goods within the relevant product market(s) from entering the market(s), taking account of, in particular but not exclusively, the extent to which:

   (i)   entry is regulated by the requirements of government authorisation or standard-setting, in any form, and any legal or regulatory controls on entry to the market(s);

   (ii) entry is influenced by the availability of raw materials;

   (iii) entry is influenced by the length of existing contracts between suppliers and customers;

   (iv) research and development and licensing patents, know-how and other rights are important;

   b describe the factors influencing entry in geographic terms: that is, the barriers that exist to prevent undertakings already producing and/or marketing goods within the relevant product market(s) outside the relevant geographic market(s) from extending sales into the relevant geographic market(s), taking account of, in particular but not exclusively, the importance of:

   (i)   trade barriers imposed by law, such as tariffs, quotas etc;

   (ii) local geographic specifications or technical requirements;

   (iii) procurement policies;

   (iv) the existence of adequate and available local distribution and retailing facilities;

   (v)   transport costs;

   (vi) strong consumer preference for local brands or products;

   c in respect of new entrants in both products and geographic terms, state whether any new undertakings have entered the product market(s) in geographic areas where the undertakings sell, during the last three years. Identify the undertakings concerned by name, address, telephone and fax numbers and, where possible, a contact name, with best estimates of market shares of each in the relevant product and geographic markets.

9.   *NEGATIVE CLEARANCE*

9.1 state reasons for seeking "negative clearance" (that is, that the Director General should conclude that the arrangement or conduct is not covered by either the Chapter I or the Chapter II prohibition). Indicate, for example, which provision or effects of the arrangement or conduct may breach the relevant prohibition, and state the reasons why it is considered that the arrangements do not have the object or effect of preventing, restricting or distorting competition within the UK to an appreciable extent, or why the undertaking does not have, or its behaviour does not abuse, a dominant position.

10. *EXEMPTION*

The criteria which are taken into account in considering notifications for exemption are set out in section 9 of the Act.

10.1 if exemption from the Chapter I prohibition is sought, explain how the arrangements contribute to improving production or distribution and/or promoting technical or economic progress, and how consumers will be allowed a fair share of those benefits. Explain how each restrictive provision in the arrangements is indispensable to these objectives, and how the arrangements do not eliminate competition in respect of a substantial part of the relevant product or geographic market concerned.

11.   *TRANSITIONAL PERIODS*

   11.1 if the arrangement is considered to benefit from any transitional periods during which the Chapter I prohibition does not apply, indicate the duration of the relevant transitional periods by reference to Schedule 13 to the Act.

12.   *OTHER INFORMATION:*

   12.1 state:

   a whether this notification should be considered as urgent. If so, give reasons;
   b details of trade publications in which advertisements seeking the views of third parties might be placed;
   c any other information you consider may be helpful.

   12.2 [fees payable . . .]

Under section 44 of the Act, it is an offence, punishable by a fine or imprisonment or both, to provide information which is false or misleading in a material particular if the undertaking or person providing it knows that it is false or misleading, or is reckless as to whether it is. If the undertaking is a body corporate, under section 72 of the Act its officers may be guilty of an offence

The notification must conclude with the following declaration which is to be signed by or on behalf of all the applicants or notifying undertakings. Unsigned notifications are invalid.

DECLARATION

The undersigned declare that all the information given above and in the . . . pages annexed hereto is correct to the best of their knowledge and belief, and that all estimates are identified as such and are their best estimates of the underlying facts.

Place and date ....

Signature ....
....

Status ....
....
.... name(s) in block capitals

PART 3:   ACKNOWLEDGEMENT OF RECEIPT

This Form will be returned to the address inserted below if the top half is completed by the undertaking lodging it.

to be completed by the undertaking making the notification

To: .... (name and address of applicant)
   ....
   ....
   ....

Your notification dated ....
concerning ....
under reference ....
involving the following undertakings:

1. ....
2. .... [and others]

---

to be completed by the Office of Fair Trading

was received on ....

and registered under reference number

.... **Please quote this number in all correspondence**

In the event that this notification is not complete in a material respect, you will be informed within one month of its receipt. If you are not informed within that time that it is considered to be incomplete, it is deemed to be effective on the date of its receipt.

PART 4   TO BE COMPLETED BY THE UNDERTAKING MAKING THE NOTIFICATION

Public Register Entry: Decision cases only

Following receipt of a notification for a decision, the Director General will place the details on the public register maintained at:

> The Office of Fair Trading
> Field House
> Breams Buildings
> London EC4A 1PR

The Director General is required to seek comments from third parties on application for a decision; he may therefore publish a notice inviting comments on the notification. The public register entry and published notice will be made without further reference to the parties. You are therefore asked to provide the information which may be used for this purpose. It is important that the answers to these questions do not contain any business secrets or other confidential information.

1. state the names of the parties to the arrangement(s) or conduct notified, as in questions 1.1 and 1.5 above;

2. give a short summary (no more than 250 words) of the nature and objectives of the arrangement(s);

3. the Standard Industrial Classification code for the relevant good(s) or service(s), if known. If the code is not known, describe the goods or services involved as fully and accurately as possible.

From the Office of Fair Trading

APPENDIX B.3   FORM EG

FORM FOR APPLICATIONS FOR EARLY GUIDANCE UNDER PARAGRAPH 7 OF SCHEDULE 13 TO THE COMPETITION ACT 1998

PART 1:   NOTES

B.3-01   *1.1 Guidance in anticipation of the coming into force of Chapter I of the Act ("early guidance") is available for agreements made during the period beginning on 9 November*

1998 *(enactment date) and ending immediately before 1 March 2000 (the date on which the Chapter I prohibition comes into force). It may be applied for under paragraph 7 of Schedule 13 to the Act. Early guidance is not available in respect of the Chapter II prohibition.* **This form cannot be used for notifications made on or after 1 March 2000; Form N must be used for such notifications.**

1.2 *Although this document is described as "a Form", it is essentially a check-list of information which must be supplied to the Director General of Fair Trading to enable him to determine an application for early guidance. Before completing the Form, reference should be made to the Early Guidance Directions of the Director General of Fair Trading issued on 26 November 1998.*

1.3 *The information must be correct and complete for the application to be effective.*

1.4 *The Form must be supplied in original version plus two copies, together with either an original or a certified copy, plus two further copies, of the agreement(s) and any relevant Annexes.*

1.5 *All applications for early guidance should be sent to the Director General of Fair Trading and marked for the attention of the "Early Guidance Co-ordination Unit".*

1.6 *The Act is enforced by the Director General of Fair Trading and, in relation to the regulated utility sectors shown in question 3.5 below, concurrently with the sector regulators; these have concurrent jurisdiction with the Director General to give early guidance. If any positive answer is given question 3.5, provide one further copy of the Form and attachments for each relevant regulator who may have concurrent jurisdiction. A copy of the Form (together with its Annexes and copies of agreements) should also be sent to the relevant regulator(s), if the agreement being notified may fall within their sector(s). In general, the relevant regulator will deal with the application. If the Director General considers that a regulator has, or may have, concurrent jurisdiction in relation to an agreement in respect of which an application for early guidance has been submitted, he will send a copy of the Form EG to the regulator(s) and inform the notifying party that he has done so.*

1.7 *Indicate clearly to which section of the Form any additional pages relate. The application* **must** *include the form of receipt at Part 3.* **Information which is regarded by the undertaking or undertakings as confidential should be clearly identified as such and placed in a separate identified annex. An explanation of why such information is regarded as confidential should also be provided.** *Applications may also be made on disk or using other electronic format: please telephone the enquiry point at the Office of Fair Trading on 0171 211 8989 before using this facility.*

1.8 **The Director General, or, if the applicant has been informed that a regulator is dealing with the application, that regulator, must be informed of any material changes which occur after application has been made and which may affect any information given in this Form.**

PART 2: INFORMATION TO BE PROVIDED BY THE UNDERTAKING NOTIFYING THE AGREEMENT

Number sections as below. In some cases, it may be possible to dispense with the requirement to provide information in all categories. This should be discussed with officials before making the application. **Information which is regarded by the undertaking(s) as confidential should be clearly identified as such and placed in a separate identified annex.**

1. *THE UNDERTAKING(S) SUBMITTING THE APPLICATION*

1.1 The identity of the undertaking submitting the application (full name and address, name of representative, telephone and fax numbers, and brief description of the undertaking or association of undertakings). For a partnership, sole trader or other unincorporated body trading under a business name, give the name(s) and address(es) of the proprietor(s) or partners. Please quote any reference which should be used;

1.2 if acting on behalf of another undertaking, state in what capacity, eg solicitor;

Where the Form is signed by a solicitor or other representative, proof of authority to act on behalf of the undertaking submitting the application must be provided.

1.3 if the application is submitted by or on behalf of more than one undertaking, indicate whether a joint representative has been appointed. If so, give the details as requested in 1.1 above in respect of the joint representative. If not, give the details in respect of any representatives who have been authorised to act on behalf of each, or either, of the parties to the agreement, indicating who they represent;

1.4 the Standard Industrial Classification code for the relevant good(s) or service(s), if known. If the code is not known, describe the goods or services involved as fully and accurately as possible;

The directions issued by the Director General require a party to an agreement who makes an application for early guidance in respect of that agreement to take all reasonable steps to notify all other parties to the agreement of whom he is aware that the application has been made. In exceptional cases, it may not be practicable to inform all non-notifying parties to the notified agreement that it has been notified, if, for example, an agreement is concluded with a large number of undertakings. The notification to such other undertakings must be made (a) in writing; and (b) within seven working days of the applicant receiving the Director General's acknowledgment of receipt of his application. The applicant must send a copy of such notification to the Director General.

1.5 the full names, addresses (by registered office, where appropriate, and principal place of business, if different), telephone and fax numbers, nature of business, and brief description of any other parties to the agreement, decision or concerted practice ("the arrangement") being notified;

1.6 details of the steps to be taken to inform any other such parties that the application has been made and indicate whether the remaining parties have received a copy of the application with confidential information and business secrets deleted. State the reasons, if it is not practicable to inform other parties of the application in accordance with the requirements outlined above.

2. PURPOSE OF THE APPLICATION

The Chapter I prohibition will not apply unless the arrangement has an "appreciable effect" on competition, and an application for early guidance will not normally be appropriate when that is not the case. Further information is given in the guideline **The Competition Act 1998: the Chapter I prohibition.**

2.1 whether the arrangement that is the subject of the application is considered to be of a type which would benefit from any exclusion from the Chapter I prohibition. Specifiy the exclusion: give reasons why you are unsure whether the arrangement will be covered by the exclusion and why an application for early guidance is considered appropriate;

2.2 specify why it is considered that the Chapter I prohibition is likely to be infringed and whether the arrangement is likely to qualify (or in the case of an individual exemption, is likely to qualify if notified) for an exemption (individual, UK block exemption, parallel, or under section 11 of the Act);

3. JURISDICTION

In general, when an arrangement is also caught by Article 85 of the EC Treaty, the Director General considers that the EC Commission is the more appropriate authority to whom notification should be made (see the guideline **The Competition Act 1998: the Chapter I prohibition**).

3.1 why the arrangement is considered to be not caught by Article 85(1);

3.2 whether the arrangement is the subject of an application to the European Commission. If so, it would assist consideration of the application if three copies of the completed Form A/B and supporting documents, and one further copy if information has been given in response to question 3.5 below, were attached. It is unnecessary to repeat information given on Form A/B, but information specific to the UK market will be necessary (following the format in question 7.1) to the extent that it has not been given on Form A/B, and should be provided separately. Supply three copies of any "comfort" letter received from the European Commission;

3.3 whether the arrangement is the subject of an application to any other national competition authority;

3.4 if the arrangement relates to transport by rail, road, inland waterway or to services ancillary to transport and is the subject of an application to the European Commission under Regulation 1017/68, it would similarly assist consideration of the application if three copies of the completed Form II and any supporting documents and one further copy if information has been given in response to question 3.5 below were attached;

3.5 whether the arrangement being notified relates to any one or more of:

    a commercial activities connected with telecommunications;

    b the shipping, conveyance or supply of gas and activities ancillary thereto;

    c commercial activities connected with the generation, transmission or supply of electricity;

    d commercial activities connected with the supply of water or securing a supply of water or with the provision or securing of sewerage services;

    e commercial activities connected with the generation, transmission or supply of electricity in Northern Ireland;

    f the conveyance, storage or supply of gas in Northern Ireland;

    g the supply of railway services.

Identify the sector regulator or regulators who may have concurrent jurisdiction with the Director General of Fair Trading to deal with the application for early guidance;

3.6 names and addresses, telephone and fax numbers, date and the details, including case references, of any previous contacts with the Office of Fair Trading, a regulator, any other national competition authority, or the EC Commission, and of any proceedings in any national court in the European Community, relating to the arrangement being notified and of any relevant previous arrangements.

4. DETAILS OF THE ARRANGEMENT

4.1 a brief description of the arrangement being notified (nature, content, purpose, date(s) and duration);

4.2 if written, attach either an original or a certified copy, together with two further copies, of the most recent version of the text of the arrangement being notified (technical details contained in know-how agreements, for example, may be omitted but omissions should be indicated); if not written, provide a full description;

4.3 identify any provisions in the arrangement which may restrict the parties in their freedom to take independent commercial decisions or to act on those decisions;

4.4 if the application relates to a standard contract, the number expected to be concluded.

5. INFORMATION ON THE PARTIES TO THE ARRANGEMENT AND THE GROUPS TO WHICH THEY BELONG

5.1 for each undertaking identified in 1.5 above, the name of a contact, together with his or her address, telephone and fax numbers, and position held in the undertaking;

5.2 the corporate groups to which each undertaking belongs and the product and/or services market(s) in which the groups are active (hereafter called "the relevant product market"); include one copy of the most recent consolidated annual report and accounts (or equivalent for unincorporated bodies) for each undertaking;

5.3 for each of the parties to the arrangement, provide a list of all undertakings belonging to the same group which are active in the same relevant product market(s), and those active in markets neighbouring the relevant product markets — that is, those which are not regarded by the consumer as fully interchangeable or substitutable for products in the defined relevant product market, as defined in question 6.1 below.

6. THE RELEVANT PRODUCT AND GEOGRAPHIC MARKETS

A relevant product market comprises all those products and/or services regarded by the consumer of the product or service as interchangeable or substitutable by reason of their characteristics, prices or intended use. The following factors are among those normally considered when determining the relevant product market and should be taken into account, together with any others considered relevant:

(i) *the degree of physical similarity between the products/services in question;*

(ii) *any differences in end-use to which the goods are or may be put;*

(iii) *differences in price between the products/services;*

(iv) *the cost of switching between two potentially competing products/services; and*

(v) *established consumer preferences for one type or category of products/service.*

The relevant geographic market is the area in which the undertakings concerned are involved in the supply of products or services in which the conditions of competition are appreciably different from neighbouring areas. The following factors are among those normally considered when determining the relevant geographic market and should be taken into account, together with any others considered relevant:

(i) *the nature and characteristics of the products or services concerned;*

(ii) *the existence of entry barriers or consumer preferences;*

(iii) *appreciable differences of the undertakings' market share or substantial price differences between neighbouring areas; and*

(iv) *transport costs.*

6.1 In the light of the relevant factors given above (which are not exhaustive), explain the definitions of the relevant product and geographic markets which should be considered, with full reasons, in particular stating the specific products or services directly or indirectly affected by the application and other goods or services that may be viewed as substitutable, with reasons. If the relevant geographic market is considered to be an area smaller, or larger, than the whole of the United Kingdom, the boundaries considered applicable, with reasons. Give reasons for all assumptions or findings, and explain how the factors outlined above have been taken into account. Further details are in the guideline *The Competition Act 1998: Market Definition;*

6.2 provide a copy of the most recent in-house long-term market studies assessing or analysing the relevant markets (including any commissioned by the undertakings from outside consultants), and give references of any external studies of the relevant product market, and, where possible, include a copy of any such studies.

7. THE POSITION OF THE UNDERTAKINGS IN THE RELEVANT PRODUCT MARKETS

The information required under this section relates to both the relevant geographic market and the relevant product market, for the groups of the parties as a whole. Market shares may be calculated either on the basis of value or volume. Justification for the figures provided must be given by reference to the sales or turnover of each of the undertakings in question. The source or sources of information should be given, and, where possible, a copy of the document from which information has been taken.

7.1 for each of the previous three calendar or financial years, as available, give:

a details of the market shares of each undertaking in the goods or services in the relevant product and geographic markets, as identified in 6.1 above, and, if different, in the UK, and in the European Community;

b estimates of market shares in the relevant product and geographic markets for each of the five main competitors of each of the undertakings, giving the undertaking's name, address, telephone and fax number, and, where possible, a contact name;

   c identify the five main customers of each of the undertakings in the relevant product and geographic markets, giving the undertaking's name, address, telephone and fax number, and, where possible, a contact name;

   d details of the undertakings' interests in, and arrangements with, any other companies competing in the relevant product and geographic market, together with details of their market shares, if known.

8. Market Entry and Potential Competition in the Relevant Product and Geographic Markets

8.1 For all relevant product and geographic markets:

   a describe the factors influencing entry into the relevant product market(s): that is, the barriers which exist to prevent undertakings not presently manufacturing goods within the relevant product market(s) from entering the market(s), taking account of, in particular but not exclusively, the extent to which:

     (i) entry is regulated by the requirements of governing authorisation or standard-setting, in any form, and any legal or regulatory controls on entry to the market(s);

     (ii) entry is influenced by the availability of raw materials;

     (iii) entry is influenced by the length of existing contracts between suppliers and customers;

     (iv) research and development and licensing patents, know-how and other rights are important;

   b describe the factors influencing entry in geographic terms: that is, the barriers that exist to prevent undertakings already producing and/or marketing goods within the relevant product market(s) outside the relevant geographic market(s) from extending sales into the relevant geographic market(s), taking account of, in particular but not exclusively, the importance of:

     (i) trade barriers imposed by law, such as tariffs, quotas etc;

     (ii) local geographical specifications or technical requirements;

     (iii) procurement policies;

     (iv) the existence of adequate and available local distribution and retailing facilities;

     (v) transport costs;

     (vi) strong consumer preference for local brands or products;

   c in respect of new entrants in both product and geographic terms, state whether any new undertakings have entered the product market(s) in geographic areas where the undertakings sell, during the last three years. Identify the undertakings concerned by name, address, telephone and fax numbers and, where possible, a contact name, with best estimates of market shares of each in the relevant product and geographic markets.

9. Negative Clearance

9.1 state reasons for seeking "negative clearance" (that is, that the Director General should conclude that the arrangement will not be covered by the Chapter I prohibition). Indicate, for example, which provision or effects of the arrangement may breach the prohibition, and state the reasons why it is considered that the arrangements do not have the object or effect of preventing, restricting or distorting competition within the UK to an appreciable extent.

10. Exemption

The criteria which will be taken into account in considering applications for exemption are set out in section 9 of the Act.

10.1 if guidance on exemption from the Chapter I prohibition is sought, explain how the arrangements contribute to improving production or distribution and/or promoting technical or economic progress, and how consumers will be allowed a fair share of those benefits. Explain how each restrictive provision in the arrangements is indispensable to these objectives, and how the arrangements to not eliminate competition in respect of a substantial part of the relevant product or geographic market concerned.

11. *TRANSITIONAL PERIODS*

11.1 if the arrangement is considered to benefit from any transitional periods during which the Chapter I prohibition does not apply, indicate the duration of the relevant transitional periods by reference to Schedule 13 to the Act.

12. *OTHER INFORMATION*

12.1 state:

    a whether this application should be considered as urgent. If so, give reasons;
    b any other information you consider may be helpful.

The application must concluded with the following declaration which is to be signed by or on behalf of all the applicants or notifying undertakings. Unsigned applications are invalid.

DECLARATION
The undersigned declare that all the information given above and in the . . . pages annexed hereto is correct to the best of their knowledge and belief, and that all estimates are identified as such and are their best estimates of the underlying facts.

Place and date ....

Signature ....
....

Status ....
....
.... name(s) in block capitals

PART 3: ACKNOWLEDGEMENT OF RECEIPT

This Form will be returned to the address inserted below if the top half is completed by the undertaking lodging it.

to be completed by the undertaking making the notification

To: .... (name and address of applicant)
    ....
    ....
    ....

Your application dated ....
concerning ....
under reference ....
involving the following undertakings:

1. ....
2. .... [and others]

to be completed by the Office of Fair Trading

was received on ....

and registered under reference number

.... **Please quote this number in all correspondence**

In the event that this application is not complete in a material respect, you will be informed within one month of its receipt. If you are not informed within that time that it is considered to be incomplete, it is deemed to be effective on the date of its receipt.

From the Office of Fair Trading

Appendix C

C.1-01 On the application of Article 85(3) of the Treaty to categories of exclusive distribution agreements

([1983] O.J. L173/1, AS AMENDED BY CORRIGENDUM [1983] O.J. L281/24)

THE COMMISSION OF THE EUROPEAN COMMUNITIES,

Having regard to the Treaty establishing the European Economic Community,

Having regard to Council Regulation No. 19/65 of 2 March 1965 on the application of Article 85(3) of the Treaty to certain categories of agreements and concerted practices, as last amended by the Act of Accession of Greece, and in particular Article 1 thereof,

Having published a draft of this Regulation,

Having consulted the Advisory Committee on Restrictive Practices and Dominant Positions,

(1) Whereas Regulation 19/65 empowers the Commission to apply Article 85(3) of the Treaty by regulation to certain categories of bilateral exclusive distribution agreements and analogous concerted practices falling within Article 85(1);

(2) Whereas experience to date makes it possible to define a category of agreements and concerted practices which can be regarded as normally satisfying the conditions laid down in Article 85(3);

(3) Whereas exclusive distribution agreements of the category defined in Article 1 of this Regulation may fall within the prohibition contained in Article 85(1) of the Treaty; whereas this will apply only in exceptional cases to exclusive agreements of this kind to which only undertakings from one Member State are party and which concern the resale of goods within that Member State; whereas, however, to the extent that such agreements may affect trade between Member States and also satisfy all the requirements set out in this Regulation there is no reason to withhold from them the benefit of the exemption by category;

(4) Whereas it is not necessary to exclude from the defined category those agreements which do not fulfil the conditions of Article 85(1) of the Treaty;

(5) Whereas exclusive distribution agreements lead in general to an improvement in distribution because the undertaking is able to concentrate its sales activities, does not need to maintain numerous business relations with a larger number of dealers and is able, by dealing with only one dealer, to overcome more easily distribution difficulties in international trade resulting from linguistic, legal and other differences;

(6) Whereas exclusive distribution agreements facilitate the promotion of sales of a product and lead to intensive marketing and to continuity of supplies while at the same time rationalizing distribution; whereas they stimulate competition between the products of different manufacturers; whereas the appointment of an exclusive distributor who will take over sales promotion, customer services and carrying of stocks is often the most effective way, and sometimes indeed the only way,

for the manufacturer to enter a market and compete with other manufacturers already present; whereas this is particular so in the case of small and medium-sized undertakings; whereas it must be left to the contracting parties to decide whether and to what extent they consider it desirable to incorporate in the agreements terms providing for the promotion of sales;

(7) Whereas, as a rule, such exclusive distribution agreements also allow consumers a fair share of the resulting benefit as they gain directly from the improvement in distribution, and their economic and supply position is improved as they can obtain products manufactured in particular in other countries more quickly and more easily;

(8) Whereas this Regulation must define the obligations restricting competition which may be included in exclusive distribution agreements; whereas the other restrictions on competition allowed under this Regulation in addition to the exclusive supply obligation produce a clear division of functions between the parties and compel the exclusive distributor to concentrate his sales efforts on the contract goods and the contract territory; whereas they are, where they are agreed only for the duration of the agreement, generally necessary in order to attain the improvement in the distribution of goods sought through exclusive distribution; whereas it may be left to the contracting parties to decide which of these obligations they include in their agreements; whereas further restrictive obligations and in particular those which limit the exclusive distributor's choice of customers or his freedom to determine his prices and conditions of sale cannot be exempted under this Regulation;

(9) Whereas the exemption by category should be reserved for agreements for which it can be assumed with sufficient certainty that they satisfy the conditions of Article 85(3) of the Treaty;

(10) Whereas it is not possible, in the absence of a case-by-case examination, to consider that adequate improvements in distribution occur where a manufacturer entrusts the distribution of his goods to another manufacturer with whom he is in competition; whereas such agreements should, therefore, be excluded from the exemption by category; whereas certain derogation's from this rule in favour of small and medium-sized undertakings can be allowed;

(11) Whereas consumers will be assured of a fair share of the benefits resulting from exclusive distribution only if parallel imports remain possible; whereas agreements relating to goods which the user can obtain only from the exclusive distributor should therefore be excluded from the exemption by category; whereas the parties cannot be allowed to abuse industrial property rights or other rights in order to create absolute territorial protection; whereas this does not prejudice the relationship between competition law and industrial property rights, since the sole object here is to determine the conditions for exemption by category;

(12) Whereas, since competition at the distribution stage is ensured by the possibility of parallel imports, the exclusive distribution agreements covered by this Regulation will not normally afford any possibility of eliminating competition in respect of a substantial part of the products in question; whereas this is also true of agreements that allot to the exclusive distributor a contract territory covering the whole of the common market;

(13) Whereas, in particular cases in which agreements or concerted practices satisfying the requirements of this Regulation nevertheless have effects incompatible with Article 85(3) of the Treaty, the Commission may withdraw the benefit of the exemption by category from the undertakings party to them;

(14) Whereas agreements and concerted practices which satisfy the conditions set out in this Regulation need not be notified; whereas an undertaking may nonetheless in a particular case where real doubt exists, request the Commission to declare whether its agreements comply with this Regulation;

(15) Whereas this Regulation does not affect the applicability of Commission Regulation 3604/82 of 23 December 1982 on the application of Article 85(3) of the Treaty to categories of specialisation agreements; whereas it does not exclude the application of Article 86 of the Treaty,

HAS ADOPTED THIS REGULATION:

Article 1

Pursuant to Article 85(3) of the Treaty and subject to the provisions of this Regulation, it is hereby declared that Article 85(1) of the Treaty shall not apply to agreements to which only two undertakings are party and whereby one party agrees with the other to supply certain goods for resale within the whole or a defined area of the common market only to that other.

Article 2

1. Apart from the obligation referred to in Article 1 no restriction on competition shall be imposed on the supplier other than the obligation not to supply the contract goods to users in the contract territory.

2. No restriction on competition shall be imposed on the exclusive distributor other than:

(a) the obligation not to manufacture or distribute goods which compete with the contract goods;

(b) the obligation to obtain the contract goods for resale only from the other party;

(c) the obligation to refrain, outside the contract territory and in relation to the contract goods, from seeking customers, from establishing any branch and from maintaining any distribution depot.

3. Article 1 shall apply notwithstanding that the exclusive distributor undertakes all or any of the following obligations:

(a) to purchase complete ranges of goods or minimum quantities;

(b) to sell the contract goods under trademarks or packed and presented as specified by the other party;

(c) to take measures for promotion of sales, in particular:

— to advertise,
— to maintain a sales network or stock of goods,
— to provide customer and guarantee services,
— to employ staff having specialised or technical training.

Article 3

Article 1 shall not apply where:

(a) manufacturers of identical goods or of goods which are considered by users as equivalent in view of their characteristics, price and intended use enter into reciprocal exclusive distribution agreements between themselves in respect of such goods;

(b) manufacturers of identical goods or of goods which are considered by users as equivalent in view of their characteristics, price and intended use enter into a non-reciprocal exclusive distribution agreement between themselves in respect of such goods unless at least one of them has a total annual turnover of no more than 100 million ECU;

(c) users can obtain the contract goods in the contract territory only from the exclusive distributor and have no alternative source of supply outside the contract territory;

(d) one or both of the parties makes it difficult for intermediaries or users to obtain the contract goods from other dealers inside the common market or, in so far as no alternative source of supply is available there, from outside the common market, in particular where one or both of them:

1. exercises industrial property rights so as to prevent dealers or users from obtaining outside, or from selling in, the contract territory properly marked or otherwise properly marketed contract goods;

2. exercises other rights or takes other measures so as to prevent dealers or users from obtaining outside, or from selling in, the contract territory contract goods.

Article 4

1. Article 3(a) and (b) shall also apply where the goods there referred to are manufactured by an undertaking connected with a party to the agreement.

2. Connected undertakings are:

(a) undertakings in which a party to the agreement, directly or indirectly:

— owns more than half the capital or business assets, or
— has the power to exercise more than half the voting rights, or
— has the power to appoint more than half the members of the supervisory board, board of directors or bodies legally representing the undertaking, or
— has the right to manage the affairs;

(b) undertakings which directly or indirectly have in or over a party to the agreement the rights or powers listed in (a);

(c) undertakings in which an undertaking referred to in (b) directly or indirectly has the rights or powers listed in (a).

3. Undertakings in which the parties to the agreement or undertakings connected with them jointly have the right or powers set out in paragraph 2(a) shall be considered to be connected with each of the parties to the agreement.

Article 5

1. For the purpose of Article 3(b), the ECU is the unit of account used for drawing up the budget of the Community pursuant to Articles 207 and 209 of the Treaty.

2. Article 1 shall remain applicable where during any period of two consecutive financial years the total turnover referred to in Article 3(b) is exceeded by no more than 10 per cent.

3. For the purpose of calculating total turnover within the meaning of Article 3(b), the turnovers achieved during the last financial year by the party to the agreement and connected undertakings in respect of all goods and services, excluding all taxes and other duties, shall be added together. For this purpose no account shall be taken of dealings between the party to the agreement and its connected undertakings or between its connected undertakings.

Article 6

The Commission may withdraw the benefit of this Regulation, pursuant to Article 7 of Regulation 19/65, when it finds in a particular case that an agreement which is exempted by this Regulation nevertheless has certain effects which are incompatible with the conditions set out in Article 85(3) of the Treaty, and in particular where:

(a) the contract goods are not subject, in the contract territory, to effective competition from identical goods or goods considered by users as equivalent in view of their characteristics, price and intended use;

(b) access by other suppliers to the different stages of distribution within the contract territory is made difficult to a significant extent;

(c) for reasons other than those referred to in Article 3(c) and (d) it is not possible for intermediaries or users to obtain supplies of the contract goods from dealers outside the contract territory on the terms there customary;

(d) the exclusive distributor:

1 without any objectively justified reason refuses to supply in the contract territory categories of purchasers who cannot obtain contract goods elsewhere on suitable terms or applies to them differing prices or conditions of sale;

2 sells the contract goods at excessively high prices.

Article 7

In the period July 1, 1983 to December 31, 1986, the prohibition in Article 85(1) of the Treaty shall not apply to agreements which were in force on July 1, 1983 or entered into force between July 1 and December 31, 1983 and which satisfy the exemption conditions of Regulation 67/67/EEC.

[The provisions of the preceding paragraph shall apply in the same way to agreements which were in force on the date of accession of the Kingdom of Spain and of the Portuguese Republic and which, as a result of accession, fall within the scope of Article 85(1) of the Treaty.]

Article 8

This Regulation shall not apply to agreements entered into for the resale of drinks in premises used for the sale and consumption of drinks or for the resale of petroleum products in service stations.

Article 9

This Regulation shall apply *mutatis mutandis* to concerted practices of the type in Article 1.

Article 10

This Regulation shall enter into force on July 1, 1983.

It shall expire on [31 December 1999].

This Regulation shall be binding in its entirety and directly applicable in all Member States.

Done at Brussels, June 22, 1983.

APPENDIX C.2   COMMISSION REGULATION 1475/95 OF JUNE 28, 1995

C.2-01   On the application of Article 85(3) of the Treaty to certain categories of motor vehicle distribution and servicing agreements

([1995] O.J. L145/25)

THE COMMISSION OF THE EUROPEAN COMMUNITIES,

Having regard to the Treaty establishing the European Community,

Having regard to Council Regulation No 19/65/EEC of 2 March 1965 on the application of Article 85(3) of the Treaty to certain categories of agreements and concerted practices, as last amended by the Act of Accession of Austria, Finland and Sweden, and in particular Article 1 thereof,

Having published a draft of this Regulation,

Having consulted the Advisory Committee on Restrictive Practices and Dominant Positions,

Whereas:

(1) Under Regulation No 19/65/EEC the Commission is empowered to declare by means of a Regulation that Article 85(3) of the Treaty applies to certain categories of agreements falling within Article 85(1) to which only two undertakings are party and by which one party agrees with the other to supply only to that other certain goods for resale within a defined area of the common market. The experience gained in dealing with many motor vehicle distribution and servicing agreements allows a category of agreement to be defined which can generally be regarded as satisfying the conditions laid down in Article 85(3). These are agreements, for a definite or an indefinite period, by which the supplying party entrusts to the reselling party the task of promoting the distribution and servicing of certain products of the motor vehicle industry in a defined area and by which the supplier undertakes to supply contract goods for resale only to the dealer, or only to a limited number of undertakings within the distribution network besides the dealer, within the contract territory,

A list of definitions for the purpose of this, Regulation is set out in Article 10.

(2) Notwithstanding that the obligations listed in Articles 1, 2 and 3 normally have as their object or effect the prevention, restriction or distortion of competition within the common market and are normally liable to affect trade between Member States, the prohibition in Article 85(1) of the Treaty may nevertheless be declared inapplicable to these agreements by virtue of Article 85(3), albeit only under certain restrictive conditions.

(3) The applicability of Article 85(1) of the Treaty to distribution and servicing agreements in the motor vehicle industry stems in particular from the fact that the restrictions on competition and obligations agreed within the framework of a manufacturer's distribution system, and listed in Articles 1 to 4 of this Regulation, are generally imposed in the same or similar form throughout the common market. The motor vehicle manufacturers cover the whole common market or substantial parts of it by means of a cluster of agreements involving similar restrictions on competition and affect in this way not only distribution and servicing within Member States but also trade between them.

(4) The exclusive and selective distribution clauses can be regarded as indispensable measures of rationalisation in the motor vehicle industry, because motor vehicles are consumer durables which at both regular and irregular intervals require expert maintenance and repair, not always in the same place. Motor vehicle manufacturers cooperate with the selected dealers and repairers in order to provide specialised servicing for the product. On grounds of capacity and efficiency alone, such a form of cooperation cannot be extended to an unlimited number of dealers and repairers. The linking of servicing and distribution must be regarded as more efficient than a separation between a distribution organisation for new vehicles on the one hand and a servicing organisation which would also distribute spare parts on the other, particularly as, before a new vehicle is delivered to the final consumer, the undertaking within the distribution system must give it a technical inspection according to the manufacturer's specification.

(5) However, obligatory recourse to the authorised network is not in all respects indispensable for efficient distribution. It should therefore be provided that the supply of contract goods to resellers may not be prohibited where they:

— belong to the same distributional system (Article 3(10)(a)), or

— purchase spare parts for their own use in effecting repairs or maintenance (Article 3(10)(b)).

Measures taken by a manufacturer or by undertakings within the distribution system with the object of protecting the selective distribution system are compatible with the exemption under this Regulation. This applies in particular to a dealer's obligation to sell vehicles to a final consumer using the services of an intermediary only where that consumer has authorised that intermediary to act as his agent (Article 3(11)).

(6) It should be possible to prevent wholesalers not belonging to the distribution system from reselling parts originating from motor vehicle manufacturers. It may be supposed that the system, beneficial to the consumer, whereby spare parts are readily available across the whole contract range, including those parts with a low turnover, could not be maintained without obligatory recourse to the authorised network.

(7) The ban on dealing in competing products may be exempted on condition that it does not inhibit the dealer from distributing vehicles of other makes in a manner which avoids all confusion between makes (Article 3(3)). The obligation to refrain from selling products of other manufacturers other than in separate sales premises, under separate management, linked to the general obligation to avoid confusion between different makes, guarantees exclusivity of distribution for each make in each place of sale. This last obligation has to be implemented in good faith by the dealer so that the promotion, sale and after-sales service cannot, in any manner, cause confusion in the eyes of the consumer or result in unfair practices on the part of the dealer with regard to suppliers of competing makes. In order to maintain the competitiveness of competing products, the separate management of different sales premises has to be carried out by distinct legal entities. Such an obligation provides an incentive for the dealer to develop sales and servicing of contract goods and thus promotes competition in the supply of those products and competing products. These provisions do not prevent the dealer from offering and providing maintenance and repair services for competing makes of motor vehicle in the same workshop, subject to the option of obliging the dealer not to allow third parties to benefit unduly from investments made by the supplier (Article 3(4)).

(8) However, bans on dealing in competing products cannot be regarded in all circumstances as indispensable to efficient distribution. Dealers must be free to obtain from third parties supplies of parts which match the quality of those offered by the manufacturer, and to use and sell them. In this regard, it can be presumed that all parts coming from the same source of production are identical in characteristics and origin; it is for spare-part manufacturers offering parts to dealers to confirm, if need be, that such parts correspond to those supplied to the manufacturer of the vehicle. Moreover, dealers must retain their freedom to choose parts which are usable in motor vehicles within the contract range and which match or exceed the quality standard. Such a limit on the ban on dealing in competing products takes account of both the importance of vehicle safety and the maintenance of effective competition (Article 3(5) and Article 4(1)(6) and (7)).

(9) The restrictions imposed on the dealer's activities outside the allotted area lead to more intensive distribution and servicing efforts in an easily supervised contract territory, to knowledge of the market based on closer contact with consumers, and to more demand-orientated supply (Article 3(8) and (9)). However, demand for contract goods must remain flexible and should not be limited on a regional basis. Dealers must not be confined to satisfying the demand for contract goods within their contract territories, but must also be able to meet demand from persons and undertakings in other areas of the common market. Advertising by dealers in a medium which is directed at customers outside the contract territory should not be prevented, because it does not run counter to the obligation to promote sales within the contract territory. The acceptable means of advertising do not include direct personal contact with the customer, whether by telephone or other form of telecommunication, door-step canvassing or by individual letter.

(10) So as to give firms greater legal certainty, certain obligations imposed on the dealer that do not stand in the way of exemption should be specified regarding the observation of minimum distribution and servicing standards (Article 4(1)(1)), regularity of orders (Article 4(1)(2)), the achievement of quantitative sales or stock targets agreed by the parties or determined by an expert third party in the event of disagreement (Article 4(1)(3) to (5)) and the arrangements made for after-sales service (Article 4(1)(6) to (9)). Such obligations are directly related to the obligations in Articles 1,

2 and 3 and influence their restrictive effect. They may therefore be exempted, for the same reasons as the latter, where they fall in individual cases under the prohibition contained in Article 85(1) of the Treaty (Article 4(2)).

(11) Pursuant to Regulation No 19/65/EEC, the conditions which must be satisfied if the declaration of inapplicability is to take effect must be specified.

(12) Under Article 5(1)(1)(a) and (b) it is a condition of exemption that the undertaking should honour the guarantee and provide free servicing, vehicle recall work, and repair and maintenance services necessary for the safe and reliable functioning of the vehicle, irrespective of where in the common market the vehicle was purchased. These provisions are intended to prevent limitation of the consumer's freedom to buy anywhere in the common market.

(13) Article 5(1)(2)(a) is intended to allow the manufacturer to build up a coordinated distribution system, but without hindering the relationship of confidence between dealers and sub-dealers. Accordingly, if the supplier reserves the right to approve appointments of sub-dealers by the dealer, he must not be allowed to withhold such approval arbitrarily.

(14) Article 5(1)(2)(b) requires the supplier not to impose on a dealer within the distribution system any requirements, as defined in Article 4(1), which are discriminatory or inequitable.

(15) Article 5(1)(2)(c) is intended to counter the concentration of the dealer's demand on the supplier which might follow from cumulation of discounts. The purpose of this provision is to allow spare-parts suppliers which do not offer as wide range of goods as the manufacturer to compete on equal terms.

(16) Article 5(1)(2)(d) makes exemption subject to the condition that the dealer must be able to purchase for customers in the common market volume-produced passenger cars with the technical features appropriate to their place of residence or to the place where the vehicle is to be registered, in so far as the corresponding model is also supplied by the manufacturer through undertakings within the distribution system in that place (Article 10(10)). This provision obviates the danger that the manufacturer and undertakings within the distribution network might make use of product differentiation as between parts of the common market to partition the market.

(17) Article 5(2) makes the exemption dependent on other minimum conditions which aim to prevent the dealer, owing to the obligations which are imposed upon him, from becoming economically over dependent on the supplier and from abandoning the competitive activity which is nominally open to him because to pursue it would be against the interests of the manufacturer or other undertakings within the distribution network.

(18) Under Article 5(2)(1), the dealer may, for objectively justified reasons, oppose the application of excessive obligations covered by Article 3(3).

(19) Article 5(2)(2) and (3) and Article 5(3) lay down minimum requirements for exemption concerning the duration and termination of the distribution and servicing agreement, because the combined effect of the investments the dealer makes in order to improve the distribution and servicing of contract goods and a short-term agreement or one terminable at short notice is greatly to increase the dealer's dependence on the supplier. In order to avoid obstructing the development of flexible and efficient distribution structures, however, the supplier should be entitled to terminate the agreement where there is a need to reorganise all or a substantial part of the network. To allow rapid settlement of any disputes, provision should be made for reference to an expert third party or arbitrator who will decide in the event of disagreement, without prejudice to the parties' right to bring the matter before a competent court in conformity with the relevant provisions of national law.

(20) Pursuant to Regulation No 19/65/EEC, the restrictions or provisions which must not be contained in the agreements, if the declaration of inapplicability of Article 85(1) of the Treaty under this Regulation is to take effect, are to be specified (Article 6(1), (1) to (5)). Moreover, practices of the parties which lead to automatic loss of the benefit of exemption when committed systematically and repeatedly shall be defined (Article 6(1)(6) to (12)).

(21) Agreements under which one motor vehicle manufacturer entrusts the distribution of his products to another must be excluded from the block exemption, because of their far-reaching impact on competition (Article 6(1), (1)).

(22) In order to ensure that the parties remain within the limits of the Regulation, any agreements whose object goes beyond the products or services referred to in Article 1 or which stipulate restrictions of competition not exempted by this Regulation should also be excluded from the exemption (Article 6(1)(2) and (3)).

(23) The exemption similarly does not apply where the parties agree between themselves obligations concerning goods covered by this Regulation which would be acceptable in the combination of obligations which is exempted by Commission Regulation (EEC) No 1983/83, for (EEC) No 1984/83, as last amended by the Act of Accession of Austria, Finland and Sweden, regarding the application of Article 85(3) of the Treaty to categories of exclusive distribution agreements and exclusive purchasing agreements respectively, but which go beyond the scope of the obligations exempted by this Regulation (Article 6(1)(4)).

(24) In order to protect dealers' investments and prevent any circumvention by suppliers of the rules governing the termination of agreements, it should be confirmed that the exemption does not apply where the supplier reserves the right to amend unilaterally during the period covered by the contract the terms of the exclusive territorial dealership granted to the dealer (Article 6(1)(5)).

(25) In order to maintain effective competition at the distribution stage, it is necessary to provide that the manufacturer or supplier will lose the benefit of exemption where he restricts the dealer's freedom to develop his own policy on resale prices (Article 6(1)(6)).

(26) The principle of a single market requires that consumers shall be able to purchase motor vehicles wherever in the Community prices or terms are most favourable and even to resell them, provided that the resale is not effected for commercial purposes. The benefits of this Regulation cannot therefore be accorded to manufacturers or suppliers who impede parallel imports or exports through measures taken in respect of consumers, authorised intermediaries or undertakings within the network (Article 6(1)(7) and (8)).

(27) So as to ensure, in the interest of consumers, effective competition on the maintenance and repair markets, the exemption must also be withheld from manufacturers or suppliers who impede independent spare part producers' and distributors' access to the markets or restrict the freedom of resellers or repairers, whether or not they belong to the network, to purchase and use such spare parts where they match the quality of the original spare parts. The dealer's right to procure spare parts with matching quality from external undertakings of his choice and the corresponding right for those undertakings to furnish spare parts to resellers of their choice, as well as their freedom to affix their trade mark or logo, are provided for subject to compliance with the industrial property rights applicable to those spare parts (Article 6(1)(9) to (11)).

(28) In order to give final consumers genuine opportunities of choice as between repairers belonging to the network and independent repairers, it is appropriate to impose upon manufacturers the obligation to give to repairers outside the network the technical information necessary for the repair and maintenance of their makes of car, whilst taking into account the legitimate interest of the manufacturer to decide itself the mode of exploitation of its intellectual property rights as well as its identified, substantial, secret know-how when granting licences to third parties. However, these rights must be exercised in a manner which avoids all discrimination or over abuse (Article 6(1)(12)).

(29) For reasons of clarity, the legal effects arising from inapplicability of the exemption in the various situations referred to in the Regulation should be defined (Article 6(2) and (3)).

(30) Distribution and servicing agreements can be exempted, subject to the conditions laid down in Articles 5 and 6, so long as the application of obligations covered by Articles 1 to 4 brings about an improvement in distribution and servicing to the benefit of the consumer and effective competition exists, not only between manufacturers' distribution systems but also to a certain extent within each system within the common market. As regards the categories of products set out in Article 1, the conditions necessary for effective competition, including competition in trade between Member

States, may be taken to exist at present, so that European consumers may be considered in general to take an equitable share in the benefit from the operation of such competition.

(31) Since the provisions of Commission Regulation (EEC) No. 123/85 of 12 December 1984 on the application of Article 85(3) of the Treaty to certain categories of motor vehicle distribution and servicing agreements, as last amended by the Act of Accession of Austria, Finland and Sweden, are applicable until 30 June 1995, provision should be made for transitional arrangements in respect of agreements still running on that date which satisfy the exemption conditions laid down by that Regulation (Article 7). The Commission's powers to withdraw the benefit of exemption or to alter its scope in a particular case should be spelled out and several important categories of cases should be listed by way of example (Article 8). Where the Commission makes use of its power of withdrawal, as provided for in Article 8(2), it should take into account any price differentials which do not principally result from the imposition of national fiscal measures or currency fluctuations between the Member States (Article 8).

(32) In accordance with Regulation No. 19/65/EEC, the exemption must be defined for a limited period. A period of seven years is appropriate for taking account of the specific characterics of the motor vehicle sector and the foreseeable changes in competition in that sector. However, the Commission will regularly appraise the application of the Regulation by drawing up a report by 31 December 2000 (Articles 11 and 13).

(33) Agreements which fulfil the conditions set out in this Regulation need not be notified. However, in the case of doubt undertakings are free to notify their agreements to the Commission in accordance with Council Regulation No. 17, as last amended by the Act of Accession of Austria, Finland and Sweden.

(34) The sector-specific character of the exemption by category for motor vehicles broadly rules out any regulations containing general exemptions by category as regards distribution. Such exclusion should be confirmed in respect of Commission Regulation (EEC) No 4087/88 of 30 November 1988 concerning the application of Article 85(3) of the Treaty to categories of franchise agreements, as last amended by the Act of Accession of Austria, Finland and Sweden, without prejudice of the right of undertakings to seek an individual exemption under Regulation No. 17. On the other hand, as regards Regulations (EEC) No. 1983/83 and (EEC) No. 1984/83, which makes provision for a more narrowly drawn framework of exemptions for undertakings, it is possible to allow them to choose. As for Commission Regulations (EEC) No. 417/85 and (EEC) No. 418/85, as last amended by the Act of Accession of Austria, Finland and Sweden, which relate to the application of Article 85(3) of the Treaty to categories of specialisation agreements and to categories of research and development agreements, respectively, but whose emphasis is not on distribution, their applicability is not called in question (Article 12).

(35) This Regulation is without prejudice to the application of Article 86 of the Treaty,

HAS ADOPTED THIS REGULATION:

Article 1

Pursuant to Article 85(3) of the Treaty it is hereby declared that subject to the conditions laid down in this Regulation Article 85(1) shall not apply to agreements to which only two undertakings are party and in which one contracting party agrees to supply, within a defined territory of the common market

— only to the other party, or

— only to the other party and to a specified number of other undertakings within the distribution system,

for the purpose of resale, certain new motor vehicles intended for use on public roads and having three or more road wheels, together with spare parts therefor.

Article 2

The exemption shall also apply where the obligation referred to in Article 1 is combined with an obligation on the supplier neither to sell contract goods to final consumers nor to provide them with servicing for contract goods in the contract territory.

Article 3

The exemption shall also apply where the obligation referred to in Article 1 is combined with an obligation on the dealer:

1. not, without the supplier's consent, to modify contract goods or correspnding goods, unless such modification has been ordered by a final consumer and concerns a particular motor vehicle within the range covered by the contrast, purchased by that final consumer;

2. not to manufacture products which compete with contract goods;

3. not to sell new motor vehicles offered by persons other than the manufacturer except on separate sales premises, under separate management, in the form of a distinct legal entity and in a manner which avoids confusion between makes;

4. not to permit a third party to benefit unduly, through any after-sales service performed in a common workshop, from investments made by a supplier, notably in equipment or the training of personnel;

5. neither to sell spare parts which compete with contract goods without matching them in quality nor to use them for repair or maintenance of contract goods or corresponding goods;

6. without the supplier's consent, neither to conclude distribution or servicing agreements with undertakings operating in the contract territory for contract goods or corresponding goods not to alter or terminate such agreements;

7. to impose upon undertakings with which the dealer has concluded agreements in accordance with point 6 obligations comparable to those which the dealer has accepted in relation to the supplier and which are covered by Articles 1 to 4 and are in conformity with Articles 5 and 6;

8. outside the contract territory:

   (a) not to maintain branches or depots for the distribution of contract goods or corresponding goods,

   (b) not to solicit customers for contract goods or corresponding goods, by personalised advertising;

9. not to entrust third parties with the distribution or servicing of contract goods or corresponding goods outside the contract territory;

10. not to supply to a reseller:

    (a) contract goods or corresponding goods unless the reseller is an undertaking within the distribution system, or

    (b) spare parts within the contract range unless the reseller uses them for the repair or maintenance of a motor vehicle;

11. not to sell motor vehicles within the contract range or corresponding goods to final consumers using the services of an intermediary unless that intermediary has prior written authority from such consumers to purchase a specified motor vehicle or where it is taken away by him, to collect it.

Article 4

1. The exemption shall apply notwithstanding any obligation whereby the dealer undertakes to:

(1) comply, in distribution, sales and after-sales servicing with minimum standards, regarding in particular;

    (a) the equipment of the business premises and the technical facilities for servicing;
    (b) the specialised, technical training of staff;
    (c) advertising;
    (d) the collection, storage and delivery of contract goods or corresponding goods and sales and after-sales servicing;
    (e) the repair and maintenance of contract goods and corresponding goods, particularly as regards the safe and reliable functioning of motor vehicles;

(2) order contract goods from the supplier only at certain times or within certain periods, provided that the interval between ordering dates does not exceed three months;

(3) endeavour to sell, within the contract territory and during a specified period, a minimum quantity of contract goods, determined by the parties by common agreement or, in the event of disagreement between the parties as to the minimum number of contractual goods to be sold annually, by an expert third party, account being taken in particular of sales previously achieved in the territory and of forecast sales for the territory and at national level;

(4) keep in stock such quantity of contract goods as may be determined in accordance with the procedure in (3);

(5) keep such demonstration vehicles within the contract range, or such number thereof, as may be determined in accordance with the procedure in (3);

(6) perform work under guarantee, free servicing and vehicle-recall work for contract goods and corresponding goods;

(7) use only spare parts within the contract range or corresponding spare parts for work under guarantee, free servicing and vehicle-recall work in respect of contract goods or corresponding goods;

(8) inform customers, in a general manner, of the extent to which spare parts from other sources might be used for the repair or maintenance of contract goods or corresponding goods;

(9) inform customers whenever spares parts from other sources have been used for the repair or maintenance of contract goods or corresponding goods.

2. The exemption shall also apply to the obligation referred to in (1) above where such obligations fall in individual cases under the prohibition contained in Article 85(1).

Article 5

1. In all cases, the exemption shall apply only if:

(1) the dealer undertakes:

    (a) in respect of motor vehicles within the contract range or corresponding thereto which have been supplied in the common market by another undertaking within the distribution network:

       — to honour guarantees and to perform free servicing and vehicle-recall work to an extent which corresponds to the dealer's obligation covered by Article 4(1)(6),
       — to carry out repair and maintenance work in accordance with Article 4(1)(1)(e);

(b) to impose upon the undertakings operating within the contract territory with which the dealer has concluded distribution and servicing agreements as provided for in Article 3(6) an obligation to honour guarantees and to perform free servicing and vehicle recall work at least to the extent to which the dealer himself is so obliged:

(2) the supplier;

  (a) does not without objectively valid reasons withhold consent to conclude, alter or terminate sub-agreements referred to in Article 3(6);

  (b) does not apply, in relation to the dealer's obligations referred to in Article 41(1), minimum requirements or criteria for estimates such that the dealer is subject to discrimination without objective reasons or is treated inequitably;

  (c) distinguishes, in any scheme for aggregating quantities or values of goods obtained by the dealer from the supplier and from connected undertakings within a specified period for the purpose of calculating discounts, at least between supplies of

    — motor vehicles within the contract range,
    — spare parts within the contract range, for supplies of which the dealer is dependent on undertakings within the distribution network, and
    — other goods;

  (d) supplies to the dealer, for the purpose of performance of a contract of sale concluded between the dealer and a final customer in the common market, any passenger car which corresponds to a model within the contract range and which is marketed by the manufacturer or with the manufacturer's consent in the Member State in which the vehicle is to be registered.

2. Where the dealer has, in accordance with Article 4(1), assumed obligations for the improvement of distribution and servicing structures, the exemption shall apply provided that:

(1) the supplier releases the dealer from the obligations referred to in Article 3(3) where the dealer shows that there are objective reasons for doing so;

(2) the agreement is for a period of at least five years or, if for an indefinite period, the period of notice for regular termination of the agreement is at least two years for both parties; this period is reduced to at least one year where:

    — the supplier is obliged by law or by special agreement to pay appropriate compensation on termination of the agreement, or
    — the dealer is a new entrant to the distribution system and the period of the agreement, or the period of notice for regular termination of the agreement, is the first agreed by that dealer;

(3) each party undertakes to give the other at least six months' prior notice of intention not to renew an agreement concluded for a definite period.

3. The conditions for exemption laid down in (1) and (2) shall not affect;

    — the right of the supplier to terminate the agreement subject to at least one year's notice in a case where it is necessary to reorganise the whole or a substantial part of the network,

    — the right of one party to terminate the agreement for cause where the other party fails to perform one of its basic obligations.

In each case, the parties must, in the event of disagreement, accept a system for the quick resolution of the dispute, such as recourse to an expert third party or an arbitrator, without prejudice to the parties' right to apply to a competent court in conformity with the provisions of national law.

Article 6

1. The exemption shall not apply where:

(1) both parties to the agreement or their connected undertakings are motor vehicle manufac-turers; or

(2) the parties link their agreement to stipulations concerning products or services other than those referred to in this Regulation or apply their agreement to such products or services; or

(3) in respect of motor vehicles having three or more road wheels, spare parts or services there-for, the parties agree restrictions of competition that are not expressly exempted by this Regulation; or

(4) in respect of motor vehicles having three or more road wheels or spare parts therefor, the parties make agreements or engage in concerted practices which are exempted from the prohibition in Article 85(1) of the Treaty under Regulations (EEC) No. 1983/83 or (EEC) No. 1984/83 to an extent exceeding the scope of this Regulation; or

(5) the parties agree that the supplier reserves the right to conclude distribution and servicing agreements for contract goods with specified further undertakings operating within the contract territory, or to alter the contract territory: or

(6) the manufacturer, the supplier or another undertaking directly or indirectly restricts the dealer's freedom to determine prices and discounts in reselling contract goods or corre-sponding goods; or

(7) the manufacturer, the supplier or another undertaking within the network directly or indi-rectly restricts the freedom of final consumers, authorised intermediaries or dealers to obtain from an undertaking belonging to the network of their choice within the common market contract goods or corresponding goods or to obtain servicing for such goods, or the freedom of final consumers to resell the contract goods or corresponding goods, when the sale is not effected for commercial purposes; or

(8) the supplier, without any objective reason, grants dealers remuneration's calculated on the basis of the place of destination of the motor vehicles resold or the place of residence of the purchaser: or

(9) the supplier directly or indirectly restricts the dealer's freedom under Article 3(5) to obtain from a third undertaking of his choice spare parts which compete with contract goods and which match their quality;

(10) the manufacturer directly or indirectly restricts the freedom of suppliers of spare-parts to supply such products to resellers of their choice, including those which are undertakings within the distribution system, provided that such parts match the quality of contract goods; or

(11) the manufacturer directly or indirectly restricts the freedom of spare-part manufacturers to place effectively and in an easily visible manner their trade mark or logo on parts sup-plied for the initial assembly or for the repair or maintenance of contract goods or corre-sponding goods; or

(12) the manufacturer refuses to make accessible, where appropriate upon payment, to repair-ers who are not undertakings within the distribution system, the technical information required for the repair or maintenance of the contractual or corresponding goods or for the implementing of environmental protection measures, provided that the information is not covered by an intellectual property right or does not constitute identified, substantial, secret know-how; in such case, the necessary technical information shall not be withheld improperly.

2. Without prejudice to the consequences for the other provisions of the agreement, in the cases specified in paragraph 1(1) to (5), the inapplicability of the exemption shall apply to all the clauses restrictive of competition contained in the agreement concerned; in the cases specified in paragraph 1(6) to (12), it shall apply only to the clauses restrictive of competition agreed respectively on behalf of the manufacturer, the supplier or another undertaking within the network which is engaged in the practice complained of.

3. Without prejudice to the consequences for the other provisions of the agreement, in the cases specified in paragraph 1(6) to (12), the inapplicability of the exemption shall only apply to the

clauses restrictive of competition agreed in favour of the manufacturer, the supplier or another undertaking within the network which appear in the distribution and servicing agreements concluded for a geographic area within the common market in which the objectionable practice distorts competition, and only for the duration of the practice complained of.

Article 7

The prohibition laid down in Article 85(1) of the Treaty shall not apply during the period from 1 October 1995 to 30 September 1996 to agreements already in force on 1 October 1995 which satisfy the conditions for exemption provided for in Commission Regulation (EEC) No. 123/85.

Article 8

The Commission may withdraw the benefit of the application of this Regulation, pursuant to Article 7 of Regulation No. 19/65/EEC, where it finds that in an individual case an agreement which falls within the scope of this Regulation nevertheless has effects which are incompatible with the provisions of Article 85(3) of the Treaty, and in particular:

(1) where, in the common market or a substantial part thereof, contract goods or corresponding goods are not subject to competition from products considered by consumers as similar by reason of their characteristics, price and intended use;

(2) where prices or conditions of supply for contract goods or for corresponding goods are continually being applied which differ substantially as between Member States, such substantial differences being chiefly due to obligations exempted by this Regulation;

(3) where the manufacturer or an undertaking within the distribution system in supplying the distributors with contract goods or corresponding goods apply, unjustifiably, discriminatory prices or sales conditions.

Article 9

This Regulation shall apply *mutatis mutandis* to concerted practices falling within the categories covered by this Regulation.

Article 10

For the purposes of this Regulation the following terms shall have the following meanings:

1. "distribution and servicing agreements" are framework agreements between two undertakings, for a definite or indefinite period, whereby the party supplying goods entrusts to the other the distribution and servicing of those goods;

2. "parties", are the undertakings which are party to an agreement within the meaning of Article 1: "the supplier" being the undertaking which supplies the contract goods, and "the dealer" the undertaking entrusted by the supplier with the distribution and servicing of contract goods;

3. the "contract territory" is the defined territory of the common market to which the obligation of exclusive supply in the meaning of Article 1 applies;

4. "contract goods" are new motor vehicles intended for use on public roads and having three or more road wheels, and spare parts therefor, which are the subject of an agreement within the meaning of Article 1;

5. the "contract range" refers to the totality of the contract goods;

6. "spare parts" are parts which are to be installed in or upon a motor vehicle so as to replace components of that vehicle. They are to be distinguished from other parts and accessories, according to trade usage;

7. the "manufacturer" is the undertaking:

(a) which manufactures or procures the manufacture of the motor vehicles in the contract range, or

(b) which is connected with an undertaking described at (a);

8. "connected undertakings" are:

(a) undertakings one of which directly or indirectly:
 — holds more than half of the capital or business assets of the other, or
 — has the power to exercise more than half the voting rights in the other, or
 — has the power to appoint more than half the members of the supervisory board, board of directors or bodies legally representing the other, or
 — has the right to manage the affairs of the other;

(b) undertakings in relation to which a third undertaking is able directly or indirectly to exercise such rights or powers as are mentioned in (a) above.

9. "undertakings within the distribution system" are, besides the parties to the agreement, the manufacturer and undertakings which are entrusted by the manufacturer or with the manufacturer's consent with the distribution of servicing of contract goods or corresponding goods;

10. a "passenger car which corresponds to a model within the contract range" is a passenger car:

— manufactured or assembled in volume by the manufacturer, and

— identical as to body style, drive-line, chassis, and type of motor with a passenger car within the contract range;

11. "corresponding goods", "corresponding motor vehicles" and "corresponding parts" are those which are similar in kind to those in the contract range, are distributed by the manufacturer or with the manufacturer's consent, and are the subject of a distribution or servicing agreement with an undertaking within the distribution system;

12. "resale" includes all transactions, by which a physical or legal person — "the reseller" — disposes of a motor vehicle which is still in a new condition and which he had previously acquired in his own name and on his own behalf, irrespective of the legal description applied under civil law or the format of the transaction which effects such resale. The terms resale shall include all leasing contracts which provide for a transfer of ownership or an option to purchase prior to the expiry of the contract;

13. "distribute" and "sell" include other forms of supply by the dealer such as leasing.

Article 11

1. The Commission will evaluate on a regular basis the application of this Regulation, particularly as regards the impact of the exempted system of distribution on price differentials of contract goods between the different Member States and on the quality of service to final users.
2. The Commission will collate the opinions of associations and experts representing the various interested parties, particularly consumer organisations.
3. The Commission will draw up a report on the evaluation of this Regulation on or before 31 December 2000, particularly taking into account the criteria provided for in paragraph 1.

Article 12

Regulation (EEC) No 4087/88 is not applicable to agreements concerning the products or services referred to in this Regulation.

Article 13

This Regulation shall enter into force on 1 July 1995.
It shall apply from 1 October 1995 until 30 September 2002.
The provisions of Regulation (EEC) No 123/85 shall continue to apply until 30 September 1995.

APPENDIX C.3 COMMISSION REGULATION 1984/83 OF JUNE 22, 1983

C.3-01 On the application of Article 85(3) of the Treaty to categories of exclusive purchasing agreements

([1983] O.J. L173/5, AS AMENDED BY CORRIGENDUM [1983] O.J. L281/24)

THE COMMISSION OF THE EUROPEAN COMMUNITIES,

Having regard to the Treaty establishing the European Economic Community,

Having regard to Council Regulation 19/65 of 2 March 1965 on the application of Article 85(3) of the Treaty to certain categories of agreements and concerted practices, as last amended by the Act of Accession of Greece, and in particular Article 1 thereof,

Having published a draft of this Regulation,

Having consulted the Advisory Committee on Restrictive Practices and Dominant Positions,

(1) Whereas Regulation 19/65 empowers the Commission to apply Article 85(3) of the Treaty by regulation to certain categories of bilateral exclusive purchasing agreements entered into for the purpose of the resale of goods and corresponding concerted practices falling within Article 85(1).

(2) Whereas experience to date makes it possible to define three categories of agreements and concerted practices which can be regarded as normally satisfying the conditions laid down in Article 85(3); whereas the first category comprises exclusive purchasing agreements short and medium duration in all sectors of the economy; whereas the other two categories comprise long-term exclusive purchasing agreements entered into for the resale of beer in premises used for the sale and consumption of drinks (beer supply agreements) and of petroleum products in service stations (service station agreements);

(3) Whereas exclusive purchasing agreements of the categories defined in this Regulation may fall within the prohibition contained in Article 85(1) of the Treaty; whereas this will often be the case with agreements concluded between undertakings from different Member States; whereas an exclusive purchasing agreement to which undertakings from only one Member State are party and which concerns the resale of goods within that Member State may also be caught by the prohibition; whereas this is in particular the case where it is one of a number of similar agreements which together may affect trade between Member States;

(4) Whereas it is not necessary expressly to exclude from the defined categories those agreements which do not fulfil the conditions of Article 85(1) of the Treaty;

(5) Whereas the exclusive purchasing agreements defined in this Regulation lead in general to an improvement in distribution; whereas they enable the supplier to plan the sales of his goods with greater precision and for a longer period and ensure that the reseller's requirements will be met on a regular basis for the duration of the agreement; whereas this allows the parties to limit the risk to them of variations in market conditions and to lower distribution costs;

(6) Whereas such agreements also facilitate the promotion of the sales of a product and lead to intensive marketing because the supplier, in consideration for the exclusive purchasing obligation, is as a rule under an obligation to contribute to the improvement of the structure of the distribution network, the quality of the promotional effort or the sales success; whereas, at the same time, they stimulate competition between the products of different manufacturers; whereas the appointment of several resellers, who are bound to purchase exclusively from the manufacturer and who take over sales promotion, customer services and carrying of stock, is often the most effective way, and sometimes the only way, for the manufacturer to penetrate a market and compete with other manufacturers already present; whereas this is particularly so in the case of small and medium-sized undertakings; whereas it must be left to the contracting parties to decide whether and to what extent they consider it desirable to incorporate in their agreements terms concerning the promotion of sales;

(7) Whereas, as a rule, exclusive purchasing agreements between suppliers and resellers also allow consumers a fair share of resulting benefit as they gain the advantages of regular supply and are able to obtain the contract goods more quickly and more easily;

(8) Whereas this Regulation must define the obligations restricting competition which may be included in an exclusive purchasing agreement; whereas the other restrictions of competition allowed under this Regulation in addition to the exclusive purchasing obligation lead to a clear division of functions between the parties and compel the reseller to concentrate his sales efforts on the contract goods; whereas they are, where they are agreed only for the duration of the agreement, generally necessary in order to attain the improvement in the distribution of goods sought through exclusive purchasing; whereas further restrictive obligations and in particular those which limit the reseller's choice of customers or his freedom to determine his prices and conditions of sale cannot be exempted under this Regulation;

(9) Whereas the exemption by categories should be reserved for agreements for which it can be assumed with sufficient certainty that they satisfy the conditions of Article 85(3) of the Treaty;

(10) Whereas it is not possible, in the absence of a case-by-case examination, to consider that adequate improvements in distribution occur where a manufacturer imposes an exclusive purchasing obligation with respect to his goods on a manufacturer with whom he is in competition; whereas such agreements should, therefore, be excluded from the exemption by categories; whereas certain derogation's from this rule in favour of small and medium-sized undertakings can be allowed;

(11) Whereas certain conditions must be attached to the exemption by categories so that access by other undertakings to the different stages of distribution can be ensured; whereas, to this end, limits must be set to the scope and to the duration of the exclusive purchasing obligation; whereas it appears appropriate as a general rule to grant the benefit of a general exemption from the prohibition on restrictive agreements only to exclusive purchasing agreements which are concluded for a specific product or range of products and for not more than five years;

(12) Whereas, in the case of beer supply agreements and service-station agreements, different rules should be laid down which take account of the particularities of the markets in question;

(13) Whereas these agreements are generally distinguished by the fact that, on the one hand the supplier confers on the reseller special commercial or financial advantages by contributing to his financing, granting him or obtaining for him a loan on favourable terms, equipping him with a site or premises for conducting his business, providing him with equipment or fittings, or undertaking other investments for his benefit and that, on the other hand, the reseller enters into a long-term exclusive purchasing obligation which in most cases is accompanied by a ban on dealing in competing products;

(14) Whereas beer supply and service-station agreements, like the other exclusive purchasing agreements dealt with in this Regulation, normally produce an appreciable improvement in distribution in which consumers are allowed a fair share of the resulting benefit;

(15) Whereas the commercial and financial advantages conferred by the supplier on the reseller make it significantly easier to establish, modernise, maintain and operate premises used for the sale and consumption of drinks and service stations; whereas the exclusive purchasing obligation and the ban on dealing in competing products imposed on the reseller incite the reseller to devote all the resources at his disposal to the sale of the contract goods; whereas such agreements lead to durable co-operation between the parties allowing them to improve or maintain the quality of the contract goods and of the services to the customer and sales efforts of the reseller; whereas they allow long-term planning of sales and consequently a cost effective organization of production and distribution; whereas the pressure of competition between products of different makes obliges the undertaking involved to determine the number and character of premises used for the sale and consumption of drinks and service stations, in accordance with the wishes of customers;

(16) Whereas consumers benefit from the improvements described in particular because they are ensured supplies of goods of satisfactory quality at fair prices and conditions while being able to choose between the products of different manufacturers;

(17) Whereas the advantages produced by beer supply agreements and service-station agreements cannot otherwise be secured to the same extent and with the same degree of certainty; whereas the exclusive purchasing obligation on the reseller and the non-competition clause imposed on him are essential components of such agreements and thus usually indispensable for the attainment of these advantages; whereas, however, this is true only as long as the reseller's obligation to purchase from the supplier is confined in the case of premises used for the sole consumption of drinks to beers and other drinks of the types offered by the supplier, and in the case of service stations to petroleum-based fuel for motor vehicles and other petroleum-based fuels; whereas the exclusive purchasing obligation for lubricants and related petroleum-based products can be accepted only on condition that the supplier provides for the reseller or finances the procurement of specific equipment for the carrying out of lubrication work; whereas this obligation should only relate to products intended for use within the service station;

(18) Whereas, in order to maintain the reseller's commercial freedom and to ensure access to the retail level of distribution on the part of other suppliers, not only the scope but also the duration of the exclusive purchasing obligation must be limited; whereas it appears appropriate to allow drinks suppliers a choice between a medium-term exclusive purchasing agreement covering a range of drinks and a long-term exclusive purchasing agreement for beer, whereas it is necessary to provide special rules for those premises used for the sale and consumption of drinks which the supplier lets to the reseller; whereas, in this case, the reseller must have the right to obtain from other undertakings, under the conditions specified in this Regulation, other drinks, except beer, supplied under the agreement or of the same type but bearing a different trademark; whereas a uniform maximum duration should be provided for service-station agreements, with the exception of tenancy agreements between the supplier and the reseller, which takes account of the long-term character of the relationship between the parties;

(19) Whereas to the extent that Member States provide, by law or administrative measures, for the same upper limit of duration for the exclusive purchasing obligation upon the reseller in service-station agreements as laid down in this Regulation but provide for a permissible duration which varies in proportion to the consideration provided by the supplier or generally provide for a shorter duration than that permitted by this Regulation, such laws or measures are not contrary to the objectives of this Regulation which, in this respect, merely sets an upper limit to the duration of service-station agreements; whereas the application and enforcement of such national laws or measures must therefore be regarded as compatible with the provisions of this Regulation;

(20) Whereas the limitations and conditions provided for in this Regulation are such as to guarantee effective competition on the markets in question; whereas, therefore, the agreements to which the exemption by category applies do not normally enable the participating undertakings to eliminate competition for a substantial part of the products in question;

(21) Whereas, in particular cases in which agreements or concerted practices satisfying the conditions of this Regulation nevertheless have effects incompatible with Article 85(3) of the Treaty, the Commission may withdraw the benefit of the exemption by category from the undertakings party thereto;

(22) Whereas agreements and concerted practices which satisfy the conditions set out in this Regulation need not be notified; whereas an undertaking may nonetheless, in a particular case where real doubt exists, request the Commission to declare whether its agreements comply with this Regulation;

(23) Whereas this Regulation does not affect the applicability of Commission Regulation 3604/82 of 23 December 1982 on the application of Article 85(3) of the Treaty to categories of specialisation agreements; whereas it does not exclude the application of Article 86 of the Treaty.

HAS ADOPTED THIS REGULATION:

TITLE I

GENERAL PROVISIONS

Article 1

Pursuant to Article 85(3) of the Treaty and subject to the conditions set out in Articles 2 to 5 of this Regulation, it is hereby declared that Article 85(1) of the Treaty shall not apply to agreements to which only two undertakings are party and whereby one party, the reseller, agrees with the other, the supplier, to purchase certain goods specified in the agreement for resale only from the supplier or from a connected undertaking or from another undertaking which the supplier has entrusted with the sale of his goods.

Article 2

1. No other restriction of competition shall be imposed on the supplier than the obligation not to distribute the contract goods or goods which compete with the contract goods in the reseller's principal sales area and at the reseller's level of distribution.

2. Apart from the obligation described in Article 1, no other restriction of competition shall be imposed on the reseller other than the obligation not to manufacture or distribute goods which compete with the contract goods.

3. Article 1 shall apply notwithstanding that the reseller undertakes any or all of the following obligations:

   (a) to purchase complete ranges of goods;

   (b) to purchase minimum quantities of goods which are subject to the exclusive purchasing obligation;

   (c) to sell the contract goods under trademarks, or packed and presented as specified by the supplier;

   (d) to take measures for the promotion of sales, in particular:

   — to advertise,
   — to maintain a sales network or stock of goods,
   — to provide customer and guarantee services,
   — to employ staff having specialised or technical training.

Article 3

Article 1 shall not apply where:

(a) manufacturers of identical goods or of goods which are considered by users as equivalent in view of their characteristics, price and intended use enter into reciprocal exclusive purchasing agreements between themselves in respect of such goods;

(b) manufacturers of identical goods or of goods which are considered by users as equivalent in view of their characteristics, price and intended use enter into a non-reciprocal exclusive purchasing agreement between themselves in respect of such goods, unless at least one of them has a total turnover of no more than 100 million ECU;

(c) the exclusive purchasing obligation is agreed for more than one type of goods where these are neither by their nature nor according to commercial usage connected to each other;

(d) the agreement is concluded for an indefinite duration or for a period of more than five years.

Article 4

1. Article 3(a) and (b) shall also apply where the goods there referred to are manufactured by an undertaking connected with a party to the agreement.

2. Connected undertakings are:

(a) undertakings in which a party to the agreement, directly or indirectly:

— owns more than half the capital or business assets, or
— has the power to exercise more than half the voting rights, or
— has the power to appoint more than half the members of the supervisory board, board of directors or bodies legally representing the undertaking, or
— has the right to manage the affairs;

(b) undertakings which directly or indirectly have in or over a party to the agreement the rights or powers listed in (a);

(c) undertakings in which an undertaking referred to in (b) directly or indirectly has the rights or powers listed in (a).

3. Undertakings in which the parties to the agreement or undertakings connected with them jointly have the rights or powers set out in paragraph 2(a) shall be considered to be connected with each of the parties to the agreement.

Article 5

1. For the purpose of Article 3(b), the ECU is the unit of account used for drawing up the budget of the Community pursuant to Articles 207 and 209 of the Treaty.

2. Article 1 shall remain applicable where during any period of two consecutive financial years the total turnover referred to in Article 3(b) is exceeded by no more than 10%.

3. For the purpose of calculating total turnover within the meaning of Article 3(b), the turnovers achieved during the last financial year by the party to the agreement and connected undertakings in respect of all goods and services, excluding all taxes and other duties, shall be added together. For this purpose, no account shall be taken of dealings between the party to the agreement and its connected undertakings or between its connected undertakings.

Title II

SPECIAL PROVISIONS FOR BEER SUPPLY AGREEMENTS

Article 6

1. Pursuant to Article 85(3) of the Treaty, and subject to Article 7 to 9 of this Regulation, it is hereby declared that Article 85(1) of the Treaty shall not apply to agreements to which only two undertakings are party and whereby one party, the reseller, agrees with the other, the supplier, in consideration for the according of special commercial or financial advantages, to purchase only from the supplier, an undertaking connected with the supplier or another undertaking entrusted by the supplier with the distribution of his goods, certain beers, or certain beers and certain other drinks, specified in the agreement for resale in premises used for the sale and consumption of drinks and designated in the agreement.

2. The declaration in paragraph 1 shall also apply where exclusive purchasing obligations of the kind described in paragraph 1 are imposed on the reseller in favour of the supplier by another undertaking which is itself not a supplier.

Article 7

1. Apart from the obligation referred to in Article 6, no restriction on competition shall be imposed on the reseller other than:

(a) the obligation not to sell beers and other drinks which are supplied by other undertakings and which are of the same type as the beers or other drinks supplied under the agreement in the premises designated in the agreement;

(b) the obligation, in the event that the reseller sells in the premises designated in the agreement beers which are supplied by other undertakings and which are of a different type from the beers supplied under the agreement, to sell such beers only in bottles, cans or other small packages, unless the sale of such beers in draught form is customary or is necessary to satisfy a sufficient demand from consumers;

(c) the obligation to advertise goods supplied by other undertakings within or outside the premises designated in the agreement only in proportion to the share of these goods in the total turnover realised in the premises.

2. Beers or other drinks are of different types where they are clearly distinguishable by their composition, appearance or taste.

Article 8

1. Article 6 shall apply where:

(a) the supplier or a connected undertaking imposes on the reseller exclusive purchasing obligations for goods other than drinks or for services;

(b) the supplier restricts the freedom of the reseller to obtain from an undertaking of his choice either services or goods for which neither an exclusive purchasing obligation nor a ban on dealing in competing products may be imposed;

(c) the agreement is concluded for an indefinite duration or for a period of more than five years and the exclusive purchasing obligation relates to specified beers and other drinks;

(d) the agreement is concluded for an indefinite duration or for a period of more than 10 years and the exclusive purchasing obligation relates only to specified beers;

(e) the supplier obliges the reseller to impose the exclusive purchasing obligation on his successor for a longer period than the reseller would himself remain tied to the supplier.

2. Where the agreement relates to premises which the supplier lets to the reseller or allows or allows the reseller to occupy on some other basis in law or in fact, the following provisions shall also apply:

(a) notwithstanding paragraphs (1)(c) and (d), the exclusive purchasing obligations and bans on dealing in competing products specified in this Title may be imposed on the reseller for the whole period for which the reseller in fact operates the premises;

(b) the agreement must provide for the reseller to have the right to obtain:

— drinks, except beer, supplied under the agreement from other undertakings where these undertakings offer them on more favourable conditions which the supplier does not meet,
— drinks, except beer, which are of the same type as those supplied under the agreement but which bear different trade marks, from other undertakings where the supplier does not offer them.

Article 9

Articles 2(1) and (3), 3(a) and (b), 4 and 5 shall apply *mutatis mutandis*.

TITLE III

SPECIAL PROVISIONS FOR SERVICE-STATION AGREEMENTS

Article 10

Pursuant to Article 85(3) of the Treaty and subject to Articles 11 to 13 of this Regulation, it is hereby declared that Article 85(1) of the Treaty shall not apply to agreements to which only two undertakings are party and whereby one party, the reseller, agrees with the other, the supplier, in consideration for the according of special commercial or financial advantages, to purchase only from the supplier, an undertaking connected with the supplier or another undertaking entrusted by the supplier with the distribution of this goods, certain petroleum-based motor vehicle fuels or certain petroleum-based motor vehicle and other fuels specified in the agreement for resale in a service station designated in the agreement.

Article 11

Apart from the obligation referred to in Article 10, no restriction on competition shall be imposed on the reseller other than:

(a) the obligation not to sell motor-vehicle fuel and other fuels which are supplied by other undertakings in the service station designated in the agreement;

(b) the obligation not to use lubricants or related petroleum-based products which are supplied by other undertakings within the service station designated in the agreement where the supplier or a connected undertaking has made available to the reseller, or financed, a lubrication bay or other motor-vehicle lubrication equipment;

(c) the obligation to advertise goods supplied by other undertakings within or outside the service station designated in the agreement only in proportion to the share of these goods in the total turnover realised in the service station;

(d) the obligation to have equipment owned by the supplier or a connected undertaking or financed by the supplier or a connected undertaking designated by him.

Article 12

1. Article 10 shall not apply where:

   (a) the supplier or a connected undertaking imposes on the reseller exclusive purchasing obligations for goods other than motor-vehicle and other fuels or for services, except in the case of the obligations referred to in Article 11(b) and (d);

   (b) the supplier restricts the freedom of the reseller to obtain from an undertaking of his choice goods or services for which under the provisions of this Title neither an exclusive purchasing obligation nor a ban on dealing in competing products may be imposed;

   (c) the agreement is concluded for an indefinite duration or for a period of more than 10 years;

   (d) the supplier obliges the reseller to impose the exclusive purchasing obligation on his successor for a longer period than the reseller would himself remain tied to the supplier.

2. Where the agreement relates to a service station which the supplier lets to the reseller, or allows the reseller to occupy on some other basis, in law or in fact, exclusive purchasing obligations or bans on dealing in competing products specified in this Title may, notwithstanding paragraph 1(c), be imposed on the reseller for the whole period for which the reseller in fact operates the premises.

Article 13

Articles 2(1) and (3), 3(a) and (b), 4 and 5 of this Regulation shall apply *mutatis mutandis*.

Title IV

MISCELLANEOUS PROVISION

Article 14

The Commission may withdraw the benefit of this Regulation, pursuant to Article 7 of Regulation 19/65, when it finds in a particular case that an agreement which is exempted by this Regulation nevertheless has certain effects which are incompatible with the conditions set out in Article 85(3) of the Treaty, and in particular where:

   (a) the contract goods are not subject, in a substantial part of the common market, to effective competition from identical goods or goods considered by users as equivalent in view of their characteristics, price and intended use;

   (b) access by of other suppliers to the different stages of distribution in a substantial part of the common market is made difficult to a significant extent;

   (c) the supplier without any objectively justified reason:

   1. refuses to supply categories of resellers who cannot obtain the contract goods elsewhere on suitable terms or applies to them differing prices or conditions of sale;
   2. applies less favourable prices or conditions of sale to resellers bound by an exclusive purchasing obligation as compared with other resellers at the same level of distribution.

Article 15

1. In the period 1 July 1983 to 31 December 1986, the prohibition in Article 85(1) of the Treaty shall not apply to agreements of the kind described in Article 1 which either were in force on 1 July 1983 or entered into force between 1 July and 31 December 1983 and which satisfy the exemption conditions under Regulation 67/67.

2. In the period 1 July 1983 to 31 December 1988, the prohibition in Article 85(1) of the Treaty shall not apply to agreements of the kinds described in Articles 6 and 10 which either were in force on 1 July 1983 or entered into force between 1 July and 31 December 1983 and which satisfy the exemption conditions of Regulation 67/67.

3. In the case of agreements of the kinds described in Articles 6 and 10, which were in force on 1 July 1983 and which expire after 31 December 1988, the prohibition in Article 85(1) of the Treaty shall not apply in the period from 1 January 1989 to the expiry of the agreement but at the latest to the expiry of this Regulation to the extent that the supplier releases the reseller, before 1 January 1989, from all obligations which would prevent the application of the exemption under Titles II and III.

[4. The provisions of the preceding paragraphs shall apply in the same way to the agreements referred to respectively in those paragraphs, which were in force on the date of accession of the Kingdom of Spain and of the Portuguese Republic and which, as a result of accession, fall within the scope of Article 85(1) of the Treaty.]

Article 16

This Regulation shall not apply to agreements by which the supplier undertakes with the reseller to supply only to the reseller certain goods for resale, in the whole or in a defined part of the Community, and the reseller undertakes with the supplier to purchase these goods only from the supplier.

Article 17

This Regulation shall not apply where the parties or connected undertakings, for the purpose of resale in one and the same premises used for the sale and consumption of drinks or service station, enter into agreements both of the kind referred to in Title I and of a kind referred to in Title II or III.

Article 18

This Regulation shall apply *mutatis mutandis* to the categories of concerted practices defined in Articles 1, 6 and 10.

Article 19

This Regulation shall enter into force on 1 July 1983. It shall expire on 31 December [1999].

This Regulation shall be binding in its entirety and directly applicable in all Member States.

Done at Brussels, June 22, 1983.

APPENDIX C.4   COMMISSION REGULATION 417/85 OF DECEMBER 19, 1984

C.4-01   On the application of Article 85(3) of the Treaty to categories of specialisation agreements

([1985] O.J. L53/1, AS AMENDED, [1993] O.J. L21/8)

THE COMMISSION OF THE EUROPEAN COMMUNITIES,

Having regard to the Treaty establishing the European Economic Community,

Having regard to Council Regulation (EEC) No. 2321/71 of 20 December 1971 on the application of Article 85(3) of the Treaty to categories of agreements , decisions and concerted practices, as last amended by the Act of Accession of Greece, and in particular Article 1 thereof,

Having published a draft of this Regulation

Having consulted the Advisory Committee on Restrictive Practices and Dominant Positions,

Whereas:

(1) Regulation (EEC) No. 2821/71 empowers the Commission to apply Article 85(3) of the Treaty by Regulation to certain categories of agreements, decisions and concerted practices falling within the scope of Article 85(1) which relate to specialisation, including agreements necessary for achieving it.

(2) Agreements on specialisation in present or future production may fall within the scope of Article 85(1).

(3) Agreements on specialisation in production generally contribute to improving the production or distribution of goods, because undertakings concerned can concentrate on the manufacture of certain products and thus operate more efficiently and supply the products more cheaply. It is likely that, given effective competition, consumers will receive a fair share of the resulting benefit.

(4) Such advantages can arise equally from agreements whereby each participant gives up the manufacture of certain products in favour of another participant and from agreements whereby the participants undertake to manufacture certain products or have them manufactured only jointly.

(5) The Regulation must specify what restrictions of competition may be included in specialisation agreements. The restrictions of competition that are permitted in the Regulation in addition to reciprocal obligations to give up manufacture are normally essential for the making and implementation of such agreements. These restrictions are therefore, in general, indispensable for the attainment of the desired advantages for the participating undertakings and consumers. It may be left to the parties to decide which of these provisions they include in their agreements.

(6) The exemption must be limited to agreements which do not give rise to the possibility of eliminating competition in respect of a substantial part of the products in question. The Regulation must therefor apply only as long as the market share and turnover of the participating undertakings do not exceed a certain limit.

(7) It is, however, appropriate to offer undertakings which exceed the turnover limit set in the Regulation a simplified means of obtaining the legal certainty provided by the block exemption. This must allow the Commission to exercise effective supervision as well as simplifying its administration of such agreements.

(8) In order to facilitate the conclusion of long-term specialisation agreements, which can have a bearing on the structure of the participating undertakings, it is appropriate to fix the period of validity of the Regulation at 13 years. If the circumstances on the basis of which the Regulation was adopted should change significantly within this period, the Commission will make the necessary amendments.

(9) Agreements, decisions and concerted practices which are automatically exempted pursuant to this Regulation need not be notified. Undertakings may none the less in an individual case request

a decision pursuant to Council Regulation No. 17, as last amended by the Act of Accession of Greece,

HAS ADOPTED THIS REGULATION:

Article 1

Pursuant to Article 85(3) of the Treaty and subject to the provisions of this Regulation, it is hereby declared that Article 85(1) of the Treaty shall not apply to agreements on specialisation whereby, for the duration of the agreement, undertakings accept reciprocal obligations:

(a) not to manufacture certain products or to have them manufactured, but to leave it to other parties to manufacture the products or have them manufactured; or

(b) to manufacture certain products or have them manufactured only jointly.

Article 2

1. [Article 1 shall also apply to the following restrictions of competition:]

(a) an obligation not to conclude with third parties specialisation agreements relating to identical products or to products considered by users to be equivalent in view of their characteristics, price and intended use;

(b) an obligation to procure products which are the subject of the specialisation exclusively from another party, a joint undertaking or an undertaking jointly charged with their manufacture, except where they are obtainable on more favourable terms elsewhere and the other party, the joint undertaking or the undertaking charged with manufacture is not prepared to offer the same terms;

[(c) and obligation to grant other parties the exclusive right, within the whole or a defined area of the common market, to distribute products which are the subject of the specialisation, provided that intermediaries and users can also obtain the products from other suppliers and the parties do not render it difficult for intermediaries or users to thus obtain the products;]

[(d) an obligation to grant one of the parties the exclusive right to distribute products which are the subject of the specialisation provided that that party does not distribute products of a third undertaking which compete with the contract products;

(e) an obligation to grant the exclusive right to distribute products which are the subject of the specialisation to a joint undertaking or to a third undertaking, provided that the joint undertaking or third undertaking does not manufacture or distribute products which compete with the contract products;

(f) an obligation to grant the exclusive right to distribute within the whole or a defined area of the common market the products which are the subject of the specialisation to joint undertakings or third undertakings which do not manufacture or distribute products which compete with the contract products, provided that users and intermediaries can also obtain the contract products from other suppliers and that neither the parties nor the joint undertakings or third undertakings entrusted with the exclusive distribution of the contract products render it difficult for users and intermediaries to thus obtain the contract products.]

2. Article 1 shall also apply where the parties undertake obligations of the types referred to in paragraph 1 but with a more limited scope than is permitted by that paragraph.

[2a. Article 1 shall not apply if restrictions of competition other than those set out in paragraphs 1 and 2 are imposed upon the parties by agreement, decision or concerted practice.]

3.Article 1 shall apply notwithstanding that any of the following obligations, in particular, are imposed:

(a) an obligation to supply other parties with products which are the subject of the specialisation and in so doing to observe minimum standards of quality;

(b) an obligation to maintain minimum stocks of products which are the subject of the specialisation and of replacement parts for them;

(c) an obligation to provide customer and guarantee services for products which are the subject of the specialisation.

Article 3

[1. Article 1 shall apply only if:

(a) the products which are the subject of the specialisation together with the participating undertakings' other products which are considered by users to be equivalent in view of their characteristics, price and intended use do not represent more than 20 per cent. of the market for all such products in the common market or a substantial part thereof; and

(b) the aggregate turnover of all the participating undertakings does not exceed ECU 1,000 million.

2. If pursuant to point (d), (e) or (f) of Article 2(1), one of the parties, a joint undertaking, a third undertaking or more than one joint undertaking or third undertaking are entrusted with the distribution of the products which are the subject of the specialisation, Article 1 shall apply only if:

(a) the products which are the subject of the specialisation together with the participating undertakings' other products which are considered by users to be equivalent in view of their characteristics, price and intended use do not represent more than 10 per cent. of the market for all such products in the common market or a substantial part thereof; and

(b) the aggregate annual turnover of all the participating undertakings does not exceed ECU 1,000 million.

3. Article 1 shall continue to apply if the market shares and turnover referred to in paragraphs 1 and 2 are exceeded during any period of two consecutive financial years by not more than one-tenth.

4. Where the limits laid down in paragraph 3 are also exceeded, Article 1 shall continue to apply for a period of six months following the end of the financial year during which they were exceeded.']

Article 4

1. The exemption provided for in Article 1 shall also apply to agreements involving participating undertakings whose aggregate turnover exceeds the limits laid down in [Article 3(1)(b), (2)(b) and (3)], on condition that the agreements in question are notified to the Commission in accordance with the provisions of Commission Regulation No. [3385], and that the Commission does not oppose such exemption within a period of six months.

2. The period of six months shall run from the date on which the notification is received by the Commission. Where, however, the notification is made by registered post, the period shall run from the date shown on the postmark of the place of posting.

3. Paragraph 1 shall apply only if:

(a) express reference is made to this Article in the notification or in a communication accompanying it; and

(b) the information furnished with the notification is complete and in accordance with the facts.

4. The benefit of paragraph 1 may be claimed for agreements notified before the entry into force of this Regulation by submitting a communication to the Commission referring expressly to this Article and to the notification. Paragraphs 2 and 3(b) shall apply *mutatis mutandis.*

5. The Commission may oppose the exemption. It shall oppose exemption if it receives a request to do so from a Member State within three months of the forwarding to the Member State of the notification referred to in paragraph 1 or of the communication referred to in paragraph 4. This request must be justified on the basis of considerations relating to the competition rules of the Treaty.

6. The Commission may withdraw the opposition to the exemption at any time. However, where the opposition was raised at the request of a Member State and this request is maintained, it may be withdrawn only after consultation of the Advisory Committee on Restrictive Practices and Dominant Positions.

7. If the opposition is withdrawn because the undertakings concerned have shown that the conditions of Article 85(3) are fulfilled, the exemption shall apply from the date of notification.

8. If the opposition is withdrawn because the undertakings concerned have amended the agreement so that the conditions of Article 85(3) are fulfilled, the exemption shall apply from the date on which the amendments take effect.

9. If the Commission opposes exemption and the opposition is not withdrawn, the effects of the notification shall be governed by the provisions of Regulation No. 17.

Article 5

1. Information acquired pursuant to Article 4 shall be used only for the purposes of this Regulation.

2. The Commission and the authorities of the Member States, their officials and other servants shall not disclose information acquired by them pursuant to this Regulation of a kind that is covered by the obligation of professional secrecy.

3. Paragraphs 1 and 2 shall not prevent publication of general information or surveys which do not contain information relating to particular undertakings or associations of undertakings.

Article 6

For the purpose of calculating total annual turnover within the meaning of Article 3(1)(b) [and (2)(b)], the turnovers achieved during the last financial year by the participating undertakings in respect of all goods and services excluding tax shall be added together. For this purpose, no account shall be taken of dealings between the participating undertakings or between these undertakings and a third undertaking jointly charged with manufacture [or sale].

Article 7

1. [For the purposes of Article 3(1) and (2), and Article 6, participating undertakings are:]

(a) undertakings party to the agreement;

(b) undertakings in which a party to the agreement, directly or indirectly:

— owns more than half the capital or business assets,

— has the power to exercise more than half the voting rights,

— has the power to appoint at least half the members of the supervisory board, board of management or bodies legally representing the undertakings, or

— has the right to manage the affairs;

(c) undertakings which directly or indirectly have in or over a party to the agreement the rights or powers listed in (b);

(d) undertakings in or over which an undertaking referred in in (c) directly or indirectly has the rights or powers listed in (b).

2. Undertakings in which the undertakings referred to in paragraph 1(a) to (d) directly or indirectly jointly have the rights or powers set out in paragraph 1(b) shall also be considered to be participating undertakings.

Article 8

The Commission may withdraw the benefit of this Regulation, pursuant to Article 7 of Regulation (EEC) No. 2821/71, where it finds in a particular case that an agreement exempted by this Regulation nevertheless has effects which are incompatible with the conditions set out in Article 85(3) of the Treaty, and in particular where:

(a) the agreement is not yielding significant results in terms of rationalisation or consumers are not receiving a fair share of the resulting benefit; or

(b) the products which are the subject of the specialisation are not subject in the common market or a substantial part thereof to effective competition from identical products or products considered by users to be equivalent in view of their characteristics, price and intended use.

Article 9

This Regulation shall apply *mutatis mutandis* to decisions of associations of undertakings and concerted practices.

Article 9a

The prohibition in Article 85(1) of the Treaty shall not apply to the specialisation agreements which were in existence at the date of the accession of the Kingdom of Spain and of the Portuguese Republic and which, by reason of this accession, fall within the scope of Article 85(1), if before July, 1, 1986, they are so amended that they comply with the conditions laid down in this Regulation.

Article 10

1. This Regulation shall enter into force on 1 March 1985. It shall apply until [31 December 2000].

2. Commission Regulation (EEC) No. 3604/82 is hereby repealed.
This Regulation shall be binding in its entirety and directly applicable in all Member States.
Done at Brussels, 19 December 1984.

APPENDIX C.5   COMMISSION REGULATION 4087/88 OF NOVEMBER 30, 1988

C.5-01   On the application of Article 85(3) of the Treaty to categories of franchise agreements

([1988] O.J. L359/46)

THE COMMISSION OF THE EUROPEAN COMMUNITIES,
Having regard to the Treaty establishing the European Economic Community,
Having regard to Council Regulation No. 19/65/EEC of 2 March 1965 on the application of Article 85(3) of the Treaty to certain categories of agreements and concerted practices, as last amended by the Act of Accession of Spain and Portugal, and in particular Article 1 thereof,
Having published a draft of this Regulation,
Having consulted the Advisory Committee on Restrictive Practices and Dominant Positions,
Whereas:

(1) Regulation No. 19/65/EEC empowers the Commission to apply Article 85(3) of the Treaty by Regulation to certain categories of bilateral exclusive agreements falling within the scope of Article 85(1) which either have as their object the exclusive distribution or exclusive purchase of goods, or include restrictions imposed in relation to the assignment or use of industrial property rights.

(2) Franchise agreements consist essentially of licences of industrial or intellectual property rights relating to trade marks or signs and know-how, which can be combined with restrictions relating to supply or purchase of goods.

(3) Several types of franchise can be distinguished according to their object: industrial franchise concerns the manufacturing of goods, distribution franchise concerns the sale of goods, and service franchise concerns the supply of services.

(4) It is possible on the basis of the experience of the Commission to define categories of franchise agreements which fall under Article 85(1) but can normally be regarded as satisfying the conditions laid down in Article 85(3). This is the case for franchise agreements whereby one of the parties supplies goods or provides services to end users. On the other hand, industrial franchise agreements should not be covered by this Regulation. Such agreements, which usually govern relationships between producers, present different characteristics than the other types of franchise. They consist of manufacturing licences based on patents and/or technical know-how, combined with trade-mark licences. Some of them may benefit from other block exemptions if they fulfil the necessary conditions.

(5) This Regulation covers franchise agreements between two undertakings, the franchisor and the franchisee, for the retailing of goods or the provision of services to end users, or a combination of these activities, such as the processing or adaptation of goods to fit specific needs of their customers. It also covers cases where the relationship between franchisor and franchisees is made through a third undertaking, the master franchisee. It does not cover wholesale franchise agreements because of the lack of experience of the Commission in that field.

(6) Franchise agreements as defined in this Regulation can fall under Article 85(1). They may in particular affect intra-Community trade where they are concluded between undertakings from different Member States or where they form the basis of a network which extends beyond the boundaries of a single Member State.

(7) Franchise agreements as defined in this Regulation normally improve the distribution of goods and/or the provision of services as they give franchisors the possibility of establishing a uniform network with limited investments, which may assist the entry of new competitors on the market, particularly in the case of small and medium-sized undertakings, thus increasing inter-brand competition. They also allow independent traders to set up outlets more rapidly and with higher chance of success than if they had to do so without the franchisor's experience and assistance. They have therefore the possibility of competing more efficiently with large distribution undertakings.

(8) As a rule, franchise agreements also allow consumers and other end users a fair share of the resulting benefit, as they combine the advantage of a uniform network with the existence of traders personally interested in the efficient operation of their business. The homogeneity of the network and the constant cooperation between the franchisor and the franchisees ensures a constant quality of the products and services. The favourable effect of franchising on interbrand competition and the fact that consumers are free to deal with any franchisee in the network guarantees that a reasonable part of the resulting benefits will be passed on to the consumers.

(9) This Regulation must define the obligations restrictive of competition which may be included in franchise agreements. This is the case in particular for the granting of an exclusive territory to the franchisees combined with the prohibition on actively seeking customers outside that territory, which allows them to concentrate their efforts on their allotted territory. The same applies to the granting of an exclusive territory to a master franchisee combined with the obligation not to conclude franchise agreements with third parties outside that territory. Where the franchisees sell or use in the process of providing services, goods manufactured by the franchisor or according to its instructions and or bearing its trade mark, an obligation on the franchisees not to sell, or use in the process of the provision of services, competing goods, makes it possible to establish a coherent network which is identified with the franchised goods. However, this obligation should only be accepted with respect to the goods which form the essential subject-matter of the franchise. It should notably not relate to accessories or spare parts for these goods.

(10) The obligations referred to above thus do not impose restrictions which are not necessary for the attainment of the abovementioned objectives. In particular, the limited territorial protection granted to the franchisees is indispensable to protect their investment.

(11) It is desirable to list in the Regulation a number of obligations that are commonly found in franchise agreements and are normally not restrictive of competition and to provide that if, because of the particular economic or legal circumstances, they fall under Article 85(1), they are also covered by the exemption. This list, which is not exhaustive, includes in particular clauses which are essential to preserve the common identity and reputation of the network or to prevent the know-how made available and the assistance given by the franchisor from benefiting competitors.

(12) The Regulation must specify the conditions which must be satisfied for the exemption to apply. To guarantee that competition is not eliminated for a substantial part of the goods which are the subject of the franchise, it is necessary that parallel imports remain possible. Therefore, cross deliveries between franchisees should always be possible. Furthermore, where a franchise network is combined with another distribution system, franchisees should be free to obtain supplies from authorised distributors. To better inform consumers, thereby helping to ensure that they receive a fair share of the resulting benefits, it must be provided that the franchisee shall be obliged to indicate its status as an independent undertaking, by any appropriate means which does not jeopardize the common identity of the franchised network. Furthermore, where the franchisees have to honour guarantees for the franchisor's goods, this obligation should also apply to goods supplied by the franchisor, other franchisees or other agreed dealers.

(13) The Regulation must also specify restrictions which may not be included in franchise agreements if these are to benefit from the exemption granted by the Regulation, by virtue of the fact that such provisions are restrictions falling under Article 85(1) for which there is no general presumption that they will lead to the positive effects required by Article 85(3). This applies in particular to market sharing between competing manufacturers, to clauses unduly limiting the franchisee's choice of suppliers or customers, and to cases where the franchisee is restricted in determining its prices. However, the franchisor should be free to recommend prices to the franchisees, where it is not prohibited by national laws and to the extent that it does not lead to concerted practices for the effective application of these prices.

(14) Agreements which are not automatically covered by the exemption because they contain provisions that are not expressly exempted by the Regulation and not expressly excluded from exemption may nonetheless generally be presumed to be eligible for application of Article 85(3). It will be possible for the Commission rapidly to establish whether this is the case for a particular agreement. Such agreements should therefore be deemed to be covered by the exemption provided for in this Regulation where they are notified to the Commission and the Commission does not oppose the application of the exemption within a specified period of time.

(15) If individual agreements exempted by this Regulation nevertheless have effects which are incompatible with Article 85(3), in particular as interpreted by the administrative practice of the Commission and the case law of the Court of Justice, the Commission may withdraw the benefit to the block exemption. This applies in particular where competition is significantly restricted because of the structure of the relevant market.

(16) Agreements which are automatically exempted pursuant to this Regulation need not be notified. Undertakings may nevertheless in a particular case request a decision pursuant to Council Regulation No. 17 as last amended by the Act of Accession of Spain and Portugal.

(17) Agreements may benefit from the provisions either of this Regulation or of another Regulation, according to their particular nature and provided that they fulfil the necessary conditions of application. They may not benefit from a combination of the provisions of this Regulation with those of another block exemption Regulation,

HAS ADOPTED THIS REGULATION:

Article 1

1. Pursuant to Article 85(3) of the Treaty and subject to the provisions of this Regulation, it is hereby declared that Article 85(1) of the Treaty shall not apply to franchise agreements to which two undertakings are party, which include one or more of the restrictions listed in Article 2.

2. The exemption provided for in paragraph 1 shall also apply to master franchise agreements to which two undertakings are party. Where applicable, the provisions of this Regulation concerning the relationship between franchisor and franchisee shall apply *mutatis mutandis* to the relationship between franchisor and master franchisee and between master franchisee and franchisee.

3. For the purposes of this Regulation:

(a) "franchise" means a package of industrial or intellectual property rights relating to trade marks, trade names, shop signs, utility models, designs, copyrights, know-how or patents, to be exploited for the resale of goods or the provision of services to end users;

(b) "franchise agreements" means an agreement whereby one undertaking, the franchisor, grants the other, the franchisee, in exchange for direct or indirect financial consideration, the right to exploit a franchise for the purposes of marketing specified types of goods and/or services; it includes at least obligations relating to:

— the use of a common name or shop sign and a uniform presentation of contract premises and/or means of transport,

— the communication by the franchisor to the franchisee of know-how,

— the continuing provision by the franchisor to the franchisee of commercial or technical assistance during the life of the agreement;

(c) "master franchise agreement" means an agreement whereby one undertaking, the franchisor, grants the other, the master franchisee, in exchange of direct or indirect financial consideration, the right to exploit a franchise for the purposes of concluding franchise agreements with third parties, the franchisees;

(d) "franchisor's goods" means goods produced by the franchisor or according to its instructions, and/or bearing the franchisor's name or trade mark;

(e) "contract premises" means the premises used for the exploitation of the franchise or, when the franchise is exploited outside those premises, the base from which the franchisee operates the means of transport used for the exploitation of the franchise (contract means of transport);

(f) "know-how" means a package of non-patented practical information, resulting from experience and testing by the franchisor, which is secret, substantial and identified;

(g) "secret" means that the know-how, as a body or in the precise configuration and assembly of its components, is not generally known or easily accessible; it is not limited in the narrow sense that each individual component of the know-how should be totally unknown or unobtainable outside the franchisor's business;

(h) "substantial" means that the know-how includes information which is of importance for the sale of goods or the provision of services to end users, and in particular for the presentation of goods for sale, the processing of goods in connection with the provision of services, methods of dealing with customers, and administration and financial management; the know-how must be useful for the franchisee by being capable, at the date of conclusion of the agreement, of improving the competitive position of the franchisee, in particular by improving the franchisee's performance or helping it to enter a new market;

(i) "identified" means that the know-how must be described in a sufficiently comprehensive manner so as to make it possible to verify that it fulfils the criteria of secrecy and substantiality; the description of the know-how can either be set out in the franchise agreement or in a separate document or recorded in any other appropriate form.

Article 2

The exemption provided for in Article shall apply to the following restrictions of competition:

(a) an obligation on the franchisor, in a defined area of the common market, the contract territory, not to:

— grant, the right to exploit all or part of the franchise to third parties,

— itself exploit the franchise, or itself market the goods or services which are the subject-matter of the franchise under a similar formula,

— itself supply the franchisor's goods to third parties;

(b) an obligation on the master franchisee not to conclude franchise agreement with third parties outside its contract territory;

(c) an obligation on the franchisee to exploit the franchise only from the contract premises;

(d) an obligation on the franchisee to refrain, outside the contract territory, from seeking customers for the goods or the services which are the subject-matter of the franchise;

(e) an obligation on the franchisee not to manufacture, sell or use in the course of the provision of services, goods competing with the franchisor's goods which are the subject-matter of the franchise; where the subject-matter of the franchise is the sale or use in the course of the provision of services both certain types of goods and spare parts or accessories therefor, that obligation may not be imposed in respect of these spare parts or accessories.

Article 3

1. Article 1 shall apply notwithstanding the presence of any of the following obligations on the franchisee, in so far as they are necessary to protect the franchisor's industrial or intellectual property rights or to maintain the common identity and reputation of the franchised network:

(a) to sell, or use in the course of the provision of services, exclusively goods matching minimum objective quality specifications laid down by the franchisor;

(b) to sell, or use in the course of the provision of services, goods which are manufactured only by the franchisor or by third parties designed by it, where it is impracticable, owing to the nature of the goods which are the subject-matter of the franchise, to apply objective quality specifications;

(c) not to engage, directly or indirectly, in any similar business in a territory where it would compete with a member of the franchised network, including the franchisor; the franchisee may be held to this obligation after the termination of the agreement, for a reasonable period which may not exceed one year, in the territory where it has exploited the franchise;

(d) not to acquire financial interests in the capital of a competing undertaking, which would give the franchisee the power to influence the economic conduct of such undertaking;

(e) to sell the goods which are the subject-matter of the franchise only to end users, to other franchisees and to resellers within other channels of distribution supplied by the manufacturer of these goods or with its consent;

(f) to use its best endeavours to sell the goods or provide the services that are the subject-matter of the franchise; to offer for sale a minimum range of goods, achieve a minimum turnover, plan its orders in advance, keep minimum stocks and provide customer and warranty services;

(g) to pay to the franchisor a specified proportion of its revenue for advertising and itself carry out advertising for the nature of which it shall obtain the franchisor's approval.

2. Article 1 shall apply notwithstanding the presence of any of the following obligations on the franchisee:

(a) not to disclose to third parties the know-how provided by the franchisor; the franchisee may be held to this obligation after termination of the agreement;

(b) to communicate to the franchisor any experience gained in exploiting the franchise and to grant it, and other franchisees, a non-exclusive licence for the know-how resulting from that experience;

(c) to inform the franchisor of infringements of licensed industrial or intellectual property rights, to take legal action against infringers or to assist the franchisor in any legal actions against infringers:

(d) not to use know-how licensed by the franchisor for purposes other than the exploitation of the franchise; the franchisee may be held to this obligation after termination of the agreement;

(e) to attend or have its staff attend training courses arranged by the franchisor;

(f) to apply the commercial methods devised by the franchisor, including any subsequent modification thereof, and use the licensed industrial or intellectual property rights;

(g) to comply with the franchisor's standards for the equipment and presentation of the contract premises and/or means of transport;

(h) to allow the franchisor to carry out checks of the contract premises and/or means of transport, including the goods sold and the services provided, and the inventory and accounts of the franchisee;

(i) not without the franchisor's consent to change the location of the contract premises;

(j) not without the franchisor's consent to assign the rights and obligations under the franchise agreement.

3. In the event that, because of particular circumstances, obligations referred to in paragraph 2 fall within the scope of Article 85(1), they shall also be exempted even if they are not accompanied by any of the obligations exempted by Article 1.

Article 4

The exemption provided for in Article 1 shall apply on condition that:

(a) the franchisee is free to obtain the goods that are the subject-matter of the franchise from other franchisees; where such goods are also distributed through another network of authorised distributors, the franchisee must be free to obtain the goods from the latter;

(b) where the franchisor obliges the franchisee to honour guarantees for the franchisor's goods, that obligation shall apply in respect of such goods supplied by any member of the franchised network or other distributors which give a similar guarantee, in the common market;

(c) the franchisee is obliged to indicate its status as an independent undertaking; this indication shall however not interfere with the common identity of the franchised network resulting in particular from the common name or shop sign and uniform appearance of the contract premises and/or means of transport.

Article 5

The exemption granted by Article 1 shall not apply where:

(a) undertakings producing goods or providing services which are identical or are considered by users as equivalent in view of their characteristics, price and intended use, enter into franchise agreements in respect of such goods or services;

(b) without prejudice to Article 2(e) and Article 3(1)(b), the franchisee is prevented from obtaining supplies of goods of a quality equivalent to those offered by the franchisor;

(c) without prejudice to Article 2(e), the franchisee is obliged to sell, or use in the process of providing services, goods manufactured by the franchisor or third parties designated by the franchisor and the franchisor refuses, for reasons other than protecting the franchisor's industrial or intellectual property rights, or maintaining the common identity and reputation of the franchised network, to designate as authorised manufacturers third parties proposed by the franchisee;

(d) the franchisee is prevented from continuing to use the licensed know-how after termination of the agreement where the know-how has become generally known or easily accessible, other than by breach of an obligation by the franchise;

(e) the franchisee is restricted by the franchisor, directly or indirectly, in the determination of sale prices for the goods or services which are the subject-matter of the franchise, without prejudice to the possibility for the franchisor of recommending sale prices;

(f) the franchisor prohibits the franchisee from challenging the validity of the industrial or intellectual property rights which form part of the franchise, without prejudice to the possibility for the franchisor of terminating the agreement in such a case;

(g) franchisees are obliged not to supply within the common market the goods or services which are the subject-matter of the franchise to end users because of their place of residence.

Article 6

1. The exemption provided for in Article 1 shall also apply to franchise agreements which fulfil the conditions laid down in Article 4 and include obligations restrictive of competition which are not covered by Articles 2 and 3(3) and do not fall within the scope of Article 5, on condition that the agreements in question are notified to the Commission in accordance with the provisions of Commission Regulation No. [3385/94] and that the Commission does not oppose such exemption within a period of six months.

2. The period of six months shall run from the date on which the notification is received by the Commission. Where, however, the notification is made by registered post, the period shall run from the date shown on the postmark of the place of posting.

3. Paragraph 1 shall apply only if:

(a) express reference is made to this Article in the notification or in a communication accompanying it; and

(b) the information furnished with the notification is complete and in accordance with the facts.

4. The benefit of paragraph 1 can be claimed for agreements notified before the entry into force of this Regulation by submitting a communication to the Commission referring expressly to this Article and to the notification. Paragraphs 2 and 3(b) shall apply *mutatis mutandis*.

5. The Commission may oppose exemption. It shall oppose exemption if it receives a request to do so from a Member State within three months of the forwarding to the Member State of the notification referred to in paragraph 1 or the communication referred to in paragraph 4. This request must be justified on the basis of considerations relating to the competition rules of the Treaty.

6. The Commission may withdraw its opposition to the exemption at any time. However, where that opposition was raised at the request of a Member State, it may be withdrawn only after consultation of the advisory Committee on Restrictive Practices and Dominant Positions.

7. If the opposition is withdrawn because the undertakings concerned have shown that the conditions of Article 85(3) are fulfilled, the exemption shall apply from the date of the notification.

8. If the opposition is withdrawn because the undertakings concerned have amended the agreement so that the conditions of Article 85(3) are fulfilled, the exemption shall apply from the date on which the amendments take effect.

9. If the Commission opposes exemption and its opposition is not withdrawn, the effects of the notification shall be governed by the provisions of Regulation No. 17.

Article 7

1. Information acquired pursuant to Article 6 shall be used only for the purposes of this Regulation.

2. The Commission and the authorities of the Member States, their officials and other servants shall not disclose information acquired by them pursuant to this Regulation of a kind that is covered by the obligation of professional secrecy.

3. Paragraphs 1 and 2 shall not prevent publication of general information or surveys which do not contain information relating to particular undertakings or associations of undertakings.

Article 8

The Commission may withdraw the benefit of this Regulation, pursuant to Article 7 of Regulation No. 19/65/EEC, where it finds in a particular case that an agreement exempted by this Regulation nevertheless has certain effects which are incompatible with the conditions laid down in Article 85(3) of the EEC Treaty, and in particular where territorial protection is awarded to the franchisee and:

(a) access to the relevant market or competition therein is significantly restricted by the cumulative effect of parallel networks of similar agreements established by competing manufacturers or distributors;

(b) the goods or services which are the subject-matter of the franchise do not face, in a substantial part of the common market, effective competition from goods or services which are identical or considered by users as equivalent in view of their characteristics, price and intended use;

(c) the parties, or one of them, prevent end users, because of their place of residence, from obtaining, directly or through intermediaries, the goods or services which are the subject-matter of the franchise within the common market, or use differences in specifications concerning those goods or services in different Member States, to isolate markets;

(d) franchisees engage in concerted practices relating to the sale prices of the goods or services which are the subject-matter of the franchise;

(e) the franchisor uses its right to check the contract premises and means of transport, or refuses its agreement to requests by the franchisee to move the contract premises or assign its rights and obligations under the franchise agreement, for reasons other than protecting the franchisor's industrial or intellectual property rights, maintaining the common identity and reputation of the franchised network or verifying that the franchisee abides by its obligations under the agreement.

Article 9

This Regulation shall enter into force on 1 February 1989.
It shall remain in force until 31 December 1999.

This Regulation shall be binding in its entirety and directly applicable in all Member States.
Done at Brussels, 30 November 1988.

APPENDIX C.6   COMMISSION NOTICE CONCERNING REGULATIONS 1983/83 AND 1984/83

C.6-01   On the application of Article 85(3) of the Treaty to categories of exclusive distribution and exclusive purchasing agreements

([1984] O.J. C101/02, AS MODIFIED, [1992] O.J. C121/2)

I. Introduction

1. Commission Regulation No. 67/67/EEC of 22 March 1967 on the application of Article 85(3) of the Treaty to certain categories of exclusive dealing agreements expired on 30 June 1983 after being in force for over 15 years. With Regulations (EEC) No. 1983/83 and (EEC) No. 1984/83, the Commission has adapted the block exemption of exclusive distribution agreements and exclusive purchasing agreements to the intervening developments in the common market and in Community law. Several of the provisions in the new Regulations are new. A certain amount of interpretative guidance is therefore called for. This will assist undertakings in bringing their agreements into line with the new legal requirements and will also help ensure that the Regulations are applied uniformly in all the Member States.

2. In determining how a given provision is to be applied, one must take into account, in addition to the ordinary meaning of the words used, the intention of the provision as this emerges from the preamble. For further guidance, reference should be made to the principles that have been evolved in the case-law of the Court of Justice of the European Communities and in the Commission's decisions on individual cases.

3. This notice sets out the main considerations which will determine the Commission's view of whether or not an exclusive distribution or purchasing agreement is covered by the block exemption. The notice is without prejudice to the jurisdiction of natural courts to apply the Regulations, although it may well be of persuasive authority in proceedings before such courts. Nor does the notice necessarily indicate the interpretation which might be given to the provisions by the Court of Justice.

II. Exclusive distribution and exclusive purchasing agreements (Regulations (EEC) No. 1983/83 and (EEC) No. 1984/83)

1. Similarities and differences

4. Regulations (EEC) No. 1983/83 and (EEC) No. 1984/83 are both concerned with exclusive agreements between two undertakings for the purpose of the resale of goods. Each deals with a particular type of such agreements. Regulation (EEC) No. 1983/83 applies to exclusive distribution agreements, Regulation (EEC) No. 1984/83 to exclusive purchasing agreements. The distinguishing feature of exclusive distribution agreements is that one party, the supplier, allots to the other, the reseller, a defined territory (the contract territory) in which the reseller has to concentrate his sales effort, and in return undertakes not to supply any other reseller in that territory. In exclusive purchasing agreements, the reseller agrees to purchase the contract goods only from the other party and not from any other supplier. The supplier is entitled to supply other resellers in the same sales area and at the same level of distribution. Unlike an exclusive distributor, the tied reseller is not protected against competition from other resellers who, like himself, receive the contract goods direct from the supplier. On the other hand, he is free of restrictions as to the area over which he may make his sales effort.

5. In keeping with their common starting point, the Regulations have many provisions that are the same or similar in both Regulations. This is true of the basic provision in Article 1, in which the respective subject-matters of the block exemption, the exclusive supply or purchasing obligation, are defined, and of the exhaustive list of restrictions of competition which may be agreed in addition to the exclusive supply or purchasing obligation (Article 2(1) and (2)), the non-exhaustive enumeration of other obligations which do not prejudice the block exemption (Article 2(3)), the inapplicability of the block exemption in principle to exclusive agreements between competing manufacturers (Article 3(a) and (b), 4 and 5), the withdrawal of the block exemption in individual cases (Article 6 of Regulation (EEC) No. 1983/83 and Article 14 of Regulation (EEC) No. 1984/83), the transitional provisions (Article 7 of Regulation (EEC) No. 1983/83 and Article 15(1) of Regulation (EEC) No. 1984/83), and the inclusion of concerted practices within the scope of the Regulations (Article 9 of Regulation (EEC) No. 1983/83 and Article 18 of Regulation (EEC) No. 1984/83). In so far as their wording permits, these parallel provisions are to be interpreted in the same way.

6. Different rules are laid down in the Regulations wherever they need to take account of matters which are peculiar to the exclusive distribution agreements or exclusive purchasing agreements respectively. This applies in Regulation (EEC) No. 1983/83, to the provisions regarding the obligation on the exclusive distributor not actively to promote sales outside the contract territory (Article 2(2)(c)) and the inapplicability of the block exemption to agreements which give the exclusive distributor absolute territorial protection (Article 3(c) and (d)) and, in Regulation (EEC) No. 1984/83, to the provisions limiting the scope and duration of the block exemption for exclusive purchasing agreements in general (Article 3(c) and (d)) and for beer-supply and service-station agreements in particular (Titles II and III).

7. The scope of the two Regulations has been defined so as to avoid any overlap (Article 16 of Regulation (EEC) No. 1984/83).

2. Basic provision

(Article 1)

8. Both Regulations apply only to agreements entered into for the purpose of the resale of goods to which not more than two undertakings are party.
(a) "For resale"

9. The notion of resale requires that the goods concerned be disposed of by the purchasing party to others in return for consideration. Agreements on the supply or purchase of goods which the purchasing party transforms or processes into other goods or uses or consumes in manufacturing other goods are not agreements for resale. The same applies to the supply of components which are combined with other components into a different product. The criterion is that with other components into a different product. The criterion is that the goods distributed by the reseller are the same as

those the other party has supplied to him for that purpose. The economic identity of the goods is not affected if the reseller merely breaks up and packages the goods in smaller quantities, or repackages them, before resale.

10. Where the reseller performs additional operations to improve the quality, durability, appearance or taste of the goods (such as rust-proofing of metals, sterilization of food or the addition of colouring matter of flavourings to drugs), the position will mainly depend on how much value the operation adds to the goods. Only a slight addition in value can be taken not to change the economic identity of the goods. In determining the precise dividing line in individual cases, trade usage in particular must be considered. The Commission applies the same principles to agreements under which the reseller is supplied with a concentrated extract for a drink which he has to dilute with water, pure alcohol or another liquid and to bottle before reselling.
(b) "Goods"

11. Exclusive agreements for the supply of services rather than the resale of goods are not covered by the Regulations. The block exemption still applies, however, where the reseller provides customer or after-sales services incidental to the resale of the goods. Nevertheless, a case where the charge for the service is higher than the price of the goods would fall outside the scope of the Regulations.

12. The hiring out of goods in return for payment comes closer, economically speaking, to a resale of goods than to provision of services. The Commission therefore regards exclusive agreements under which the purchasing party hires out or leases to others the goods supplied to him as covered by the Regulations.
(c) "Only two undertakings party"

13. To be covered by the block exemption, the exclusive distribution or purchasing agreement must be between only one supplier and one reseller in each case. Several undertakings forming one economic unit count as one undertaking.

14. This limitation on the number of undertakings that may be party relates solely to the individual agreement. A supplier does not lose the benefit of the block exemption if he enters into exclusive distribution or purchasing agreements covering the same goods with several resellers.

15. The supplier may delegate the performance of his contractual obligations to a connected or independent undertaking which he has entrusted with the distribution of his goods, so that the reseller has to purchase the contract goods from the latter undertaking. This principle is expressly mentioned only in Regulation (EEC) No. 1984/83 (Article 1, 6 and 10), because the question of delegation arises mainly in connection with exclusive purchasing agreements. It also applies, however, to exclusive distribution agreements under Regulation (EEC) No. 1983/83.

16. The involvement of undertakings other than the contracting parties must be confined to the execution of deliveries. The parties may accept exclusive supply or purchase obligations only for themselves, and not impose them on third parties, since otherwise more than two undertakings would be party to the agreement. The obligation of the parties to ensure that the obligations they have accepted are respected by connected undertakings is, however, covered by the block exemption.

3. Other restrictions on competition that are exempted

(Article 2(1) and (2))

17. Apart from the exclusive supply obligation (Regulation (EEC) No. 1983/83) or exclusive purchase obligation (Regulation (EEC) No. 1984/83), obligations defined in Article 1 which must be present if the block exemption is to apply, the only other restrictions of competition that may be agreed by the parties are those set out in Article 2(1) and (2). If they agree on further obligations restrictive of competition, the agreement as a whole is no longer covered by the block exemption and requires individual exemption. For example, an agreement will exceed the bounds of the Regulations if the parties relinquish the possibility of independently determining their prices or conditions of business or undertake to refrain from, or even prevent, cross-border trade, which the

Regulations expressly state must not be impeded. Among other clauses which in general are not permissible under the Regulations are those which impede the reseller in his free choice of customers.

18. The obligations restrictive of competition that are exempted may be agreed only for the duration of the agreement. This also applies to restrictions accepted by the supplier or reseller on competing with the other party.

4. Obligations upon the reseller which do not prejudice the block exemption

(Article 2(3))

19. The obligations cited in this provision are examples of clauses which generally do not restrict competition. Undertakings are therefore free to include one, several or all of these obligations in their agreements. However, the obligations may not be formulated or applied in such a way as to take on the character of restrictions of competition that are not permitted. To forestall this danger, Article 2(3)(b) of Regulation (EEC) No. 1984/83 expressly allows minimum purchase obligations only for goods that are subject to an exclusive purchasing obligation.

20. As part of the obligation to take measures for promotion of sales and in particular to maintain a distribution network (Article 2(3)(c) of Regulation (EEC) No. 1983/83 and Article 2(3)(d) of Regulation (EEC) No. 1984/83), the reseller may be forbidden to supply the contract goods to unsuitable dealers. Such clauses are unobjectionable if admission to the distribution network is based on objective criteria of a qualitative nature relating to the professional qualifications of the owner of the business or his staff or the suitability of his business premises, if the criteria are the same for all potential dealers, and if the criteria are actually applied in a non-discriminatory manner. Distribution systems which do not fulfil these conditions are not covered by the block exemption.

5. Inapplicability of the block exemption to exclusive agreements between competing manufacturers

(Articles 3(a) and (b), 4 and 5)

21. The block exemption does not apply if either the parties themselves or undertakings connected with them are manufacturers, manufacture goods belonging to the same product market, and enter into exclusive distribution or purchasing agreements with one another in respect of those goods. Only identical or equivalent goods are regarded as belonging to the same product market. The goods in question must be interchangeable. Whether or not this is the case must be judged from the vantage point of the user, normally taking the characteristics, price and intended use of the goods together. In certain cases, however, goods can form a separate market on the basis of their characteristics, their price or their intended use alone. This is true especially where consumer preferences have developed. The above provisions are applicable regardless of whether or not the parties or the undertakings connected with them are based in the Community and whether or not they are already actually in competition with one another in the relevant goods inside or outside the Community.

22. In principle, both reciprocal and non-reciprocal exclusive agreements between competing manufacturers are not covered by the block exemption and are therefore subject to individual scrutiny of their compatibility with Article 85 of the Treaty, but there is an exception for non-reciprocal agreements of the abovementioned kind where one or both of the parties are undertakings with a total annual turnover of no more than 100 million ECU (Article 3(b)). Annual turnover is used as a measure of the economic strength of the undertakings involved. Therefore, the aggregate turnover from goods and services of all types, and not only from the contract goods, is to be taken. Turnover taxes and other turnover-related levies are not included in turnover. Where a party belongs to a group of connected undertakings, the world-wide turnover of the group, excluding intragroup sales (Article 5(3)), is to be used.

23. The total turnover limit can be exceeded during any period of two successive financial years by up to 10 per cent. without loss of the block exemption. The block exemption is lost if, at the end of the second financial year, the total turnover over the preceding two years has been over 220 million ECU (Article 5(2)).

6. Withdrawal of the block exemption in individual cases

(Article 6 of Regulation (EEC) No. 1983/83 and Article 14 of Regulation (EEC) No. 1984/83)

24. The situations described are meant as illustrations of the sort of situations in which the Commission can exercise its powers under Article 7 of Council Regulation No. 19/65/EEC to withdraw a block exemption. The benefit of the block exemption can only be withdrawn by a decision in an individual case following proceedings under Regulation No. 17. Such a decision cannot have retroactive effect. It may be coupled with an individual exemption subject to conditions or obligations or, in an extreme case, with the finding of an infringement and an order to bring it to an end.

7. Transitional provisions

(Article 7 of Regulation (EEC) No. 1983/83 and Article 15(1) of Regulation (EEC) No. 1984/83)

25. Exclusive distribution or exclusive purchasing agreements which were concluded and entered into force before 1 January 1984 continue to be exempted under the provisions of Regulation No. 67/67/EEC until 31 December 1986. Should the parties wish to apply such agreements beyond 1 January 1987, they will either have to bring them into line with the provisions of the new Regulations or to notify them to the Commission. Special rules apply in the case of beer-supply and service-station agreements (see paragraphs 64 and 65 below).

8. Concerted practices

(Article 9 of Regulation (EEC) No. 1983/83 and Article 18 of Regulation (EEC) No. 1984/83)

26. These provisions bring within the scope of the Regulations exclusive distribution and purchasing arrangements which are operated by undertakings but are not the subject of a legally-binding agreement.

III. Exclusive distribution agreements (Regulation (EEC) No. 1983/83)

1. Exclusive supply obligation

(Article 1)

27. The exclusive supply obligation does not prevent the supplier from providing the contract goods to other resellers who afterwards sell them in the exclusive distributor's territory. It makes no difference whether the other dealers concerned are established outside or inside the territory. The supplier is not in breach of his obligation to the exclusive distributor provided that he supplies the resellers who wish to sell the contract goods in the territory only at their request and that the goods are handed over outside the territory. It does not matter whether the reseller takes delivery of the goods himself or through an intermediary, such as a freight forwarder. However, supplies of this nature are only permissible if the reseller and not the supplier pays the transport costs of the goods into the contract territory.

28. The goods supplied to the exclusive distributor must be intended for resale, in the contract territory. This basic requirement does not, however, mean that the exclusive distributor cannot sell

the contract goods to customers outside his contract territory should he receive orders from them. Under Article 2(2)(c), the supplier can prohibit him only from seeking customers in other areas, but not from supplying them.

29. It would also be incompatible with the Regulation for the exclusive distributor to be restricted to supplying only certain categories of customers (*e.g.* specialist retailers) in his contract territory and prohibited from supplying other categories (*e.g.* department stores), which are supplied by other resellers appointed by the supplier for that purpose.

2. Restriction on competition by the supplier

(Article 2(1))

30. The restriction on the supplier himself, supplying the contract goods to final users in the exclusive distributor's contract territory need not be absolute. Clauses permitting the supplier to supply certain customers in the territory—with or without payment of compensation to the exclusive distributor—are compatible with the block exemption provided the customers in question are not resellers. The supplier remains free to supply the contract goods outside the contract territory to final users based in the territory. In this case the position is the same as for dealers (see paragraph 27 above).

3. Inapplicability of the block exemption in cases of absolute territorial protection

(Articles 3(c) and (d)).

31. The block exemption cannot be claimed for agreements that give the exclusive distributor absolute territorial protection. If the situation described in Article 3(c) obtains, the parties must ensure either that the contract goods can be sold in the contract territory by parallel importers or that users have a real possibility of obtaining them from undertakings outside the contract territory, if necessary outside the Community, at the prices and on the terms there prevailing. The supplier can represent an alternative source of supply for the purposes of this provision if he is prepared to supply the contract goods on request to final users located in the contract territory.

32. Article 3(d) is chiefly intended to safeguard the freedom of dealers and users to obtain the contract goods in other Member States. Action to impede imports into the Community from third countries will only lead to loss of the block exemption if there are no alternative sources of supply in the Community. This situation can arise especially where the exclusive distributor's contract territory covers the whole or the major part of the Community.

33. The block exemption ceases to apply as from the moment that either of the parties takes measures to impede parallel imports into the contract territory. Agreements in which the supplier undertakes with the exclusive distributor to prevent his other customers from supplying into the contract territory are ineligible for the block exemption from the outset. This is true even if the parties agree only to prevent imports into the Community from third countries. In this case it is immaterial whether or not there are alternative sources of supply in the Community. The inapplicability of the block exemption follows from the mere fact that the agreement contains restrictions on competition which are not covered by Article 2(1).

IV. Exclusive purchasing agreements (Regulation (EEC) No. 1984/83)

1. Structure of the Regulation

34. Title I of the Regulation contains general provisions for exclusive purchasing agreements and Titles II and III special provisions for beer supply and service-station agreements. The latter types

of agreement are governed exclusively by the special provisions, some of which (Articles 9 and 13), however, refer to some of the general provisions, Article 17 also excludes the combination of agreements of the kind referred to in Title I with those of the kind referred to in Titles II or III to which the same undertakings or undertakings connected with them are party. To prevent any avoidance of the special provisions for beer-supply and service-station agreements, it is also made clear that the provisions governing the exclusive distribution of goods do not apply to agreements entered into for the resale of drinks on premises used for the sale or consumption of beer or for the resale of petroleum products in service stations (Article 8 of Regulation (EEC) No. 1983/83).

2. Exclusive purchasing obligation

(Article 1)

35. The Regulation only covers agreements whereby the reseller agrees to purchase all his requirements for the contract goods from the other party. If the purchasing obligation relates to only part of such requirements, the block exemption does not apply. Clauses which allow the reseller to obtain the contract goods from other suppliers, should these sell them more cheaply or on more favourable terms than the other party are still covered by the block exemption. The same applies to clauses releasing the reseller from his exclusive purchasing obligation should the other party be unable to supply.

36. The contract goods must be specified by brand or denomination in the agreement. Only if this is done will it be possible to determine the precise scope of the reseller's exclusive purchasing obligation (Article 1) and of the ban on dealing in competing products (Article 2(2)).

3. Restriction on competition by the supplier

(Article 2(1))

37. This provision allows the reseller to protect himself against direct competition from the supplier in his principal sales area. The reseller's principal sales area is determined by his normal business activity. It may be more closely defined in the agreement. However, the supplier cannot be forbidden to supply dealers who obtain the contract goods outside this area and afterwards resell them to customers inside it or to appoint other resellers in the area.

4. Limits of the block exemption

(Article 3(c) and (d))

38. Article 3(c) provides that the exclusive purchasing obligation can be agreed for one or more products, but in the latter case the products must be so related as to be thought of as belonging to the same range of goods. The relationship can be founded on technical (e.g., a machine, accessories and spare parts for it) or commercial grounds (e.g. several products used for the same purpose) or on usage in the trade (different goods that are customarily offered for sale together). In the latter case, regard must be had to the usual practice at the reseller's level of distribution on the relevant market, taking into account all relevant dealers and not only particular forms of distribution. Exclusive purchasing agreements covering goods which do not belong together can only be exempted from the competition rules by an individual decision.

39. Under Article 3(d), exclusion purchasing agreements concluded for an indefinite period are not covered by the block exemption. Agreements which specify a fixed term but are automatically renewable unless one of the parties gives notice to terminate are to be considered to have been concluded for an indefinite period.

V. Beer-supply agreements (Title II of Regulation (EEC) No. 1984/83)

1. Agreements of minor importance

40. It is recalled that the Commission's notice on agreements of minor importance states that the Commission holds the view that agreements between undertakings do not fall under the prohibition of Article 85(1) of the EEC Treaty if certain conditions as regards market share and turnover are met by the undertakings concerned. Thus, it is evident that when an undertaking, brewery or wholesaler, surpasses the limits as laid down in the above notice, the agreements concluded by it may all under Article 85(1) of the EEC Treaty. The notice, however, does not apply where in a relevant market competition is restricted by the cumulative effects of parallel networks of similar agreements which would not individually fall under Article 85(1) of the EEC Treaty if the notice as applicable. Since the markets for beer will frequently be characterized by the existence of cumulative effects, it seems appropriate to determine which agreements can nevertheless be considered *de minimis*.

The Commission is of the opinion that an exclusive beer supply agreement concluded by a brewery, in the sense of Article 6, and including Article 8(2) of Regulation (EEC) 1984/83 does not, in general, fall under Article 85(1) of the EEC Treaty if

— the market share of that brewery is not higher than 1% on the national market for the resale of beer in premises used for the sale and consumption of drinks, and
— if that brewery does not produce more than 200 000 hl of beer per annum.

However, these principles do not apply if the agreement in question is concluded for more than 7 and a half years in as far as it covers beer and other drinks, and for 15 years if it covers only beer.

In order to establish the market share of the brewery and its annual production, the provisions of Article 4(2) of Regulation (EEC) 1984/83 apply.

As regards exclusive beer supply agreements in the sense of Article 6, and including Article 8(2) of Regulation (EEC) 1984/83 which are concluded by wholesalers, the above principles apply *mutatis mutandis* by taking account of the position of the brewery whose beer is the main subject of the agreement in question.

The present communication does not preclude that in individual cases even agreements between undertakings which do not fulfill the above criteria, in particular where the number of outlets tied to them is limited as compared to the number of outlets existing on the market, may still have only a negligible effect on trade between Member States or on competition, and would therefore not be caught by Article 85(1) of the EEC Treaty.

Neither does this communication in any Prejudge the application of nation law to the agreements covered by it.

2. Exclusive purchasing obligation

(Article 6)

41. The beers and other drinks covered by the exclusive purchasing obligation must be specified by brand or denomination in the agreement. An exclusive purchasing obligation can only be imposed on the reseller for drinks which the supplier carries at the time the contract takes effect and provided that they are supplied in the quantities required, at sufficiently regular intervals and at prices and on conditions allowing normal sales to the consumer. Any extension of the exclusive purchasing obligation to drinks not specified in the agreement requires an additional agreement, which must likewise satisfy the requirements of Title II of the Regulation. A change in the brand or denomination of a drink which in other respects remains unchanged does not constitute such an extension of the exclusive purchasing obligation.

42. The exclusive purchasing obligation can be agreed in respect of one or more premises used for the sale and consumption of drinks which the reseller runs at the time the contract takes effect. The name and location of the premises must be stated in the agreement. Any extension of the exclusive purchasing obligation to other such premises requires an additional agreement, which must likewise satisfy the provisions of Title II of the Regulation.

43. The concept of "premises used for the sale and consumption of drinks" covers any licensed premises used for this purpose. Private clubs are also included. Exclusive purchasing agreements

between the supplier and the operator of an off-licence shop are governed by the provisions of Title I of the Regulation.

44. Special commercial or financial advantages are those going beyond what the reseller could normally expect under an agreement. The explanations given in the 13th recital are illustrations. Whether or not the supplier is affording the reseller special advantages depends on the nature, extent and duration of the obligation undertaken by the parties. In doubtful cases usage in the trade is the decisive element.

45. The reseller can enter into exclusive purchasing obligations both with a brewery in respect of beers of a certain type and with a drinks wholesaler in respect of beers of another types and/or other drinks. The two agreements can be combined into one document. Article 6 also covers cases where the drinks wholesaler performs several functions at once: signing the first agreement on the brewery's and the second on his own behalf and also undertaking delivery of all the drinks. The provisions of Title II do not apply to the contractual relations between the brewery and the drinks wholesaler.

46. Article 6(2) makes the block exemption also applicable to cases in which the supplier affords the owner of premises financial or other help in equipping them as a public house, restaurant, etc., and in return the owner imposes on the buyer or tenant of the premise an exclusive purchasing obligation in favour of the supplier. A similar situation, economically speaking, is the transmission of an exclusive purchasing obligation from the owner of a public house to his successor. Under Article 8(1)(e) this is also, in principle, permissible.

3. Other restrictions of competition that are exempted

(Article 7)

47. The list of permitted obligations given in Article 7 is exhaustive. If any further obligations restricting competition are imposed on the reseller, the exclusive purchasing agreement as a whole is no longer covered by the block exemption.

48. The obligation referred to in paragraph 1(a) applies only so long as the supplier is able to supply the beers or other drinks specified in the agreement and subject to the exclusive purchasing obligation in sufficient quantities to cover the demand the reseller anticipates for the products from his customers.

49. Under paragraph 1(b), the reseller is entitled to sell beer of other types in draught form if the other party has tolerated this in the past. If this is not the case, the reseller must indicate that there is sufficient demand from his customers to warrant the sale of other draught beers. The demand must be deemed sufficient if it can be satisfied without a simultaneous drop in sales of the beers specified in the exclusive purchasing agreement. It is definitely not sufficient if sales of the additional draught beer turn out to be slow that there is a danger of its quality deteriorating. It is for the reseller to assess the potential demand of his customers for other types of beer; after all, he bears the risk if his forecasts are wrong.

50. The provision in paragraph 1(c) is not only intended to ensure the possibility of advertising products supplied by other undertakings to the minimum extent necessary in any given circumstances. The advertising of such products should also reflect their relative importance *vis-à-vis* the competing products of the supplier who is party to the exclusive purchasing agreement. Advertising for products which the public house has just begun to sell may not be excluded or unduly impeded.

51. The Commission believes that the designations of types customary in inter-State trade and within the individual Member States may afford useful pointers to the interpretation of Article 7(2). Nevertheless the alternative criteria stated in the provision itself are decisive. In doubtful cases, whether or not two beers are clearly distinguishable by their composition, appearance or taste depends on custom at the place where the public house is situated. The parties may, if they wish, jointly appoint an expert to decide the matter.

4. Agreements excluded from the block exemption

(Article 8)

52. The reseller's right to purchase drinks from third parties may be restricted only to the extent allowed by Articles 6 and 7. In his purchases of goods other than drinks and in his procurement of services which are not directly connected with the supply of drinks by the other party, the reseller must remain free to choose his supplier. Under Article 8(1)(a) and (b), any action by the other party or by an undertaking connected with or appointed by him or acting at his instigation or with his agreement to prevent the reseller exercising his rights in this regard will entail the loss of the block exemption. For the purposes of these provisions it makes no difference whether the reseller's freedom is restricted by contract, informal understanding, economic pressures or other practical measures.

53. The installation of amusement machines in tenanted public houses may by agreement be made subject to the owner's permission. The owner may refuse permission on the ground that this would impair the character of the premises or he may restrict the tenant to particular types of machines. However, the practice of some owners of tenanted public houses to allow the tenant to conclude contracts for the installation of such machines only with certain undertakings which the owner recommends is, as a rule, incompatible with this Regulation, unless the undertakings are selected on the basis of objective criteria of a qualitative nature that are the same for all potential providers of such equipment and are applied in a non-discriminatory manner. Such criteria may refer to the reliability of the undertaking and its staff and the quality of the services it provides. The supplier may not prevent a public house tenant from purchasing amusement machines rather than renting them.

54. The limitation of the duration of the agreement in Article 8(1)(c) and (d) does not affect the parties' right to renew their agreement in accordance with the provisions of Title II of the Regulation.

55. Article 8(2)(b) must be interpreted in the light both of the aims of the Community competition rules and of the general legal principle whereby contracting parties must exercise their rights in good faith.

56. Whether or not a third undertaking offers certain drinks covered by the exclusive purchasing obligation on more favourable terms than the other party for the purposes of the first indent of Article 8(2)(b) is to be judged in the first instance on the basis of a comparison of prices. This should take into account the various factors that go to determine the prices. If a more favourable offer is available and the tenant wishes to accept it, he must inform the other party of his intentions without delay so that the other party has an opportunity of matching the terms offered by the third undertaking. If the other party refuses to do so or fails to let the tenant have his decision within a short period, the tenant is entitled to purchase the drinks from the other undertaking. The Commission will ensure that exercise of the brewery's or drinks wholesaler's right to match the prices quoted by another supplier does not make it significantly harder for other suppliers to enter the market.

57. The tenant's right provided for in the second indent of Article 8(2)(b) to purchase drinks or another brand or denomination from third undertakings obtains in cases where the other party does not offer them. Here the tenant is not under a duty to inform the other party of his intentions.

58. The tenant's rights arising from Article 8(2)(b) override any obligation to purchase minimum quantities imposed upon him under Article 9 in conjunction with Article 2(3)(b) to the extent that this is necessary to allow the tenant full exercise of those rights.

VI. Service-station agreements (Title III of Regulation (EEC) No. 1984/83)

1. Exclusive purchasing obligation

(Article 10)

59. The exclusive purchasing obligation can cover either motor vehicle fuels (*e.g.*, petrol, diesel fuel, LPG, kerosene) alone or motor vehicle fuels and other fuels, (*e.g.*, heating oil, bottled gas, paraffin). All the goods concerned must be petroleum-based products.

60. The motor vehicle fuels covered by the exclusive purchasing obligations must be for use in motor-powered land or water vehicles or aircraft. The term "service station" is to be interpreted in a correspondingly wide sense.

61. The Regulation applies to petrol stations adjoining public roads and fuelling installations on private property not open to public traffic.

2. Other restrictions on competition that are exempted

(Article 11)

62. Under Article 11(b) only the use of lubricants and related petroleum-based products supplied by other undertakings can be prohibited. This provision refers to the servicing and maintenance of motor vehicles, *i.e.* to the reseller's activity in the field of provision of services. It does not affect the reseller's freedom to purchase the said products from other undertakings for resale in the service station. the petroleum-based products related to lubricants referred to in paragraph (b) are additives and brake fluids.

63. For the interpretation of Article 11(c), the considerations stated in paragraph 49 above apply by analogy.

3. Agreements excluded from the block exemption

(Article 12)

64. These provisions are analogous to those of Article 8(1)(a), (b), (d) and (e) and 8(2)(a). Reference is therefore made to paragraphs 51 and 53 above.

VII. Transitional provisions for beer-supply and service-station agreements (Article 15(2) and (3))

65. Under Article 15(2), all beer-supply and service-station agreements which were concluded and entered into force before 1 January 1984 remain covered by the provision of Regulation No. 67/67/EEC until 31 December 1988. From 1 January 1989 they must comply with the provisions of Titles II and III of Regulation (EEC) No. 1984/83. Under Article 15(3), in the case of agreements which were in force on 1 July 1983, the same principle applies except that the 10-year maximum duration for such agreements laid down in Article 8(1)(d) and Article 12(1)(c) may be exceeded.

66. The sole requirement for the eligible beer-supply and service-station agreements to continue to enjoy the block exemption beyond 1 January 1989 is that they be brought into line with the new provisions. It is left to the undertakings concerned how they do so. One way is for the parties to agree to amend the original agreement, another for the supplier unilaterally to release the reseller from all obligations that would prevent the application of the block exemption after 1 January 1989. The latter method is only mentioned in Article 15(3) in relation to agreements in force on 1 July 1983. However, there is no reason why this possibility should not also be open to parties to agreements entered into between 1 July 1983 and 1 January 1984.

67. Parties lose the benefit of application of the transitional provisions if they extend the scope of their agreement as regards persons, places or subject matter, or incorporate into it additional obligations restrictive of competition. The agreement then counts as a new agreement. The same applies if the parties substantially change the nature or extent of their obligations to one another. A substantial change in this sense includes a revision of the purchase price of the goods supplied to the reseller or of the rent for a public house or service station which goes beyond mere adjustment to the changing economic environment.

Appendix D

D.1-01 On the application of Article 85(3) of the Treaty to categories of research and development agreements

([1985] O.J. L53/5, AS AMENDED, [1993] O.J. L21/10)

THE COMMISSION OF THE EUROPEAN COMMUNITIES,

Having regard to the Treaty establishing the European Economic Community,

Having regard to Council Regulation (EEC) No. 2821/71 of 20 December 1971 on the application of Article 85(3) of the Treaty to categories of agreements, decisions and concerted practices, as last amended by the Act of Accession of Greece, and in particular Article 1 thereof,

Having published a draft of this Regulation,

Having consulted the Advisory Committee on Restrictive Practices and Dominant Positions,

Whereas:

(1) Regulation (EEC) No.2821/71 empowers the Commission to apply Article 85(3) of the Treaty by Regulation to certain categories of agreements, decisions and concerted practices falling within the scope of Article 85(1) which have as their object the research and development of products or processes up to the stage of industrial application, and exploitation of the results, including provisions regarding industrial property rights and confidential technical knowledge.

(2) As stated in the Commission's 1968 notice, concerning agreements, decisions and concerted practices in the field of cooperation between enterprises, agreements on the joint execution of research work or the joint development of the results of the research, up to but not including the stage of industrial application, generally do not fall within the scope of Article 85(1) of the Treaty. In certain circumstances, however, such as where the parties agree not to carry out other research and development in the same field, thereby forgoing the opportunity of gaining competitive advantages over the other parties, such agreements may fall within Article 85(1) and should therefore not be excluded from this Regulation.

(3) Agreements providing for both joint research and development and joint exploitation of the results may fall within Article 85(1) because the parties jointly determine how the products developed are manufactured or the processes developed are applied or how related intellectual property rights or know-how are exploited.

(4) Cooperation in research and development and in the exploitation of the results generally promotes technical and economic progress by increasing the dissemination of technical knowledge between the parties and avoiding duplication of research and development work, by stimulating new advances through the exchange of complementary technical knowledge, and by rationalizing the manufacture of the products or application of the processes arising out of the research and development. These aims can be achieved only where the research and development programme and its objectives are clearly defined and each of the parties is given the opportunity of exploiting any of the results of the programme that interest it; where universities or research institutes participate and are not interested in the industrial exploitation of the results, however, it may be agreed that they may use the said results solely for the purpose of further research.

(5) Consumers can generally be expected to benefit from the increased volume and effectiveness of research and development through the introduction of new or improved products or services or the reduction of prices brought about by new or improved processes.

(6) This Regulation must specify the restrictions of competition which may be included in the exempted agreements. The purpose of the permitted restrictions is to concentrate the research activities of the parties in order to improve their chances of success, and to facilitate the introduction of new products and services onto the market. These restrictions are generally necessary to secure the desired benefits for the parties and consumers.

(7) The joint exploitation of results can be considered as the natural consequence of joint research and development. It can take different forms ranging from manufacture to the exploitation of intellectual property rights or know-how that substantially contributes to technical or economic progress. In order to attain the benefits and objectives described above and to justify the restrictions of competition which are exempted, the joint exploitation must relate to products or processes for which the use of the results of the research and development is decisive. Joint exploitation is not therefore justified where it relates to improvements which were not made within the framework of a joint research and development programme but under an agreement having some other principal objective, such as the licensing of intellectual property rights, joint manufacture or specialization, and merely containing ancillary provisions on joint research and development.

(8) The exemption granted under the Regulation must be limited to agreements which do not afford the undertakings the possibility of eliminating competition in respect of a substantial part of the products in question. In order to guarantee that several independent poles of research can exist in the common market in any economic sector, it is necessary to exclude from the block exemption agreements between competitors whose combined share of the market for products capable of being improved or replaced by the results of the research and development exceeds a certain level at the time the agreement is entered into.

(9) In order to guarantee the maintenance of effective competition during joint exploitation of the results, it is necessary to provide that the block exemption will cease to apply if the parties' combined shares of the market for the products arising out of the joint research and development become too great. However, it should be provided that the exemption will continue to apply, irrespective of the parties' market shares, for a certain period after the commencement of joint exploitation, so as to await stabilization of their market shares, particularly after the introduction of an entirely new product, and to guarantee a minimum period of return on the generally substantial investments involved.

(10) Agreements between undertakings which do not fulfil the market share conditions laid down in the Regulation may, in appropriate cases, be granted an exemption by individual decision, which will in particular take account of world competition and the particular circumstances prevailing in the manufacture of high technology products.

(11) It is desirable to list in the Regulation a number of obligations that are commonly found in research and development agreements but that are normally not restrictive of competition and to provide that, in the event that, because of the particular economic or legal circumstances, they should fall within Article 85(1), they also would be covered by the exemption. This list is not exhaustive.

(12) The Regulation must specify what provisions may not be included in agreements if these are to benefit from the block exemption by virtue of the fact that such provisions are restrictions falling within Article 85(1) for which there can be no general presumption that they will lead to the positive effects required by Article 85(3).

(13) Agreements which are not automatically covered by the exemption because they include provisions that are not expressly exempted by the Regulation and are not expressly excluded from exemption are none the less capable of benefiting from the general presumption of compatibility with Article 85(3) on which the block exemption is based. It will be possible for the Commission rapidly to establish whether this is the case for a particular agreement. Such an agreement should therefore be deemed to be covered by the exemption provided for in this Regulation where it is notified to the Commission and the Commission does not oppose the application of the exemption within a specified period of time.

(14) Agreements covered by this Regulation may also take advantage of provisions contained in other block exemption Regulations of the Commission, and in particular Regulation (EEC) No.

417/85 on specialization agreements, Regulation (EEC) No. 1983/83 on exclusive distribution agreements, Regulation (EEC) No. 1984/83, on exclusive purchasing agreements and Regulation (EEC) No. 2349/84, on patent licensing agreements, if they fulfil the conditions set out in these Regulations. The provisions of the aforementioned Regulations are, however, not applicable in so far as this Regulation contains specific rules.

(15) If individual agreements exempted by this Regulation nevertheless have effects which are incompatible with Article 85(3), the Commission may withdraw the benefit of the block exemption.

(16) The Regulation should apply with retroactive effect to agreements in existence when the Regulation comes into force where such agreements already fulfil its conditions or are modified to do so. The benefit of these provisions may not be claimed in actions pending at the date of entry into force of this Regulation, nor may it be relied on as grounds for claims for damages against third parties.

(17) Since research and development cooperation agreements are often of a long-term nature, especially where the cooperation extends to the exploitation of the results, it is appropriate to fix the period of validity of the Regulation at 13 years. If the circumstances on the basis of which the Regulation was adopted should change significantly within the period, the Commission will make the necessary amendments.

(18) Agreements which are automatically exempted pursuant to this Regulation need not be notified. Undertakings may nevertheless in a particular case request a decision pursuant to Council Regulation No. 17, as last mentioned by the Act of Accession of Greece,

HAS ADOPTED THIS REGULATION:

Article 1

1. Pursuant to Article 85(3) of the Treaty and subject to the provisions of this Regulation, it is hereby declared that Article 85(1) of the Treaty shall not apply to agreements entered into between undertakings for the purpose of:

(a) joint research and development of products or processes and joint exploitation of the results of that research and development;

(b) joint exploitation of the results of research and development of products or processes jointly carried out pursuant to a prior agreement between the same undertakings; or

(c) joint research and development of products or processes excluding joint exploitation of the results, in so far as such agreements fall within the scope of Article 85(1).

2. For the purposes of this Regulation:

(a) *research and development of products or processes* mean the acquisition of technical knowledge and the carrying out of theoretical analysis, systematic study or experimentation, including experimental production, technical testing of products or processes, the establishment of the necessary facilities and the obtaining of intellectual property rights for the results;

(b) *contract processes* means processes arising out of the research and development;

(c) *contract products* means products or services arising out of the research and development or manufactured or provided applying the contract processes;

(d) *exploitation of the results* means the manufacture of the contract products or the application of the contract processes or the assignment or licensing of intellectual property rights or the communication of know-how required for such manufacture or application;

(e) *technical knowledge* means technical knowledge which is either protected by an intellectual property right or is secret (know-how).

3. Research and development of the exploitation of the results are carried out *jointly* where:

(a) the work involved is:
—carried out by a joint team, organisation or undertaking,
—jointly entrusted to a third party, or
—allocated between the parties by way of specialisation in research, development or production;

(b) the parties collaborate in any way in the assignment or the licensing of intellectual property rights or the communication of know-how, within the meaning of paragraph 2(d), to third parties.

Article 2

The exemption provided for in Article 1 shall apply on condition that:

(a) the joint research and development work is carried out within the framework of a programme defining the objectives of the work and the field in which it is to be carried out;

(b) all the parties have access to the results of the work;

(c) where the agreement provides only for joint research and development, each party is free to exploit the results of the joint research and development and any pre-existing technical knowledge necessary therefor independently;

(d) the joint exploitation relates only to results which are protected by intellectual property rights or constitute know-how which substantially contributes to technical or economic progress and that the results are decisive for the manufacture of the contract products or the application of the contract processes;

(e) (repealed by Regulation 151/93);

(f) undertakings charged with manufacture by way of specialisation in production are required to fulfil orders for supplies from all the parties.

Article 3

1. Where the parties are not competing manufacturers of products capable of being improved or replaced by the contract products, the exemption provided for in Article 1 shall apply for the duration of the research and development programme and, where the results are jointly exploited, for five years from the time the contract products are first put on the market within the common market.

2. Where two or more of the parties are competing manufacturers within the meaning of paragraph 1, the exemption provided for in Article 1 shall apply for the period specified in paragraph 1 only if, at the time the agreement is entered into, the parties' combined production of the products capable of being improved or replaced by the contract products does not exceed 20 per cent. of the market for such products in the common market or a substantial part thereof.

3. After the end of the period referred to in paragraph 1, the exemption provided for in Article 1 shall continue to apply as long as the production of the contract products together with the parties' combined production of other products which are considered by users to be equivalent in view of their characteristics, price and intended use does not exceed 20 per cent. of the total market for such products in the common market or a substantial part thereof. Where contract products are components used by the parties of the manufacture of other products, reference shall be made to the markets for such of those latter products for which the components represent a significant part.

[3a. Where one of the parties, a joint undertaking, a third undertaking or more than one joint undertaking or third undertaking are entrusted with the distribution of the products which are the subject of the agreement under Article 4(1)(fa), (fb) or (fc), the exemption provided for in Article 1 shall apply only if the parties production of the products referred to in paragraphs 2 and 3 does not exceed 10 per cent. of the market for all such products in the common market or a substantial part thereof.']

[4. The exemption provided for in Article 1 shall continue to apply where the market shares referred to in paragraphs 3 and 4 are exceeded during any period of two consecutive financial years by not more than one-tenth.

5. Where the limits laid down in paragraph 5 are also exceeded, the exemption provided for in Article 1 shall continue to apply for a period of six months following the end of the financial year during which they were exceeded.']

Article 4

1. The exemption provided for in Article 1 shall also apply to the following restrictions of competition imposed on the parties:

(a) an obligation not to carry out independently research and development in the field to which the programme relates or in a closely connected field during the execution of the programme;

(b) an obligation not to enter into agreements with third parties on research and development in the field to which the programme relates or in a closely connected field during the execution of the programme;

(c) an obligation to procure the contract products exclusively from parties, joint organizations or undertakings or third parties, jointly charged with their manufacture;

(d) an obligation not to manufacture the contract products or apply the contract processes in territories reserved for other parties;

(e) an obligation to restrict the manufacture of the contract products or application of the contract processes to one or more technical fields of application, except where two or more of the parties are competitors within the meaning of Article 3 at the time the agreement is entered into;

(f) an obligation not to pursue, for a period of five years from the time the contract products are first put on the market within the common market, an active policy of putting the products on the market in territories reserved for other parties, and in particular not to engage in advertising specifically aimed at such territories or to establish any branch or maintain any distribution depot there for the distribution of the products, provided that users and intermediaries can obtain the contract products from other suppliers and the parties do not render it difficult for intermediaries and users to thus obtain the products;

[(fa) an obligation to grant one of the parties the exclusive right to distribute the contract products, provided that that party does not distribute products manufactured by a third producer which compete with the contract products;

(fb) an obligation to grant the exclusive right to distribute the contract products to a joint undertaking or a third undertaking, provided that the joint undertaking or third undertaking does not manufacture or distribute products which compete with the contract products;

(fc) an obligation to grant the exclusive right to distribute the contract products in the whole or a defined area of the common market to joint undertakings or third undertakings which do not manufacture or distribute products which compete with the contract products, provided that users and intermediaries are also able to obtain the contract products from other suppliers and neither the parties nor the joint undertakings or third undertakings entrusted with the exclusive distribution of the contract products render it difficult for users and intermediaries to thus obtain the contract products.]

(g) an obligation on the parties to communicate to each other any experience they may gain in exploiting the results and to grant each other non-exclusive licences for inventions relating to improvements or new applications.

2. The exemption provided for in Article 1 shall also apply where in a particular agreement the parties undertake obligations of the types referred to in paragraph 1 but with a more limited scope than is permitted by that paragraph.

Article 5

1. Article 1 shall apply notwithstanding that any of the following obligations, in particular, are imposed on the parties during the currency of the agreement:

(a) an obligation to communicate patented or non-patented technical knowledge necessary for the carrying out of the research and development programme for the exploitation of its results;

(b) an obligation not to use any know-how received from another party for purposes other than carrying out the research and development programme and the exploitation of its results;

(c) an obligation to obtain and maintain in force intellectual property rights for the contract products or processes;

(d) an obligation to preserve the confidentiality of any know-how received or jointly developed under the research and development programme; this obligation may be imposed even after the expiry of the agreement;

(e) an obligation:
  (i) to inform other parties of infringements of their intellectual property rights,
  (ii) to take legal action against infringers, and
  (iii) to assist in any such legal action or share with the other parties in the cost thereof;

(f) an obligation to pay royalties or render services to other parties to compensate for unequal contributions to the joint research and development or unequal exploitation of its results;

(g) an obligation to share royalties received from third parties with other parties;

(h) an obligation to supply other parties with minimum quantities of contract products and to observe minimum standards of quality.

2. In the event that, because of particular circumstances, the obligations referred to in paragraph 1 fall within the scope of Article 85(1), they also shall be covered by the exemption. The exemption provided for in this paragraph shall also apply where in a particular agreement the parties undertake obligations of the types referred to in paragraph 1 but with a more limited scope than is permitted by that paragraph.

Article 6

The exemption provided for in Article 1 shall not apply where the parties, by agreement, decision or concerted practice:

(a) are restricted in their freedom to carry out research and development independently or in cooperation with third parties in a field unconnected with that to which the programme relates or, after its completion, in the field to which the programme relates or in a connected field;

(b) are prohibited after completion of the research and development programme from challenging the validity of intellectual property rights which the parties hold in the common market and which are relevant to the programme or, after the expiry of the agreement, from challenging the validity of intellectual property rights which the parties hold in the common market and which protect the results of the research and development;

(c) are restricted as to the quantity of the contract products they may manufacture or sell or as to the number of operations employing the contract process they may carry out;

(d) are restricted in their determination of prices, components of prices or discounts when selling the contract products to third parties;

(e) are restricted as to the customers they may serve, without prejudice to Article 4(1)(e);

(f) are prohibited from putting the contract products on the market or pursuing an active sales policy for them in territories within the common market that are reserved for other parties after the end of the period referred to in Article 4(1)(f);

[(g) are required not to grant licences to third parties to manufacture the contract products or to apply the contract processes even though the exploitation by the parties themselves of the results of the joint research and development is not provided for or does not take place.]

(h) are required:
  —to refuse without any objectively justified reason to meet demand from users or dealers established in their respective territories who would market the contract products in other territories within the common market, or
  —to make it difficult for users or dealers to obtain the contract products from other dealers within the common market, and in particular to exercise intellectual property rights or take measures so as to prevent users or dealers from obtaining, or from putting on the market within the common market, products which have been lawfully put on the market within the common market by another party or with its consent.

Article 7

1. The exemption provided for in this Regulation shall also apply to agreements of the kinds described in Article 1 which fulfil the conditions laid down in Articles 2 and 3 and which contain obligations restrictive of competition which are not covered by Articles 4 and 5 and do not fall within the scope of Article 6, on condition that the agreements in question are notified to the Commission in accordance with the provisions of Commission Regulation No. [3385/94], and that the Commission does not oppose such exemption within a period of six months.

2. The period of six months shall run from the date on which the notification is received by the Commission. Where, however, the notification is made by registered post, the period shall run from the date shown on the postmark of the place of posting.

3. Paragraph 1 shall apply only if:

(a) express reference is made to this Article in the notification or in a communication accompanying it, and

(b) the information furnished with the notification is complete and in accordance with the facts.

4. The benefit of paragraph 1 may be claimed for agreements notified before the entry into force of this Regulation by submitting a communication to the Commission referring expressly to this Article and to the notification. Paragraphs 2 and 3(b) shall apply *mutatis mutandis*.

5. The Commission may oppose the exemption. It shall oppose exemption if it receives a request to do so from a Member State within three months of the forwarding to the Member State of the notification referred to in paragraph 1 or of the communication referred to in paragraph 4. This request must be justified on the basis of considerations relating to the competition rules of the Treaty.

6. The Commission may withdraw the opposition to the exemption at any time. However, where the opposition was raised at the request of a Member State and this request is maintained, it may be withdrawn only after consultation of the Advisory Committee on Restrictive Practices and Dominant Positions.

7. If the opposition is withdrawn because the undertakings concerned have shown that the conditions of Article 85(3) are fulfilled, the exemption shall apply from the date of notification.

8. If the opposition is withdrawn because the undertakings concerned have amended the agreement so that the conditions of Article 85(3) are fulfilled, the exemption shall apply from the date on which the amendments take effect.

9. If the Commission opposes exemption and the opposition is not withdrawn, the effects of the notification shall be governed by the provisions of Regulation No. 17.

Article 8

1. Information acquired pursuant to Article 7 shall be used only for the purposes of this Regulation.

2. The Commission and the authorities of the Member States, their officials and other servants shall not disclose information acquired by them pursuant to this Regulation of a kind that is covered by the obligation of professional secrecy.

3. Paragraphs 1 and 2 shall not prevent publication of general information or surveys which do not contain information relating to particular undertakings or associations of undertakings.

Article 9

1. The provisions of this Regulation shall also apply to rights and obligations which the parties create for undertakings connected with them. The market shares held and the actions and measures taken by connected undertakings shall be treated as those of the parties themselves.

2. Connected undertakings for the purposes of this Regulation are:

  (a) undertakings in which a party to the agreement, directly or indirectly:
     — owns more than half the capital or business assets,
     — has the power to exercise more than half the voting rights,
     — has the power to exercise more than half the members of the supervisory board, board of directors or bodies legally representing the undertakings, or
     — has the right to manage the affairs;
  (b) undertakings which directly have in or over a party to the agreement the rights or powers listed in (a);
  (c) undertakings in or over which an undertaking referred to in (b) directly or indirectly has the rights or powers listed in (a);

3. Undertakings in which the parties to the agreement or undertakings connected with them jointly have, directly or indirectly, the rights or powers set out in paragraph 2(a) shall be considered to be connected with each of the parties to the agreement.

Article 10

The Commission may withdraw the benefit of this Regulation, pursuant to Article 7 of Regulation (EEC) No. 2821/71, where it finds in a particular case that an agreement exempted by this Regulation nevertheless has certain effects which are incompatible with the conditions laid down in Article 85(3) of the Treaty, and in particular where:

  (a) the existence of the agreement substantially restricts the scope for third parties to carry out research and development in the relevant field because of the limited research capacity available elsewhere;

(b) because of the particular structure of supply, the existence of the agreement substantially restricts the access of third parties to the market for the contract products;

(c) without any objectively valid reason, the parties do not exploit the results of the joint research and development;

(d) the contract products are not subject in the whole or a substantial part of the common market to effective competition from identical products or products considered by users as equivalent in view of their characteristics, price and intended use.

Article 11

1. In this case of agreements notified to the Commission before 1 March 1985, the exemption provided for in Article 1 shall have retroactive effect from the time at which the conditions for application of this Regulation were fulfilled or, where the agreement does not fall within Article 4(2)(3)(b) of Regulation No. 17, not earlier than the date of notification.

2. In the case of agreements existing on March 13, 1962 and notified to the Commission before February 1, 1963, the exemption shall have retroactive effect from the time at which the conditions for application of this Regulation were fulfilled.

3. Where agreements which were in existence on March 13, 1962 and which were notified to the Commission before February 1, 1963, or which are covered by Article 4(2)(3)(b) of Regulation No. 17 and were notified to the Commission before January 1, 1967, and amended before September 1, 1985 so as to fulfil the conditions for application of this Regulation, such amendment being communicated to the Commission before October 1, 1985, the prohibition laid down in Article 85(1) of the Treaty shall not apply in respect of the period prior to the amendment. The communication of amendments shall take effect from the date of their receipt by the Commission. Where the communication is sent by registered post, it shall take effect from the date shown on the postmark of the place of posting.

4. In the case of agreements to which Article 85 of the Treaty applies as a result of the accession of the United Kingdom, Ireland and Denmark, paragraphs 1 to 3 shall apply except that the relevant dates shall be January 1, 1973 instead of March 13, 1962 and July 1, 1973 instead of February 1, 1963 and January 1, 1967.

5. In the case of agreements to which Article 85 of the Treaty applies as a result of the accession of Greece, paragraphs 1 to 3 shall apply except that the relevant dates shall be January 1, 1981 instead of March 13, 1962 and July 1, 1981 instead of February 1, 1963 and January 1, 1967.

[6. As regards agreements to which Article 83 of the Treaty applies as a result of the accession of the Kingdom of Spain and of the Portuguese Republic, paragraphs 1 to 3 shall apply except that the relevant dates should be January 1, 1986 instead of March 13, 1962 and July 1, 1986 instead of February 1, 1963, January 1, 1967, March 1, 1985 and September 1, 1985. The amendment made to the agreements in accordance with the provisions of paragraph 3 need not be notified to the Commission.]

Article 12

This Regulation shall apply *mutatis mutandis* to decisions of associations of undertakings.

Article 13

This Regulation shall enter into force on March 1, 1985.
It shall apply until [December 31, 2000].

This Regulation shall be binding in its entirety and directly applicable in all Member States. Done at Brussels, December 19, 1984.

APPENDIX D.2   COMMISSION REGULATION 240/96 OF JANUARY 31, 1996

D.2-01 On the application of Article 85(3) of the Treaty to certain categories of technology transfer agreements

([1996] O.J. L31/2)

THE COMMISSION OF THE EUROPEAN COMMUNITIES,

Having regard to the Treaty establishing the European Community,
Having regard to Council Regulation No. 19/65/EEC of 2 March 1965 on the application of Article 85(3) of the Treaty to certain categories of agreements and concerted practices, as last amended by the Act of Accession of Austria, Finland and Sweden, and in particular Article 1 thereof,
Having published a draft of this Regulation,
After consulting the Advisory Committee on Restrictive Practices and Dominant Positions,
Whereas:

(1) Regulation No. 19/65/EEC empowers the Commission to apply Article 85(3) of the Treaty by regulation to certain categories of agreements and concerted practices falling within the scope of Article 85(1) which include restrictions imposed in relation to the acquisition or use of industrial property rights—in particular of patents, utility models, designs or trademarks—or to the rights arising out of contracts for assignment of, or the right to use, a method of manufacture of knowledge relating to use or to the application of industrial processes.

(2) The Commission has made use of this power by adopting Regulation (EEC) No. 2349/84 of 23 July 1984 on the application of Article 85(3) of the Treaty to certain categories of patent licensing agreements, as last amended by Regulation (E.C.) No. 2131/95, and Regulation (EEC) No. 556/89 of 30 November 1988 on the application of Article 85(3) of the Treaty to certain categories of know-how licensing agreements, as last amended by the Act of Accession of Austria, Finland and Sweden.

(3) These two block exemptions ought to be combined into a single regulation covering technology transfer agreements, and the rules governing patent licensing agreements and agreements for the licensing of know-how ought to be harmonized and simplified as far as possible, in order to encourage the dissemination of technical knowledge in the Community and to promote the manufacture of technically more sophisticated products. In those circumstances Regulation (EEC) No. 556/89 should be repealed.

(4) The Regulation should apply to the licensing of Member States' own patents, Community patents and European patents ("pure" patent licensing agreements). It should also apply to agreements for the licensing of non-patented technical information such as descriptions of manufacturing processes, recipes, formulae, designs or drawings, commonly termed "know-how" ("pure" know-how licensing agreements) and to combined patent and know-how licensing agreements, ("mixed" agreements), which are playing an increasingly important role in the transfer of technology. For the purposes of this Regulation, a number of terms are defined in Article 10.

(5) Patent or know-how licensing agreements are agreements whereby one undertaking which holds a patent or know-how ("the licensor") permits another undertaking ("the licensee") to exploit the patent thereby licensed, or communicates the know-how to it, in particular for purposes of manufacture, use or putting on the market. In the light of experience acquired so far, it is possible to define a category of licensing agreements covering all or part of the common market which are capable of falling within the scope of Article 85(1) but which can normally be regarded as satisfying the conditions laid down in Article 85(3), where patents are necessary for the achievement of the objects of the licensed technology by a mixed agreement or where know-how—whether it is

ancillary to patents or independent of them—is secret, substantial and identified in any appropriate form. These criteria are intended only to ensure that the licensing of the know-how or the grant of the patent licence justifies a block exemption of obligations restricting competition. This is without prejudice to the right of the parties to include in the contract provisions regarding other obligations, such as the obligation to pay royalties, even if the block exemption no longer applies.

(6) It is appropriate to extend the scope of this Regulation to pure or mixed agreements containing the licensing of intellectual property rights other than patents (in particular, trademarks, design rights and copyright, especially software protection), when such additional licensing contributes to the achievement of the objects of the licensed technology and contains only ancillary provisions.

(7) Where such pure or mixed licensing agreements contain not only obligations relating to territories within the common market but also obligations relating to non-member countries, the presence of the latter does not prevent this Regulation from applying to the obligations relating to territories within the common market. Where licensing agreements for non-member countries or for territories which extend beyond the frontiers of the Community have effects within the common market which may fall within the scope of Article 85(1), such agreements should be covered by this Regulation to the same extent as would agreements for territories within the common market.

(8) The objective being to facilitate the dissemination of technology and the improvement of manufacturing processes, this Regulation should apply only where the licensee himself manufactures the licensed products or has them manufactured for his account, or where the licensed product is a service, provides the service himself or has the service provided for his account, irrespective of whether or not the licensee is also entitled to use confidential information provided by the licensor for the promotion and sale of the licensed product. The scope of this Regulation should therefore exclude agreements solely for the purpose of sale. Also to be excluded from the scope of this Regulation are agreements relating to marketing know-how communicated in the context of franchising arrangements and certain licensing agreements entered into in connection with arrangements such as joint ventures or patent pools and other arrangements in which a licence is granted in exchange for other licences not related to improvements to or new applications of the licensed technology. Such agreements pose different problems which cannot at present be dealt with in a single regulation (Article 5).

(9) Given the similarity between sale and exclusive licensing, and the danger that the requirements of this Regulation might be evaded by presenting as assignments what are in fact exclusive licenses restrictive of competition, this Regulation should apply to agreements concerning the assignment and acquisition of patents or know-how where the risk associated with exploitation remains with the assignor. It should also apply to licensing agreements in which the licenser is not the holder of the patent or know-how but is authorised by the holder to grant the licence (as in the case of sub-licences) and to licensing agreements in which the parties' rights or obligations are assumed by connected undertakings (Article 6).

(10) Exclusive licensing agreements, *i.e.* agreements in which the licensor undertakes not to exploit the licensed technology in the licensed territory himself or to grant further licences there, may not be in themselves incompatible with Article 85(1) where they are concerned with the introduction and protection of a new technology in the licensed territory, by reason of the scale of the research which has been undertaken, of the increase in the level of competition, in particular inter-brand competition, and of the competitiveness of the undertakings concerned resulting from the dissemination of innovation within the Community. In so far as agreements of this kind fall, in other circumstances, within the scope of Article 85(1), it is appropriate to include them in Article 1 in order that they may also benefit from the exemption.

(11) The exemption of export bans on the licensor and on the licensees does not prejudice any developments in the case law of the Court of Justice in relation to such agreements, notably with respect to Articles 30 to 36 and Article 85(1). This is also the case, in particular, regarding the prohibition on the licensee from selling the licensed product in territories granted to other licensees (passive competition).

(12) The obligations listed in Article 1 generally contribute to improving the production of goods and to promoting technical progress. They make the holders of patents or know-how more willing to grant licences and licensees more inclined to undertake the investment required to manufacture,

use and put on the market a new product or to use a new process. Such obligations may be permitted under this Regulation in respect of territories where the licensed product is protected by patents as long as these remain in force.

(13) Since the point at which the know-how ceases to be secret can be difficult to determine, it is appropriate, in respect of territories where the licensed technology comprises know-how only, to limit such obligations to a fixed number of years. Moreover, in order to provide sufficient periods of protection, it is appropriate to take as the starting point for such periods the date on which the product is first put on the market in the Community by a licensee.

(14) Exemption under Article 85(3) of longer periods of territorial protection for know-how agreements, in particular in order to protect expensive and risky investment or where the parties were not competitors at the date of the grant of the licence, can be granted only by individual decision. On the other hand, parties are free to extend the term of their agreements in order to exploit any subsequent improvement and to provide for the payment of additional royalties. However, in such cases, further periods of territorial protection may be allowed only starting from the date of licensing of the secret improvements in the Community, and by individual decision. Where the research for improvements results in innovations which are distinct from the licensed technology the parties may conclude a new agreement benefiting from an exemption under this Regulation.

(15) Provision should also be made for exemption of an obligation on the licensee not to put the product on the market in the territories of other licensees, the permitted period for such an obligation (this obligation would ban not just active competition but passive competition too) should, however, be limited to a few years from the date on which the licensed product is first put on the market in the Community by a licensee, irrespective of whether the licensed technology comprises know-how, patents or both in the territories concerned.

(16) The exemption of territorial protection should apply for the whole duration of the periods thus permitted, as long as the patents remain in force or the know-how remains secret and substantial. The parties to a mixed patent and know-how licensing agreement must be able to take advantage in a particular territory of the period of protection conferred by a patent or by the know-how, whichever is the longer.

(17) The obligations listed in Article 1 also generally fulfil the other conditions for the application for the application of Article 85(3). Consumers will, as a rule, be allowed a fair share of the benefit resulting from the improvement in the supply of goods on the market. To safeguard this effect, however, it is right to exclude from the application of Article 1 cases where the parties agree to refuse to meet demand from users or resellers within their respective territories who would resell for export, or to take other steps to impede parallel imports. The obligations referred to above thus only impose restrictions which are indispensable to the attainment of their objectives.

(18) It is desirable to list in this Regulation a number of obligations that are commonly found in licensing agreements but are normally not restrictive of competition, and to provide that in the event that because of the particular economic or legal circumstances they should fall within Article 85(1), they too will be covered by the exemption. This list, in Article 2, is not exhaustive.

(19) This Regulation must also specify what restrictions or provisions may not be included in licensing agreements if there are to benefit from the block exemption. The restrictions listed in Article 3 may fall under the prohibition of Article 85(1), but in their case there can be no general presumption that, although they relate to the transfer of technology, they will lead to the positive effects required by Article 85(3), as would be necessary for the granting of a block exemption. Such restrictions can be declared exempt only by an individual decision, taking account of the market position of the undertakings concerned and the degree of concentration on the relevant market.

(20) The obligations on the licensee to cease using the licensed technology after the termination of the agreement (Article 2(1)(3)) and to make improvements available to the licensor (Article 2(1)(4)) do not generally restrict competition. The post-term use ban may be regarded as a normal feature of licensing, as otherwise the licensor would be forced to transfer his know-how or patents in perpetuity. Undertakings by the licensee to grant back to the licensor a licence for improvements to the licensed know-how and/or patents are generally not restrictive of competition if the licensee is entitled by the contract to share in future experience and inventions made by the licensor. On the

other hand, a restrictive effect on competition arises where the agreement obliges the licensee to assign to the licensor rights to improvements of the originally licensed technology that he himself has brought about (Article 3(6)).

(21) The list of clauses which do not prevent exemption also includes an obligation on the licensee to keep paying royalties until the end of the agreement independently of whether or not the licensed know-how has entered into the public domain through the action of third parties or of the licensee himself (Article 2(1)(7)). Moreover, the parties must be free, in order to facilitate payment, to spread the royalty payments for the use of the licensed technology over a period extending beyond the duration of the licensed patents, in particular by setting lower royalty rates. As a rule, parties do not need to be protected against the foreseeable financial consequences of an agreement freely entered into, and they should therefore be free to choose the appropriate means of financing the technology transfer and sharing between them the risks of such use. However, the setting of rates of royalty so as to achieve one of the restrictions listed in Article 3 renders the agreement ineligible for the block exemption.

(22) An obligation on the licensee to restrict his exploitation of the licensed technology to one or more technical fields of application ("fields of use") or to one or more product markets is not caught by Article 85(1) either, since the licenser is entitled to transfer the technology only for a limited purpose (Article 2(1)(8)).

(23) Clauses whereby the parties allocate customers within the same technological field of use or the same product market, either by an actual prohibition on supplying certain classes of customer or through an obligation with an equivalent effect, would also render the agreement ineligible for the block exemption where the parties are competitors for the contract products (Article 3(4)). Such restrictions between undertakings which are not competitors remain subject to the opposition procedure. Article 3 does not apply to cases where the patent or know-how licence is granted in order to provide a single customer with a second source of supply. In such a case, a prohibition on the second licensee from supplying persons other than the customer concerned is an essential condition for the grant of a second licence, since the purpose of the transaction is not to create an independent supplier in the market. The same applies to limitations on the qualities the licensee may supply to the customer concerned (Article 2(1)(13)).

(24) Besides the clauses already mentioned, the list of restrictions which render the block exemption inapplicable also includes restrictions regarding the selling prices of the licensed product or the quantities to be manufactured or sold, since they seriously limit the extent to which the licensee can exploit the licensed technology and since quantity restrictions particularly may have the same effect as export bans (Article 3(1) and (5)). This does not apply where a licence is granted for use of the technology in specific production facilities and where both a specific technology is communicated for the setting-up, operation and maintenance of these facilities and the licensee is allowed to increase the capacity of the facilities or to set up further facilities for its own use on normal commercial terms. On the other hand, the licensee may lawfully be prevented from using the transferred technology to set up facilities for third parties, since the purpose of the agreement is not to permit the licensee to give other producers access to the licensor's technology while it remains secret or protected by patent (Article 2(1)(12)).

(25) Agreements which are not automatically covered by the exemption because they contain provisions that are not expressly exempted by this Regulation and not expressly excluded from exemption, including those listed in Article 4(2), may, in certain circumstances, nonetheless be presumed to be eligible for application of the block exemption. It will be possible for the Commission rapidly to establish whether this is the case on the basis of the information undertakings are obliged to provide under Commission Regulation (E.C.) No. 3385/94. The Commission may waive the requirement to supply specific information required in form A/B but which it does not deem necessary. The Commission will generally be content with communication of the text of the agreement and with an estimate, based on directly available data, of the market structure and of the licensee's market share. Such agreements should therefore be deemed to be covered by the exemption provided for in this Regulation where they are notified to the Commission and the Commission does not oppose the application of the exemption within a specified period of time.

(26) Where agreements exempted under this Regulation nevertheless have effects incompatible with Article 85(3), the Commission may withdraw the block exemption, in particular where the

licensed products are not faced with real competition in the licensed territory (Article 7). This could also be the case where the licensee has a strong position on the market. In assessing the competition the Commission will pay special attention to cases where the licensee has more than 40 per cent of the whole market for the licensed products and of all the products or services which customers consider interchangeable or substitutable on account of their characteristics, prices and intended use.

(27) Agreements which come within the terms of Articles 1 and 2 and which have neither the object nor the effect of restricting competition in any other way need no longer be notified. Nevertheless, undertakings will still have the right to apply in individual cases for negative clearance or for exemption under Article 85(3) in accordance with Council Regulation No. 17, as last amended by the Act of Accession of Austria, Finland and Sweden. They can in particular notify agreements obliging the licensor not to grant other licences in the territory, where the licensee's market share exceeds or is likely to exceed 40 per cent.

HAS ADOPTED THIS REGULATION

Article 1

1. Pursuant to Article 85(3) of the Treaty and subject to the conditions set out below, it is hereby declared that Article 85(1) of the Treaty shall not apply to pure patent licensing or know-how licensing agreements and to mixed patent and know-how licensing agreements, including those agreements containing ancillary provisions relating to intellectual property rights other than patents, to which only two undertakings are party and which include one or more of the following obligations:

(1) an obligation on the licensor not to license other undertakings to exploit the licensed technology in the licensed territory;

(2) an obligation on the licensor not to exploit the licensed technology in the licensed territory himself;

(3) an obligation on the licensee not to exploit the licensed technology in the territory of the licensor within the common market;

(4) an obligation on the licensee not to manufacture or use the licensed product, or use the licensed process, in territories within the common market which are licensed to other licensees;

(5) an obligation on the licensee not to pursue an active policy of putting the licensed product on the market in the territories within the common market which are licensed to other licensees, and in particular not to engage in advertising specifically aimed at those territories or to establish any branch or maintain a distribution depot there;

(6) an obligation on the licensee not to put the licensed product on the market in the territories licensed to other licensees within the common market in response to unsolicited orders;

(7) an obligation on the licensee to use only the licensor's trademark or get up to distinguish the licensed product during the term of the agreement, provided that the licensee is not prevented from identifying himself as the manufacturer of the licensed products;

(8) an obligation on the licensee to limit his production of the licensed product to the quantities he requires in manufacturing his own products and to sell the licensed product only as an integral part of or a replacement part for his own products or otherwise in connection with the sale of his own products, provided that such quantities are freely determined by the licensee.

2. Where the agreement is a pure patent licensing agreement, the exemption of the obligations referred to in paragraph 1 is granted only to the extent that and for as long as the licensed product is protected by parallel patents, in the territories respectively of the licensee (points (1), (2), (7) and (8)), the licensor (point (3)) and other licensees (points (4) and (5)). The exemption of the obligation referred to in point (6) of paragraph 1 is granted for a period not exceeding five years from the date when the licensed product is first put on the market within the common market by one of the

licensees, to the extent that and for as long as, in these territories, this product is protected by parallel patents.

3. Where the agreement is a pure know-how licensing agreement, the period for which the exemption of the obligations referred to in points (1) to (5) of paragraph 1 is granted may not exceed ten years from the date when the licensed product is first put on the market within the common market by one of the licensees.

The exemption of the obligation referred to in point (6) of paragraph 1 is granted for a period not exceeding five years from the date when the licensed product is first put on the market within the common market by one of the licensees.

The obligations referred to in points (7) and (8) of paragraph 1 are exempted during the lifetime of the agreement for as long as the know-how remains secret and substantial.

However, the exemption in paragraph 1 shall apply only where the parties have identified in any appropriate form the initial know-how and any subsequent improvements to it which become available to one party and are communicated to the other party pursuant to the terms of the agreement and to the purpose thereof, and only for as long as the know-how remains secret and substantial.

4. Where the agreement is a mixed patent and know-how licensing agreement, the exemption of the obligations referred to in points (1) to (5) of paragraph 1 shall apply in Member States in which the licensed technology is protected by necessary patents for as long as the licensed product is protected in those Member States by such patents if the duration of such protection exceeds the periods specified in paragraph 3.

The duration of the exemption provided in point (6) of paragraph 1 may not exceed the five-year period provided for in paragraphs 2 and 3.

However, such agreements qualify for the exemption referred to in paragraph 1 only for as long as the patents remain in force or to the extent that the know-how is identified and for as long as it remains secret and substantial whichever period is the longer.

5. The exemption provided for in paragraph 1 shall also apply where in a particular agreement the parties undertake obligations of the types referred to in that paragraph but with a more limited scope than is permitted by that paragraph.

Article 2

1. Article 1 shall apply notwithstanding the presence in particular of any of the following clauses, which are generally not restrictive of competition:

(1) an obligation on the licensee not to divulge the know-how communicated by the licensor; the licensee may be held to this obligation after the agreement has expired;

(2) an obligation on the licensee not to grant sublicences or assign the licence;

(3) an obligation on the licensee not to exploit the licensed know-how or patents after termination of the agreement in so far and as long as the know-how is still secret or the patents are still in force;

(4) an obligation on the licensee to grant to the licensor a licence in respect of his own improvements to or his new applications of the licensed technology, provided:
   — that, in the case of severable improvements, such a licence is not exclusive, so that the licensee is free to use his own improvements or to license them to third parties, in so far as that does not involve disclosure of the know-how communicated by the licensor that is still secret,
   — and that the licensor undertakes to grant an exclusive or non-exclusive licence of his own improvements to the licensee;

(5) an obligation on the licensee to observe minimum quality specifications, including technical specifications, for the licensed product or to procure goods or services from the licensor or from an undertaking designated by the licensor, in so far as these quality specifications, products or services are necessary for:

(a) a technically proper exploitation of the licensed technology; or

(b) ensuring that the product of the licensee conforms to the minimum quality specifications that are applicable to the licensor and other licensees:

and to allow the licensor to carry out related checks;

(6) obligations:

(a) to inform the licensor of misappropriation of the know-how or of infringements of the licensed patents; or
(b) to take or to assist the licensor in taking legal action against such misappropriation or infringements;

(7) an obligation on the licensee to continue paying the royalties:

(a) until the end of the agreement in the amounts, for the periods and according to the methods freely determined by the parties, in the event of the know-how becoming publicly known other than by action of the licensor, without prejudice to the payment of any additional damages in the event of the know-how becoming publicly known by the action of the licensee in breach of the agreement;
(b) over a period going beyond the duration of the licensed patents, in order to facilitate payment;

(8) an obligation on the licensee to restrict his exploitation of the licensed technology to one or more technical fields of application covered by the licensed technology or to one or more product markets;

(9) an obligation on the licensee to pay a minimum royalty or to produce a minimum quantity of the licensed product or to carry out a minimum number of operations exploiting the licensed technology;

(10) an obligation on the licensor to grant the licensee any more favourable terms that the licensor may grant to another undertaking after the agreement is entered into;

(11) an obligation on the licensee to mark the licensed product with an indication of the licensor's name or of the licensed patent;

(12) an obligation on the licensee not to use the licensor's technology to construct facilities for third parties; this is without prejudice to the right of the licensee to increase the capacity of his facilities or to set up additional facilities for his own use on normal commercial terms, including the payment of additional royalties;

(13) an obligation on the licensee to supply only a limited quantity of the licensed product to a particular customer, where the licence was granted so that the customer might have a second source of supply inside the licensed territory; this provision shall also apply where the customer is the licensee, and the licence which was granted in order to provide a second source of supply provides that the customer is himself to manufacture the licensed products or to have them manufactured by a subcontractor;

(14) a reservation by the licensor of the right to exercise the rights conferred by a patent to oppose the exploitation of the technology by the licensee outside the licensed territory;

(15) a reservation by the licensor of the right to terminate the agreement if the licensee contests the secret or substantial nature of the licensed know-how or challenges the validity of licensed patents within the common market belonging to the licensor or undertakings connected with him;

(16) a reservation by the licensor of the right to terminate the licence agreement of a patent if the licensee raises the claim that such a patent is not necessary;

(17) an obligation on the licensee to use his best endeavours to manufacture and market the licensed product;

(18) a reservation by the licensor of the right to terminate the exclusivity granted to the licensee and to stop licensing improvements to him when the licensee enters into competition within the common market with the licensor, with undertakings connected with the licensor or with other undertakings in respect of research and development, production, use or distribution of competing products, and to require the licensee to prove that the licensed

know-how is not being used for the production of products and the provision of services other than those licensed.

2. In the event that, because of particular circumstances, the clauses referred to in paragraph 1 fall within the scope of Article 85(1), they shall also be exempted even if they are not accompanied by any of the obligations exempted by Article 1.

3. The exemption in paragraph 2 shall also apply where an agreement contains clauses of the types referred to in paragraph 1 but with a more limited scope than is permitted by that paragraph.

Article 3

Article 1 and Article 2(2) shall not apply where:

(1) one party is restricted in the determination of prices, components of prices or discounts for the licensed products;

(2) one party is restricted from competing within the common market with the other party, with undertakings connected with the other party or with other undertakings in respect of research and development, production, use or distribution of competing products without prejudice to the provisions of Article 2(1) (17) and (18);

(3) one or both of the parties are required without any objectively justified reason:

    (a) to refuse to meet orders from users or resellers in their respective territories who would market products in other territories within the common market;

    (b) to make it difficult for uses or resellers to obtain the products from other resellers within the common market, and in particular to exercise intellectual property rights or take measures so as to prevent users or resellers from obtaining outside, or from putting on the market in the licensed territory products which have been lawfully put on the market within the common market by the licensor or with his consent;

or do so as a result of a concerted practice between them;

(4) the parties were already competing manufactures before the grant of the licence and one of them is restricted, within the same technical field of use or within the same product market, as to the customers he may serve, in particular by being prohibited from supplying certain classes of user, employing certain forms of distribution or, with the aim of sharing customers, using certain types of packaging for the products, save as provided in Article 1(1)(7) and Article 2(1)(13);

(5) the quantity of the licensed products one party may manufacture or sell or the number of operations exploiting the licensed technology he may carry out are subject to limitations, save as provided in Article (1)(8) and Article 2(1)(13);

(6) the licensee is obliged to assign in whole or in part to the licensor rights to improvements to or new applications of the licensed technology;

(7) the licensor is required, albeit in separate agreements or through automatic prolongation of the initial duration of the agreement by the inclusion of any new improvements, for a period exceeding that referred to in Article 1(2) and (3) not to license other undertakings to exploit the licensed technology in the licensed territory, or a party is required for a period exceeding that referred to in Article 1(2) and (3) or Article 1(4) not to exploit the licensed technology in the territory of the other party or of other licensees.

Article 4

1. The exemption provided for in Articles I and 2 shall also apply to agreements containing obligations restrictive of competition which are not covered by those Articles and do not fall within the scope of Article 3, on condition that the agreements in question are notified to the Commission in accordance with the provisions of Articles 1, 2 and 3 of Regulation (E.C.) No. 3385/94 and that the Commission does not oppose such exemption within a period of four months.

2. Paragraph 1 shall apply, in particular, where:

(a) the licensee is obliged at the time the agreement is entered into to accept quality specifications or further licences or to procure goods or services which are not necessary for a technically satisfactory exploitation of the licensed technology or for ensuring that the production of the licensee conforms to the quality standards that are respected by the licensor and other licensees,

(b) the licensee is prohibited from contesting the secrecy or the substantiality of the licensed know-how or from challenging the identity of patents licensed within the common market belonging to the licensor or undertakings connected with him.

3. The period of four months referred to in paragraph 1 shall run from the date on which the notification takes effect in accordance with Article 4 of Regulation (E.C.) No. 3385/94.

4. The benefit of paragraphs 1 and 2 may be claimed for agreements notified before the entry into force of this Regulation by submitting a communication to the Commission referring expressly to this Article and to the notification. Paragraph 3 shall apply *mutatis mutandis*.

5. The Commission may oppose the exemption within a period of four months. It shall oppose exemption if it receives a request to do so from a Member State within two months of the transmission to the Member State of the notification referred to in paragraph 1 or of the communication referred to in paragraph 4. This request must be justified on the basis of considerations relating to the competition rules of the Treaty.

6. The Commission may withdraw the opposition to the exemption at any time. However, where the opposition was raised at the request of a Member State and this request is maintained, it may be withdrawn only after consultation of the Advisory Committee on Restrictive Practices and Dominant Positions.

7. If the opposition is withdrawn because the undertakings concerned have shown that the conditions of Article 85(3) are satisfied, the exemption shall apply from the date of notification.

8. If the opposition is withdrawn because the undertakings concerned have amended the agreement so that the conditions of Article 85(3) are satisfied, the exemption shall apply from the date on which the amendments take effect.

9. If the Commission opposes exemption and the opposition is not withdrawn, the effects of the notification shall be governed by the provisions of Regulation No. 17.

Article 5

This Regulation shall not apply to:

(1) agreements between members of a patent or know-how pool which relate to the pooled technologies;

(2) licensing agreements between competing undertakings which hold interests in a joint venture, or between one of them and the joint venture, if the licensing agreements relate to the activities of the joint venture;

(3) agreements under which one party grants the other a patent and/or know-how licence and in exchange the other party, albeit in separate agreements or through connected undertakings, grants the first party a patent, trademark or know-how licence or exclusive sales rights, where the parties are competitors in relation to the products covered by those agreements;

(4) licensing agreements containing provisions relating to intellectual property rights other than patents which are not ancillary;

(5) agreements entered into solely for the purpose of sale.

2. This Regulation shall nevertheless apply:

(1) to agreements to which paragraph 1(2) applies, under which a parent undertaking grants the joint venture a patent or know-how licence, provided that the licensed products and the other goods and services of the participating undertakings which are considered by users to be interchangeable or substitutable in view of their characteristics, price and intended use represent:
— in case of a licence limited to production, not more than 20 per cent, and
— in case of a licence covering production and distribution, not more than 10 per cent;
of the market for licensed products and all interchangeable or substitutable goods and services;

(2) to agreements to which paragraph 1(1) applies and to reciprocal licences within the meaning of paragraph 1(3), provided the parties are not subject to any territorial restriction within the common market with regard to the manufacture, use or putting on the market of the licensed products or to the use of the licensed or pooled technologies.

3. This Regulation shall continue to apply where, for two consecutive financial years, the market shares in paragraph 2(1) are not exceeded by more than one-tenth; where that limit is exceeded, this Regulation shall continue to apply for a period of six months from the end of the year in which the limit was exceeded.

Article 6

This Regulation shall also apply to:

(1) agreements where the licensor is not the holder of the know-how or the patentee, but is authorized by the holder or the patentee to grant a licence;

(2) assignments of know-how, patents or both where the risk associated with exploitation remains with the assignor, in particular where the sum payable in consideration of the assignment is dependent on the turnover obtained by the assignee in respect of products made using the know-how or the patents, the quantity of such products manufactured or the number of operations carried out employing the know-how or the patents;

(3) licensing agreements in which the rights or obligations of the licensor or the licensee are assumed by undertakings connected with them.

Article 7

The Commission may withdraw the benefit of this Regulation, pursuant to Article 7 of Regulation No. 19/65/EEC, where it finds in a particular case that an agreement exempted by this Regulation nevertheless has certain effects which are incompatible with the conditions laid down in Article 85(3) of the Treaty, and in particular where:

(1) the effect of the agreement is to prevent the licensed products from being exposed to effective competition in the licensed territory from identical goods or services or from goods or services considered by users as interchangeable or substitutable in view of their characteristics, price and intended use, which may in particular occur where the licensee's market share exceeds 40 per cent;

(2) without prejudice to Article 1(1) (6), the licensee refuses, without any objectively justified reason, to meet unsolicited orders from users or resellers in the territory of other licensees;

(3) the parties:

(a) without any objectively justified reason, refuse to meet orders from users or resellers in their respective territories who would market the products in other territories within the common market; or

(b) make it difficult for users or resellers to obtain the products from other resellers within the common market, and in particular where they exercise intellectual property rights or take measures so as to prevent resellers or users from obtaining outside, or from putting on the market in the licensed territory products which have been lawfully put on the market within the common market by the licensor or with his consent;

(4) the parties were competing manufacturers at the date of the grant of the licence and obligations on the licensee to produce a minimum quantity or to use his best endeavours as referred to in Article 2(1), (9) and (17) respectively have the effect of preventing the licensee from using competing technologies.

Article 8

1. For purposes of this Regulation:

(a) patent applications;

(b) utility models,

(c) applications for registration of utility models;

(d) topographies of semiconductor products;

(e) *certificats d'utilité* and *certificats d'addition* under French law;

(f) applications for *certificats d'utilité* and *certificats d'addition* under French law;

(g) supplementary protection certificates for medicinal products or other products for which such supplementary protection certificates may be obtained;

(h) plant breeder's certificates,

shall be deemed to be patents.

2. This Regulation shall also apply to agreements relating to the exploitation of an invention if an application within the meaning of paragraph 1 is made in respect of the invention for a licensed territory after the date when the agreements were entered into but within the time-limits set by the national law or the international convention to be applied.

3. This Regulation shall furthermore apply to pure patent or know-how licensing agreements or to mixed agreements whose initial duration is automatically prolonged by the inclusion of any new improvements, whether patented or not, communicated by the licensor, provided that the licensee has the right to refuse such improvements or each party has the right to terminate the agreement at the expiry of the initial term of an agreement and at least every three years thereafter.

Article 9

1. Information acquired pursuant to Article 4 shall be used only for the purposes of this Regulation.

2. The Commission and the authorities of the Member States, their officials and other servants shall not disclose information acquired by them pursuant to this Regulation of the kind covered by the obligation of professional secrecy.

3. The provisions of paragraphs 1 and 2 shall not prevent publication of general information or surveys which do not contain information relating to particular undertakings or associations of undertakings.

Article 10

For purposes of this Regulation:

(1) "know-how' means a body of technical information that is secret, substantial and identified in any appropriate form;

(2) "secret" means that the know-how package as a body or in the precise configuration and assembly of its components is not generally known or easily accessible, so that part of its value consists in the lead which the licensee gains when it is communicated to him; it is not limited to the narrow sense that each individual component of the know-how should be totally unknown or unobtainable outside the licensor's business;

(3) "substantial" means that the know-how includes information which must be useful, *i.e.* can reasonably be expected at the date of conclusion of the agreement to be capable of improving the competitive position of the licensee, for example by helping him to enter a new market or giving him an advantage in competition with other manufacturers or providers of services who do not have access to the licensed secret know-how or other comparable secret know-how;

(4) "identified" means that the know-how is described or recorded in such a manner as to make it possible to verify that it satisfies the criteria of secrecy and substantiality and to ensure that the licensee is not unduly restricted in his exploitation of his own technology, to be identified the know-how can either be set out in the licence agreement or in a separate document or recorded in any other appropriate form at the latest when the know-how is transferred or shortly thereafter, provided that the separate document or other record can be made available if the need arises;

(5) "necessary patents" are patents where a licence under the patent is necessary for the putting into effect of the licensed technology in so far as, in the absence of such a licence, the realisation of the licensed technology would not be possible or would be possible only to a lesser extent or in more difficult or costly conditions. Such patents must therefore be of technical, legal or economic interest to the licensee;

(6) "licensing agreement" means pure patent licensing agreements and pure know-how licensing agreements as well as mixed patent and know-how licensing agreements;

(7) "licensed technology" means the initial manufacturing know-how or the necessary product and process patents, or both, existing at the time the first licensing agreement is concluded, and improvements subsequently made to the know-how or patents, irrespective of whether and to what extent they are exploited by the parties or by other licensees;

(8) "the licensed products" are goods or services the production or provision of which requires the use of the licensed technology'

(9) "the licensee's market share" means the proportion which the licensed products and other goods or services provided by the licensee, which are considered by users to be interchangeable or substitutable for the licensed products in view of their characteristics, price and intended use, represent the entire market for the licensed products and all other interchangeable or substitutable goods and services in the common market or a substantial part of it;

(10) "exploitation" refers to any use of the licensed technology in particular in the production, active or passive sales in a territory even if not coupled with manufacture in that territory, or leasing of the licensed products;

(11) "the licensed territory" is the territory covering all or at least part of the common market where the licensee is entitled to exploit the licensed technology;

(12) "territory of the licensor" means territories in which the licensor has not granted any licences for patents and/or know-how covered by the licensing agreement;

(13) "parallel patents" means patents which, in spite of the divergences which remain in the absence of any unification of national rules concerning industrial property, protect the same invention in various Member States;

(14) "connected undertakings" means:

  (a) undertakings in which a party to the agreement, directly or indirectly:
    — owns more than half the capital or business assets, or
    — has the power to exercise more than half the voting rights, or
    — has the power to appoint more than half the members of the supervisory board, board of directors or bodies legally representing the undertaking, or
    — has the right to manage the affairs of the undertaking;
  (b) undertakings which, directly or indirectly, have in or over a party to the agreement the rights or powers listed in (a);
  (c) undertakings in which an undertaking referred to in (b), directly or indirectly, has the rights or powers listed in (a);
  (d) undertakings in which the parties to the agreement or undertakings connected with them jointly have the rights or powers listed in (a): such jointly controlled undertakings are considered to be connected with each of the parties to the agreement;

(15) "ancillary provisions" are provisions relating to the exploitation of intellectual property rights other than patents, which contain no obligations restrictive of competition other than those also attached to the licensed know-how or patents and exempted under this Regulation;

(16) "obligation" means both contractual obligation and a concerted practice;

(17) "competing manufacturers" or manufacturers of "competing products" means manufacturers who sell products which, in view of their characteristics, price and intended use, are considered by users to be interchangeable or substitutable for the licensed products.

Article 11

1. Regulation (EEC) No. 556/89 is hereby repealed with effect from 1 April 1996.

2. Regulation (EEC) No. 2349/84 shall continue to apply until 31 March 1996.

3. The prohibition in Article 85(1) of the Treaty shall not apply to agreements in force on 31 March 1996 which fulfil the exemption requirements laid down by Regulation (EEC) No. 2349/84 or (EEC) No. 556/89.

Article 12

1. The Commission shall undertake regular assessments of the application of this Regulation, and in particular of the opposition procedure provided for in Article 4.

2. The Commission shall draw up a report on the operation of this Regulation before the end of the fourth year following its entry into force and shall, on that basis, assess whether any adaptation of the Regulation is desirable.

Article 13

This Regulation shall enter into force on 1 April 1996.

It shall apply until 31 March 2006.

Article 11(2) of this Regulation shall, however, enter into force on January 1, 1996.

This Regulation shall be binding in its entirety and directly applicable in all member States.

Done at Brussels, 31 January 1996.

Appendix E

PART IV

E.1-01   FUNCTIONS OF DIRECTOR AND COMMISSION IN RELATION TO MONOPOLY SITUATIONS AND UNCOMPETITIVE PRACTICES

Powers for Director to require information

44.—(1) Where it appears to the Director that there are grounds for believing—

(a) that a monopoly situation may exist in relation to the supply of goods or services of any description, or in relation to exports of goods of any description from the United Kingdom, and

(b) that in accordance with the following provisions of this Part of this Act he would not be precluded from making a monopoly reference to the Commission with respect to the existence or possible existence of that situation,

the Director, for the purpose of assisting him in determining whether to make a monopoly reference with respect to the existence or possible existence of that situation, may exercise the powers conferred by the next following subsection.

(2) In the circumstances and for the purpose mentioned in the preceding subsection the Director may require any person who supplies or produces goods of the description in question in the United Kingdom, or to whom any such goods are supplied in the United Kingdom, or (as the case may be) any person who supplies services of that description in the United Kingdom, or for whom any such services are so supplied, to furnish to the Director such information as the Director may consider necessary with regard to—

(a) the value, cost, price or quantity of goods of that description supplied or produced by that person, or of goods of that description supplied to him, or (as the case may be) the value, cost price or extent of the services of that description supplied by that person or of the services of that description supplied for him, or

(b) the capacity of any undertaking carried on by that person to supply, produce or make use of goods of that description, or (as the case may be) to supply or make use of services of that description, or

(c) the number of persons employed by that person wholly or partly on work related to the supply, production or use of goods of that description, or (as the case may be) the supply or use of services of that description.

45.—(1) Where it appears to the Director that there are grounds for believing—

(a) that a complex monopoly situation may exist in relation to the supply of goods or services of any description, or in relation to exports of goods of any description from the United Kingdom, and

(b) that in accordance with the following provisions of this Part of this Act he would not be precluded from making a monopoly reference to the Commission with respect to the existence or possible existence of that situation, the Director may formulate proposals for requiring specified persons to furnish information to him in accordance with the proposals for the purpose of assisting him in determining whether to make a monopoly reference with respect to the existence or possible existence of that situation.

(2) The persons specified in any such proposals shall be persons appearing to the Director to be, or to be included among, those who, in relation to the production or supply of goods or to the supply of services of the description in question, or in relation to exports from the United Kingdom of goods of the description in question,—

(a) may be parties to any such agreement as is mentioned in paragraph (d) of section 6(1) or paragraph (d) of section 7(1) of this Act (or mentioned in either of those paragraphs as modified by section 9(2) of this Act) or may be parties to any such agreement as is mentioned in subsection (2) or subsection (3) of section 8 of this Act, or

(b) may be conducting their respective affairs as mentioned in section 6(2) or in section 7(2) of this Act.

(3) Any such proposals shall also specify the description of goods or services in question, and—

(a) in a case falling within paragraph (a) of subsection (2) of this section, shall indicate the particular respects in which it appears to the Director that any agreement in question may be such an agreement as is referred to in that paragraph, or

(b) in a case falling within paragraph (b) of that subsection, shall indicate the particular respects in which it appears to the Director that the persons specified in the proposals may be conducting their respective affairs in a manner referred to in that paragraph,

and shall state what information the Director proposes that the persons specified in the proposals should be required to furnish for the purpose of indicating whether, in those respects, they are parties to such an agreement, or are so conducting their respective affairs, and, if so, of indicating in what circumstances they are parties to such an agreement or are so conducting their affairs.

(4) Where the Director has formulated proposals under this section, he may submit those proposals to the Secretary of State for approval; and if the Secretary of State approves the proposals, with or without modifications, the Director may require any person specified in the proposals to furnish to the Director such information as the Director may specify in accordance with the proposals, or, if the proposals have been approved with modifications, in accordance with the proposals as so modified.

46.—(1) Any power conferred on the Director by the preceding provisions of this Part of this Act to require a person to furnish information shall be exercisable by notice in writing served on that person.

(2) Any person who refuses or wilfully neglects to furnish to the Director information required by such a notice shall be guilty of an offence and shall be liable on summary conviction to a fine not exceeding £400.

(3) Any person who, in furnishing information required by such a notice, makes a statement which he knows to be false in a material particular, or recklessly makes a statement which is false in a material particular, shall be guilty of an offence and shall be liable—

(a) on summary conviction, to a fine not exceeding £400;

(b) on conviction on indictment, to imprisonment for a term not exceeding two years or to a fine or to both.

Monopoly references

47.—(1) A monopoly reference—

(a) shall specify the description of goods or services to which it relates;

(b) in the case of a reference relating to goods, shall state whether it relates to the supply of goods or to exports of goods from the United Kingdom or to both; and

(c) if, for the purposes of the reference, considerations is to be limited to a part of the United Kingdom, shall specify the part of the United Kingdom to which consideration is to be limited,

and (subject to the next following subsection) shall be framed in one or other of the ways specified in section 48 or section 49 of this Act.

(2) A monopoly reference (whether it falls within section 48 or within section 49 of this Act) may be so framed as to require the Commission to exclude from consideration, or to limit consideration to,—

(a) such agreements as are mentioned in paragraph (d) of section 6(1) or paragraph (d) of section 7(1) of this Act (or in either of those paragraphs as modified by section 9(2) of this Act) or as are mentioned in subsection (2) or subsection (3) of section 8 of this Act, or

(b) agreements or practices whereby persons conduct their affairs as mentioned in section 6(2) or section 7(2) of this Act,

or to exclude from consideration, or to limit consideration to, such one or more agreements or practices falling within paragraph (a) or paragraph (b) of this subsection as are specified in the reference.

48. A monopoly reference may be so framed as to require the Commission only to investigate and report on the questions whether a monopoly situation exists in relation to the matters set out in the reference in accordance with section 47 of this Act and, if so,—

(a) by virtue of which provisions of sections 6 to 8 of this Act that monopoly situation is to be taken to exist;

(b) in favour of what person or persons that monopoly situation exists;

(c) whether any steps (by way of uncompetitive practices or otherwise) are being taken by that person or those persons for the purpose of exploiting or maintaining the monopoly situation and, if so, by what uncompetitive practices or in what other way; and

(d) whether any action or omission on the part of that person or those persons is attributable to the existence of the monopoly situation and, if so, what action or omission and in what way it is so attributable;

and a monopoly reference so framed is in this Act referred to as a "monopoly reference limited to the facts".

49.—(1) A monopoly reference may be so framed as to require the Commission to investigate and report on the question whether a monopoly situation exists in relation to the matters set out in the reference in accordance with section 47 of this Act and, if so, to investigate and report—

(a) on the questions mentioned in paragraphs (a) to (d) of section 48 of this Act, and

(b) on the question whether any facts found by the Commission in pursuance of their investigations under the preceding provisions of this subsection operate, or may be expected to operate, against the public interest.

(2) A monopoly reference may be so framed as to require the Commission to investigate and report on the questions whether a monopoly situation exists in relation to the matters set out in the reference in accordance with section 47 of this Act and, if so,—

(a) by virtue of which provisions of sections 6 to 8 of this Act that monopoly situation is to be taken to exist;

(b) in favour of what person or persons that monopoly situation exists; and

(c) whether any action or omission on the part of that person or those persons in respect of matters specified in the reference for the purposes of this paragraph operates, or may be expected to operate, against the public interest.

(3) For the purpose of subsection (2)(c) of this section any matter may be specified in a monopoly reference if it relates to any of the following, that is to say—

(a) prices charged, or proposed to be charged, for goods or services of the description specified in the reference;

(b) any recommendation or suggestion made as to such prices;

(c) any refusal to supply goods or services of the description specified in the reference;

(d) any preference given to any person (whether by way of discrimination in respect of prices or in respect of priority of supply or otherwise) in relation to the supply of goods or services of that description;

and any matter not falling within any of the preceding paragraphs may be specified for those purposes in a monopoly reference if, in the opinion of the person or persons making the reference, it is of a kind such that (if a monopoly situation is found to exist) that matter might reasonably be regarded as a step taken for the purpose of exploiting or maintaining that situation or as being attributable to the existence of that situation.

(4) A monopoly reference framed in either of the ways mentioned in subsections (1) and (2) of this section is in this Act referred to as a "monopoly reference not limited to the facts".

50.—(1) Where it appears to the Director that a monopoly situation exists or may exist in relation to—

(a) the supply of goods of any description, or

(b) the supply of services of any description, or

(c) exports of goods of any description from the United Kingdom, either generally or to any particular market,

the Director, subject to section 12 of this Act and to the following provisions of this section, may if he thinks fit make a monopoly reference to the Commission with respect to the existence or possible existence of such a monopoly situation.

(2) No monopoly reference shall be made by the Director with respect to the existence or possible existence of a monopoly situation in relation to the supply of goods or services of any description specified in Part I of Schedule 5 or in Part I of Schedule 7 to this Act.

(3) Notwithstanding anything in subsections (30 and (4) of section 10 of this Act—

(a) for the purposes of any monopoly reference made by the Director the supply of goods or services of any description specified in the first column of Part II of Schedule 5 or of Part II of Schedule 7 to this Act in any manner specified in relation to that description of goods or services in the second column of Part II of the relevant Schedule shall be taken to be a separate form of supply, and

(b) any monopoly reference made by the Director in relation to the supply of goods or services of any such description shall be limited so as to exclude that form of supply.

(4) For the purposes of any monopoly reference made by the Director in relation to goods of any description specified in the first column of Part III of Schedule 7 to this Act—

(a) the supply of goods of that description in Northern Ireland in any manner specified in relation to that description of goods in the second column of that Part of that Schedule shall be taken to be a separate form of supply, and, notwithstanding anything in section 10(3) and (4) of this Act, any monopoly reference so made in relation to the supply of goods of any such description in Northern Ireland shall be limited so as to exclude that form of supply, and

(b) for the purposes of any such monopoly reference the Director shall so exercise his powers under section 9 of this Act as to comply with the requirements of the preceding paragraph.

(5) The Secretary of State may by order made by statutory instrument vary any of the provisions of Schedule 7 to this Act, either by adding one or more further entries or by altering or deleting any entry for the time being contained in it; and any reference in this Act to that Schedule shall be construed as a reference to that Schedule as for the time being in force.

(6) On making a monopoly reference to the Commission, the Director shall send a copy of it to the Secretary of State; and if, before the end of the period of fourteen days from the day on which the reference is first published in the Gazette in accordance with section 53 of this Act, the Secretary of State directs the Commission not to proceed with that reference,—

(a) the Commission shall not proceed with that reference, but

(b) nothing in the preceding paragraph shall prevent the Commission from proceeding with any subsequent monopoly reference, notwithstanding that it relates wholly or partly to the same matters.

51.—(1) Subject to the following provisions of this section, the Secretary of State, or the Secretary of State and any other Minister acting jointly, where it appears to him or them that a monopoly situation exists or may exist in relation to—

(a) the supply of goods of any description, or

(b) the supply of services of any description, or

(c) exports of goods of any description from the United Kingdom, either generally or to any particular market,

may, if the Secretary of State (or, in the case of joint action by the Secretary of State and another Minister, each of them) thinks fit, make a monopoly reference to the Commission with respect to the existence or possible existence of such a monopoly situation.

(2) Where it appears to the Secretary of State that a monopoly situation exists or may exist as mentioned in the preceding subsection, and that the goods or services in question are of a description specified in Part I of, or in the first column of Part II of, Schedule 5 or Schedule 7 to this Act, the Secretary of State shall not make a monopoly reference with respect to the existence or possible existence of that situation except jointly with such one or more of the Ministers mentioned in the next following subsection as appear to him to have functions directly relating—

(a) to the supply of goods or services of that description in the area (whether consisting of the whole or part of the United Kingdom) in relation to which the question arises, or

(b) to exports of goods of that description from the United Kingdom,

as the case may be.

(3) The Ministers referred to in subsection (2) of this section are the Secretary of State for Scotland, the Secretary of State for Wales, the Secretary of State for Northern Ireland, the Secretary of State for the Environment, the Minister of Agriculture, Fisheries and Food, the Minister of Agriculture, Fisheries and Food, the Minister of Agriculture for Northern Ireland, the Minister of Commerce for Northern Ireland and the Minister of Posts and Telecommunications.

(4) Where it appears to the Secretary of State that a monopoly situation exists or may exist as mentioned in subsection (1) of this section in relation to the supply in Northern Ireland of goods

of a description specified in the first column of Part III of Schedule 7 to this Act, the Secretary of State shall not make a monopoly reference with respect to the existence or possible existence of that situation except jointly with the Minister of Agriculture for Northern Ireland.

52.—(1) Subject to the following provisions of this section, the Director may at any time vary a monopoly reference made by him, and the Secretary of State (or, in the case of a monopoly reference made by the Secretary of State jointly with one or more other Ministers, the Secretary of State and that Minister or those Ministers acting jointly) may vary a monopoly reference made by him or them.

(2) A monopoly reference not limited to the facts shall not be varied so as to become a monopoly reference limited to the facts; but (subject to the following provisions of this section) a monopoly reference limited to the facts may be varied so as to become a monopoly reference not limited to the facts, whether the Commission have already reported on the reference as originally made or not.

(3) A monopoly reference made by the Director shall not be varied so as to become a reference which he is precluded from making by any provisions of section 50 of this Act.

(4) On varying a monopoly reference made by him, the Director shall send a copy of the variation to the Secretary of State; and if, before the end of the period of fourteen days from the day on which the variation is first published in the Gazette in accordance with the next following section, the Secretary of State directs the Commission not to give effect to the variation,—

(a) the Commission shall proceed with the reference as if that variation had not been made, but

(b) nothing in the preceding paragraph shall prevent the Commission from proceeding with any subsequent monopoly reference, or from giving effect to any subsequent variation, notwithstanding that it relates wholly or partly to the matters to which that variation related.

(5) In this section and in sections 53 to 55 of this Act "Minister" includes the Minister of Agriculture for Northern Ireland.

53.—(1) On making a monopoly reference, or a variation of a monopoly reference, the Director or, as the case may be, the Secretary of State (or, in the case of a monopoly reference or variation made by the Secretary of State acting jointly with one or more other Ministers, the Secretary of State and that Minister or those Ministers acting jointly) shall arrange for the reference or variation to be published in full in the Gazette, and shall arrange for the reference or variation to be published in such other manner as he or they may think most suitable for bringing it to the attention of persons who, in his or their opinion, would be affected by it.

(2) Where the Secretary of State gives a direction under section 50(6) of this Act with respect to a monopoly reference, or gives a direction under section 52(4) of this Act with respect to a variation of a monopoly reference, the Secretary of State shall arrange for the direction to be published in the Gazette and otherwise in the same manner as the monopoly reference or variation was published in accordance with the preceding subsection.

(3) In this section "the Gazette" means the London, Edinburgh and Belfast Gazettes, except that, in relation to a monopoly reference under which consideration is limited to a particular part of the United Kingdom in accordance with section 9 of this Act (including a reference under which consideration is required to be so limited by section 50(4)(b) of this Act), it means such one or more of those Gazettes as are appropriate to that part of the United Kingdom.

(4) In sections 50 and 52 of this Act any reference to publication in the Gazette is a reference to publication in the London Gazette, the Edinburgh Gazette or the Belfast Gazette, whichever first occurs.

54.—(1) A report of the Commission on a monopoly reference—

(a) if the reference was made by the Director, shall be made to the Secretary of State, and

(b) in any other case, shall be made to the Minister or Ministers by whom the reference was made.

(2) In making their report on a monopoly reference, the Commission shall include in it definite conclusions on the questions comprised in the reference, together with—

(a) such an account of their reasons for those conclusions, and

(b) such a survey of the general position with respect to the subject-matter of the reference, and of the developments which have led to that position,

as in their opinion are expedient for facilitating a proper understanding of those questions and of their conclusions.

(3) Where, on a monopoly reference not limited to the facts, the Commission find that a monopoly situation exists and that facts found by the Commission in pursuance of their investigations under subsection (1) or subsection (2) of section 49 of this Act operate, or may be expected to operate, against the public interest, the report shall specify those facts, and the conclusions to be included in the report, in so far as they relate to the operation of those facts, shall specify the particular effects, adverse to the public interest, which in their opinion those facts have or may be expected to have; and the Commission—

(a) shall, as part of their investigations, consider what action (if any) should be taken for the purpose of remedying or preventing those adverse effects, and

(b) may, if they think fit, include in their report recommendations as to such action.

(4) In paragraph (a) of subsection (3) of this section the reference to action to be taken for the purpose mentioned in that paragraph is a reference to action to be taken for that purpose either—

(a) by one or more Ministers (including Ministers or departments of the Government of Northern Ireland) or other public authorities, or

(b) by the person or (as the case may be) one or more of the persons in whose favour, in accordance with the findings of the Commission, the monopoly situation in question exists.

(5) Where, on a monopoly reference not limited to the facts, the Commission find—

(a) that a monopoly situation exists, and

(b) that the person (or, if more than one, any of the persons) in whose favour it exists is a party to an agreement to which Part I of the Act of 1956 applies,

the Commission, in making their report on that reference, shall exclude from their consideration the question whether the provisions of that agreement, in so far as they are provisions by virtue of which it is an agreement to which Part I of that Act applies, operate, or may be expected to operate, against the public interest; and subsection (3) of this section, in so far as it refers to facts found by the Commission in pursuance of their investigations, shall have effect subject to the provisions of this subsection.

55.—(1) A monopoly reference shall specify a period within which the Commission are to report on the reference; and, if a report of the Commission on the reference—

(a) is not made before the end of the period so specified, or

(b) if one or more extended periods are allowed under the next following subsection, is not made before the end of that extended period or of the last of those extended periods, as the case may be.

the reference shall cease to have effect and no action, or (if action has already been taken) no further action, shall be taken in relation to that reference under this Act.

(2) Directions may be given—

    (a) in the case of a monopoly reference made by the Director or by the Secretary of State otherwise than jointly with one or more Ministers, by the Secretary of State, or

    (b) in the case of a monopoly reference made by the Secretary of State jointly with one or more other Ministers, by the Secretary of State and that Minister or those Ministers acting jointly,

allowing to the Commission such extended period for the purpose of reporting on the reference as may be specified in the directions, or, if the period has already been extended once or more than once by directions under this subsection, allowing to the Commission such further extended period for that purpose as may be so specified.

56.—(1) The provisions of this section shall have effect where a report of the Commission on a monopoly reference not limited to the facts has been laid before Parliament in accordance with the provisions of Part VII of this Act, and the conclusions of the Commission set out in the report, as so laid,—

    (a) include conclusions to the effect that a monopoly situation exists and that facts found by the Commission in pursuance of their investigations under section 49 of this Act operate, or may be expected to operate, against the public interest, and

    (b) specify particular effects, adverse to the public interest, which in their opinion those facts have or may be expected to have.

(2) In the circumstances mentioned in the preceding subsection the appropriate Minister may (subject to subsection (6) of this section) by order made by statutory instrument exercise such one or more of the powers specified in Parts I and II of Schedule 8 to this Act as he considers it requisite to exercise for the purpose of remedying or preventing the adverse effects specified in the report as mentioned in the preceding subsection; and those powers may be so exercised to such extent and in such manner as the appropriate Minister considers requisite for that purpose.

(3) In determining whether, or to what extent or in what manner, to exercise any of those powers, the appropriate Minister shall take into account any recommendations included in the report of the Commission in pursuance of section 54(3)(b) of this Act and any advice given by the Director under section 88 of this Act.

(4) Subject to the next following subsection, in this section "the appropriate Minister" means the Secretary of State.

(5) Where, in any such report as is mentioned in subsection (1) of this section, the person or one of the persons specified as being the person or persons in whose favour the monopoly situation in question exists is a body corporate fulfilling the following conditions, that is to say—

    (a) that the affairs of the body corporate are managed by its members, and

    (b) that by virtue of an enactment those members are appointed by a Minister.

then for the purpose of making any order under this section in relation to that body corporate (but not for the purpose of making any such order in relation to any other person) "the appropriate Minister" in this section means the Minister by whom members of that body corporate are appointed.

(6) In relation to any such body corporate as is mentioned in subsection (5) of this section, the powers exercisable by virtue of subsection (2) of this section shall not include the powers specified in Part II of Schedule 8 to this Act.

PART V

MERGERS

Newspaper merger references

57.—(1) In this Part of this Act—

   (a) "newspaper" means a daily, Sunday or local (other than daily or Sunday) newspaper cir-
       culating wholly or mainly in the United Kingdom or in a part of the United Kingdom;

   (b) "newspaper proprietor" includes (in addition to an actual proprietor of a newspaper) any
       person having a controlling interest in a body corporate which is a newspaper proprietor,
       and any body corporate in which a newspaper proprietor has a controlling interest;

and any reference to the newspapers of a newspaper proprietor includes all newspapers in relation
to which he is a newspaper proprietor and, in the case of a body corporate, all newspapers in relation to which a person having a controlling interest in that body corporate is a newspaper proprietor.

(2) In this Part of this Act "transfer of a newspaper or of newspaper assets" means any of the
following transactions, that is to say—

   (a) any transaction (whether involving a transfer or not) by virtue of which a person would
       become, or would acquire the right to become, a newspaper proprietor in relation to a
       newspaper;

   (b) any transfer of assets necessary to the continuation of a newspaper as a separate news-
       paper (including goodwill or the right to use the name of the newspaper);

   (c) any transfer of plant or premises used in the publication of a newspaper, other than a
       transfer made without a view to a change in the ownership or control of the newspaper
       or to its ceasing publication;

and "the newspaper concerned in the transfer", in relation to any transaction falling within paragraph (a), paragraph (b) or paragraph (c) of this subsection, means the newspaper in relation to
which (as mentioned in that paragraph) the transaction is or is to be effected.

(3) In this Part of this Act "average circulation per day of publication", in relation to a newspaper, means its average circulation for the appropriate period, ascertained by dividing the number
of copies to which its circulation amounts for that period by the number of days on which the newspaper was published during that period (circulation being calculated on the basis of actual sales in
the United Kingdom of the newspaper as published on those days); and for the purpose of this subsection "the appropriate period"—

   (a) in a case in which an application is made for consent under the next following section,
       means the period of six months ending six weeks before the date of the application, or

   (b) in a case in which a transfer or purported transfer is made without any such application
       for consent, means the period of six months ending six weeks before the date of the trans-
       fer or purported transfer.

(4) For the purposes of this section a person has a controlling interest in a body corporate if (but
only if) he can, directly or indirectly, determine the manner in which one-quarter of the votes which
could be cast at a general meeting of the body corporate are to be cast on matters, and in circumstances, not of such a description as to bring into play any special voting rights or restrictions on
voting rights.

58.—(1) Subject to the following provisions of this section, a transfer of a newspaper or of newspaper assets to a newspaper proprietor whose newspapers have an average circulation per day of

publication amounting, together with that of the newspaper concerned in the transfer, to 500,000 or more copies shall be unlawful and void, unless the transfer is made with written consent given (conditionally or unconditionally) by the Secretary of State.

(2) Except as provided by subsections (3) and (4) of this section and by section 60(3) of this Act, the consent of the Secretary of State under the preceding subsection shall not be given in respect of a transfer until after the Secretary of State has received a report on the matter from the Commission.

(3) Where the Secretary of State is satisfied that the newspaper concerned in the transfer is not economic as a going concern and as a separate newspaper, then—

(a) if he is also satisfied that, if the newspaper is to continue as a separate newspaper, the case is one of urgency, he may give his consent to the transfer without requiring a report from the Commission under this section;

(b) if he is satisfied that the newspaper is not intended to continue as a separate newspaper, he shall give his consent to the transfer, and shall give it unconditionally, without requiring such a report.

(4) If the Secretary of State is satisfied that the newspaper concerned in the transfer has an average circulation per day of publication of not more than 25,000 copies, he may give his consent to the transfer without requiring a report from the Commission under this section.

(5) The Secretary of State may by order made by statutory instrument provide, subject to any transitional provisions contained in the order, that for any number specified in subsection (1) or subsection (4) of this section (whether as originally enacted or as previously varied by an order under this subsection) there shall be substituted such other number as is specified in the order.

(6) In this section "satisfied" means satisfied by such evidence as the Secretary of State may require.

59.—(1) Where an application is made to the Secretary of State for his consent to a transfer of a newspaper or of newspaper assets, the Secretary of State, subject to the next following subsection, shall, within one month after receiving the application, refer the matter to the Commission for investigation and report.

(2) The Secretary of State shall not make a reference to the Commission under the preceding subsection in a case where—

(a) by virtue of subsection (3) of section 58 of this Act he is required to give his consent unconditionally without requiring a report from the Commission under this section, or

(b) by virtue of subsection (3) or subsection (4) of that section he has power to give his consent without requiring such a report from the Commission, and determines to exercise that power,

or where the application is expressed to depend on the operation of subsection (3) or subsection (4) of that section.

(3) On a reference made to them under this section (in this Act referred to as a "newspaper merger reference") the Commission shall report to the Secretary of State whether the transfer in question may be expected to operate against the public interest, taking into account all matters which appear in the circumstances to be relevant and, in particular, the need for accurate presentation of news and free expression of opinion.

60.—(1) A report of the Commission on a newspaper merger reference shall be made before the end of the period of three months beginning with the date of the reference or of such further period (if any) as the Secretary of State may allow for the purpose in accordance with the next following subsection.

(2) The Secretary of State shall not allow any further period for a report on such a reference except on representations made by the Commission and on being satisfied that there are special reasons why the report cannot be made within the original period of three months; and the Secretary of State shall allow only one such further period on any one reference, and no such further period shall be longer than three months.

(3) If on such a reference the Commission have not made their report before the end of the period specified in subsection (1) or of any further period allowed under subsection (2) of this section, the Secretary of State may, without waiting for the report, give his consent to the transfer to which the reference relates.

61.—(1) In making their report on a newspaper merger reference, the Commission shall include in it definite conclusions on the questions comprised in the reference, together with—

    (a) such an account of their reasons for those conclusions, and

    (b) such a survey of the general position with respect to the transfer of a newspaper or of newspaper assets to which the reference relates, and of the developments which have led to that position,

as in their opinion are expedient for facilitating a proper understanding of those questions and of their conclusions.

(2) Where on such a reference the Commission find that the transfer of a newspaper or of newspaper assets in question might operate against the public interest, the Commission shall consider whether any (and, if so, what) conditions might be attached to any consent to the transfer in order to prevent the transfer from so operating, and may, if they think fit, include in their report recommendations as to such conditions.

62.—(1) Any person who is knowingly concerned in, or privy to, a purported transfer of a newspaper or of newspaper assets which is unlawful by virtue of section 58 of this Act shall be guilty of an offence.

(2) Where under that section the consent of the Secretary of State is given to a transfer of a newspaper or of newspaper assets, but is given subject to one or more conditions, any person who is knowingly concerned in, or privy to, a breach of that condition, or of any of those conditions, as the case may be, shall be guilty of an offence.

(3) A person guilty of an offence under this section shall be liable, on conviction on indictment, to imprisonment for a term not exceeding two years or to a fine or to both.

(4) No proceedings for an offence under this section shall be instituted—

    (a) in England or Wales, except by, or with the consent of, the Director of Public Prosecutions, or

    (b) in Northern Ireland, except by, or with the consent of, the Director of Public Prosecutions for Northern Ireland.

Other merger references

63.—(1) Sections 64 to 75 of this Act shall have effect in relation to merger references other than newspaper merger references; and accordingly in those sections "merger reference" shall be construed—

    (a) as not including a reference made under section 59 of this Act, but

    (b) as including any merger reference relating to a transfer of a newspaper or of newspaper assets, if the reference is made under section 64 or section 75 of this Act in a case falling within section 59(2) of this Act.

(2) In the following provisions of this Part of this Act "enterprise" means the activities, or part of the activities, of a business.

64.—(1) A merger reference may be made to the Commission by the Secretary of State where it appears to him that it is or may be the fact that two or more enterprises (in this section referred to as "the relevant enterprises"), of which one at least was carried on in the United Kingdom or by or under the control of a body corporate incorporated in the United Kingdom, have, at a time or in circumstances falling within subsection (4) of this section, ceased to be distinct enterprises, and that either—

(a) as a result, the condition specified in subsection (2) or in subsection (3) of this section prevails, or does so to a greater extent, with respect to the supply of goods or services of any description, or

(b) the value of the assets taken over exceeds £5 million.

(2) The condition referred to in subsection (1)(a) of this section, in relation to the supply of goods of any description, is that at least one-quarter of all the goods of that description which are supplied in the United Kingdom, or in a substantial part of the United Kingdom, either—

(a) are supplied by one and the same person or are supplied to one and the same person, or

(b) are supplied by the persons by whom the relevant enterprises (so far as they continue to be carried on) are carried on, or are supplied to those persons.

(3) The condition referred to in subsection (1)(a) of this section, in relation to the supply of services of any description, is that the supply of services of that description in the United Kingdom, or in a substantial part of the United Kingdom, is, to the extent of at least one-quarter, either—

(a) supply by one and the same person, or supply for one and the same person, or

(b) supply by the persons by whom the relevant enterprises (so far as they continue to be carried on) are carried on, or supply for those persons.

(4) For the purposes of subsection (1) of this section enterprises shall be taken to have ceased to be distinct enterprises at a time or in circumstances falling within this subsection if either—

(a) they did so not earlier than six months before the date on which the merger reference relating to them is to be made, or

(b) they did so under or in consequence of arrangements or transactions which were entered into without prior notice being given to the Secretary of State or to the Director of material facts about the proposed arrangements or transactions and in circumstances in which those facts had not been made public, and notice of those facts was not given to the Secretary of State or to the Director or made public more than six months before the date mentioned in the preceding paragraph.

(5) In determining whether to make a merger reference to the Commission the Secretary of State shall have regard, with a view to the prevention or removal of uncertainty, to the need for making a determination as soon as is reasonably practicable.

(6) On making a merger reference, the Secretary of State shall arrange for it to be published in such manner as he thinks most suitable for bringing it to the attention of persons who in his opinion would be affected by it.

(7) The Secretary of State may by order made by statutory instrument provide, subject to any transitional provisions contained in the order, that for the sum specified in subsection (1)(b) of this section (whether as originally enacted or as previously varied by an order under this subsection) there shall be substituted such other sum (not being less than £5 million) as is specified in the order.

(8) The fact that two or more enterprises have ceased to be distinct enterprises in the circumstances described in subsection (1) of this section (including in those circumstances the result specified in paragraph (a), or fulfilment of the condition specified in paragraph (a), or fulfilment of the condition specified in paragraph (b), of that subsection) shall, for the purposes of this Act, be regarded as creating a merger situation qualifying for investigation; and in this Act "merger situation qualifying for investigation" and any reference to the creation of such a situation shall be construed accordingly.

(9) In this section "made public" means so publicised as to be generally known or readily ascertainable.

65.—(1) For the purposes of this Part of this Act any two enterprises shall be regarded as ceasing to be distinct enterprises if either—

(a) they are brought under common ownership or common control (whether or not the business to which either of them formerly belonged continues to be carried on under the same or different ownership or control), or

(b) either of the enterprises ceases to be carried on at all and does so in consequence of any arrangements or transaction entered into to prevent competition between the enterprises.

(2) For the purposes of the preceding subsection enterprises shall (without prejudice to the generality of the words "common control" in that subsection) be regarded as being under common control if they are—

(a) enterprises of interconnected bodies corporate, or

(b) enterprises carried on by two or more bodies corporate of which one and the same person or group of persons has control or

(c) an enterprise carried on by a body corporate and an enterprise carried on by a person or group of persons having control of that body corporate.

(3) A person or group of persons able, directly or indirectly, to control or materially to influence the policy of a body corporate, or the policy of any person in carrying on an enterprise, but without having a controlling interest in that body corporate or in that enterprise, may for the purposes of subsections (1) and (2) of this section be treated as having control of it.

(4) For the purposes of subsection (1)(a) of this section, in so far as it relates to bringing two or more enterprises under common control, a person or group of persons may be treated as bringing an enterprise under his or their control if—

(a) being already able to control or materially to influence the policy of the person carrying on the enterprise, that person or group of persons acquires a controlling interest in the enterprise or, in the case of an enterprise carried on by a body corporate, acquires a controlling interest in that body corporate, or

(b) being already able materially to influence the policy of the person carrying on the enterprise, that person or group of persons becomes able to control that policy.

66.—(1) Where under or in consequence of the same arrangements or transaction, or under or in consequence of successive arrangements or transactions between the same parties or interests, successive events to which this subsection applies occur within a period of two years, then for the purposes of a merger reference those events may, if the Secretary of State thinks fit, be treated as having occurred simultaneously on the date on which the latest of them occurred.

(2) The preceding subsection applies to any event whereby, under or in consequence of the arrangements or the transaction or transactions in question, any enterprises cease as between themselves to be distinct enterprises.

(3) For the purposes of subsection (1) of this section any arrangements or transactions may be treated by the Secretary of State as arrangements or transactions between the same interests if it

appears to him to be appropriate that they should be so treated, having regard to the persons who are substantially concerned in them.

(4) Subject to the preceding provisions of this section, the time at which any two enterprises cease to be distinct enterprises, where they do so under or in consequence of any arrangements or transactions not having immediate effect, or having immediate effect in part only, shall be taken to be the time when the parties to the arrangements or transaction become bound to such extent as will result, on effect being given to their obligations, in the enterprises ceasing to be distinct enterprises.

(5) In accordance with subsection (4) of this section (but without prejudice to the generality of that subsection) for the purpose of determining the time at which any two enterprises cease to be distinct enterprises no account shall be taken of any option or other conditional right until the option is exercised or the condition is satisfied.

67.—(1) The provisions of this section shall have effect for the purposes of section 64(1)(b) of this Act.

(2 Subject to subsection (4) of this section, the value of the assets taken over—

(a) shall be determined by taking the total value of the assets employed in, or appropriated to, the enterprises which cease to be distinct enterprises, except any enterprise which remain under the same ownership and control, or if none of the enterprises remains under the same ownership and control, then that one of the enterprises having the assets with the highest value, and

(b) shall be so determined by reference to the values at which, on the enterprises ceasing to be distinct enterprises or (if they have not then done so) on the making of the merger reference to the Commission, the assets stand in the books of the relevant business, less any relevant provisions for depreciation, renewals or diminution in value.

(3) For the purposes of subsection (2) of this section any assets of a body corporate which, on a change in the control of the body corporate or of any enterprise of it, are dealt with in the same way as assets appropriated to any such enterprise shall be treated as appropriated to that enterprise.

(4) Where in accordance with subsection (1) of section 66 of this Act events to which that subsection applies are treated as having occurred simultaneously, subsection (2) of this section shall apply with such adjustments as appear to the Secretary of State or to the Commission to be appropriate.

68.—(1) In relation to goods or services of any description which are the subject of different forms of supply—

(a) references in subsection (2) of section 64 of this Act to the supply of goods, or

(b) references in subsection (3) of that section to the supply of services,

shall be construed in whichever of the following ways appears to the Secretary of State or the Commission, as the case may be, to be appropriate in all the circumstances, that is to say, as references to any of those forms of supply taken separately, to all those forms of supply taken together, or to any of those forms of supply taken in groups.

(2) For the purposes of the preceding subsection the Secretary of State or the Commission may treat goods or services as being the subject of different forms of supply whenever the transactions in question differ as to their nature, their parties, their terms or their surrounding circumstances, and the difference is one which, in the opinion of the Secretary of State or of the Commission, as the case may be, ought for the purposes of that subsection to be treated as a material difference.

(3) For the purpose of determining whether the proportion of one-quarter mentioned in subsection (2) or subsection (3) of section 64 of this Act is fulfilled with respect to goods or services of any description, the Secretary of State or the Commission, as the case may be, shall apply such criter-

ion (whether it be value or cost or price or quantity or capacity or number of workers employed or some other criterion, of whatever nature) or such combination of criteria as may appear to the Secretary of State or the Commission to be most suitable in all the circumstances.

(4) The criteria for determining when goods or services can be treated, for the purposes of section 64 of this Act, as goods or services of a separate description shall be such as in any particular case the Secretary of State thinks most suitable in the circumstances of that case.

69.—(1) Subject to the following provisions of this Part of this Act, on a merger reference the Commission shall investigate and report on the questions—

(a) whether a merger situation qualifying for investigation has been created, and

(b) if so, whether the creation of that situation operates, or may be expected to operate, against the public interest.

(2) A merger reference may be so framed as to require the Commission, in relation to the question whether a merger situation qualifying for investigation has been created, to exclude from consideration paragraph (a) of subsection (1) of section 64 of this Act, or to exclude from consideration paragraph (b) of that subsection, or to exclude one of those paragraphs if the Commission find the other satisfied.

(3) In relation to the question whether any such result as is mentioned in section 64(1)(a) of this Act has arisen, a merger reference may be so framed as to require the Commission to confine their investigation to the supply of goods or services in a specified part of the United Kingdom.

(4) A merger reference may require the Commission, if they find that a merger situation qualifying for investigation has been created, to limit their consideration thereafter to such elements in, or possible consequences of, the creation of that situation as may be specified in the reference, and to consider whether, in respect only of those elements or possible consequences, the situation operates, or may be expected to operate, against the public interest.

70.—(1) Every merger reference shall specify a period (not being longer than six months beginning with the date of the reference) within which a report on the reference is to be made; and a report of the Commission on a merger reference shall not have effect, and no action shall be taken in relation to it under this Act, unless the report is made before the end of that period or of such further period (if any) as may be allowed by the Secretary of State in accordance with the next following subsection.

(2) The Secretary of State shall not allow any further period for a report on a merger reference except on representations made by the Commission and on being satisfied that there are special reasons why the report cannot be made within the period specified in the reference; and the Secretary of State shall allow only one such further period on any one reference, and no such further period shall be longer than three months.

71.—(1) Subject to the following provisions of this section, the Secretary of State may at any time vary a merger reference made under section 69(4) of this Act.

(2) A merger reference made under section 69(4) of this Act shall not be so varied that it ceases to be a reference limited in accordance with that subsection.

(3) Without prejudice to the powers of the Secretary of State under section 70 of this Act, a merger reference shall not be varied so as to specify a period within which a report on the reference is to be made which is different from the period specified in the reference in accordance with that section.

72.—(1) In making their report on a merger reference, the Commission shall include in it definite conclusions on the questions comprised in the reference, together with—

(a) such an account of their reasons for those conclusions, and

(b) such a survey of the general position with respect to the subject-matter of the reference, and of the developments which have led to that position,

as in their opinion are expedient for facilitating a proper understanding of those questions and of their conclusions.

(2) Where on a merger reference the Commission find that a merger situation qualifying for investigation has been created and that the creation of that situation operates or may be expected to operate against the public interest (or, in a case falling within subsection (4) of section 69 of this Act, find that one or more elements in or consequences of that situation which were specified in the reference in accordance with that subsection so operate or may be expected so to operate) the Commission shall specify in their report the particular effects, adverse to the public interest, which in their opinion the creation of that situation (or, as the case may be, those elements in or consequences of it) have or may be expected to have; and the Commission—

(a) shall, as part of their investigation, consider what action (if any) should be taken for the purpose of remedying or preventing those adverse effects, and

(b) may, if they think fit, include in their report recommendations as to such action.

(3) In paragraph (a) of subsection (2) of this section the reference to action to be taken for the purpose mentioned in that paragraph is a reference to action to be taken for that purpose either—

(a) by one or more Ministers (including Ministers or departments of the Government of Northern Ireland) or other public authorities, or

(b) by one or more persons specified in the report as being persons carrying on, owning or controlling any of the enterprises which, in accordance with the conclusions of the Commission, have ceased to be distinct enterprises.

73.—(1) The provisions of this section shall have effect where a report of the Commission on a merger reference has been laid before Parliament in accordance with the provisions of Part VII of this Act, and the conclusions of the Commission set out in the report, as so laid,—

(a) include conclusions to the effect that a merger situation qualifying for investigation has been created and that its creation, or particular elements in or consequences of it specified in the report, operate or may be expected to operate against the public interest, and

(b) specify particular effects, adverse to the public interest, which in the opinion of the Commission the creation of that situation, or (as the case may be) those elements in or consequences of it, have or may be expected to have.

(2) In the circumstances mentioned in the preceding subsection the Secretary of State may by order made by statutory instrument exercise such one or more of the powers specified in Parts I and II of Schedule 8 to this Act as he may consider it requisite to exercise for the purpose of remedying or preventing the adverse effects specified in the report as mentioned in the preceding subsection; and those powers may be so exercised to such extent and in such manner as the Secretary of State considers requisite for that purpose.

(3) In determining whether, or to what extent or in what manner, to exercise any of those powers, the Secretary of State shall take into account any recommendations included in the report of the Commission in pursuance of section 72(2)(b) of this Act and any advice given by the Director under section 88 of this Act.

74.—(1) Where a merger reference has been made to the Commission, and does not impose on the Commission a limitation under section 69(4) of this Act, then, with a view to preventing action to which this subsection applies, the Secretary of State, subject to subsection (3) of this section, may by order made by statutory instrument—

(a) prohibit or restrict the doing of things which in his opinion would constitute action to which this subsection applies, or

(b) impose on any person concerned obligations as to the carrying on of any activities of the safeguarding of any assets, or

(c) provide for the carrying on of any activities on the safeguarding of any assets either by the appointment of a person to conduct or supervise the conduct of any activities (on such terms and with such powers as may be specified or described in the order) or in any other manner, or

(d) exercise any of the powers which, by virtue of paragraph 12 of Schedule 8 to this Act, are exercisable by an order under section 73 of this Act.

(2) In relation to a merger reference the preceding subsection applies to any action which might prejudice the reference or impede the taking of any action under this Act which may be warranted by the Commission's report on the reference.

(3) No order shall be made under this section in respect of a merger reference after whichever of the following events first occurs, that is to say—

(a) the time (including any further period) allowed to the Commission for making a report on the reference expires without their having made such a report;

(b) the period of forty days beginning with the day on which a report of the Commission on the reference is laid before Parliament expires.

(4) An order under this section made in respect of a merger reference (if it has not previously ceased to have effect) shall cease to have effect on the occurrence of whichever of those events first occurs, but without prejudice to anything previously done under the order.

(5) Subsection (4) of this section shall have effect without prejudice—

(a) to the operation, in relation to any such order, of section 134(1) of this Act, or

(b) to the operation of any order made under section 73 of this Act which exercises the same or similar powers to those exercised by the order under this section.

7.—(1) A merger reference may be made to the Commission by the Secretary of State where it appears to him that it is or may be the fact that arrangements are in progress or in contemplation which, if carried into effect, will result in the creation of a merger situation qualifying for investigation.

(2) Subject to the following provisions of this section, on a merger reference under this section the Commissions shall proceed in relation to the prospective and (if events so require) the actual results of the arrangements proposed or made as, in accordance with the preceding provisions of this Part of this Act, they could proceed if the arrangements in question had actually been made, and the results in question had followed immediately before the date of the reference under this section.

(3) A merger reference under this section may require the Commission, if they find that a merger situation qualifying for investigation has been created, or will be created if the arrangements in question are carried into effect, to limit their consideration thereafter to such elements in, or possible consequences of, the creation of that situation as may be specified in the reference, and to consider whether, in respect only of those elements or possible consequences, the situation might be expected to operate against the public interest.

(4) In relation to a merger reference under this section, sections 66, 67, 69, 71, 72, 73 and 74 of this Act shall apply subject to the following modifications, that is to say—

(a) section 66 shall apply with the necessary adaptations in relation to enterprises which will or may cease to be distinct enterprises under or in consequence of arrangements not yet carried into effect or not yet fully carried into effect;

(b) in section 67(4) the reference to subsection (1) of section 66 shall be construed as a reference to that subsection as modified in accordance with the preceding paragraph;

(c) in section 69, subsection (1) shall be construed as modified by subsection (2) of this section; in subsections (2) and (3) any reference to the question whether a merger situation qualifying for investigation has been created, or whether a result mentioned in section 64(1)(a) of this Act has arisen, shall be construed as including a reference to the question whether such a situation will be created or such a result will arise if the arrangements in question are carried into effect; and subsection (4) of that section shall not apply;

(d) in section 71, in section 72(2) and in section 74(1), the references to section 69(4) of this Act shall be construed as references to subsection (3) of this section; and

(e) in section 73(1), the reference to conclusions to the effect that a merger situation qualifying for investigation has been created shall be construed as including a reference to conclusions to the effect that such a situation will be created if the arrangements in question are carried into effect.

(5) If, in the course of their investigations on a merger reference under this section, it appears to the Commission that the proposal to make arrangements such as are mentioned in the reference has been abandoned, the Commission—

(a) shall, if the Secretary of State consents, lay the reference aside, but

(b) shall in that case furnish to the Secretary of State such information as he may require as to the results until then of the investigations.

Supplementary

76. It shall be the duty of the Director—

(a) to take all such steps as are reasonably practicable for keeping himself informed about actual or prospective arrangements or transactions which may constitute or result in the creation of merger situations qualifying for investigation, and

(b) to make recommendations to the Secretary of State as to any action under this Part of this Act which in the opinion of the Director it would be expedient for the Secretary of State to take in relation to any such arrangements or transactions.

77.—(1) For the following purposes, that is to say—

(a) for the purpose of determining under section 57(1) of this Act whether a person is a newspaper proprietor and, if so, which newspapers are his newspapers;

(b) for the purpose of determining under section 65 of this Act whether any two enterprises have been brought under common ownership or common control; and

(c) for the purpose of determining what activities are carried on by way of business by any one person, in so far as that question arises in the application, by virtue of an order under section 73 of this Act, of paragraph 14 of Schedule 8 to this Act,

associated persons, and any bodies corporate which they or any of them control, shall (subject to the next following subsection) be treated as one person.

(2) The preceding subsection shall not have effect—

(a) for the purpose mentioned in paragraph (a) of that subsection so as to exclude from section 58 of this Act any case which would otherwise fall within that section, or

(b) for the purpose mentioned in paragraph (b) of the preceding subsection so as to exclude from section 65 of this Act any case which would otherwise fall within that section.

(3) A merger reference other than a newspaper merger reference (whether apart from this section the reference could be made or not) may be so framed as to exclude from consideration, either altogether or for any specified purpose or to any specified extent, any matter which, apart from this section, would not have been taken into account on that reference.

(4) For the purposes of this section the following persons shall be regarded as associated with one another, that is to say—

(a) any individual and that individual's husband or wife and any relative, or husband or wife of a relative, of that individual or of that individual's husband or wife;

(b) any person in his capacity as trustee of a settlement and the settlor or grantor and any person associated with the settlor or grantor;

(c) persons carrying on business in partnership and the husband or wife and relatives of any of them;

(d) any two or more persons acting together to secure or exercise control of a body corporate or other association or to secure control of any enterprise or assets.

(5) The reference in subsection (1) of this section to bodies corporate which associated persons control shall be construed as follows, that is to say—

(a) in its application for the purpose mentioned in paragraph (a) of that subsection, "control" in that reference means having a controlling interest within the meaning of section 57(4) of this Act, and

(b) in its application for any other purpose mentioned in subsection (1) of this section, "control" in that reference shall be construed in accordance with section 65(3) and (4) of this Act.

(6) In this section "relative" means a brother, sister, uncle, aunt, nephew, niece, lineal ancestor or descendant (the stepchild or illegitimate child of any person, or anyone adopted by a person, whether legally or otherwise, as his child, being taken into account as a relative or to trace a relationship in the same way as that person's child); and references to a wife or husband shall include a former wife or husband and a reputed wife or husband.

PART VI

REFERENCES TO COMMISSION OTHER THAN MONOPOLY AND MERGER REFERENCES

78.—(1) The Secretary of State, or the Secretary of State and any other Minister acting jointly, may at any time require the Commission to submit to him or them a report on the general effect on the public interest—

(a) of practices of a specified class which, in his or their opinion, are commonly adopted as a result of, or for the purpose of preserving, monopoly situations, or

(b) of any specified practices which appear to him or them to be uncompetitive practices.

(2) The Secretary of State, or the Secretary of State and any other Minister acting jointly, may also at any time require the Commission to submit to him or them a report on the desirability of action of any specified description for the purpose of remedying or preventing effects, adverse to the public interest, which result or might result from monopoly situations or from any such practices as are mentioned in the preceding subsection.

(3) The matters to be taken into consideration by the Commission on any reference under this section shall not include any provisions of any agreement in so far as they are provisions by virtue of which it is an agreement to which Part I of the Act of 1956 applies.

79.—(1) The Secretary of State, or the Secretary of State and any other Minister acting jointly, may at any time refer to the Commission the questions—

(a) whether a practice of a description specified in the reference exists and, if so, whether it is a restrictive labour practice, and

(b) if it exists and is a restrictive labour practice, whether it operates or may be expected to operate against the public interest and, if so, what particular effects, adverse to the public interest, it has or may be expected to have.

(2) A reference under this section may refer those questions to the Commission either—

(a) in relation to commercial activities in the United Kingdom generally, or

(b) in relation to such commercial activities in the United Kingdom as consist of the supply of goods of a description specified in the reference, or of the supply of services of a description so specified, or of the export from the United Kingdom of goods of a description so specified.

(3) The Commission shall examine any questions referred to them under this section and shall report to the Minister or Ministers who referred them to the Commission.

(4) For the purposes of their functions under subsection (3) of this section the Commission shall disregard anything which appears to them to have been done, or omitted to be done, in contemplation or furtherance of an industrial dispute within the meaning of the Industrial Relations Act 1971.

(5) In this section "restrictive labour practice" means any practice whereby restrictions or other requirements, not being restrictions or requirements relating exclusively to rates of remuneration, operate in relation to the employment of workers in any commercial activities in the United Kingdom or in relation to work done by any such workers, and are restrictions or requirements which—

(a) could be discontinued without thereby contravening the provisions of an enactment or of any instrument having effect by virtue of an enactment, and

(b) are not necessary for, or are more stringent than is necessary for, the efficient conduct of those activities.

80. A reference made under this Part of this Act may at any time be varied by the Minister or Ministers by whom the reference was made.

PART VII

PROVISIONS RELATING TO REFERENCES TO ADVISORY COMMITTEE OR TO COMMISSION

81.—(1) The Advisory Committee, in carrying out an investigation on a reference to which section 17 of this Act applies, and the Commission, in carrying out an investigation on a reference made to them under this Act (whether it is a monopoly reference or a merger reference or a reference under Part VI of this Act),—

(a) shall take into consideration any representations made to them by persons appearing to them to have a substantial interest in the subject-matter of the reference, or by bodies appearing to them to represent substantial numbers of persons who have such an interest, and

(b) unless in all the circumstances they consider it not reasonably necessary or not reasonably practicable to do so, shall permit any such person or body to be heard orally by the Advisory Committee or the Commission, as the case may be, or by a member of the Committee or of the Commission nominated by them for that purpose.

(2) Subject to subsection (1) of this section, the Advisory Committee or the Commission may determine their own procedure for carrying out any investigation on a reference under this Act, and in particular may determine—

(a) the extent, if any, to which persons interested or claiming to be interested in the subject-matter of the reference are allowed to be present or to be heard, either by themselves or by their representatives, or to cross-examine witnesses or otherwise take part in the investigation, and

(b) the extent, if any, to which the sittings of the Advisory Committee or of the Commission are to be held in public.

(3) In determining their procedure under subsection (2) of this section, and, in the case of the Commission, in exercising any powers conferred on them by section 85 of this Act, the Advisory Committee or the Commission, as the case may be, shall act in accordance with any general directions which may from time to time be given to them by the Secretary of State.

(4) The Secretary of State shall lay before each House of Parliament a copy of any directions given by him under subsection (3) of this section.

82.—(1) In making any report under this Act the Advisory Committee or the Commission shall have regard to the need for excluding, so far as that is practicable,—

(a) any matter which relates to the private affairs of an individual, where the publication of that matter would or might, in their opinion, seriously and prejudicially affect the interests of that individual, and

(b) any matter which relates specifically to the affairs of a particular body of persons, whether corporate or uncorporate, where publication of that matter would or might, in the opinion of the Advisory Committee or of the Commission, as the case may be, seriously and prejudicially affect the interests of that body, unless in their opinion the inclusion of that matter relating specifically to that body is necessary for the purposes of the report

(2) For the purposes of the law relating to defamation, absolute privilege shall attach to any report of the Advisory Committee or of the Commission under this Act.

(3) Subject to the next following subsection, if—

(a) on a reference to the Advisory Committee under this Act, or

(b) on a reference to the Commission, other than a monopoly reference limited to the facts,

a member of the Advisory Committee or of the Commission, as the case may be, dissents from any conclusions contained in the report on the reference as being conclusions of the Committee or of the Commission, the report shall, if that member so desires, include a statement of his dissent and of his reasons for dissenting.

(4) In relation to a report made by a group of members of the Commission in pursuance of paragraph 10 or paragraph 11 of Schedule 3 to this Act, subsection (3) of this section shall have effect subject to paragraph 14(1) of that Schedule.

83.—(1) The Minister or Ministers to whom any report of the Advisory Committee on a reference to which section 17 of this Act applies, or any report of the Commission under this Act, is made shall lay a copy of the report before each House of Parliament, and shall arrange for the report to be published in such manner as appears to the Minister or Ministers to be appropriate.

(2) If such a report is presented by command of Her Majesty to either House of Parliament otherwise than at or during the time of a sitting of that House, the presentation of the report shall for the purposes of this section be treated as the laying of a copy of it before that House by the Minister or Ministers to whom the report was made.

(3) If it appears to the Minister or Ministers to whom any report of the Advisory Committee or of the Commission under this Act is made that the publication of any matter in the report would be against the public interest, the Minister or Ministers shall exclude that matter from the copies of the report as laid before Parliament and from the report as published under this section.

(4) Any reference in this Act to a report of the Advisory Committee or of the Commission as laid before Parliament shall be construed as a reference to the report in the form in which copies of it are laid (or by virtue of subsection (2) of this section are treated as having been laid) before each House of Parliament under this section.

PART VIII

ADDITIONAL PROVISIONS RELATING TO REFERENCES TO COMMISSION

84.—(1) In determining for any purposes to which this section applies whether any particular matter operates, or may be expected to operate, against the public interest, the Commission shall take into account all matters which appear to them in the particular circumstances to be relevant and, among other things, shall have regard to the desirability—

(a) of maintaining and promoting effective competition between persons supplying goods and services in the United Kingdom;

(b) of promoting the interests of consumers, purchasers and other users of goods and services in the United Kingdom in respect of the prices charged for them and in respect of their quality and the variety of goods and services supplied;

(c) of promoting, through competition, the reduction of costs and the development and use of new techniques and new products, and of facilitating the entry of new competitors into existing markets;

(d) of maintaining and promoting the balanced distribution of industry and employment in the United Kingdom; and

(e) of maintaining and promoting competitive activity in markets outside the United Kingdom on the part of producers of goods, and of suppliers of goods and services, in the United Kingdom.

(2) This section applies to the purposes of any functions of the Commission under this Act other than functions to which section 59(3) of this Act applies.

85.—(1) For the purposes of any investigation on a reference made to them under this Act the Commission may, by notice in writing signed on their behalf by any of their members or by their secretary,—

(a) require any person to attend at a time and place specified in the notice, and to give evidence to the Commission or a member of the Commission nominated by them for the purpose, or

(b) require any person to produce, at a time and place specified in the notice, to the Commission or to any person nominated by the Commission for the purpose, any documents which are specified or described in the notice and which are documents in his custody or under his control and relating to any matter relevant to the investigation, or

(c) require any person carrying on any business to furnish to the Commission such estimates, returns or other information as may be specified or described in the notice, and specify the time, the manner and the form in which any such estimates, returns or information are to be furnished.

(2) For the purposes of any such investigation the Commission, or a member of the Commission nominated by them for that purpose, may take evidence on oath, and for that purpose may administer oaths.

(3) No person shall be compelled for the purpose of any such investigation to give any evidence or produce any document which he could not be compelled to give or produce in civil proceedings before the court or, in complying with any requirement for the furnishing of information, to give any information which he could not be compelled to give in evidence in such proceedings.

(4) No person shall be required, in obedience to a notice under subsection (1) of this section, to go more than ten miles from his place of residence unless the necessary expenses of his attendance are paid or tendered to him.

(5) Any person who refuses or, without reasonable excuse, fails to do anything duly required of him by a notice under subsection (1) of this section shall be guilty of an offence and liable on summary conviction to a fine not exceeding £400.

(6) Any person who—

(a) wilfully alters, suppresses or destroys any document which he has been required by any such notice to produce, or

(b) in furnishing any estimate, return or other information required of him under any such notice, makes any statement which he knows to be false in a material particular or recklessly makes any statement which is false in a material particular,

shall be guilty of an offence and liable on summary conviction to a fine not exceeding £400 or, on conviction on indictment, to imprisonment for a term not exceeding two years or to a fine or to both.

(7) If a person makes default in complying with a notice under subsection (1) of this section, the court may, on the application of the Secretary of State, make such order as the court thinks fit for requiring the default to be made good; and any such order may provide that all the costs or expenses of and incidental to the application shall be borne by the person in default or by any officers of a company or other association who are responsible for its default.

(8) In this section "the court"—

(a) in relation to England and Wales, means the High Court;

(b) in relation to Scotland, means the Court of Session; and

(c) in relation to Northern Ireland, means the High Court or a judge of the High Court.

86.—(1) Subject to the next following subsection, a copy of every report of the Commission on a monopoly reference, or on a merger reference other than a newspaper merger reference, shall be transmitted by the Commission to the Director; and the Minister or Ministers to whom any such report is made shall take account of any advice given to him or them by the Director with respect to a report of which a copy is transmitted to the Director under this section.

(2) The preceding subsection shall not apply to a report made on a monopoly reference, where the reference was made by a Minister or Ministers and (by virtue of any of the provisions of section 50 of this Act) could not have been made by the Director.

(3) In this section "Minister" includes the Minister of Agriculture for Northern Ireland and the Minister of Commerce for Northern Ireland.

87.—(1) Where under section 83 of this Act the Secretary of State lays before Parliament a copy of a report of the Commission on a newspaper merger reference, then—

(a) if before laying it the Secretary of State has consented to the transfer of a newspaper or of newspaper assets to which the report relates, he shall annex a copy of that consent to the copy of the report laid before Parliament, or

(b) if he subsequently consents to that transfer, he shall thereupon lay before Parliament a copy of that consent.

(2) Where the persons to whom a report of the Commission is made under this Act include the Minister of Agriculture for Northern Ireland, that Minister shall lay a copy of the report before the Senate and House of Commons of Northern Ireland, and shall arrange for it to be published in Northern Ireland in such manner as appears to him to be appropriate.

(3) If a report to which subsection (2) of this section applies is presented by command of the Governor of Northern Ireland to the Senate or House of Commons of Northern Ireland otherwise than at or during the time of a sitting of the Senate or of that House, as the case may be, the presentation of the report shall for the purposes of that subsection be treated as the laying of a copy of it before the Senate or that House as required by that subsection.

88.—(1) Where a report of the Commission on a monopoly reference, or on a merger reference other than a newspaper merger reference, as laid before Parliament,—

(a) in the case of a monopoly reference, sets out such conclusions as are mentioned in section 56(1) of this Act, or

(b) in the case of a merger reference, sets out such conclusions as are mentioned in section 73(1) or in section 75(4)(e) of this Act,

and a copy of the report is transmitted to the Director under section 86 of this Act, it shall be the duty of the Director, if requested by the appropriate Minister or Ministers to do so, to consult the relevant parties with a view to obtaining from them undertakings to take action indicated in the request made to the Director as being action requisite, in the opinion of the appropriate Minister or Ministers, for the purpose of remedying or preventing the adverse effects specified in the report.

(2) The Director shall report to the appropriate Minister or Ministers the outcome of his consultations under the preceding subsection; and if any undertaking is given by any of the relevant parties to take action indicated in the request made to the Director as mentioned in that subsection (in this section referred to as an "appropriate undertaking") the Minister to whom the undertaking is given shall furnish particulars of it to the Director.

(3) Where in his consultations under subsection (1) of this section the Director seeks to obtain an appropriate undertaking from any of the relevant parties, and either—

(a) he is satisfied that no such undertaking is likely to be given by that party within a reasonable time, or

(b) having allowed such time as in his opinion is reasonable for the purpose, he is satisfied that no such undertaking has been given by that party,

the Director shall give such advice to the appropriate Minister or Ministers as he may think proper in the circumstances (including, if the Director thinks fit, advice with respect to the exercise by the appropriate Minister or Ministers of his or their powers under section 56 or section 73 of this Act, as the case may be).

(4) Where the Director has made a report under subsection (2) of this section, and particulars of an undertaking given by any of the relevant parties have been furnished to the Director in accordance with that subsection, it shall be the duty of the Director—

(a) to keep under review the carrying out of that undertaking, and from time to time to consider whether, by reason of any change of circumstances, it needs to be varied or to be superseded by a new undertaking, and

(b) if it appears to him that it has not been or is not being fulfilled, or needs to be varied or superseded, to give such advice to the appropriate Minister or Ministers as he may think proper in the circumstances.

(5) Where, in consequence of a report of which a copy is transmitted to the Director under section 86 of this Act, an order is made under section 56 or section 73 of this Act in relation to any of the matters to which the report relates, it shall be the duty of the Director to keep under review the action (if any) taken in compliance with that order, and from time to time to consider whether, by

reason of any change of circumstances, the order should be varied or should be superseded by a new order, and—

(a) if it appears to him that the order has in any respect not been complied with, to consider whether any action (by way of proceedings in accordance with section 93 of this Act or otherwise) should be taken for the purpose of securing compliance with the order, and (where in his opinion it is appropriate to do so) to take such action himself or give advice to any Minister or other person by whom such action might be taken, or

(b) if it appears to him that the order needs to be varied, or to be superseded by a new order, to give such advice to the appropriate Minister or Ministers as he may think proper in the circumstances.

(6) In this section "the relevant parties"—

(a) in relation to a report of the Commission on a monopoly reference, means the person or persons specified in the report as being the person or persons in whose favour the monopoly situation in question exists;

(b) in relation to a report of the Commission on a merger reference under section 75 of this Act, which includes a finding that a merger situation qualifying for investigation will be created if the arrangements in question are carried into effect, means any person indicated in the report as being a person by whom in accordance with the arrangements any assets are to be taken over;

(c) in relation to a report of the Commission on a merger reference, other than a newspaper merger reference or a reference falling within paragraph (b) of this subsection, means the persons specified in the report as being persons carrying on, owning or controlling any of the enterprises which, in accordance with the conclusions of the Commission, have ceased to be distinct enterprises;

and, in relation to a report of the Commission, "the appropriate Minister or Ministers" means the Minister or Ministers to whom the report is made, "undertaking" means an undertaking given to that Minister or to one of those Ministers, as the case may be, and, in subsections (3) and (5) of this section, the references to section 73 of this Act shall be construed as including references to that section as applied by section 75(4) of this Act.

89.—(1) The provisions of this section shall have effect where—

(a) in the circumstances specified in subsection (1) of section 56 of this Act the Secretary of State makes, or has under consideration the making of, an order under that section exercising any of the powers specified in Part II of Schedule 8 to this Act, or

(b) in the circumstances specified in subsection (1) of section 73 of this Act the Secretary of State makes, or has under consideration the making of, an order under that section exercising any of those powers;

and in those provisions "the principal order" means the order which the Secretary of State makes, or has it under consideration to make, as mentioned in paragraph (a) or paragraph (b) of this subsection.

(2) With a view to achieving the purpose for which any of the powers specified in Part II of that Schedule are, or are proposed to be, exercised by the principal order, the Secretary of State may by order made by statutory instrument exercise any of the powers mentioned in the next following subsection.

(3) An order under this section may—

(a) prohibit or restrict the doing of things which, in the opinion of the Secretary of State, might impede the operation of the principal order or, where it has not yet been made, might be an impediment to making it;

(b) impose on any person concerned obligations as to the carrying on of any activities or the safeguarding of any assets;

(c) provide for the carrying on of any activities or the safeguarding of any assets either by the appointment of a person to conduct or supervise the conduct of any activities (on such terms and with such powers as may be specified or described in the order under this section) or in any other manner.

90.—(1) This section applies to any order under section 56, section 73, section 74 or section 89 of this Act.

(2) Any such order declaring anything to be unlawful may declare it to be unlawful either for all persons or for such persons as may be specified or described in the order.

(3) Nothing in any such order shall have effect so as to apply to any person in relation to his conduct outside the United Kingdom unless that person is—

(a) a citizen of the United Kingdom and Colonies, or

(b) a body corporate incorporated under the law of the United Kingdom or of a part of the United Kingdom, or

(c) a person carrying on business in the United Kingdom, either alone or in partnership with one or more other persons,

but, in the case of a person falling within paragraph (a), paragraph (b) or paragraph (c) of this sub-section, any such order may extend to acts or omissions outside the United Kingdom.

(4) An order to which this section applies may extend so as to prohibit the carrying out of agreements already in existence on the date on which the order is made.

(5) Nothing in any order to which this section applies shall have effect so a to restrict the doing of anything for the purpose of restraining an infringement of a United Kingdom patent or so as to restrict any person as to the conditions which he attaches to a licence to do anything the doing of which would, but for the licence, be an infringement of a United Kingdom patent.

(6) Nothing in any such order shall affect the conduct of a board established under a scheme made under the Agricultural Marketing Act 1958 or under the Agricultural Marketing Act (Northern Ireland) 1964.

(7) An order to which this section applies may authorise the Minister making the order to give directions to a person specified in the direction, or to the holder for the time being of an office so specified in any company or association,—

(a) to take such steps within his competence as may be specified or described in the directions for the purpose of carrying out, or securing compliance with, the order, or

(b) to do or refrain from doing anything so specified or described which he might be required by the order to do or refrain from doing,

and may authorise that Minister to vary or revoke any directions so given.

91.—(1) No order to which section 90 of this Act applies and which exercises any of the powers specified in Part II of Schedule 8 to this Act, and no order varying or revoking any such order, shall be made unless a draft or the order has been laid before Parliament and approved by a resolution of each House of Parliament; and the provisions of Schedule 9 to this Act shall have effect with respect to the procedure to be followed before laying before Parliament a draft of any such order.

(2) Before making any order under section 56 or section 73 of this Act other than any such order as is mentioned in the preceding subsection, the Minister proposing to make the order shall publish, in such manner as appears to him to be appropriate, a notice—

(a) stating his intention to make the order;

(b) indicating the nature of the provisions to be embodied in the order; and

(c) sttaing that any person whose interests are likely to be affected by the order, and who is desirous of making representations in respect of it, should do so in writing (stating his interest and the grounds on which he wishes to make the representations) before a date specified in the notice (that date being not earlier than the end of the period of thirty days beginning with the day on which publication of the notice is completed);

and the Minister shall not make the order before the date specified in the notice in accordance with paragraph (c) of this subsection and shall consider any representations duly made to him in accordance with the notice before that date.

92.—(1) For the purpose of determining whether to make an order to which section 90 of this Act applies whereby any powers are to be exercised in relation to a company or association, or for the purpose of obtaining information on which to exercise by or under any such order any powers in relation to a company or association, the Secretary of State may appoint an inspector to investigate and report to him on any such matters falling within the next following subsection as are specified or described in the appointment.

(2) The matters which may be so specified or described are any matters which, in the case of a company registered under the Companies Act 1948,—

(a) could in accordance with sections 165 and 166 of that Act be investigated by an inspector appointed under section 165 of that Act, or

(b) could in accordance with section 172 of that Act, or in accordance with any provisions as applied by subsection (5) of that section, be investigated by an inspector appointed under that section.

(3) For purposes connected with any investigation made by an inspector appointed under this section—

(a) section 167 (or that section as applied by section 172(5)) of the Companies Act 1948 shall have effect as it has effect for the purposes of any investigation under section 165 or section 172 of that Act, and

3 (b) the provisions of that Act referred to in this and the last preceding subsection shall be taken to extend throughout the United Kingdom.

93.—(1) No criminal proceedings shall, by virtue of the making of an order to which section 90 of this Act applies, lie against any person on the grounds that he has committed, or aided, abetted, counselled or procured the commission of, or conspired or attempted to commit, or incited others to commit, any contravention of the order.

(2) Nothing in the preceding subsection shall limit any right of any person to bring civil proceedings in respect of any contravention or apprehended contravention of any such order, and (without prejudice to the generality of the preceding words) compliance with any such order shall be enforceable by civil proceedings by the Crown for an injunction or interdict or for any other appropriate relief.

(3) If any person makes default in complying with any directions given under section 90(7) of this Act, the court may, on the application of the Secretary of State, make an order requiring him to make good the default within a time specified in the order, or, if the directions related to anything to be done in the management or administration of a company or association, requiring the company or association or any officer of it to do so.

(4) Any order of the court under subsection (3) of this section may provide that all the costs or expenses of or incidental to the application for the order shall be borne by any person in default or by any officers of a company or association who are responsible for its default.

(5) In this section "the court"—

(a) in relation to England and Wales, means the High Court;

(b) in relation to Scotland, menas the Court of Session; and

(c) in relation to Northern Ireland, means the High Court or a judge of the High Court.

SCHEDULE 8   Sections 56, 73, 74, 77, 89 and 91.

POWERS EXERCISABLE BY ORDERS UNDER SECTION 56 AND 73

PART I

POWERS EXERCISABLE IN ALL CASES

1. Subject to paragraph 3 of this Schedule, an order under section 56 or section 73 of this Act (in this Schedule referred to as an "order") may declare it to be unlawful, except to such extent and in such circumstances as may be provided by or under the order, to make or to carry out any such agreement as may be specified or described in the order.

2. Subject to the next following paragraph, an order may require any party to any such agreement as may be specified or described in the order to terminate the agreement within such time as may be so specified, either wholly or to such extent as may be so specified.

3.—(1) An order shall not by virtue of paragraph 1 of this Schedule declare it to be unlawful to make any agreement in so far as, if made, it would be an agreement to which Part I of the Act of 1956 would apply.

(2) An order shall not by virtue of paragraph 1 or paragraph 2 of this Schedule declare it to be unlawful to carry out, or require any person to terminate, an agreement in so far as it is an agreement to which Part I of the Act of 1956 applies.

(3) An order shall not by virtue of either of those paragraphs declare it to be unlawful to make or to carry out, or require any person to terminate, an agreement in so far as, if made, it would relate, or (as the case may be) in so far as it relates, to the terms and conditions of employment of any workers, or to the physical conditions in which any workers are required to work.

(4) In this paragraph "terms and conditions of employment" has the meaning assigned to it by section 167(1) of the Industrial Relations Act 1971.

4. An order may declare it to be unlawful, except to such extent and in such circumstances as may be provided by or under the order, to withhold or to agree to withhold or to threaten to withhold, or to procure others to withhold or to agree to withhold or threaten to withhold, from any such persons as may be specified or described in the order, any supplies or services so specified or described or any orders for such supplies or services (whether the withholding is absolute or is to be effectual only in particular circumstances).

5. An order may declare it to be unlawful, except to such extent and in such circumstances as may be provided by or under the order, to require, as a condition of the supplying of goods or services to any person,—

(a) the buying of any goods, or

(b) the making of any payment in respect of services other than the goods or services supplied, or

(c) the doing of any other such matter as may be specified or described in the order.

6. An order may declare it to be unlawful, except to such extent and in such circumstances as may be provided by or under the order,—

(a) to discriminate in any manner specified or described in the order between any persons in the prices charged for goods or services so specified or described, or

(b) to do anything so specified or described which appears to the appropriate Minister to amount to such discrimination,

or to procure others to do any of the things mentioned in sub-paragraph (a) or sub-paragraph (b) of this paragraph.

7. An order may declare it to be unlawful, except to such extent and in such circumstances as may be provided by or under the order,—

(a) to give or agree to give in other ways any such preference in respect of the supply of goods or services, or the giving of orders for goods or services, as may be specified or described in the order, or

(b) to do anything so specified or described which appears to the appropriate Minister to amount to giving such preference,

or to procure others to do any of the things mentioned in sub-paragraph (a) or sub-paragraph (b) of this paragraph.

8. An order may declare it to be unlawful, except to such extent and in such circumstances as may be provided by or under the order, to charge for goods or services supplied prices differing from those in any published list or notification, or to do anything specified or described in the order which appears to the appropriate Minister to amount to charging such prices.

9. An order may require a person supplying goods or services to publish a list of or otherwise notify prices, with or without such further information as may be specified or described in the order.

10.—(1) Subject to the following provisions of this paragraph, an order may, to such extent and in such circumstances as may be provided by or under the order, regulate the prices to be charged for any goods or services specified or described in the order.

(2) An order shall not exercise the power conferred by the preceding sub-paragraph in respect of goods or services of any description unless the matters specified in the relevant report as being those which in the opinion of the Commission operate, or may be expected to operate, against the public interest relate, or include matters relating, to the prices charged for goods or services of that description.

(3) In this paragraph "the relevant report", in relation to an order, means the report of the Commission in consequence of which the order is made, in the form in which that report is laid before Parliament.

11. An order may declare it to be unlawful, except to such extent and in such circumstances as may be provided by or under the order, for any person, by publication or otherwise, to notify, to persons supplying goods or services, prices recommended or suggested as appropriate to be charged by those persons for those goods or services.

12.—(1) An order may prohibit or restrict the acquisition by any person of the whole or part of the undertaking or assets of another person's business, or the doing of anything which will or may have a result to which this paragraph applies, or may require that, if such an acquisition is made of anything is done which has such a result, the persons concerned or any of them shall thereafter observe any prohibitions or restrictions imposed by or under the order.

(2) This paragraph applies to any result which consists in two or more bodies corporate becoming interconnected bodies corporate.

(3) Where an order is made in consequence of a report of the Commission under section 72 of this Act, or is made under section 74 of this Act, this paragraph also applies to any result (other than that specified in sub-paragraph (2) of this paragraph) which, in accordance with section 65 of this Act, consists in two or more enterprises ceasing to be distinct enterprises.

13. In this Part of this Schedule "the appropriate Minister", in relation to an order, means the Minister by whom the order is made.

PART II

POWERS EXERCISABLE EXCEPT IN CASES FALLING WITHIN SECTION 56(6)

14. An order may provide for the division of any business by the sale of any part of the undertaking or assets or otherwise (for which purpose all the activities carried on by way of business by any one person or by any two or more interconnected bodies corporate may be treated as a single business), or for the division of any group of interconnected bodies corporate, and for all such matters as may be necessary to effect or take account of the division, including—

(a) the transfer or vesting of property, rights, liabilities or obligations;

(b) the adjustment of contracts, whether by discharge or reduction of any liability or obligation or otherwise;

(c) the creation, allotment, surrender or cancellation of any shares, stock or securities;

(d) the formation or winding up of a company or other association, corporate or unincorporate, or the amendment of the memorandum and articles or other instruments regulating any company or association;

(e) the extent to which, and the circumstances in which, provisions of the order affecting a company or association in its share capital, constitution or other matters may be altered by the company or association, and the registration under any enactment of the order by companies or associations so affected;

(f) the continuation, with any necessary change of parties, of any legal proceedings.

15. In relation to an order under section 73 of this Act, the reference in paragraph 14 of this Schedule to the division of a business as mentioned in that paragraph shall be construed as including a reference to the separation, by the sale of any part of any undertaking or assets concerned or other means, of enterprises which are under common control otherwise than by reason of their being enterprises of interconnected bodies corporate.

Index